STRANGER THAN LIFE

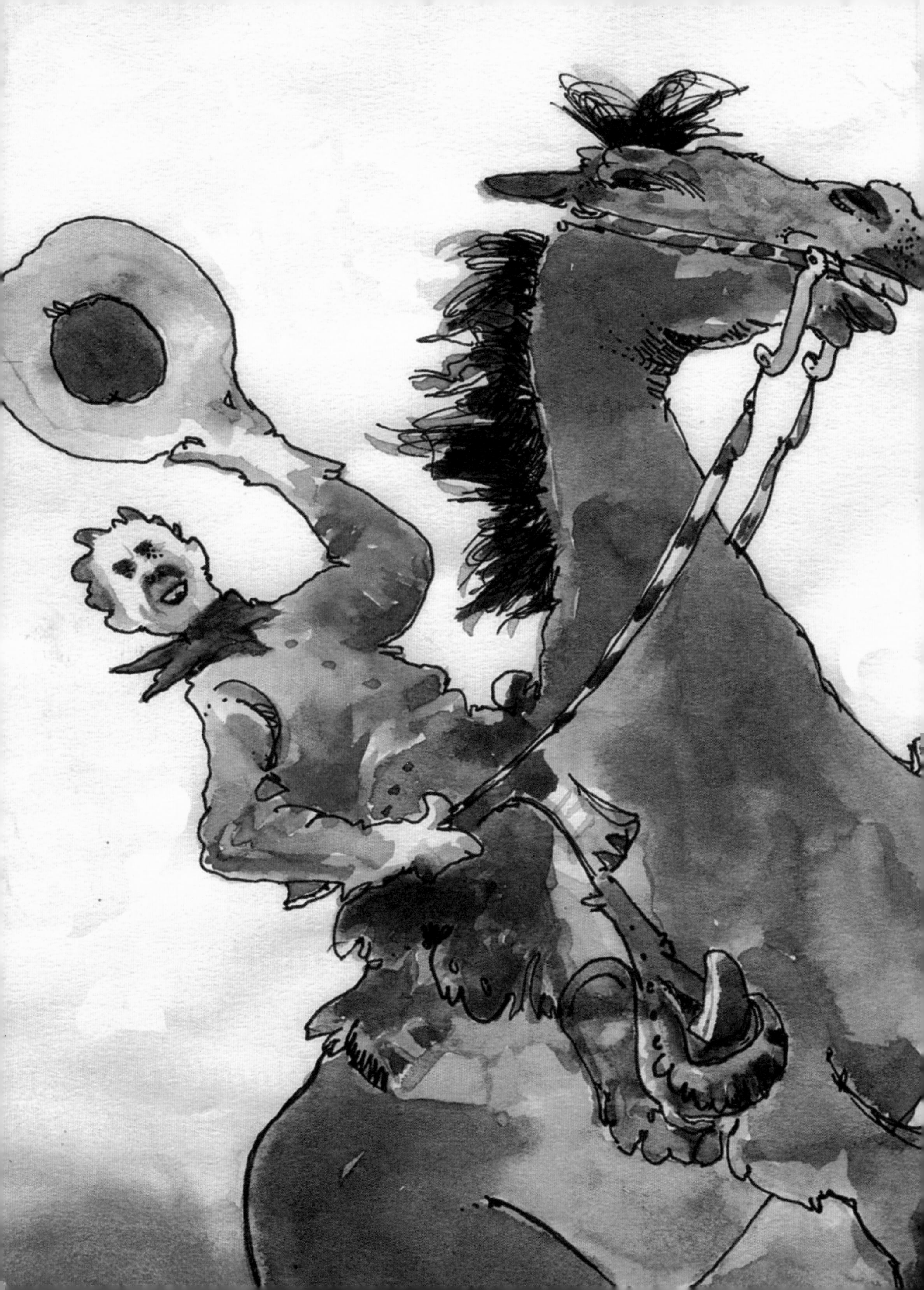

MK Brown

STRANGER than LIFE

CARTOONS AND COMICS

1970–2013

FANTAGRAPHICS BOOKS

Dedicated to Kalia, Sarah, and Benjamin Kliban, and to the memory of Gunard Solberg and B. Kliban.

With many thanks to Gary Groth, Mary Bisbee-Beek, Louise Kollenbaum, Bill Griffith, Roz Chast, Dick Daniels, and Cristofer Morley.

Fantagraphics Books
7563 Lake City Way NE
Seattle, Washington 98115

Editor: Gary Groth
Associate Publisher: Eric Reynolds
Publisher: Gary Groth

To receive a free full-color catalog of comics, graphic novels, and prose novels, including work by other cartooning geniuses, call 1-800-657-1100, or visit fantagraphics.com.

First Fantagraphics Books Edition: February 2014

ISBN 978-1-60699-708-6

Printed in China

TABLE OF CONTENTS

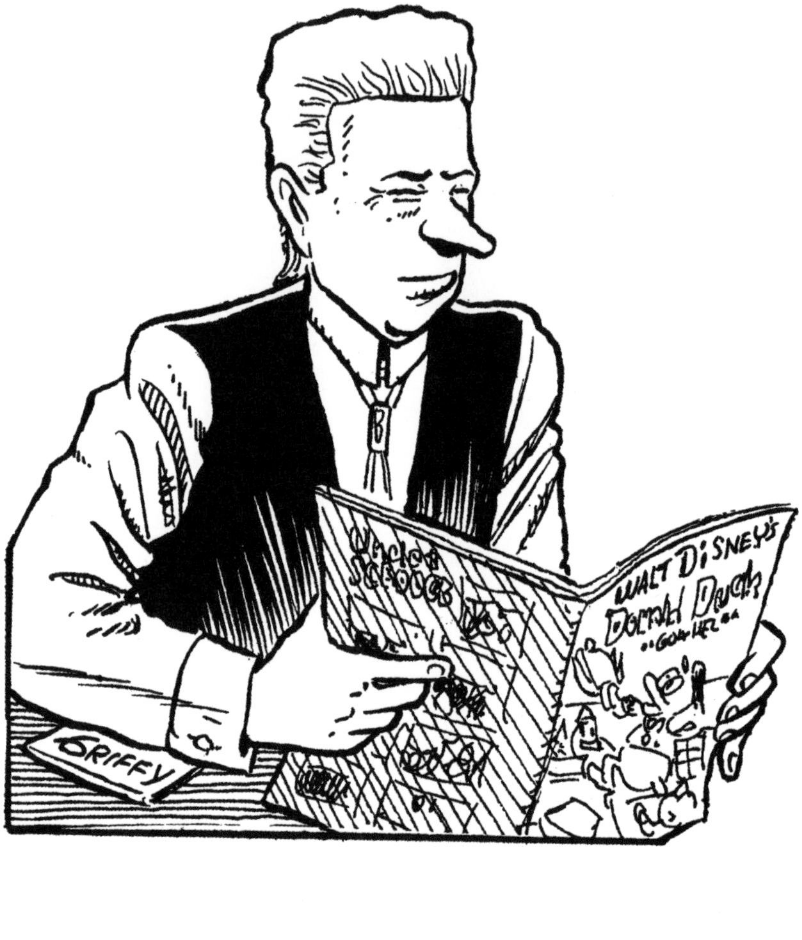
WALT DISNEY'S
GRIFFY

HERE'S MY CHECKLIST FOR EVERYTHING I WANT IN A CARTOONIST:

- Funny, but in a knowing, subtle way.

- Self-effacing, yet more than willing to vent a personal opinion.

- Channels anger and annoyance at society into keen social observation.

- Strong in the writing department, with an ear for the rhythm and idiosyncrasy of speech. Characters come with backstories.

- Easy-to-read lettering, full of personality.

- All the people in the strips don't look like they came from the same two parents.

- Deals with absurd, oddball things, but is not an absurd oddball away from the drawing table.

- Can really draw the hell out of: clothing folds, faces, perspective, cars, main streets, furniture, water, horses, pigs, shoes, snakes, insects, rocket ships, hair, and food.

- Chronicles the times we live in but does so in a way that doesn't "date."

- Juxtaposition, juxtaposition, juxtaposition.

- Makes the personal universal, makes the universal personal.

- Everything flows. No connective tissue is left out.

- Could have just as easily been a famous screenwriter, a 19th-century French watercolorist, or an exceptionally creative hair stylist.

- Pleasantly distorts human anatomy.

- Turns the orderly world we think we all live in upside down, shakes up our perceptions of normality—then hands everything back to us profoundly altered in some way only our subconscious minds truly understand.

- Really knows how to end a story.

Hey. I think I just summed up the wonderful, funny, insightful, beautifully crafted, stranger-than-life comics of M.K. Brown! Best of all—they're all together in this one gorgeous volume.

Now check out that pig snout on p. 209.

—Bill Griffith

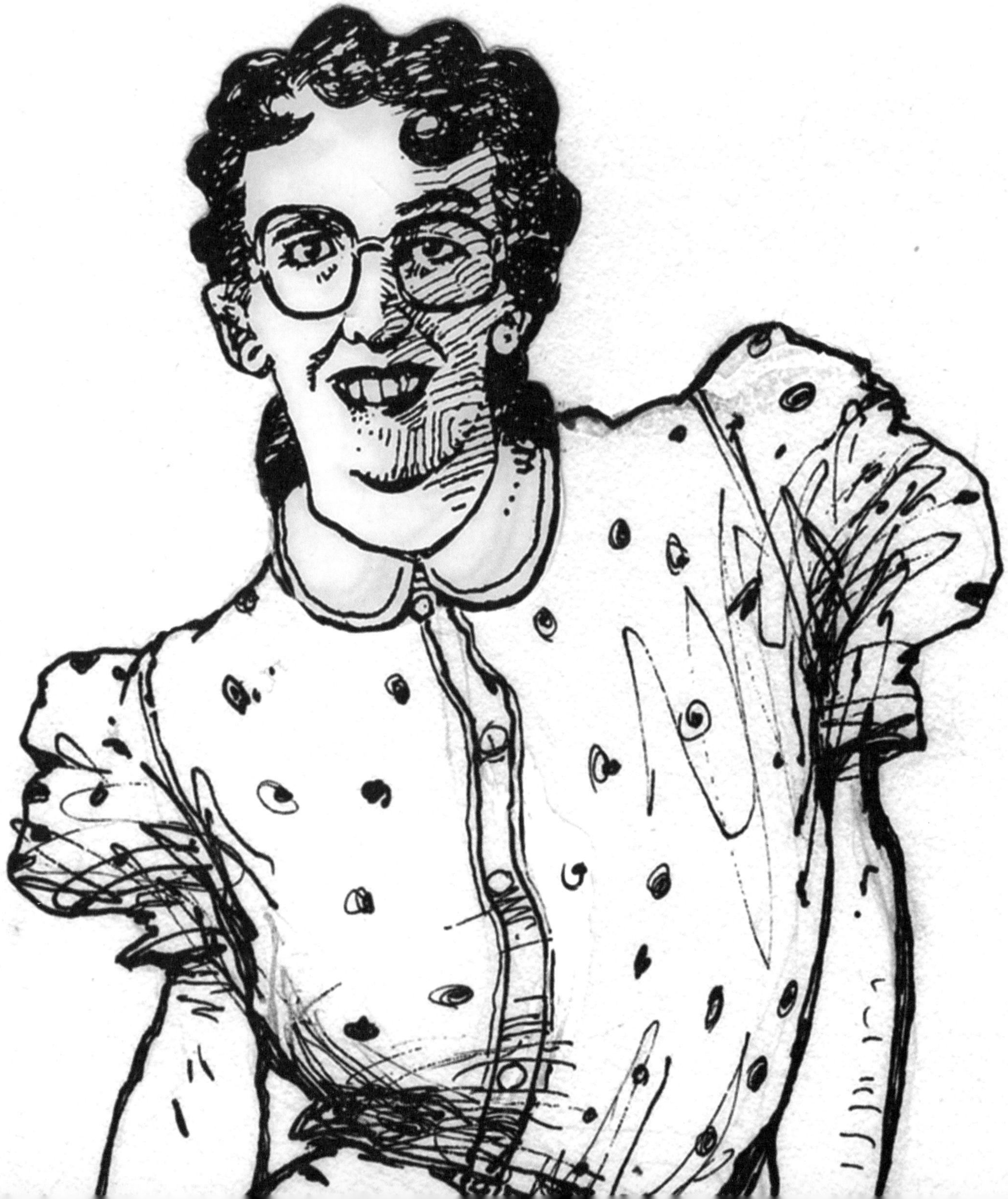

These cartoons are from the early '70s to the present, so you will see some changes in drawing styles. I have put them into categories that are either very obvious or weirdly fitting that they should be there.

As we all know, cartooning requires enough independence and self-absorption to spend hours drawing alone with only a radio and a cat for company, often without a clue as to what happens next, yet remaining perfectly entertained. Of course, it also demands a certain degree of craft in order to be understood, especially when the idea is, shall we say, *complicated*.

Cartooning also contains the lunacy component, which maintains that if one person (oneself) can see the humor or truth or strangeness in something (thus the value in drawing it), others will too, and if they don't, well, we can't help that.

And so, in the spirit of independent thinking and drawing without fear, or because of it, I am pleased to present these pages both to new readers and to those loyal folks who have, over the years, challenged me with provocative inquiries, such as this one from Mr. Osborne in Cyberville: "Why do so many of your characters have heads shaped like Lake Superior?"

I trust that questions of this caliber will be addressed within these covers, and that you will have a safe and pleasant journey through *Stranger Than Life*.

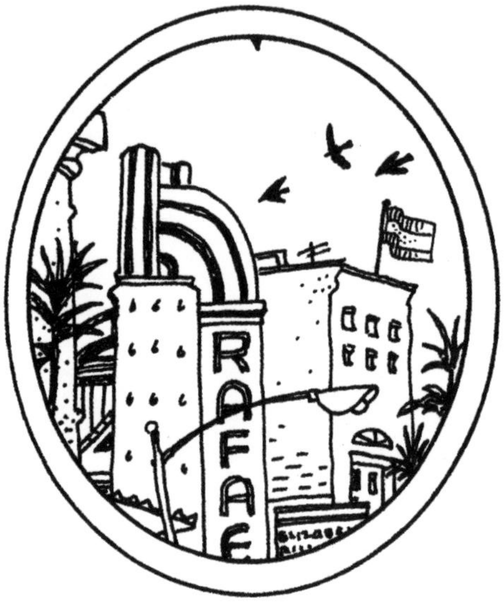
RAFAE

Housepeople

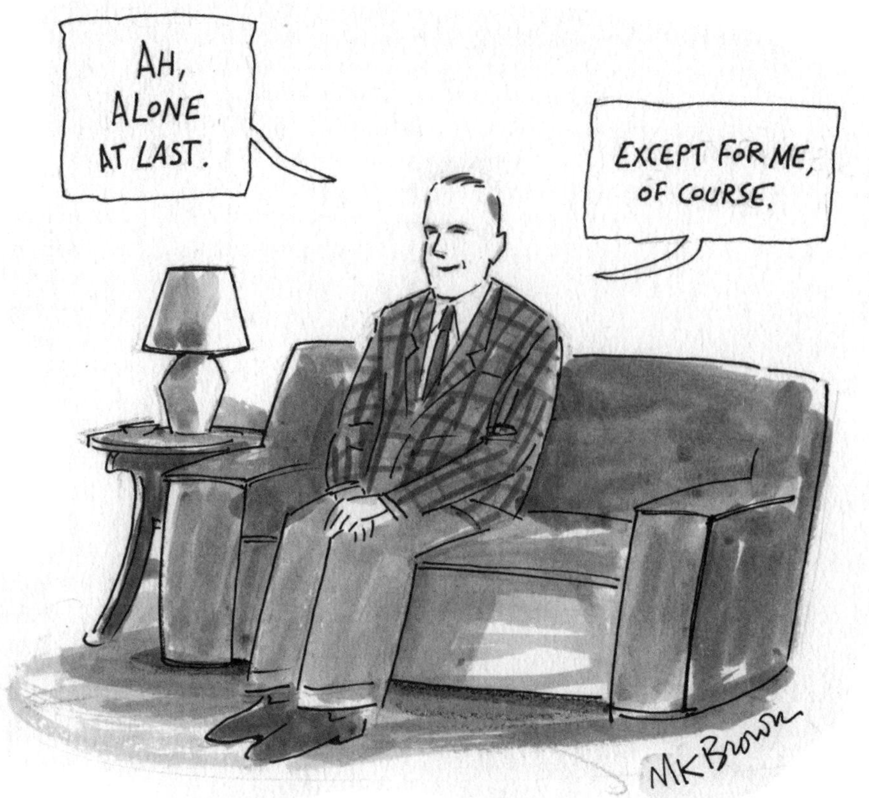
AH, ALONE AT LAST.
EXCEPT FOR ME, OF COURSE.
MK Brown

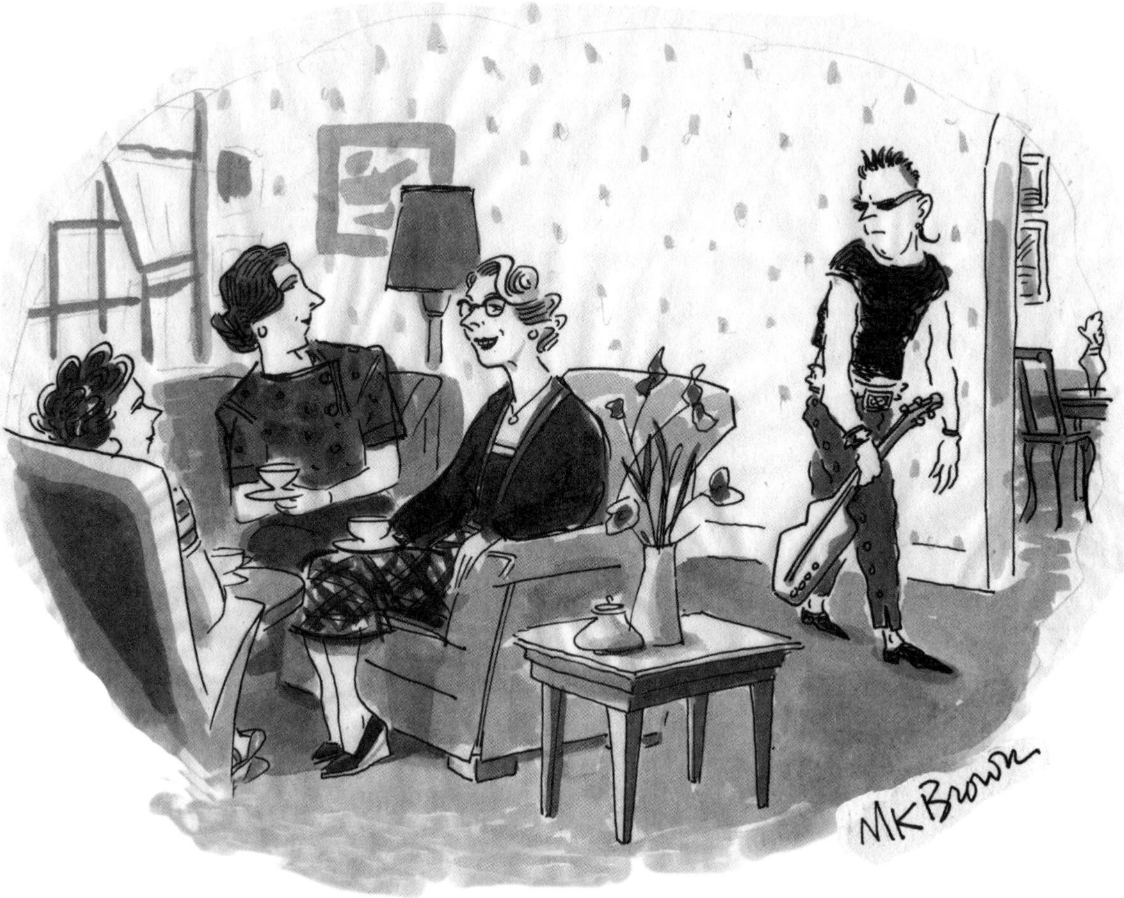
MK Brown

Barry is thinking of joining a rock group.

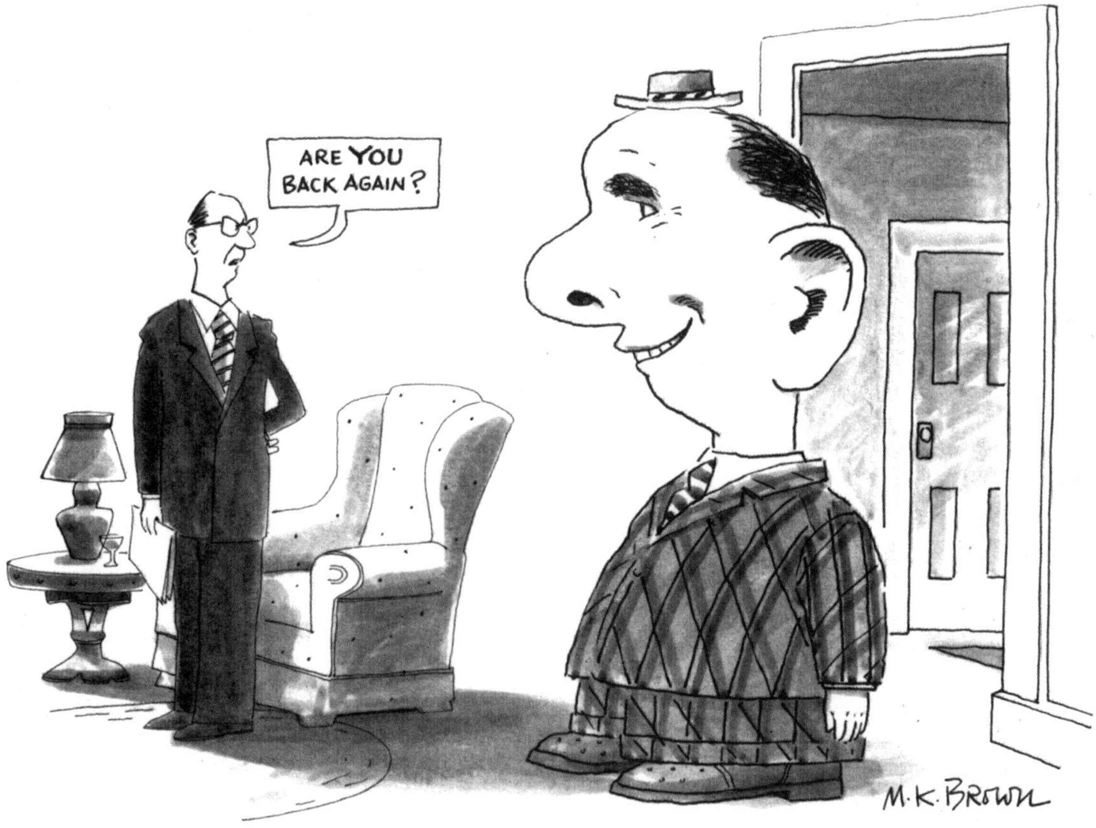
ARE YOU BACK AGAIN?
M.K. BROWN

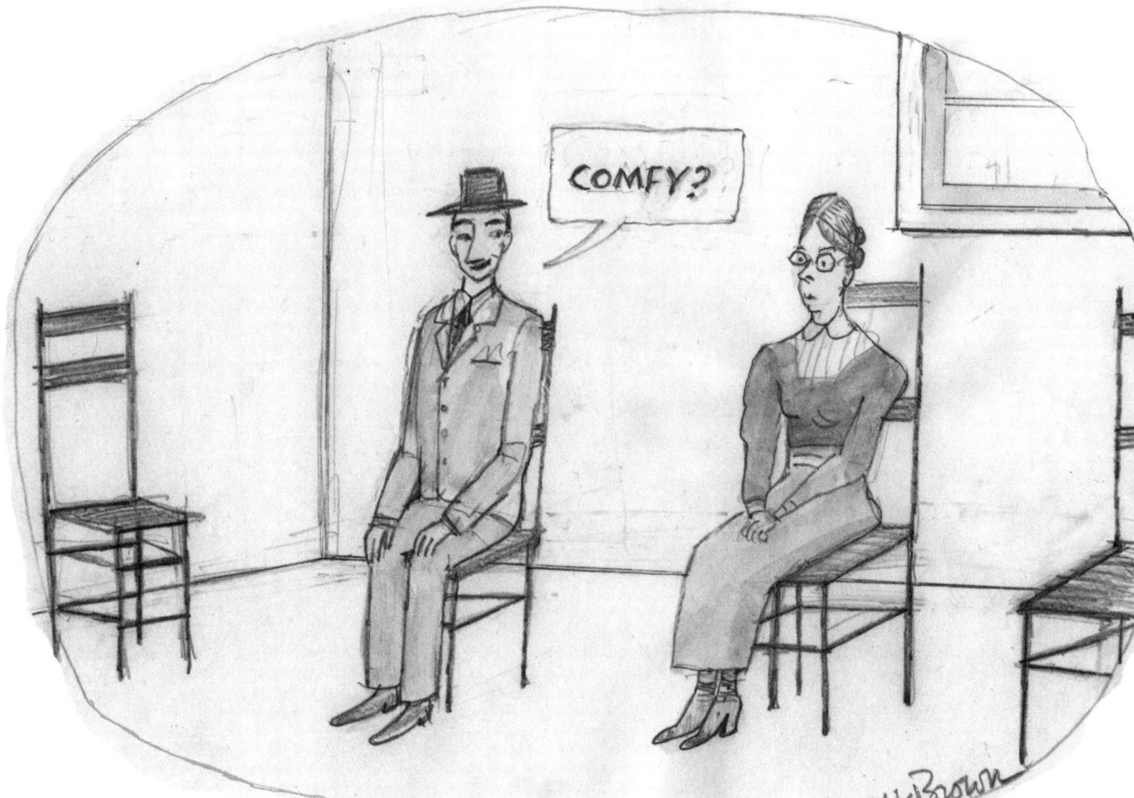
COMFY?
MKBrown

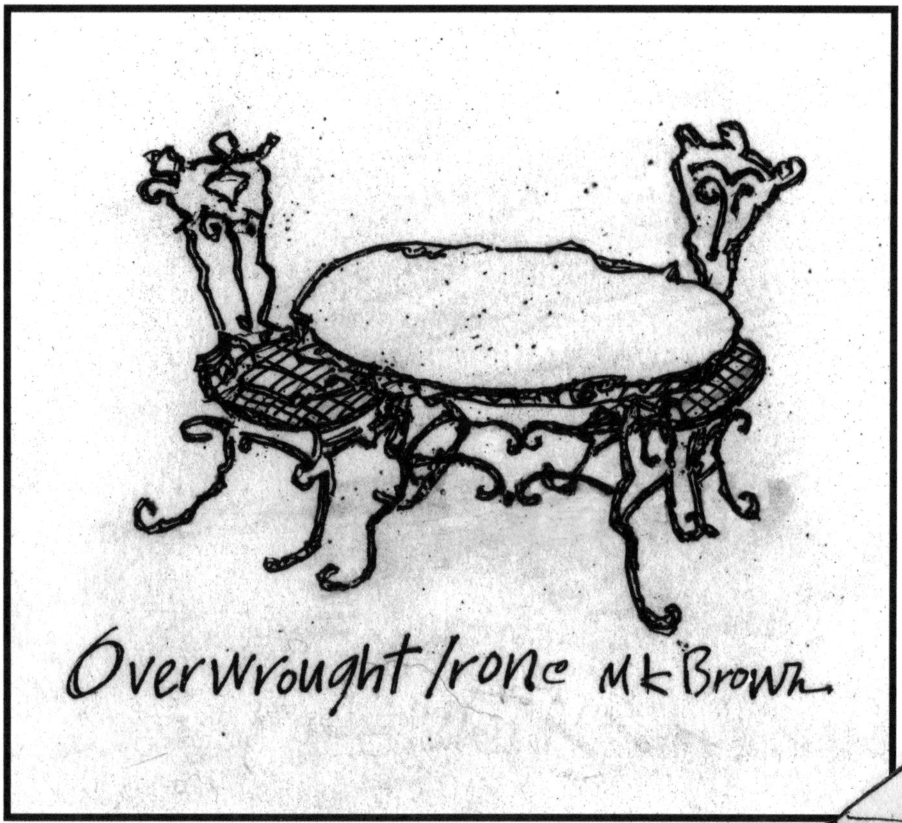
Overwrought Irone MKBrown

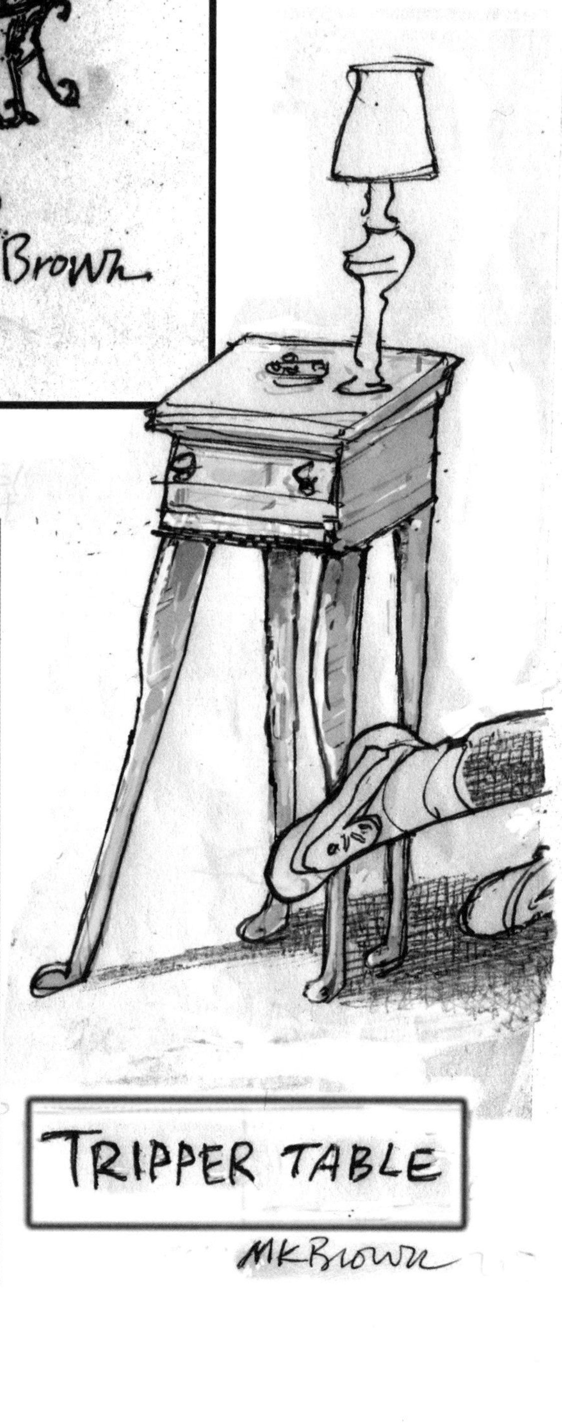
TRIPPER TABLE
MKBrown

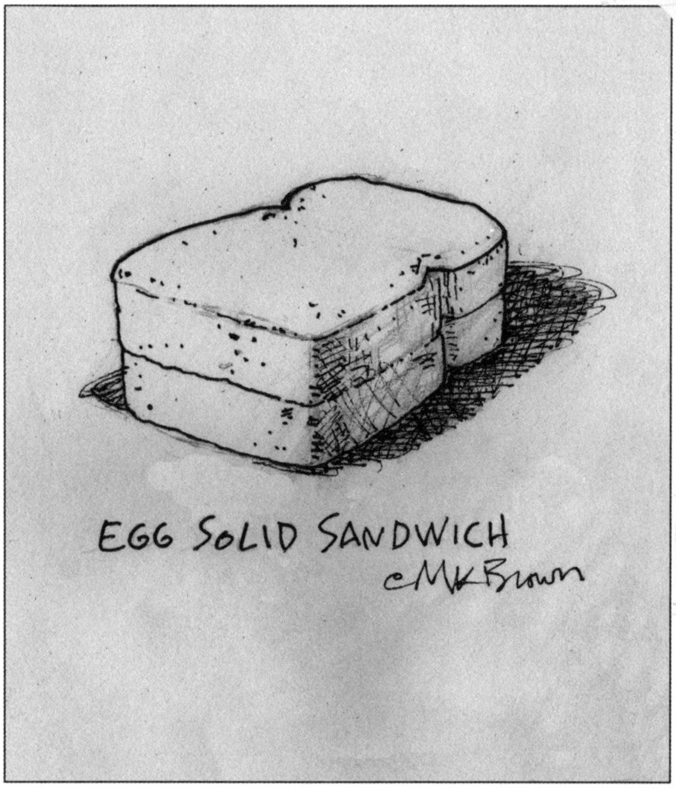
EGG SOLID SANDWICH
©MKBrown

I was angry with Billie Jean King.

She was one of the publishers at *Women's Sports* at the time, a magazine to which I often contributed, and they had recently lost an original cartoon of mine, "Camel Racing in the Desert."

Although she had nothing to do with its disappearance, when I saw a photo of Billie Jean King in a magazine ad, I decided to use her for the main character in a new cartoon I was doing for *Playgirl*, of all things.

Nothing really bad happened to Ms. King when she was sucked up into space in the middle of the party, and I felt better about losing an original watercolor.

This turned out to be the only original cartoon that was ever lost in many years of mailing them to different magazines. During some difficult times at the *National Lampoon*, only two were returned with coffee cup stains and cut-off borders. Most were treated with great respect.

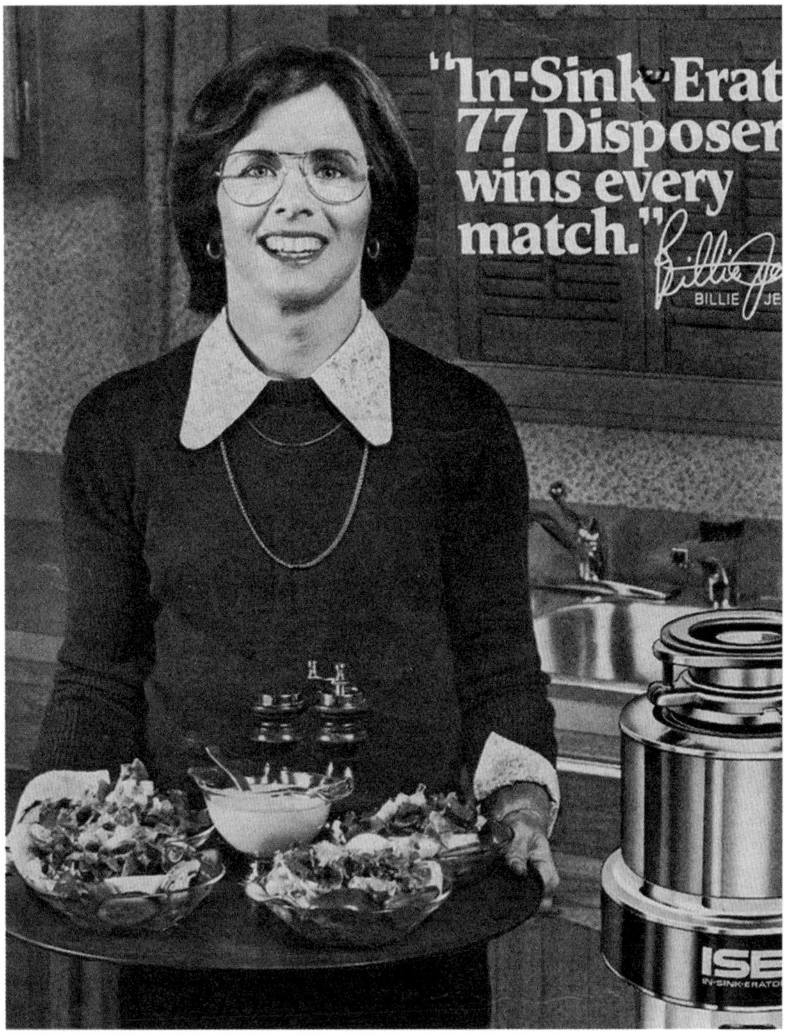
"In-Sink-Erat
77 Disposer
wins every
match."
BILLIE JE
ISE

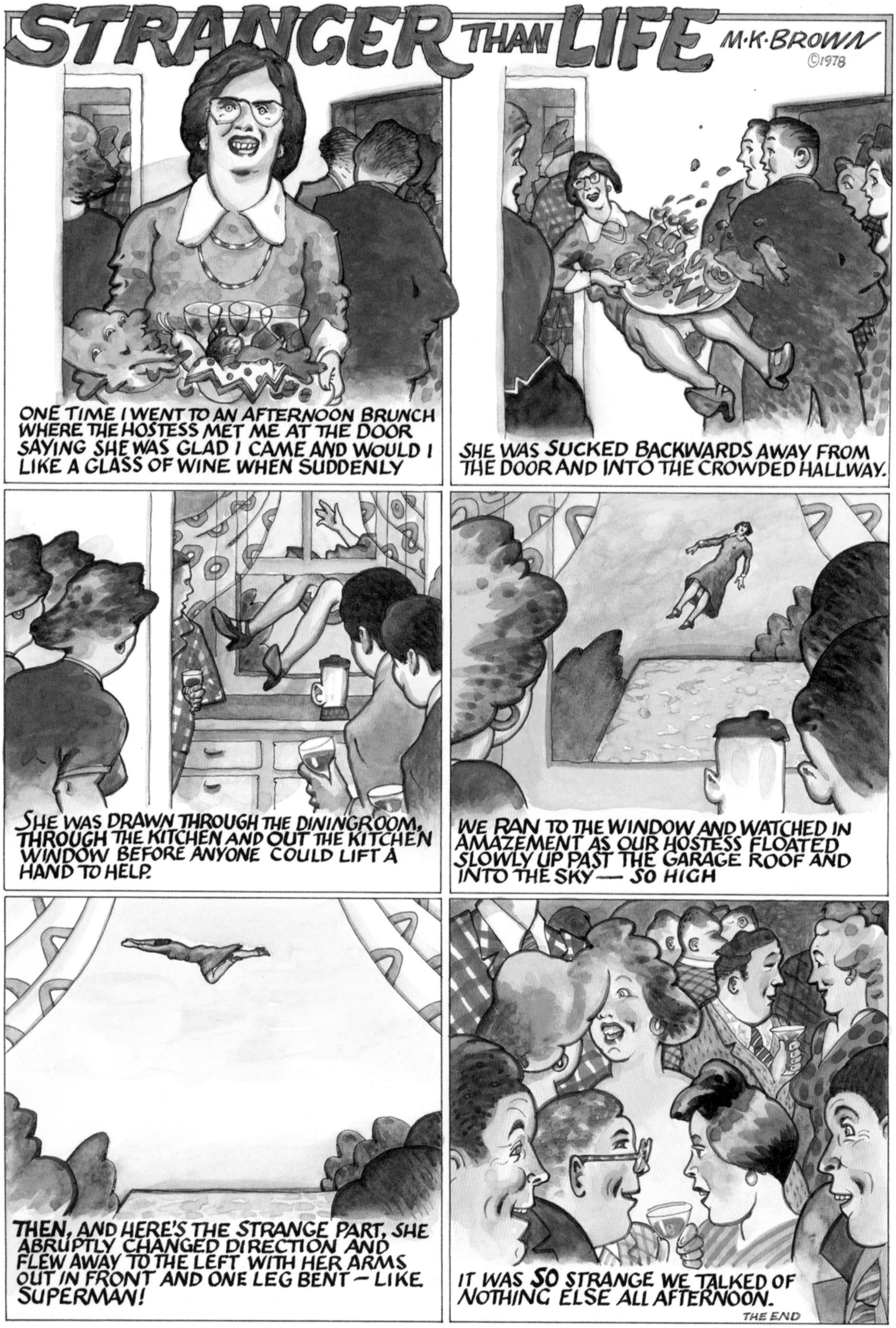
STRANGER THAN LIFE
M·K·BROWN
©1978
ONE TIME I WENT TO AN AFTERNOON BRUNCH WHERE THE HOSTESS MET ME AT THE DOOR SAYING SHE WAS GLAD I CAME AND WOULD I LIKE A GLASS OF WINE WHEN SUDDENLY
SHE WAS SUCKED BACKWARDS AWAY FROM THE DOOR AND INTO THE CROWDED HALLWAY.
SHE WAS DRAWN THROUGH THE DININGROOM, THROUGH THE KITCHEN AND OUT THE KITCHEN WINDOW BEFORE ANYONE COULD LIFT A HAND TO HELP.
WE RAN TO THE WINDOW AND WATCHED IN AMAZEMENT AS OUR HOSTESS FLOATED SLOWLY UP PAST THE GARAGE ROOF AND INTO THE SKY — SO HIGH
THEN, AND HERE'S THE STRANGE PART, SHE ABRUPTLY CHANGED DIRECTION AND FLEW AWAY TO THE LEFT WITH HER ARMS OUT IN FRONT AND ONE LEG BENT — LIKE SUPERMAN!
IT WAS SO STRANGE WE TALKED OF NOTHING ELSE ALL AFTERNOON.
THE END

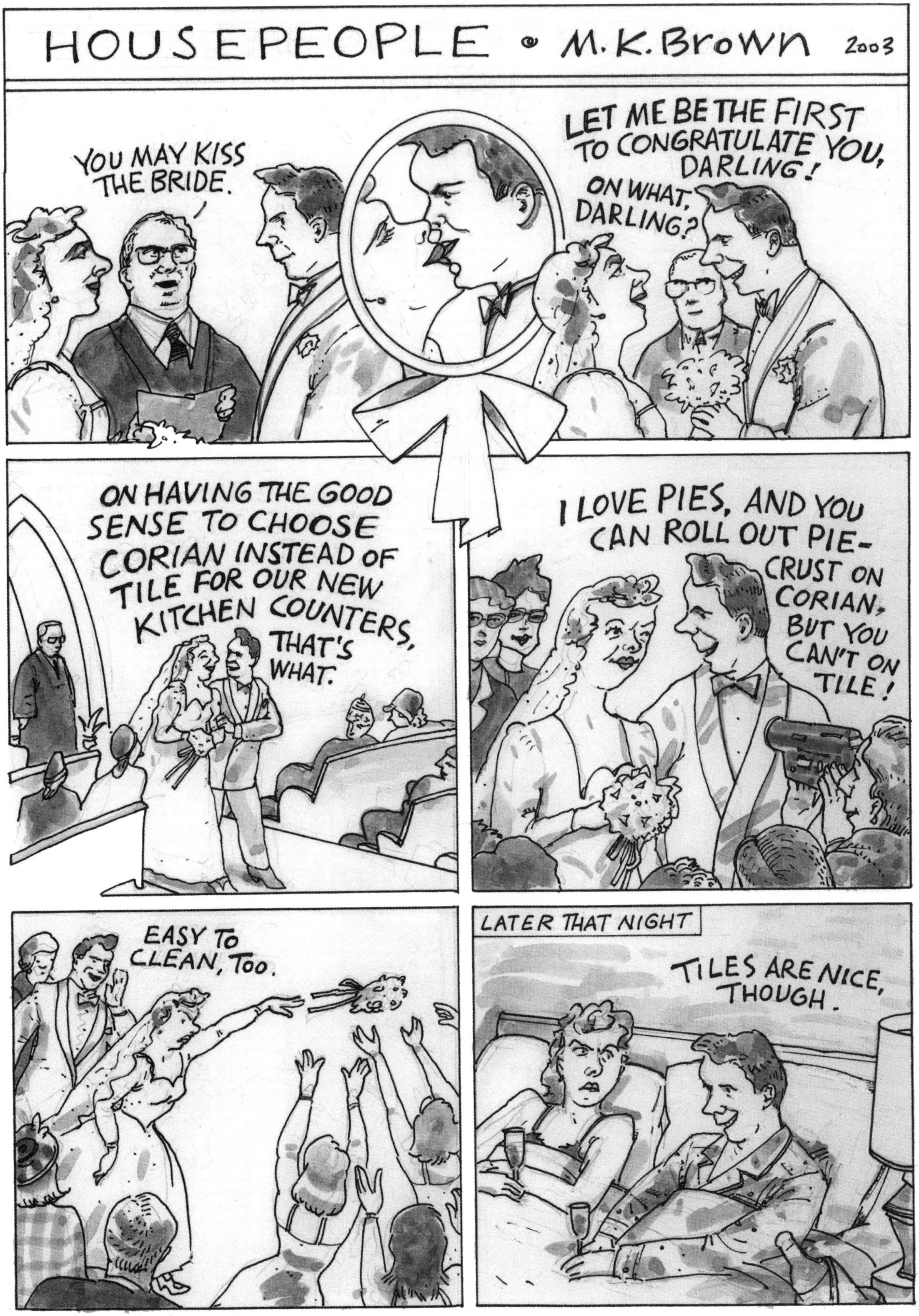
HOUSEPEOPLE • M.K. Brown 2003
YOU MAY KISS THE BRIDE.
LET ME BE THE FIRST TO CONGRATULATE YOU, DARLING!
ON WHAT, DARLING?
ON HAVING THE GOOD SENSE TO CHOOSE CORIAN INSTEAD OF TILE FOR OUR NEW KITCHEN COUNTERS,
THAT'S WHAT.
I LOVE PIES, AND YOU CAN ROLL OUT PIE-CRUST ON CORIAN, BUT YOU CAN'T ON TILE!
EASY TO CLEAN, TOO.
LATER THAT NIGHT
TILES ARE NICE, THOUGH.

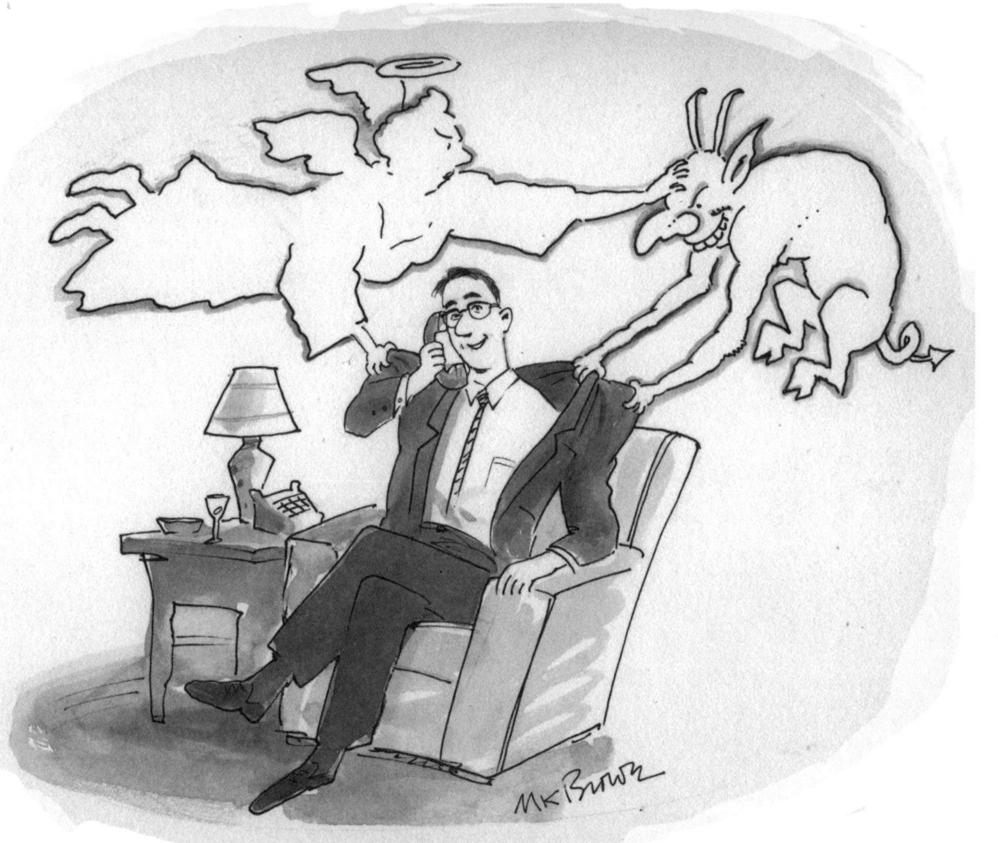

Oh, not much. What's new with you?

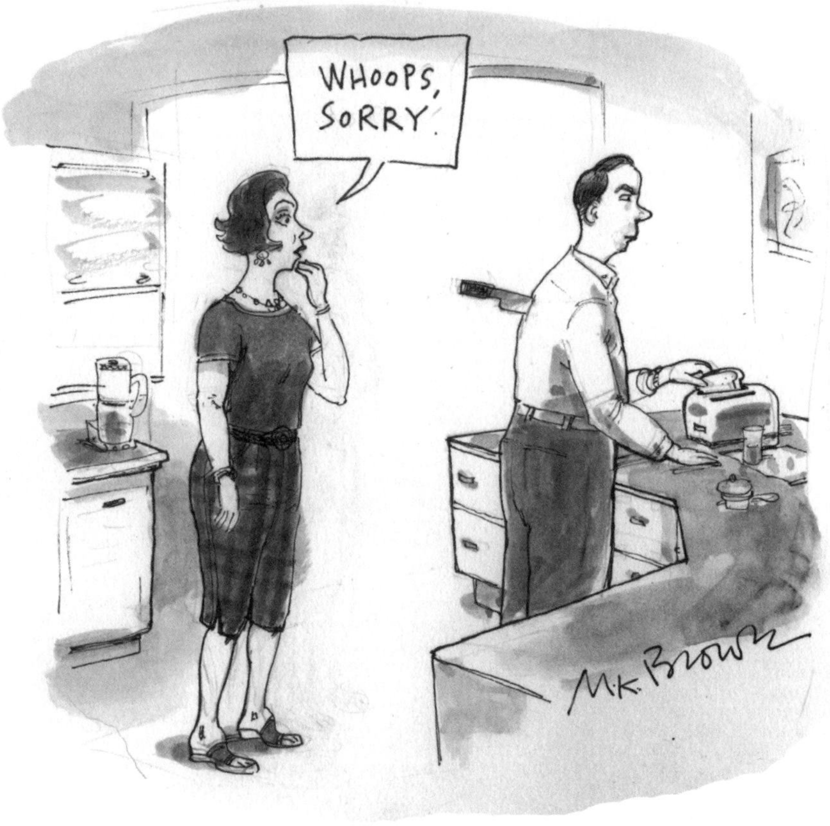
WHOOPS, SORRY

HOW TO
MAKE A PAIR OF PANTS IN 20 MINUTES

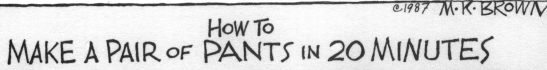

THIS IS YOUR FABRIC: THIRTY-SEVEN YARDS OF SILK BROCADE FROM CHINA.

NATURALLY, EACH YARD REPRESENTS A PART OF THE BODY, WHICH IS RELATED TO ANOTHER PART OF THE BODY.

Sides of neck

Palm

Toe

Frontal

Cubital fossa

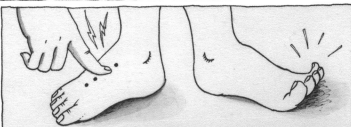

THEREFORE, FINGER PRESSURE ON ANY ONE OF THESE PARTS WILL STIMULATE A REACTION ELSEWHERE, OFTEN FAVORABLY—SO, LET'S GET GOING ON THESE PANTS!

(1) PANTS ARE MADE FOR WALKING

MEASURE YOUR STRIDE, AND THE TIME IT TAKES FROM ONE PART OF TOWN TO ANOTHER.

two three four

NO FAIR CHEATING

(5) PANTS ARE ALSO MADE FOR SITTING

SIT STILL FOR A WHILE ON SOMETHING UNCOMFORTABLE

MAKE ADJUSTMENTS

HERE →

HERE →

AND HERE →

(6) CUT OUT ALL PATTERN PIECES THAT LOOK LIKE PANTS. DISCARD THE REST. STITCH AND PRESS.

NOW IT'S PARTY TIME!

Whoops, sorry.

DRY-CLEAN ONLY BUT WHAT THE HECK

Pammy and I are thinking of getting into heroin.

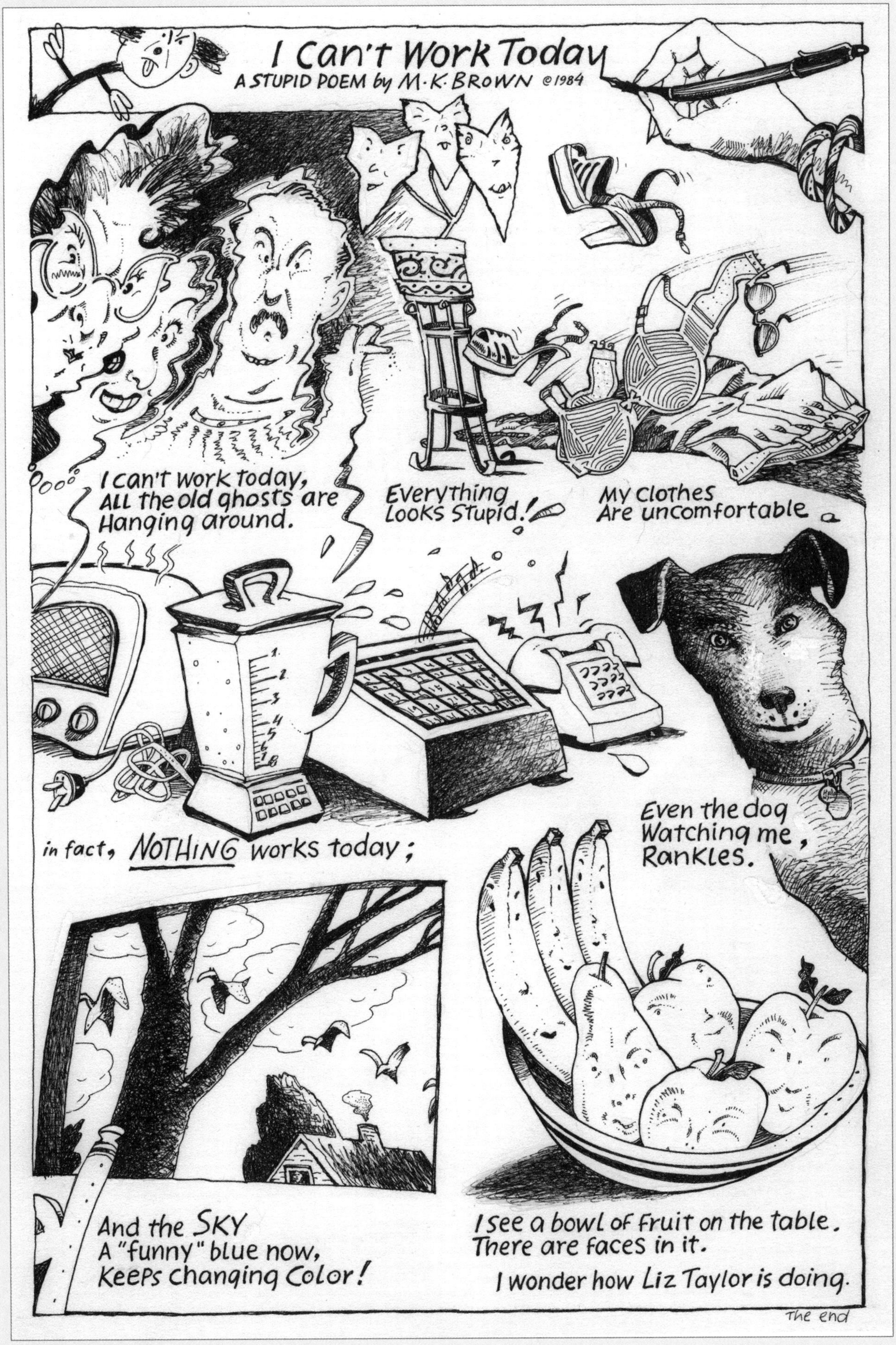

I Can't Work Today
A STUPID POEM by M·K·BROWN ©1984
I can't work today,
All the old ghosts are
Hanging around.
Everything
Looks Stupid!
My Clothes
Are uncomfortable
in fact, NOTHING works today;
Even the dog
Watching me,
Rankles.
And the SKY
A "funny" blue now,
Keeps changing Color!
I see a bowl of Fruit on the table.
There are faces in it.
I wonder how Liz Taylor is doing.
The end

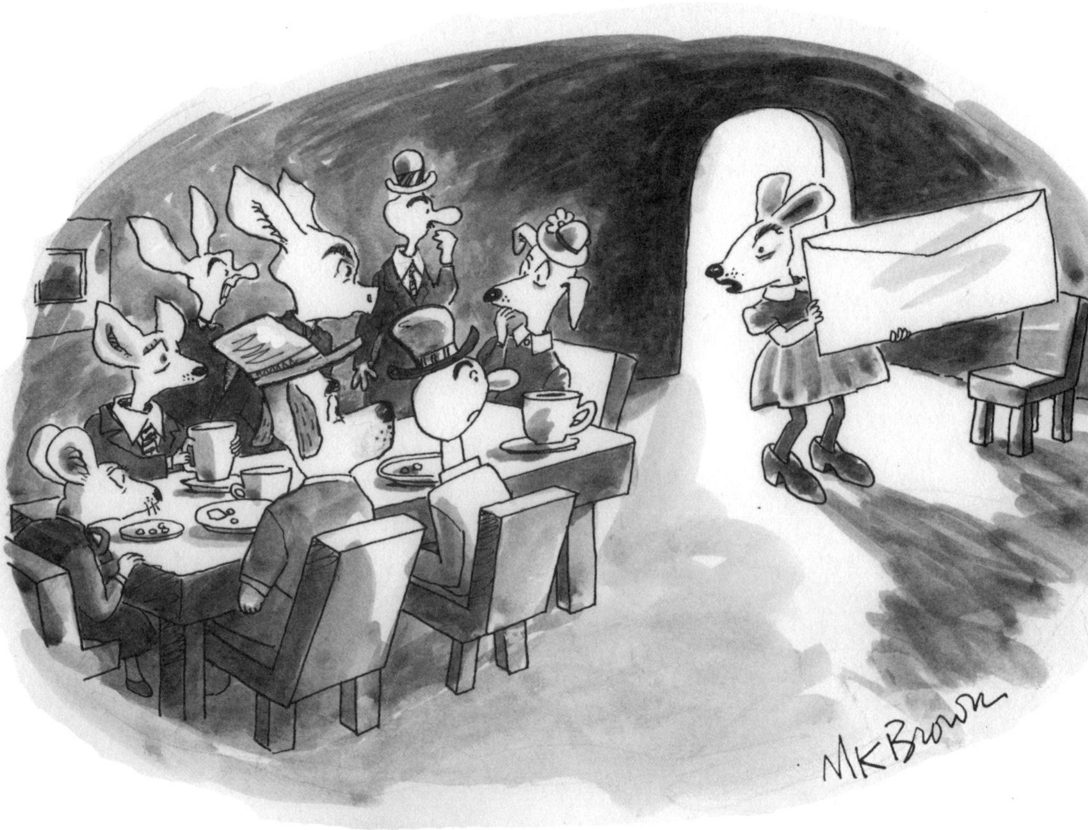
MKBrown

It's from Publishers Clearing House!

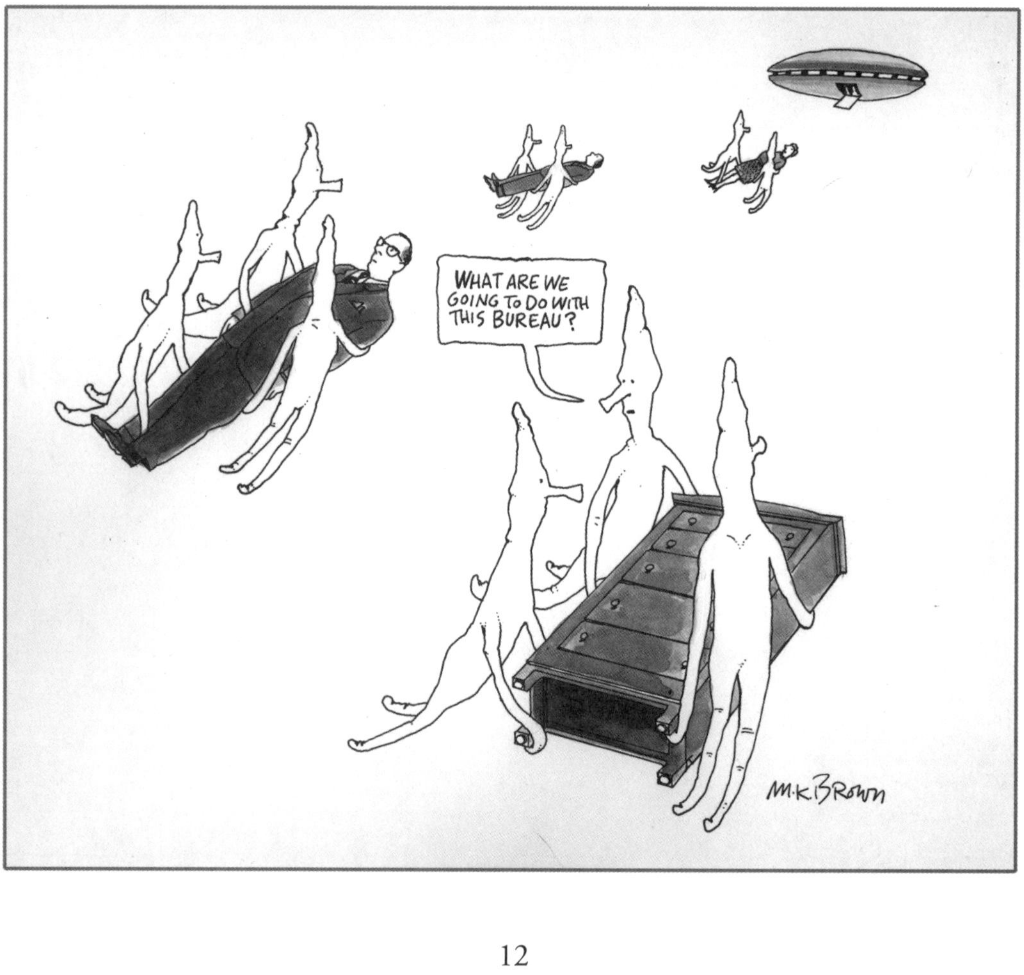
WHAT ARE WE GOING TO DO WITH THIS BUREAU?
M.K.Brown

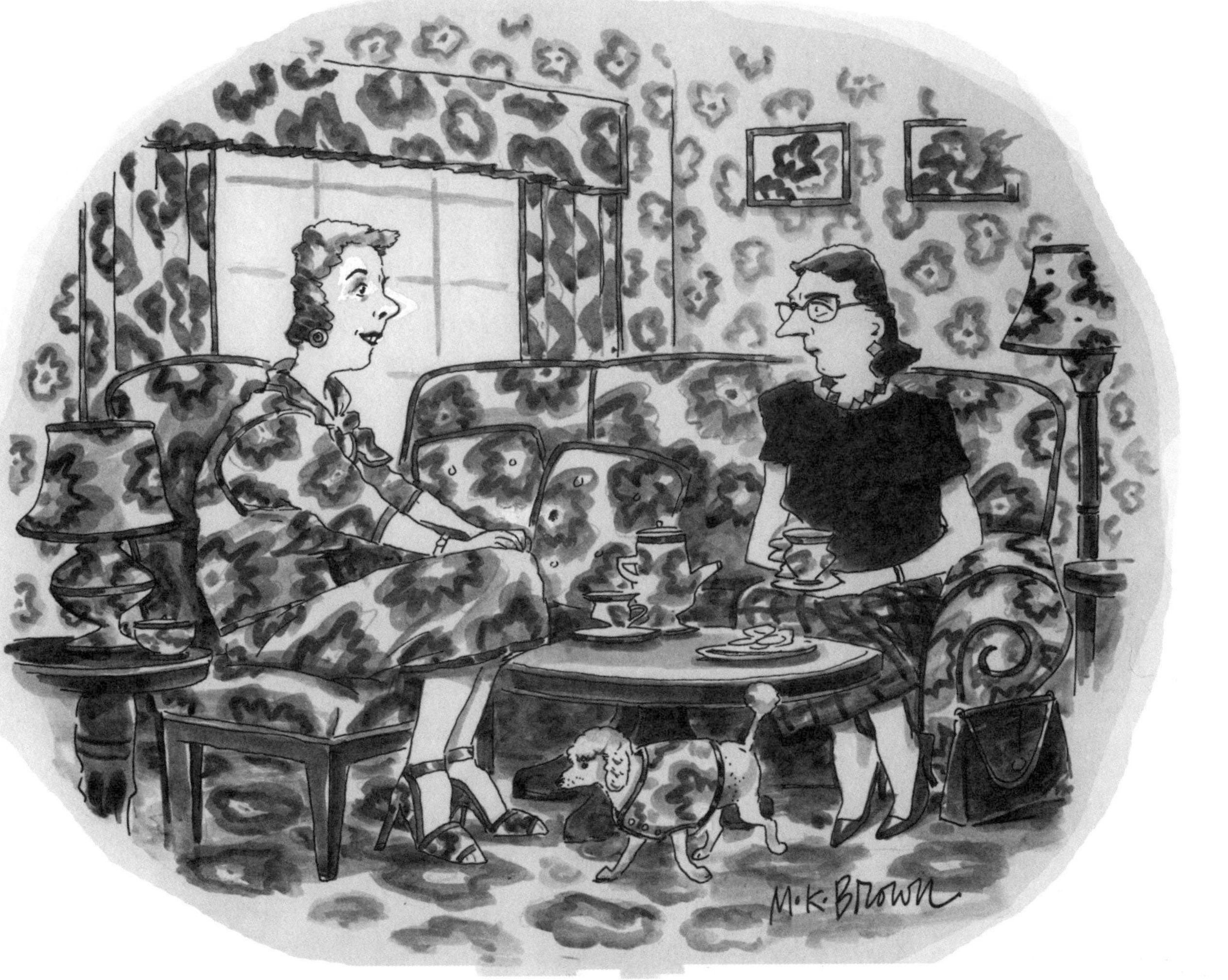
M·K·BROWN

It all began with wanting matching shoes and purse.

The words "snakes in the bathroom" came out of the air and I wrote them down. The phrase held a certain menace in a tropical sort of way. I wondered how the snakes got there, theoretically speaking, and practically speaking, how one would get them out.

When cartoon editor Sam Gross called from *National Lampoon* to ask if I had any ideas for a five-page color piece, I said, "How about snakes in the bathroom?"

He said, "Great!"

Because of creative editors like Sam Gross and Brian McConnachie, it was a pleasure to work with the magazine for so many years.

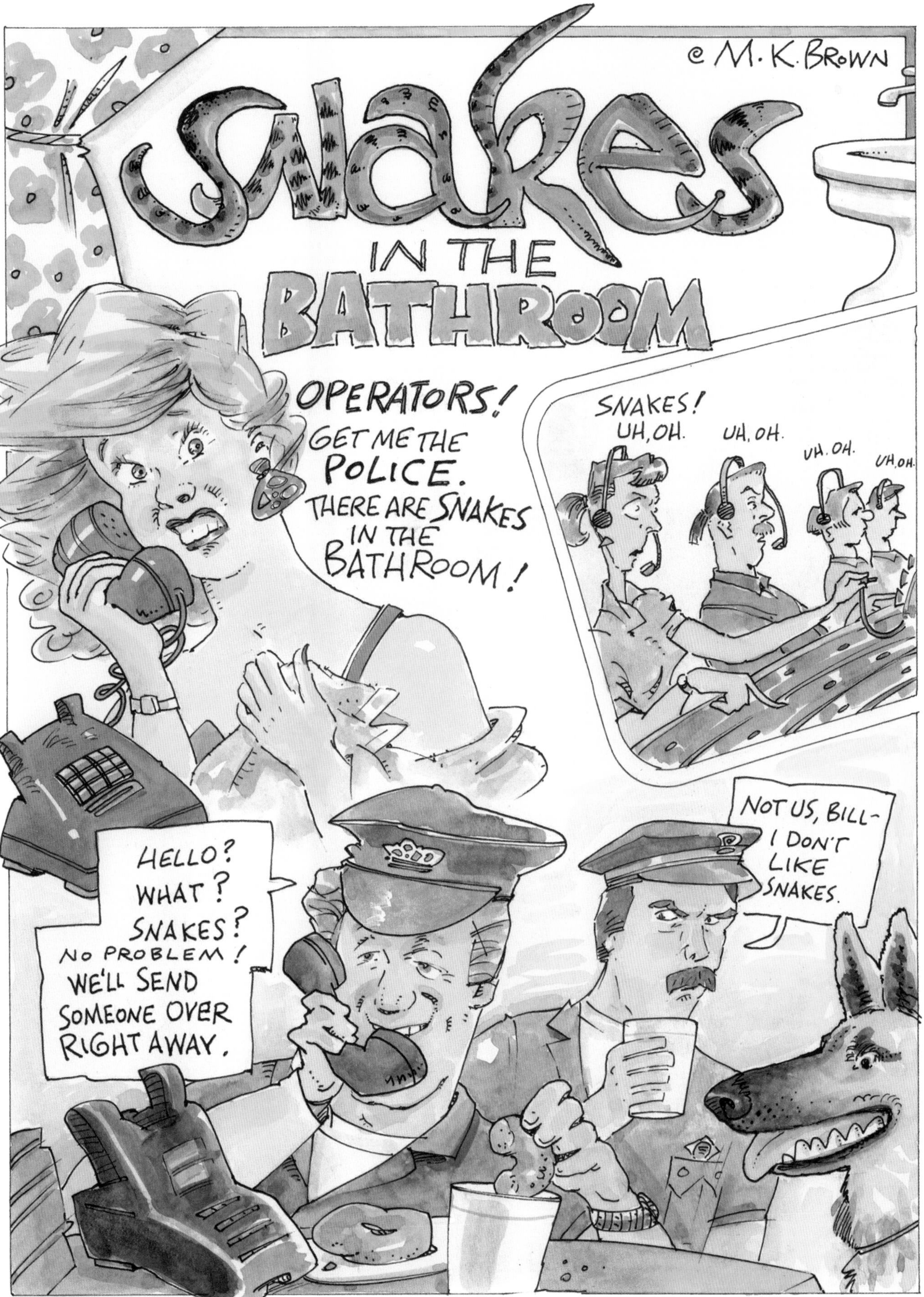
© M. K. BROWN
SNAKES IN THE BATHROOM
OPERATORS! GET ME THE POLICE. THERE ARE SNAKES IN THE BATHROOM!
SNAKES! UH, OH.
UH, OH.
UH, OH.
UH, OH.
HELLO? WHAT? SNAKES? NO PROBLEM! WE'LL SEND SOMEONE OVER RIGHT AWAY.
NOT US, BILL- I DON'T LIKE SNAKES.

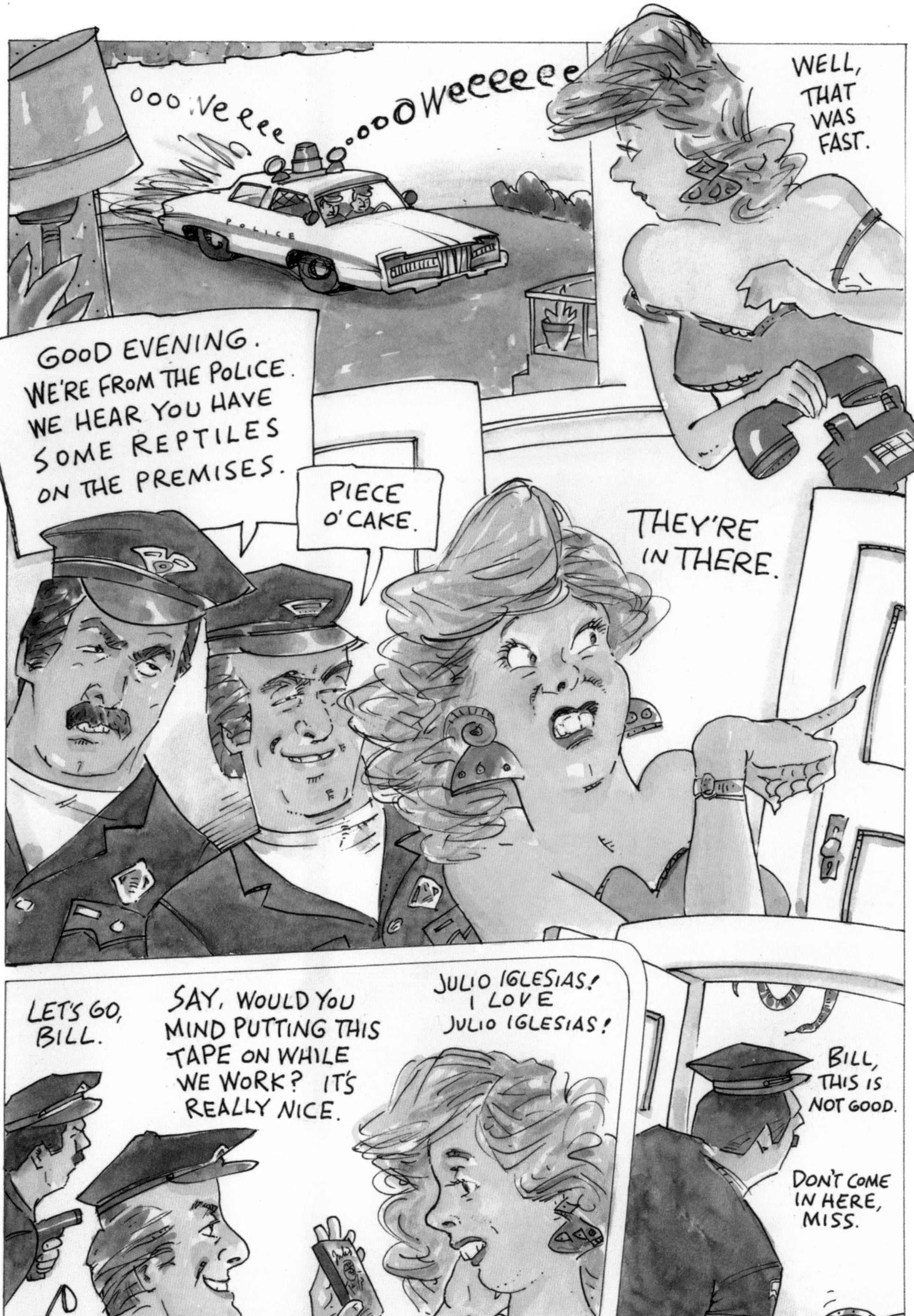
oooWeeee...oooWeeeeee
WELL, THAT WAS FAST.
GOOD EVENING. WE'RE FROM THE POLICE. WE HEAR YOU HAVE SOME REPTILES ON THE PREMISES.
PIECE O' CAKE.
THEY'RE IN THERE.
LET'S GO, BILL.
SAY, WOULD YOU MIND PUTTING THIS TAPE ON WHILE WE WORK? IT'S REALLY NICE.
JULIO IGLESIAS! I LOVE JULIO IGLESIAS!
BILL, THIS IS NOT GOOD.
DON'T COME IN HERE, MISS.

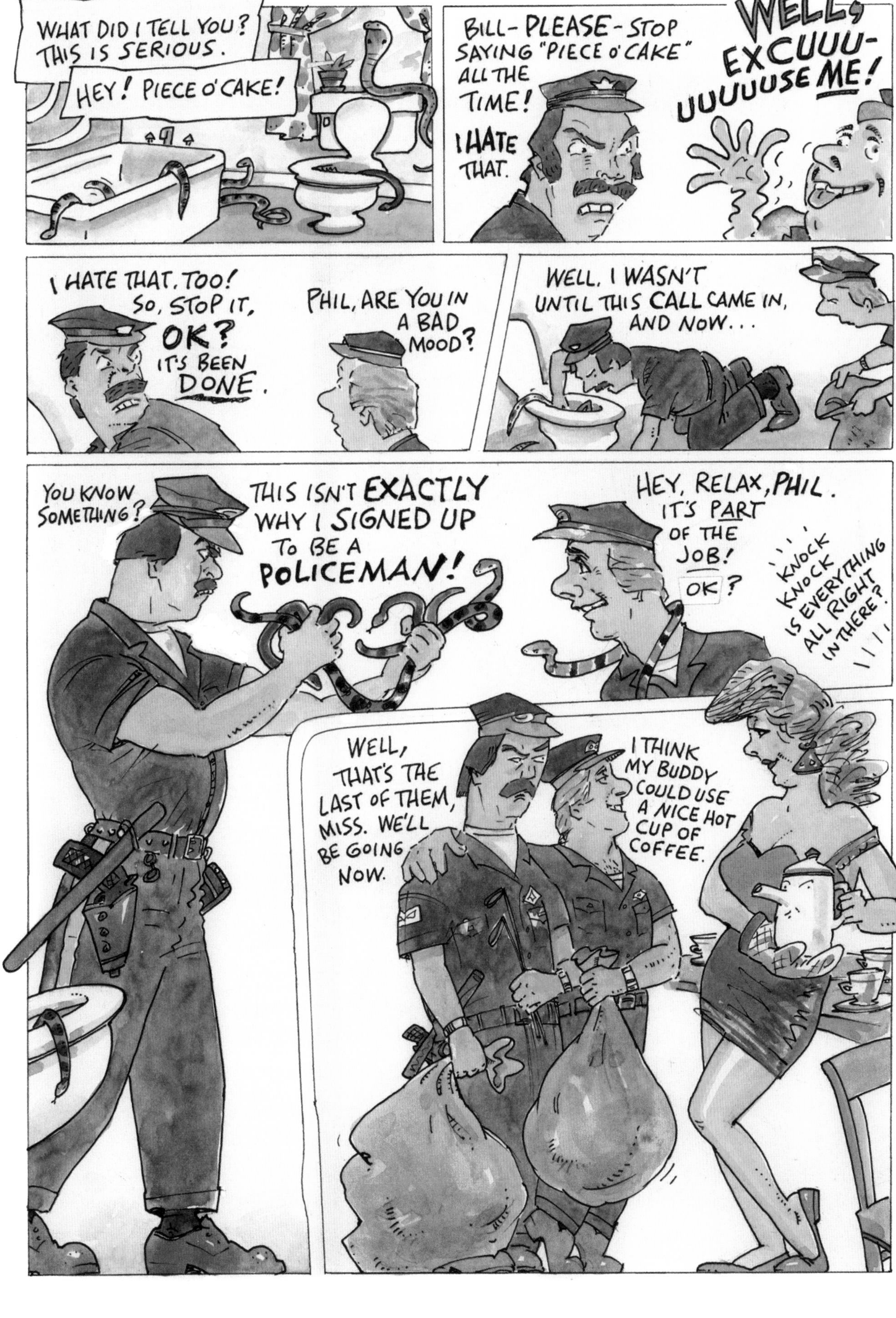
WHAT DID I TELL YOU? THIS IS SERIOUS.
HEY! PIECE O'CAKE!
BILL - PLEASE - STOP SAYING "PIECE O'CAKE" ALL THE TIME!
I HATE THAT.
WELL, EXCUUUUUUUUSE ME!
I HATE THAT, TOO! SO, STOP IT, OK? IT'S BEEN DONE.
PHIL, ARE YOU IN A BAD MOOD?
WELL, I WASN'T UNTIL THIS CALL CAME IN, AND NOW...
YOU KNOW SOMETHING?
THIS ISN'T EXACTLY WHY I SIGNED UP TO BE A POLICEMAN!
HEY, RELAX, PHIL. IT'S PART OF THE JOB!
OK?
KNOCK KNOCK
IS EVERYTHING ALL RIGHT IN THERE?
WELL, THAT'S THE LAST OF THEM, MISS. WE'LL BE GOING NOW.
I THINK MY BUDDY COULD USE A NICE HOT CUP OF COFFEE.

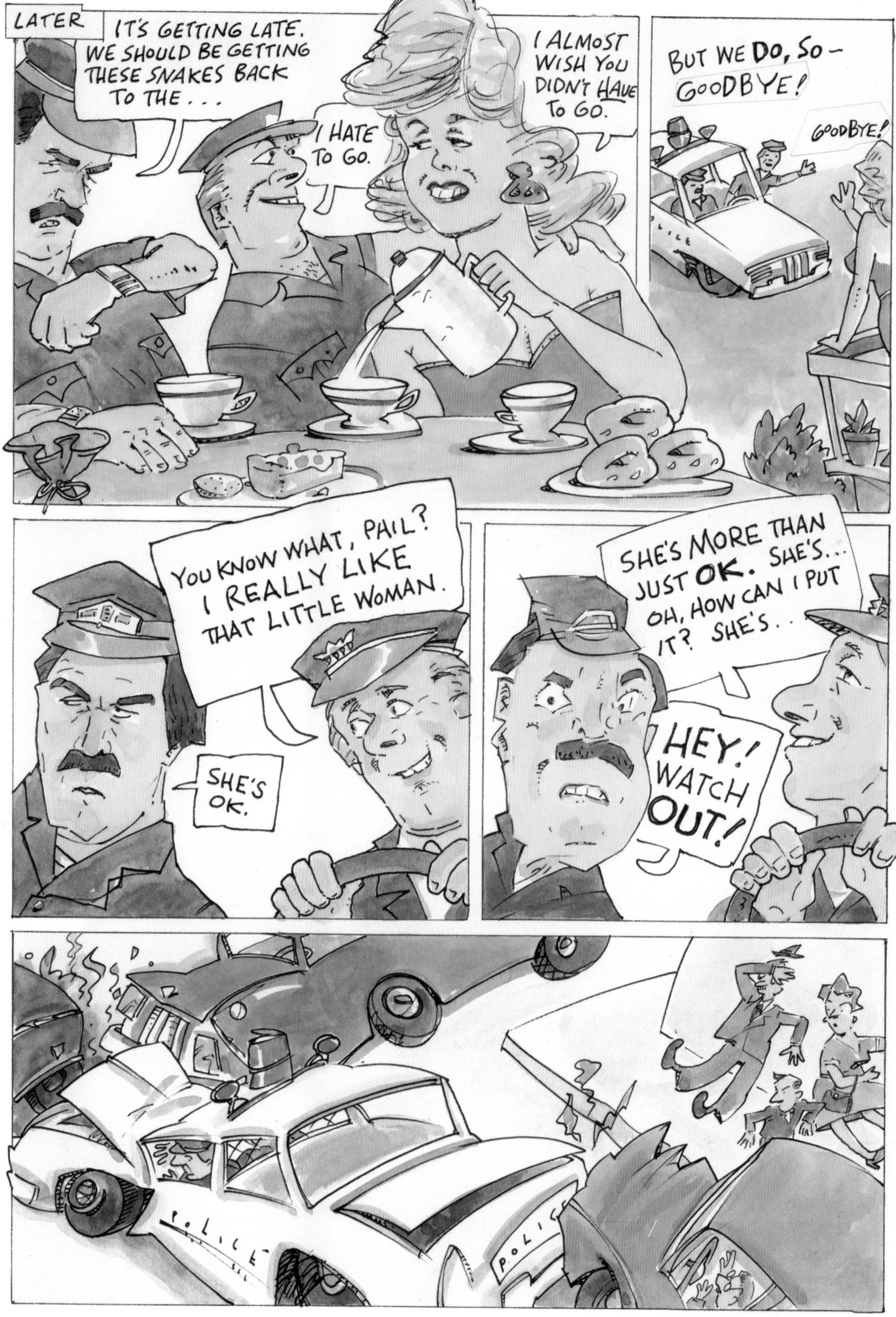
LATER
IT'S GETTING LATE. WE SHOULD BE GETTING THESE SNAKES BACK TO THE . . .
I HATE TO GO.
I ALMOST WISH YOU DIDN'T HAVE TO GO.
BUT WE DO, SO – GOODBYE!
GOODBYE!
POLICE
YOU KNOW WHAT, PAIL? I REALLY LIKE THAT LITTLE WOMAN.
SHE'S OK.
SHE'S MORE THAN JUST OK. SHE'S... OH, HOW CAN I PUT IT? SHE'S . . .
HEY! WATCH OUT!
POLICE
POLICE

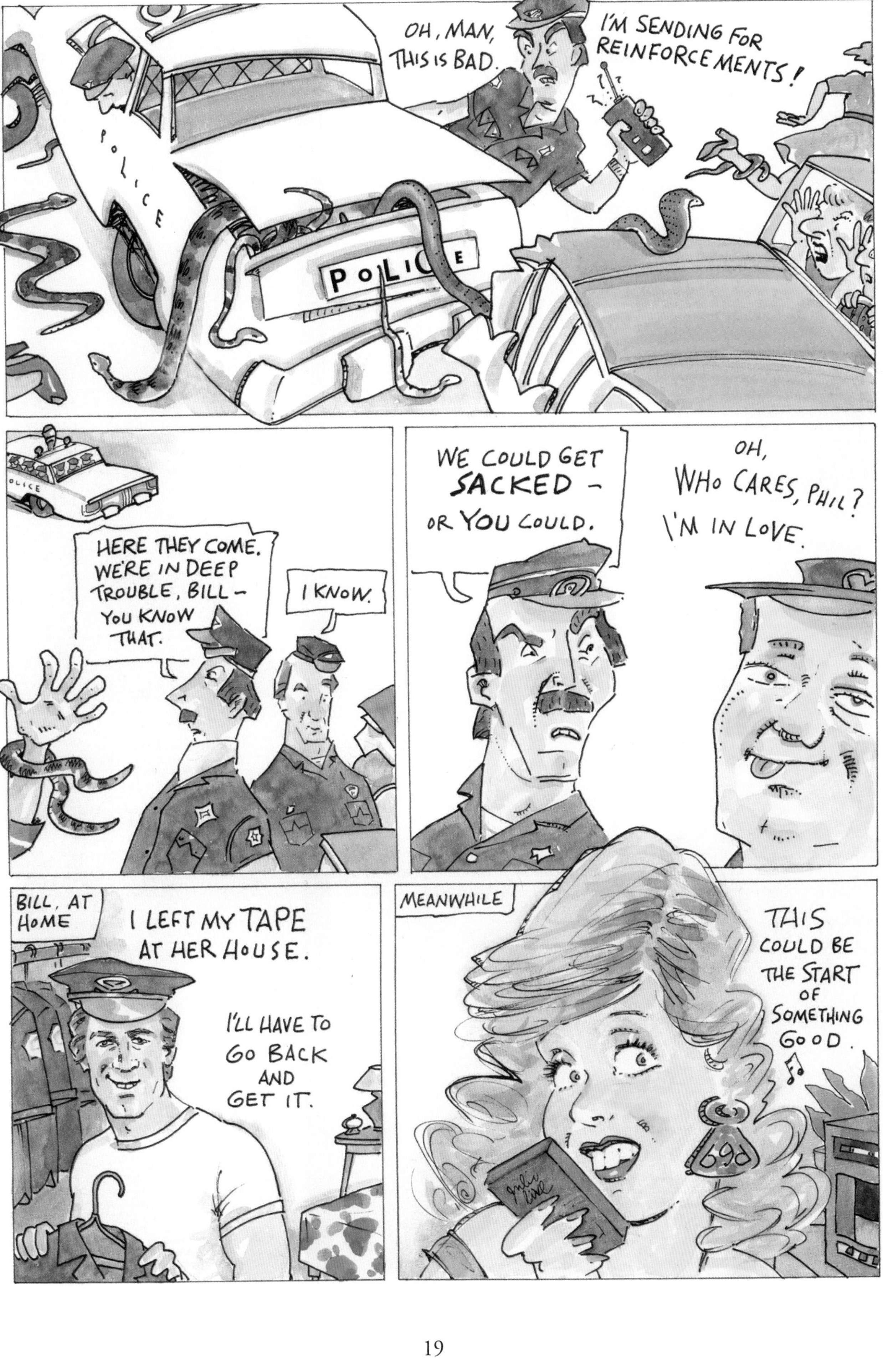

OH, MAN, THIS IS BAD.
I'M SENDING FOR REINFORCEMENTS!
POLICE
POLICE
POLICE
HERE THEY COME. WE'RE IN DEEP TROUBLE, BILL - YOU KNOW THAT.
I KNOW.
WE COULD GET SACKED - OR YOU COULD.
OH, WHO CARES, PHIL? I'M IN LOVE.
BILL, AT HOME
I LEFT MY TAPE AT HER HOUSE.
I'LL HAVE TO GO BACK AND GET IT.
MEANWHILE
THIS COULD BE THE START OF SOMETHING GOOD.

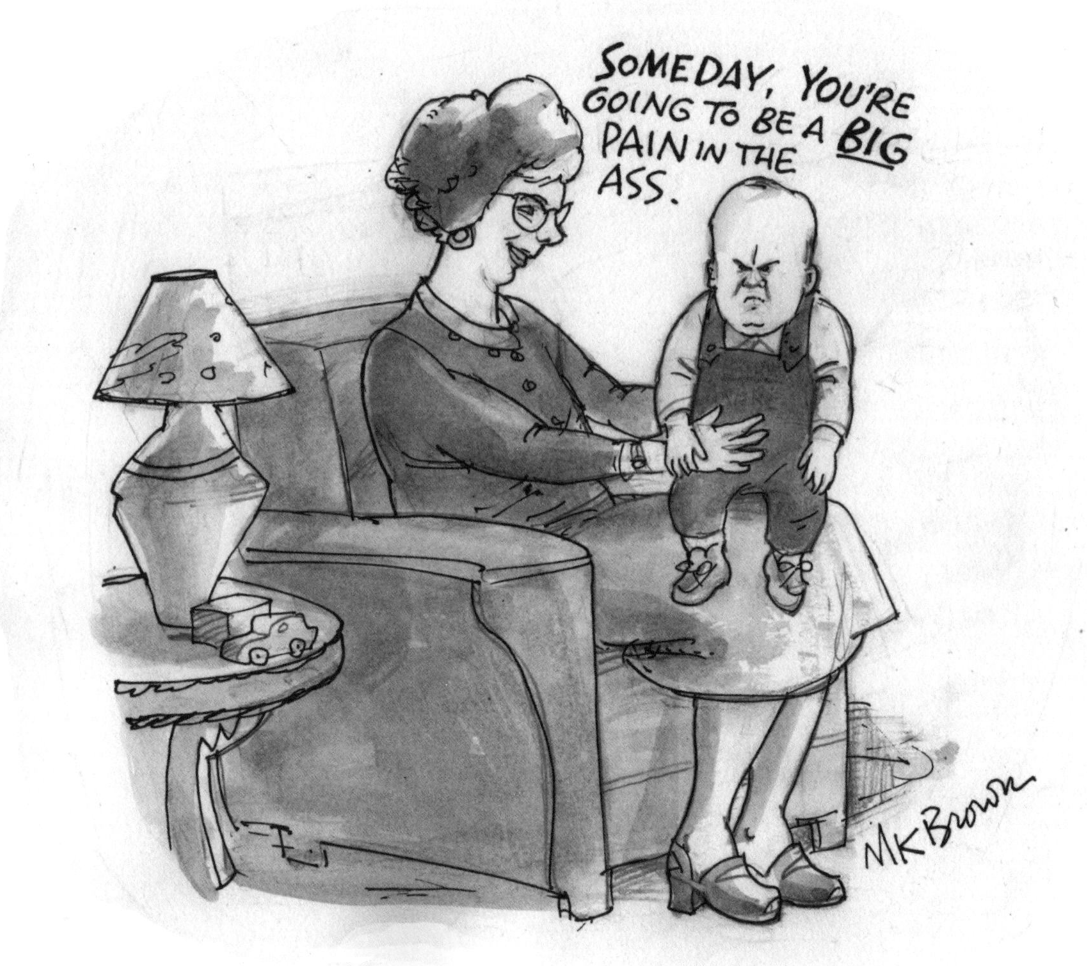
SOMEDAY, YOU'RE GOING TO BE A BIG PAIN IN THE ASS.
MKBrown

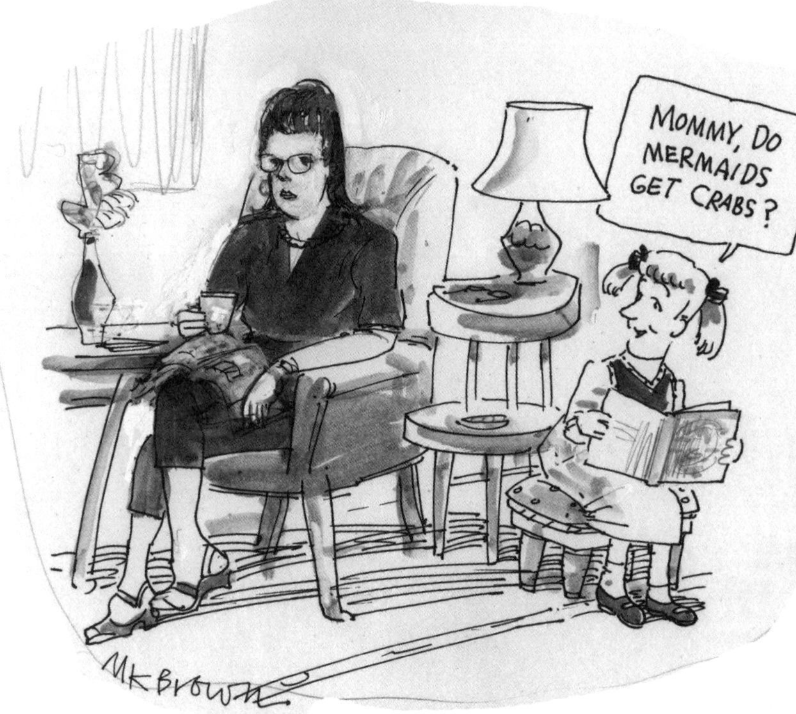
MOMMY, DO MERMAIDS GET CRABS?
MKBrown

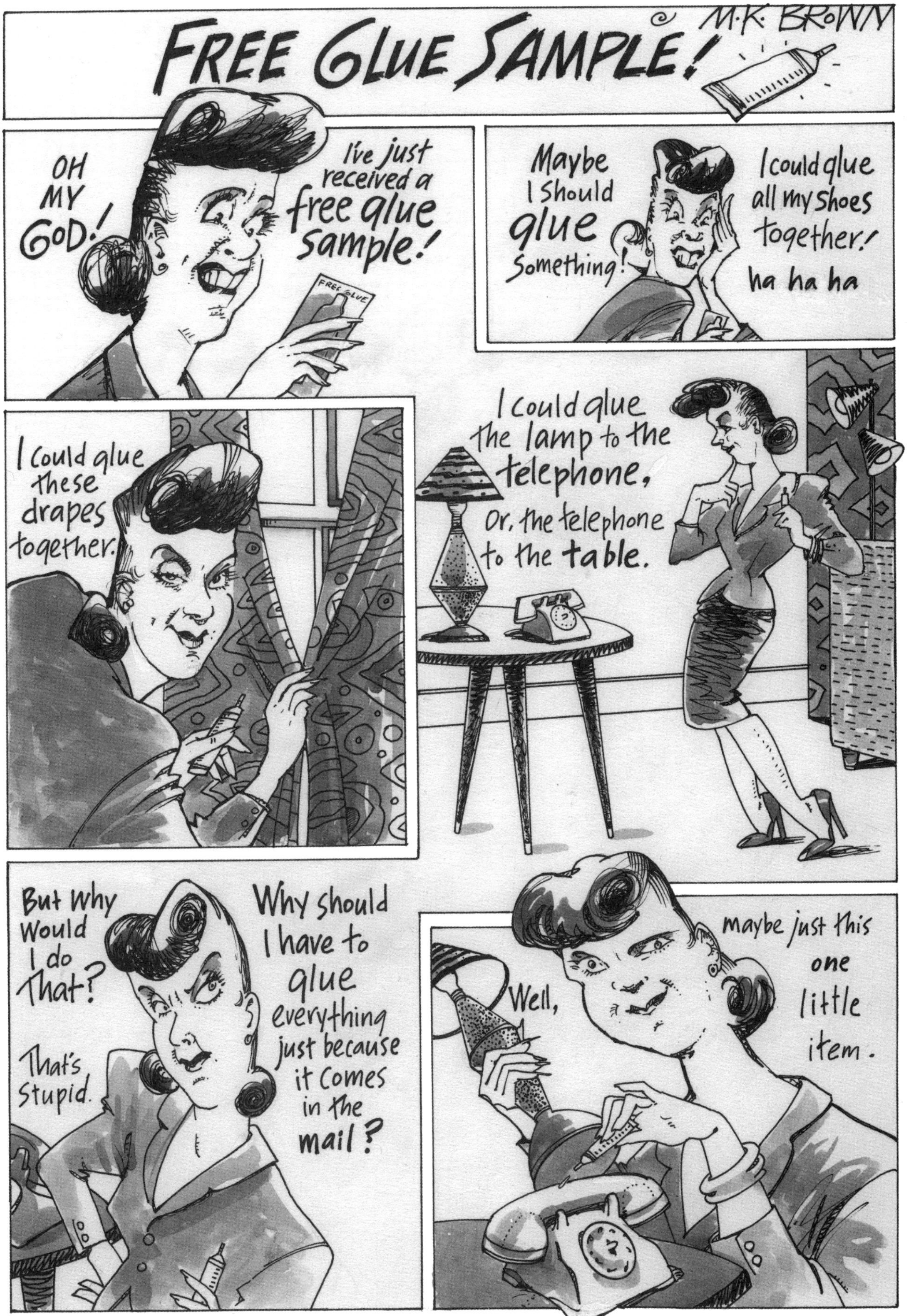
FREE GLUE SAMPLE!
© M.K. BROWN
OH MY GOD!
I've just received a free glue sample!
FREE GLUE
Maybe I Should glue Something!
I could glue all my shoes together!
ha ha ha
I could glue these drapes together.
I could glue the lamp to the telephone,
Or, the telephone to the table.
But Why Would I do That?
That's Stupid.
Why Should I have to glue everything just because it comes in the mail?
Well,
maybe just this one little item.

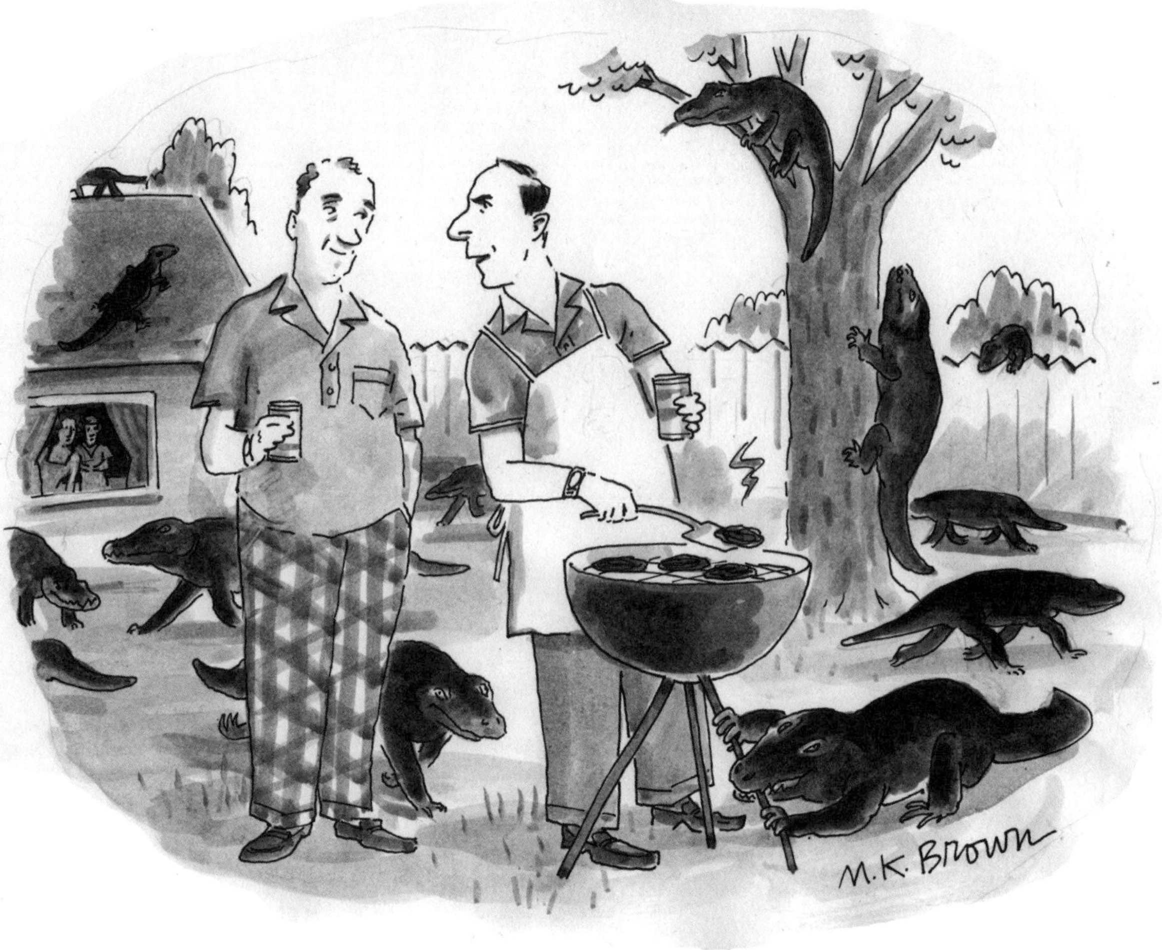
M.K. BROWN

We'd cook out more often if it weren't for these damned monitor lizards.

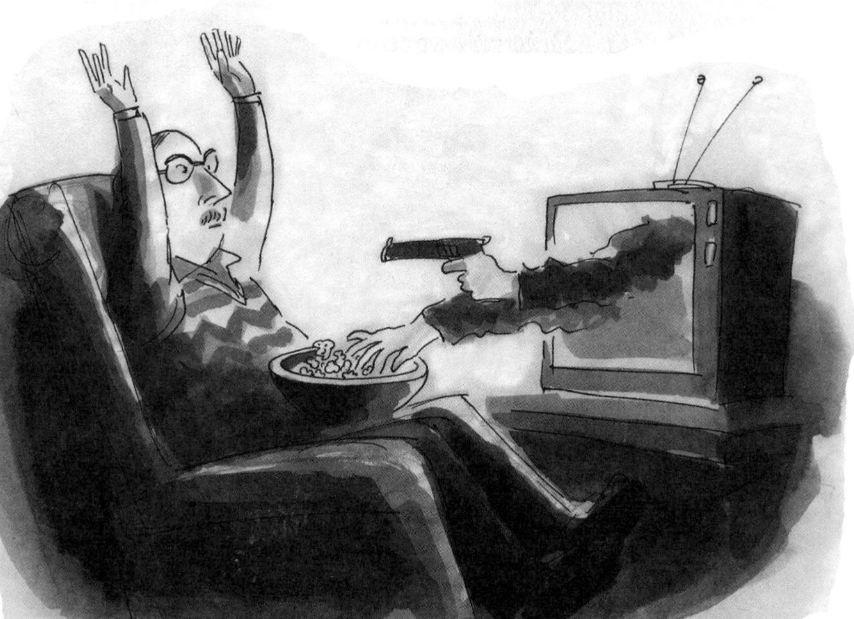

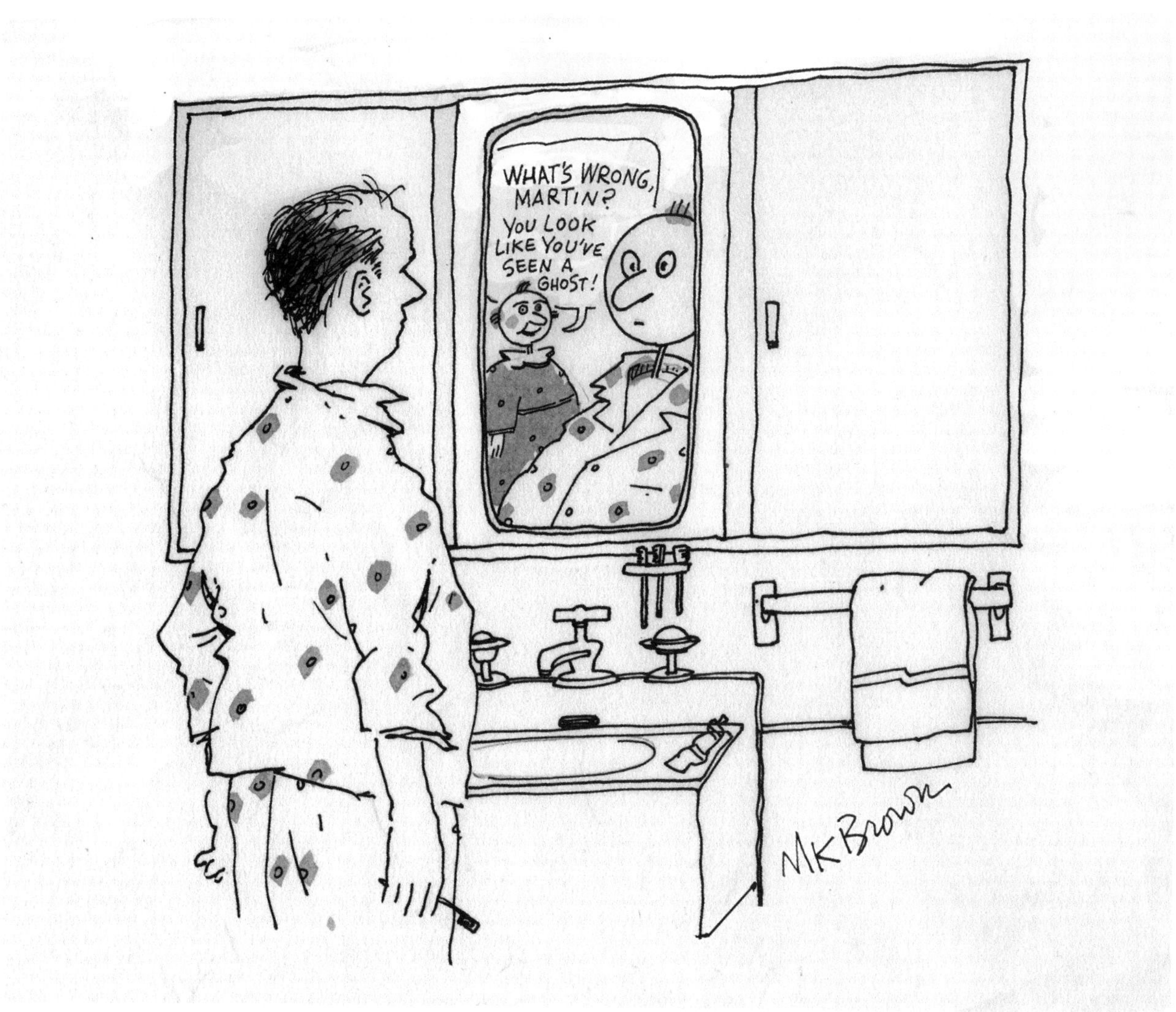
WHAT'S WRONG, MARTIN? YOU LOOK LIKE YOU'VE SEEN A GHOST!
MK BROWN

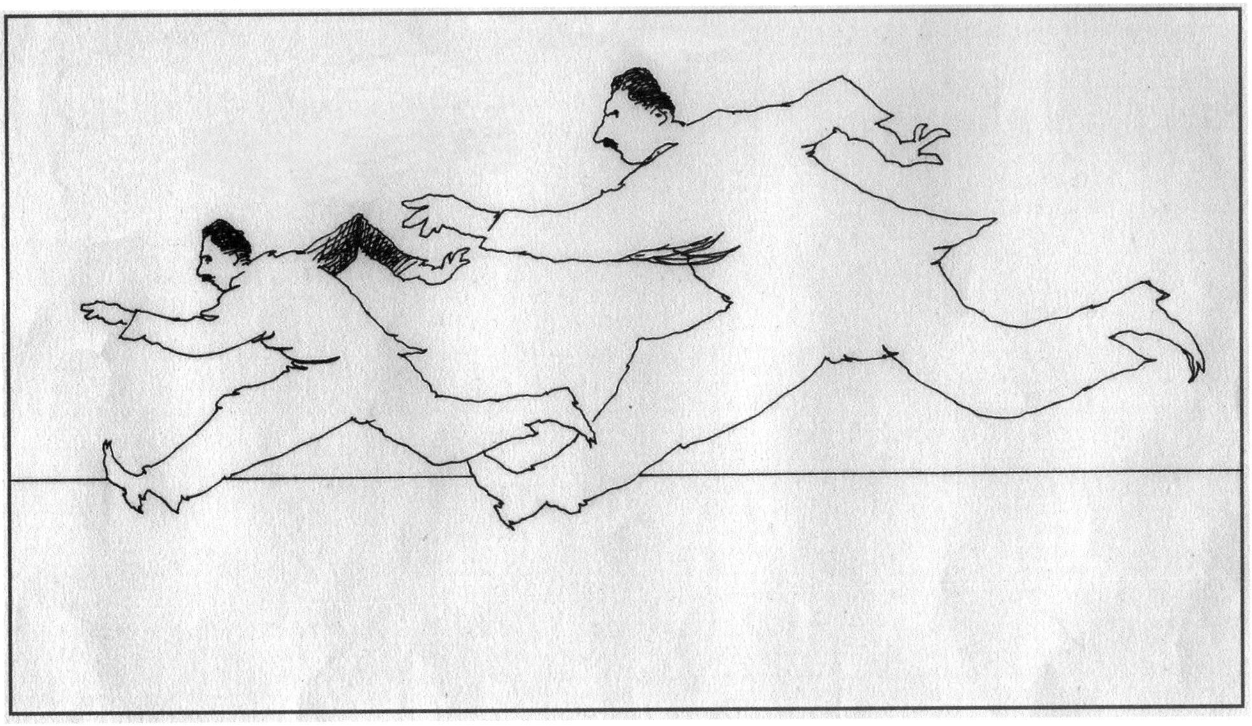

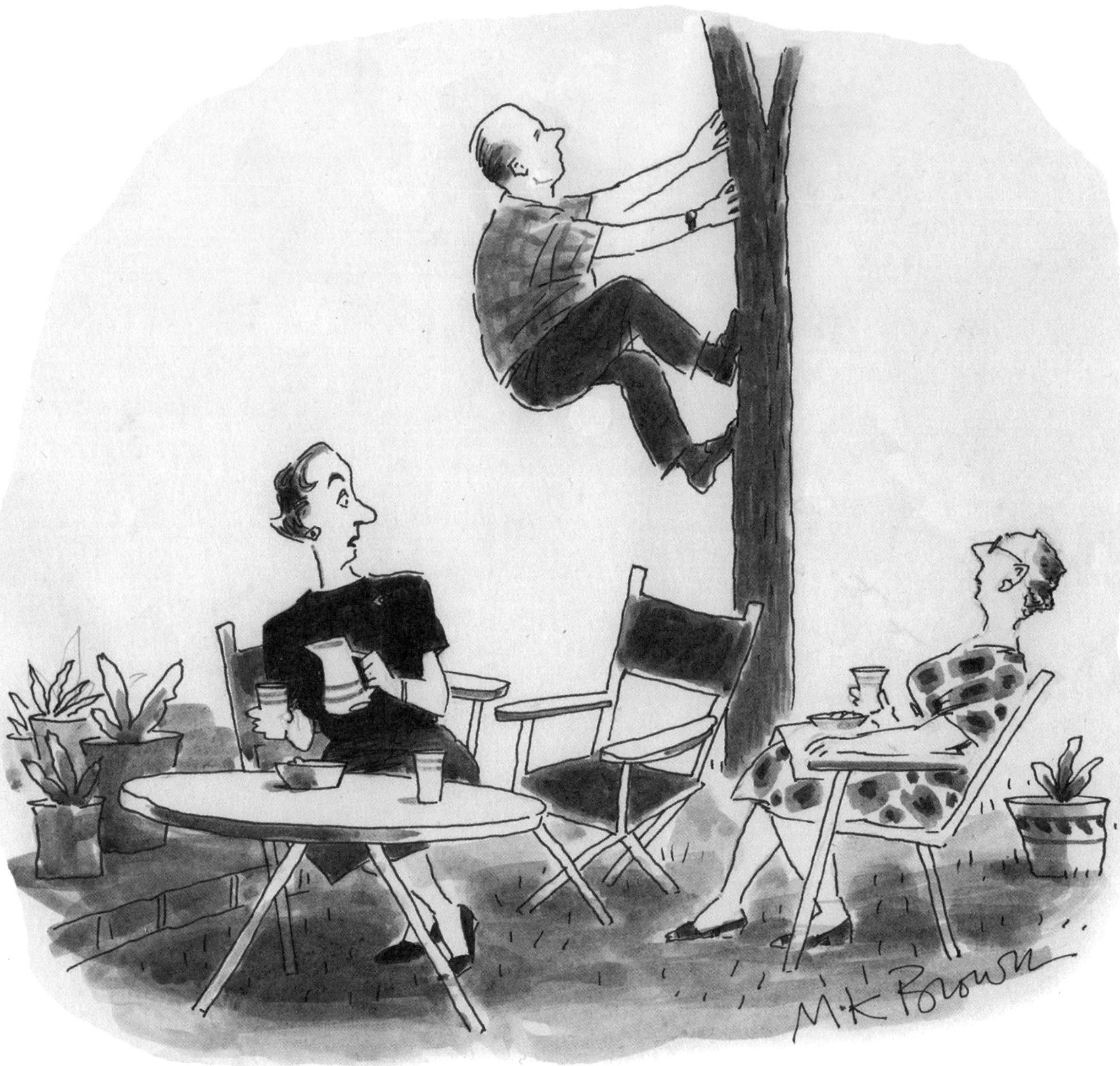
M.K. Brown

Where is *he* going?

It's just a lot yellower than we expected.

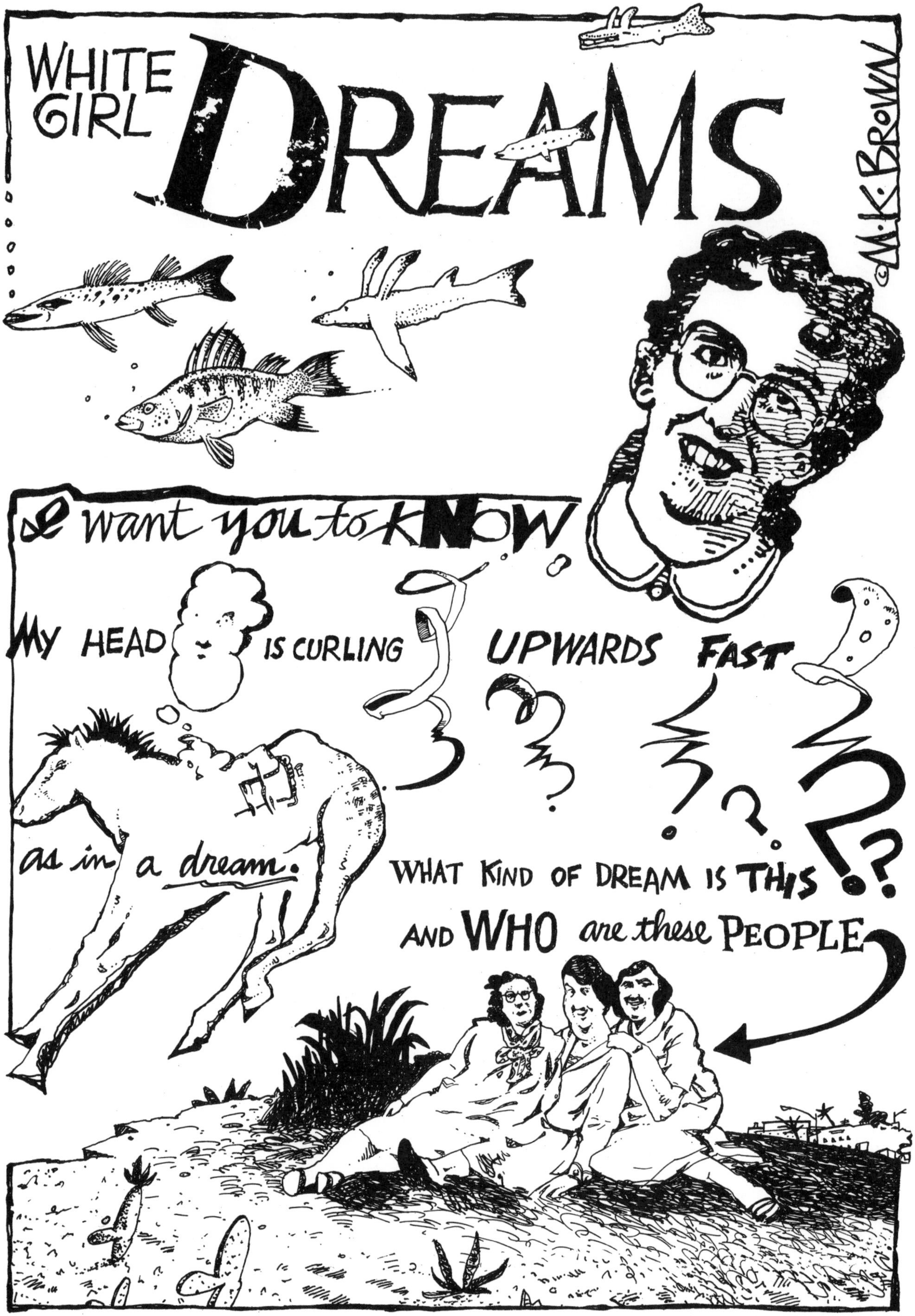
WHITE GIRL DREAMS
©M.K. BROWN
I want you to KNOW
MY HEAD IS CURLING UPWARDS FAST
as in a dream.
WHAT KIND OF DREAM IS THIS ?!?
AND WHO are these PEOPLE ?

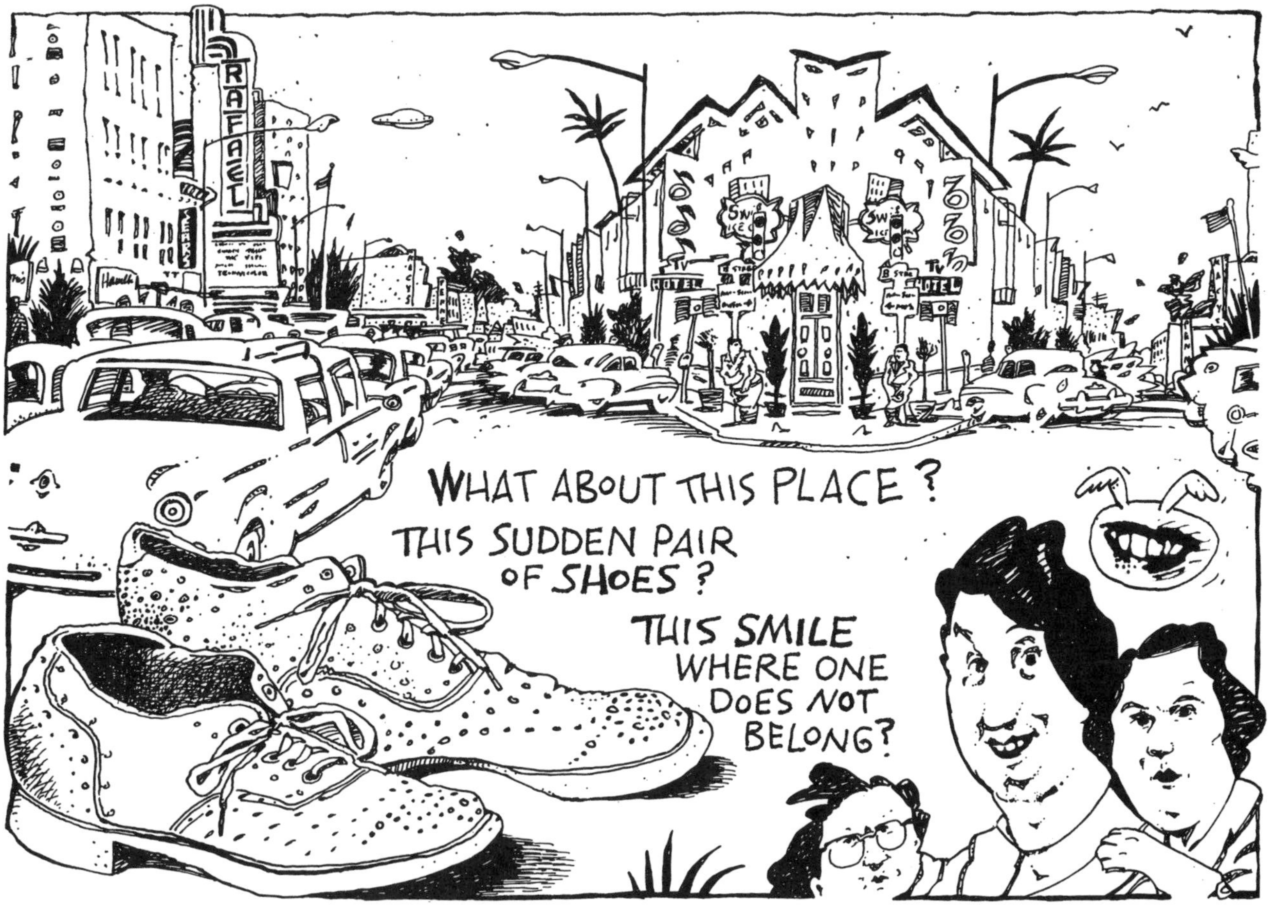
RAFAEL
HOTEL
HOTEL
WHAT ABOUT THIS PLACE?
THIS SUDDEN PAIR OF SHOES?
THIS SMILE WHERE ONE DOES NOT BELONG?

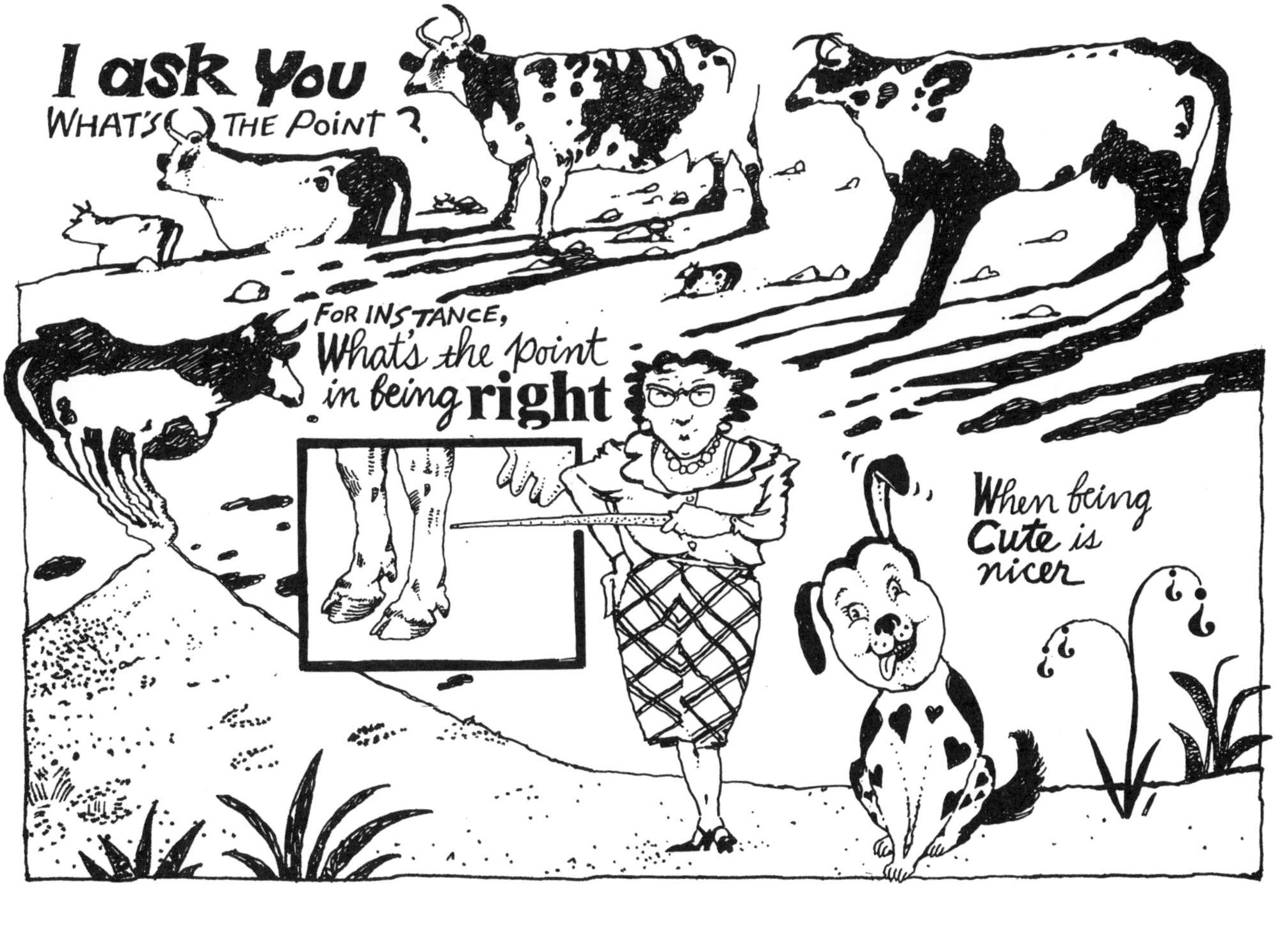
I ask You
WHAT'S THE POINT?
FOR INSTANCE,
What's the point in being right
When being Cute is nicer

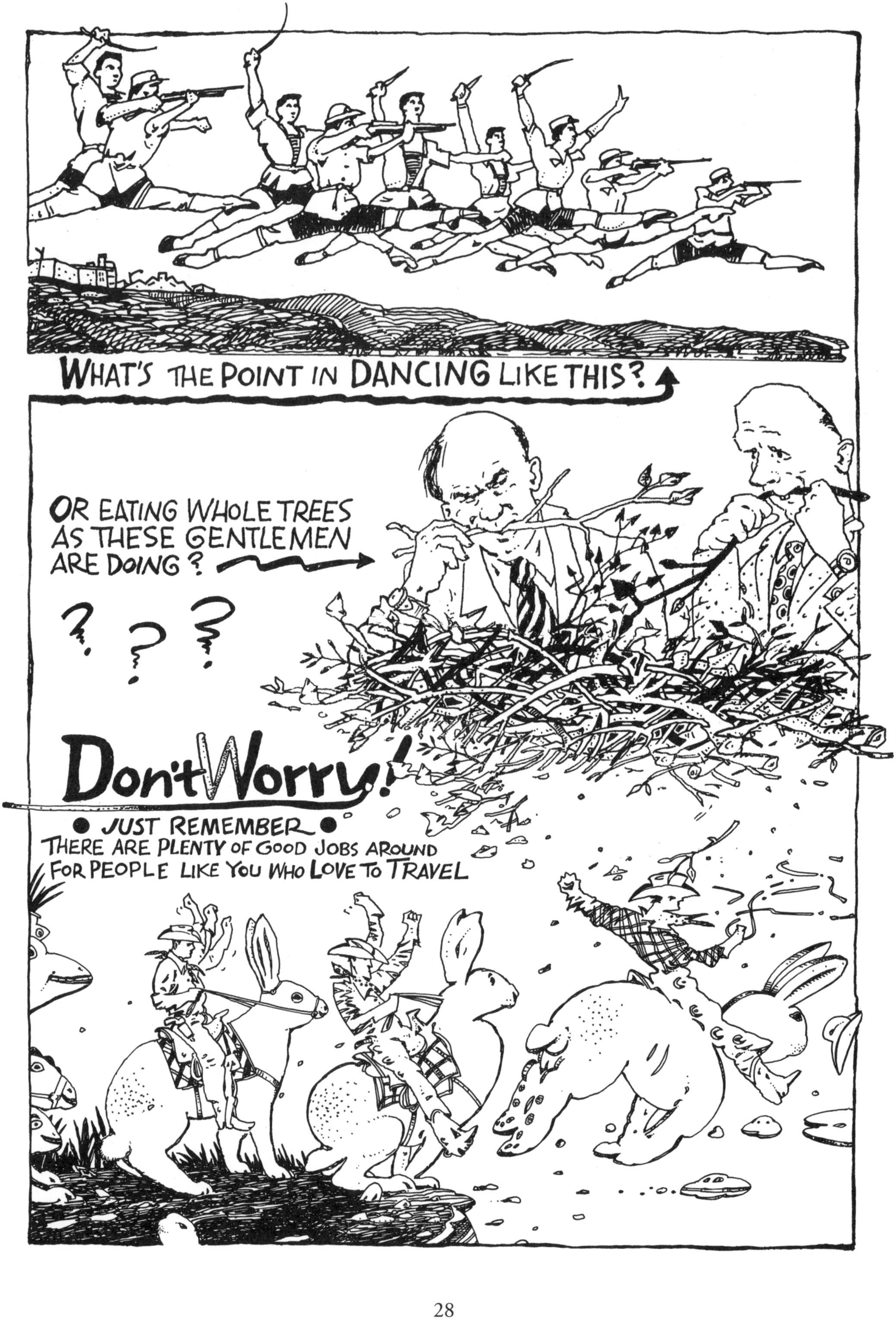

WHAT'S THE POINT IN DANCING LIKE THIS?
OR EATING WHOLE TREES AS THESE GENTLEMEN ARE DOING?
???
Don't Worry!
JUST REMEMBER
THERE ARE PLENTY OF GOOD JOBS AROUND FOR PEOPLE LIKE YOU WHO LOVE TO TRAVEL

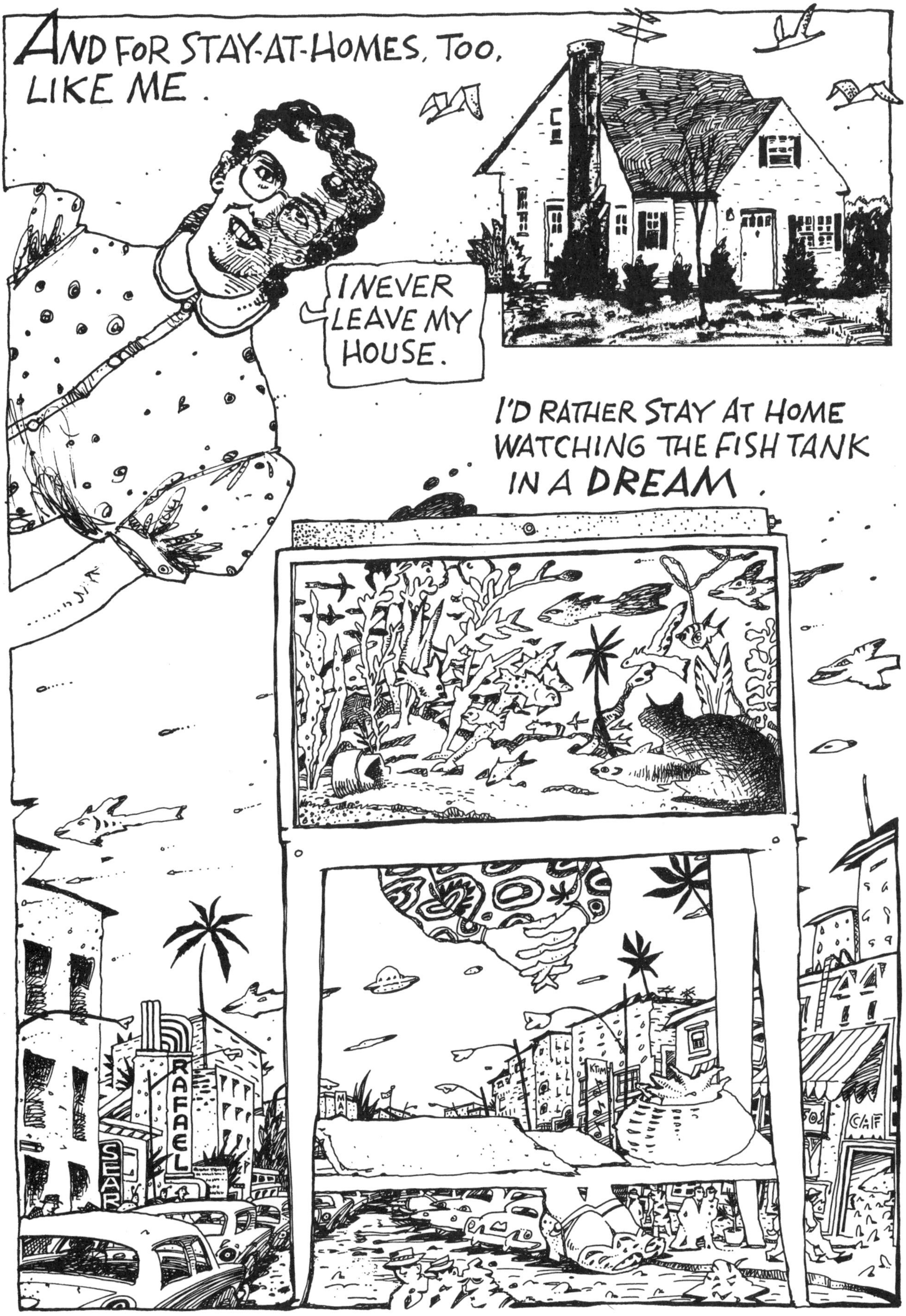
AND FOR STAY-AT-HOMES, TOO, LIKE ME.
I NEVER LEAVE MY HOUSE.
I'D RATHER STAY AT HOME WATCHING THE FISH TANK IN A DREAM.
RAFAEL

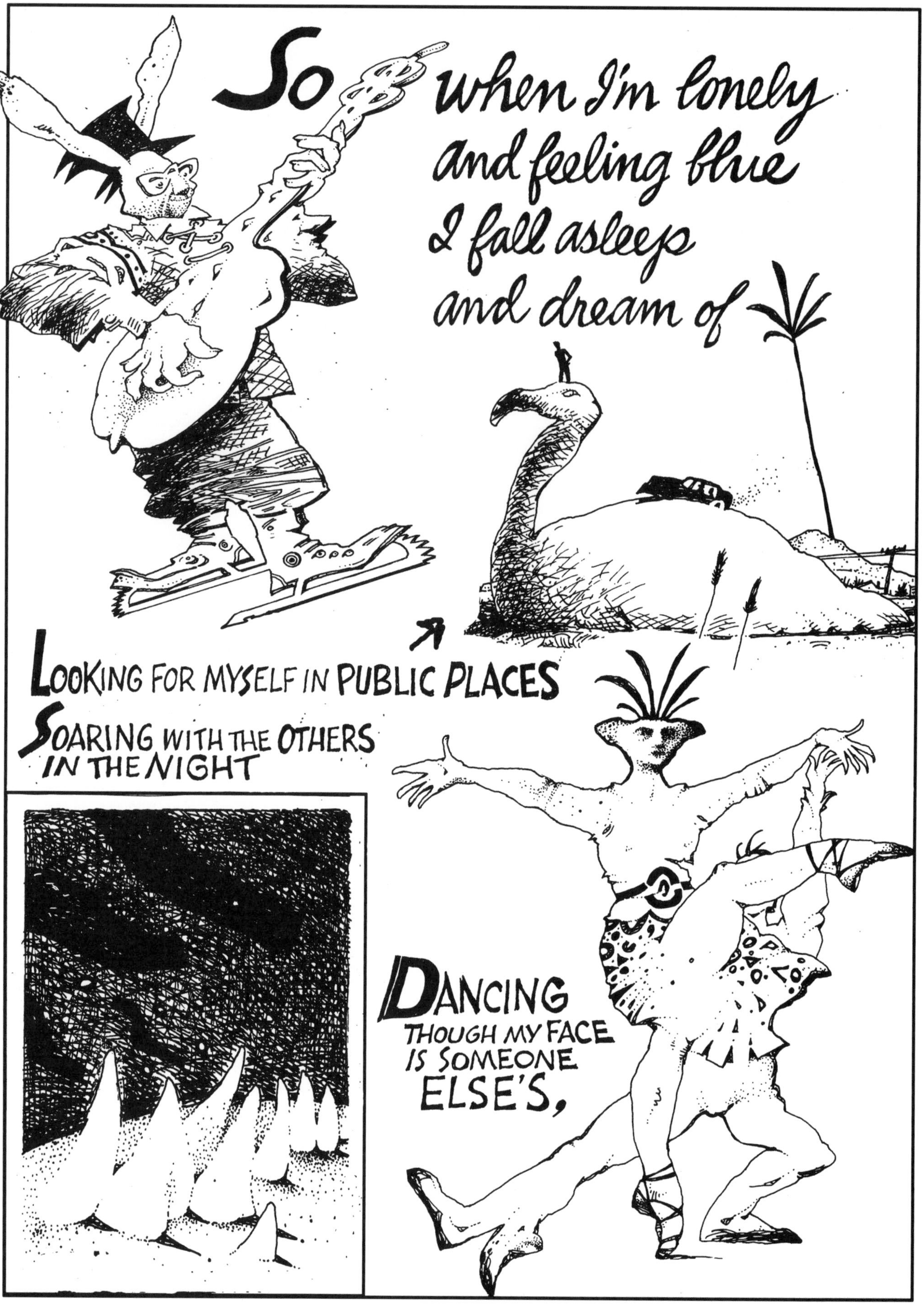

So when I'm lonely
and feeling blue
I fall asleep
and dream of
LOOKING FOR MYSELF IN PUBLIC PLACES
SOARING WITH THE OTHERS IN THE NIGHT
DANCING THOUGH MY FACE IS SOMEONE ELSE'S,

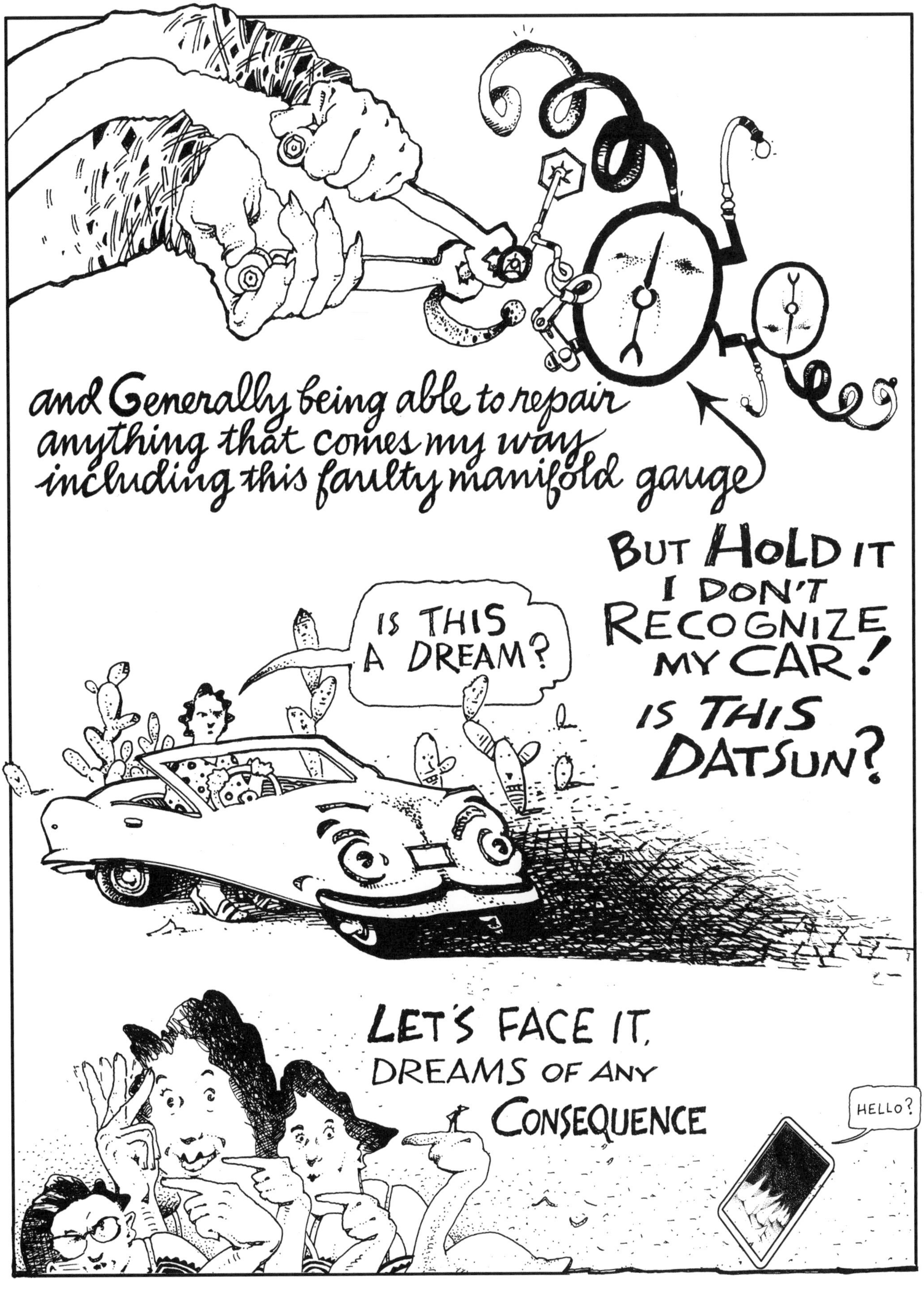

and Generally being able to repair anything that comes my way including this faulty manifold gauge
BUT HOLD IT I DON'T RECOGNIZE MY CAR!
IS THIS A DREAM?
IS THIS DATSUN?
LET'S FACE IT, DREAMS OF ANY CONSEQUENCE
HELLO?

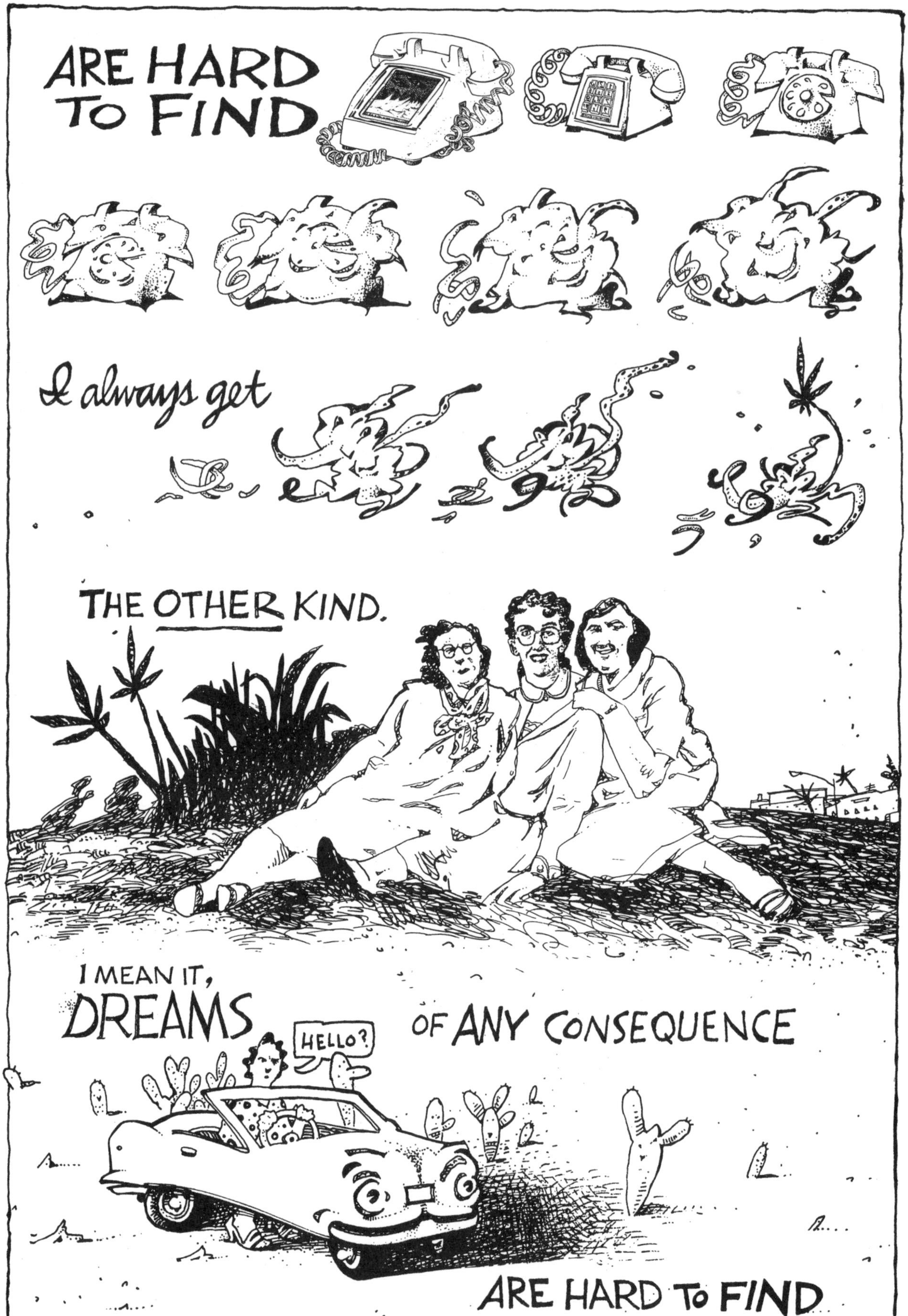
ARE HARD TO FIND
I always get
THE OTHER KIND.
I MEAN IT, DREAMS
HELLO?
OF ANY CONSEQUENCE
ARE HARD TO FIND

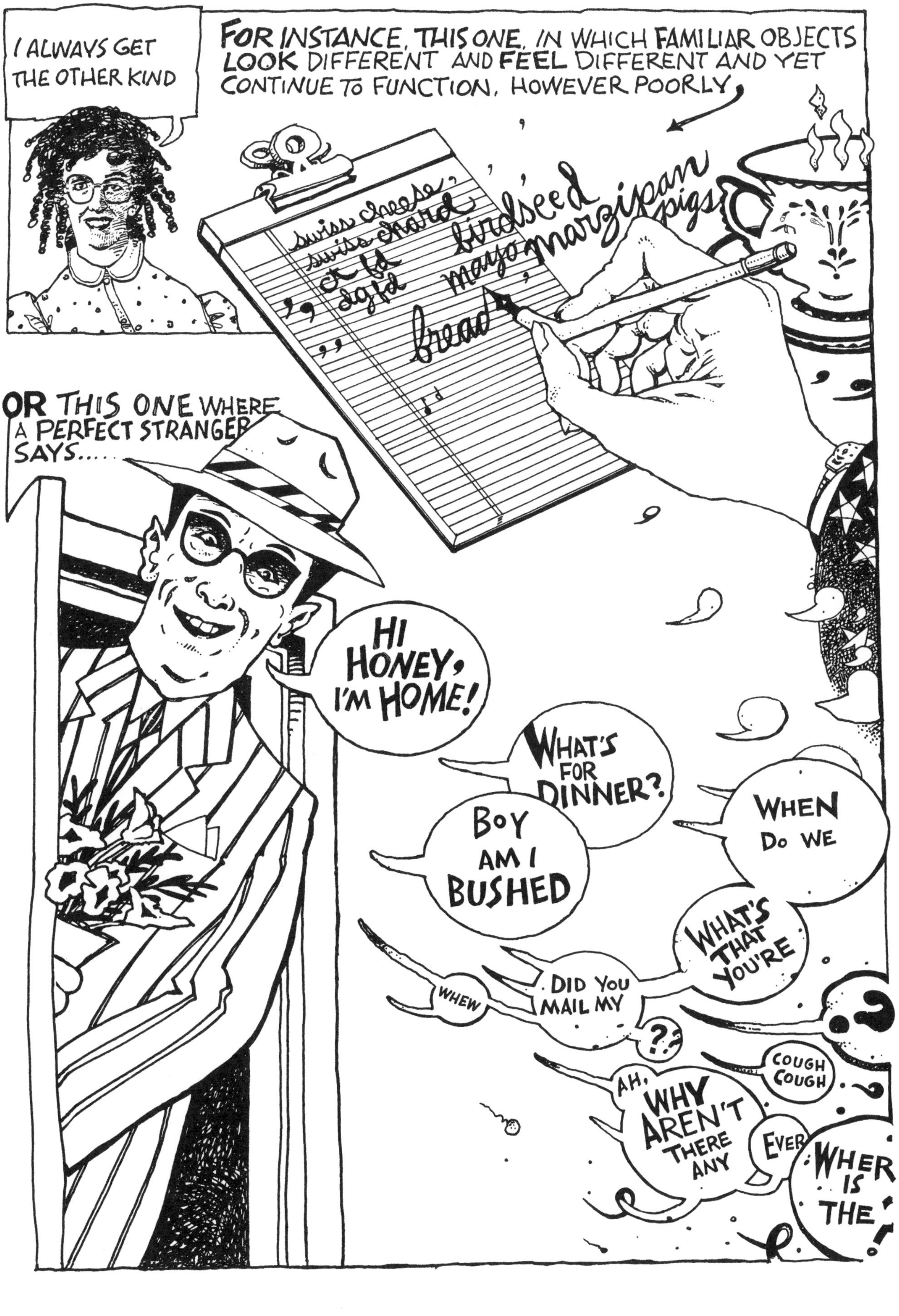

I ALWAYS GET THE OTHER KIND
FOR INSTANCE, THIS ONE, IN WHICH FAMILIAR OBJECTS LOOK DIFFERENT AND FEEL DIFFERENT AND YET CONTINUE TO FUNCTION, HOWEVER POORLY,
swiss cheese
swiss chard
birdseed
marzipan
pigs
mayo
bread
OR THIS ONE WHERE A PERFECT STRANGER SAYS....
HI HONEY, I'M HOME!
WHAT'S FOR DINNER?
BOY AM I BUSHED
WHEN DO WE
WHAT'S THAT YOU'RE
WHEW
DID YOU MAIL MY
AH, WHY AREN'T THERE ANY
COUGH COUGH
EVER
WHER IS THE

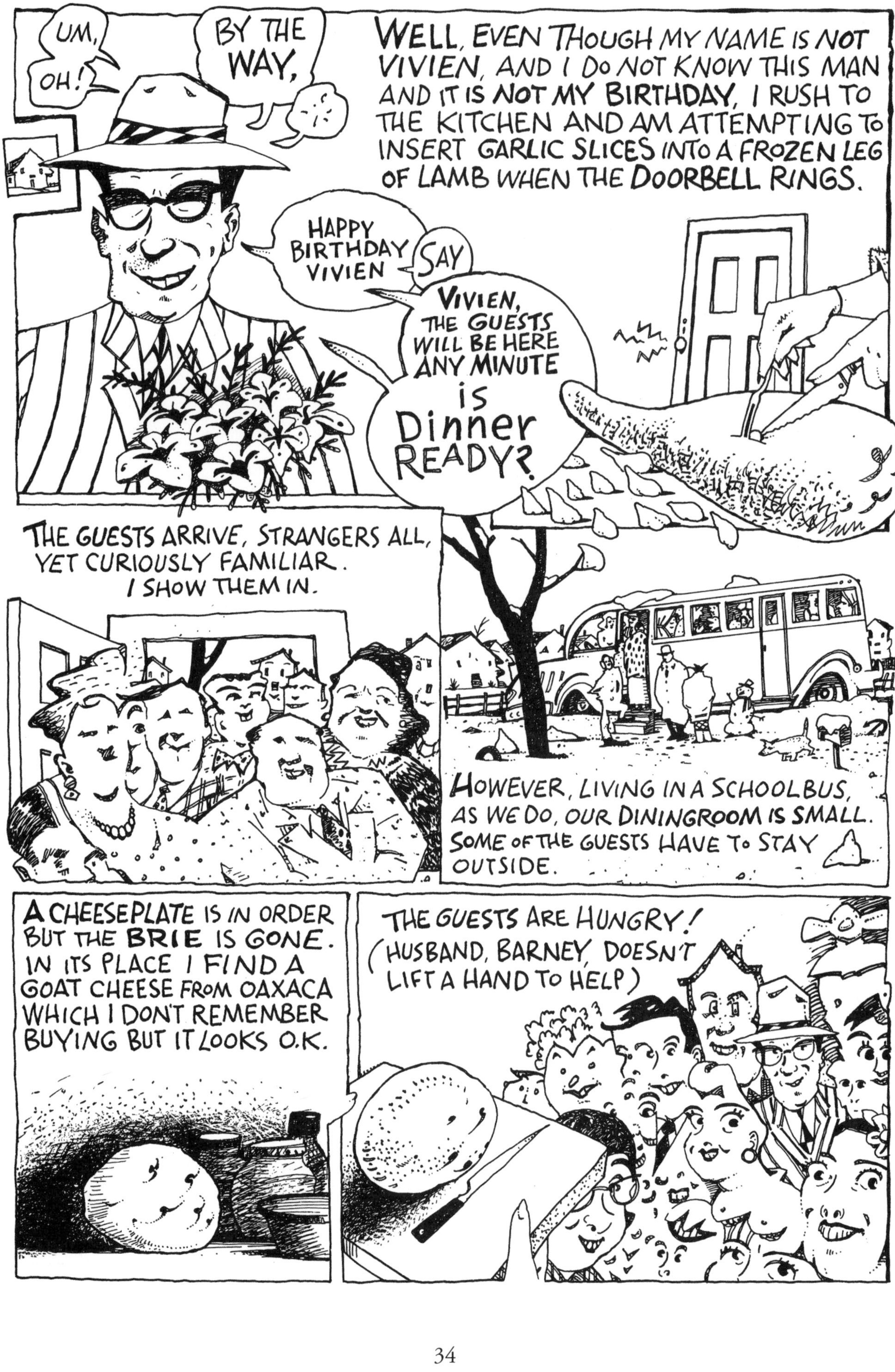
UM, OH!
BY THE WAY,
WELL, EVEN THOUGH MY NAME IS NOT VIVIEN, AND I DO NOT KNOW THIS MAN AND IT IS NOT MY BIRTHDAY, I RUSH TO THE KITCHEN AND AM ATTEMPTING TO INSERT GARLIC SLICES INTO A FROZEN LEG OF LAMB WHEN THE DOORBELL RINGS.
HAPPY BIRTHDAY VIVIEN
SAY
VIVIEN, THE GUESTS WILL BE HERE ANY MINUTE
is Dinner READY?
THE GUESTS ARRIVE, STRANGERS ALL, YET CURIOUSLY FAMILIAR. I SHOW THEM IN.
HOWEVER, LIVING IN A SCHOOLBUS, AS WE DO, OUR DININGROOM IS SMALL. SOME OF THE GUESTS HAVE TO STAY OUTSIDE.
A CHEESEPLATE IS IN ORDER BUT THE BRIE IS GONE. IN ITS PLACE I FIND A GOAT CHEESE FROM OAXACA WHICH I DON'T REMEMBER BUYING BUT IT LOOKS O.K.
THE GUESTS ARE HUNGRY! (HUSBAND, BARNEY, DOESN'T LIFT A HAND TO HELP)

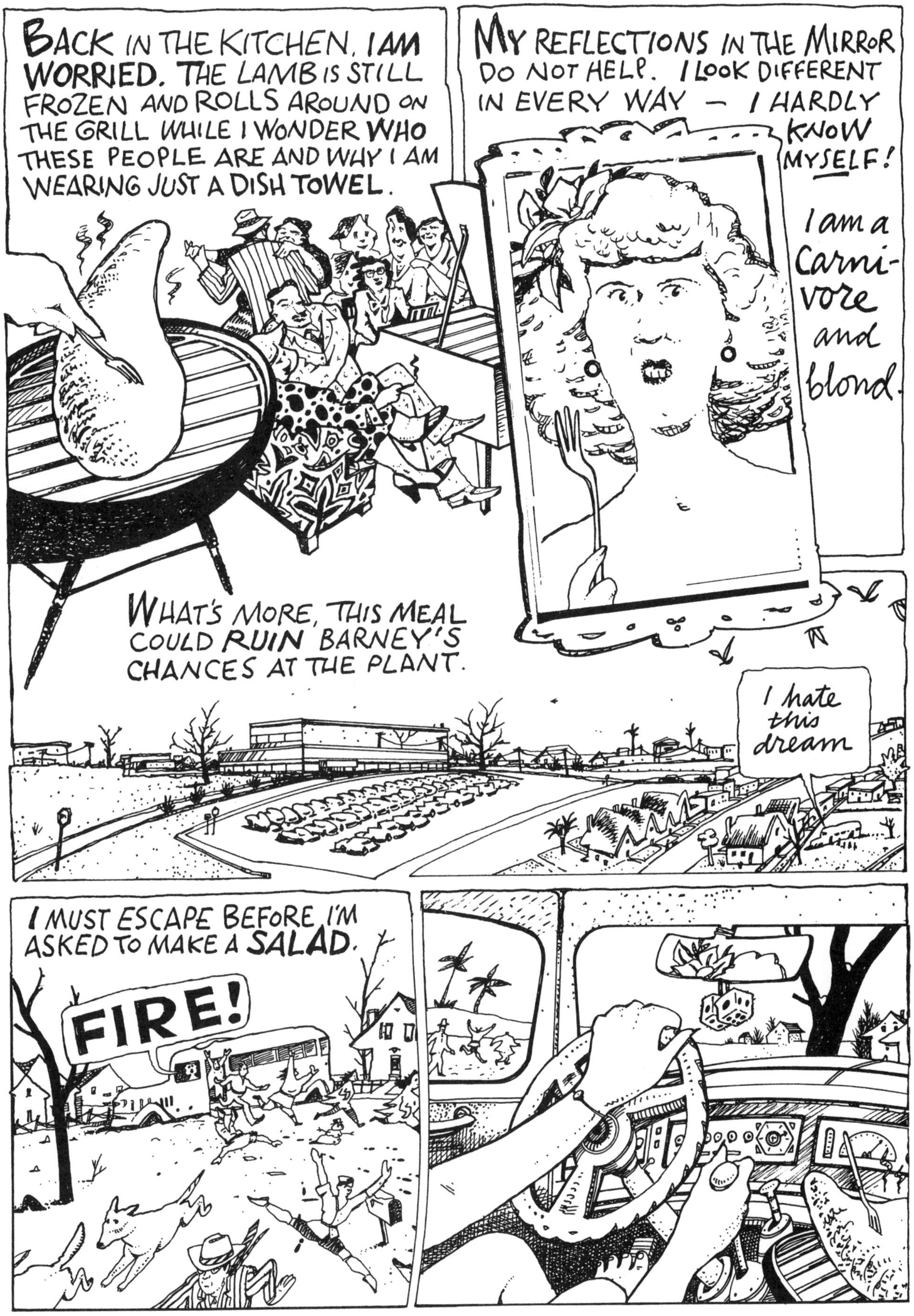
BACK IN THE KITCHEN, I AM WORRIED. THE LAMB IS STILL FROZEN AND ROLLS AROUND ON THE GRILL WHILE I WONDER WHO THESE PEOPLE ARE AND WHY I AM WEARING JUST A DISH TOWEL.
MY REFLECTIONS IN THE MIRROR DO NOT HELP. I LOOK DIFFERENT IN EVERY WAY — I HARDLY KNOW MYSELF!
I am a Carnivore and blond.
WHAT'S MORE, THIS MEAL COULD RUIN BARNEY'S CHANCES AT THE PLANT.
I hate this dream
I MUST ESCAPE BEFORE I'M ASKED TO MAKE A SALAD.
FIRE!

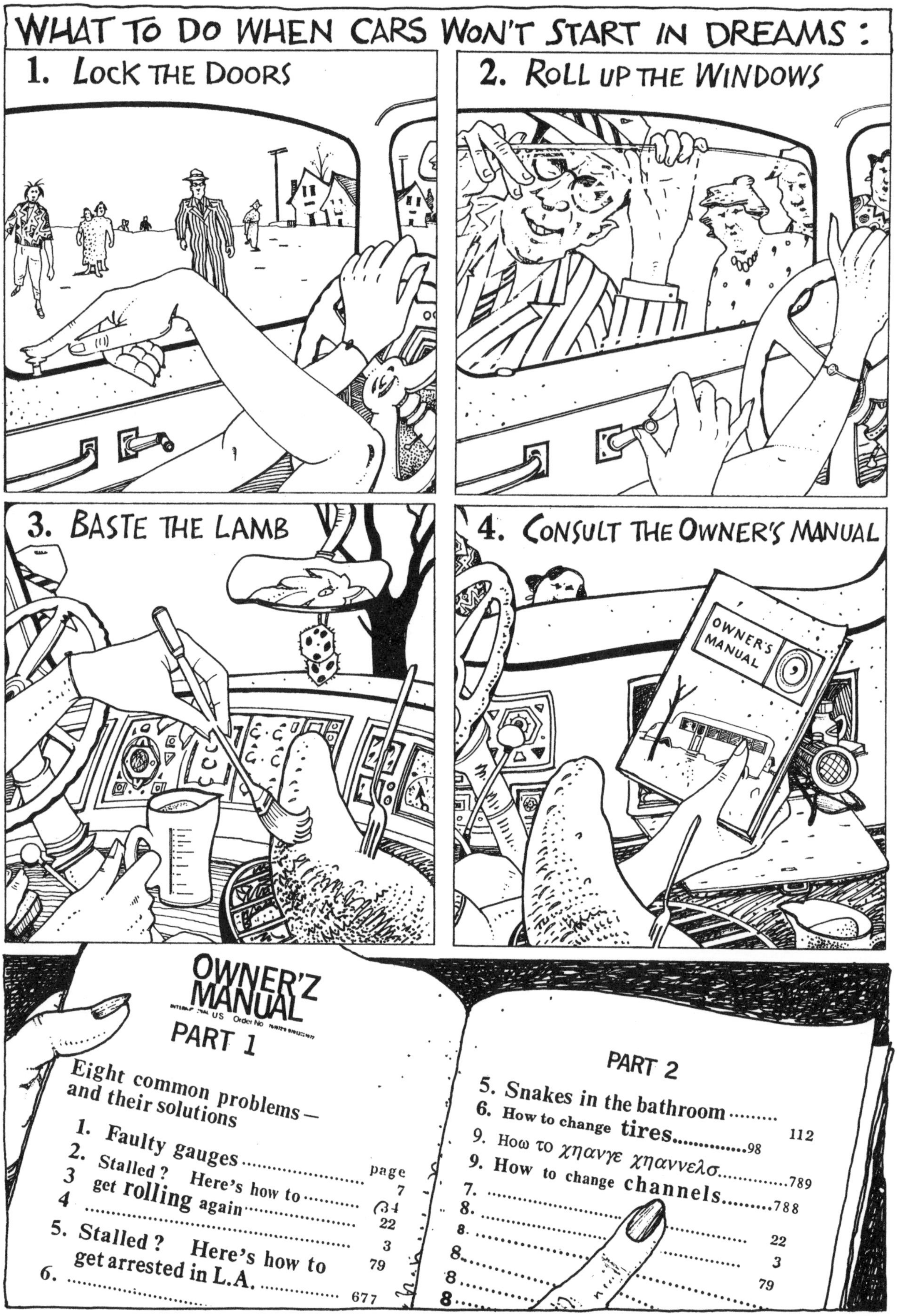
WHAT TO DO WHEN CARS WON'T START IN DREAMS:
1. LOCK THE DOORS
2. ROLL UP THE WINDOWS
3. BASTE THE LAMB
4. CONSULT THE OWNER'S MANUAL
OWNER'S MANUAL
OWNER'Z MANUAL
US Order No
PART 1
Eight common problems — and their solutions
page
1. Faulty gauges 7
2. Stalled? Here's how to
3 get rolling again 34
4 22
3
5. Stalled? Here's how to get arrested in L.A. 79
6. 677
PART 2
5. Snakes in the bathroom 112
6. How to change tires 98
9. Ηοω το χηανγε χηαννελσ 789
9. How to change channels 788
7.
8. 22
8. 3
8. 79
8.

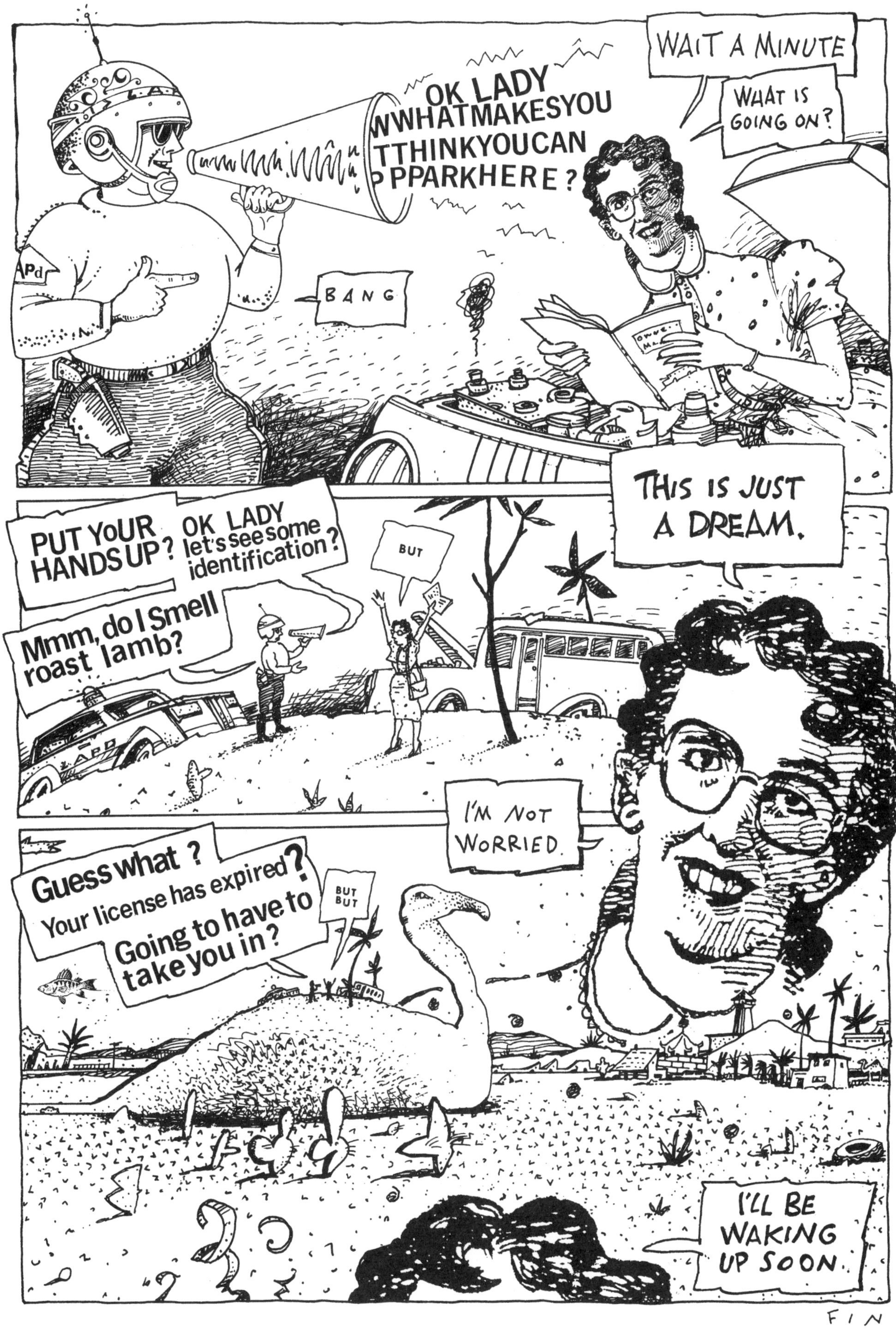
OK LADY
WWHATMAKESYOU
TTHINKYOUCAN
PPARKHERE?
WAIT A MINUTE
WHAT IS GOING ON?
BANG
THIS IS JUST A DREAM.
PUT YOUR HANDS UP?
OK LADY let's see some identification?
BUT
Mmm, do I Smell roast lamb?
I'M NOT WORRIED
Guess what?
Your license has expired?
Going to have to take you in?
BUT BUT
I'LL BE WAKING UP SOON.
FIN

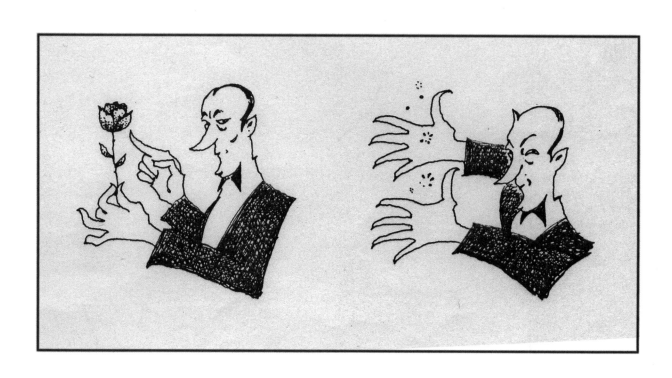

In the Workplace

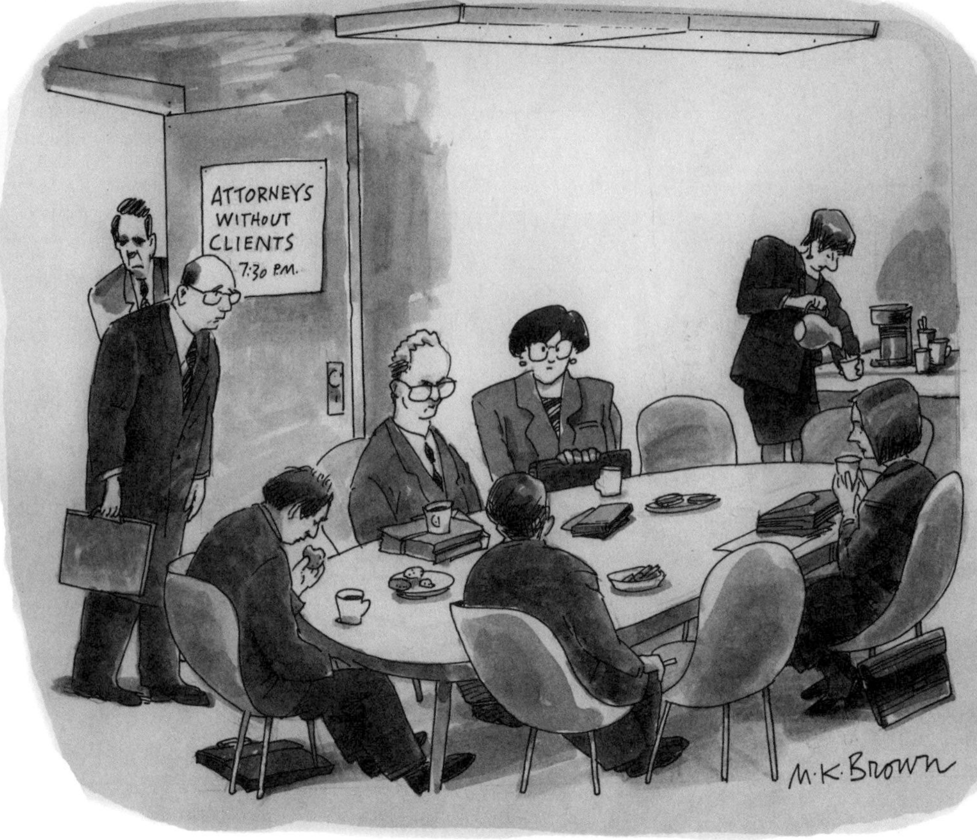
ATTORNEYS
WITHOUT
CLIENTS
7:30 P.M.
M.K. BROWN

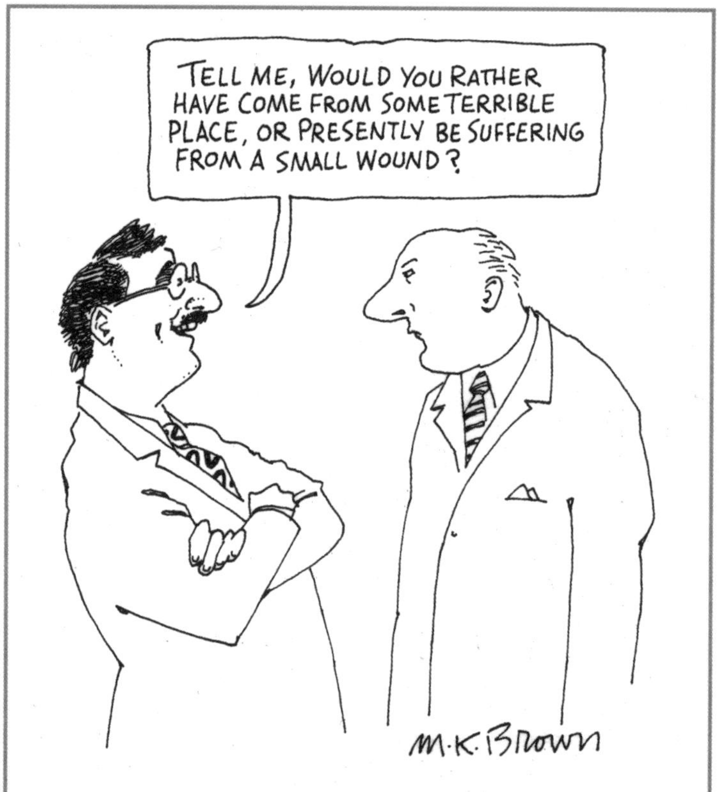
TELL ME, WOULD YOU RATHER HAVE COME FROM SOME TERRIBLE PLACE, OR PRESENTLY BE SUFFERING FROM A SMALL WOUND?
M.K. BROWN

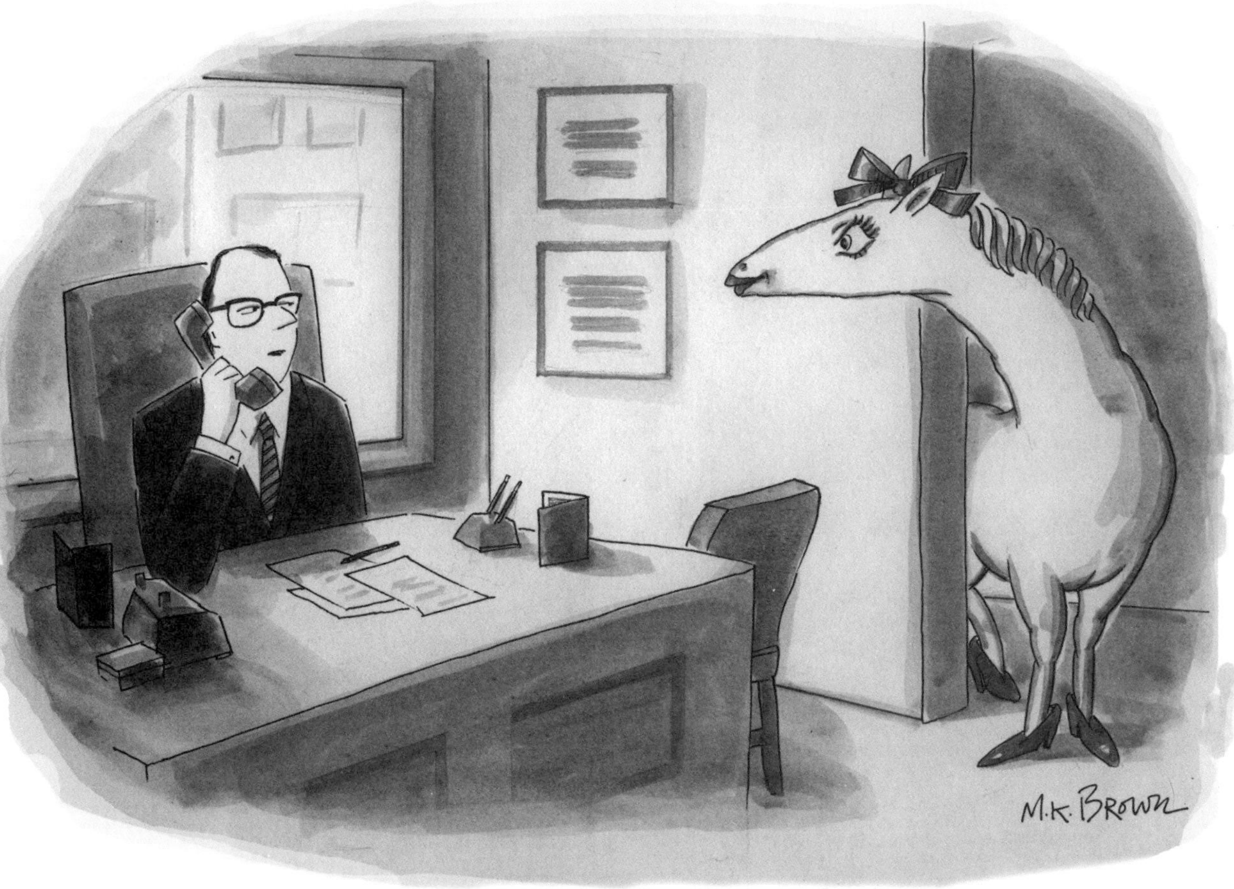
M.K. BROWN

I may have to cut this short, BK, and get back to you.

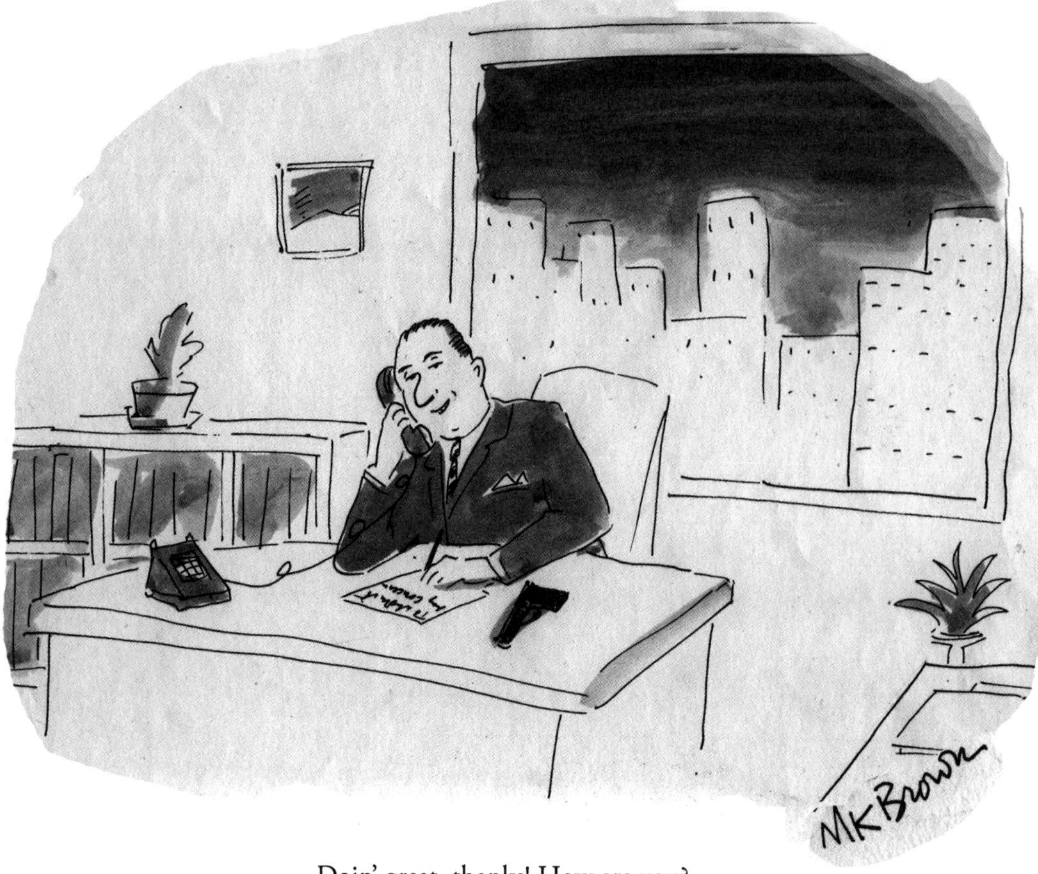
MK Brown

Doin' great, thanks! How are you?

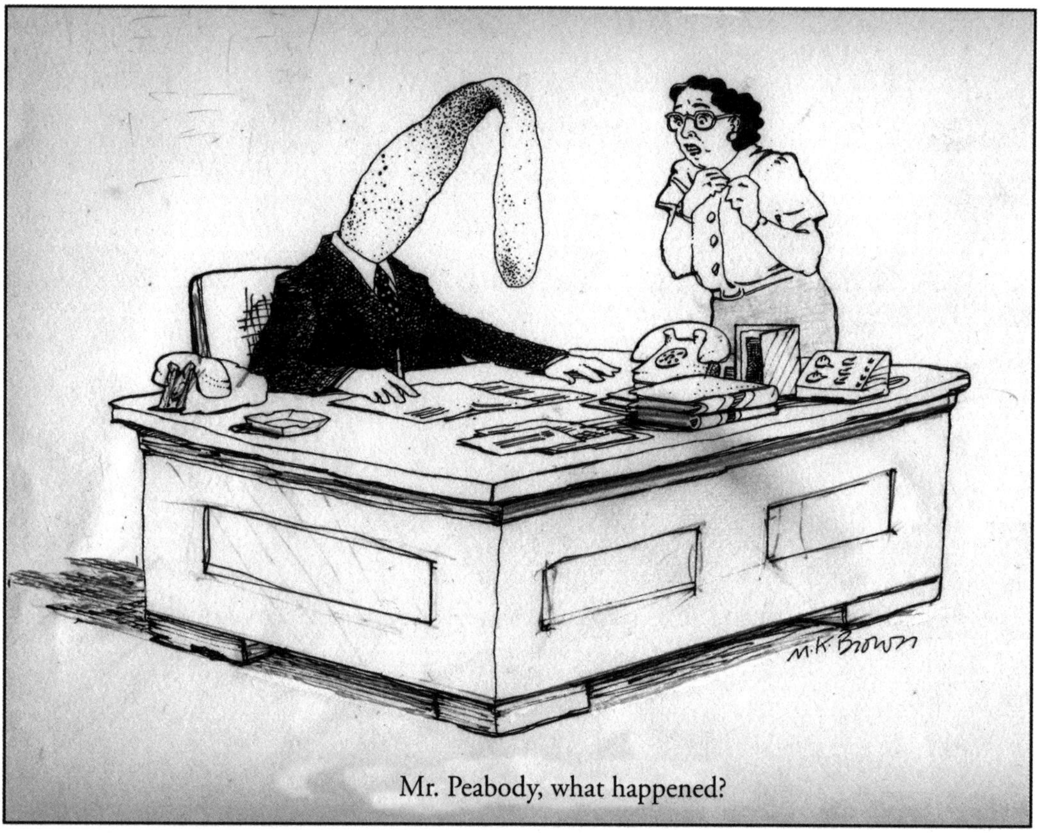
M.K. Brown

Mr. Peabody, what happened?

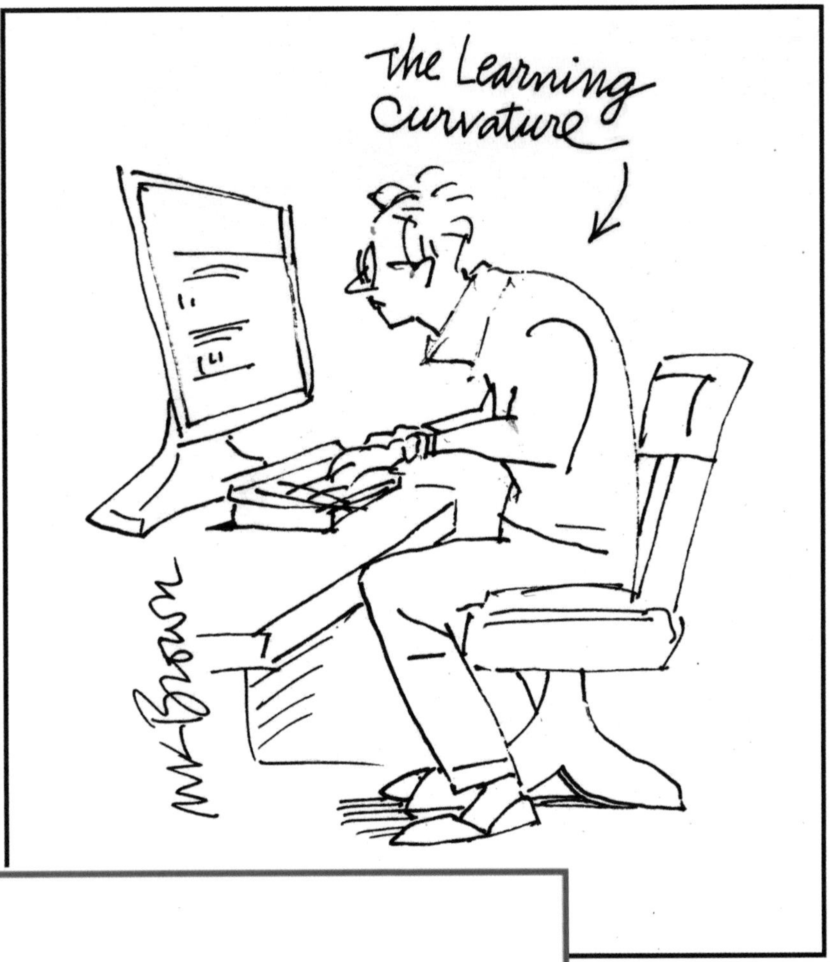
The Learning Curvature
MK Brown

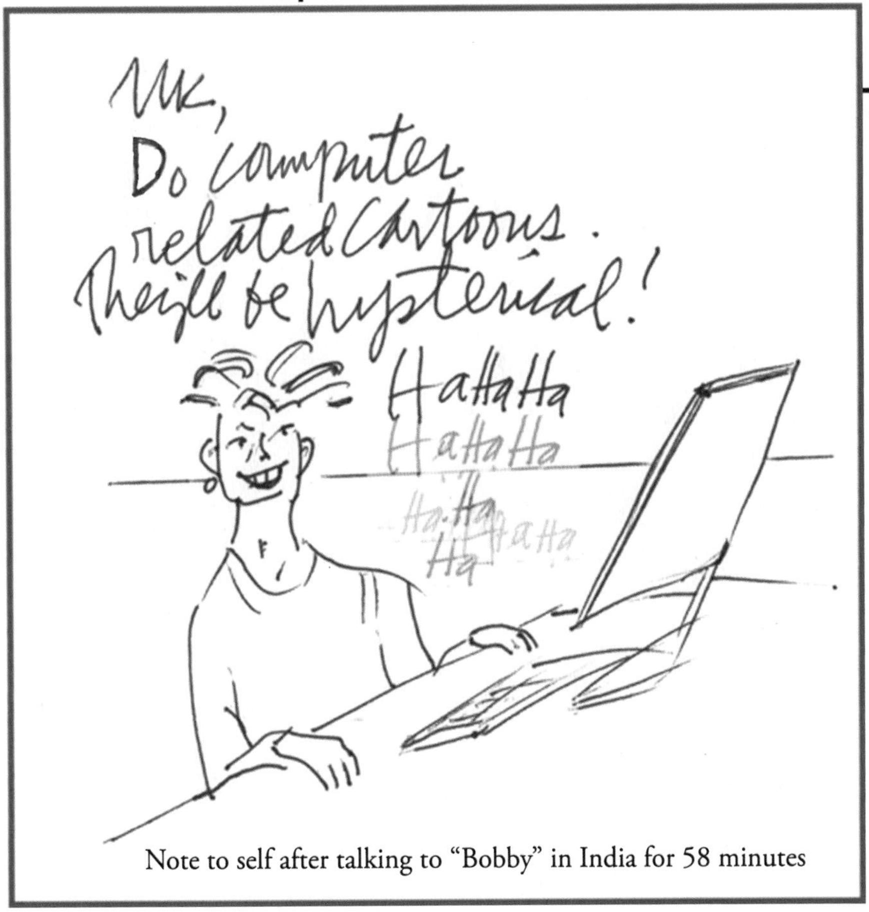
MK,
Do computer related cartoons. They'll be hysterical!
HaHaHa
HaHaHa
HaHa
Ha
HaHa

Note to self after talking to "Bobby" in India for 58 minutes

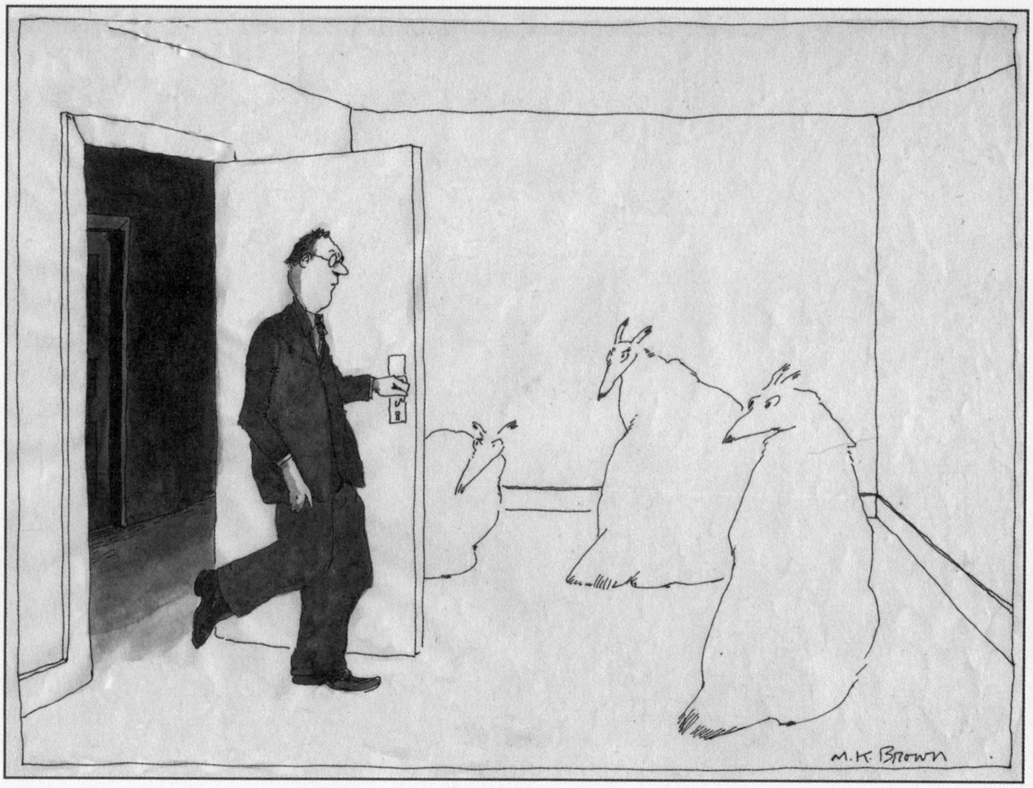
M.K. BROWN

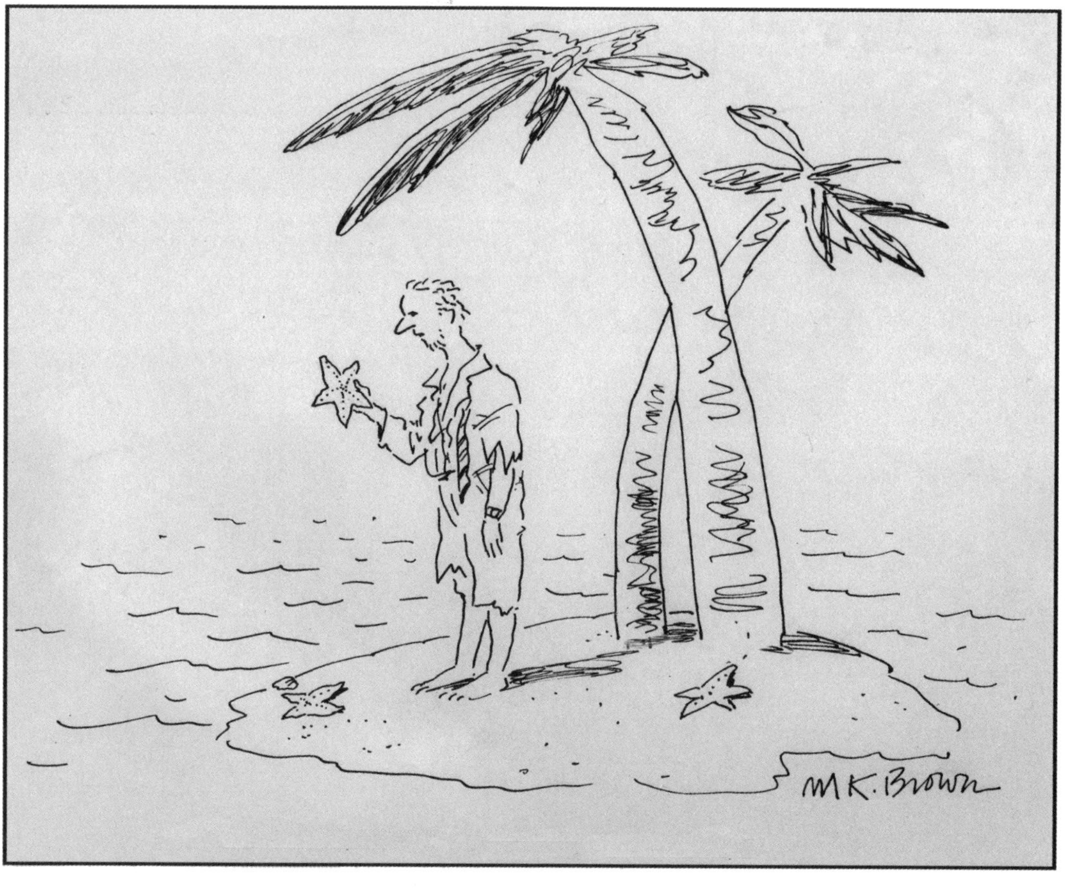
M.K. BROWN

I think I'll go type this up.

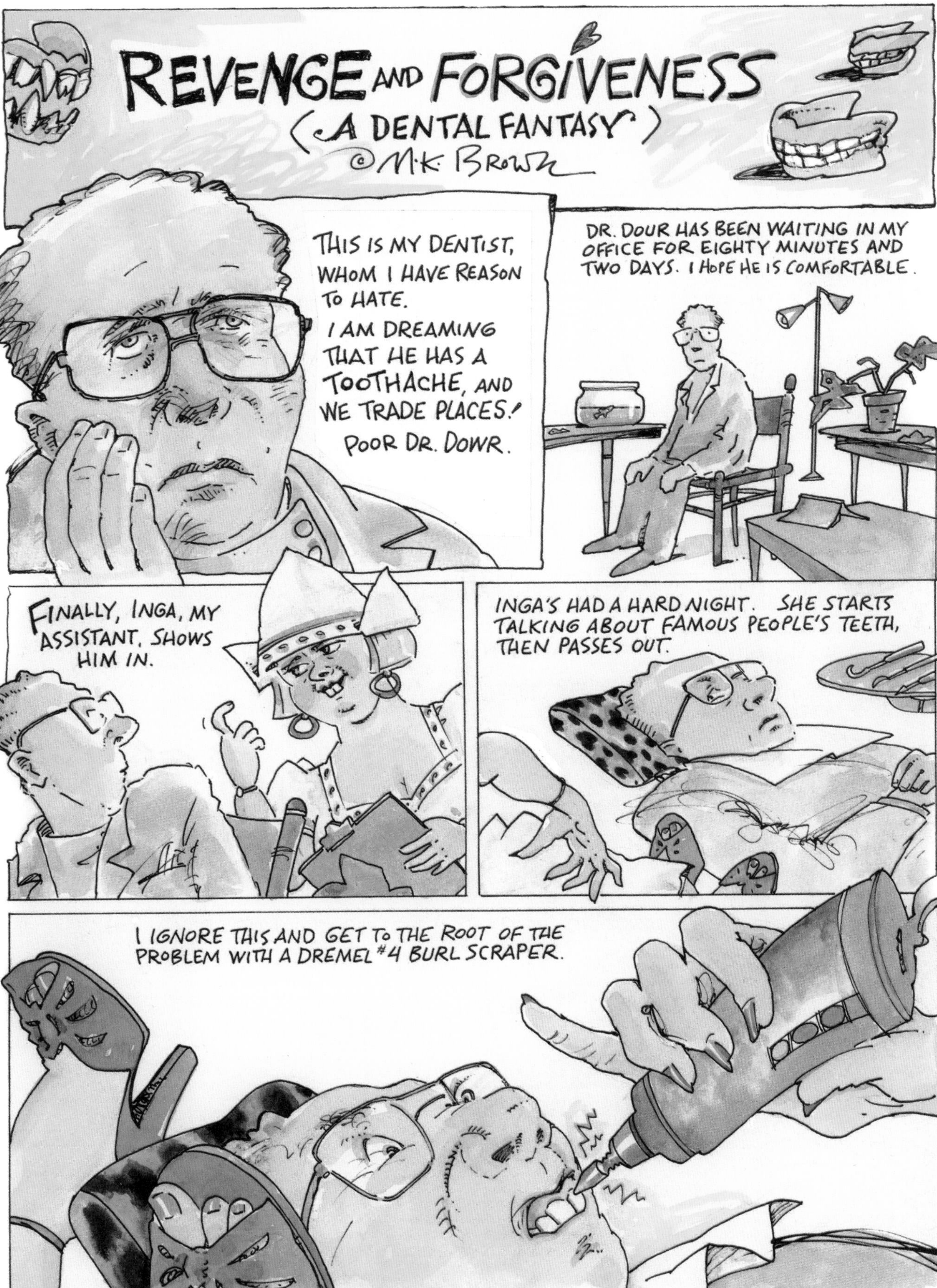
REVENGE AND FORGIVENESS
(A DENTAL FANTASY)
©M.K. BROWN
THIS IS MY DENTIST, WHOM I HAVE REASON TO HATE.
I AM DREAMING THAT HE HAS A TOOTHACHE, AND WE TRADE PLACES!
POOR DR. DOWR.
DR. DOUR HAS BEEN WAITING IN MY OFFICE FOR EIGHTY MINUTES AND TWO DAYS. I HOPE HE IS COMFORTABLE.
FINALLY, INGA, MY ASSISTANT, SHOWS HIM IN.
INGA'S HAD A HARD NIGHT. SHE STARTS TALKING ABOUT FAMOUS PEOPLE'S TEETH, THEN PASSES OUT.
I IGNORE THIS AND GET TO THE ROOT OF THE PROBLEM WITH A DREMEL #4 BURL SCRAPER.

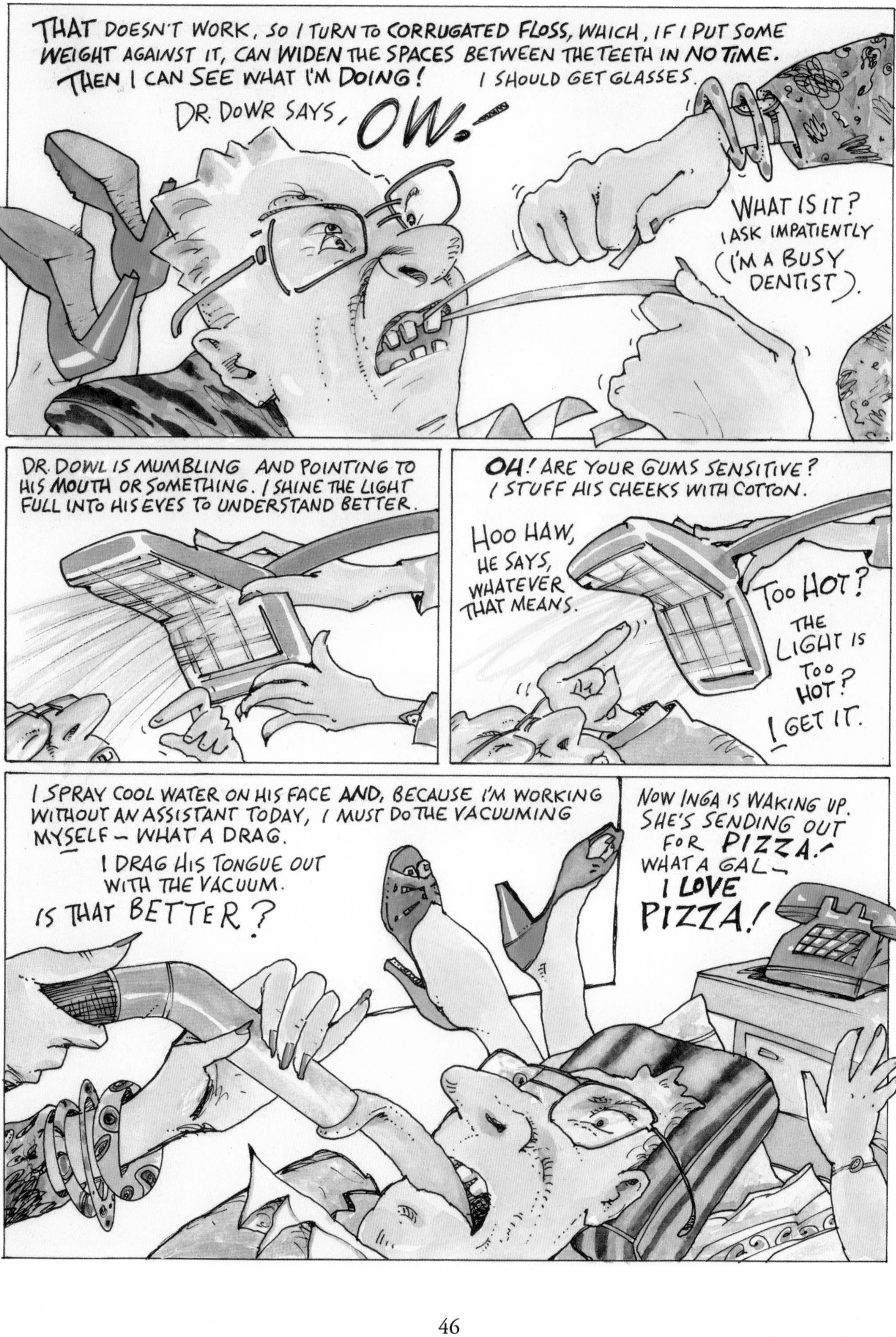

THAT DOESN'T WORK, SO I TURN TO CORRUGATED FLOSS, WHICH, IF I PUT SOME WEIGHT AGAINST IT, CAN WIDEN THE SPACES BETWEEN THE TEETH IN NO TIME. THEN I CAN SEE WHAT I'M DOING!
I SHOULD GET GLASSES.
DR. DOWR SAYS, OW!
WHAT IS IT? I ASK IMPATIENTLY (I'M A BUSY DENTIST).
DR. DOWL IS MUMBLING AND POINTING TO HIS MOUTH OR SOMETHING. I SHINE THE LIGHT FULL INTO HIS EYES TO UNDERSTAND BETTER.
OH! ARE YOUR GUMS SENSITIVE? I STUFF HIS CHEEKS WITH COTTON.
HOO HAW, HE SAYS, WHATEVER THAT MEANS.
TOO HOT? THE LIGHT IS TOO HOT? I GET IT.
I SPRAY COOL WATER ON HIS FACE AND, BECAUSE I'M WORKING WITHOUT AN ASSISTANT TODAY, I MUST DO THE VACUUMING MYSELF – WHAT A DRAG.
I DRAG HIS TONGUE OUT WITH THE VACUUM.
IS THAT BETTER?
NOW INGA IS WAKING UP. SHE'S SENDING OUT FOR PIZZA! WHAT A GAL – I LOVE PIZZA!

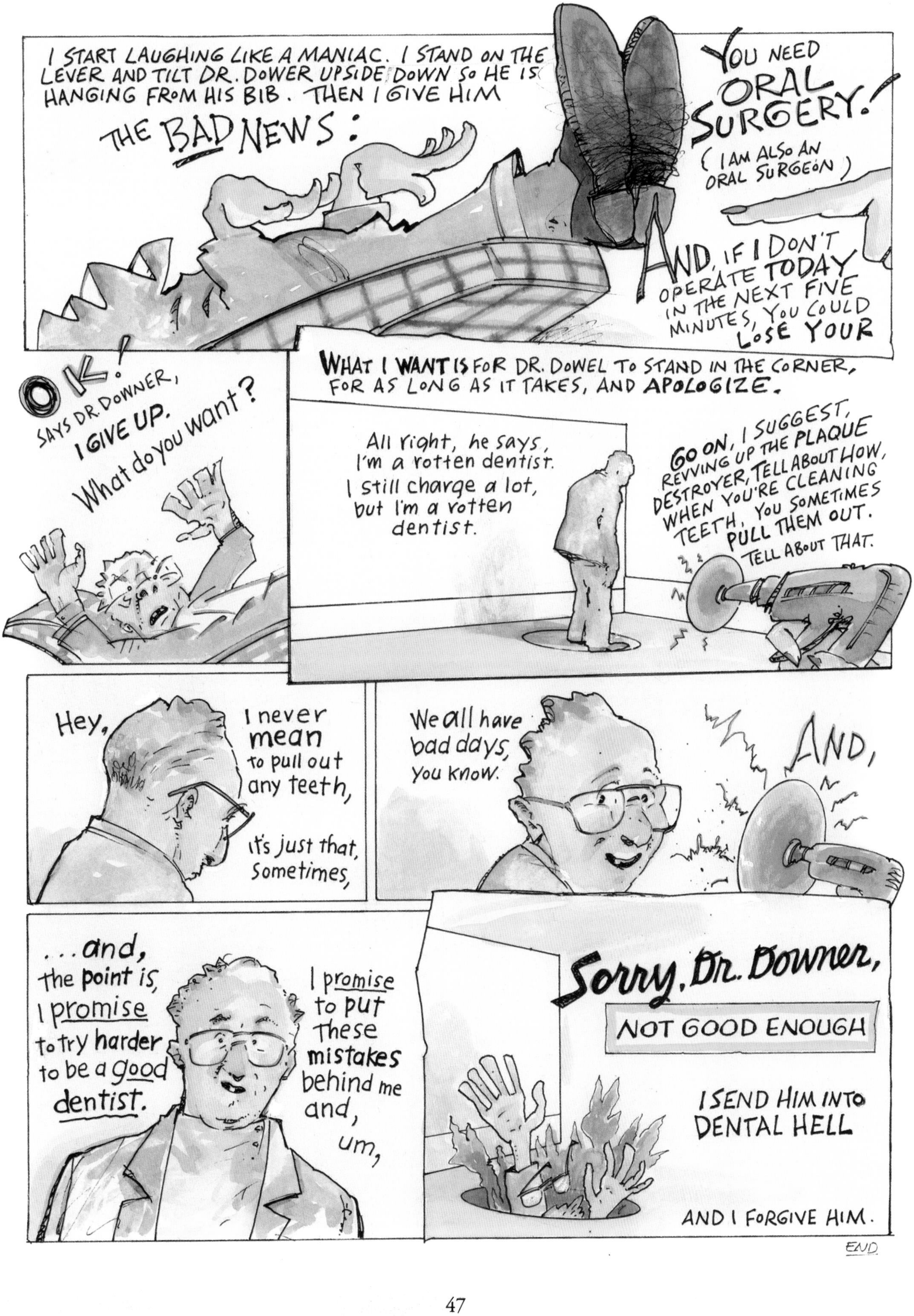
I START LAUGHING LIKE A MANIAC. I STAND ON THE LEVER AND TILT DR. DOWER UPSIDE DOWN SO HE IS HANGING FROM HIS BIB. THEN I GIVE HIM
THE BAD NEWS:
YOU NEED ORAL SURGERY!
(I AM ALSO AN ORAL SURGEON)
AND, IF I DON'T OPERATE TODAY IN THE NEXT FIVE MINUTES, YOU COULD LOSE YOUR
OK! SAYS DR. DOWNER, I GIVE UP.
What do you want?
WHAT I WANT IS FOR DR. DOWEL TO STAND IN THE CORNER, FOR AS LONG AS IT TAKES, AND APOLOGIZE.
All right, he says, I'm a rotten dentist. I still charge a lot, but I'm a rotten dentist.
GO ON, I SUGGEST, REVVING UP THE PLAQUE DESTROYER, TELL ABOUT HOW, WHEN YOU'RE CLEANING TEETH, YOU SOMETIMES PULL THEM OUT. TELL ABOUT THAT.
Hey,
I never mean to pull out any teeth,
it's just that, Sometimes,
We all have bad days, you know.
AND,
. . . and, the point is, I promise to try harder to be a good dentist.
I promise to put these mistakes behind me and,
um,
Sorry, Dr. Downer,
NOT GOOD ENOUGH
I SEND HIM INTO DENTAL HELL
AND I FORGIVE HIM.
END

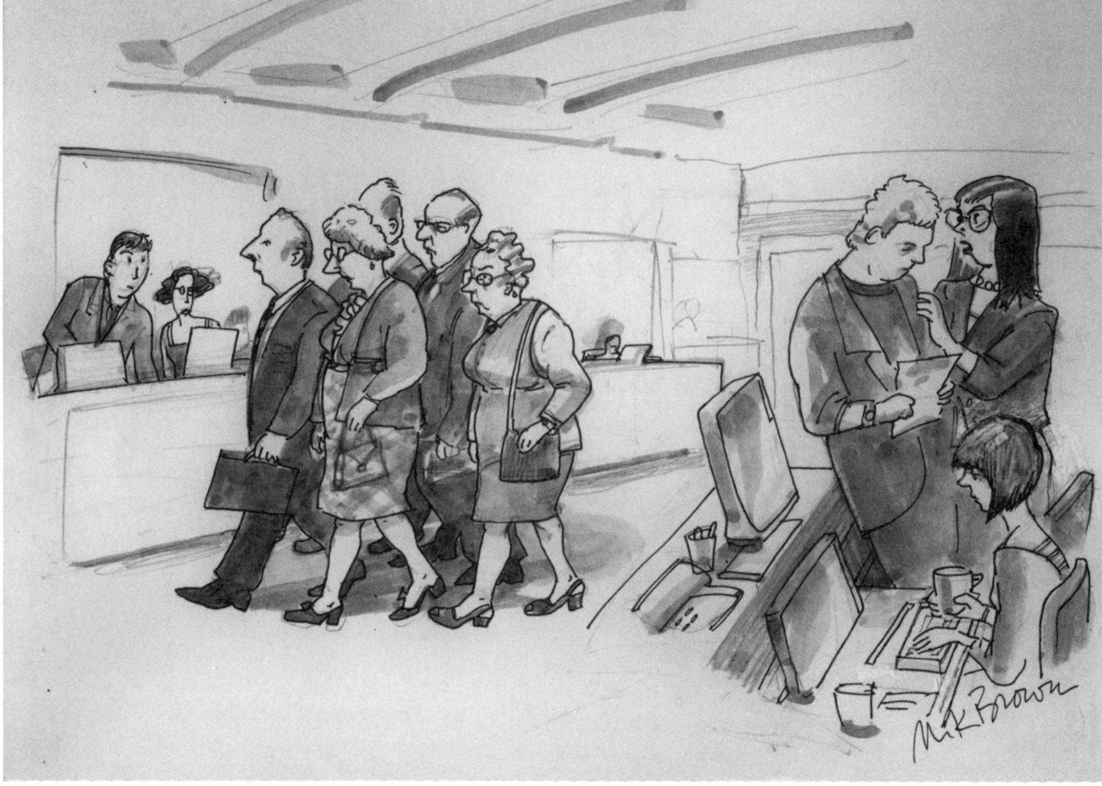
M.K. Brown

Oh, my God. Old people.

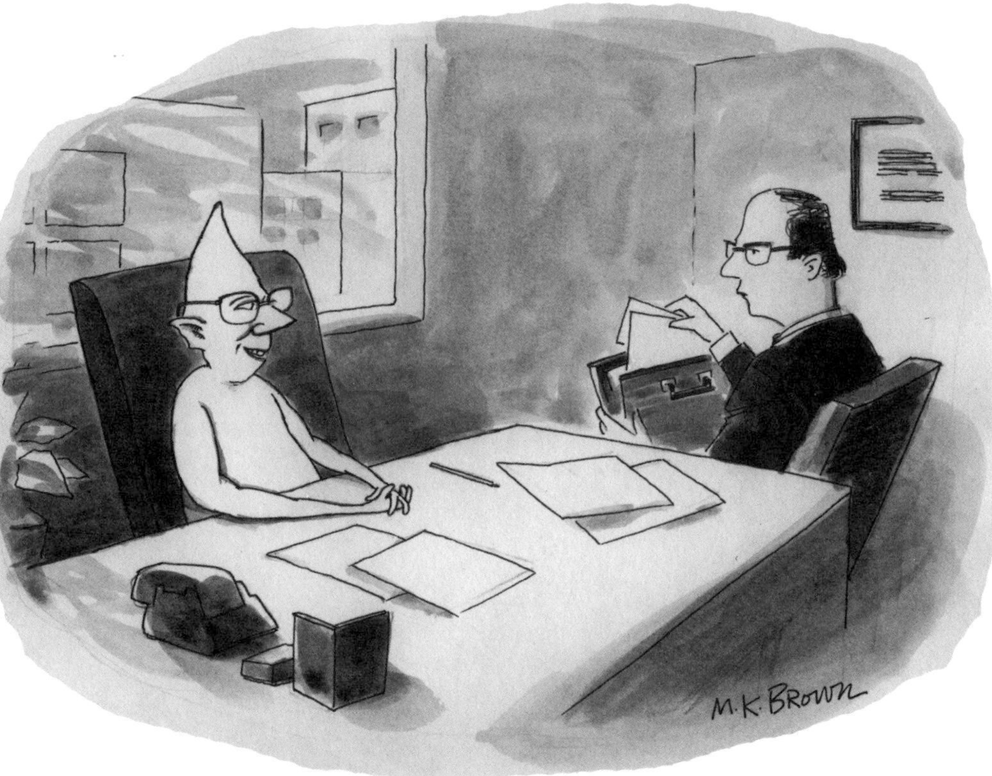
M.K. BROWN

Actually, I'm not Mr. Weintraub. I'm just, sort of, taking over for awhile.

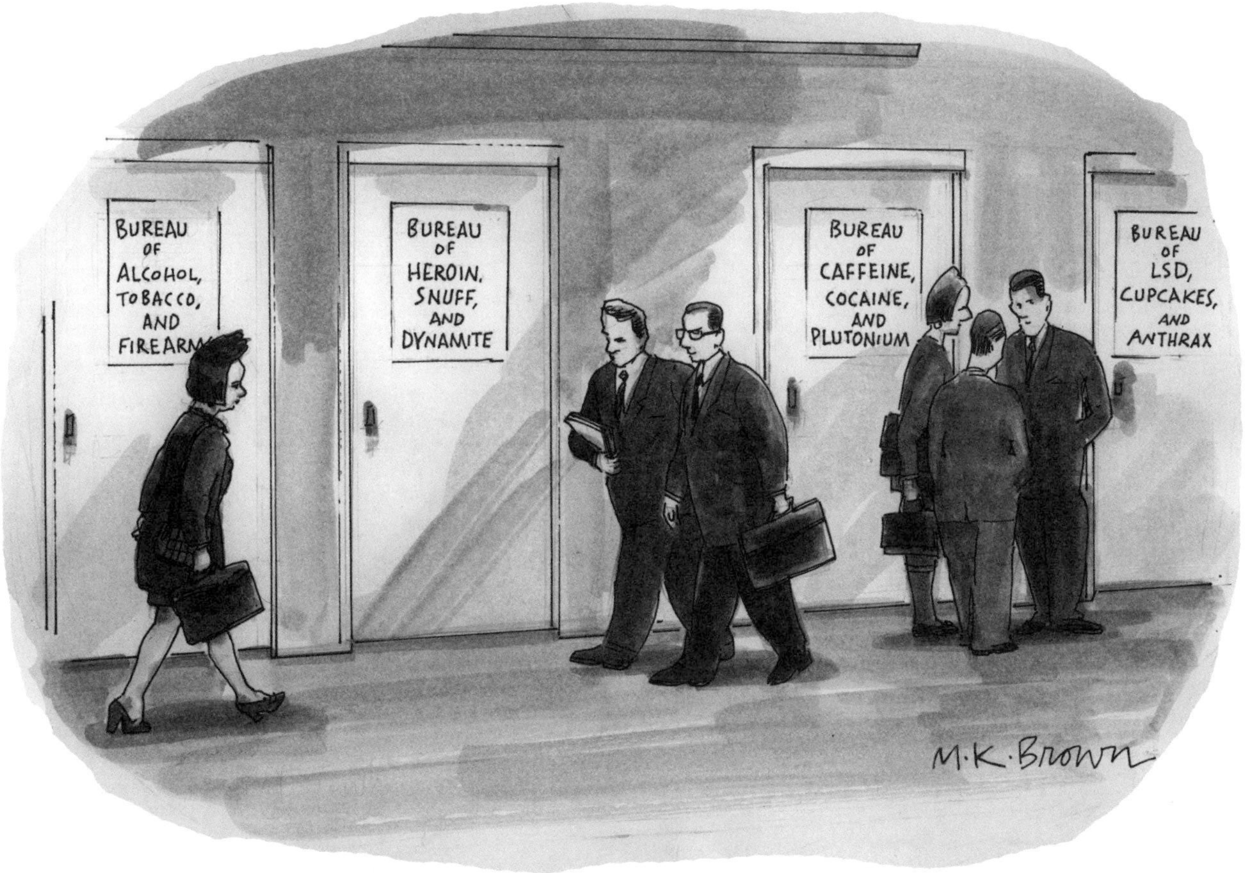
BUREAU OF ALCOHOL, TOBACCO, AND FIREARMS
BUREAU OF HEROIN, SNUFF, AND DYNAMITE
BUREAU OF CAFFEINE, COCAINE, AND PLUTONIUM
BUREAU OF LSD, CUPCAKES, AND ANTHRAX
M.K. BROWN

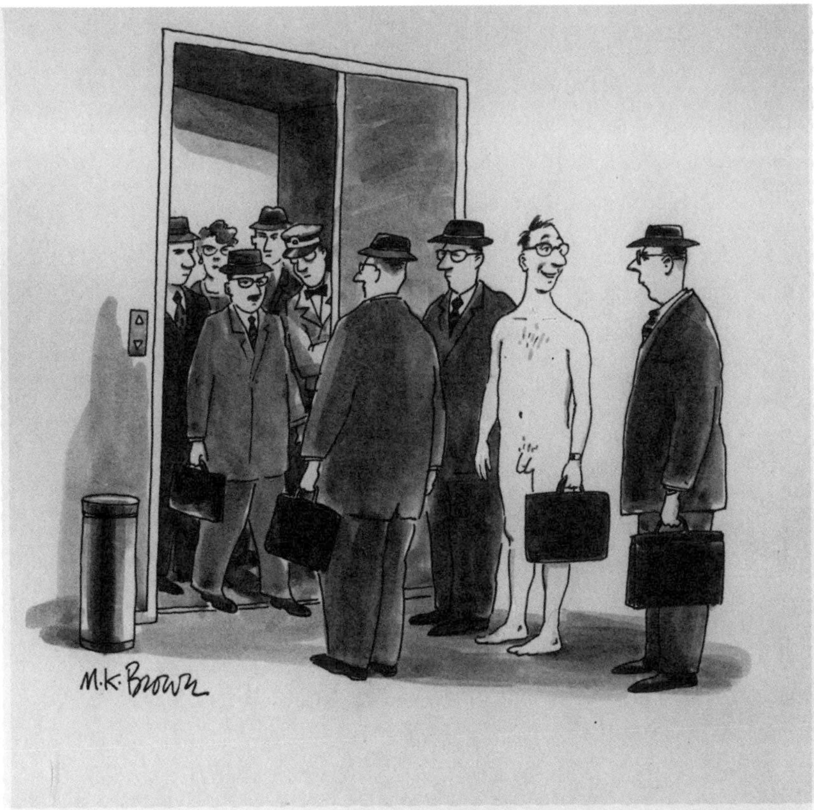
M.K. BROWN

Did you ever have a day when you just couldn't stand to get dressed?

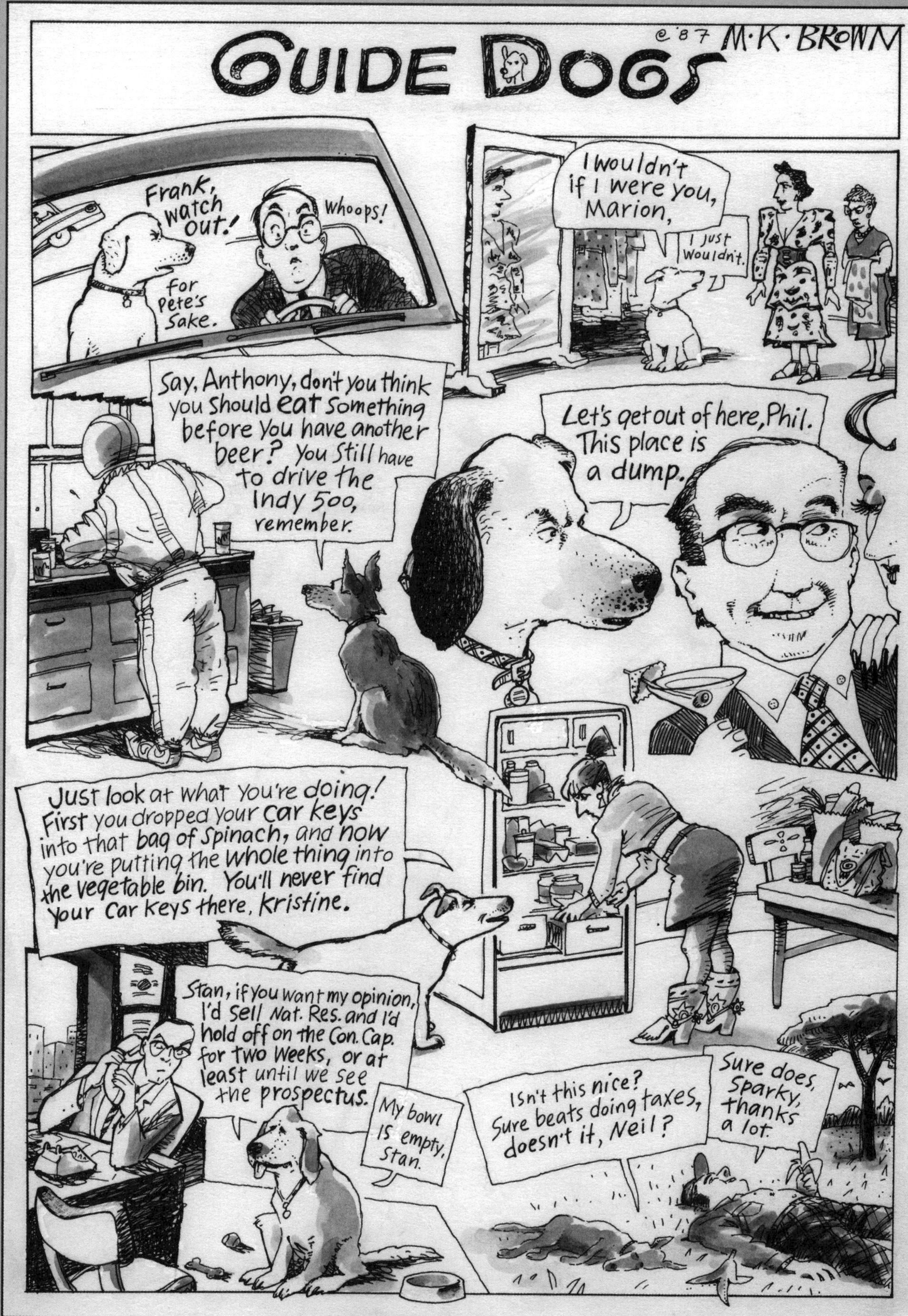

GUIDE DOGS
©'87 M·K·BROWN
Frank, watch out!
Whoops!
For Pete's Sake.
I wouldn't if I were you, Marion,
I just wouldn't.
Say, Anthony, don't you think you should eat something before you have another beer? You still have to drive the Indy 500, remember.
Let's get out of here, Phil. This place is a dump.
Just look at what you're doing! First you dropped your car keys into that bag of spinach, and now you're putting the whole thing into the vegetable bin. You'll never find your car keys there, Kristine.
Stan, if you want my opinion, I'd sell Nat. Res. and I'd hold off on the Con. Cap. for two weeks, or at least until we see the prospectus.
My bowl is empty, Stan.
Isn't this nice? Sure beats doing taxes, doesn't it, Neil?
Sure does, Sparky, thanks a lot.

Russ de la Rocca – Worm Trainer of the Americas
OK, SHIRLEY. THIS IS YOUR LAST CHANCE
ARE YOU READY?
HUP HUP!
GET UP, SHIRLEY!
GOOD GIRL!
UP!
?,
!
SHIRLEY! GET UP!
OR YOU KNOW WHAT WILL HAPPEN.
?
TOO BAD FOR SHIRLEY. EVERYBODY GETS A DOUGHNUT BUT SHIRLEY.
!
M.K. BROWN

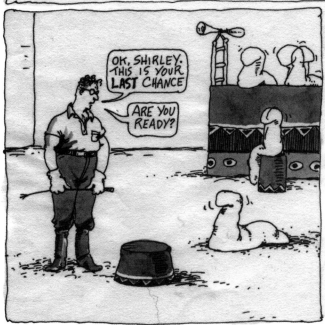

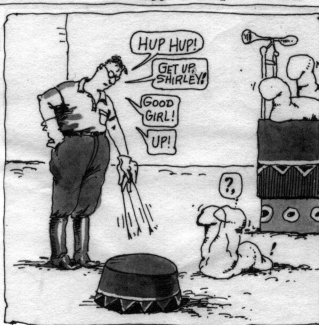

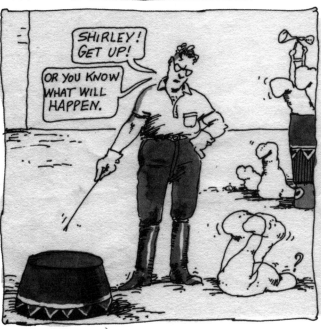

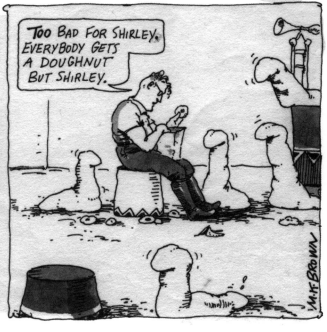

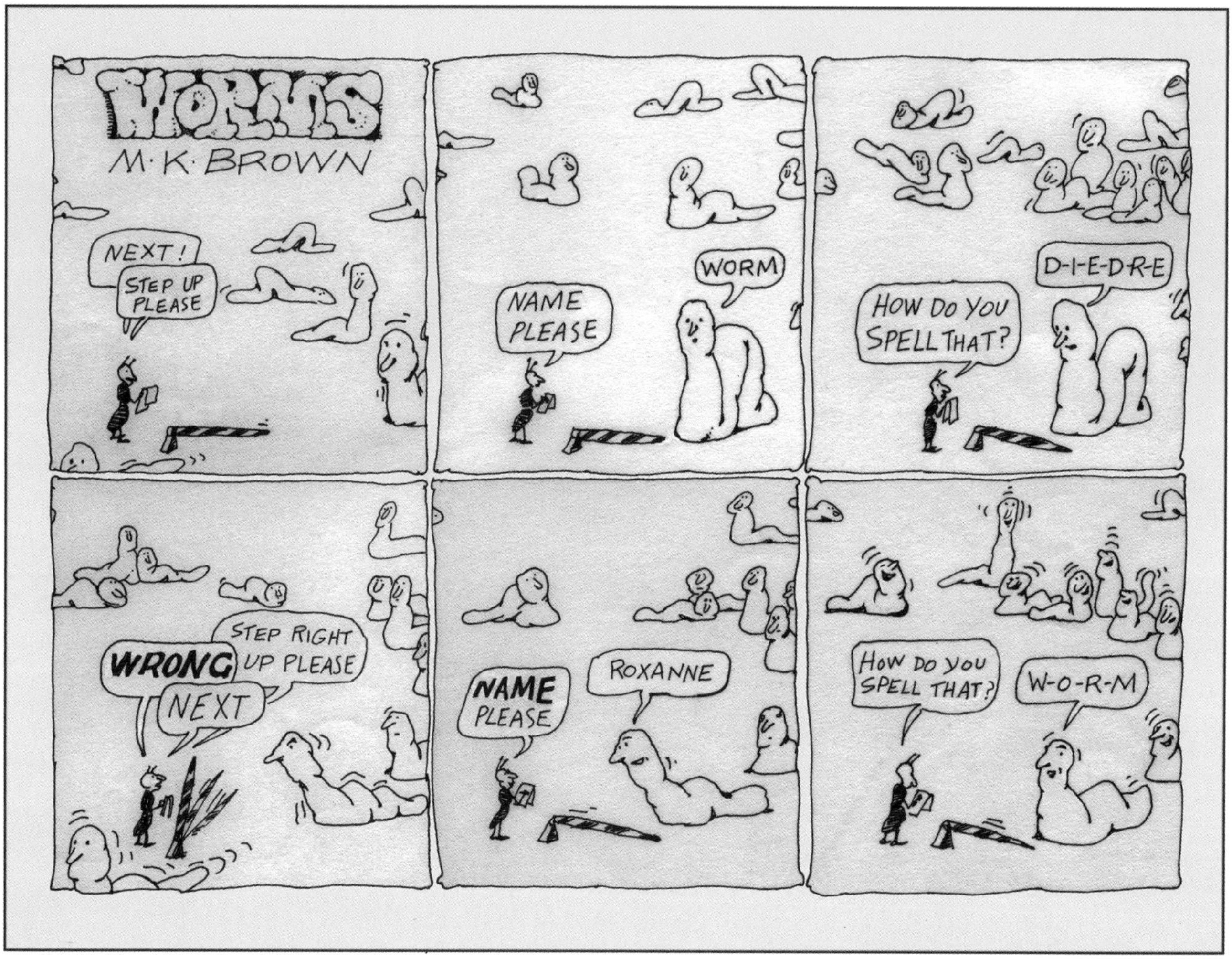
WORMS
M·K·BROWN
NEXT!
STEP UP PLEASE
NAME PLEASE
WORM
HOW DO YOU SPELL THAT?
D-I-E-D-R-E
WRONG
NEXT
STEP RIGHT UP PLEASE
NAME PLEASE
ROXANNE
HOW DO YOU SPELL THAT?
W-O-R-M

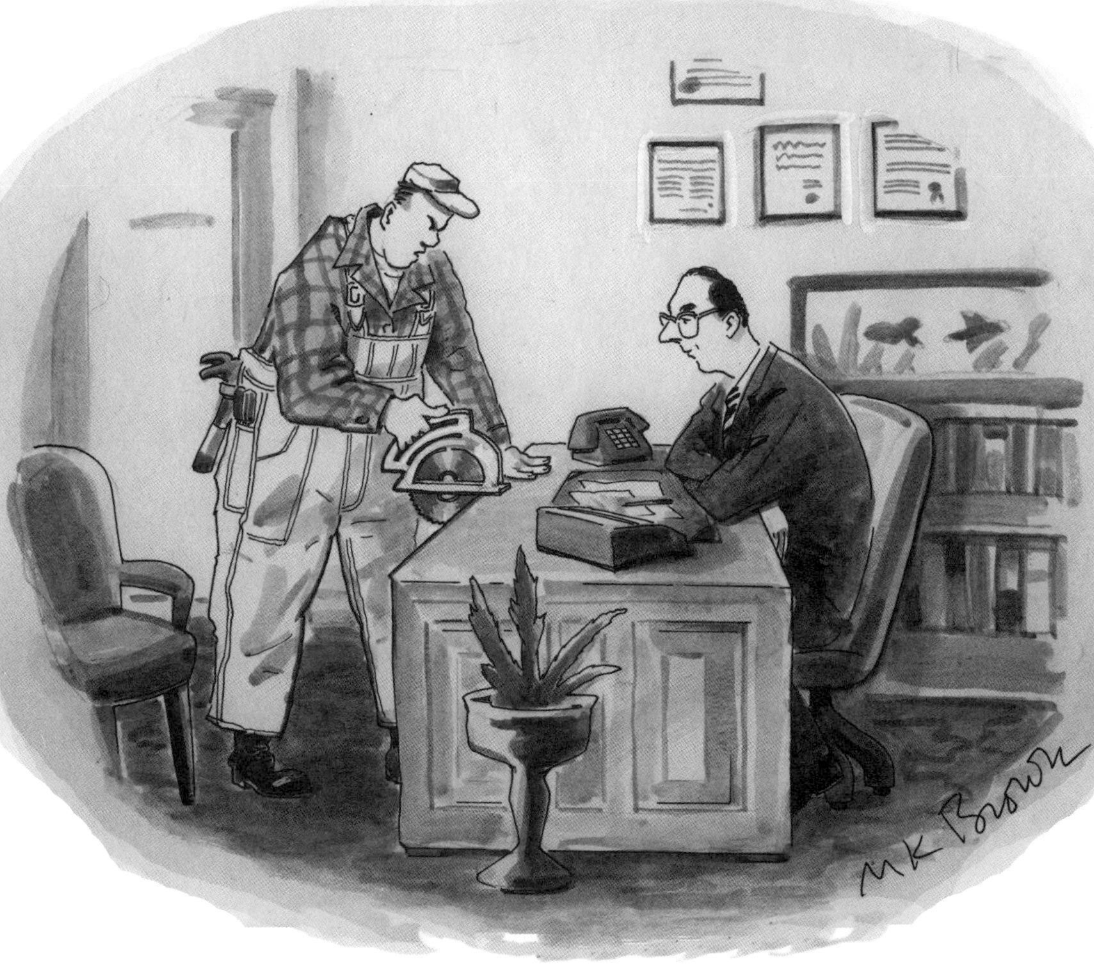
MK Brown

I still don't feel right about this, Mr. Bernstein.

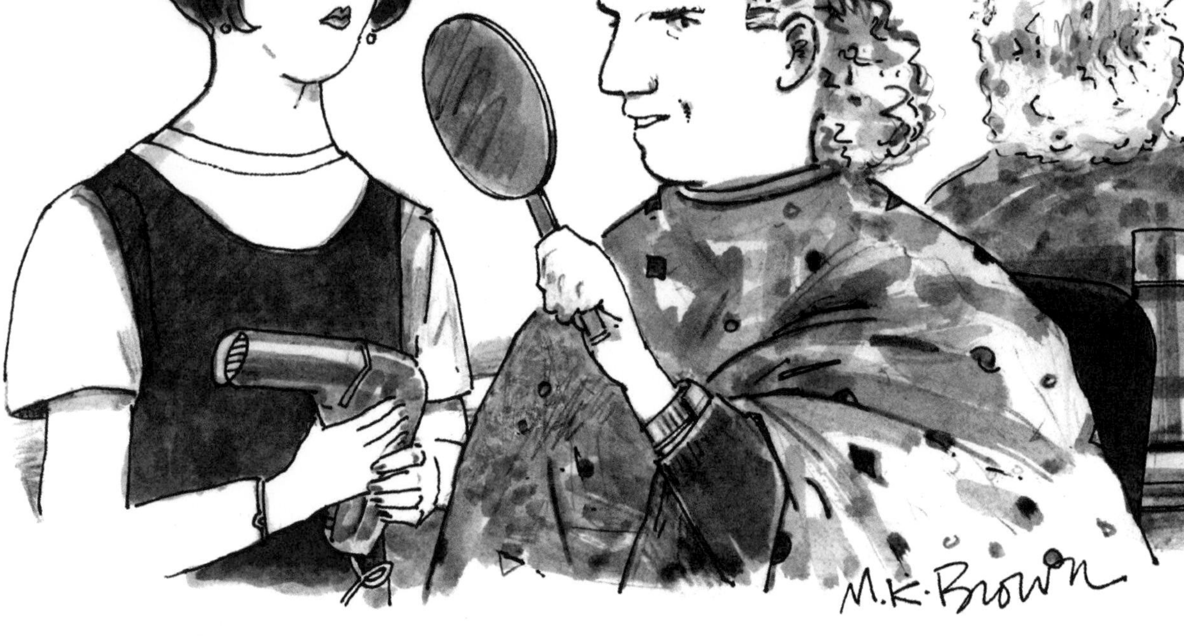
M.K.Brown

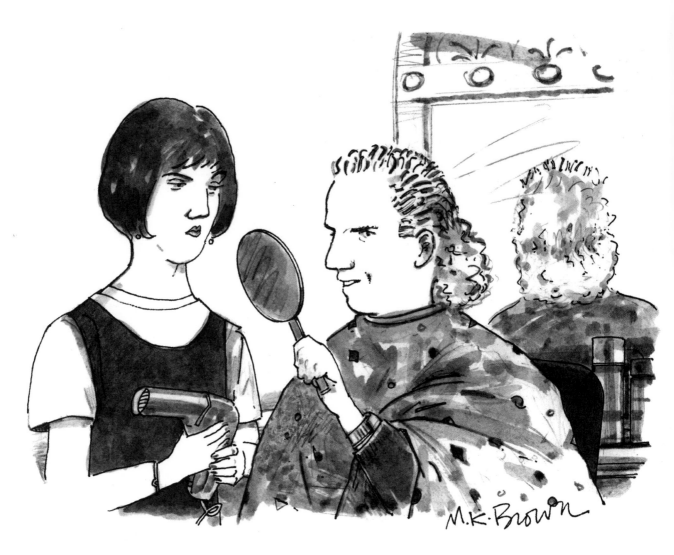

No, leave it long in the back so I can look like a nincompoop.

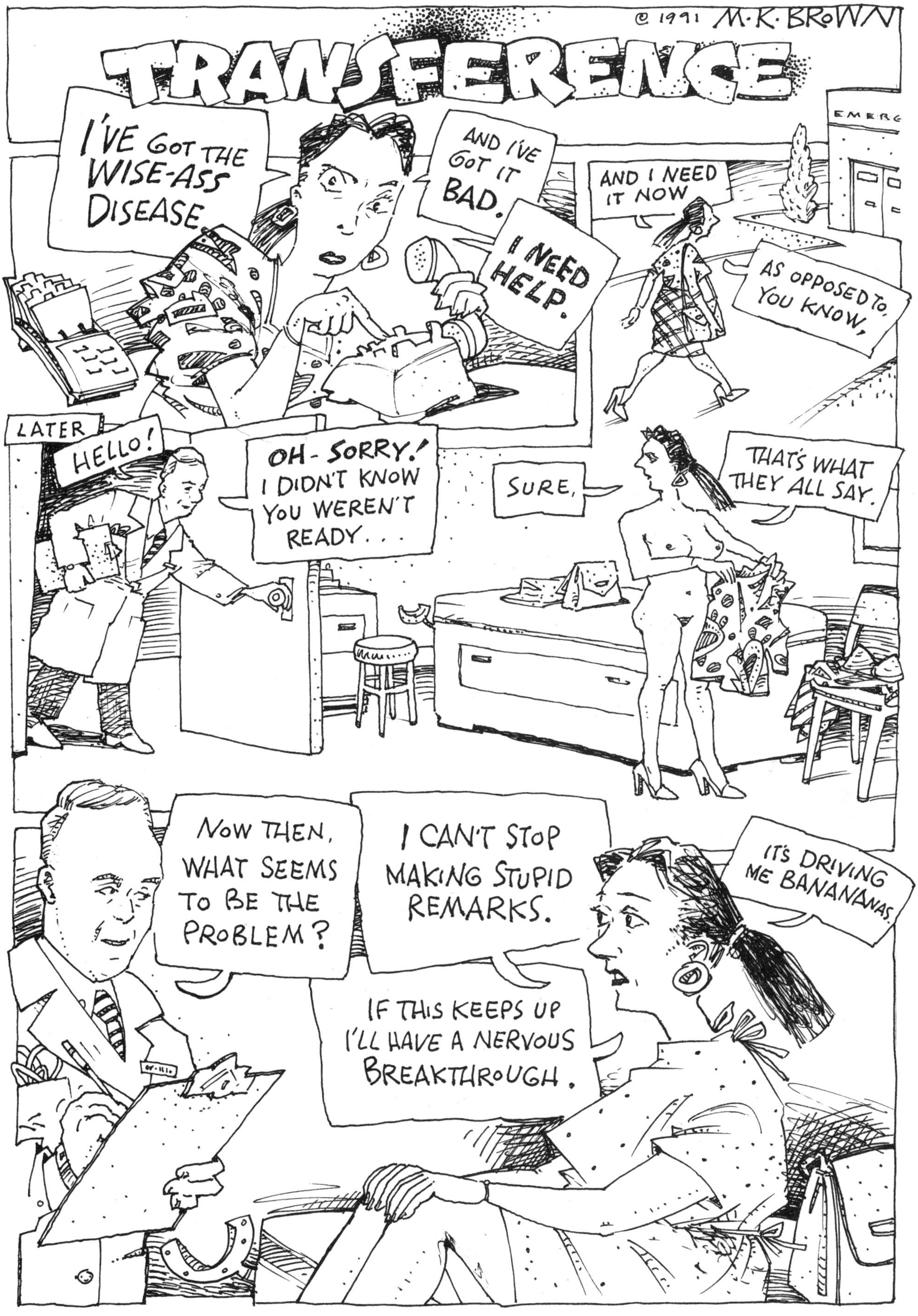
© 1991 M·K·BROWN
TRANSFERENCE
I'VE GOT THE WISE-ASS DISEASE.
AND I'VE GOT IT BAD.
I NEED HELP.
AND I NEED IT NOW
AS OPPOSED TO, YOU KNOW,
LATER
HELLO!
OH - SORRY! I DIDN'T KNOW YOU WEREN'T READY . . .
SURE,
THAT'S WHAT THEY ALL SAY.
NOW THEN, WHAT SEEMS TO BE THE PROBLEM?
I CAN'T STOP MAKING STUPID REMARKS.
IT'S DRIVING ME BANANANANAS.
IF THIS KEEPS UP I'LL HAVE A NERVOUS BREAKTHROUGH.

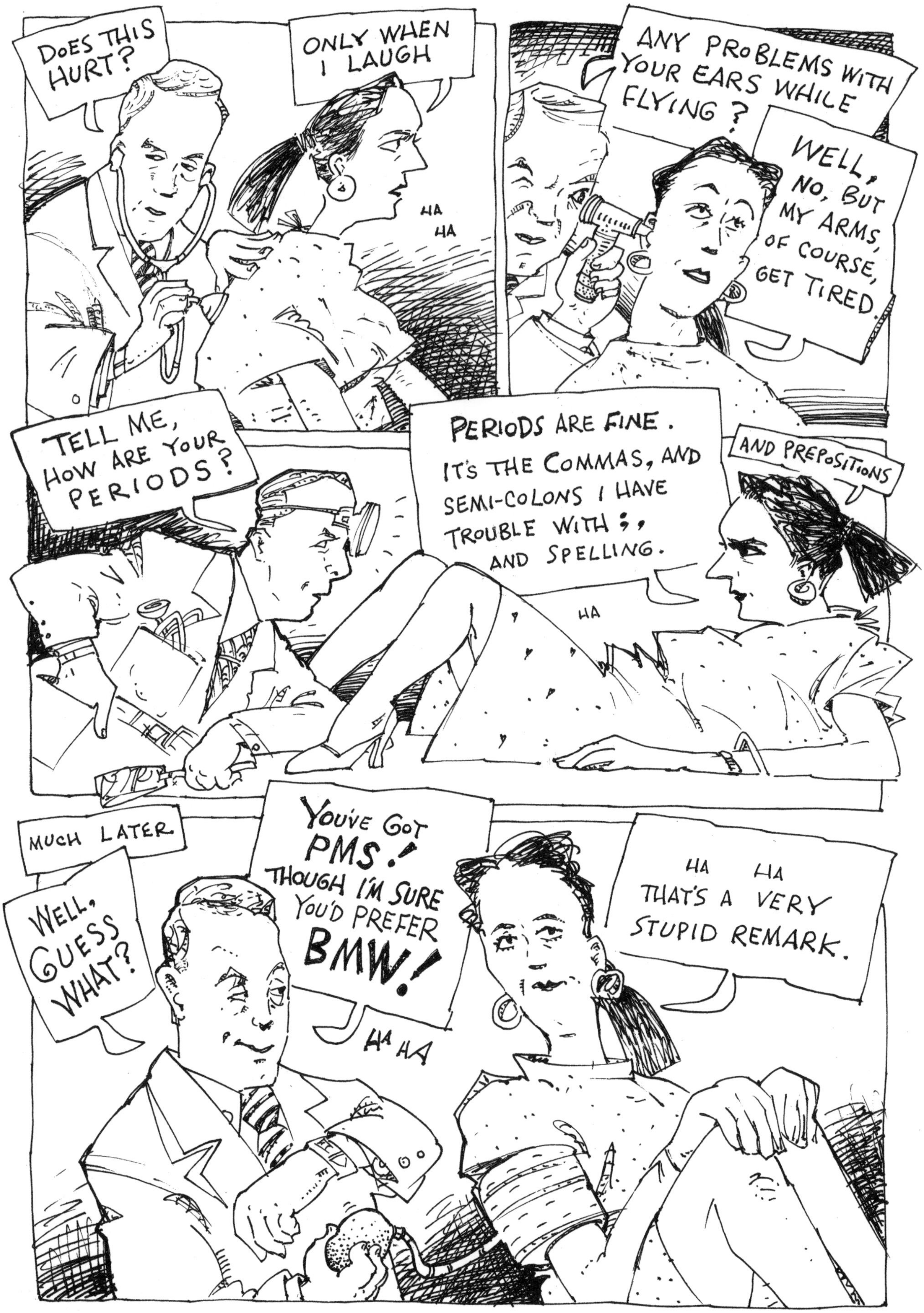
DOES THIS HURT?
ONLY WHEN I LAUGH
HA HA
ANY PROBLEMS WITH YOUR EARS WHILE FLYING?
WELL, NO, BUT MY ARMS, OF COURSE, GET TIRED.
TELL ME, HOW ARE YOUR PERIODS?
PERIODS ARE FINE. IT'S THE COMMAS, AND SEMI-COLONS I HAVE TROUBLE WITH ;, AND SPELLING.
AND PREPOSITIONS
HA
MUCH LATER.
WELL, GUESS WHAT?
YOU'VE GOT PMS! THOUGH I'M SURE YOU'D PREFER BMW!
HA HA
HA HA THAT'S A VERY STUPID REMARK.

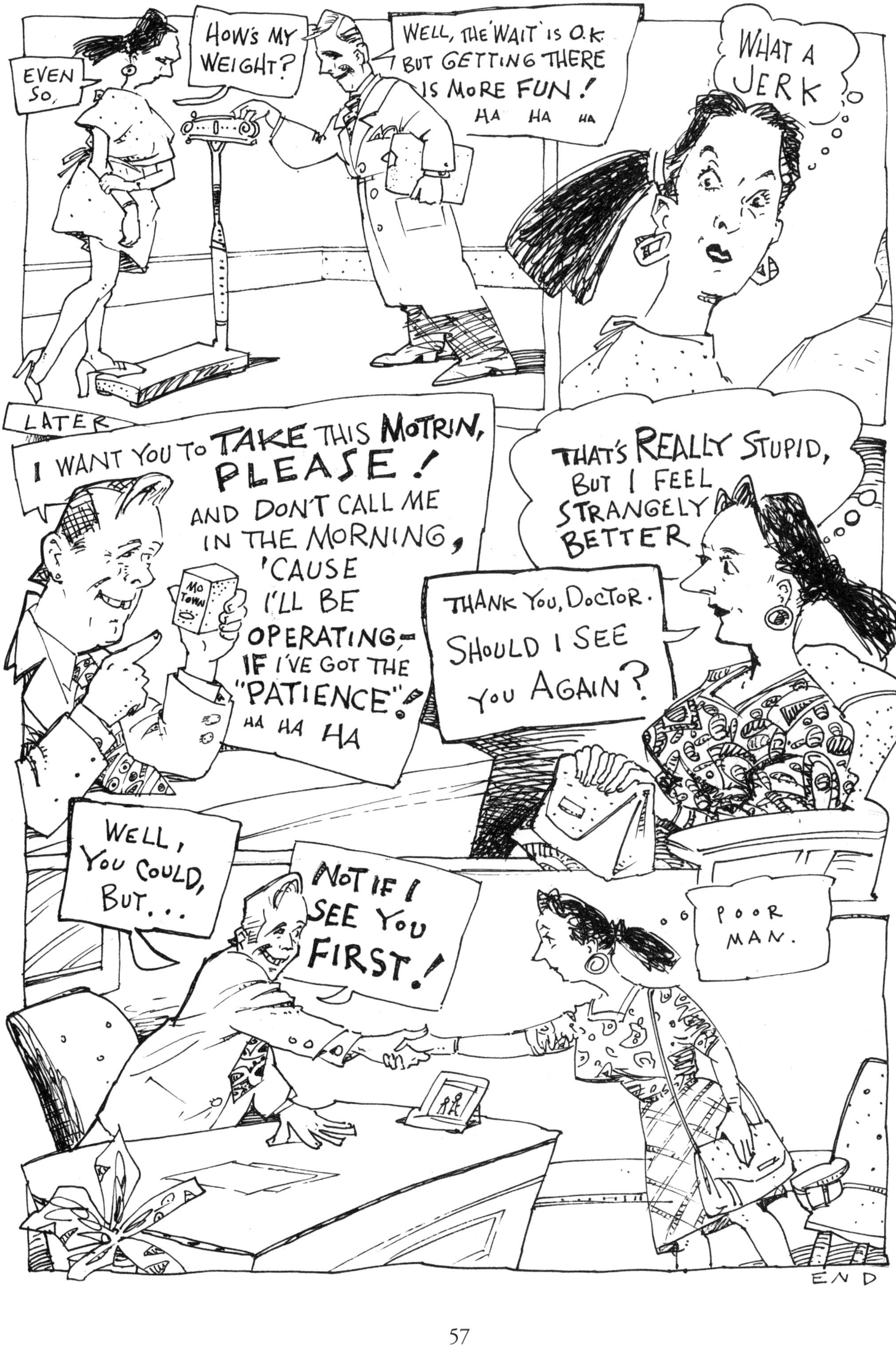
EVEN SO,
HOW'S MY WEIGHT?
WELL, THE 'WAIT' IS O.K. BUT GETTING THERE IS MORE FUN! HA HA HA
WHAT A JERK
LATER
I WANT YOU TO TAKE THIS MOTRIN, PLEASE! AND DON'T CALL ME IN THE MORNING, 'CAUSE I'LL BE OPERATING— IF I'VE GOT THE "PATIENCE"! HA HA HA
MO TOWN
THAT'S REALLY STUPID, BUT I FEEL STRANGELY BETTER
THANK YOU, DOCTOR. SHOULD I SEE YOU AGAIN?
WELL, YOU COULD, BUT...
NOT IF I SEE YOU FIRST!
POOR MAN.
END

An annoying fly circled low and pulled in for a landing on my drawing board one summer afternoon. I could see immediately that it had a bad attitude, hovering and dive-bombing on purpose. I was working on new ideas for cartoons but now I couldn't think. So, I drew the fly, its nasty smirk and taunting posture, and put the sketch up on my wall. Shortly after the fly itself had escaped, the idea for "Fly Brothers in Hollywood" was hatched. I pitched it to the *Lampoon* editor and got the gig.

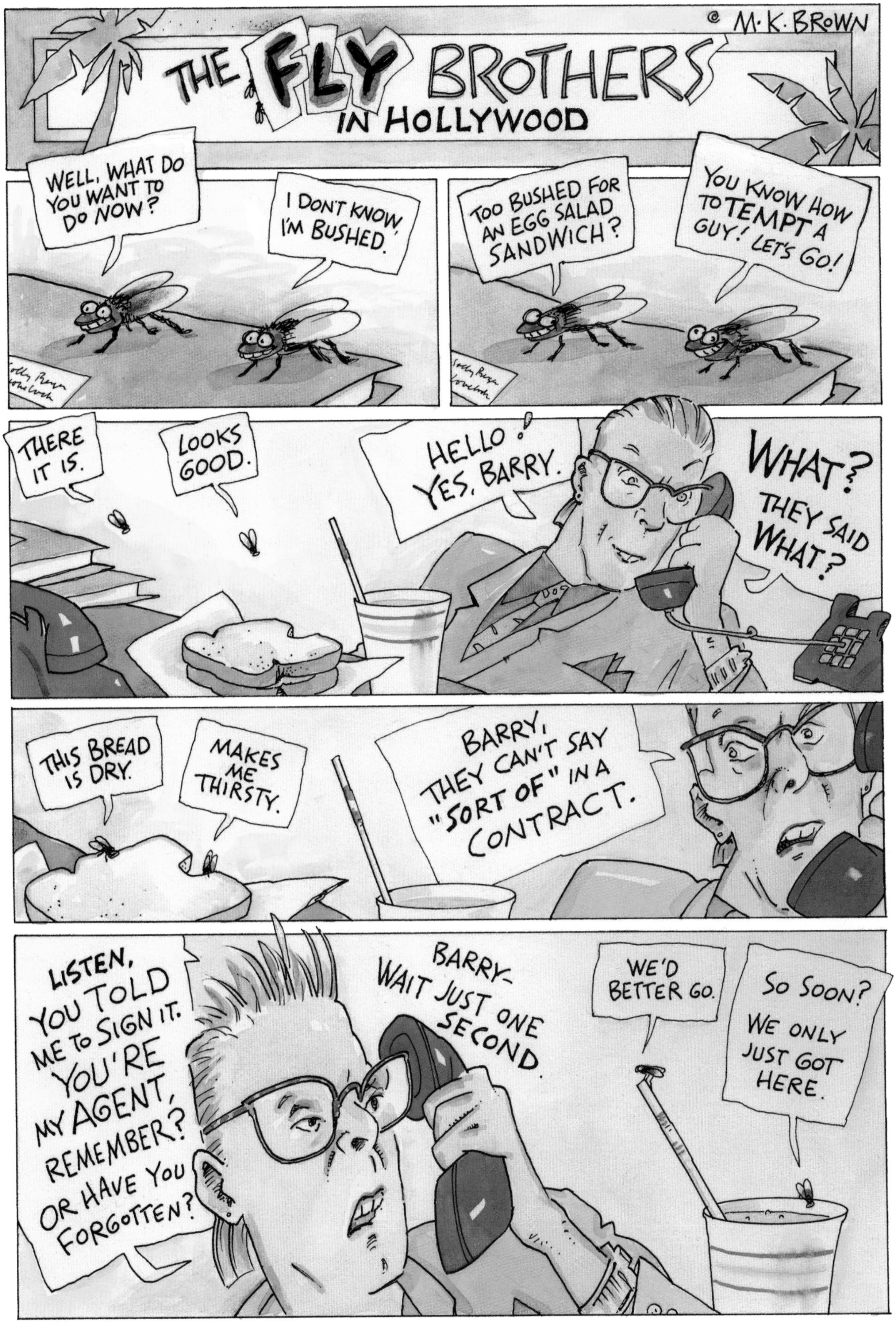

© M·K·BROWN
THE FLY BROTHERS IN HOLLYWOOD
WELL, WHAT DO YOU WANT TO DO NOW?
I DON'T KNOW, I'M BUSHED.
TOO BUSHED FOR AN EGG SALAD SANDWICH?
YOU KNOW HOW TO TEMPT A GUY! LET'S GO!
THERE IT IS.
LOOKS GOOD.
HELLO! YES, BARRY.
WHAT? THEY SAID WHAT?
THIS BREAD IS DRY.
MAKES ME THIRSTY.
BARRY, THEY CAN'T SAY "SORT OF" IN A CONTRACT.
LISTEN, YOU TOLD ME TO SIGN IT. YOU'RE MY AGENT, REMEMBER? OR HAVE YOU FORGOTTEN?
BARRY- WAIT JUST ONE SECOND.
WE'D BETTER GO.
SO SOON? WE ONLY JUST GOT HERE.

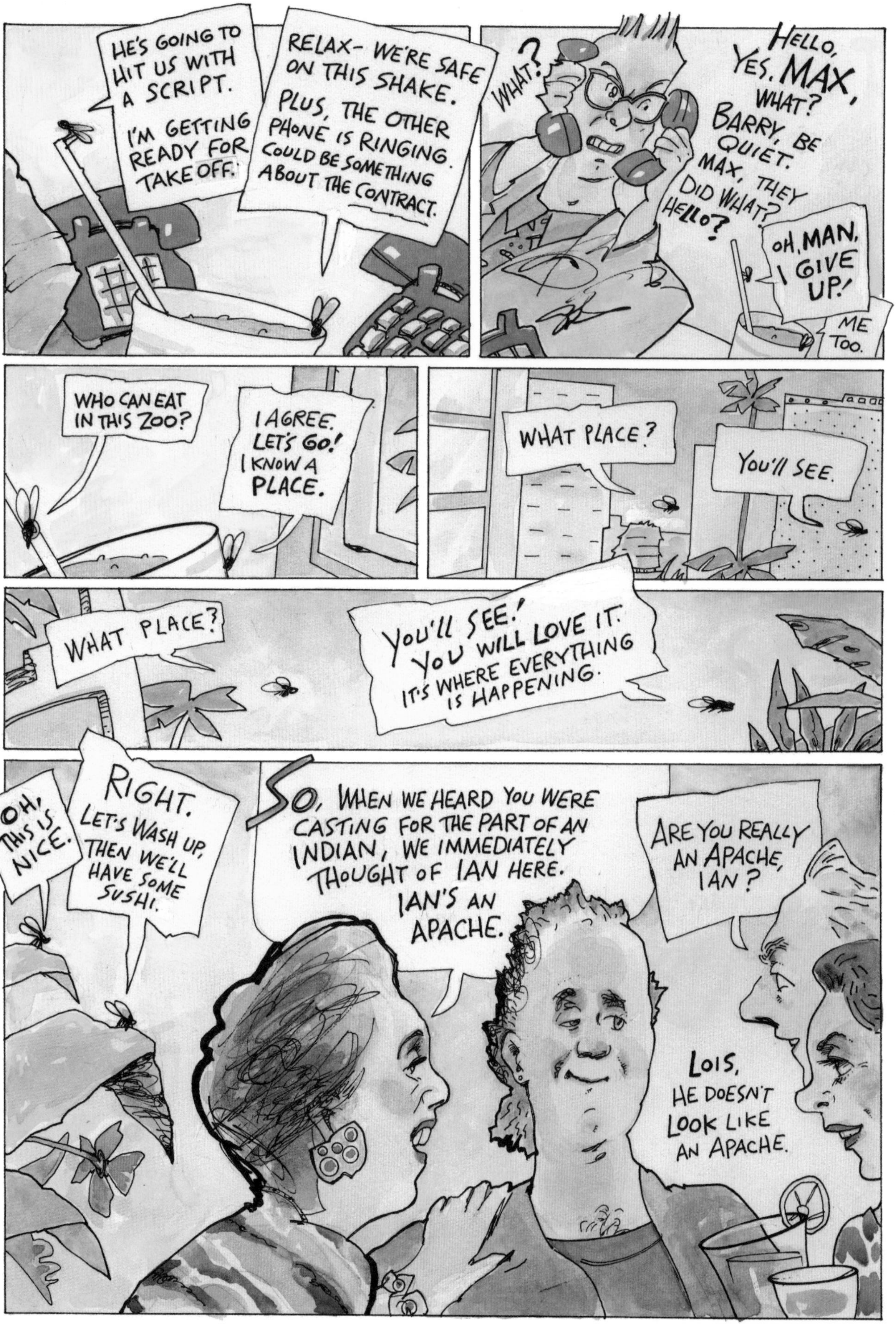

HE'S GOING TO HIT US WITH A SCRIPT.
I'M GETTING READY FOR TAKE OFF.
RELAX- WE'RE SAFE ON THIS SHAKE.
PLUS, THE OTHER PHONE IS RINGING. COULD BE SOMETHING ABOUT THE CONTRACT.
WHAT?
HELLO, YES. MAX, WHAT? BARRY, BE QUIET. MAX, THEY DID WHAT? HELLO?
OH, MAN, I GIVE UP!
ME TOO.
WHO CAN EAT IN THIS ZOO?
I AGREE. LET'S GO! I KNOW A PLACE.
WHAT PLACE?
YOU'LL SEE.
WHAT PLACE?
YOU'LL SEE! YOU WILL LOVE IT. IT'S WHERE EVERYTHING IS HAPPENING.
OH, THIS IS NICE.
RIGHT. LET'S WASH UP, THEN WE'LL HAVE SOME SUSHI.
SO, WHEN WE HEARD YOU WERE CASTING FOR THE PART OF AN INDIAN, WE IMMEDIATELY THOUGHT OF IAN HERE. IAN'S AN APACHE.
ARE YOU REALLY AN APACHE, IAN?
LOIS, HE DOESN'T LOOK LIKE AN APACHE.

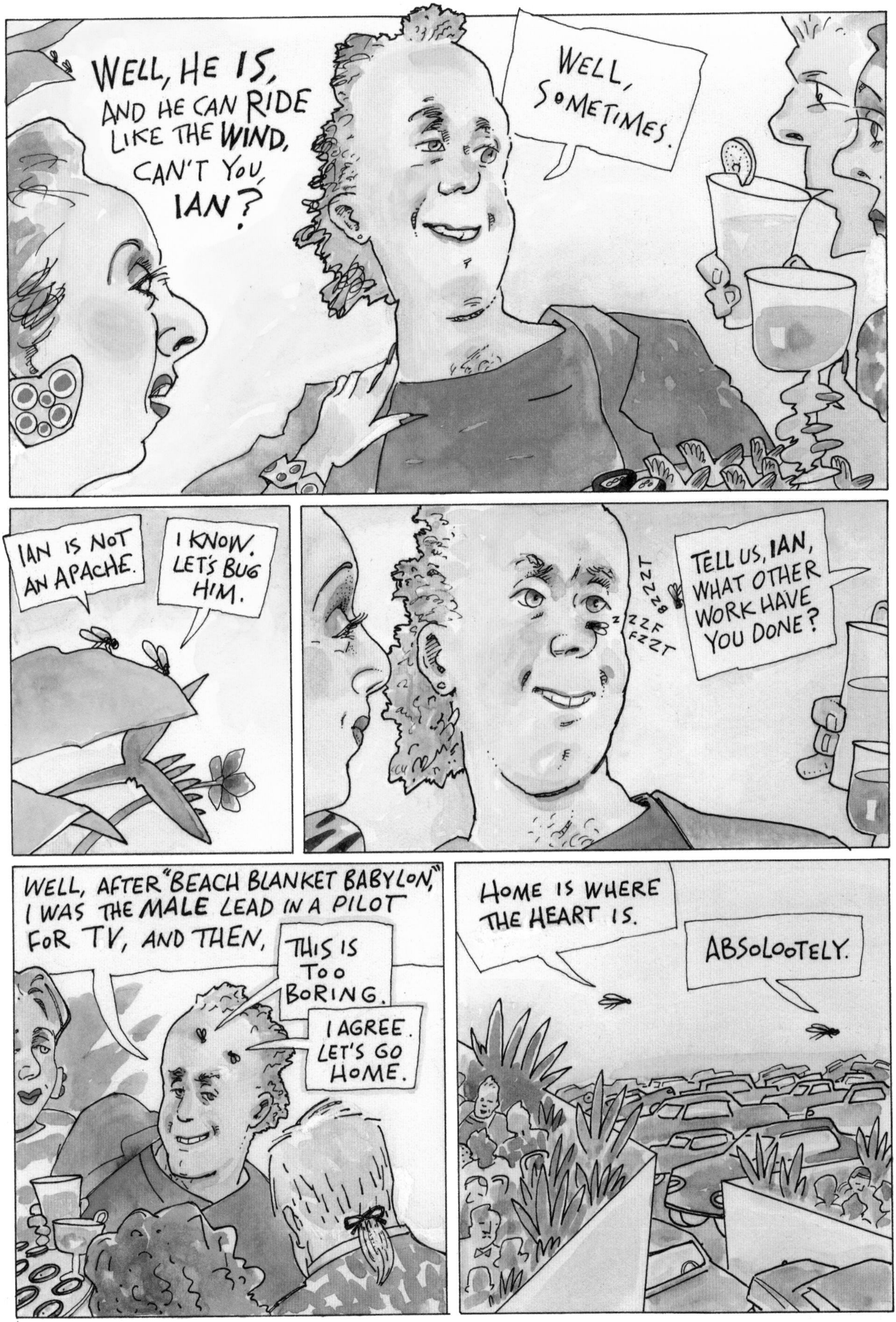
WELL, HE IS, AND HE CAN RIDE LIKE THE WIND, CAN'T YOU, IAN?
WELL, SOMETIMES.
IAN IS NOT AN APACHE.
I KNOW. LET'S BUG HIM.
ZZZZB
ZZZF FZZT
TELL US, IAN, WHAT OTHER WORK HAVE YOU DONE?
WELL, AFTER "BEACH BLANKET BABYLON," I WAS THE MALE LEAD IN A PILOT FOR TV, AND THEN,
THIS IS TOO BORING.
I AGREE. LET'S GO HOME.
HOME IS WHERE THE HEART IS.
ABSOLOOTELY.

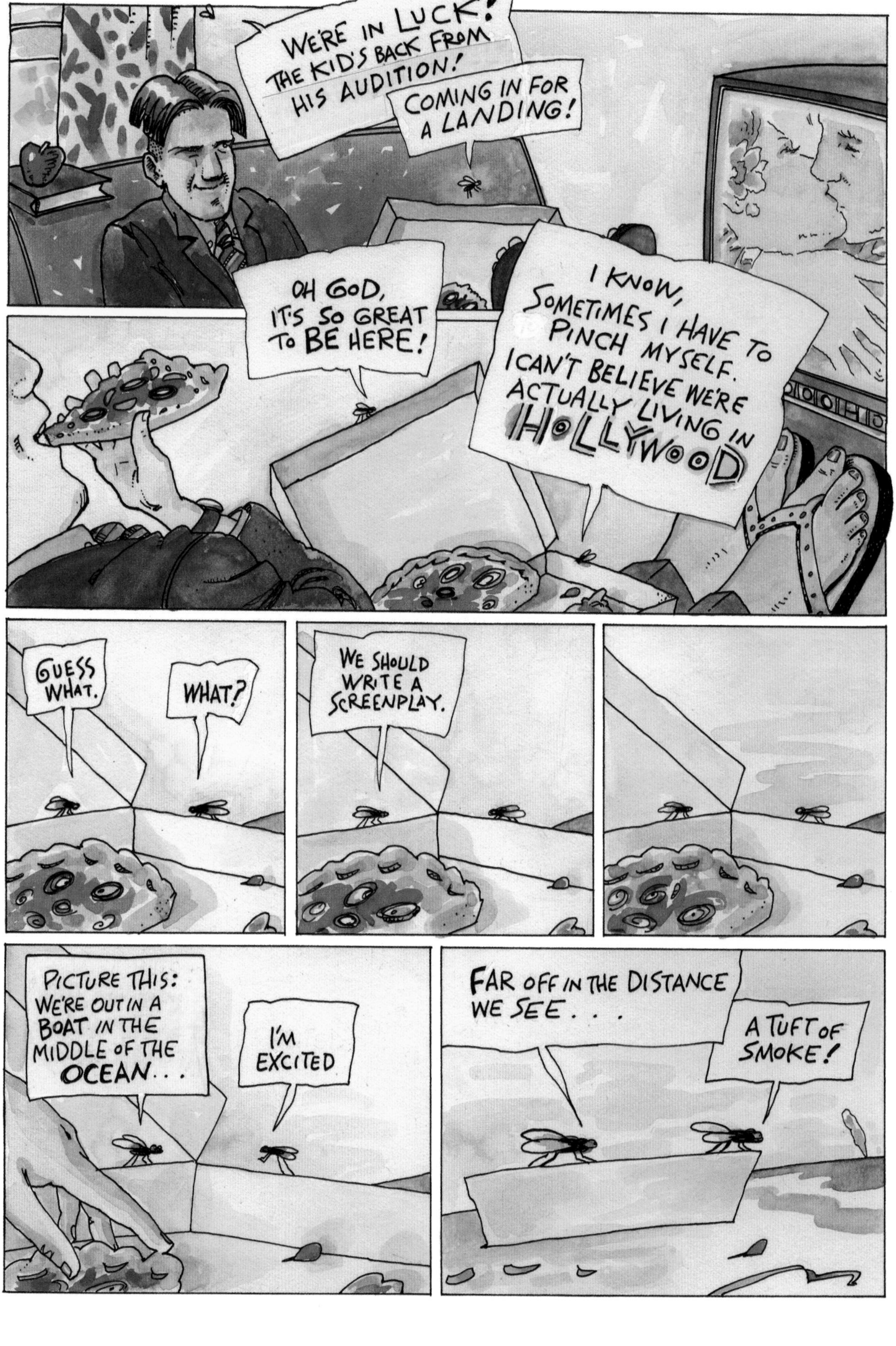
WE'RE IN LUCK! THE KID'S BACK FROM HIS AUDITION!
COMING IN FOR A LANDING!
OH GOD, IT'S SO GREAT TO BE HERE!
I KNOW, SOMETIMES I HAVE TO PINCH MYSELF. I CAN'T BELIEVE WE'RE ACTUALLY LIVING IN HOLLYWOOD
GUESS WHAT.
WHAT?
WE SHOULD WRITE A SCREENPLAY.
PICTURE THIS: WE'RE OUT IN A BOAT IN THE MIDDLE OF THE OCEAN...
I'M EXCITED
FAR OFF IN THE DISTANCE WE SEE...
A TUFT OF SMOKE!

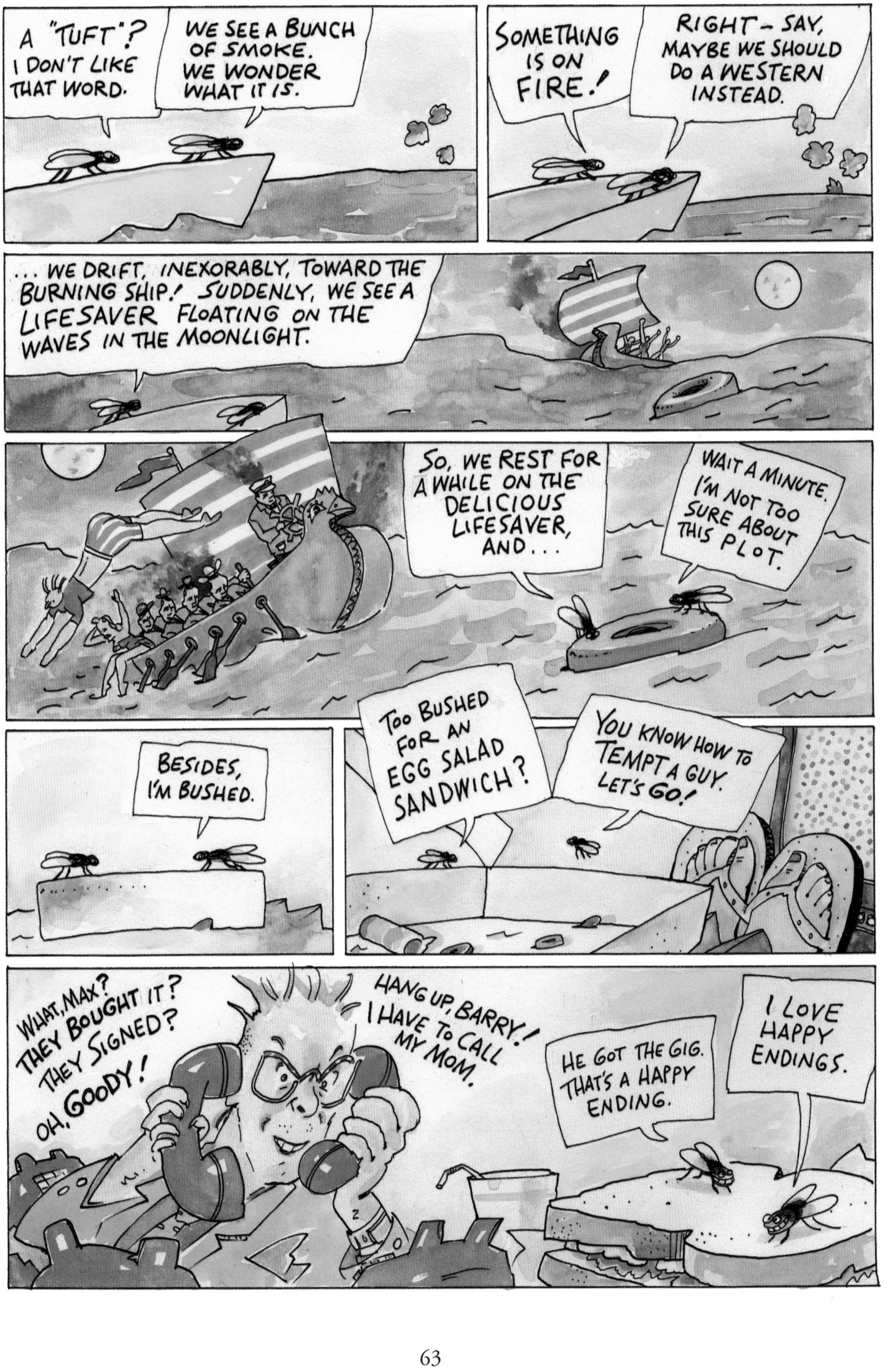
A "TUFT"? I DON'T LIKE THAT WORD.
WE SEE A BUNCH OF SMOKE. WE WONDER WHAT IT IS.
SOMETHING IS ON FIRE!
RIGHT - SAY, MAYBE WE SHOULD DO A WESTERN INSTEAD.
... WE DRIFT, INEXORABLY, TOWARD THE BURNING SHIP! SUDDENLY, WE SEE A LIFESAVER FLOATING ON THE WAVES IN THE MOONLIGHT.
SO, WE REST FOR A WHILE ON THE DELICIOUS LIFESAVER, AND...
WAIT A MINUTE. I'M NOT TOO SURE ABOUT THIS PLOT.
BESIDES, I'M BUSHED.
TOO BUSHED FOR AN EGG SALAD SANDWICH?
YOU KNOW HOW TO TEMPT A GUY. LET'S GO!
WHAT, MAX? THEY BOUGHT IT? THEY SIGNED? OH, GOODY!
HANG UP, BARRY! I HAVE TO CALL MY MOM.
HE GOT THE GIG. THAT'S A HAPPY ENDING.
I LOVE HAPPY ENDINGS.

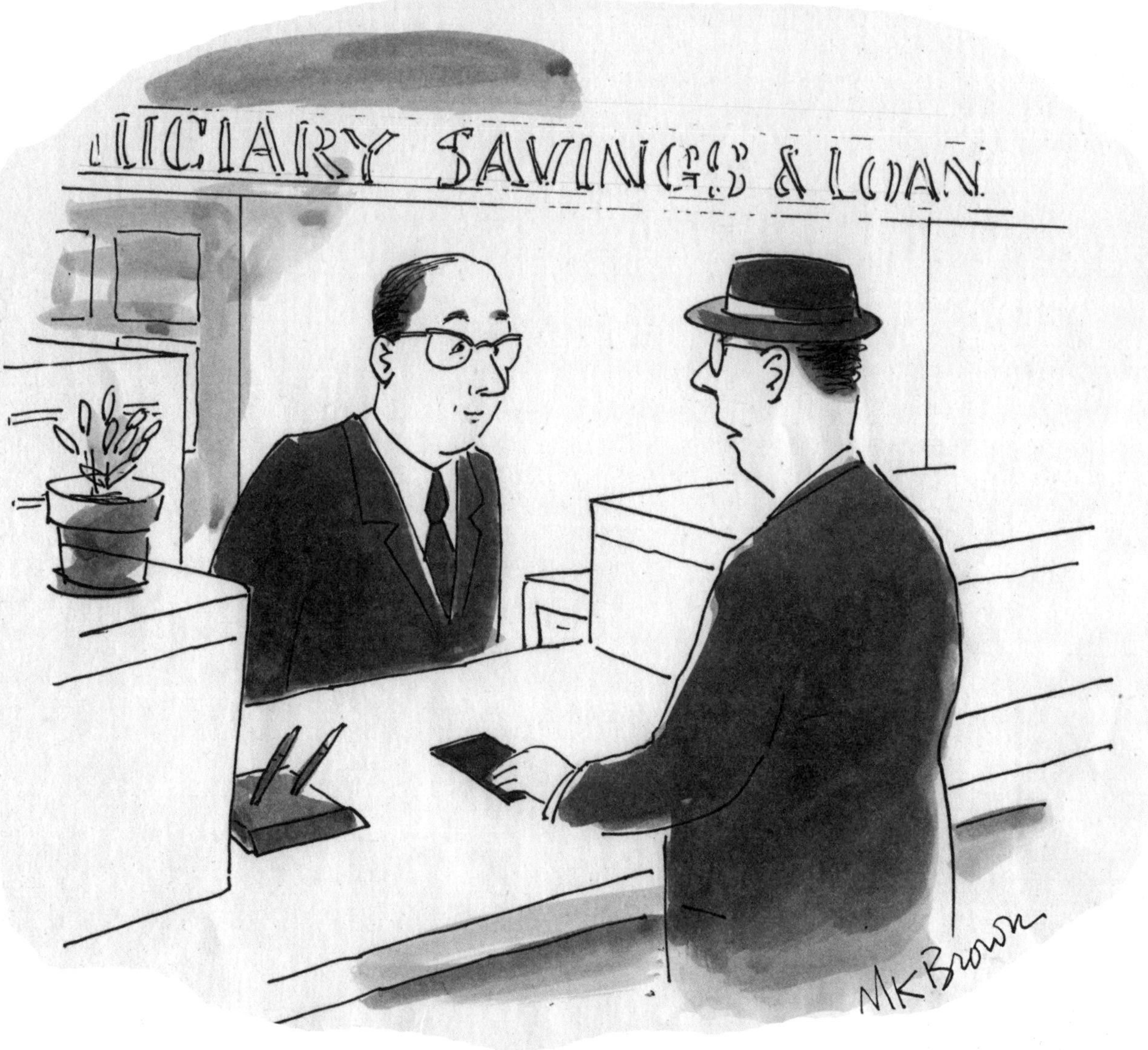
SAVINGS & LOAN
MK Brown

I don't want a kiss. I want my money.

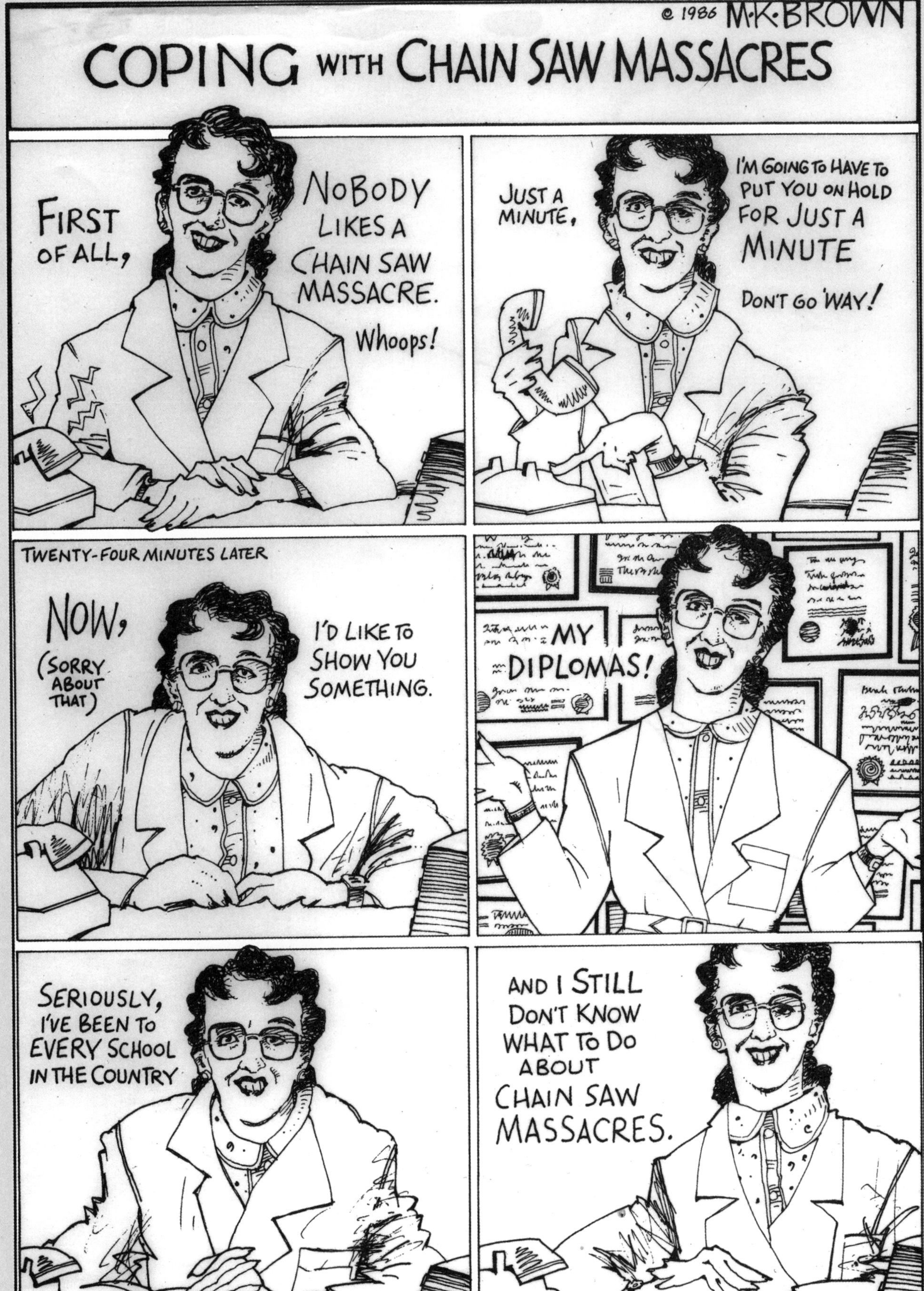
© 1986 M·K·BROWN
COPING WITH CHAIN SAW MASSACRES
FIRST OF ALL,
NOBODY LIKES A CHAIN SAW MASSACRE.
Whoops!
JUST A MINUTE,
I'M GOING TO HAVE TO PUT YOU ON HOLD FOR JUST A MINUTE
DON'T GO 'WAY!
TWENTY-FOUR MINUTES LATER
NOW,
(SORRY ABOUT THAT)
I'D LIKE TO SHOW YOU SOMETHING.
MY DIPLOMAS!
SERIOUSLY, I'VE BEEN TO EVERY SCHOOL IN THE COUNTRY
AND I STILL DON'T KNOW WHAT TO DO ABOUT CHAIN SAW MASSACRES.

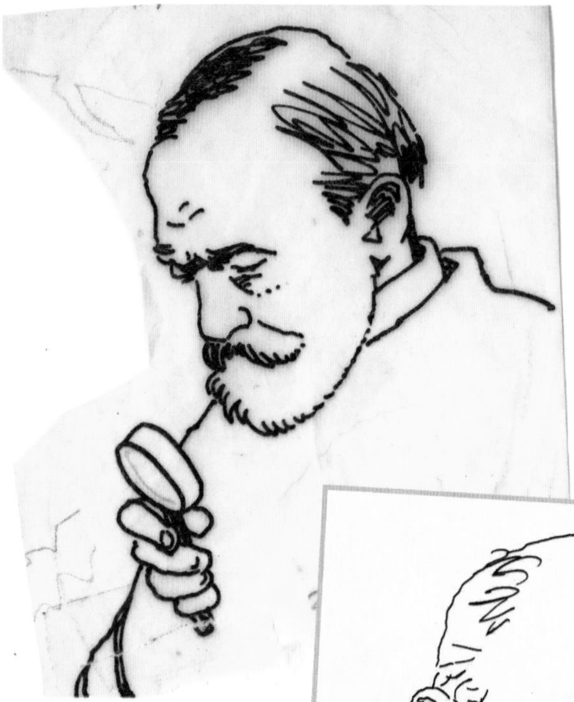
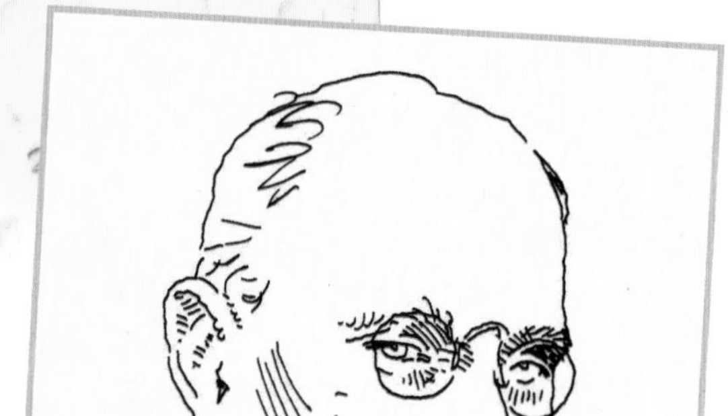

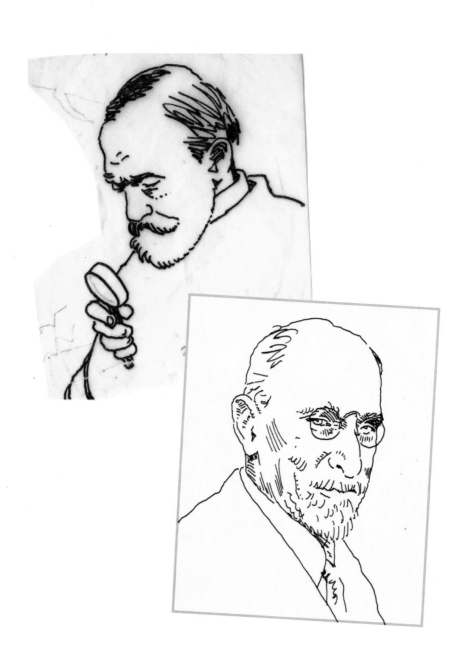

Science and Technology

"I like to draw things I don't understand so that others don't understand them also."

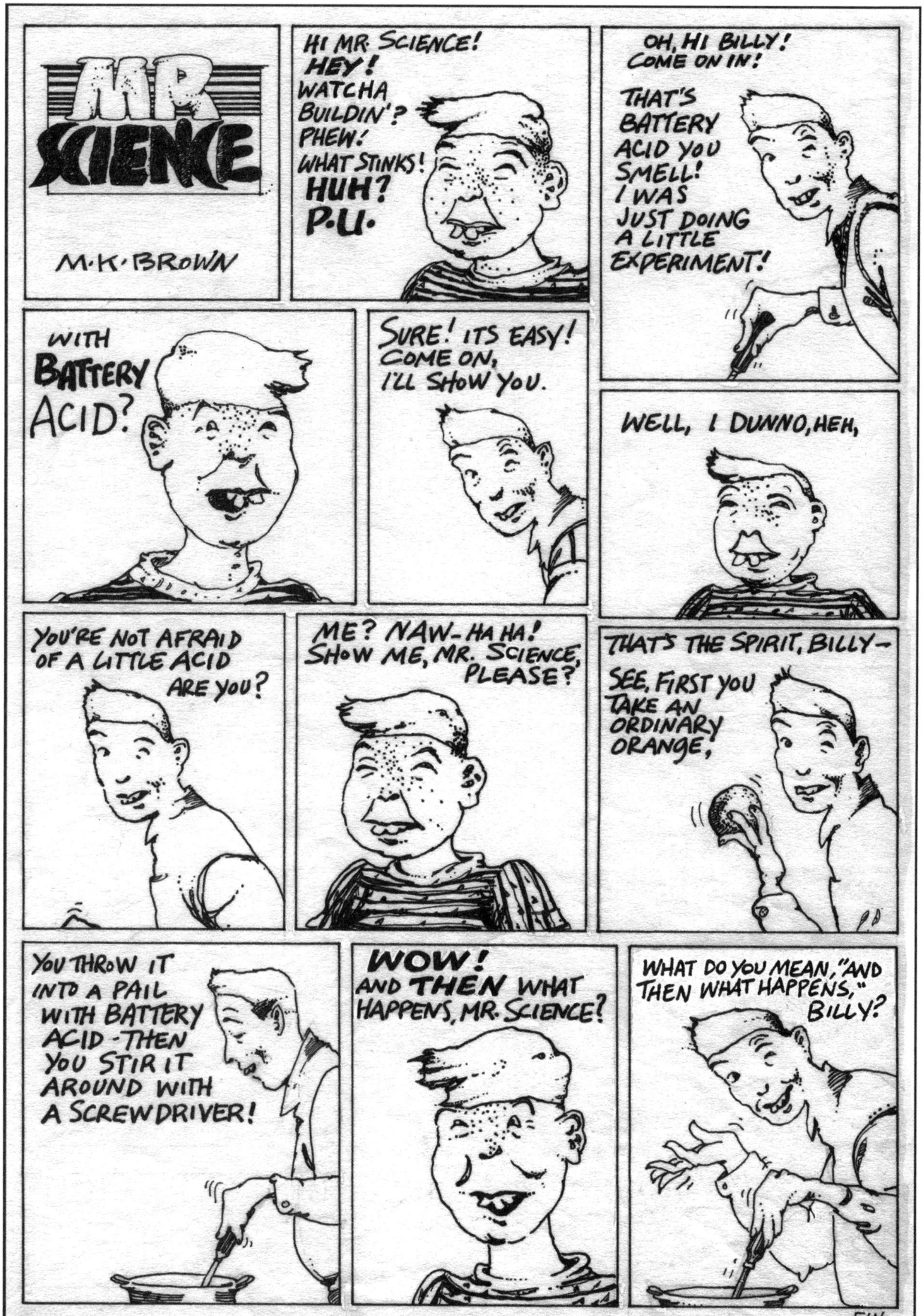
MR SCIENCE
M.K. BROWN
HI MR. SCIENCE! HEY! WATCHA BUILDIN'? PHEW! WHAT STINKS! HUH? P.U.
OH, HI BILLY! COME ON IN!
THAT'S BATTERY ACID YOU SMELL! I WAS JUST DOING A LITTLE EXPERIMENT!
WITH BATTERY ACID?
SURE! ITS EASY! COME ON, I'LL SHOW YOU.
WELL, I DUNNO, HEH,
YOU'RE NOT AFRAID OF A LITTLE ACID ARE YOU?
ME? NAW- HA HA! SHOW ME, MR. SCIENCE, PLEASE?
THAT'S THE SPIRIT, BILLY-
SEE, FIRST YOU TAKE AN ORDINARY ORANGE,
YOU THROW IT INTO A PAIL WITH BATTERY ACID - THEN YOU STIR IT AROUND WITH A SCREWDRIVER!
WOW! AND THEN WHAT HAPPENS, MR. SCIENCE?
WHAT DO YOU MEAN, "AND THEN WHAT HAPPENS," BILLY?
FIN

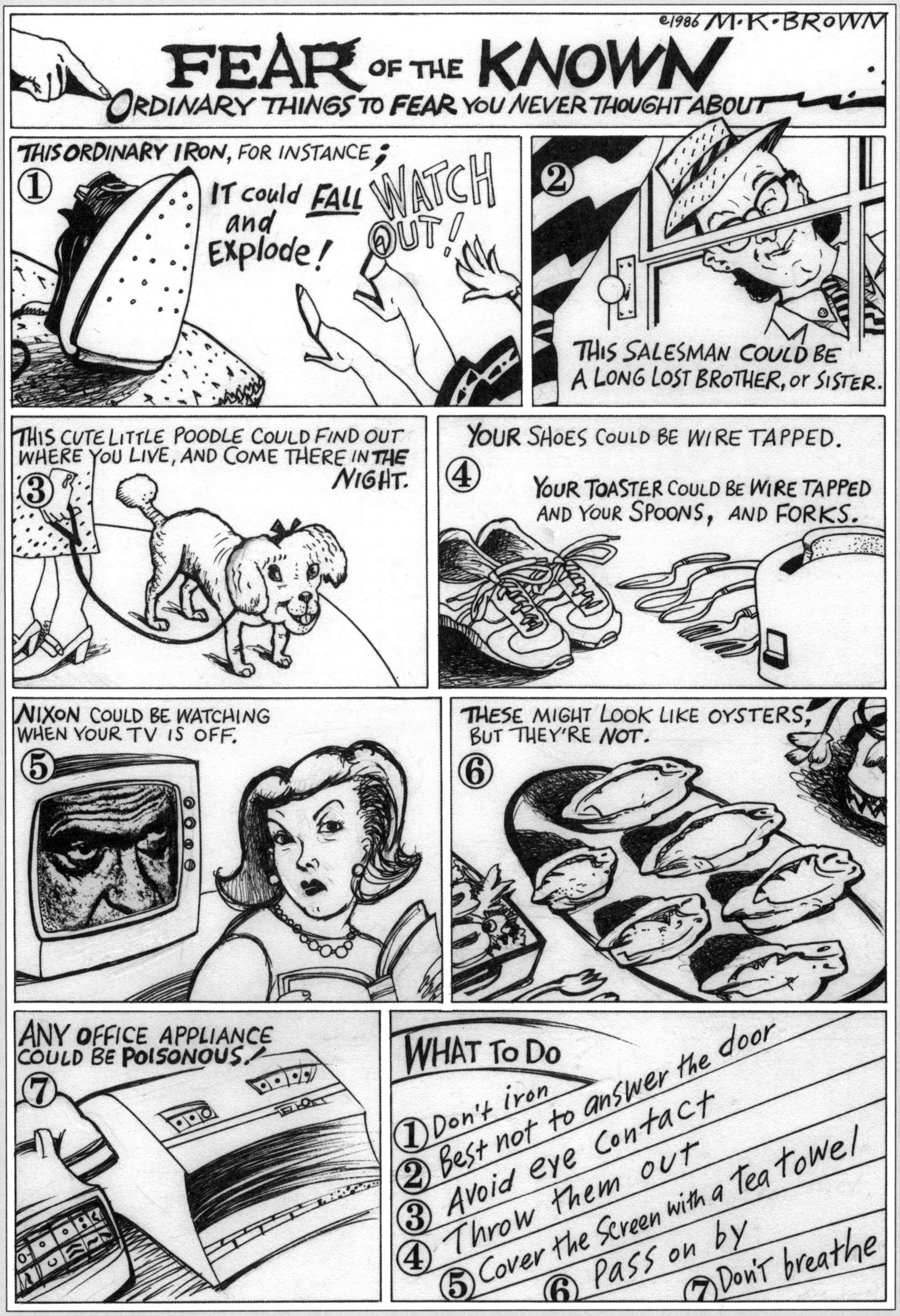
©1986 M·K·BROWN
FEAR OF THE KNOWN
ORDINARY THINGS TO FEAR YOU NEVER THOUGHT ABOUT
THIS ORDINARY IRON, FOR INSTANCE;
1
IT could FALL and Explode!
WATCH OUT!
2
THIS SALESMAN COULD BE A LONG LOST BROTHER, or SISTER.
THIS CUTE LITTLE POODLE COULD FIND OUT WHERE YOU LIVE, AND COME THERE IN THE NIGHT.
3
YOUR SHOES COULD BE WIRE TAPPED.
4
YOUR TOASTER COULD BE WIRE TAPPED AND YOUR SPOONS, AND FORKS.
NIXON COULD BE WATCHING WHEN YOUR TV IS OFF.
5
THESE MIGHT LOOK LIKE OYSTERS, BUT THEY'RE NOT.
6
ANY OFFICE APPLIANCE COULD BE POISONOUS!
7
WHAT To Do
1 Don't iron
2 Best not to answer the door
3 Avoid eye contact
4 Throw them out
5 Cover the Screen with a Tea towel
6 Pass on by
7 Don't breathe

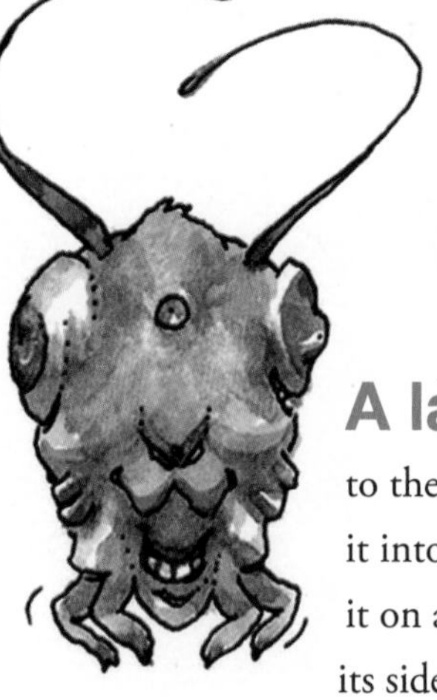

A large grasshopper was clinging to the living room drapes one hot summer day. I slid it into a jar, took it out to the garden, and placed it on a wide succulent leaf, where it collapsed onto its side. I nudged it upright so it could balance on its chest and stomach, and was admiring the handsome Lincoln Continental / jade green color and intricate armature—when I realized it must be very thirsty.

I put some water into a cup and brought it out. Grasshopper had not moved. I placed a drop on the leaf by its head and soon a dark, thin tube unfurled, sucking up half the drop. It dipped again and the drop disappeared. A second drop was also consumed.

The grasshopper seemed to pull itself together now: standing firmly on its legs and even beginning to wash up a bit, maybe getting ready for takeoff. I wanted to see it closer before departure so I brought out my large, round magnifying glass. I lowered it to within a few inches from the grasshopper and was thrilled to see the details of its limbs and wings. I slowly worked my way up the body to the boxy head, which suddenly turned toward me with that alien face. Yikes! We both gasped: I, at the oddly intelligent features from another species staring back at me, and it, recoiling in obvious shock at this hovering apparition. In a flash it flew up into a tall bay tree.

When I went inside to look at myself in the mirror, peering through the magnifying glass, I saw the reason for its hasty flight. I was a predatory monster with one huge eye, worse than any grasshopper nightmare. Though very sorry to have caused such fright, my interest was tweaked enough to do some research into its anatomy. And that's how the following cartoon began. Of course, one thing leads to another and cartoons often start one way and end elsewhere.

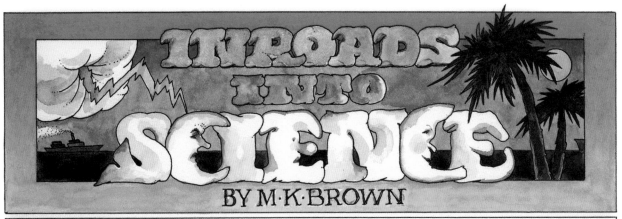

INROADS INTO SCIENCE

BY M·K·BROWN

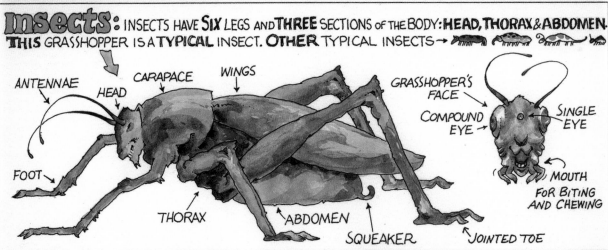

Insects: INSECTS HAVE **SIX** LEGS AND **THREE** SECTIONS OF THE BODY: **HEAD, THORAX & ABDOMEN.** **THIS** GRASSHOPPER IS A **TYPICAL** INSECT. **OTHER** TYPICAL INSECTS →

ANTENNAE
HEAD
CARAPACE
WINGS
FOOT
THORAX
ABDOMEN
SQUEAKER
JOINTED TOE

GRASSHOPPER'S FACE
COMPOUND EYE
SINGLE EYE
MOUTH FOR BITING AND CHEWING

IN **SOME** PARTS OF THE WORLD **INSECTS** ARE USED FOR **TRANSPORTATION**, AS IN **HAWAII**, WHERE **IDEAL** **CONDITIONS** ENCOURAGE **COLOSSAL** GROWTH. HERE, A LITTLE DUTCH GIRL ON A **GIANT** **CICADA** SHELL **NARROWLY MISSES** THE KIND OF **TRAGIC ACCIDENT** WHICH CAN SPOIL A VACATION.

INSECTS, HOWEVER, AREN'T THE **ONLY** THING TO **FLOURISH** IN **HAWAII**. **THIS THOUGHTLESS** FISHERMAN (ONCE A PALE AND **BITTER BOY**) **IS**, IN FACT, HAVING THE **TIME OF HIS LIFE** IN BEAUTIFUL **MAUI,** THE *"LAND OF THE* **GIANT BANANA"**.

NOT USED FOR **EATING**, MAUI'S **GIANT BANANAS** FUNCTION **SOLELY** AS TOURIST ATTRACTION AND ARE, IN FACT, A **BURDEN** UPON THOSE ENTRUSTED TO THEIR **CARE. THIS** FIELD OF **BANANAS** IS **READY** FOR **HARVEST**, AND, AS ALWAYS AT THIS TIME OF YEAR, THE **AIR** IS **CHARGED** WITH **DANGER**....

I'M SCARED.

I'M SCARED, I TELL YOU.

NOW JOHN, DON'T START.

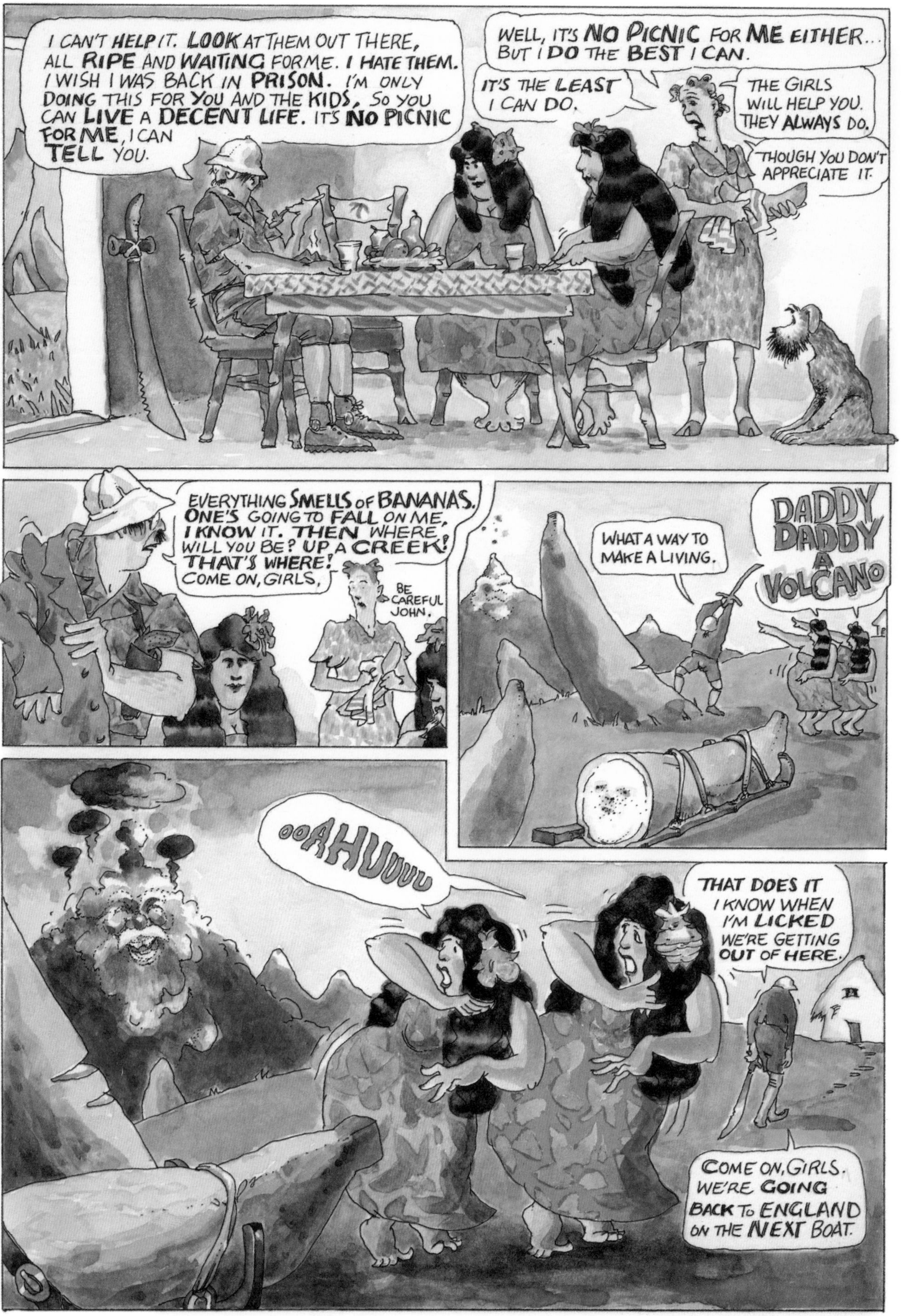
I CAN'T HELP IT. LOOK AT THEM OUT THERE, ALL RIPE AND WAITING FOR ME. I HATE THEM. I WISH I WAS BACK IN PRISON. I'M ONLY DOING THIS FOR YOU AND THE KIDS, SO YOU CAN LIVE A DECENT LIFE. IT'S NO PICNIC FOR ME, I CAN TELL YOU.
WELL, IT'S NO PICNIC FOR ME EITHER... BUT I DO THE BEST I CAN.
IT'S THE LEAST I CAN DO.
THE GIRLS WILL HELP YOU. THEY ALWAYS DO.
THOUGH YOU DON'T APPRECIATE IT.
EVERYTHING SMELLS OF BANANAS. ONE'S GOING TO FALL ON ME, I KNOW IT. THEN WHERE WILL YOU BE? UP A CREEK! THAT'S WHERE! COME ON, GIRLS.
BE CAREFUL JOHN.
WHAT A WAY TO MAKE A LIVING.
DADDY DADDY A VOLCANO
ooAHUuuuu
THAT DOES IT I KNOW WHEN I'M LICKED WE'RE GETTING OUT OF HERE.
COME ON, GIRLS. WE'RE GOING BACK TO ENGLAND ON THE NEXT BOAT.

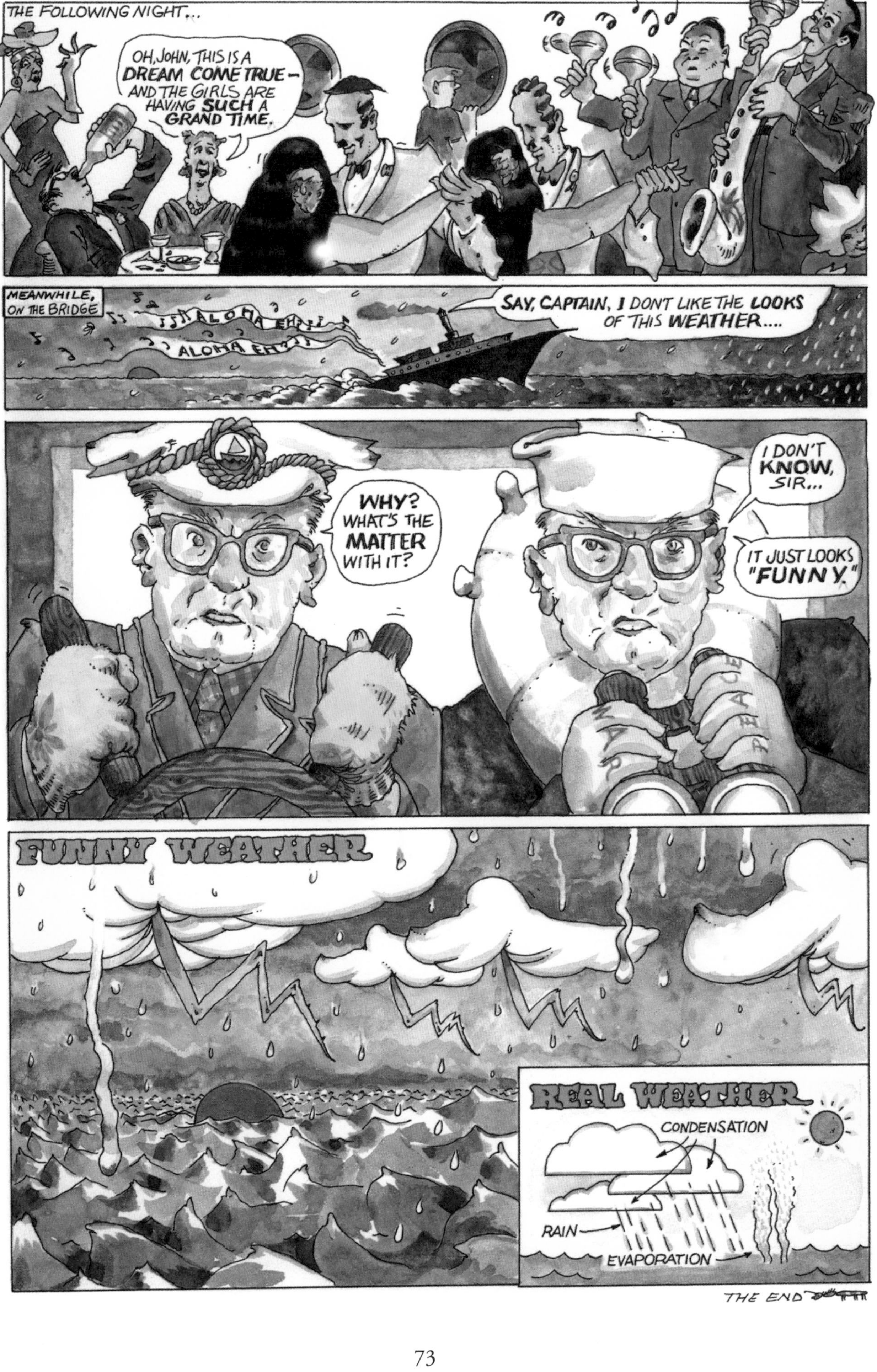
THE FOLLOWING NIGHT...
OH, JOHN, THIS IS A DREAM COME TRUE - AND THE GIRLS ARE HAVING SUCH A GRAND TIME.
MEANWHILE, ON THE BRIDGE
ALOHA EH!
ALOHA EH!
SAY, CAPTAIN, I DONT LIKE THE LOOKS OF THIS WEATHER....
WHY? WHAT'S THE MATTER WITH IT?
I DON'T KNOW, SIR...
IT JUST LOOKS "FUNNY."
WAR
PEACE
FUNNY WEATHER
REAL WEATHER
CONDENSATION
RAIN
EVAPORATION
THE END

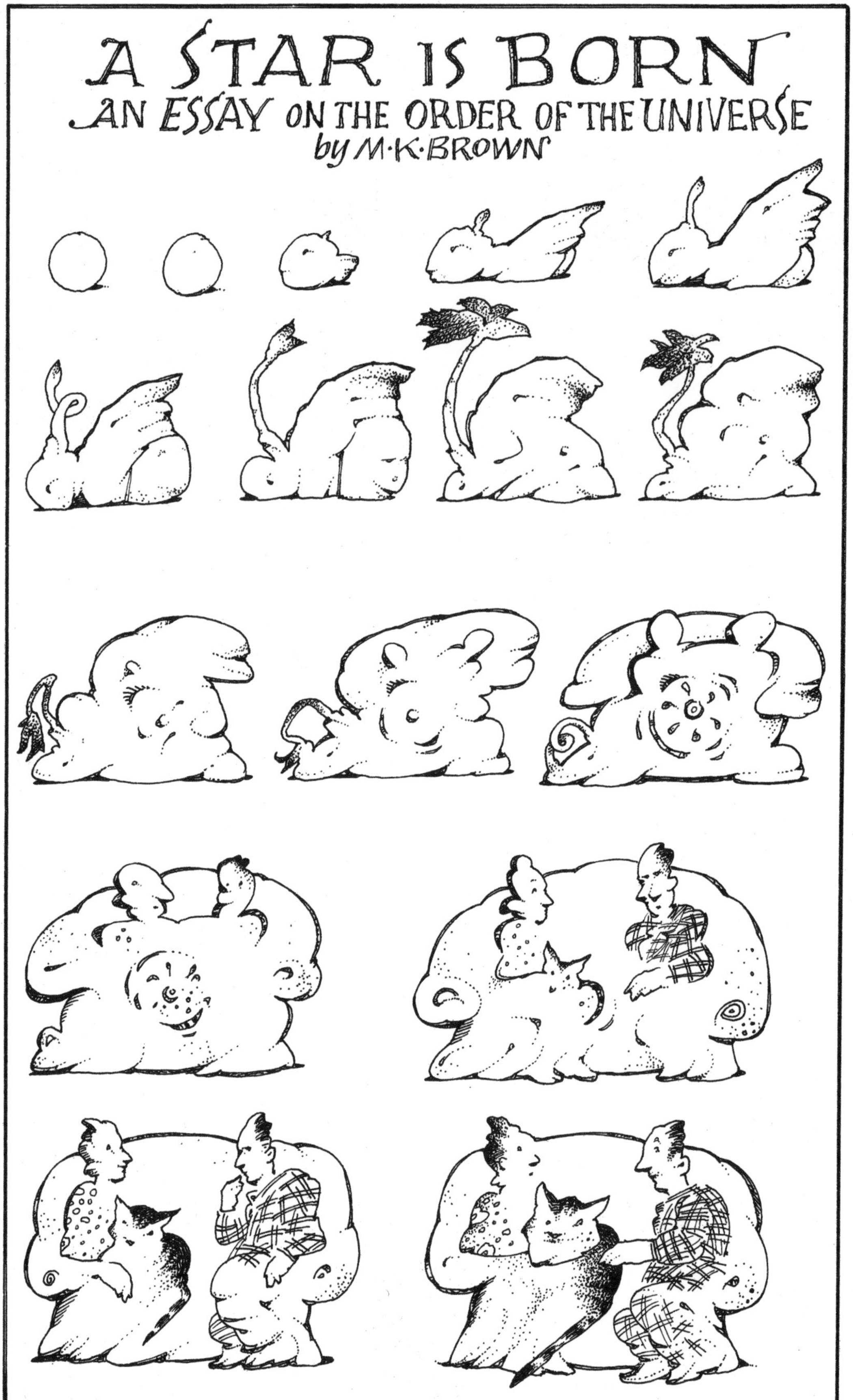
A STAR IS BORN
AN ESSAY ON THE ORDER OF THE UNIVERSE
by M·K·BROWN

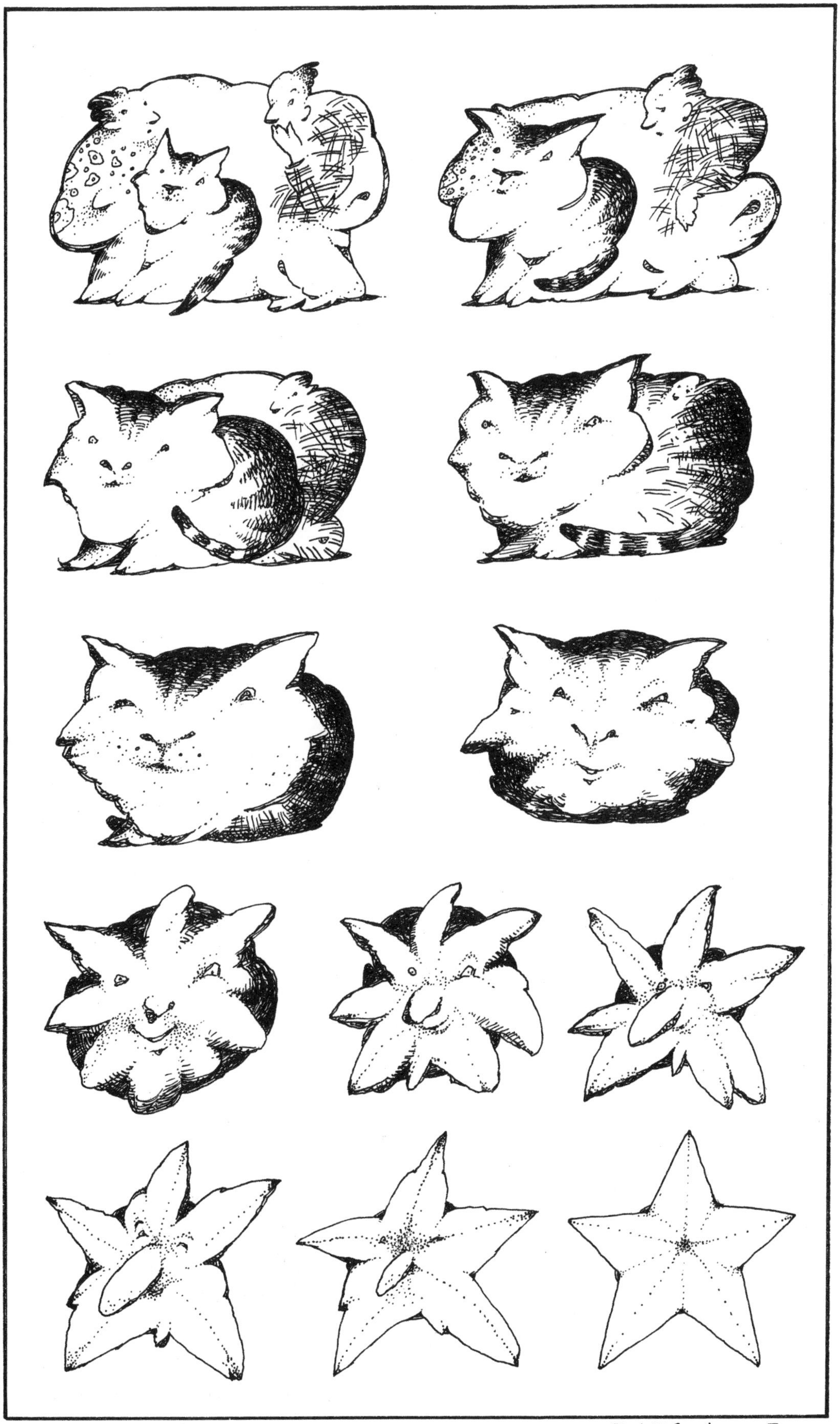

©'78 M.K.B.

The idea for "Women, What Do They Want?" surfaced late one feverish Saturday night after spinning 'round and 'round to the Bee Gees' "Disco Inferno." I am particularly fond of the '80s shoulder pads in this cartoon, something I could never get the hang of.

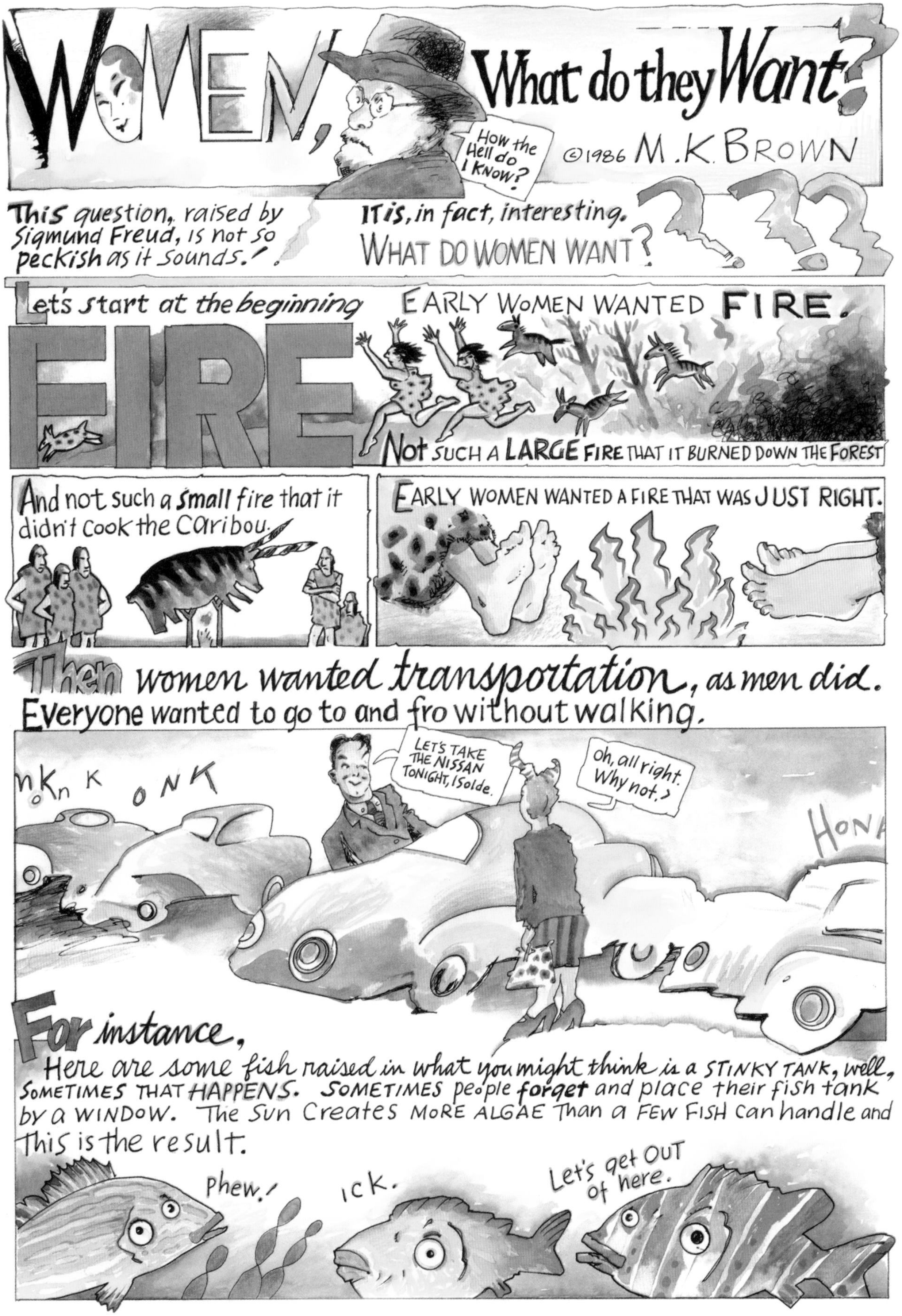
WOMEN, What do they Want?
How the Hell do I know?
©1986 M.K.BROWN
This question, raised by Sigmund Freud, is not so peckish as it sounds.!
IT is, in fact, interesting.
WHAT DO WOMEN WANT?
Let's start at the beginning
FIRE
EARLY WOMEN WANTED FIRE.
Not SUCH A LARGE FIRE THAT IT BURNED DOWN THE FOREST
And not such a small fire that it didn't cook the Caribou.
EARLY WOMEN WANTED A FIRE THAT WAS JUST RIGHT.
Then women wanted transportation, as men did.
Everyone wanted to go to and fro without walking.
nKn K ONK
LET'S TAKE THE NISSAN TONIGHT, Isolde.
Oh, all right. Why not.
HON
For instance,
Here are some fish raised in what you might think is a STINKY TANK, well, SOMETIMES THAT HAPPENS. SOMETIMES people forget and place their fish tank by a WINDOW. The Sun Creates MORE ALGAE Than a FEW FISH can handle and This is the result.
Phew.!
ick.
Let's get OUT of here.

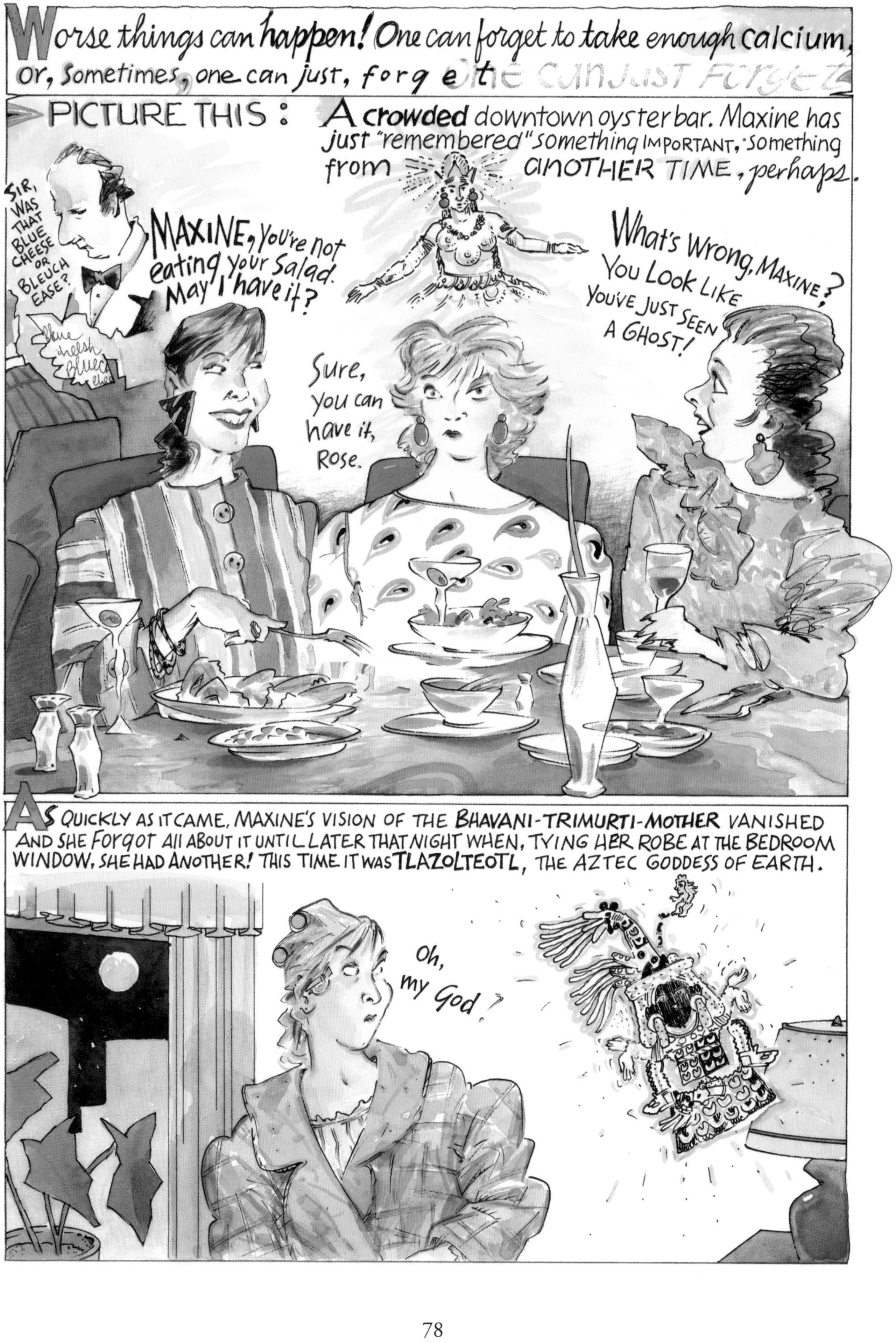
Worse things can happen! One can forget to take enough calcium,
or, Sometimes, one can just, forg e t one can just forget
PICTURE THIS: A crowded downtown oyster bar. Maxine has just "remembered" something IMPORTANT, something from ANOTHER TIME, perhaps.
SIR, WAS THAT BLUE CHEESE OR BLEUCH EASE?
MAXINE, you're not eating your Salad. May I have it?
What's Wrong, MAXINE? You Look LIKE You've JUST SEEN A GHOST!
Sure, you can have it, Rose.
AS QUICKLY AS IT CAME, MAXINE'S VISION OF THE BHAVANI-TRIMURTI-MOTHER VANISHED AND SHE Forgot All ABOUT IT UNTIL LATER THAT NIGHT WHEN, TYING HER ROBE AT THE BEDROOM WINDOW, SHE HAD ANOTHER! THIS TIME IT WAS TLAZOLTEOTL, THE AZTEC GODDESS OF EARTH.
Oh, my God?

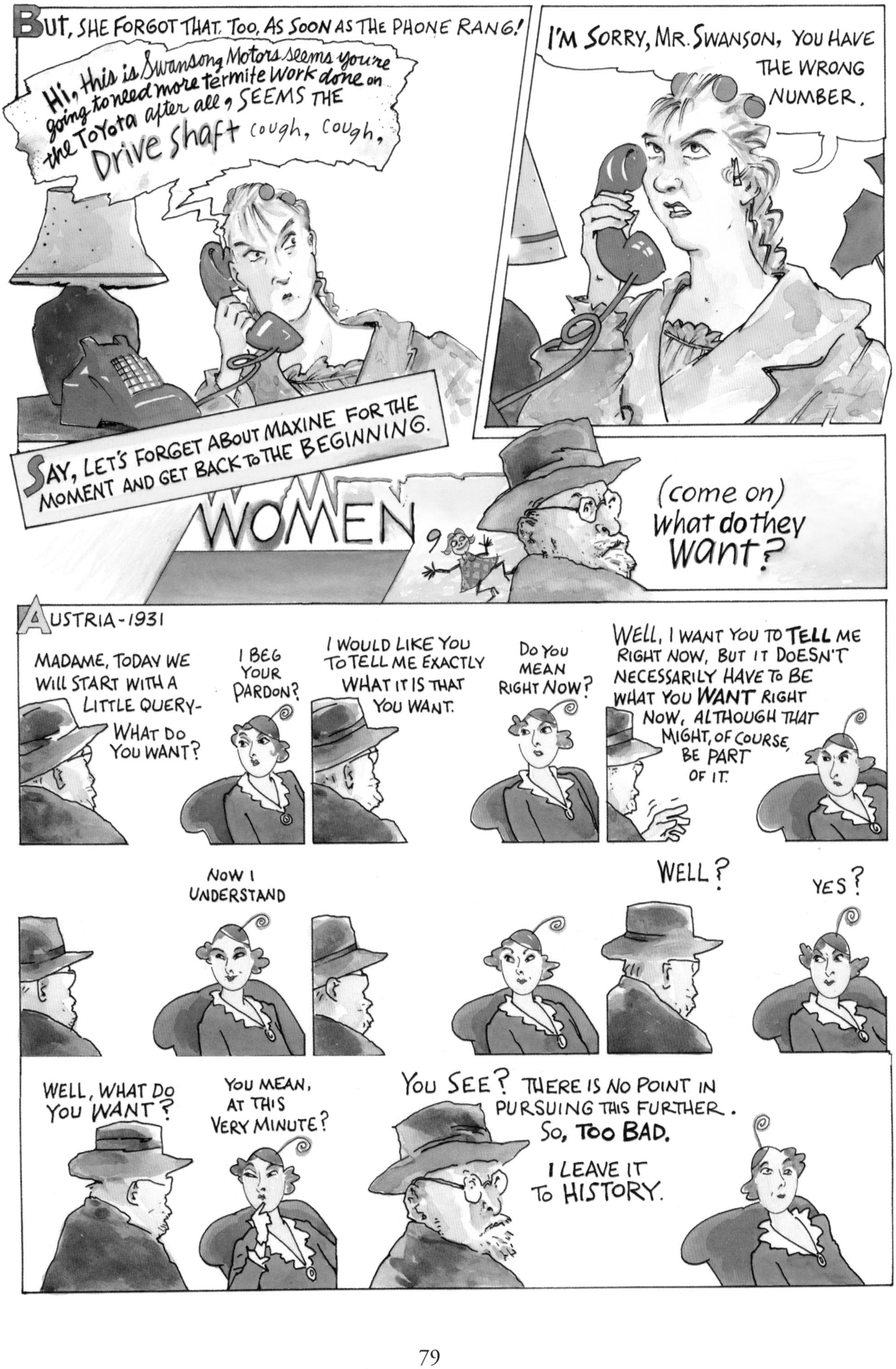
BUT, SHE FORGOT THAT, TOO, AS SOON AS THE PHONE RANG!
Hi, this is Swansong Motors seems you're going to need more termite work done on the Toyota after all, SEEMS THE Drive shaft cough, cough,
I'M SORRY, MR. SWANSON, YOU HAVE THE WRONG NUMBER.
SAY, LET'S FORGET ABOUT MAXINE FOR THE MOMENT AND GET BACK TO THE BEGINNING.
WOMEN
(come on) what do they want?
AUSTRIA - 1931
MADAME, TODAY WE WILL START WITH A LITTLE QUERY- WHAT DO YOU WANT?
I BEG YOUR PARDON?
I WOULD LIKE YOU TO TELL ME EXACTLY WHAT IT IS THAT YOU WANT.
DO YOU MEAN RIGHT NOW?
WELL, I WANT YOU TO TELL ME RIGHT NOW, BUT IT DOESN'T NECESSARILY HAVE TO BE WHAT YOU WANT RIGHT NOW, ALTHOUGH THAT MIGHT, OF COURSE, BE PART OF IT.
NOW I UNDERSTAND
WELL?
YES?
WELL, WHAT DO YOU WANT?
YOU MEAN, AT THIS VERY MINUTE?
YOU SEE? THERE IS NO POINT IN PURSUING THIS FURTHER. SO, TOO BAD.
I LEAVE IT TO HISTORY.

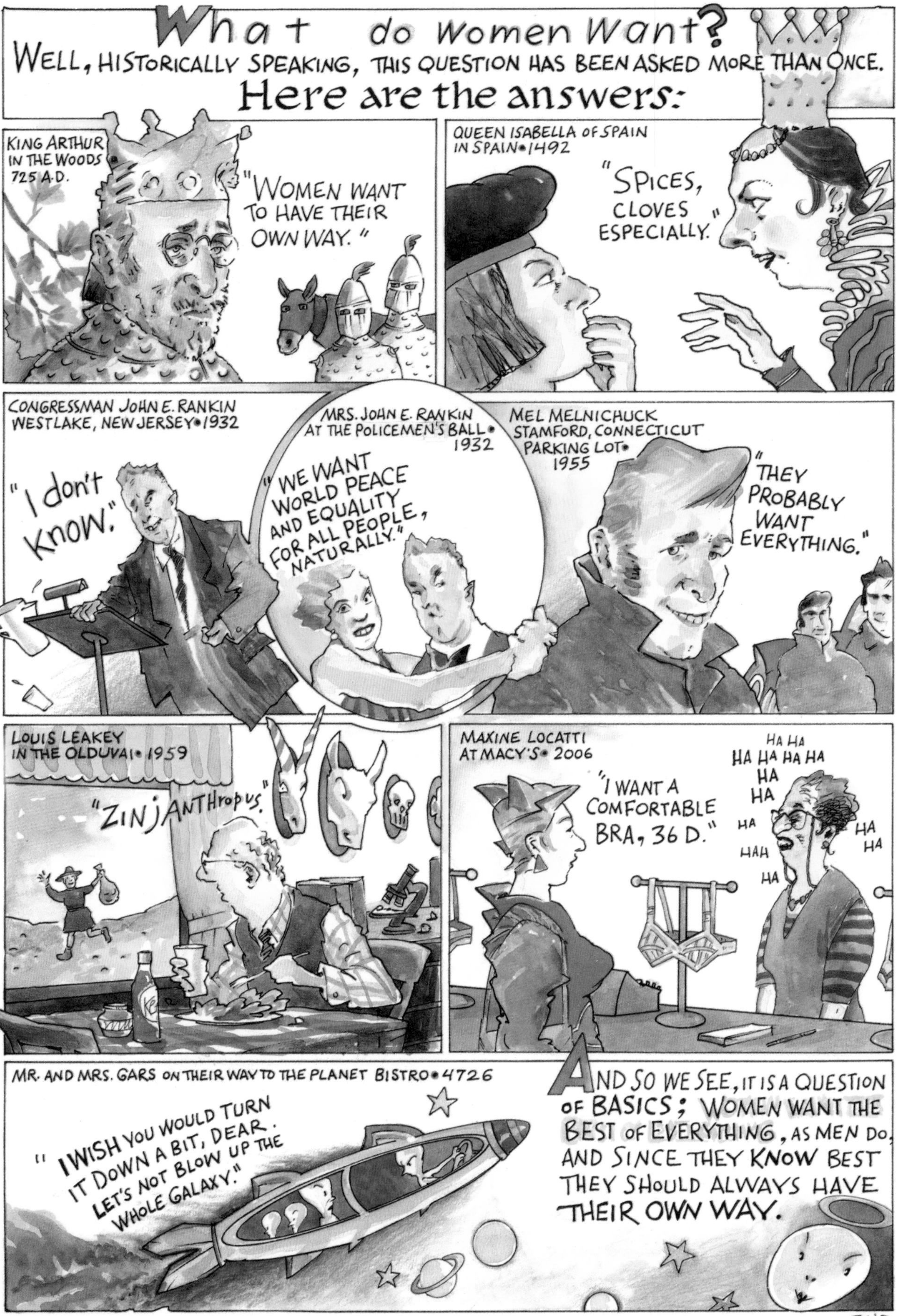
What do Women Want?
WELL, HISTORICALLY SPEAKING, THIS QUESTION HAS BEEN ASKED MORE THAN ONCE.
Here are the answers:
KING ARTHUR IN THE WOODS 725 A.D.
"WOMEN WANT TO HAVE THEIR OWN WAY."
QUEEN ISABELLA OF SPAIN IN SPAIN • 1492
"SPICES, CLOVES ESPECIALLY."
CONGRESSMAN JOHN E. RANKIN WESTLAKE, NEW JERSEY • 1932
"I don't know."
MRS. JOHN E. RANKIN AT THE POLICEMEN'S BALL • 1932
"WE WANT WORLD PEACE AND EQUALITY FOR ALL PEOPLE, NATURALLY."
MEL MELNICHUCK STAMFORD, CONNECTICUT PARKING LOT • 1955
"THEY PROBABLY WANT EVERYTHING."
LOUIS LEAKEY IN THE OLDUVAI • 1959
"ZINJANTHropus."
MAXINE LOCATTI AT MACY'S • 2006
"I WANT A COMFORTABLE BRA, 36 D."
HA HA HA HA HA HA HA HA HA HA HA HAH HA
MR. AND MRS. GARS ON THEIR WAY TO THE PLANET BISTRO • 4726
"I WISH YOU WOULD TURN IT DOWN A BIT, DEAR. LET'S NOT BLOW UP THE WHOLE GALAXY."
AND SO WE SEE, IT IS A QUESTION OF BASICS; WOMEN WANT THE BEST OF EVERYTHING, AS MEN DO, AND SINCE THEY KNOW BEST THEY SHOULD ALWAYS HAVE THEIR OWN WAY.
END

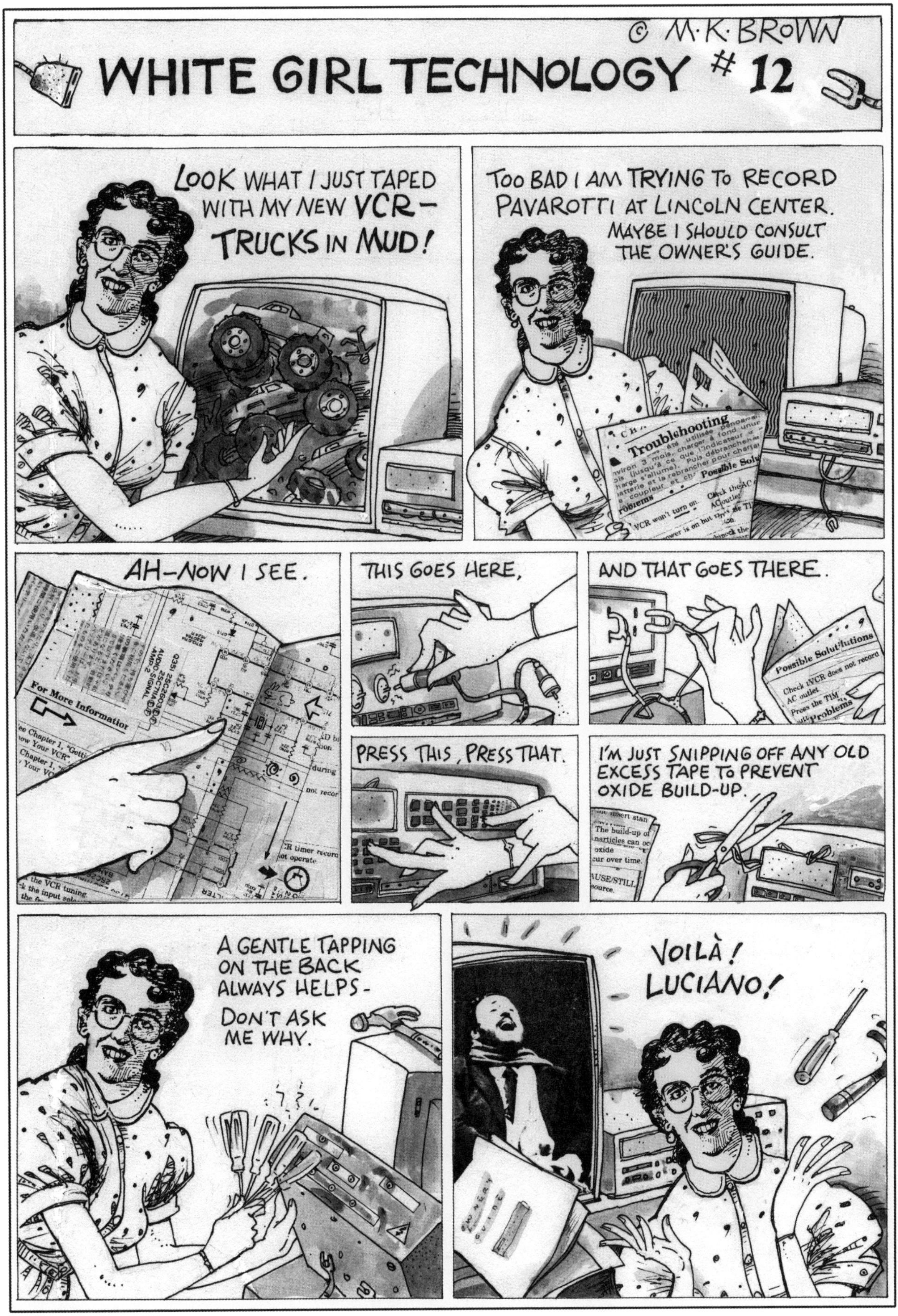
© M.K. BROWN
WHITE GIRL TECHNOLOGY # 12
LOOK WHAT I JUST TAPED WITH MY NEW VCR – TRUCKS IN MUD!
TOO BAD I AM TRYING TO RECORD PAVAROTTI AT LINCOLN CENTER.
MAYBE I SHOULD CONSULT THE OWNER'S GUIDE.
Troubleshooting
Possible Solutions
AH – NOW I SEE.
For More Information
THIS GOES HERE,
AND THAT GOES THERE.
Possible Solutions
PRESS THIS, PRESS THAT.
I'M JUST SNIPPING OFF ANY OLD EXCESS TAPE TO PREVENT OXIDE BUILD-UP.
A GENTLE TAPPING ON THE BACK ALWAYS HELPS –
DON'T ASK ME WHY.
VOILÀ! LUCIANO!

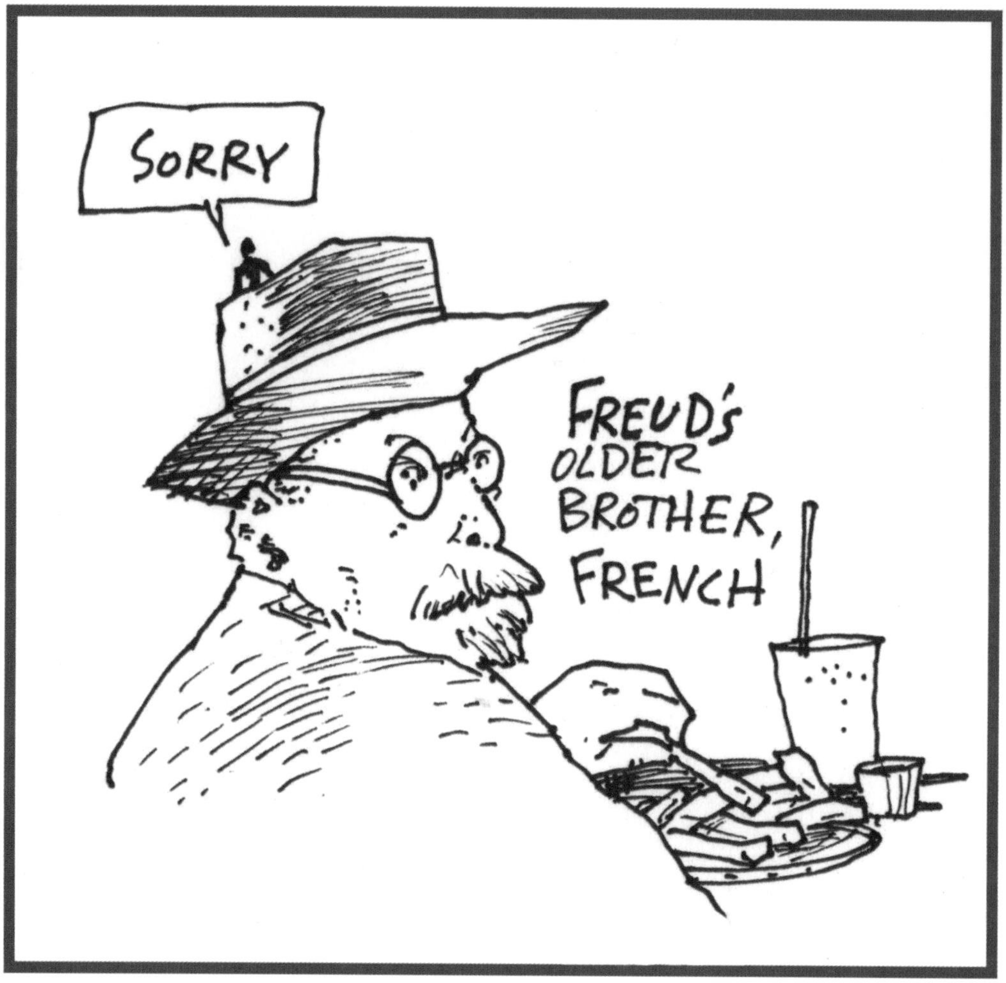
SORRY
FREUD's OLDER BROTHER, FRENCH

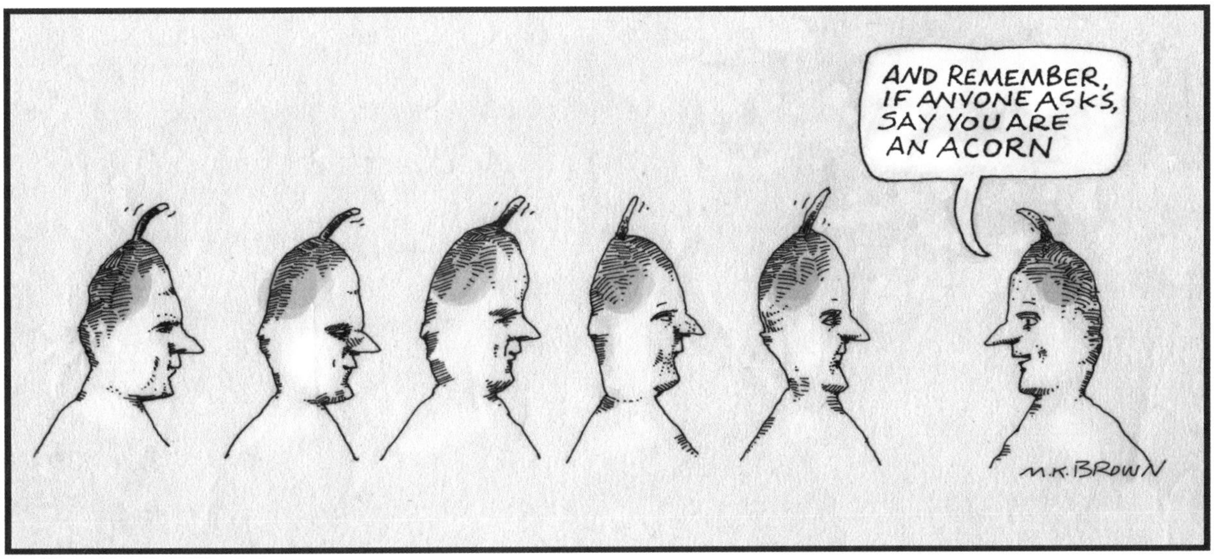
AND REMEMBER, IF ANYONE ASKS, SAY YOU ARE AN ACORN
M.K. BROWN

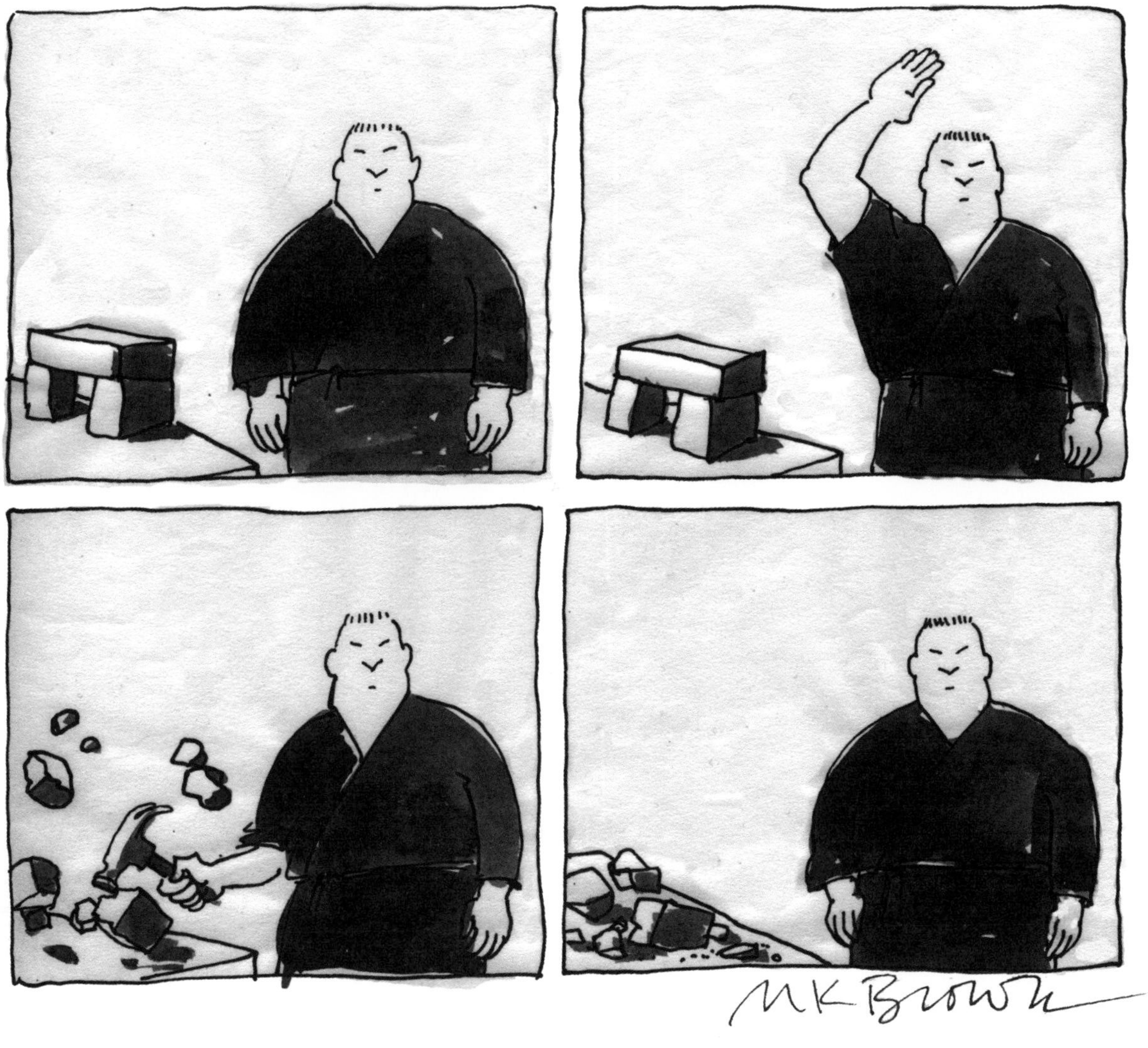
M K BROWN

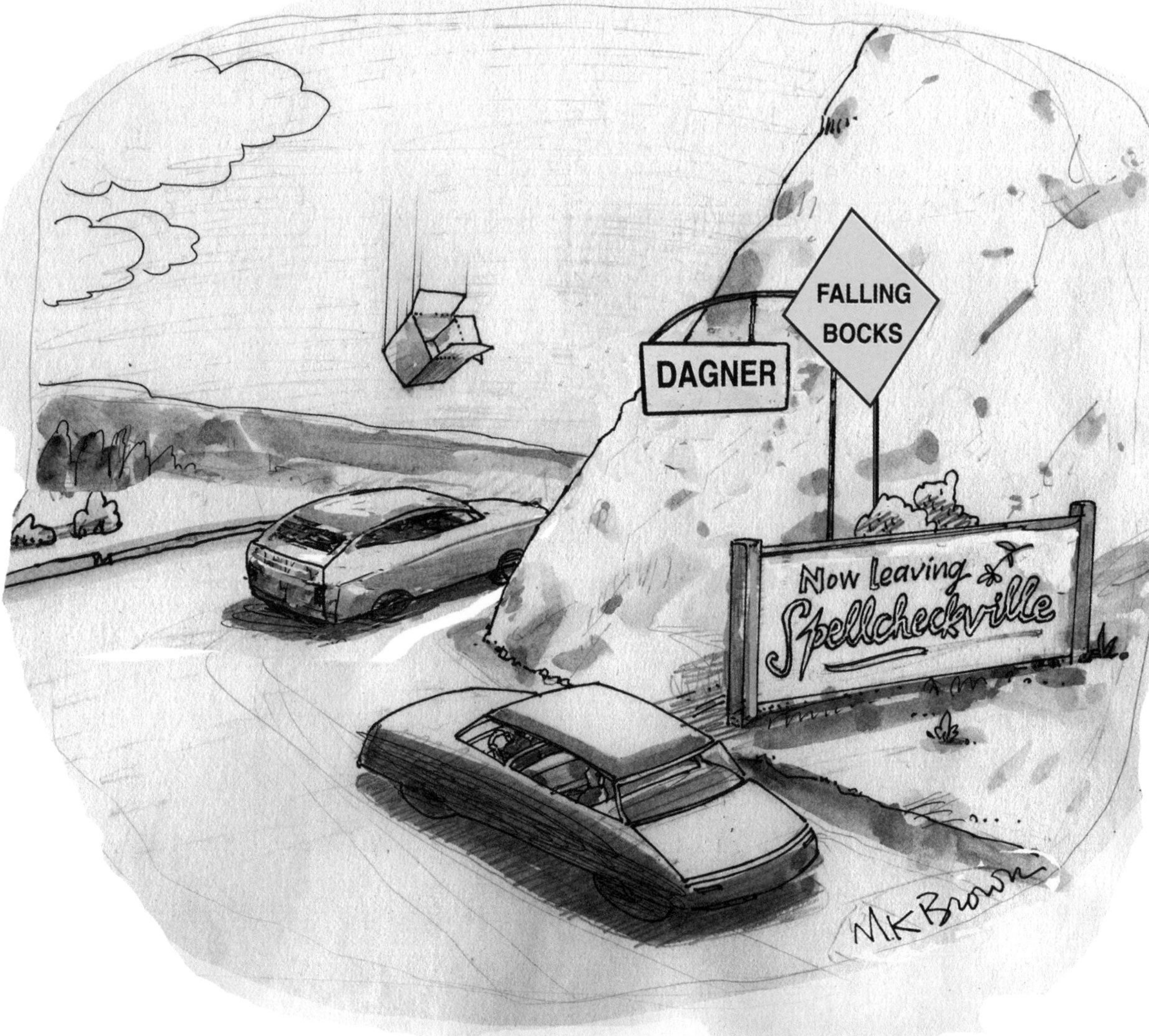
DAGNER
FALLING BOCKS
Now leaving Spellcheckville
M.K.Brown

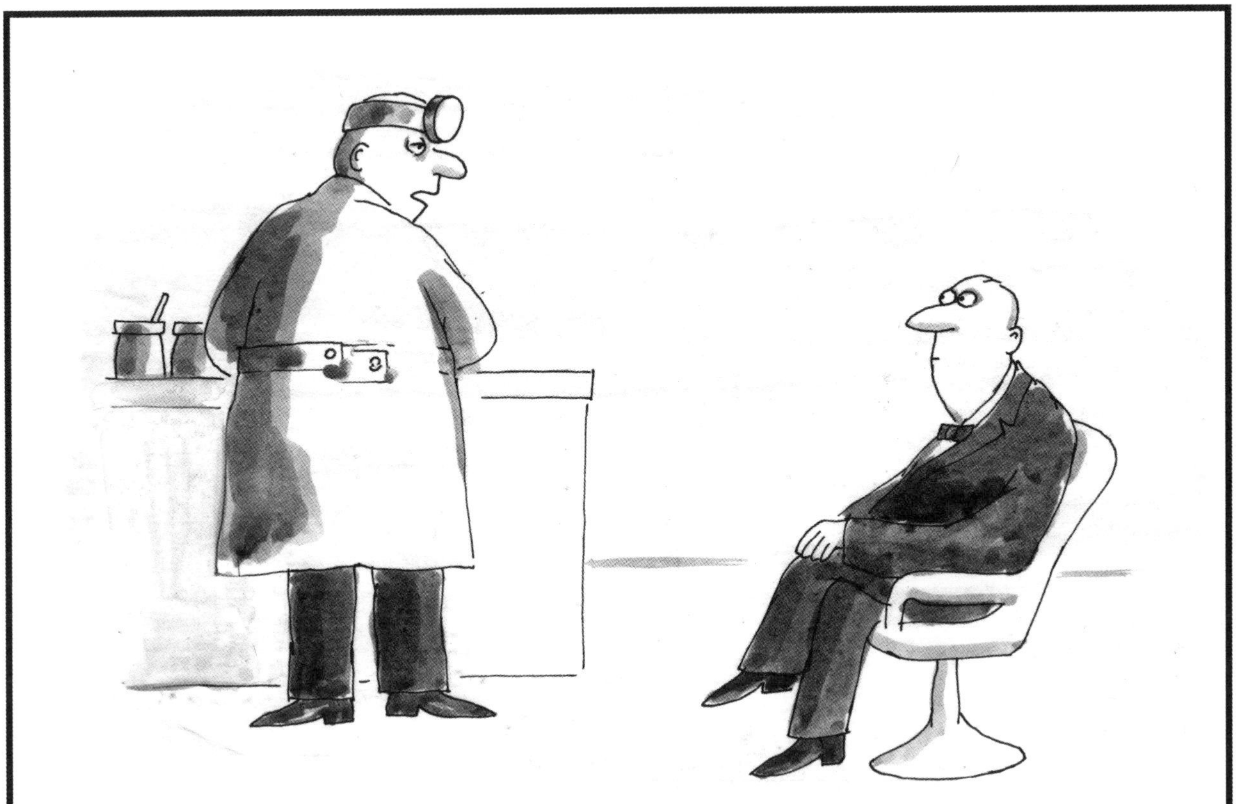

Now, this may be a little painful, Mr. Fenton.

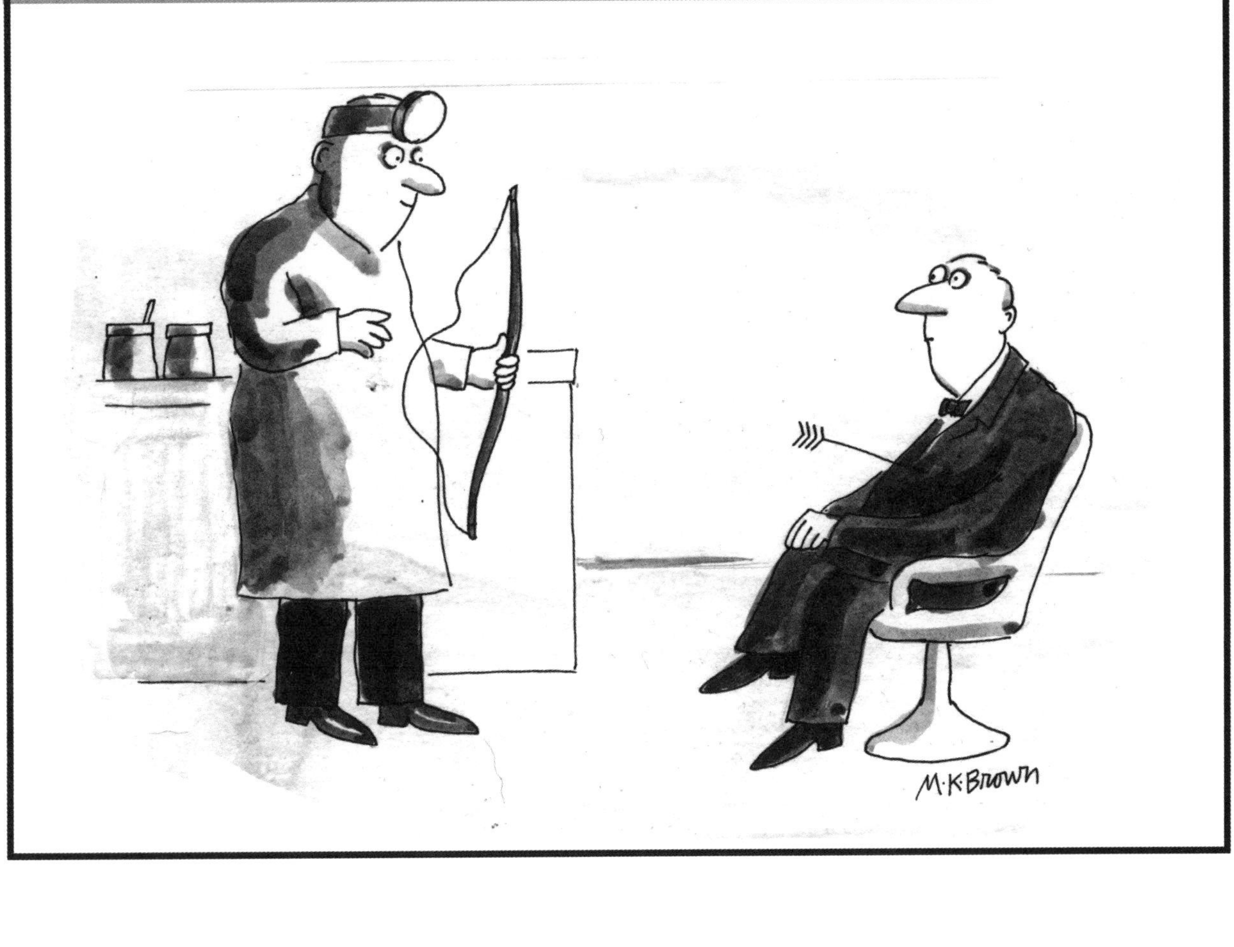
M.K.Brown

He's eating the tinfoil and everything!

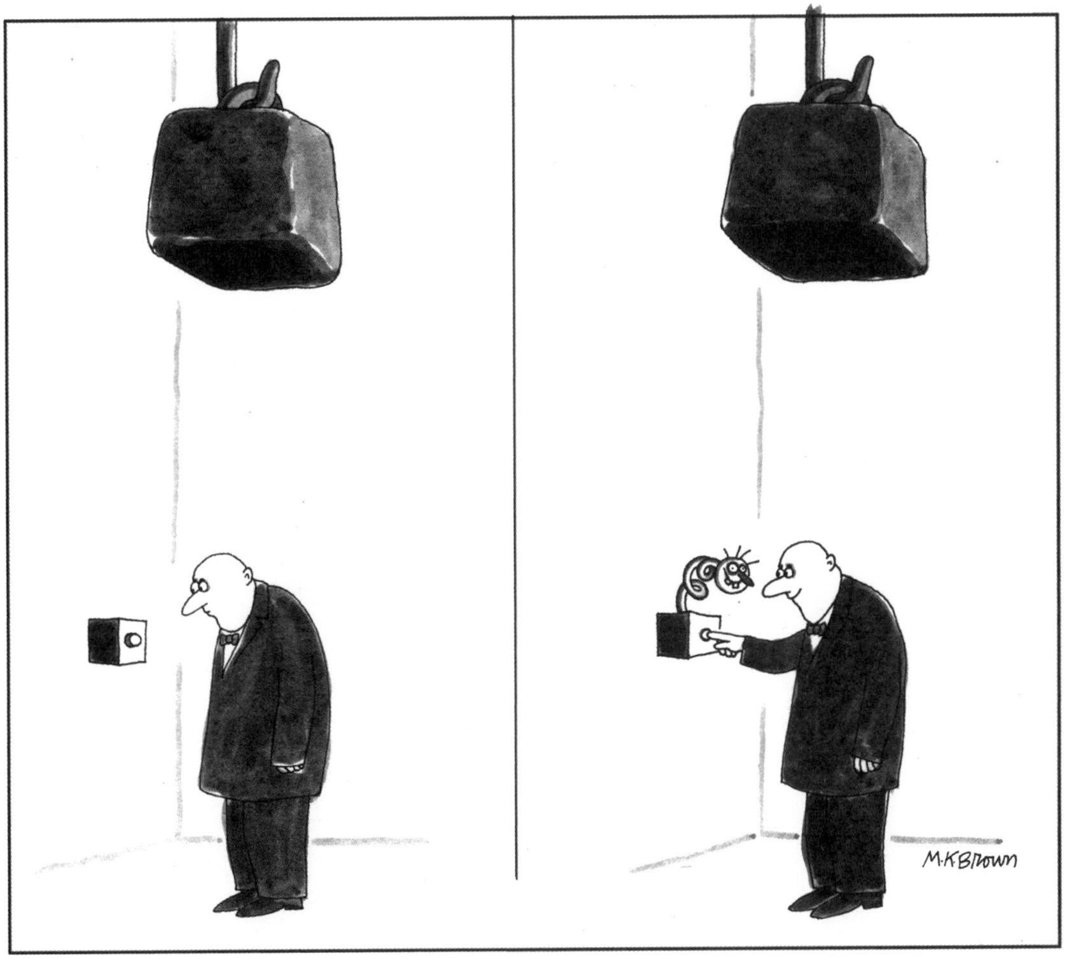
M.K.Brown

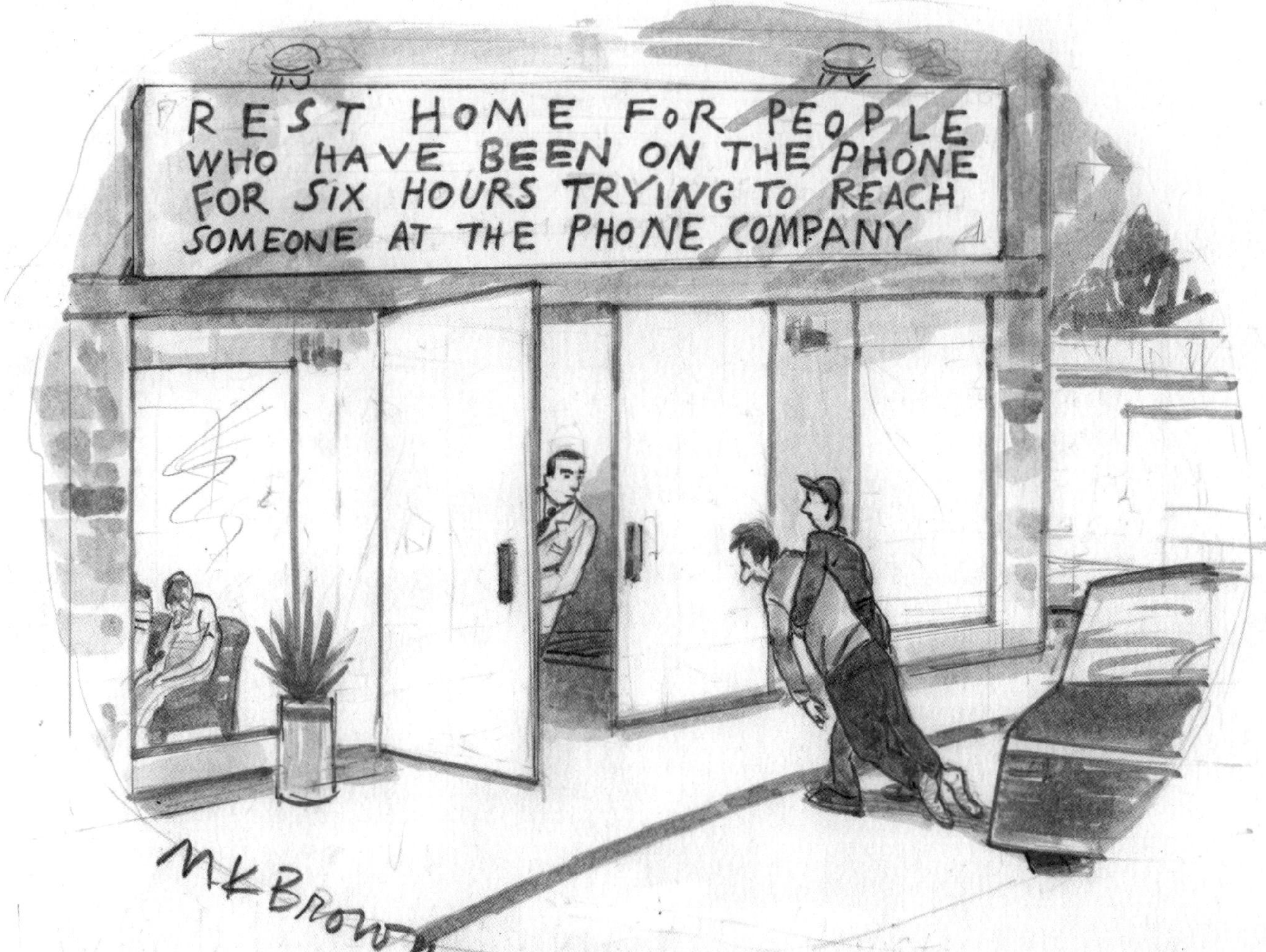
REST HOME FOR PEOPLE WHO HAVE BEEN ON THE PHONE FOR SIX HOURS TRYING TO REACH SOMEONE AT THE PHONE COMPANY
MKBROWN

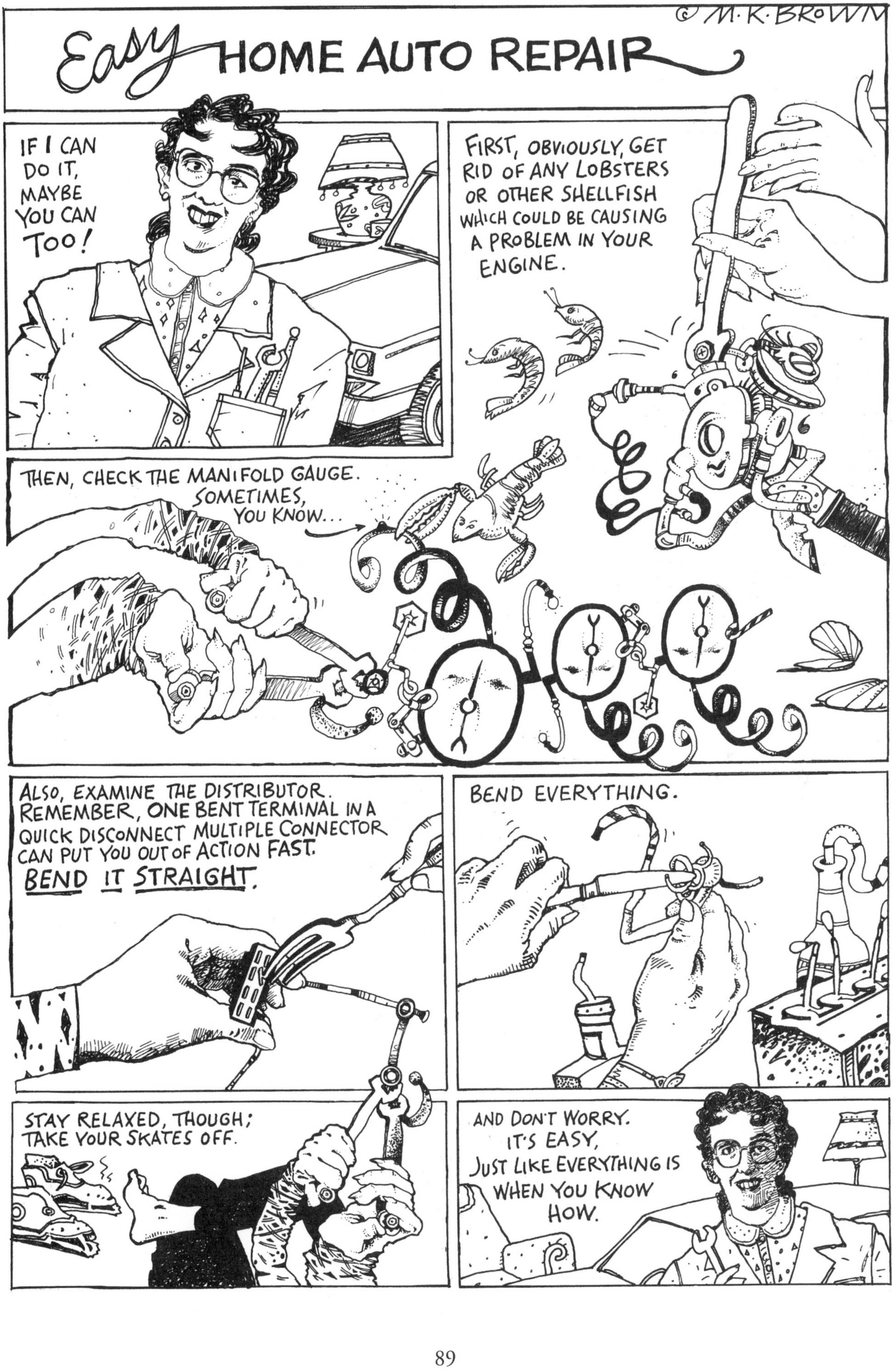
© M.K. BROWN
EASY HOME AUTO REPAIR
IF I CAN DO IT, MAYBE YOU CAN TOO!
FIRST, OBVIOUSLY, GET RID OF ANY LOBSTERS OR OTHER SHELLFISH WHICH COULD BE CAUSING A PROBLEM IN YOUR ENGINE.
THEN, CHECK THE MANIFOLD GAUGE. SOMETIMES, YOU KNOW...
ALSO, EXAMINE THE DISTRIBUTOR. REMEMBER, ONE BENT TERMINAL IN A QUICK DISCONNECT MULTIPLE CONNECTOR CAN PUT YOU OUT OF ACTION FAST. BEND IT STRAIGHT.
BEND EVERYTHING.
STAY RELAXED, THOUGH; TAKE YOUR SKATES OFF.
AND DON'T WORRY. IT'S EASY, JUST LIKE EVERYTHING IS WHEN YOU KNOW HOW.

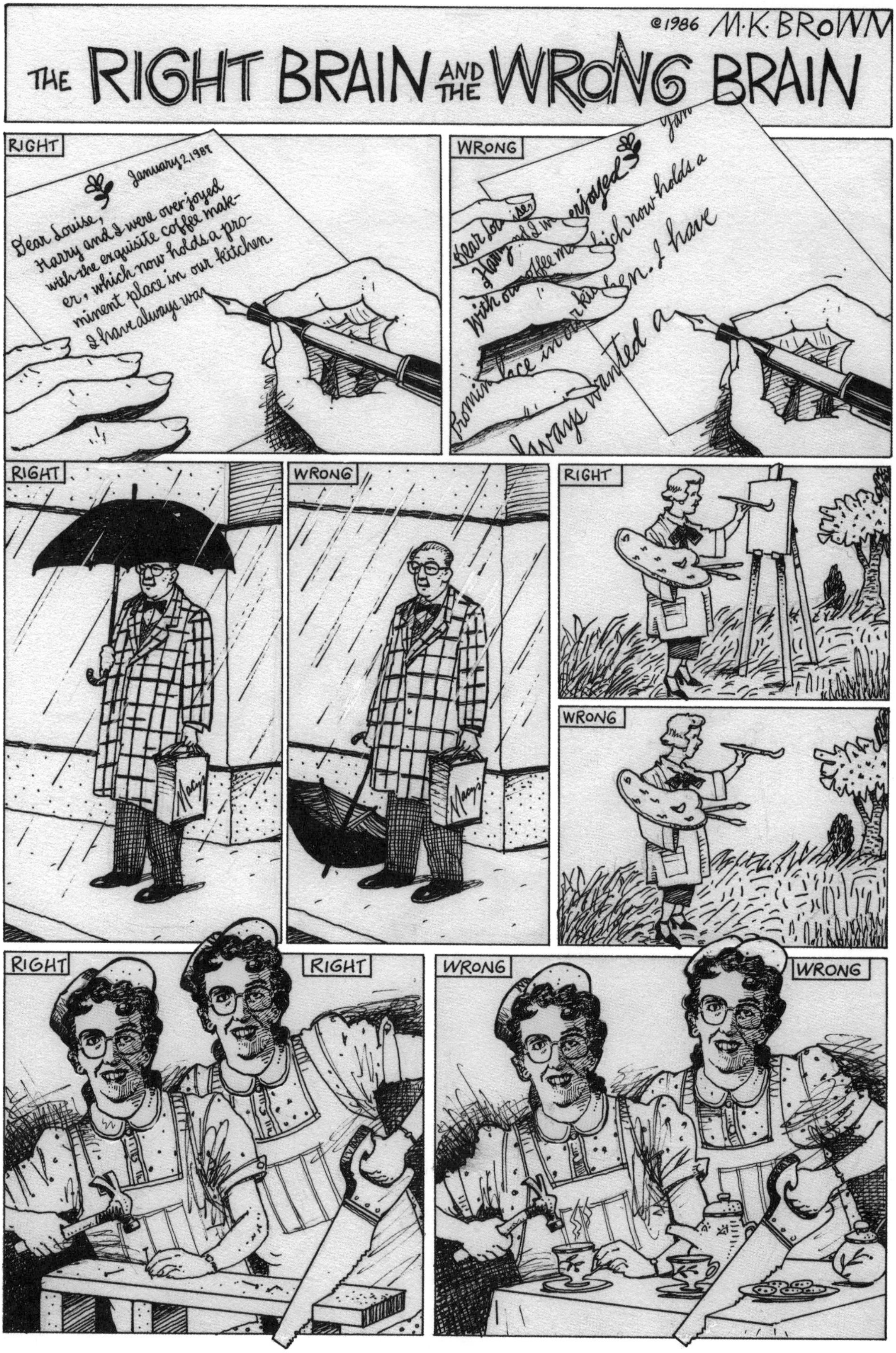
©1986 M·K·BROWN
THE RIGHT BRAIN AND THE WRONG BRAIN
RIGHT
January 2, 1987
Dear Louise,
Harry and I were overjoyed
with the exquisite coffee mak-
er, which now holds a pro-
minent place in our kitchen.
I have always wa
WRONG
enjoyed
now holds a
I have
wanted a
RIGHT
Macy's
WRONG
Macy's
RIGHT
WRONG
RIGHT
RIGHT
WRONG
WRONG

A Seedy Part of Town

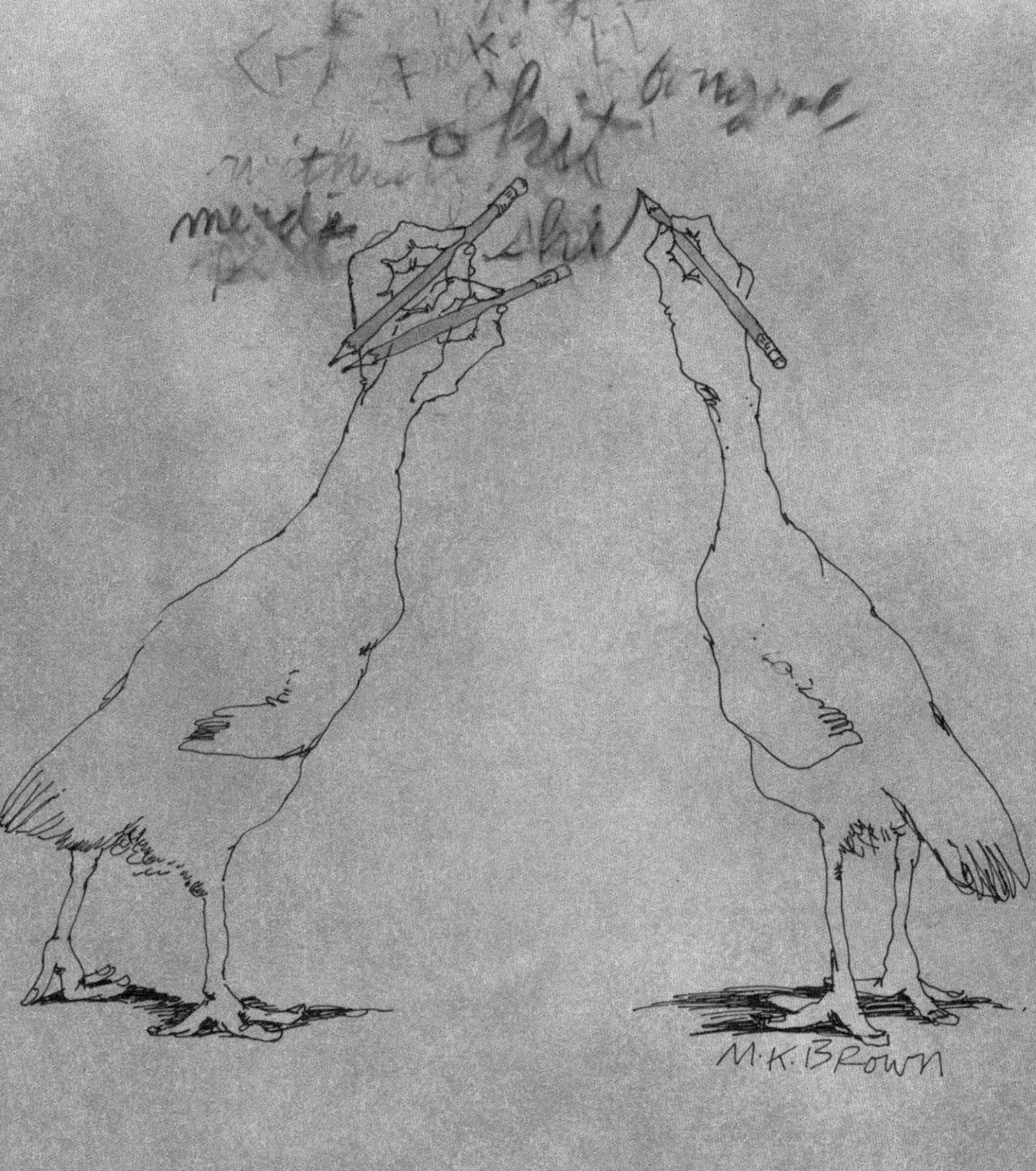
shit
merde
M.K. BROWN

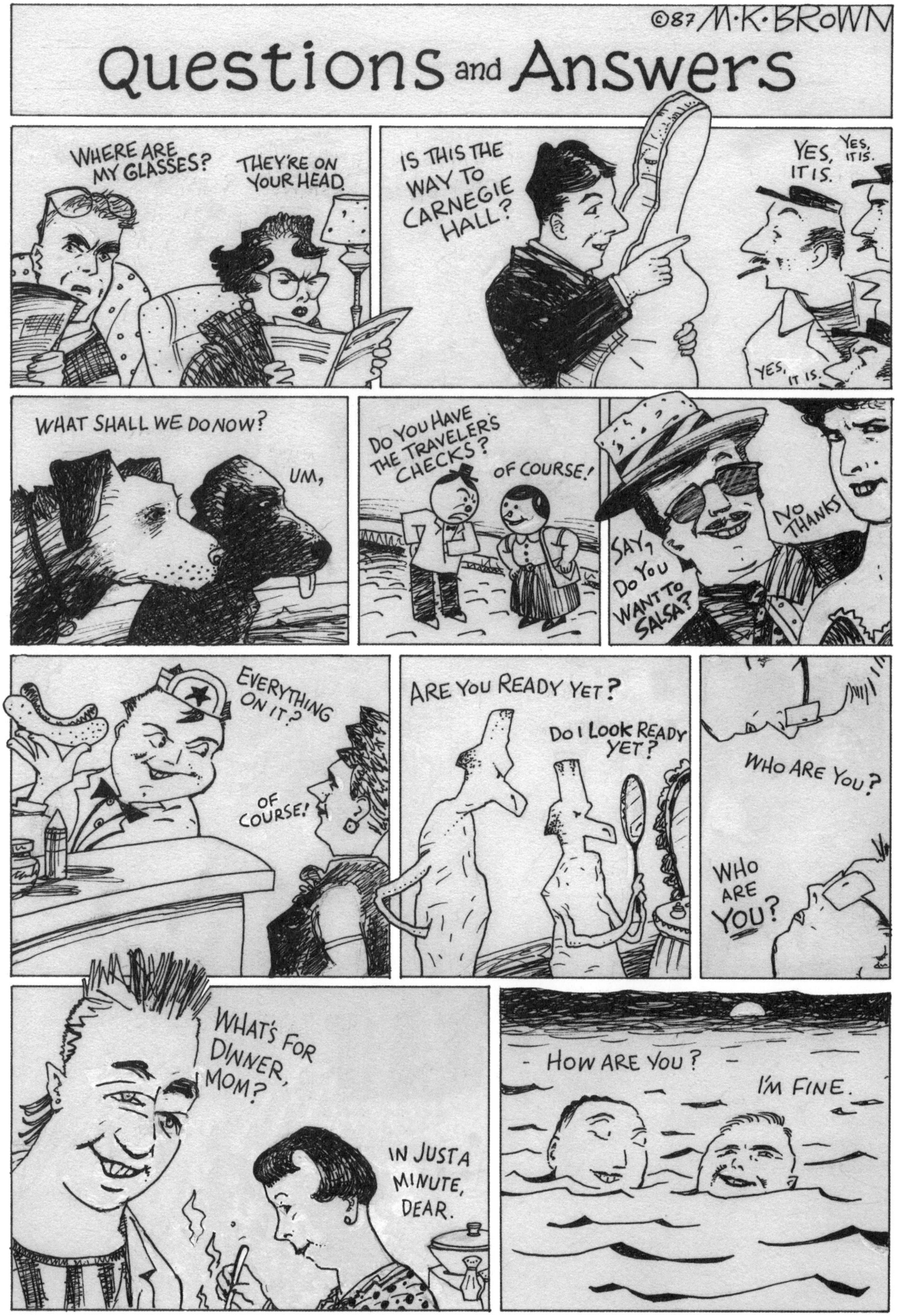
©87 M·K·BROWN
Questions and Answers
WHERE ARE MY GLASSES?
THEY'RE ON YOUR HEAD.
IS THIS THE WAY TO CARNEGIE HALL?
YES, IT IS.
YES, IT IS.
YES, IT IS.
WHAT SHALL WE DO NOW?
UM,
DO YOU HAVE THE TRAVELER'S CHECKS?
OF COURSE!
SAY, DO YOU WANT TO SALSA?
NO THANKS
EVERYTHING ON IT?
OF COURSE!
ARE YOU READY YET?
DO I LOOK READY YET?
WHO ARE YOU?
WHO ARE YOU?
WHAT'S FOR DINNER, MOM?
IN JUST A MINUTE, DEAR.
HOW ARE YOU?
I'M FINE.

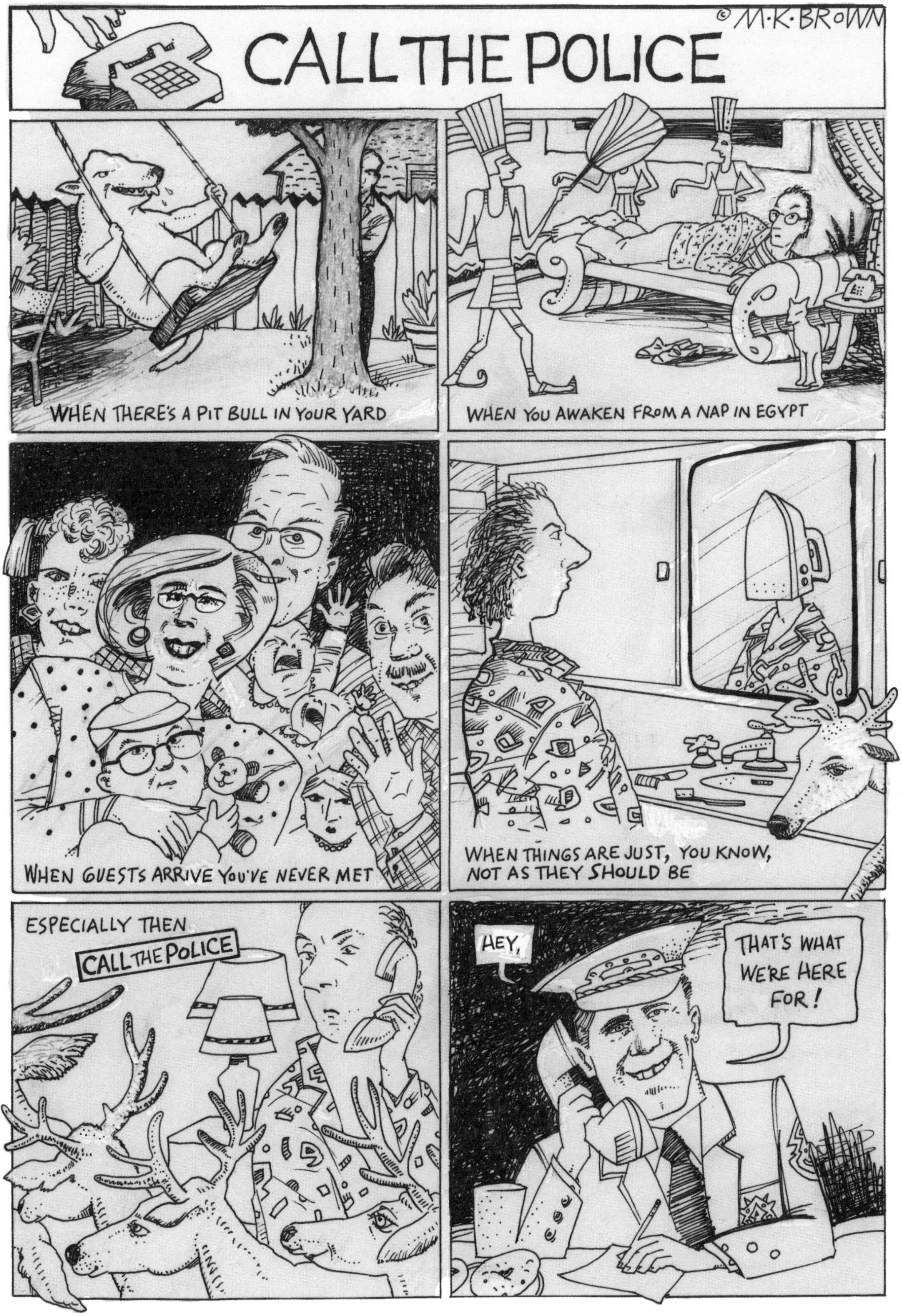

© M·K·BROWN
CALL THE POLICE
WHEN THERE'S A PIT BULL IN YOUR YARD
WHEN YOU AWAKEN FROM A NAP IN EGYPT
WHEN GUESTS ARRIVE YOU'VE NEVER MET
WHEN THINGS ARE JUST, YOU KNOW, NOT AS THEY SHOULD BE
ESPECIALLY THEN
CALL THE POLICE
HEY,
THAT'S WHAT WE'RE HERE FOR!

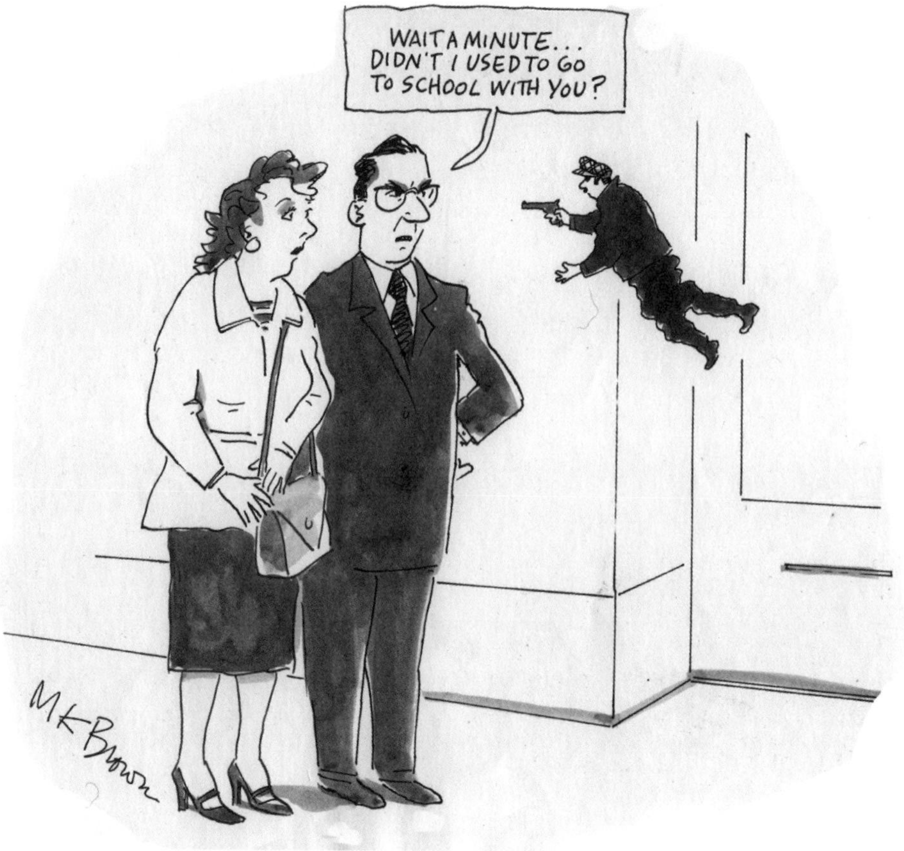
WAIT A MINUTE...
DIDN'T I USED TO GO
TO SCHOOL WITH YOU?
MK Brown

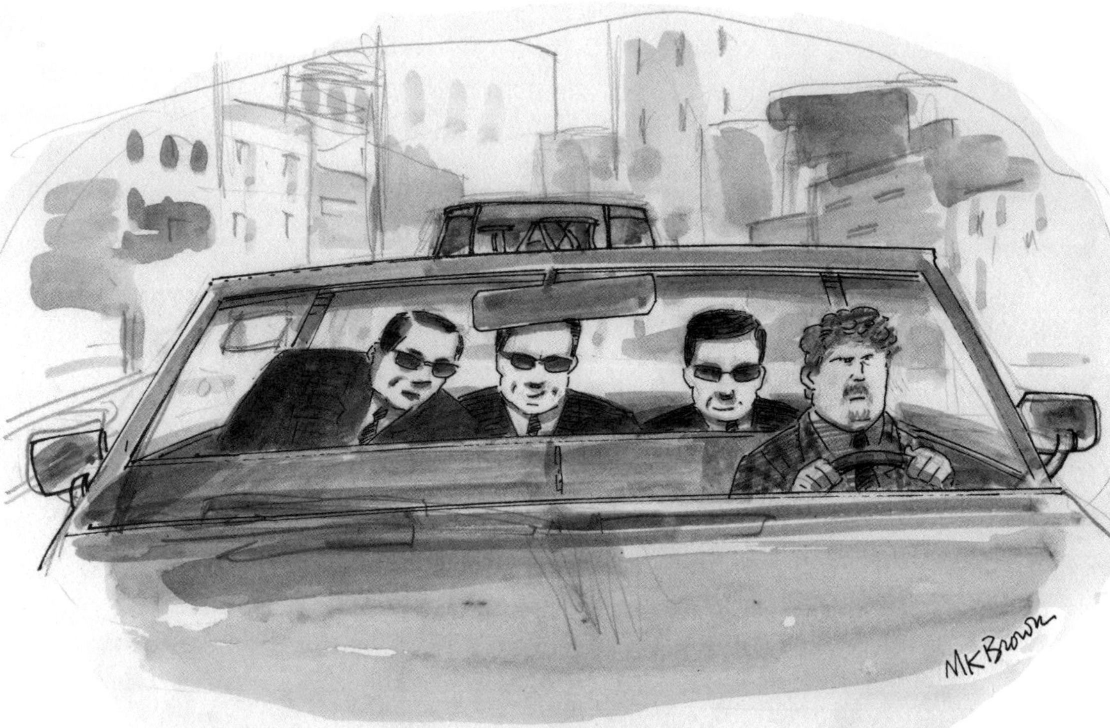
TAXI
MK Brown

Driver, stop at the next Chinese take-over, I mean take-out. Ha, ha.

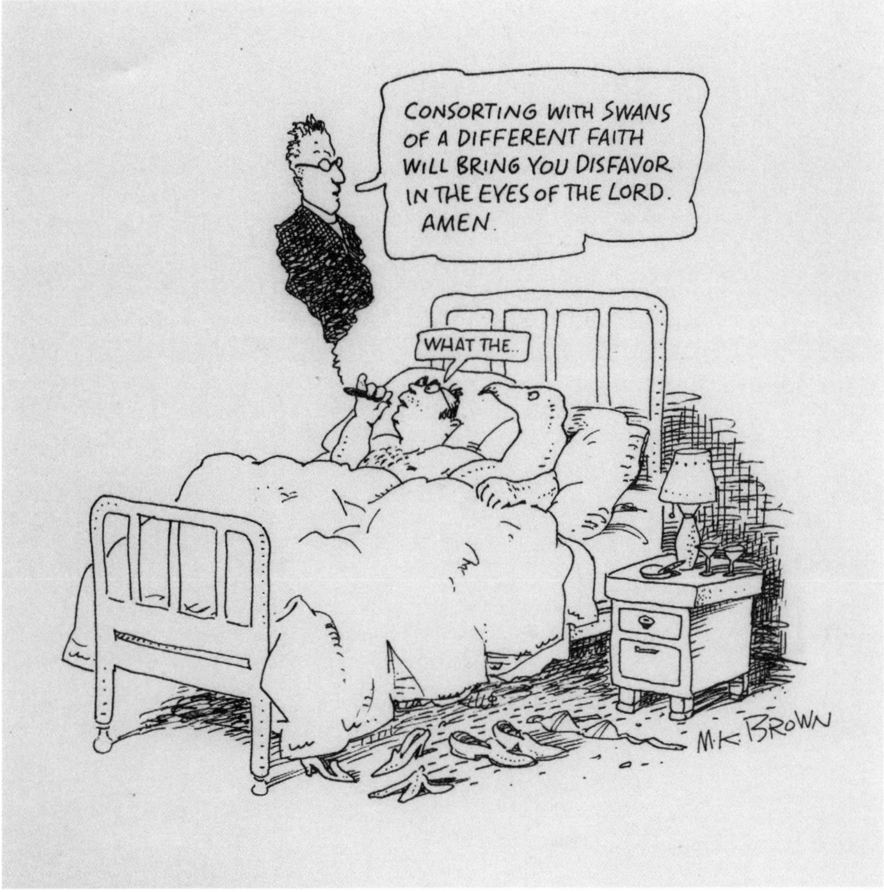
CONSORTING WITH SWANS OF A DIFFERENT FAITH WILL BRING YOU DISFAVOR IN THE EYES OF THE LORD. AMEN.
WHAT THE..
M.K. BROWN

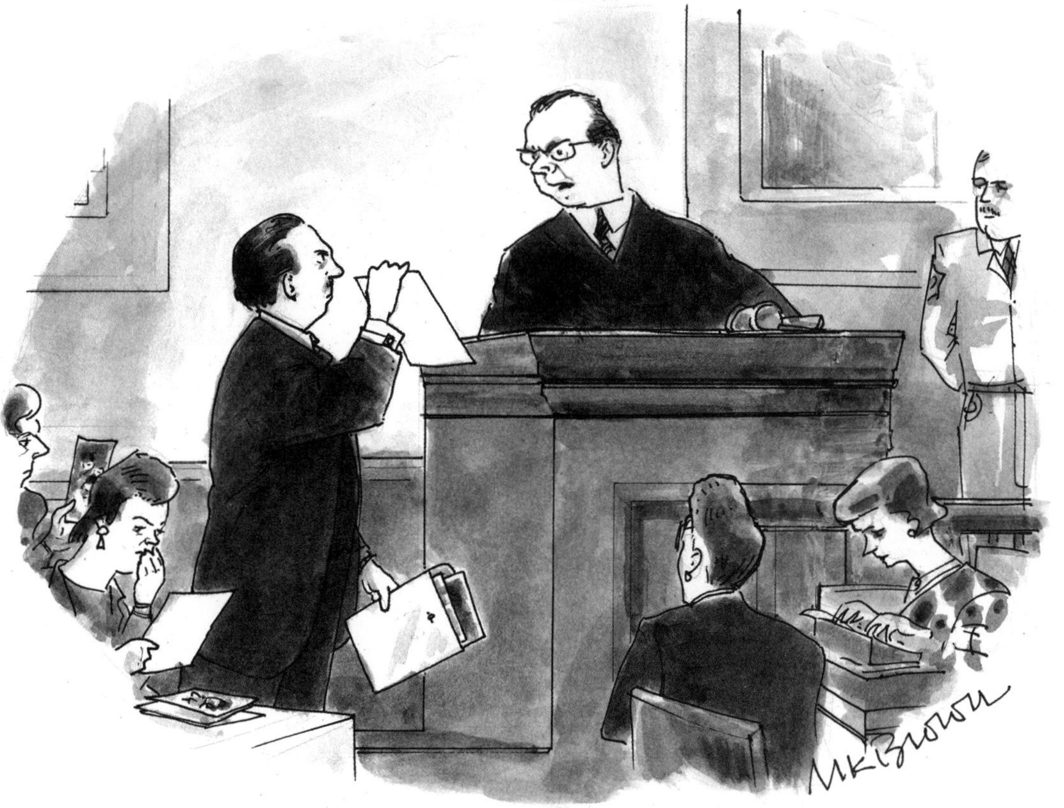
MK BROWN

I was young. I needed the work.

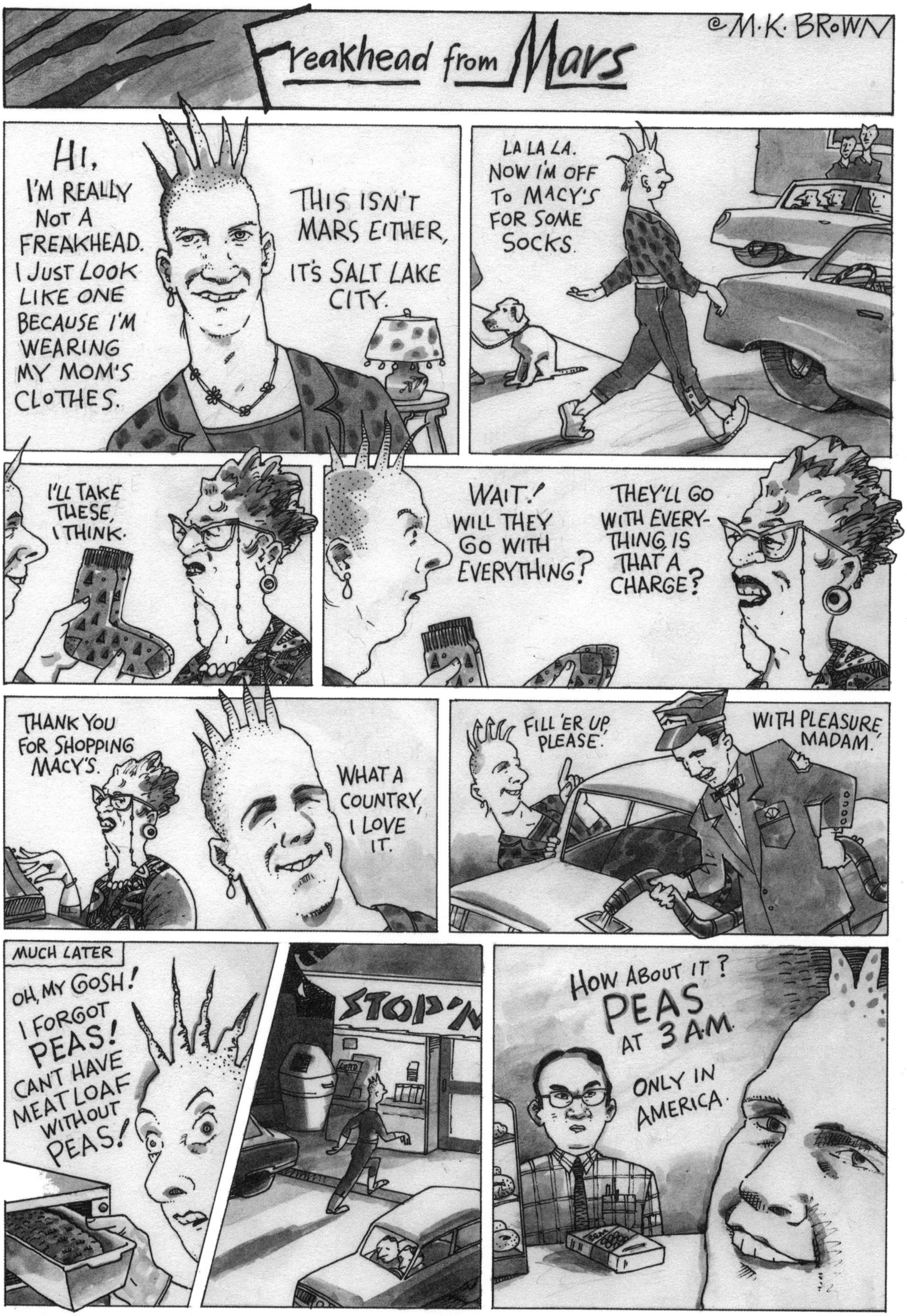
Freakhead from Mars
©M.K. BROWN
HI, I'M REALLY NOT A FREAKHEAD. I JUST LOOK LIKE ONE BECAUSE I'M WEARING MY MOM'S CLOTHES.
THIS ISN'T MARS EITHER,
IT'S SALT LAKE CITY.
LA LA LA. NOW I'M OFF TO MACY'S FOR SOME SOCKS.
I'LL TAKE THESE, I THINK.
WAIT! WILL THEY GO WITH EVERYTHING?
THEY'LL GO WITH EVERYTHING. IS THAT A CHARGE?
THANK YOU FOR SHOPPING MACY'S.
WHAT A COUNTRY, I LOVE IT.
FILL 'ER UP, PLEASE.
WITH PLEASURE, MADAM.
MUCH LATER
OH, MY GOSH! I FORGOT PEAS! CAN'T HAVE MEAT LOAF WITHOUT PEAS!
STOP 'N
HOW ABOUT IT? PEAS AT 3 AM.
ONLY IN AMERICA.

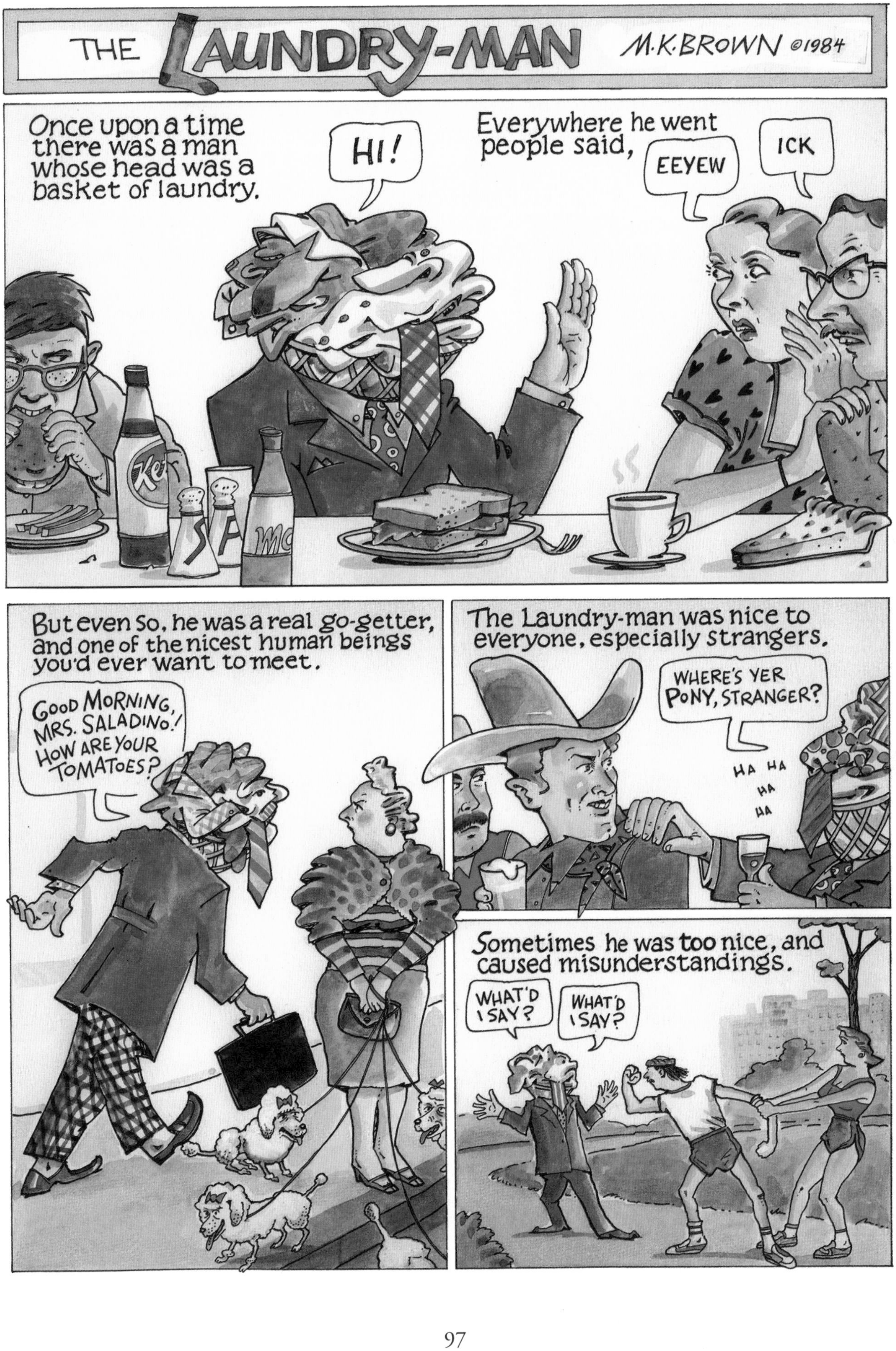
THE LAUNDRY-MAN
M.K.BROWN ©1984
Once upon a time there was a man whose head was a basket of laundry.
HI!
Everywhere he went people said,
EEYEW
ICK
But even so, he was a real go-getter, and one of the nicest human beings you'd ever want to meet.
GOOD MORNING, MRS. SALADINO! HOW ARE YOUR TOMATOES?
The Laundry-man was nice to everyone, especially strangers.
WHERE'S YER PONY, STRANGER?
HA HA HA HA
Sometimes he was too nice, and caused misunderstandings.
WHAT'D I SAY?
WHAT'D I SAY?

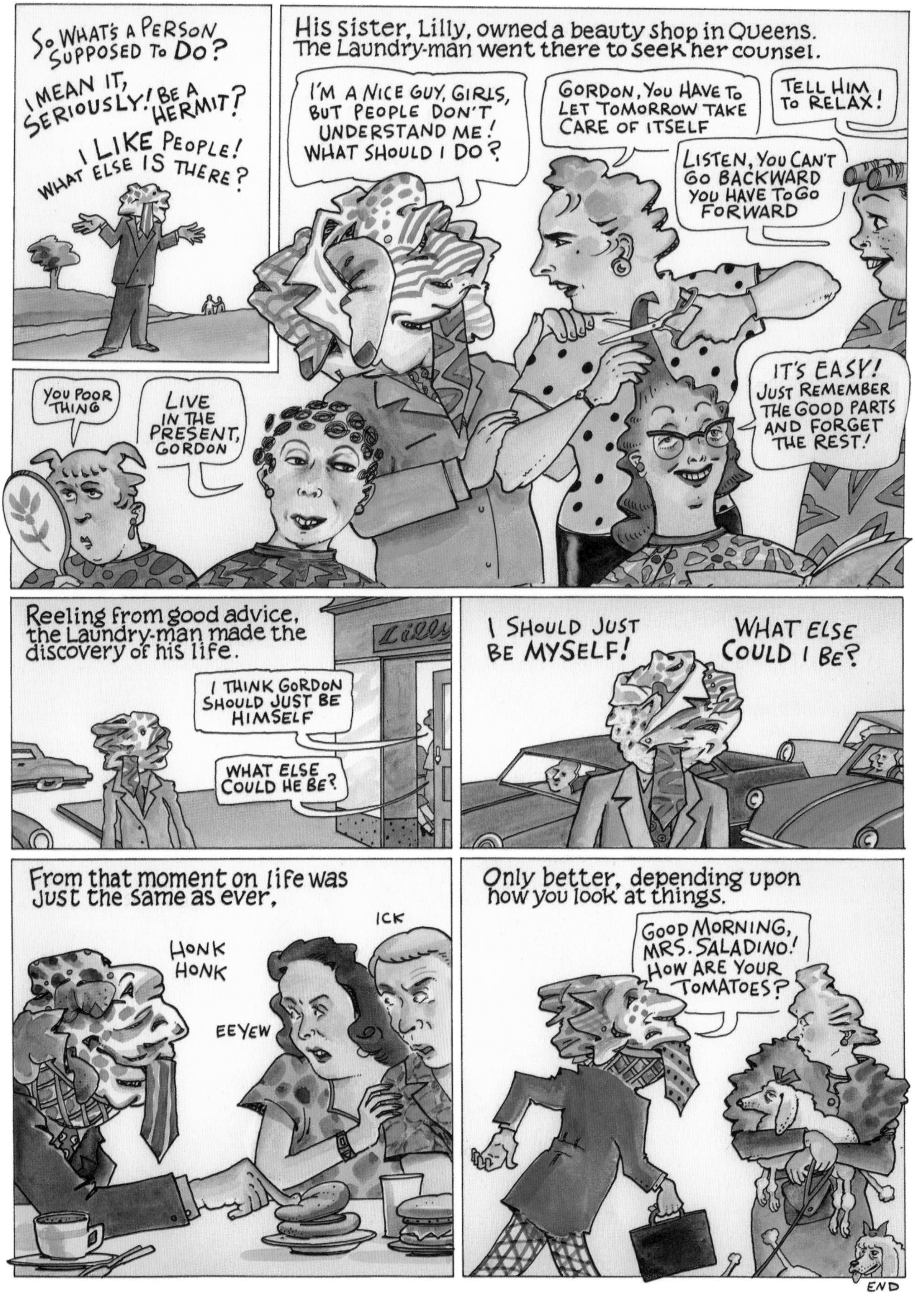
SO WHAT'S A PERSON SUPPOSED TO DO?
I MEAN IT, SERIOUSLY! BE A HERMIT?
I LIKE PEOPLE! WHAT ELSE IS THERE?
His sister, Lilly, owned a beauty shop in Queens. The Laundry-man went there to seek her counsel.
I'M A NICE GUY, GIRLS, BUT PEOPLE DON'T UNDERSTAND ME! WHAT SHOULD I DO?
GORDON, YOU HAVE TO LET TOMORROW TAKE CARE OF ITSELF
TELL HIM TO RELAX!
LISTEN, YOU CAN'T GO BACKWARD YOU HAVE TO GO FORWARD
YOU POOR THING
LIVE IN THE PRESENT, GORDON
IT'S EASY! JUST REMEMBER THE GOOD PARTS AND FORGET THE REST!
Reeling from good advice, the Laundry-man made the discovery of his life.
I THINK GORDON SHOULD JUST BE HIMSELF
WHAT ELSE COULD HE BE?
I SHOULD JUST BE MYSELF!
WHAT ELSE COULD I BE?
From that moment on life was just the same as ever,
ICK
HONK HONK
EEYEW
Only better, depending upon how you look at things.
GOOD MORNING, MRS. SALADINO! HOW ARE YOUR TOMATOES?
END

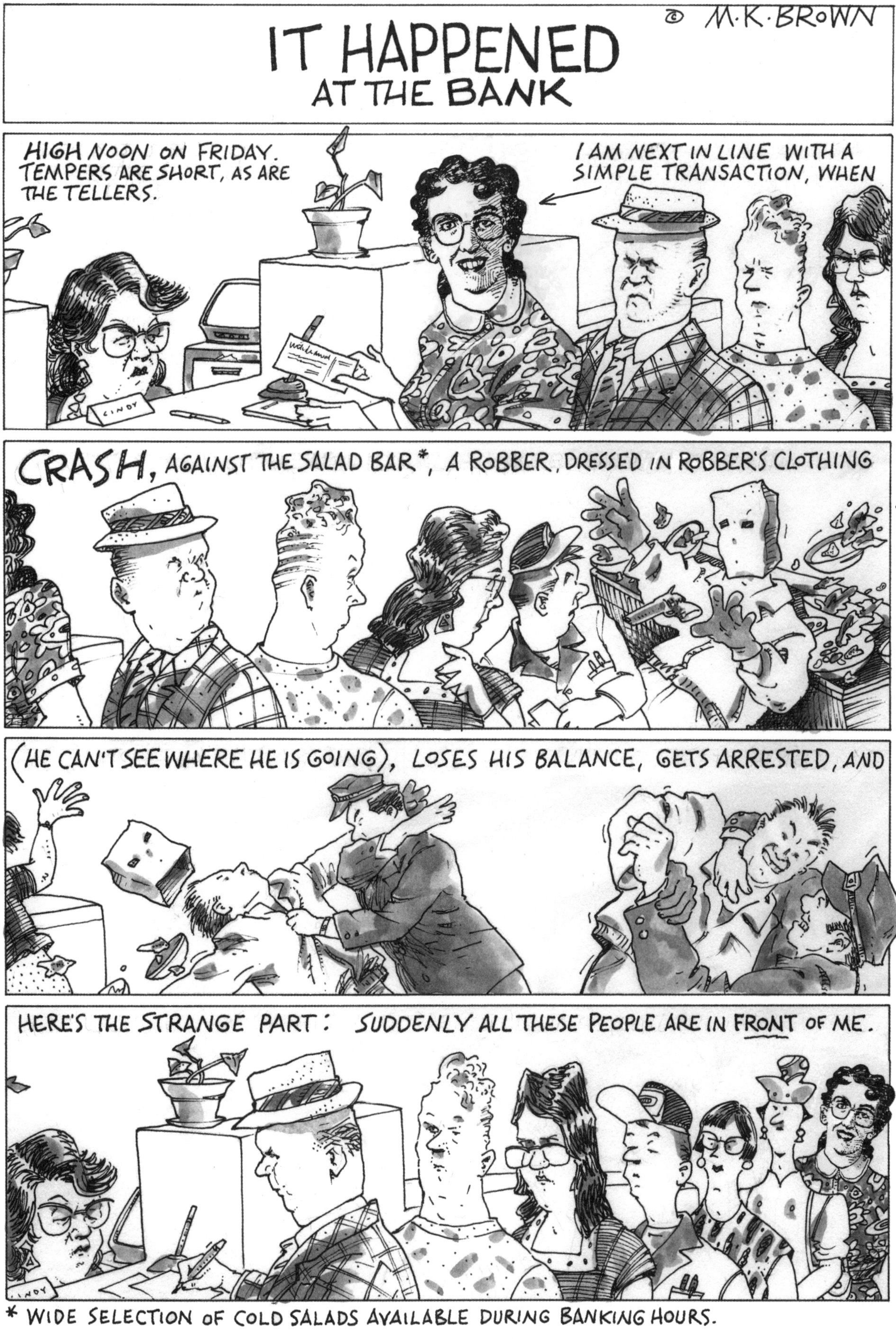
IT HAPPENED AT THE BANK
© M.K. BROWN
HIGH NOON ON FRIDAY. TEMPERS ARE SHORT, AS ARE THE TELLERS.
I AM NEXT IN LINE WITH A SIMPLE TRANSACTION, WHEN
CRASH, AGAINST THE SALAD BAR*, A ROBBER, DRESSED IN ROBBER'S CLOTHING
(HE CAN'T SEE WHERE HE IS GOING), LOSES HIS BALANCE, GETS ARRESTED, AND
HERE'S THE STRANGE PART: SUDDENLY ALL THESE PEOPLE ARE IN FRONT OF ME.
* WIDE SELECTION OF COLD SALADS AVAILABLE DURING BANKING HOURS.

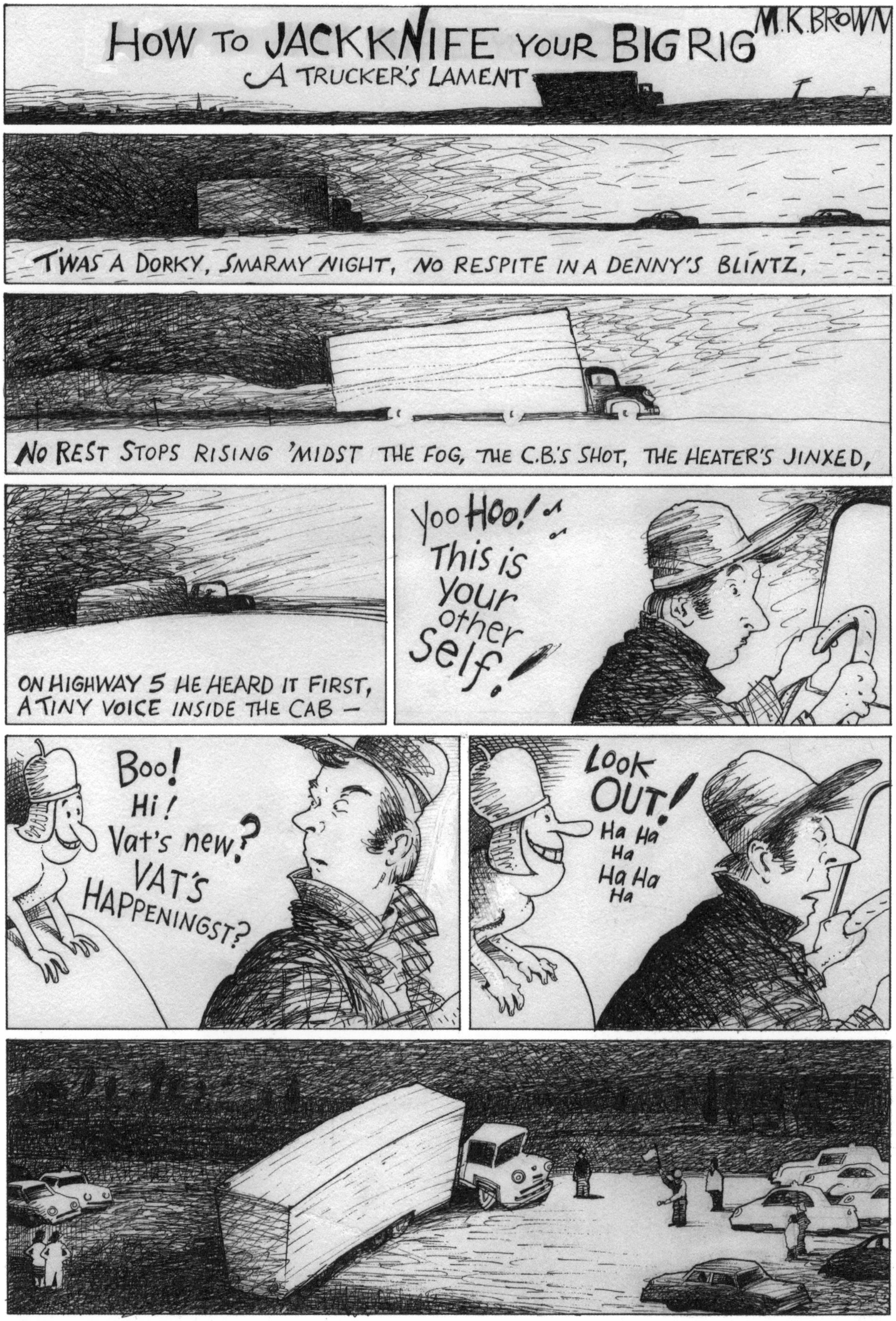
HOW TO JACKKNIFE YOUR BIGRIG
A TRUCKER'S LAMENT
M.K.BROWN
T'WAS A DORKY, SMARMY NIGHT, NO RESPITE IN A DENNY'S BLINTZ,
NO REST STOPS RISING 'MIDST THE FOG, THE C.B.'S SHOT, THE HEATER'S JINXED,
ON HIGHWAY 5 HE HEARD IT FIRST, A TINY VOICE INSIDE THE CAB —
Yoo Hoo! This is your other Self!
Boo! Hi! Vat's new? VAT'S HAPPENINGST?
LOOK OUT! Ha Ha Ha Ha Ha Ha

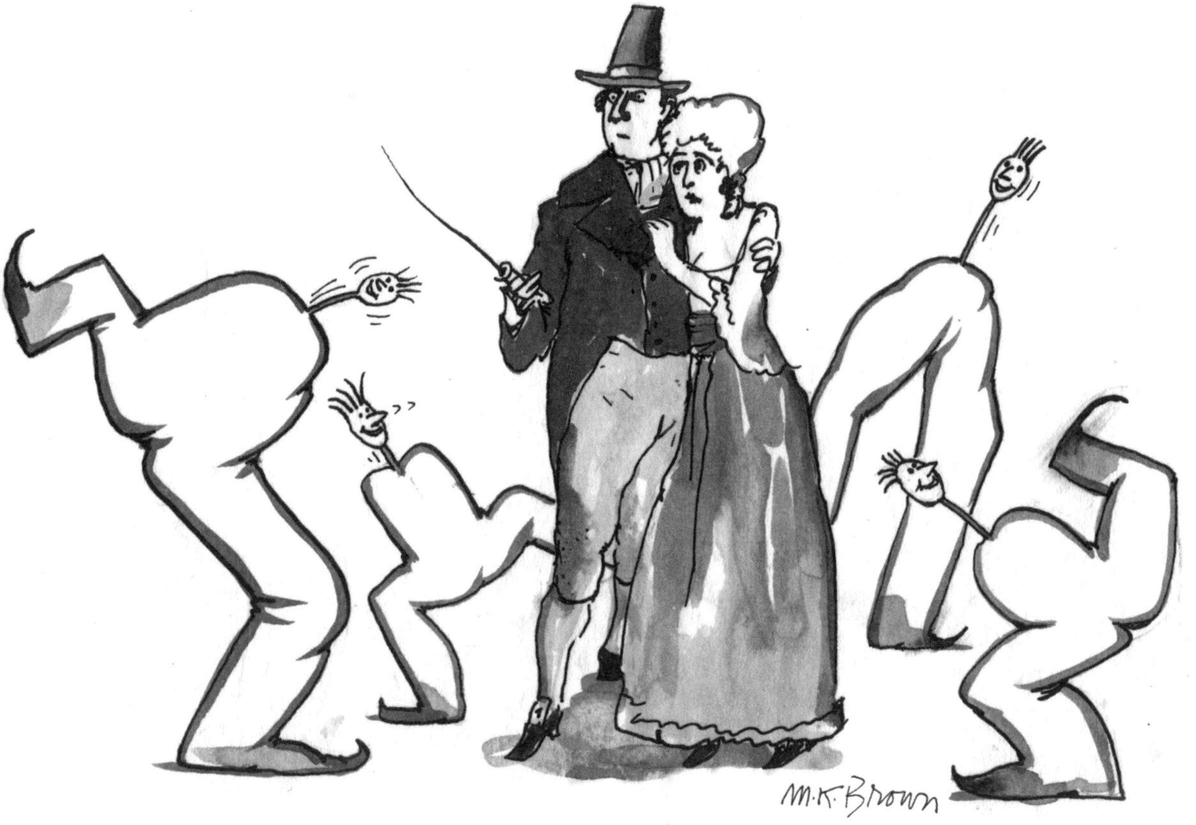
M.K. BROWN

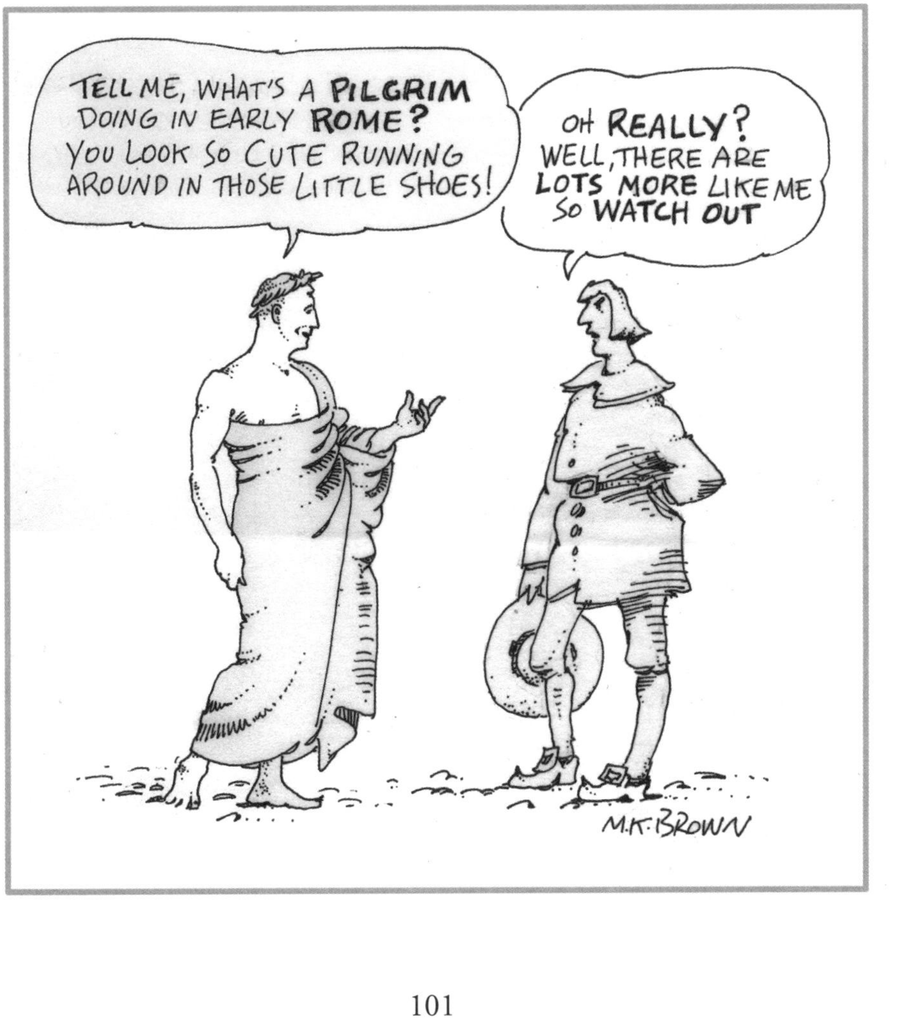
TELL ME, WHAT'S A PILGRIM DOING IN EARLY ROME? YOU LOOK SO CUTE RUNNING AROUND IN THOSE LITTLE SHOES!
OH REALLY? WELL, THERE ARE LOTS MORE LIKE ME SO WATCH OUT
M.K. BROWN

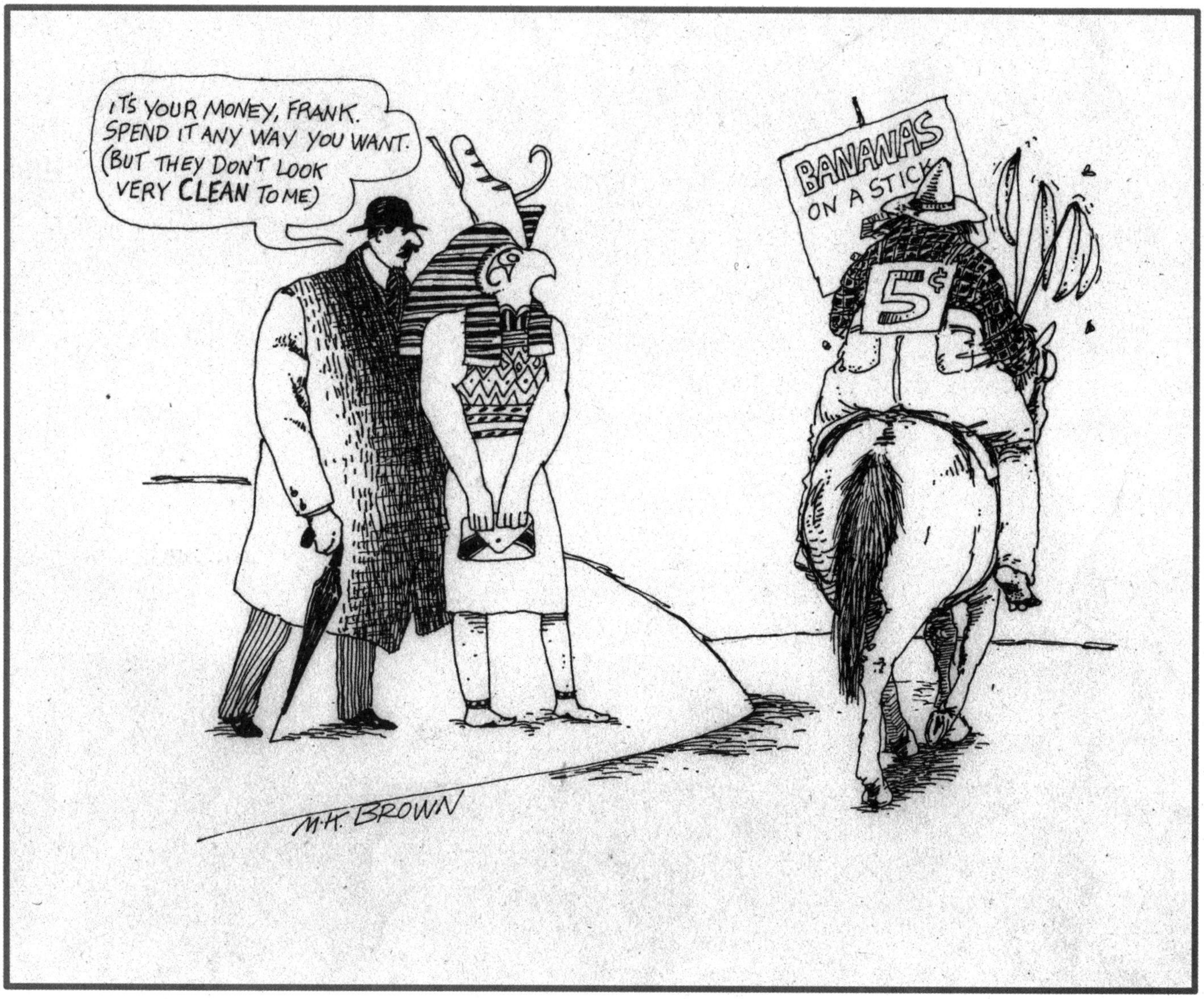
IT'S YOUR MONEY, FRANK. SPEND IT ANY WAY YOU WANT. (BUT THEY DON'T LOOK VERY CLEAN TO ME)
BANANAS ON A STICK
5¢
M.K. BROWN

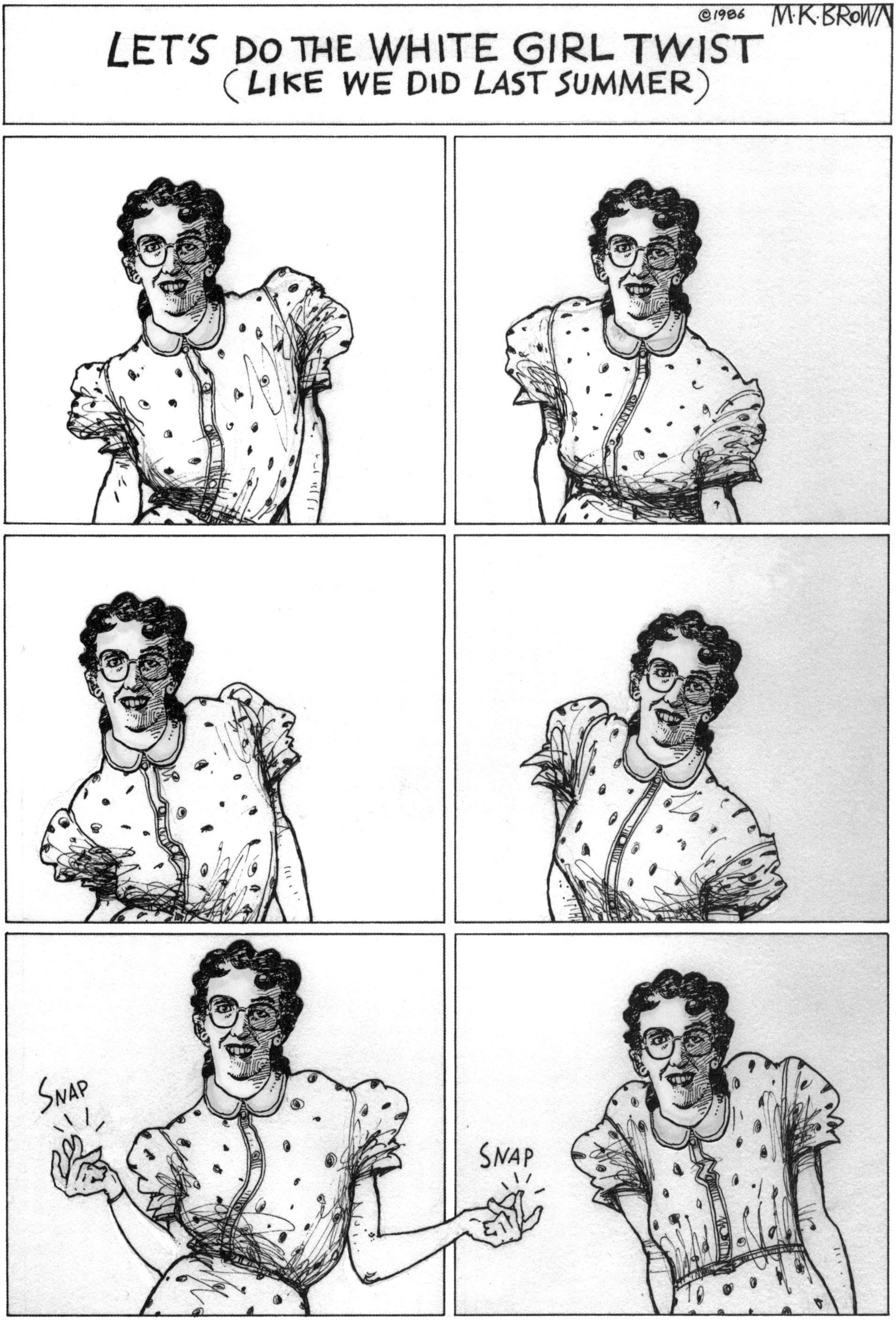
©1986 M·K·BROWN
LET'S DO THE WHITE GIRL TWIST
(LIKE WE DID LAST SUMMER)
SNAP
SNAP

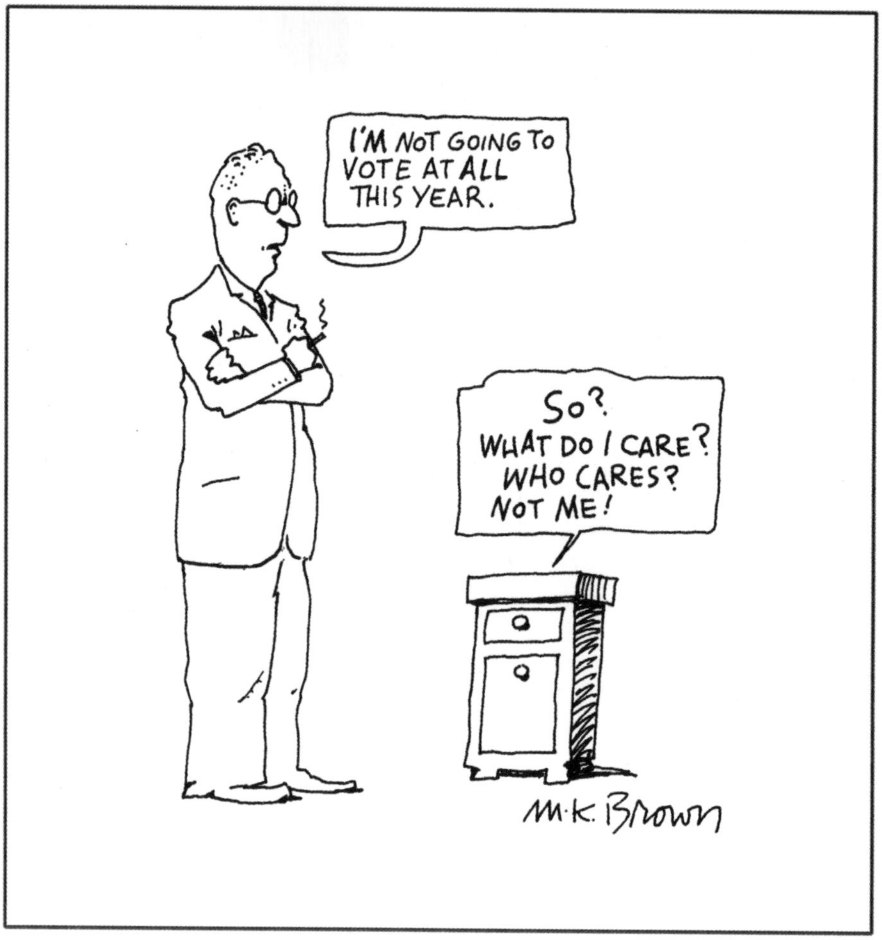
I'M NOT GOING TO VOTE AT ALL THIS YEAR.
SO? WHAT DO I CARE? WHO CARES? NOT ME!
M.K. BROWN

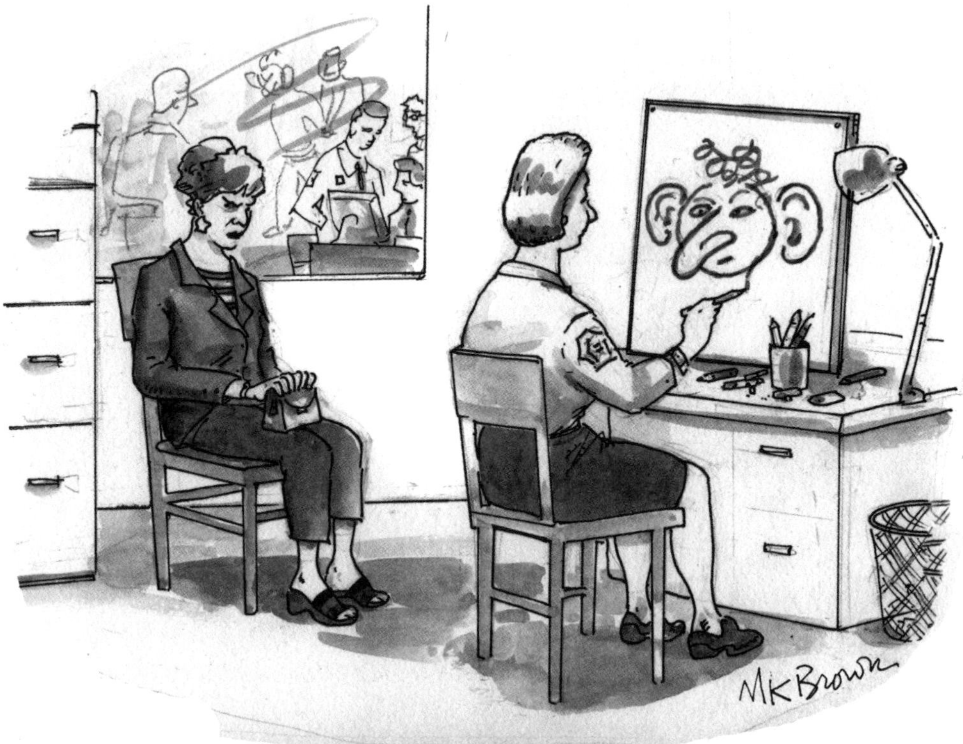
MK Brown

He had little squinty eyes and curly hair and a long nose, and his ears stuck out and...

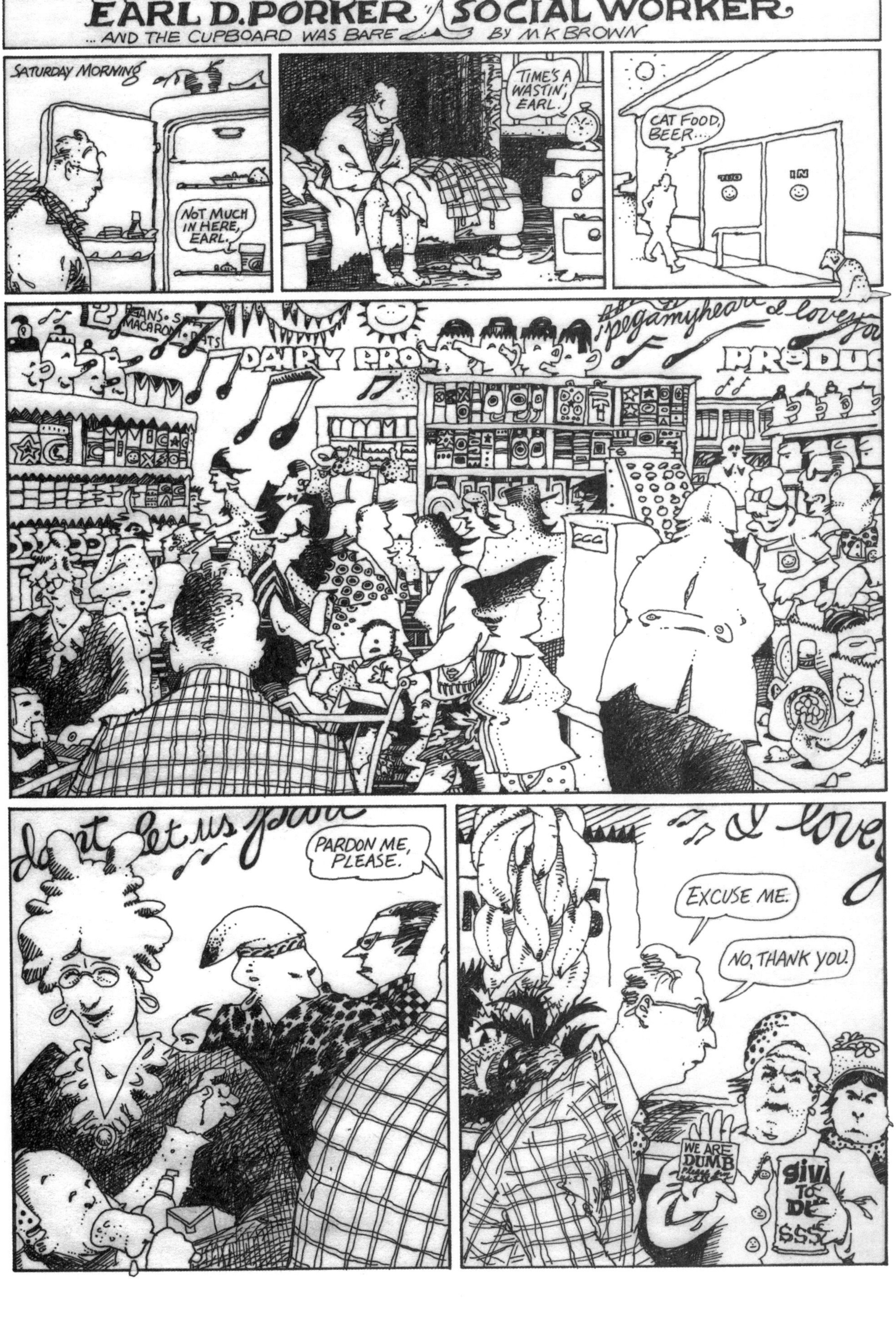

EARL D. PORKER SOCIAL WORKER
... AND THE CUPBOARD WAS BARE
BY M.K BROWN
SATURDAY MORNING
NOT MUCH IN HERE, EARL.
TIME'S A WASTIN', EARL.
CAT FOOD, BEER...
OUT
IN
DAIRY PRO
PRODUC
PARDON ME, PLEASE.
EXCUSE ME.
NO, THANK YOU.
WE ARE DUMB

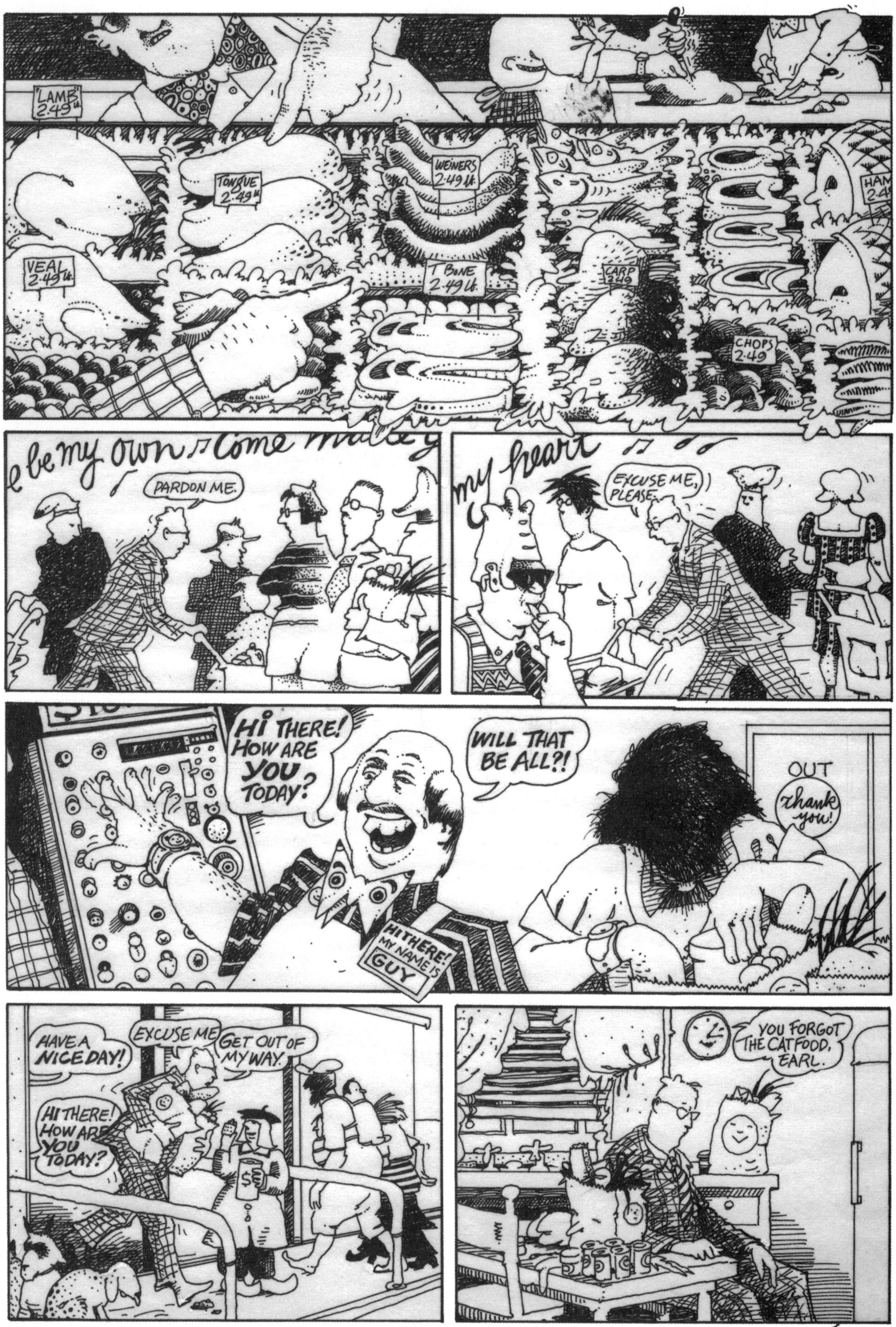
LAMB 2.49 lb.
TONGUE 2.49 lb.
WEINERS 2.49 lb.
VEAL 2.49 lb.
T BONE 2.49 lb.
CARP 2.49
CHOPS 2.49
e be my own ♫ Come make y
PARDON ME.
my heart
EXCUSE ME, PLEASE.
HI THERE! HOW ARE YOU TODAY?
WILL THAT BE ALL?!
OUT
thank you!
HI THERE! MY NAME IS GUY
HAVE A NICE DAY!
EXCUSE ME
GET OUT OF MY WAY.
HI THERE! HOW ARE YOU TODAY?
YOU FORGOT THE CAT FOOD, EARL.
THE END

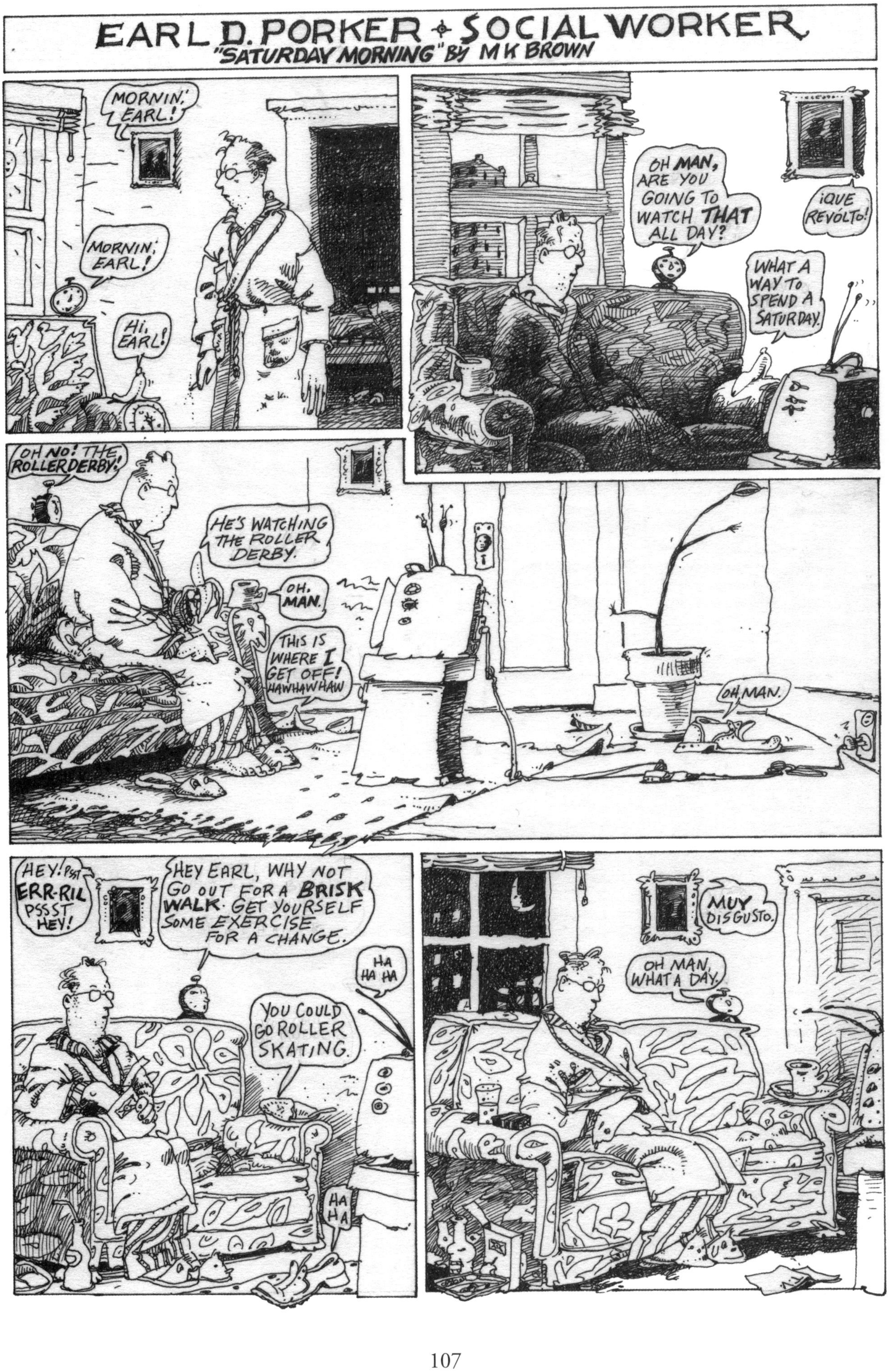
EARL D. PORKER ✦ SOCIAL WORKER
"SATURDAY MORNING" BY M K BROWN
MORNIN', EARL!
MORNIN', EARL!
HI, EARL!
OH MAN, ARE YOU GOING TO WATCH THAT ALL DAY?
¡QUE REVÓLTO!
WHAT A WAY TO SPEND A SATURDAY.
OH NO! THE ROLLERDERBY!
HE'S WATCHING THE ROLLER DERBY.
OH, MAN.
THIS IS WHERE I GET OFF! HAWHAWHAW
OH, MAN.
HEY! PSST ERR-RIL PSSSST HEY!
HEY EARL, WHY NOT GO OUT FOR A BRISK WALK. GET YOURSELF SOME EXERCISE FOR A CHANGE.
HA HA HA
YOU COULD GO ROLLER SKATING.
HA HA
MUY DISGUSTO.
OH MAN, WHAT A DAY.

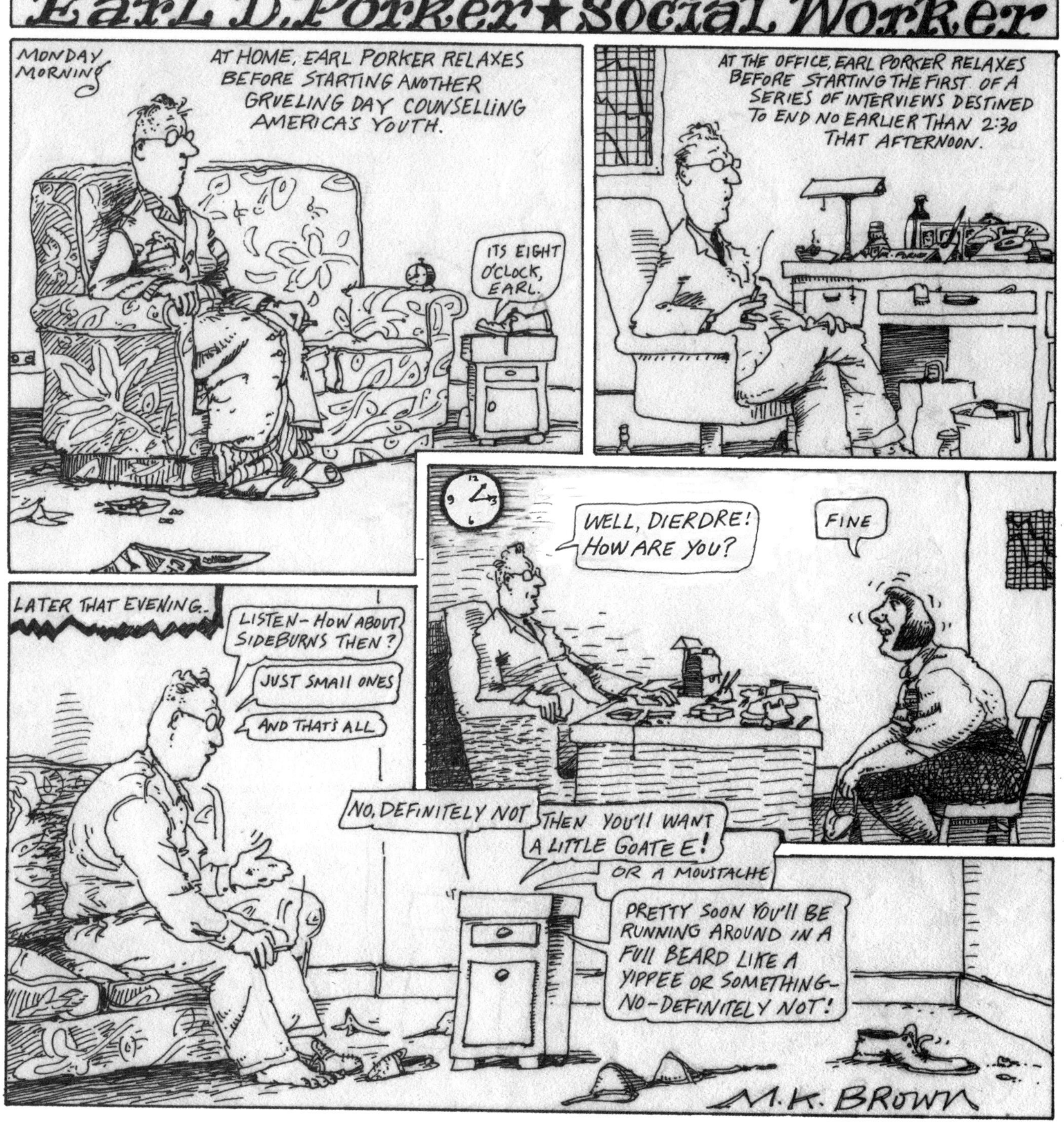
Earl D. Porker ★ Social Worker
MONDAY MORNING
AT HOME, EARL PORKER RELAXES BEFORE STARTING ANOTHER GRUELING DAY COUNSELLING AMERICA'S YOUTH.
ITS EIGHT O'CLOCK, EARL.
AT THE OFFICE, EARL PORKER RELAXES BEFORE STARTING THE FIRST OF A SERIES OF INTERVIEWS DESTINED TO END NO EARLIER THAN 2:30 THAT AFTERNOON.
WELL, DIERDRE! HOW ARE YOU?
FINE
LATER THAT EVENING..
LISTEN- HOW ABOUT SIDEBURNS THEN?
JUST SMALL ONES
AND THAT'S ALL
NO, DEFINITELY NOT
THEN YOU'LL WANT A LITTLE GOATE E!
OR A MOUSTACHE
PRETTY SOON YOU'LL BE RUNNING AROUND IN A FULL BEARD LIKE A YIPPEE OR SOMETHING- NO-DEFINITELY NOT!
M.K. BROWN

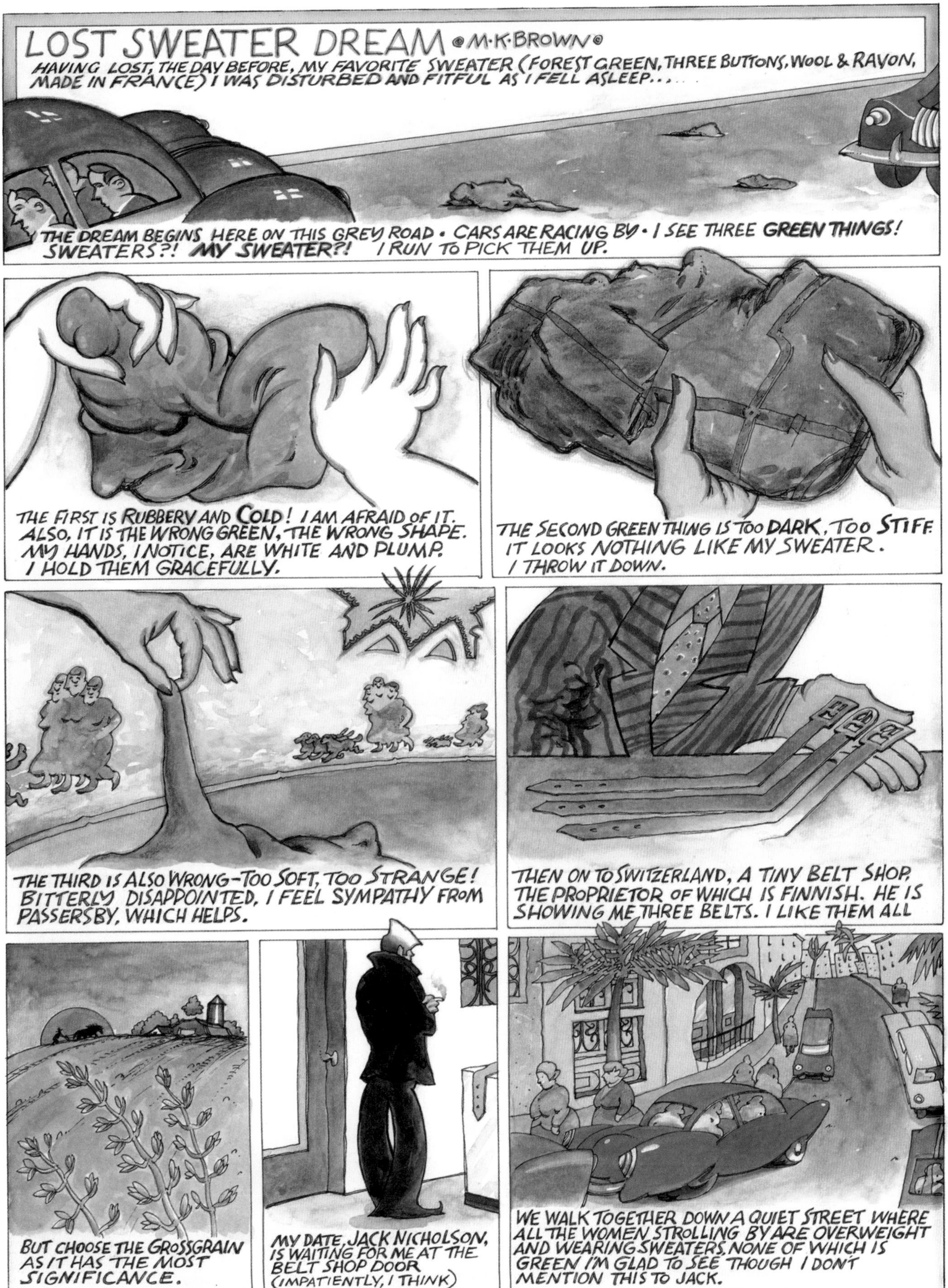
LOST SWEATER DREAM
M·K·BROWN
HAVING LOST, THE DAY BEFORE, MY FAVORITE SWEATER (FOREST GREEN, THREE BUTTONS, WOOL & RAYON, MADE IN FRANCE) I WAS DISTURBED AND FITFUL AS I FELL ASLEEP......
THE DREAM BEGINS HERE ON THIS GREY ROAD • CARS ARE RACING BY • I SEE THREE GREEN THINGS! SWEATERS?! MY SWEATER?! I RUN TO PICK THEM UP.
THE FIRST IS RUBBERY AND COLD! I AM AFRAID OF IT. ALSO, IT IS THE WRONG GREEN, THE WRONG SHAPE. MY HANDS, I NOTICE, ARE WHITE AND PLUMP. I HOLD THEM GRACEFULLY.
THE SECOND GREEN THING IS TOO DARK, TOO STIFF. IT LOOKS NOTHING LIKE MY SWEATER. I THROW IT DOWN.
THE THIRD IS ALSO WRONG-TOO SOFT, TOO STRANGE! BITTERLY DISAPPOINTED, I FEEL SYMPATHY FROM PASSERSBY, WHICH HELPS.
THEN ON TO SWITZERLAND, A TINY BELT SHOP, THE PROPRIETOR OF WHICH IS FINNISH. HE IS SHOWING ME THREE BELTS. I LIKE THEM ALL
BUT CHOOSE THE GROSSGRAIN AS IT HAS THE MOST SIGNIFICANCE.
MY DATE, JACK NICHOLSON, IS WAITING FOR ME AT THE BELT SHOP DOOR (IMPATIENTLY, I THINK)
WE WALK TOGETHER DOWN A QUIET STREET WHERE ALL THE WOMEN STROLLING BY ARE OVERWEIGHT AND WEARING SWEATERS, NONE OF WHICH IS GREEN I'M GLAD TO SEE THOUGH I DON'T MENTION THIS TO JACK.

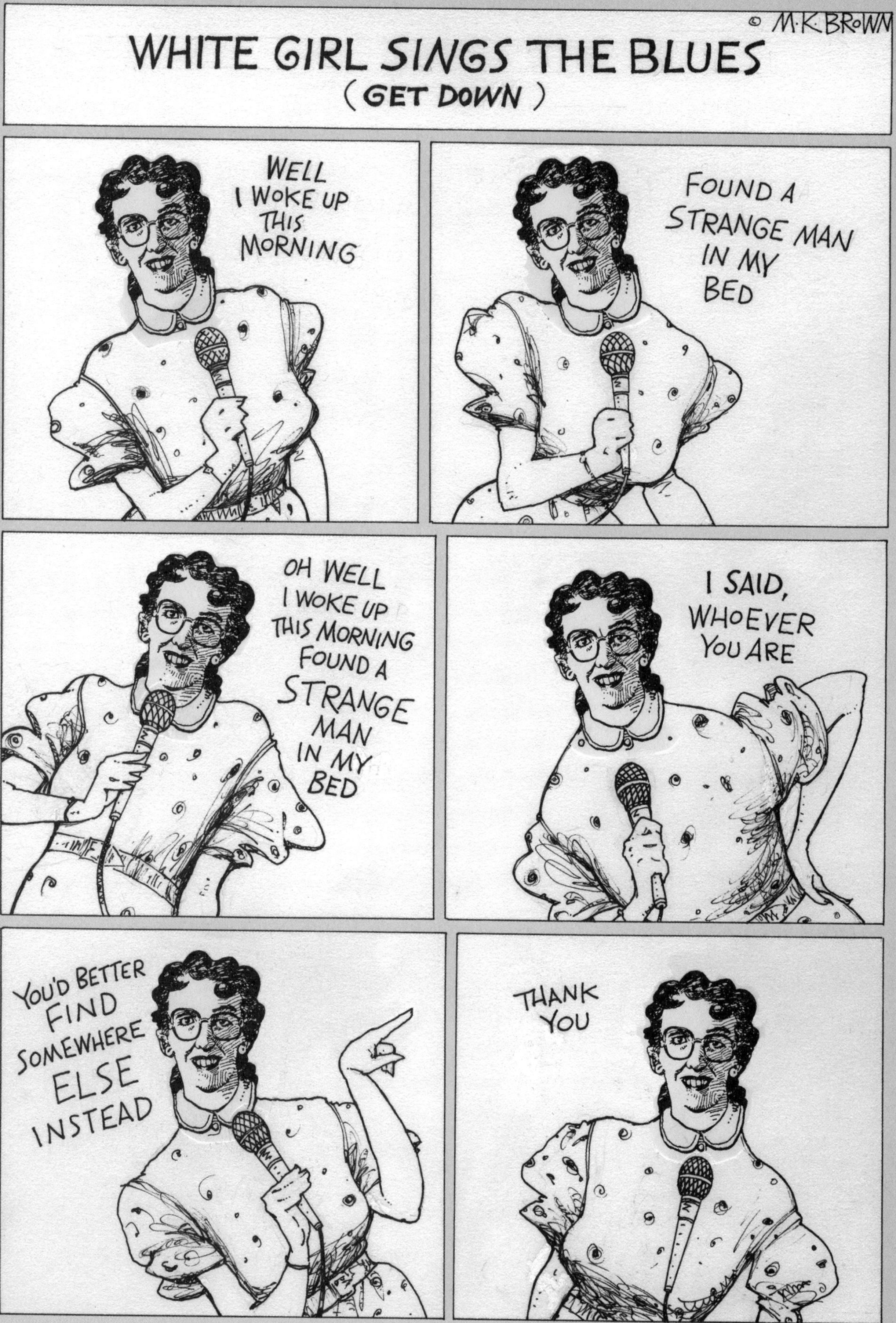
© M.K. BROWN
WHITE GIRL SINGS THE BLUES
(GET DOWN)
WELL I WOKE UP THIS MORNING
FOUND A STRANGE MAN IN MY BED
OH WELL I WOKE UP THIS MORNING FOUND A STRANGE MAN IN MY BED
I SAID, WHOEVER YOU ARE
YOU'D BETTER FIND SOMEWHERE ELSE INSTEAD
THANK YOU

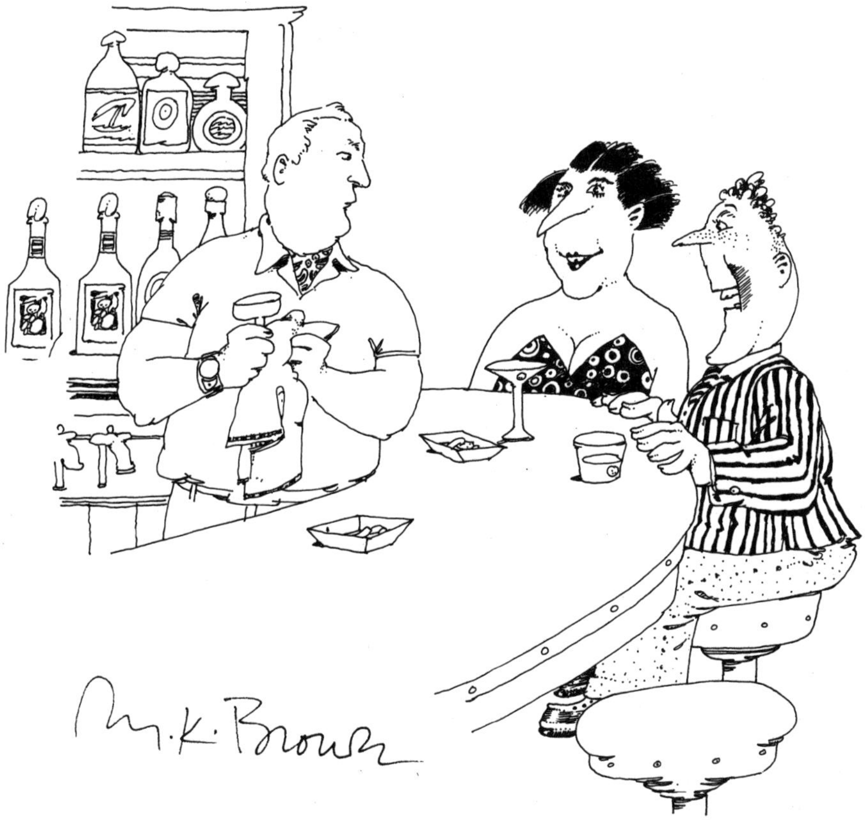
M.K. Brown

Heck, no! We're not crazy! Why? Do we look crazy?

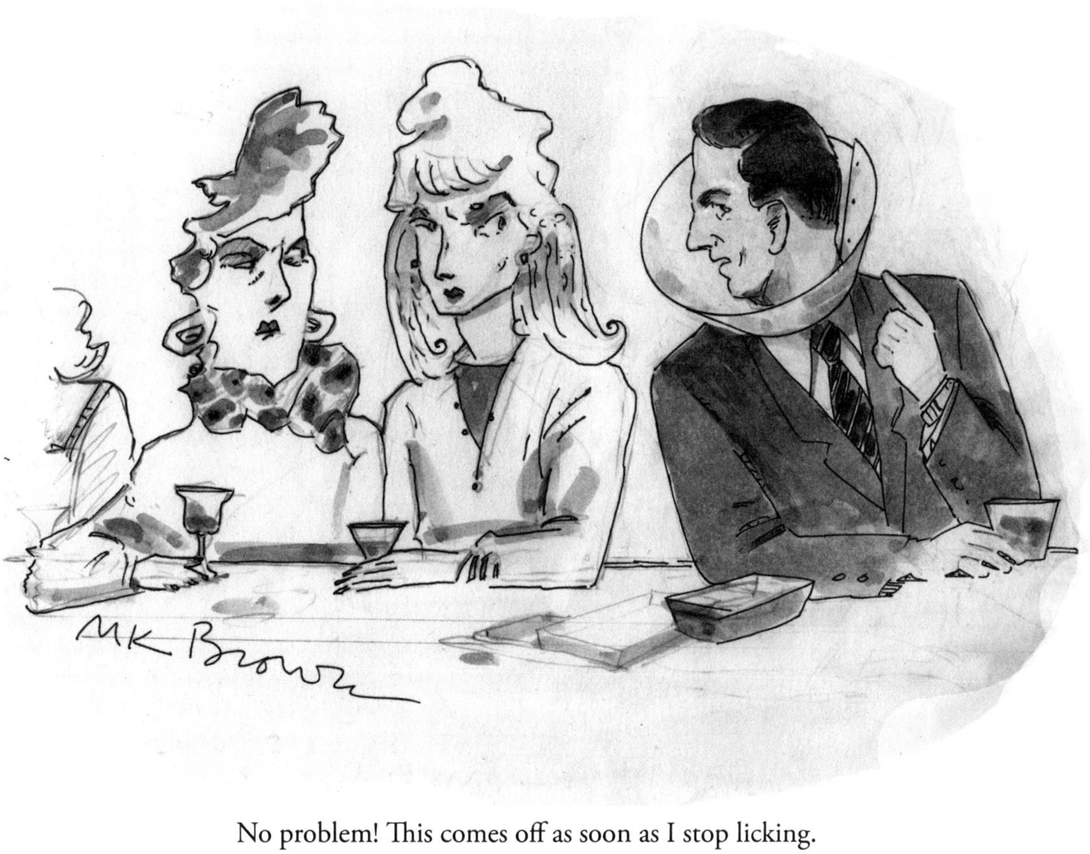
MK Brown

No problem! This comes off as soon as I stop licking.

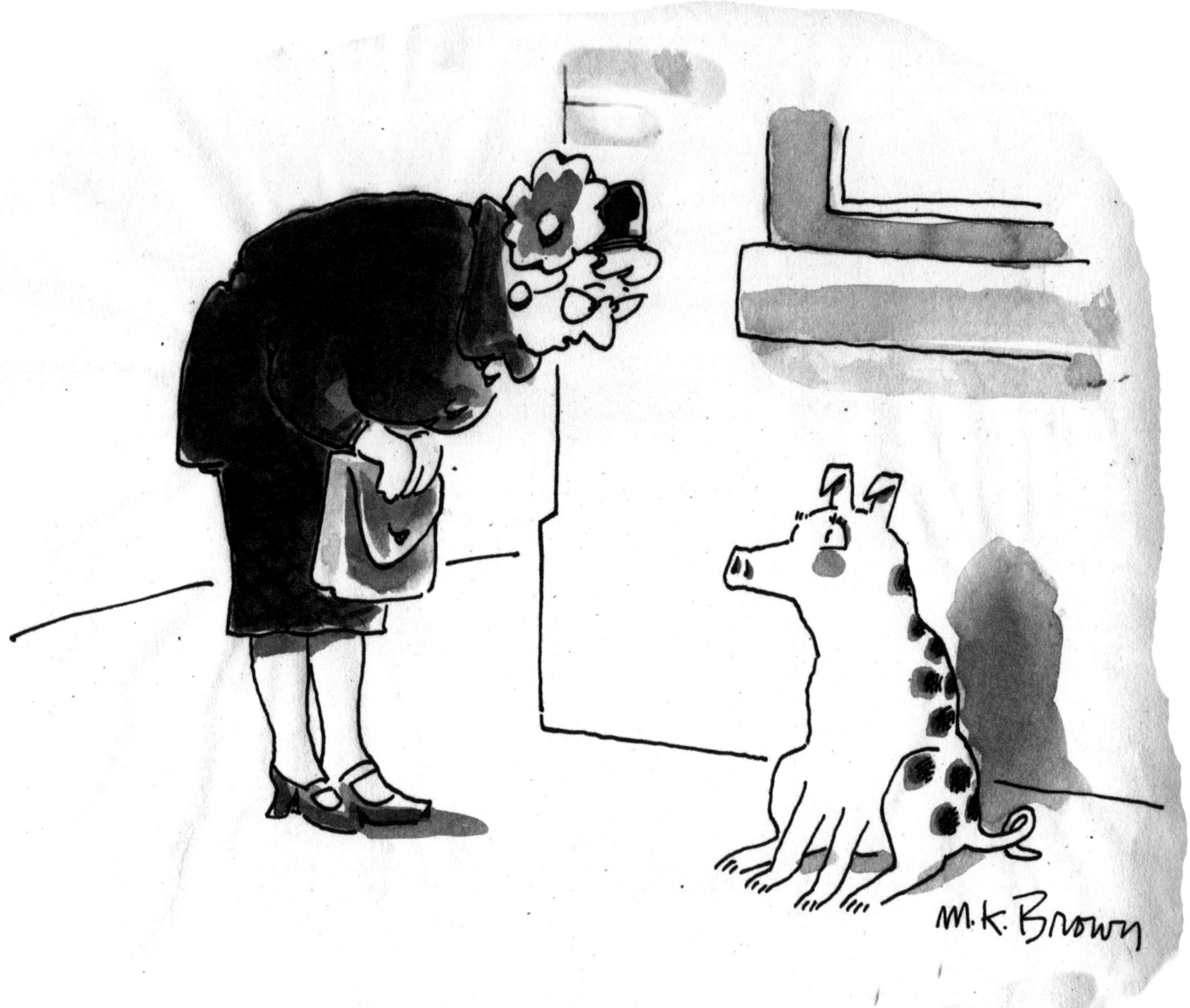
M.K. Brown

You poor thing. Are you a pig or a dog?

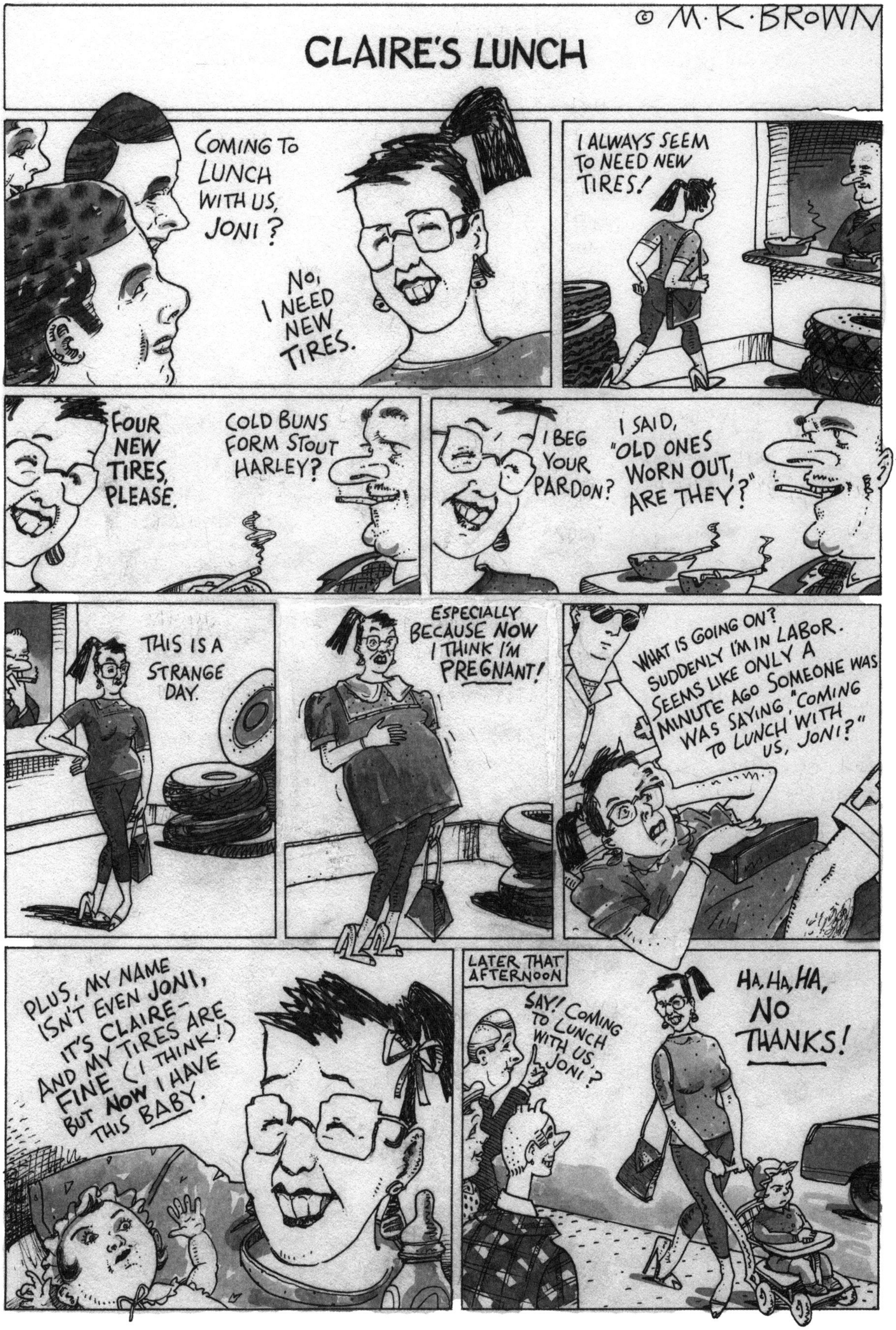
© M·K·BROWN
CLAIRE'S LUNCH
COMING TO LUNCH WITH US, JONI?
NO, I NEED NEW TIRES.
I ALWAYS SEEM TO NEED NEW TIRES!
FOUR NEW TIRES, PLEASE.
COLD BUNS FORM STOUT HARLEY?
I BEG YOUR PARDON?
I SAID, "OLD ONES WORN OUT, ARE THEY?"
THIS IS A STRANGE DAY.
ESPECIALLY BECAUSE NOW I THINK I'M PREGNANT!
WHAT IS GOING ON? SUDDENLY I'M IN LABOR. SEEMS LIKE ONLY A MINUTE AGO SOMEONE WAS SAYING, "COMING TO LUNCH WITH US, JONI?"
PLUS, MY NAME ISN'T EVEN JONI, IT'S CLAIRE– AND MY TIRES ARE FINE (I THINK!) BUT NOW I HAVE THIS BABY.
LATER THAT AFTERNOON
SAY! COMING TO LUNCH WITH US, JONI?
HA, HA, HA, NO THANKS!

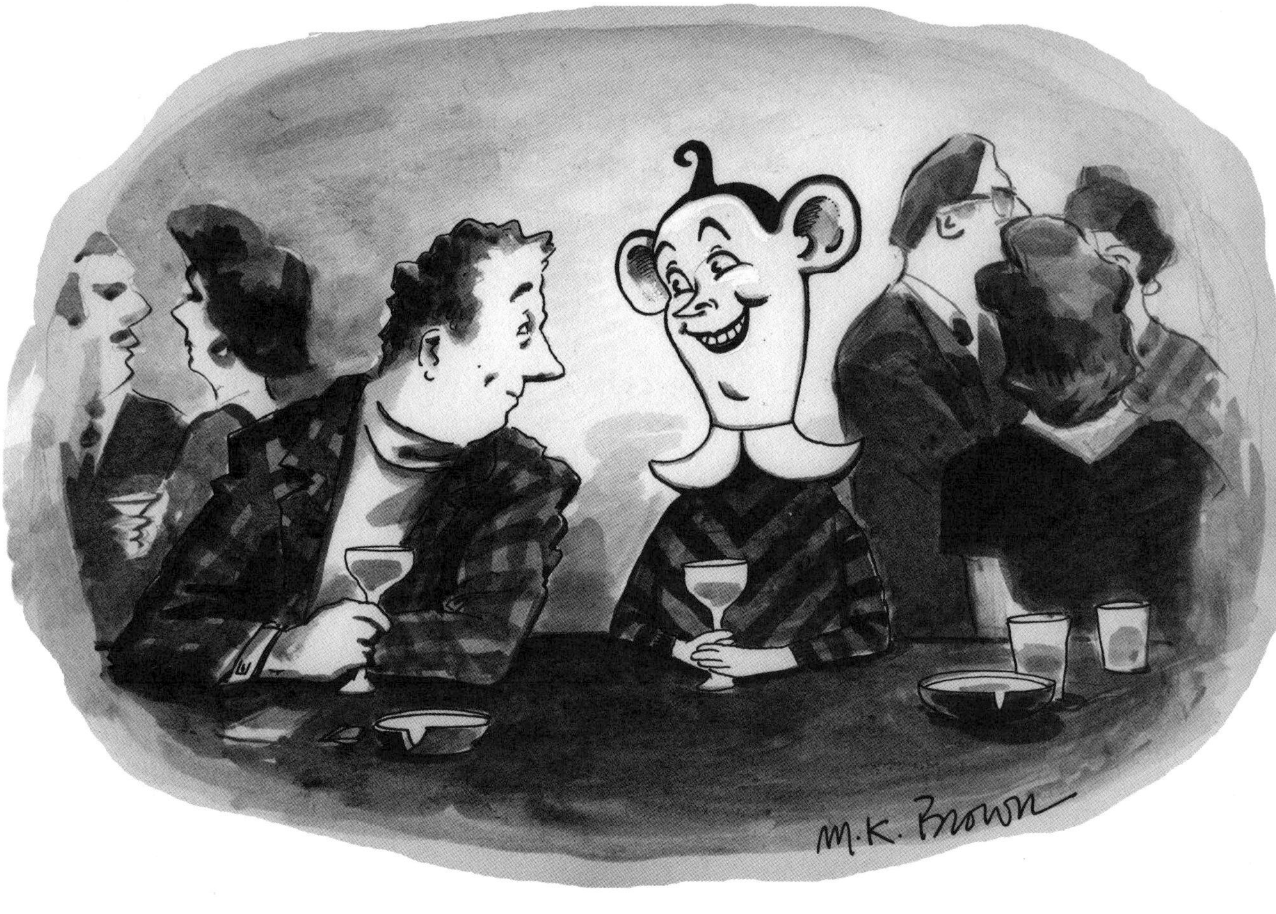
M.K. Brown

Yes, I come here every night!

Romance and Social Studies

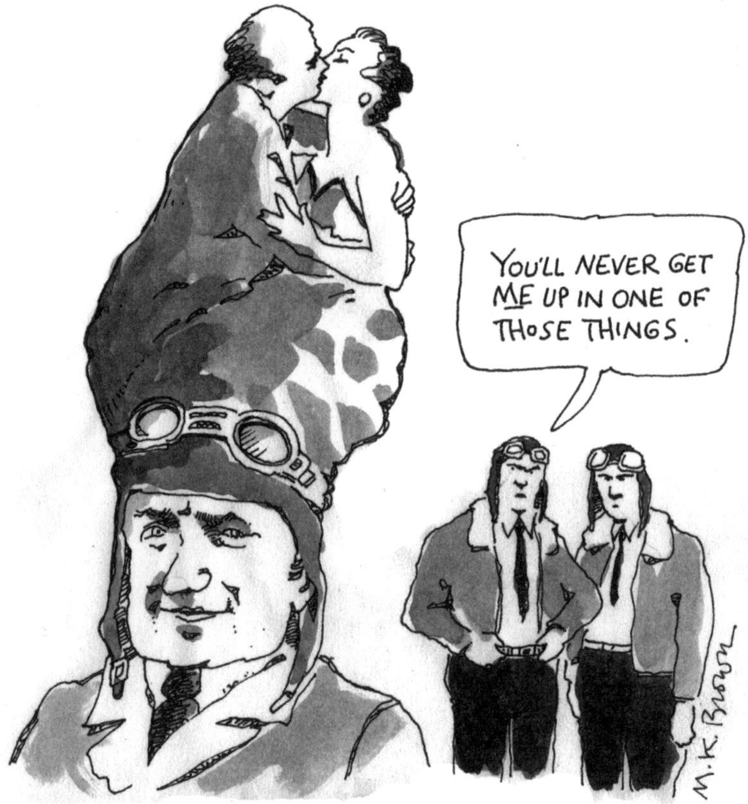
YOU'LL NEVER GET ME UP IN ONE OF THOSE THINGS.
M.K. BROWN

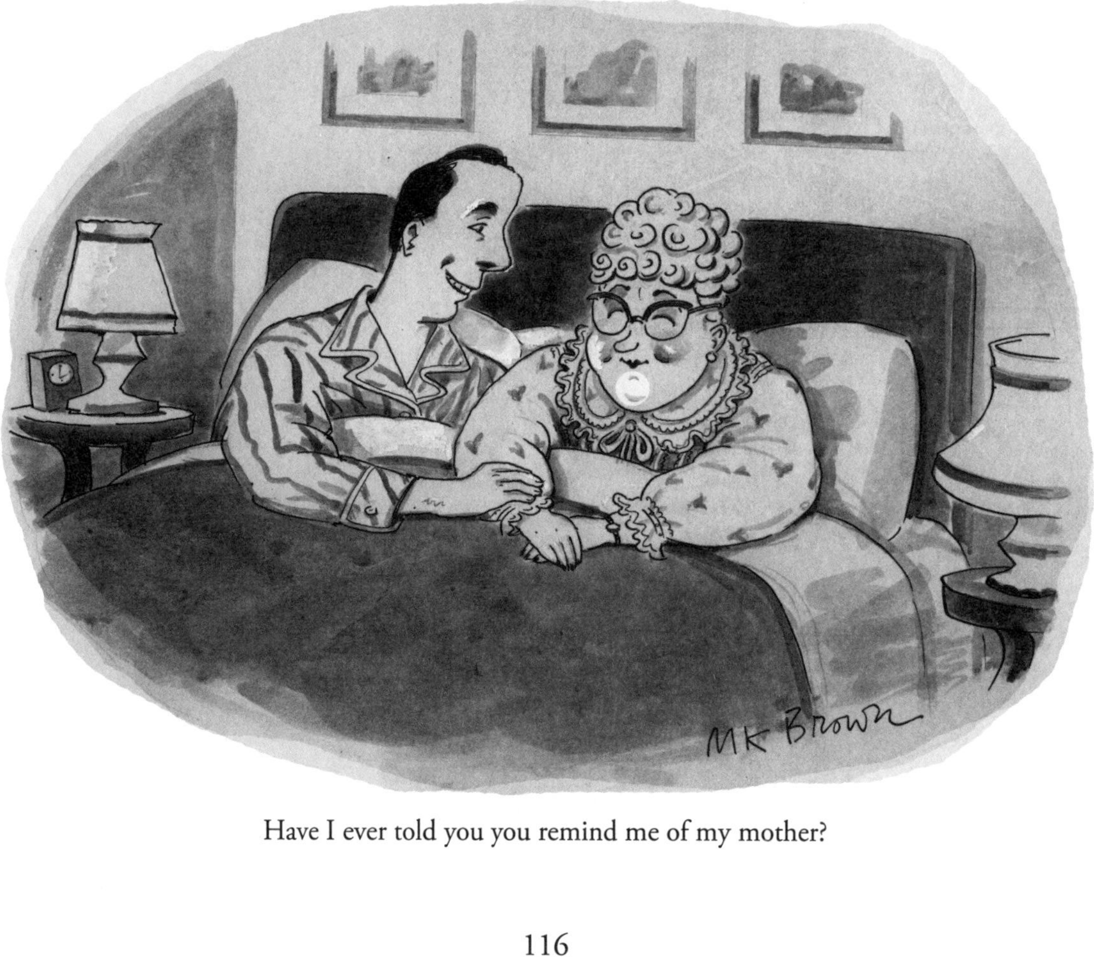
MK BROWN

Have I ever told you you remind me of my mother?

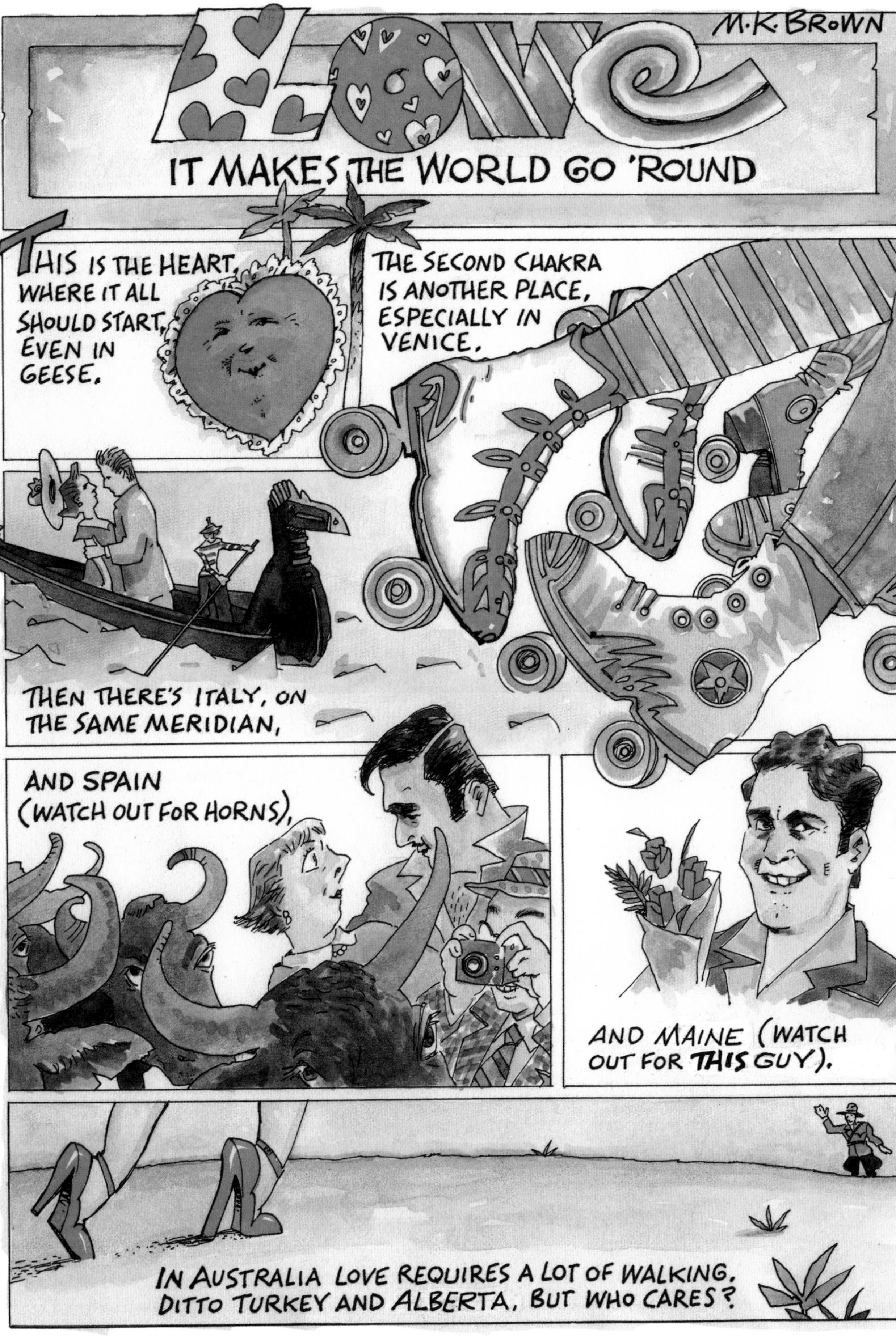
M.K. BROWN
LOVE
IT MAKES THE WORLD GO 'ROUND
THIS IS THE HEART, WHERE IT ALL SHOULD START, EVEN IN GEESE.
THE SECOND CHAKRA IS ANOTHER PLACE, ESPECIALLY IN VENICE.
THEN THERE'S ITALY, ON THE SAME MERIDIAN,
AND SPAIN (WATCH OUT FOR HORNS),
AND MAINE (WATCH OUT FOR THIS GUY).
IN AUSTRALIA LOVE REQUIRES A LOT OF WALKING, DITTO TURKEY AND ALBERTA, BUT WHO CARES?

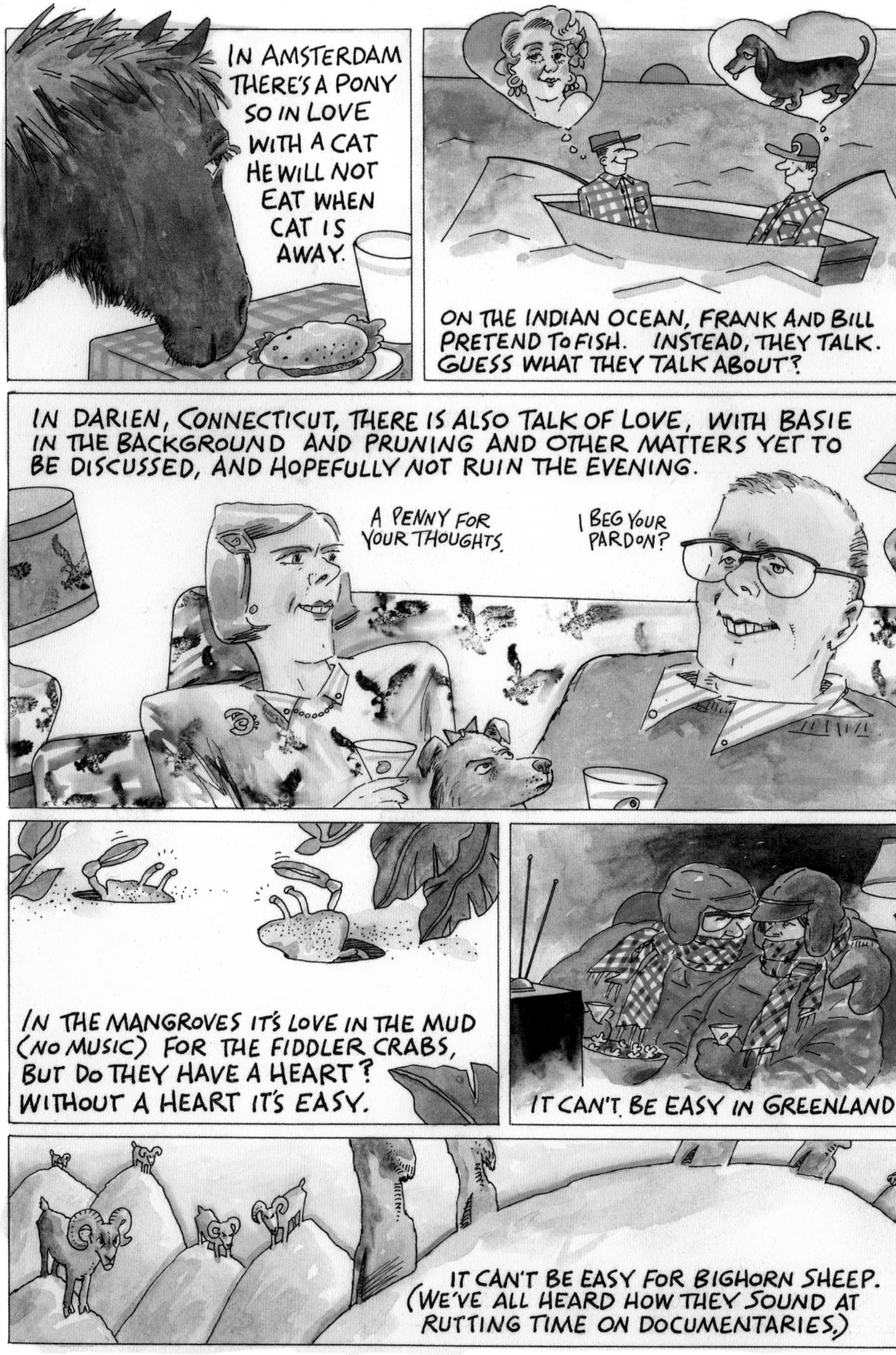
IN AMSTERDAM THERE'S A PONY SO IN LOVE WITH A CAT HE WILL NOT EAT WHEN CAT IS AWAY.
ON THE INDIAN OCEAN, FRANK AND BILL PRETEND TO FISH. INSTEAD, THEY TALK. GUESS WHAT THEY TALK ABOUT?
IN DARIEN, CONNECTICUT, THERE IS ALSO TALK OF LOVE, WITH BASIE IN THE BACKGROUND AND PRUNING AND OTHER MATTERS YET TO BE DISCUSSED, AND HOPEFULLY NOT RUIN THE EVENING.
A PENNY FOR YOUR THOUGHTS.
I BEG YOUR PARDON?
IN THE MANGROVES IT'S LOVE IN THE MUD (NO MUSIC) FOR THE FIDDLER CRABS, BUT DO THEY HAVE A HEART? WITHOUT A HEART IT'S EASY.
IT CAN'T BE EASY IN GREENLAND.
IT CAN'T BE EASY FOR BIGHORN SHEEP. (WE'VE ALL HEARD HOW THEY SOUND AT RUTTING TIME ON DOCUMENTARIES.)

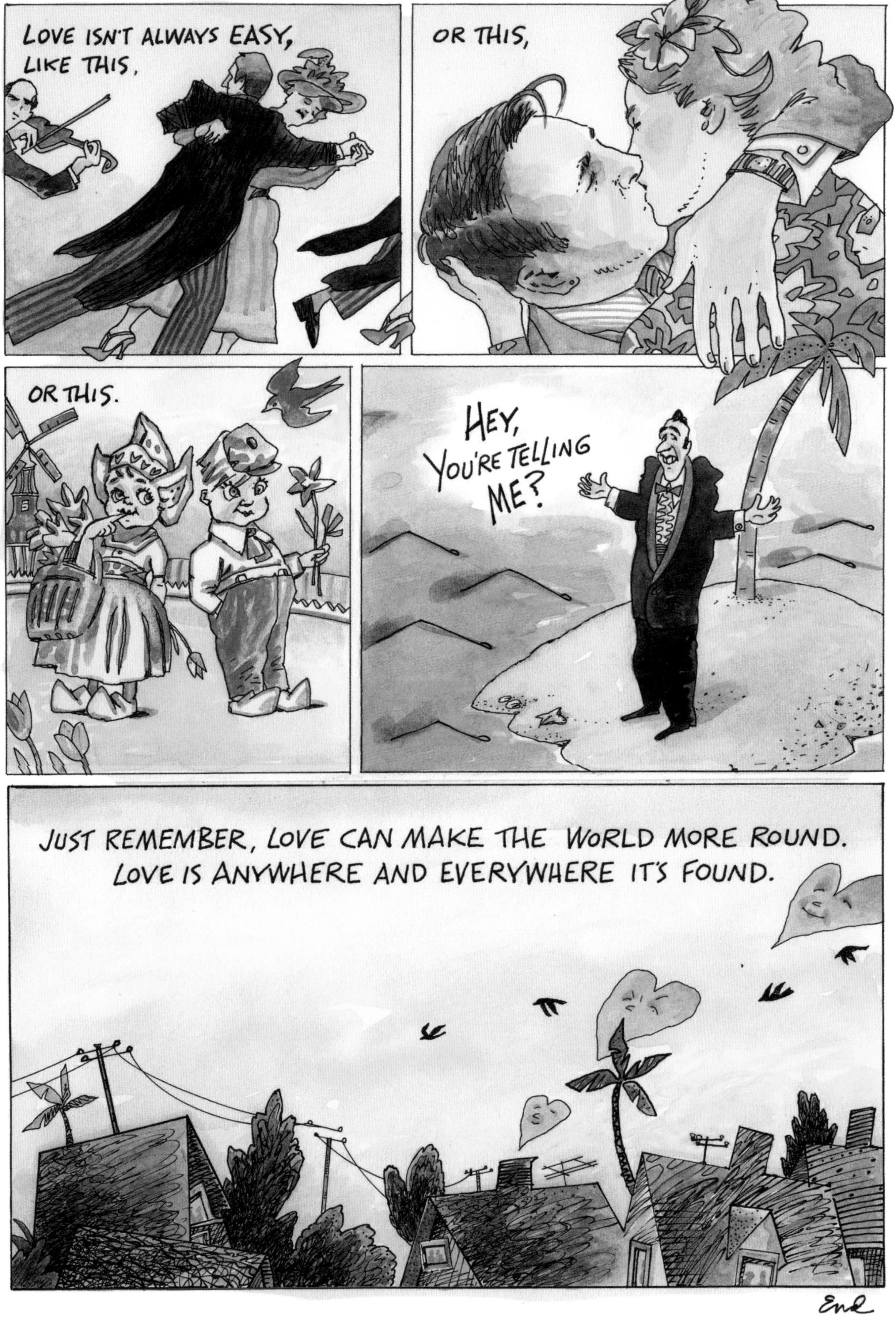
LOVE ISN'T ALWAYS EASY,
LIKE THIS,
OR THIS,
OR THIS.
HEY, YOU'RE TELLING ME?
JUST REMEMBER, LOVE CAN MAKE THE WORLD MORE ROUND.
LOVE IS ANYWHERE AND EVERYWHERE IT'S FOUND.
End

Funny the way things turn out, isn't it Stuart?

Rather stingy with the primroses, aren't you, Roger?

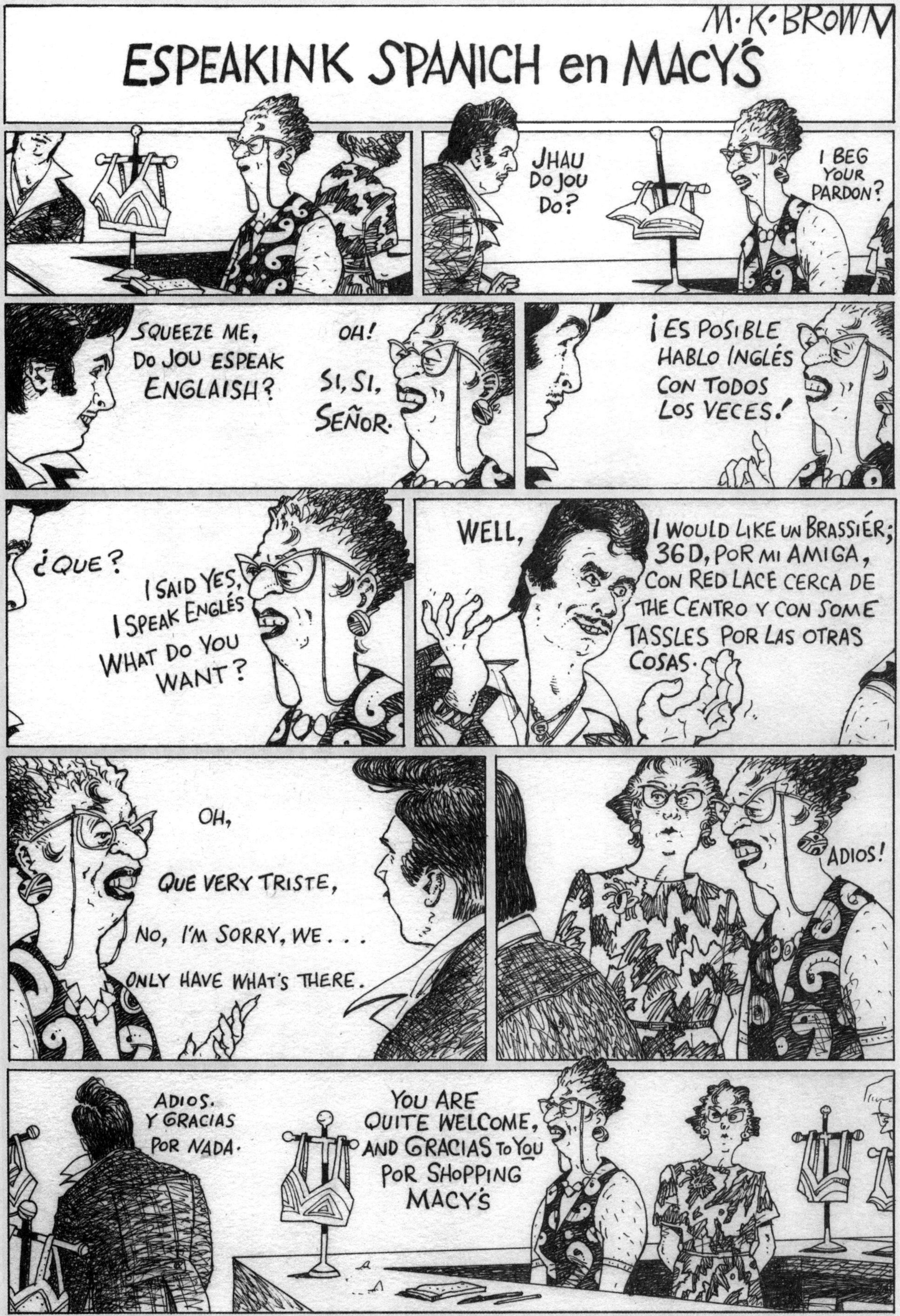
M.K. BROWN
ESPEAKINK SPANICH en MACY'S
JHAU DO JOU DO?
I BEG YOUR PARDON?
SQUEEZE ME, DO JOU ESPEAK ENGLAISH?
OH!
SI, SI, SEÑOR.
¡ES POSIBLE HABLO INGLÉS CON TODOS LOS VECES!
¿QUE?
I SAID YES, I SPEAK ENGLÉS WHAT DO YOU WANT?
WELL,
I WOULD LIKE UN BRASSIÉR; 36D, POR MI AMIGA, CON RED LACE CERCA DE THE CENTRO Y CON SOME TASSLES POR LAS OTRAS COSAS.
OH,
QUE VERY TRISTE,
NO, I'M SORRY, WE . . .
ONLY HAVE WHAT'S THERE.
ADIOS!
ADIOS. Y GRACIAS POR NADA.
YOU ARE QUITE WELCOME, AND GRACIAS TO YOU POR SHOPPING MACY'S

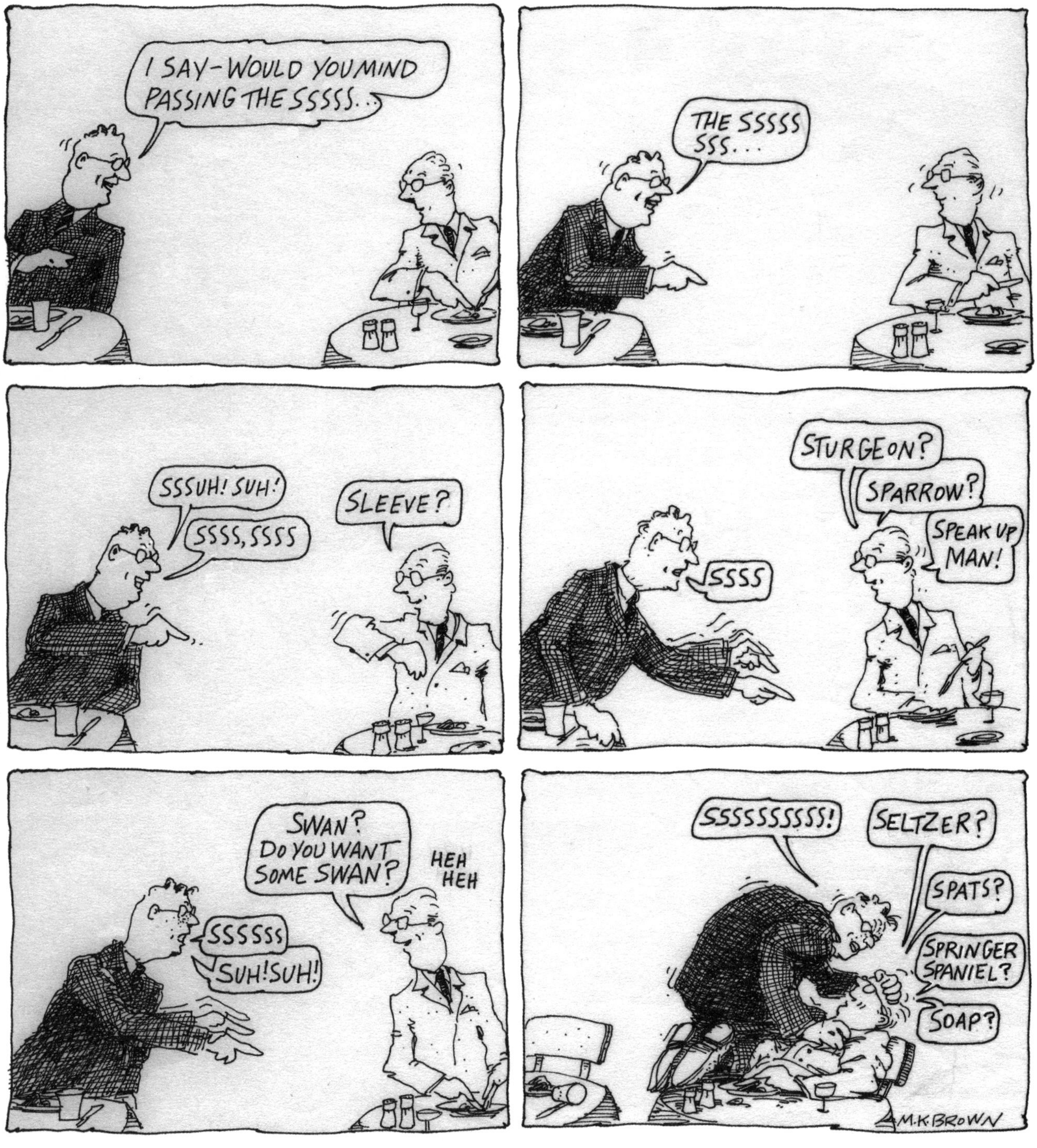
I SAY-WOULD YOU MIND PASSING THE SSSSS...
THE SSSSS SSS...
SSSUH! SUH!
SSSS, SSSS
SLEEVE?
SSSS
STURGEON?
SPARROW?
SPEAK UP MAN!
SSSSSS
SUH! SUH!
SWAN? DO YOU WANT SOME SWAN?
HEH HEH
SSSSSSSSSS!
SELTZER?
SPATS?
SPRINGER SPANIEL?
SOAP?
M.K.BROWN

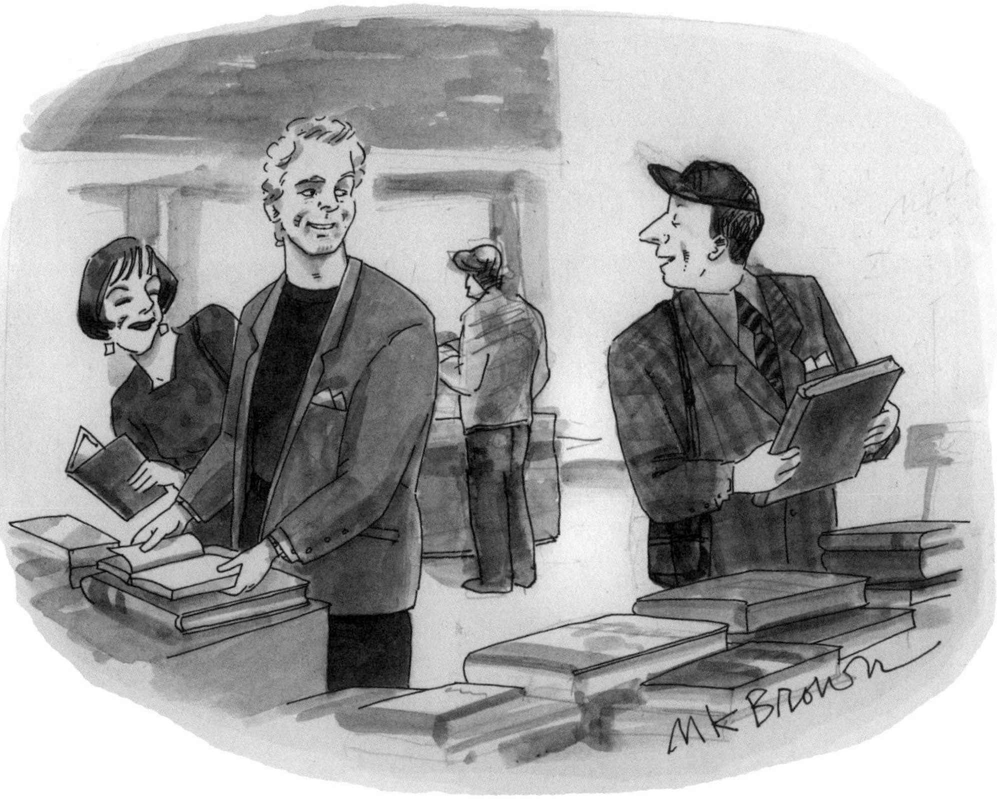

Hal! Sandra! I didn't recognize you with your new heads.

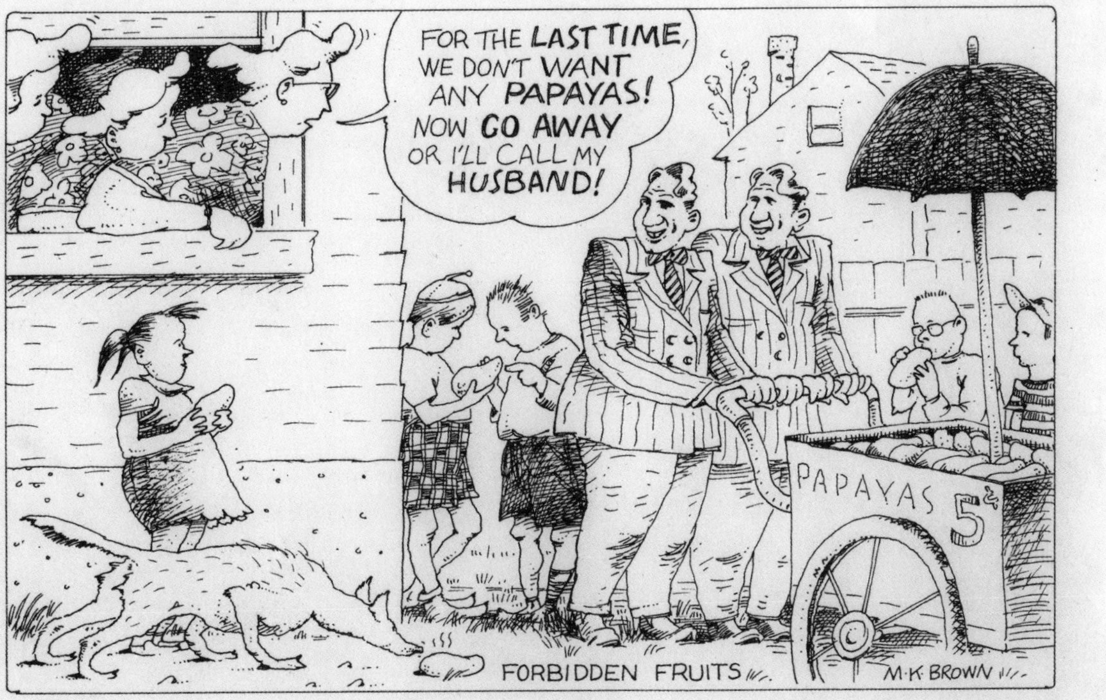
FOR THE LAST TIME, WE DON'T WANT ANY PAPAYAS! NOW GO AWAY OR I'LL CALL MY HUSBAND!
PAPAYAS 5¢
FORBIDDEN FRUITS
M·K·BROWN

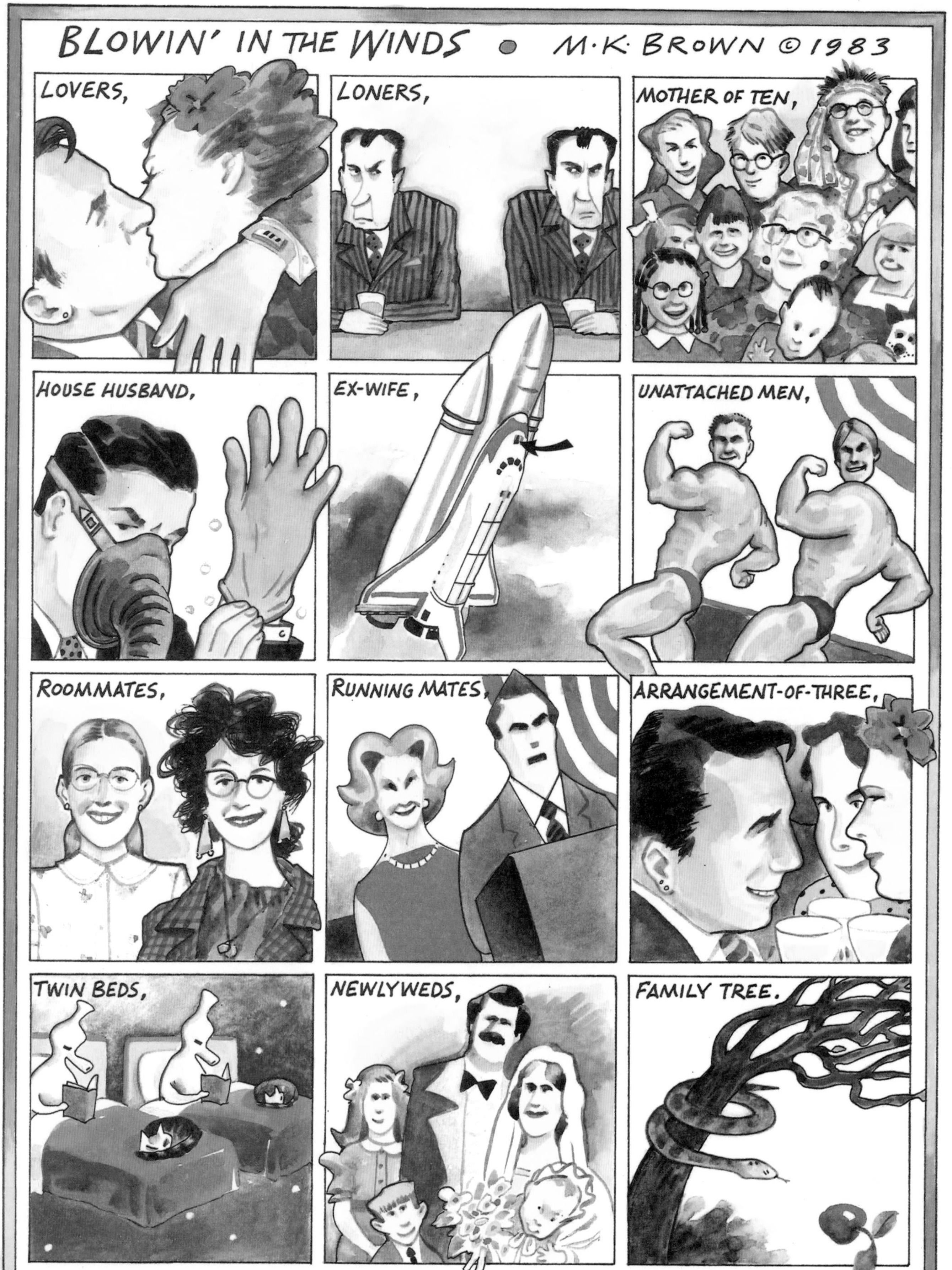
BLOWIN' IN THE WINDS • M·K· BROWN ©1983
LOVERS,
LONERS,
MOTHER OF TEN,
HOUSE HUSBAND,
EX-WIFE,
UNATTACHED MEN,
ROOMMATES,
RUNNING MATES,
ARRANGEMENT-OF-THREE,
TWIN BEDS,
NEWLYWEDS,
FAMILY TREE.

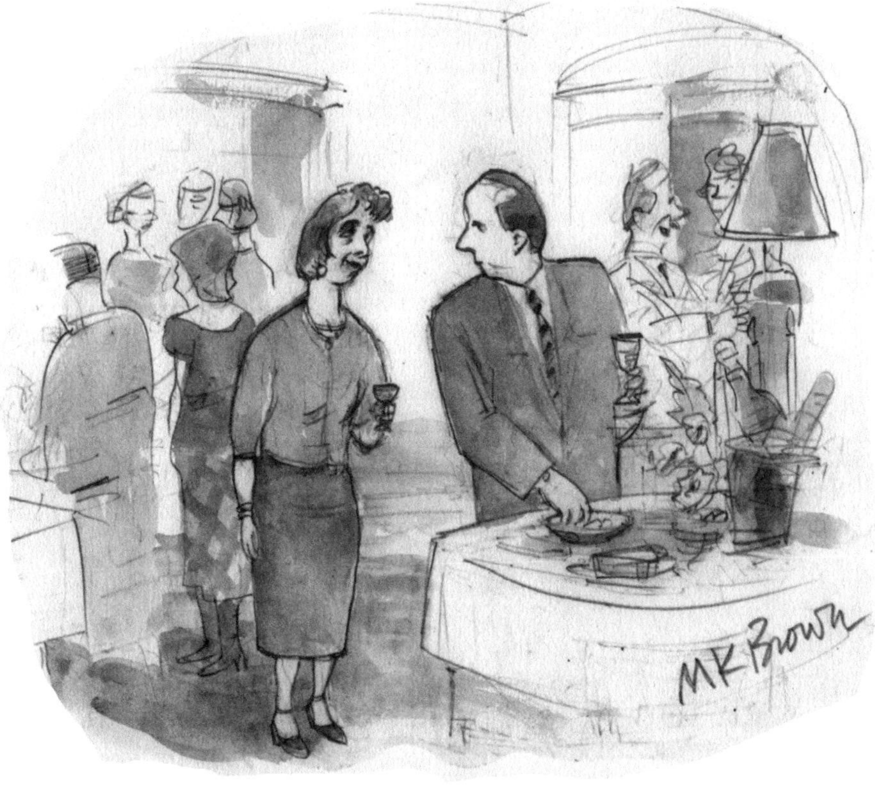
MKBrown

My name is Jean. I'll be your downer for the evening.

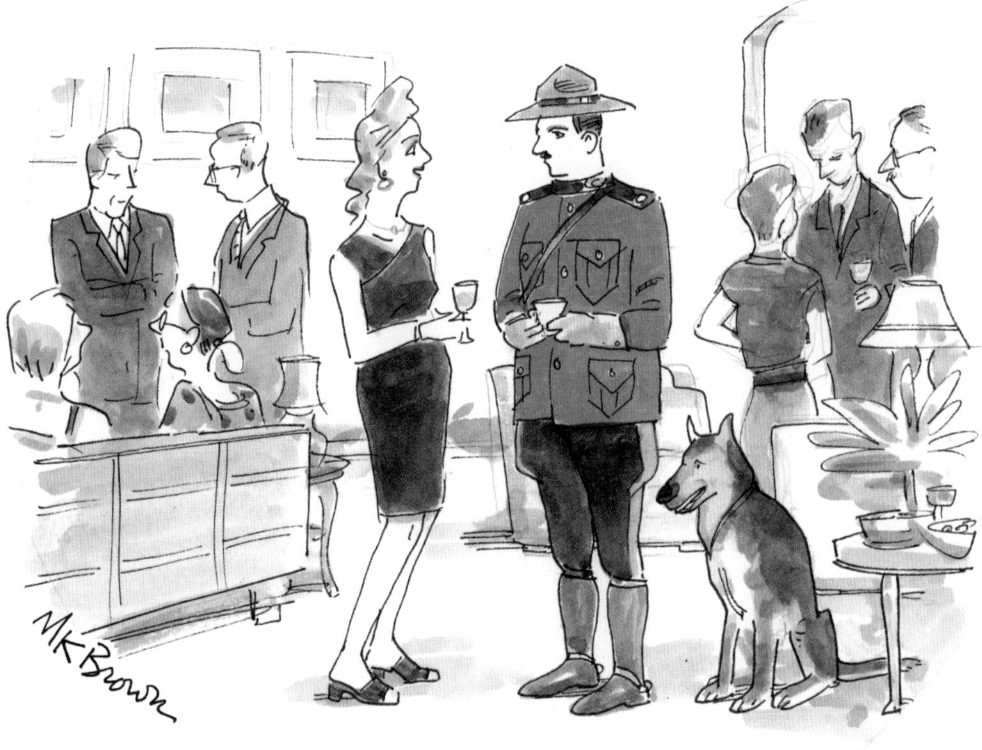
MKBrown

Enough about me. What do *you* do, Stan?

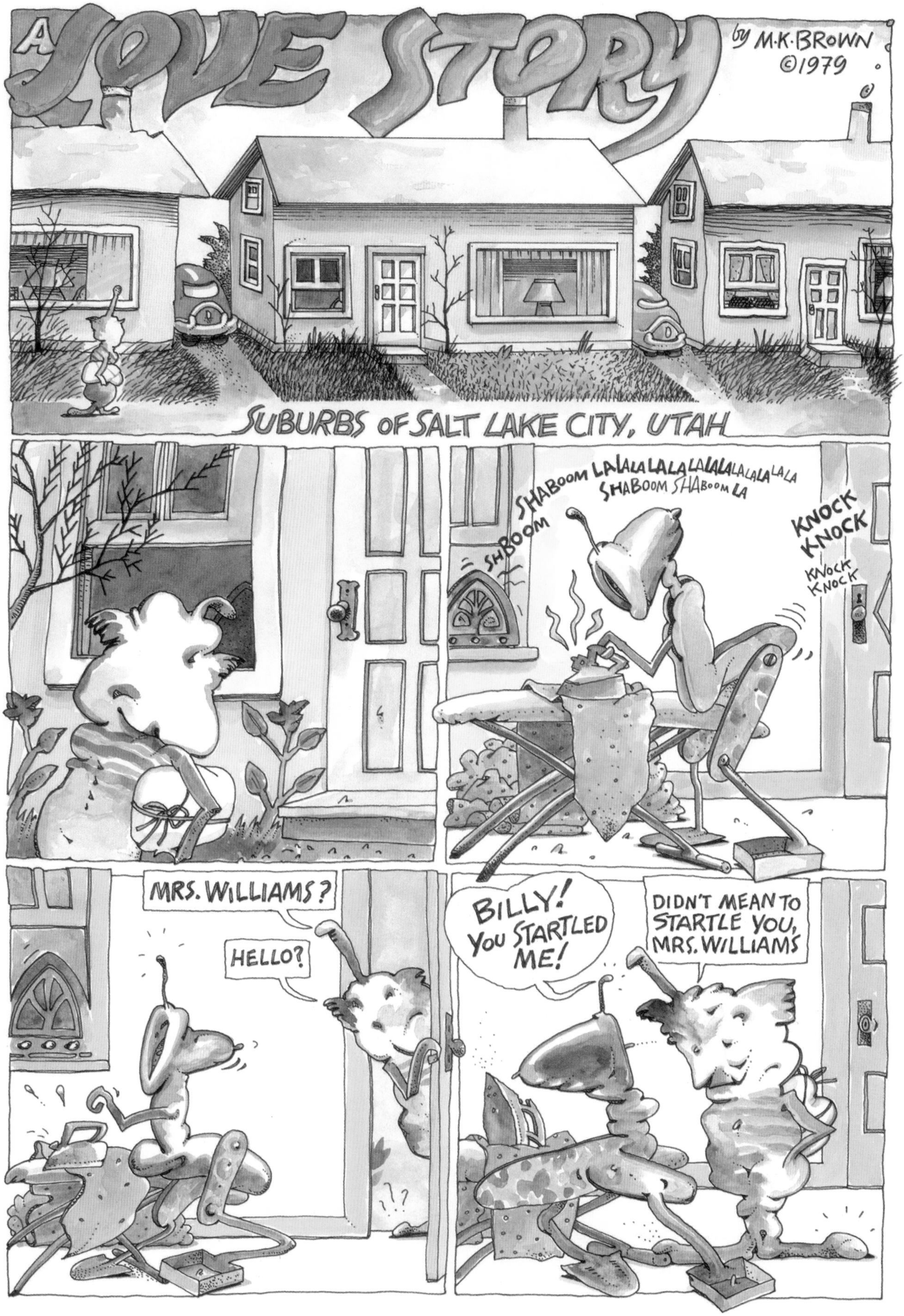
A LOVE STORY
by M.K. BROWN ©1979
SUBURBS OF SALT LAKE CITY, UTAH
SHABOOM SHABOOM LALALALALALALALALALALALALA SHABOOM SHABOOM LA
KNOCK KNOCK
KNOCK KNOCK
MRS. WILLIAMS?
HELLO?
BILLY! YOU STARTLED ME!
DIDN'T MEAN TO STARTLE YOU, MRS. WILLIAMS

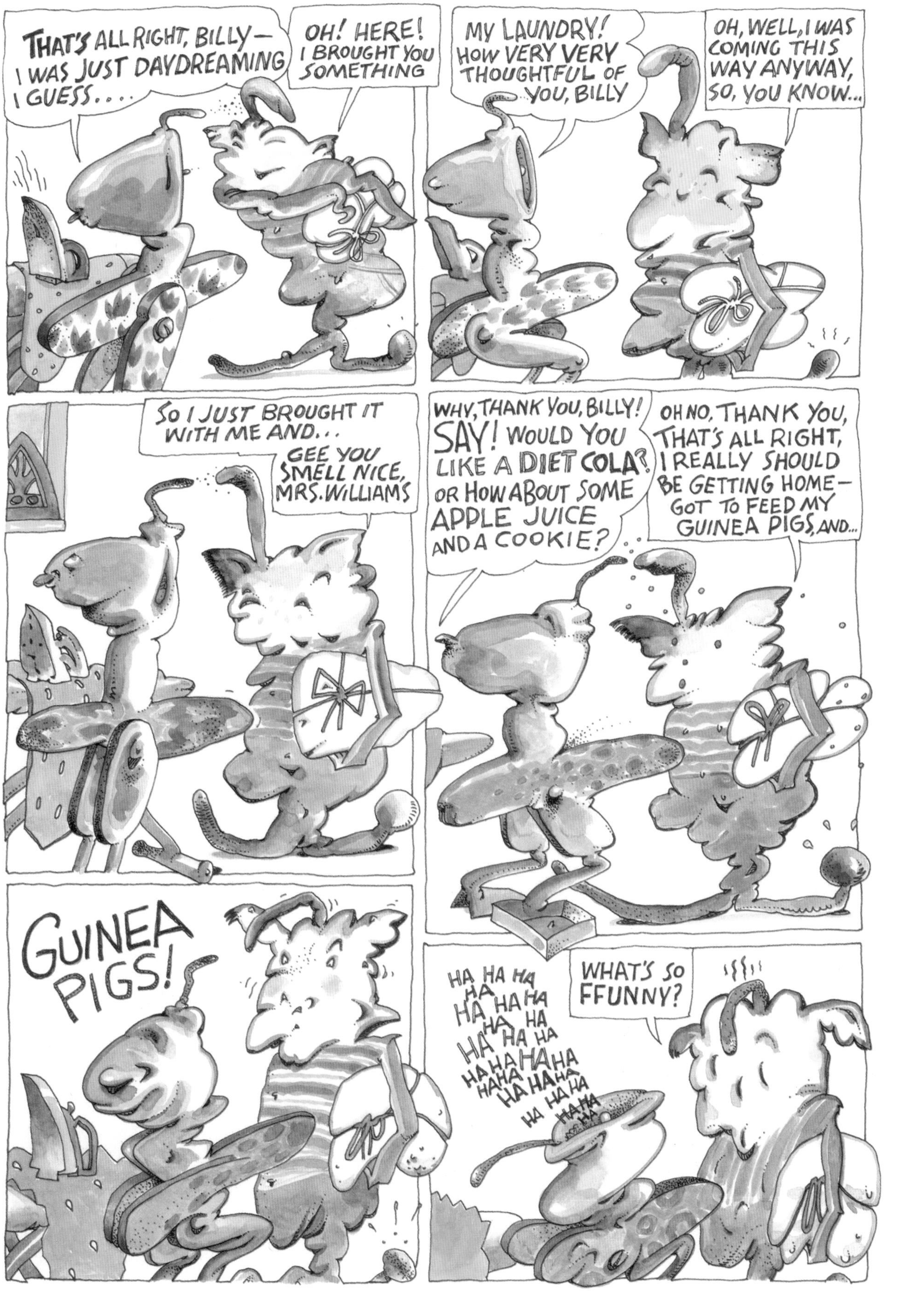

THAT'S ALL RIGHT, BILLY— I WAS JUST DAYDREAMING I GUESS....
OH! HERE! I BROUGHT YOU SOMETHING
MY LAUNDRY! HOW VERY VERY THOUGHTFUL OF YOU, BILLY
OH, WELL, I WAS COMING THIS WAY ANYWAY, SO, YOU KNOW...
SO I JUST BROUGHT IT WITH ME AND...
GEE YOU SMELL NICE, MRS. WILLIAMS
WHY, THANK YOU, BILLY! SAY! WOULD YOU LIKE A DIET COLA? OR HOW ABOUT SOME APPLE JUICE AND A COOKIE?
OH NO, THANK YOU, THAT'S ALL RIGHT, I REALLY SHOULD BE GETTING HOME— GOT TO FEED MY GUINEA PIGS, AND...
GUINEA PIGS!
HA HA HA HA HA HA HA HA HA HA HA HA HA HA HA HA HA HA HA HA HA HAHA HAHA HA HA HA HA HA HA HA HA
WHAT'S SO FFUNNY?

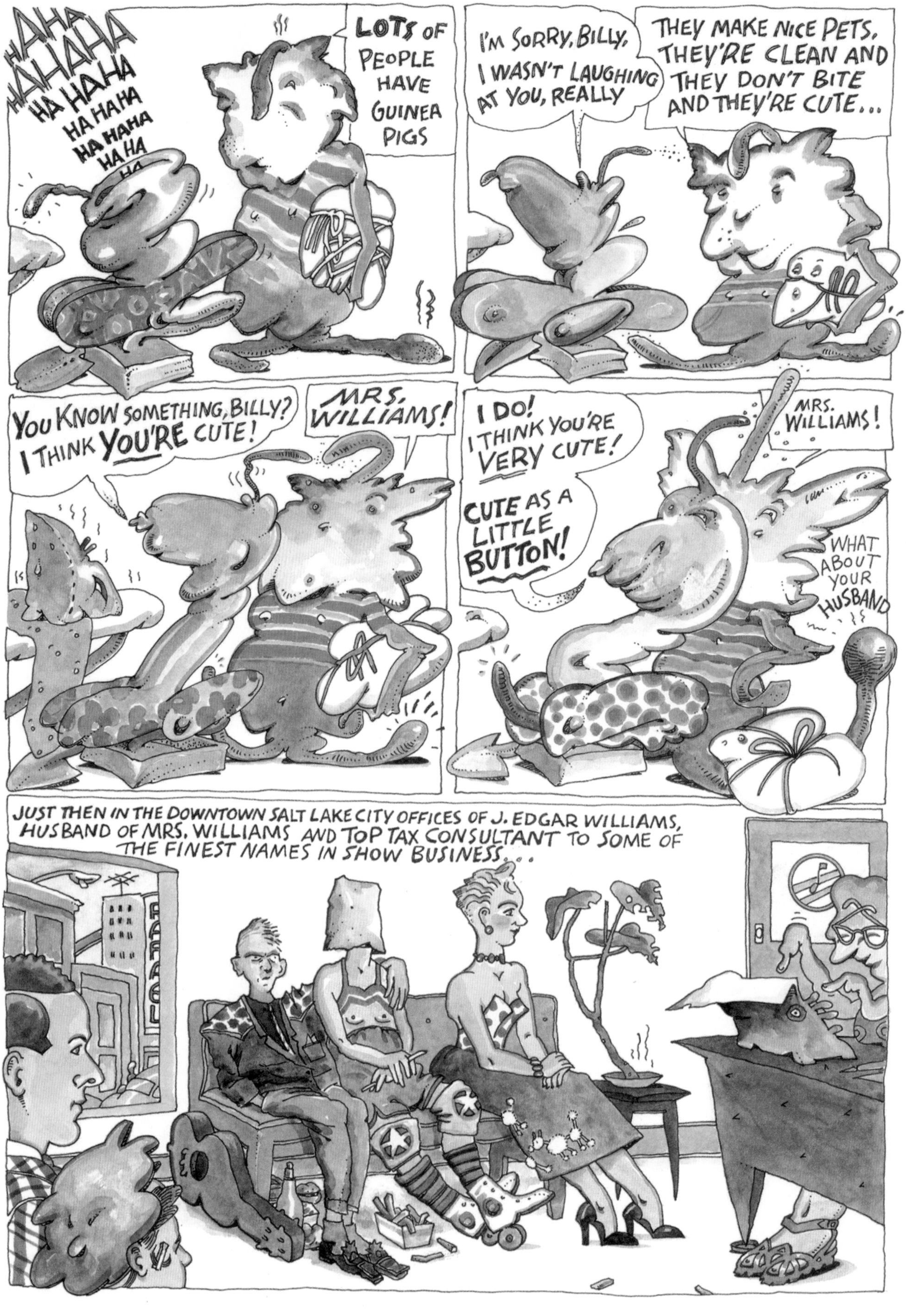
HAHAHA HAHAHA HAHAHA HA HAHA HA HAHA HA HAHA HA HA HA
LOTS OF PEOPLE HAVE GUINEA PIGS
I'M SORRY, BILLY, I WASN'T LAUGHING AT YOU, REALLY
THEY MAKE NICE PETS, THEY'RE CLEAN AND THEY DON'T BITE AND THEY'RE CUTE...
YOU KNOW SOMETHING, BILLY? I THINK YOU'RE CUTE!
MRS. WILLIAMS!
I DO! I THINK YOU'RE VERY CUTE!
CUTE AS A LITTLE BUTTON!
MRS. WILLIAMS!
WHAT ABOUT YOUR HUSBAND
JUST THEN IN THE DOWNTOWN SALT LAKE CITY OFFICES OF J. EDGAR WILLIAMS, HUSBAND OF MRS. WILLIAMS AND TOP TAX CONSULTANT TO SOME OF THE FINEST NAMES IN SHOW BUSINESS...

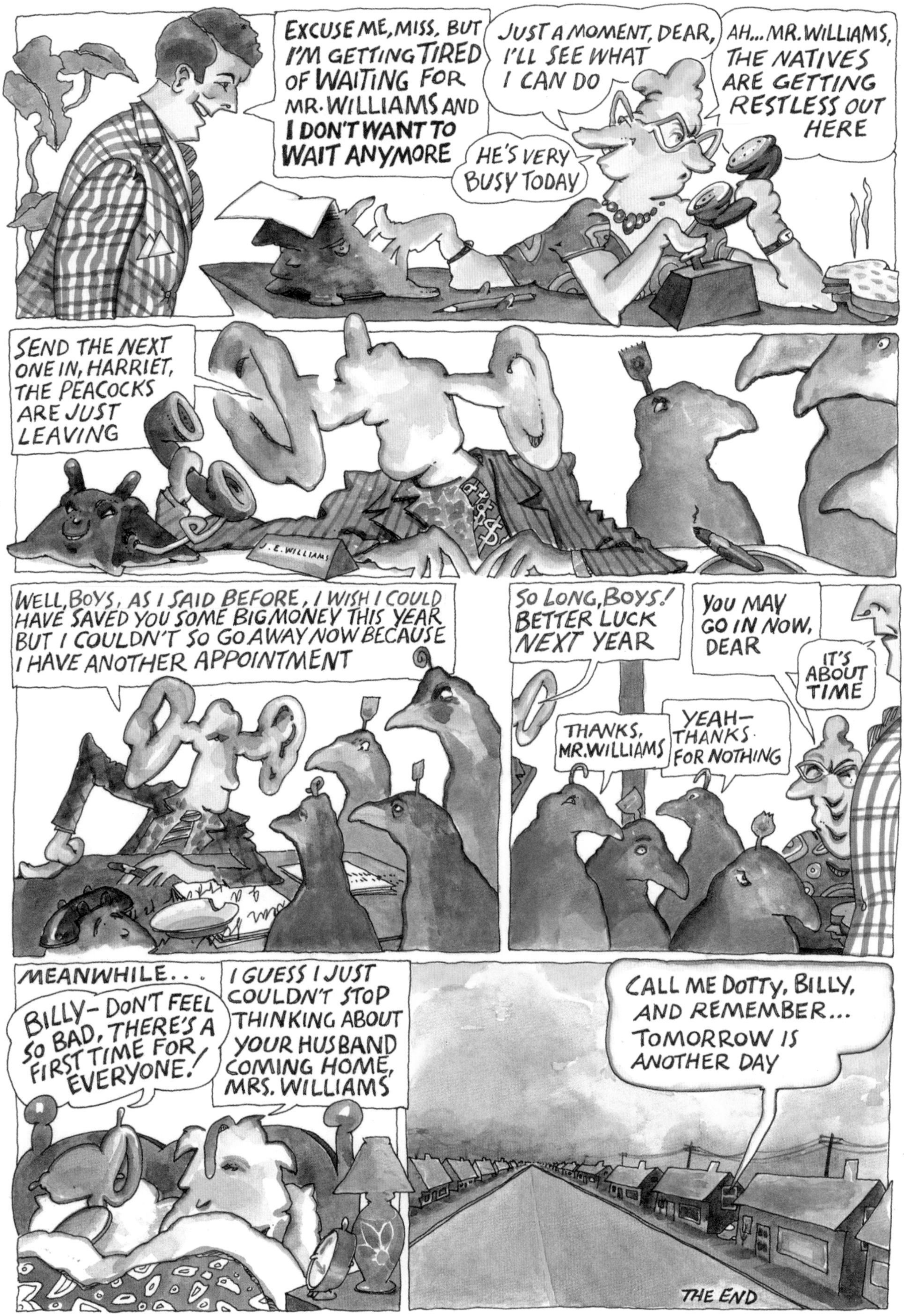
EXCUSE ME, MISS. BUT I'M GETTING TIRED OF WAITING FOR MR. WILLIAMS AND I DON'T WANT TO WAIT ANYMORE
JUST A MOMENT, DEAR, I'LL SEE WHAT I CAN DO
HE'S VERY BUSY TODAY
AH... MR. WILLIAMS, THE NATIVES ARE GETTING RESTLESS OUT HERE
SEND THE NEXT ONE IN, HARRIET, THE PEACOCKS ARE JUST LEAVING
J. E. WILLIAMS
WELL, BOYS, AS I SAID BEFORE, I WISH I COULD HAVE SAVED YOU SOME BIG MONEY THIS YEAR BUT I COULDN'T SO GO AWAY NOW BECAUSE I HAVE ANOTHER APPOINTMENT
SO LONG, BOYS! BETTER LUCK NEXT YEAR
THANKS, MR. WILLIAMS
YEAH— THANKS FOR NOTHING
YOU MAY GO IN NOW, DEAR
IT'S ABOUT TIME
MEANWHILE. . .
BILLY- DON'T FEEL SO BAD, THERE'S A FIRST TIME FOR EVERYONE!
I GUESS I JUST COULDN'T STOP THINKING ABOUT YOUR HUSBAND COMING HOME, MRS. WILLIAMS
CALL ME DOTTY, BILLY, AND REMEMBER... TOMORROW IS ANOTHER DAY
THE END

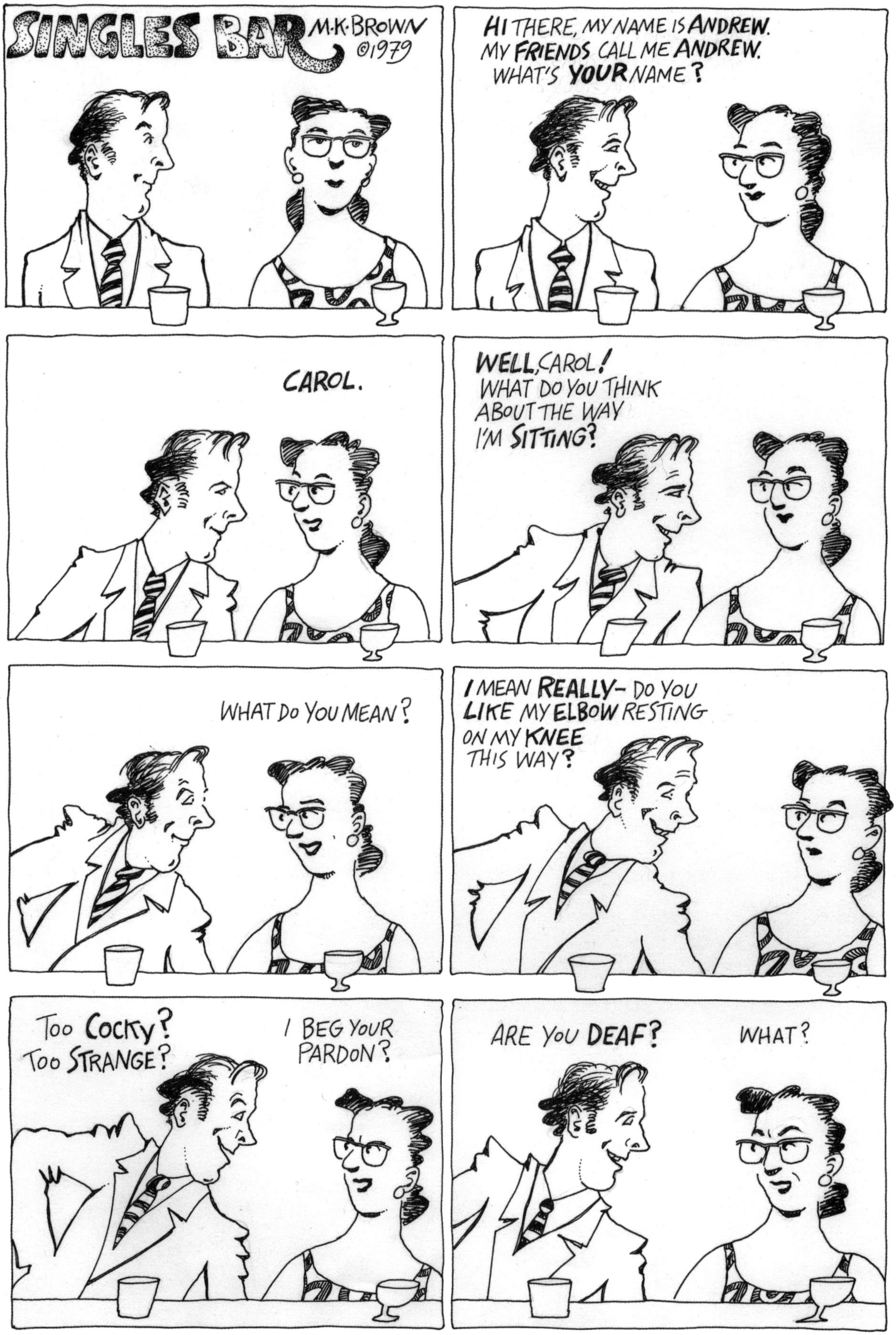
SINGLES BAR
M.K. BROWN ©1979
HI THERE, MY NAME IS ANDREW. MY FRIENDS CALL ME ANDREW. WHAT'S YOUR NAME?
CAROL.
WELL, CAROL! WHAT DO YOU THINK ABOUT THE WAY I'M SITTING?
WHAT DO YOU MEAN?
I MEAN REALLY- DO YOU LIKE MY ELBOW RESTING ON MY KNEE THIS WAY?
Too COCKY? Too STRANGE?
I BEG YOUR PARDON?
ARE YOU DEAF?
WHAT?

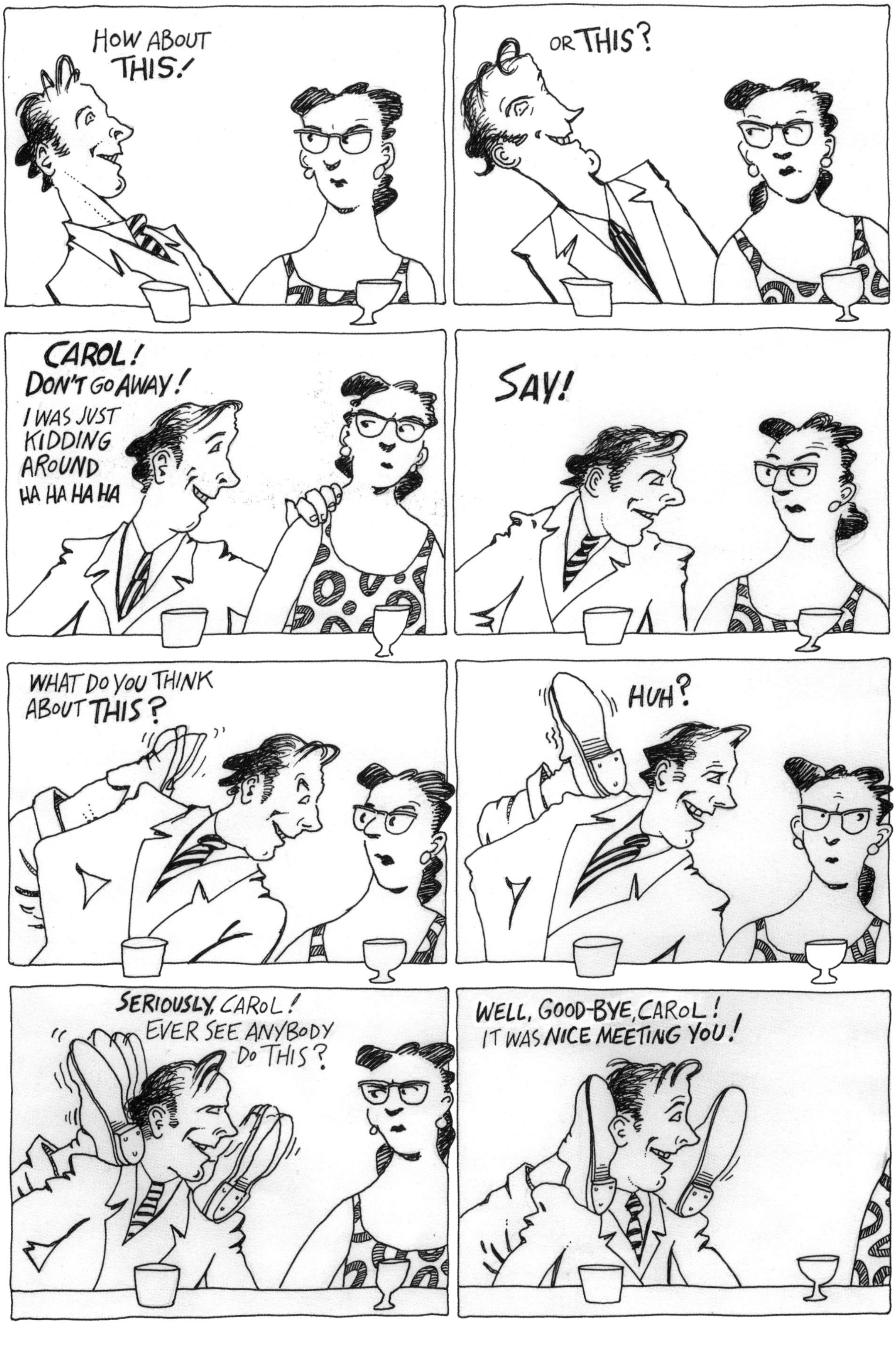
HOW ABOUT THIS!
OR THIS?
CAROL! DON'T GO AWAY! I WAS JUST KIDDING AROUND HA HA HA HA
SAY!
WHAT DO YOU THINK ABOUT THIS?
HUH?
SERIOUSLY, CAROL! EVER SEE ANYBODY DO THIS?
WELL, GOOD-BYE, CAROL! IT WAS NICE MEETING YOU!

My friend Judy from North Carolina is an avid reader of bodice-rippers and, knowing I'm not, challenged me to make a gothic romance cartoon. She then kindly offered to define the crucial ingredients of the genre. I took mental notes and did my best with the following tale, "A Promise to Remember."

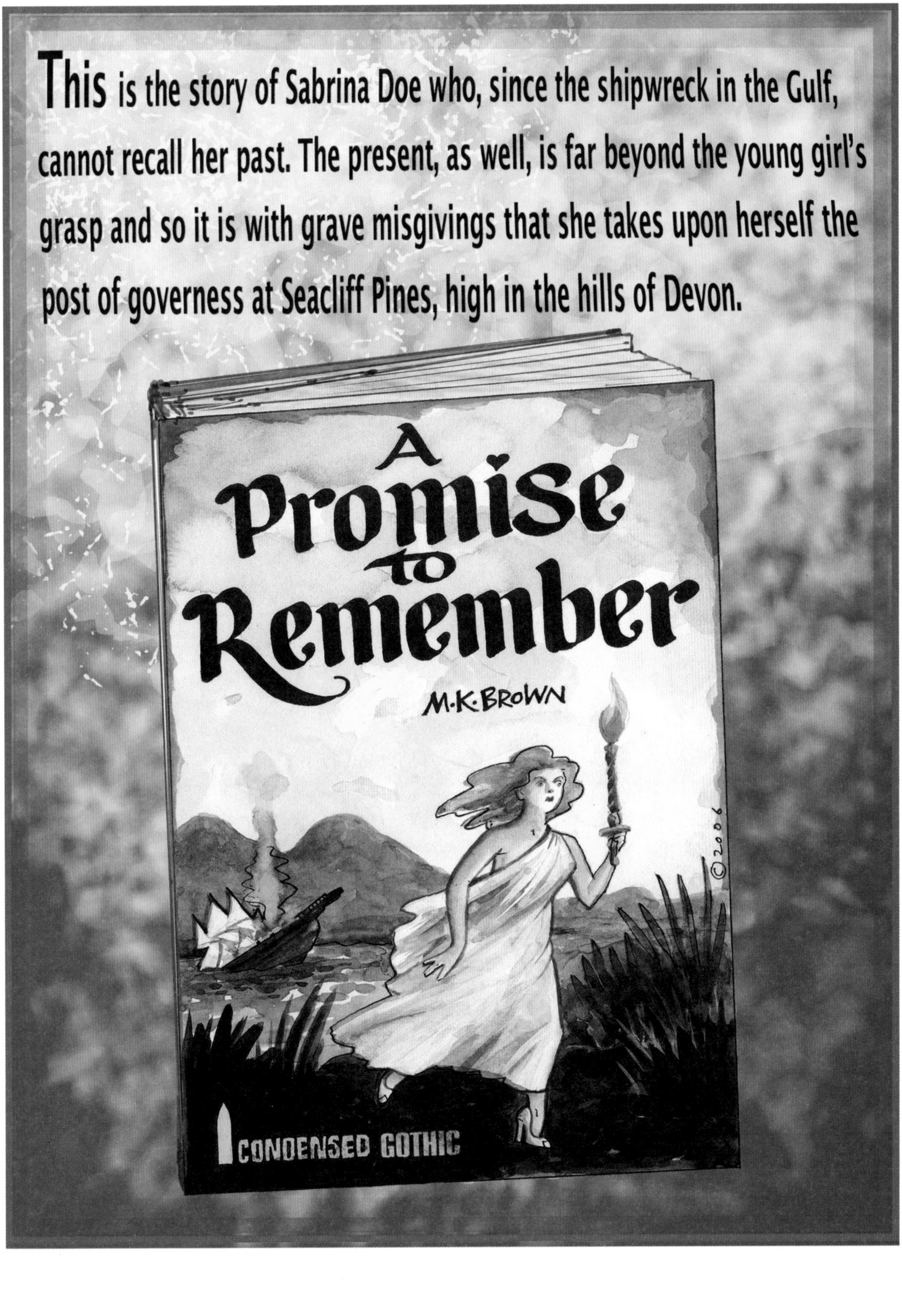
This is the story of Sabrina Doe who, since the shipwreck in the Gulf, cannot recall her past. The present, as well, is far beyond the young girl's grasp and so it is with grave misgivings that she takes upon herself the post of governess at Seacliff Pines, high in the hills of Devon.
A Promise to Remember
M.K. BROWN
©2006
CONDENSED GOTHIC

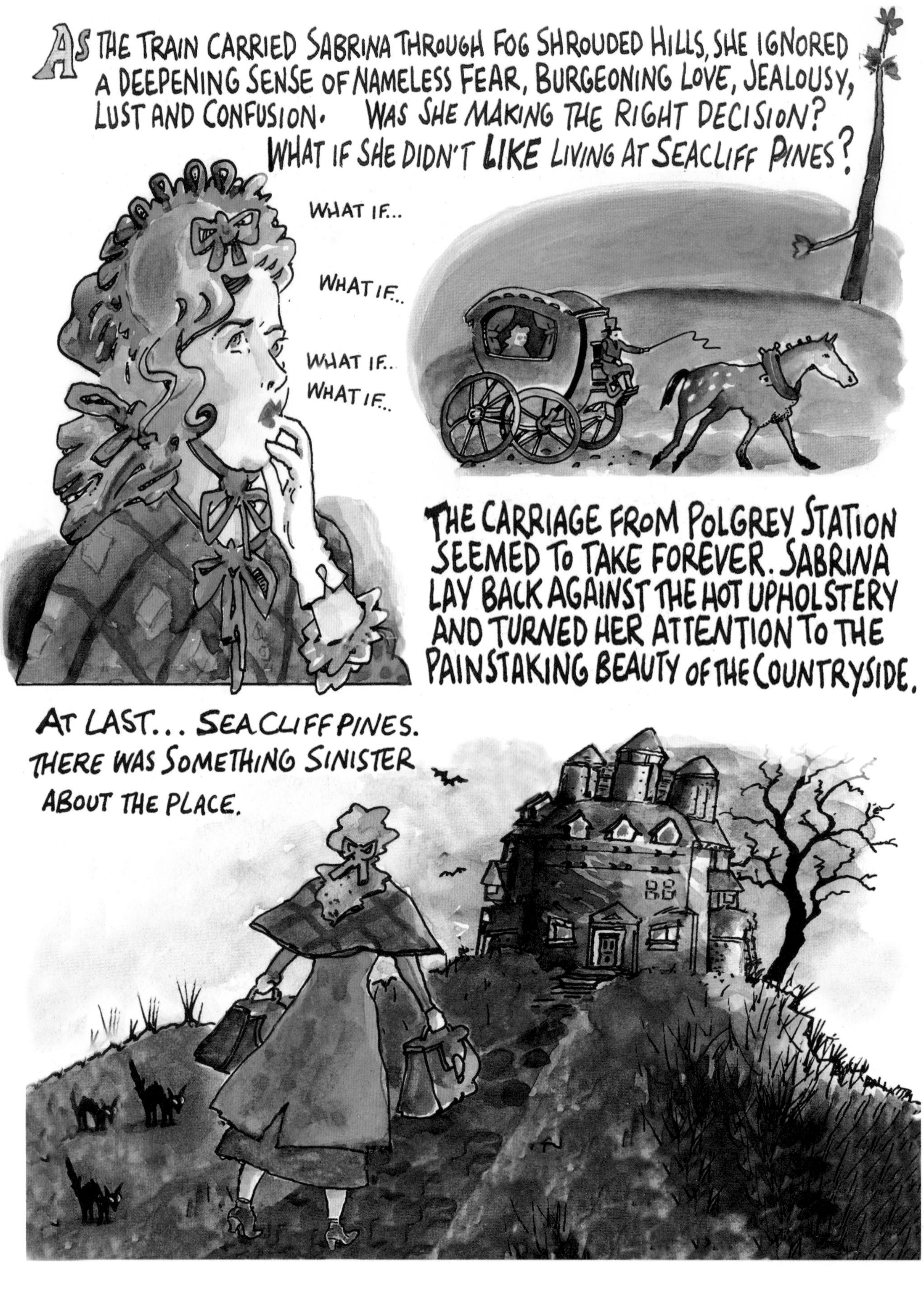

AS THE TRAIN CARRIED SABRINA THROUGH FOG SHROUDED HILLS, SHE IGNORED A DEEPENING SENSE OF NAMELESS FEAR, BURGEONING LOVE, JEALOUSY, LUST AND CONFUSION. WAS SHE MAKING THE RIGHT DECISION? WHAT IF SHE DIDN'T LIKE LIVING AT SEACLIFF PINES?
WHAT IF...
WHAT IF..
WHAT IF..
WHAT IF..
THE CARRIAGE FROM POLGREY STATION SEEMED TO TAKE FOREVER. SABRINA LAY BACK AGAINST THE HOT UPHOLSTERY AND TURNED HER ATTENTION TO THE PAINSTAKING BEAUTY OF THE COUNTRYSIDE.
AT LAST... SEACLIFF PINES. THERE WAS SOMETHING SINISTER ABOUT THE PLACE.

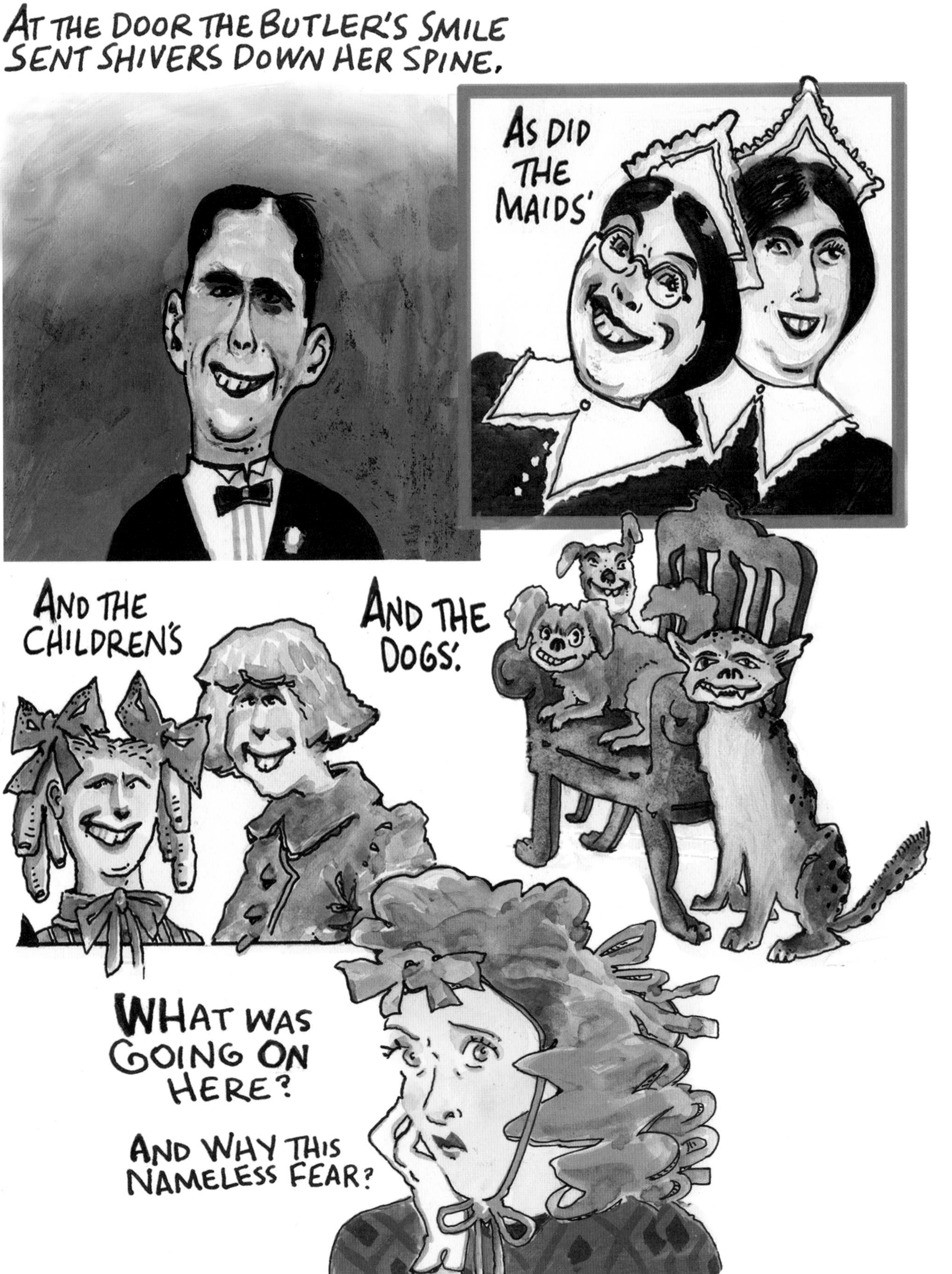
AT THE DOOR THE BUTLER'S SMILE SENT SHIVERS DOWN HER SPINE.
AS DID THE MAIDS'
AND THE CHILDREN'S
AND THE DOGS'.
WHAT WAS GOING ON HERE?
AND WHY THIS NAMELESS FEAR?

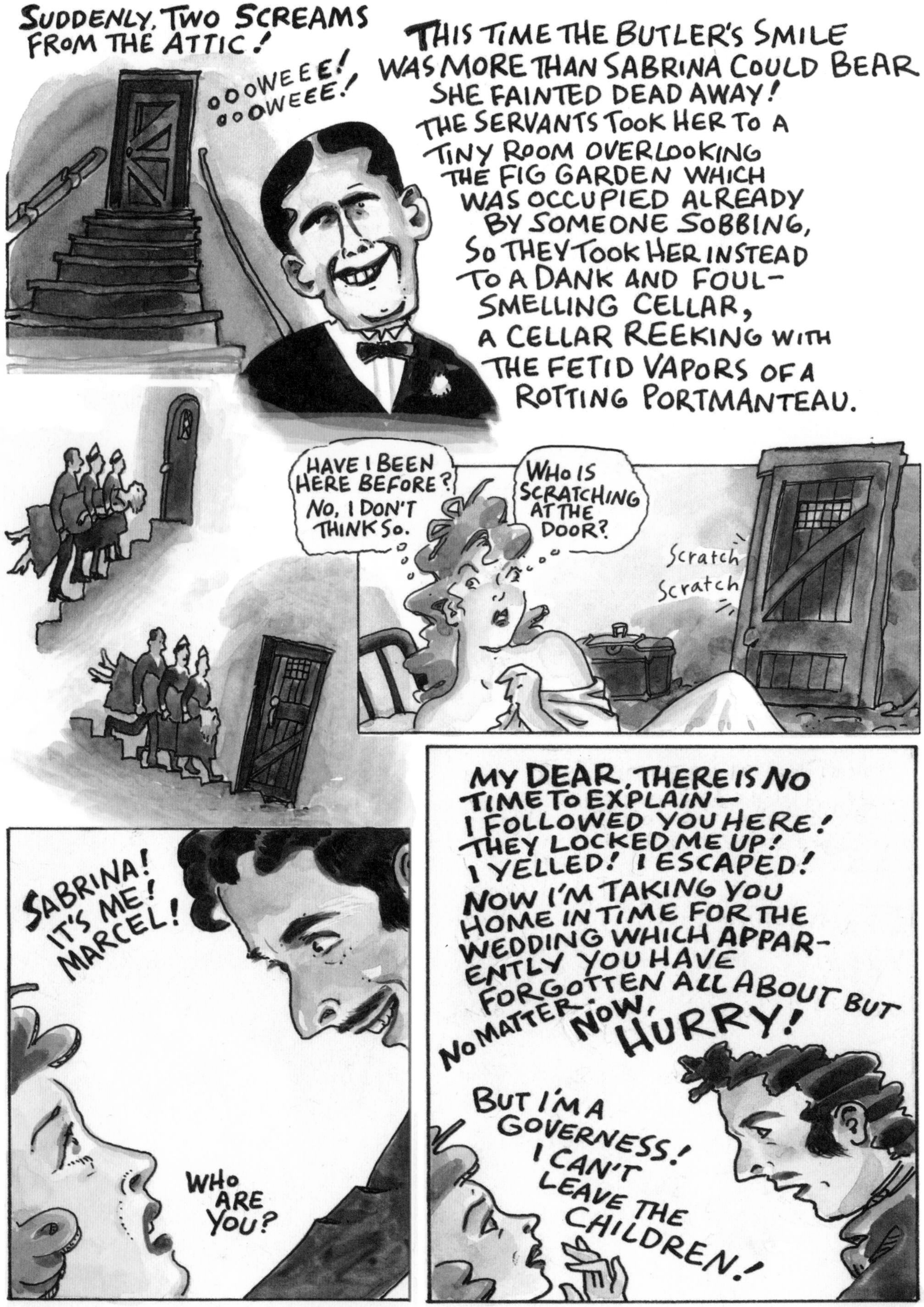

SUDDENLY, TWO SCREAMS FROM THE ATTIC!
OOOWEEE! OOOWEEE!
THIS TIME THE BUTLER'S SMILE WAS MORE THAN SABRINA COULD BEAR SHE FAINTED DEAD AWAY! THE SERVANTS TOOK HER TO A TINY ROOM OVERLOOKING THE FIG GARDEN WHICH WAS OCCUPIED ALREADY BY SOMEONE SOBBING, SO THEY TOOK HER INSTEAD TO A DANK AND FOUL-SMELLING CELLAR, A CELLAR REEKING WITH THE FETID VAPORS OF A ROTTING PORTMANTEAU.
HAVE I BEEN HERE BEFORE? NO, I DON'T THINK SO.
WHO IS SCRATCHING AT THE DOOR?
Scratch
Scratch
MY DEAR, THERE IS NO TIME TO EXPLAIN— I FOLLOWED YOU HERE! THEY LOCKED ME UP! I YELLED! I ESCAPED! NOW I'M TAKING YOU HOME IN TIME FOR THE WEDDING WHICH APPARENTLY YOU HAVE FORGOTTEN ALL ABOUT BUT NO MATTER NOW, HURRY!
SABRINA! IT'S ME! MARCEL!
WHO ARE YOU?
BUT I'M A GOVERNESS! I CAN'T LEAVE THE CHILDREN!

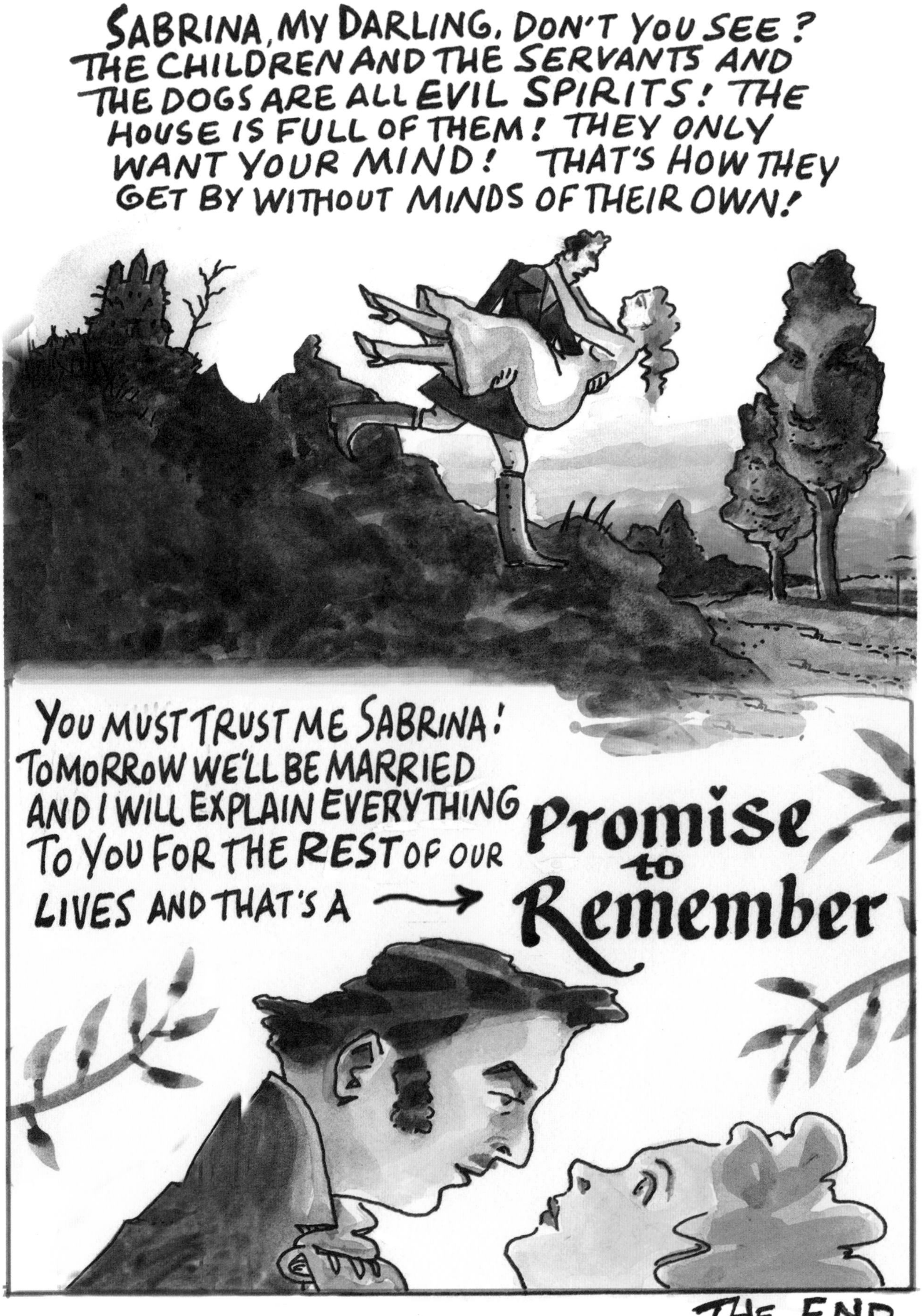
SABRINA, MY DARLING, DON'T YOU SEE? THE CHILDREN AND THE SERVANTS AND THE DOGS ARE ALL EVIL SPIRITS! THE HOUSE IS FULL OF THEM! THEY ONLY WANT YOUR MIND! THAT'S HOW THEY GET BY WITHOUT MINDS OF THEIR OWN!
YOU MUST TRUST ME SABRINA! TOMORROW WE'LL BE MARRIED AND I WILL EXPLAIN EVERYTHING TO YOU FOR THE REST OF OUR LIVES AND THAT'S A →
Promise to Remember
THE END

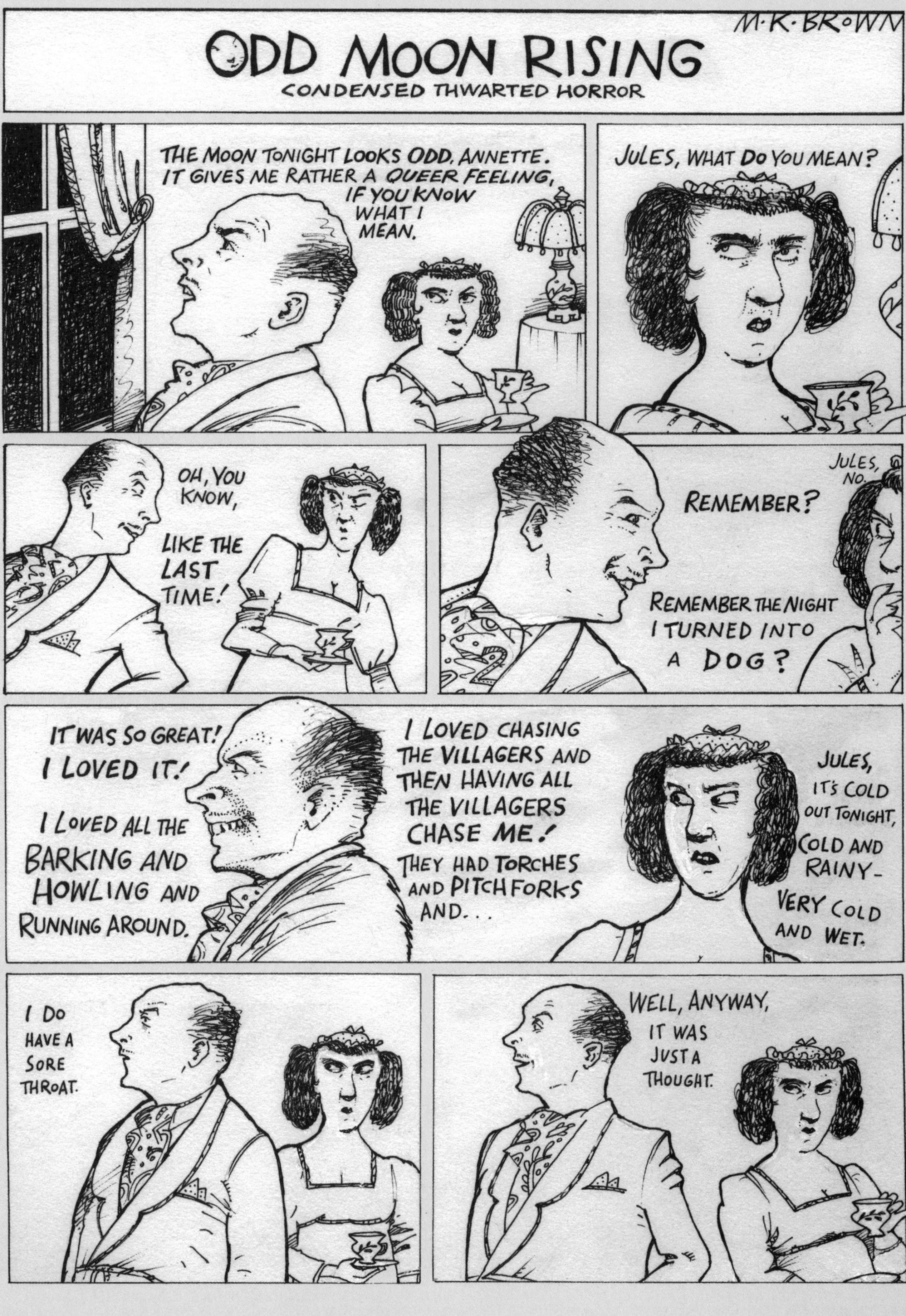
M·K·BROWN
ODD MOON RISING
CONDENSED THWARTED HORROR
THE MOON TONIGHT LOOKS ODD, ANNETTE. IT GIVES ME RATHER A QUEER FEELING, IF YOU KNOW WHAT I MEAN.
JULES, WHAT DO YOU MEAN?
OH, YOU KNOW, LIKE THE LAST TIME!
REMEMBER?
JULES, NO.
REMEMBER THE NIGHT I TURNED INTO A DOG?
IT WAS SO GREAT! I LOVED IT!
I LOVED ALL THE BARKING AND HOWLING AND RUNNING AROUND.
I LOVED CHASING THE VILLAGERS AND THEN HAVING ALL THE VILLAGERS CHASE ME!
THEY HAD TORCHES AND PITCHFORKS AND...
JULES, IT'S COLD OUT TONIGHT, COLD AND RAINY-
VERY COLD AND WET.
I DO HAVE A SORE THROAT.
WELL, ANYWAY, IT WAS JUST A THOUGHT.

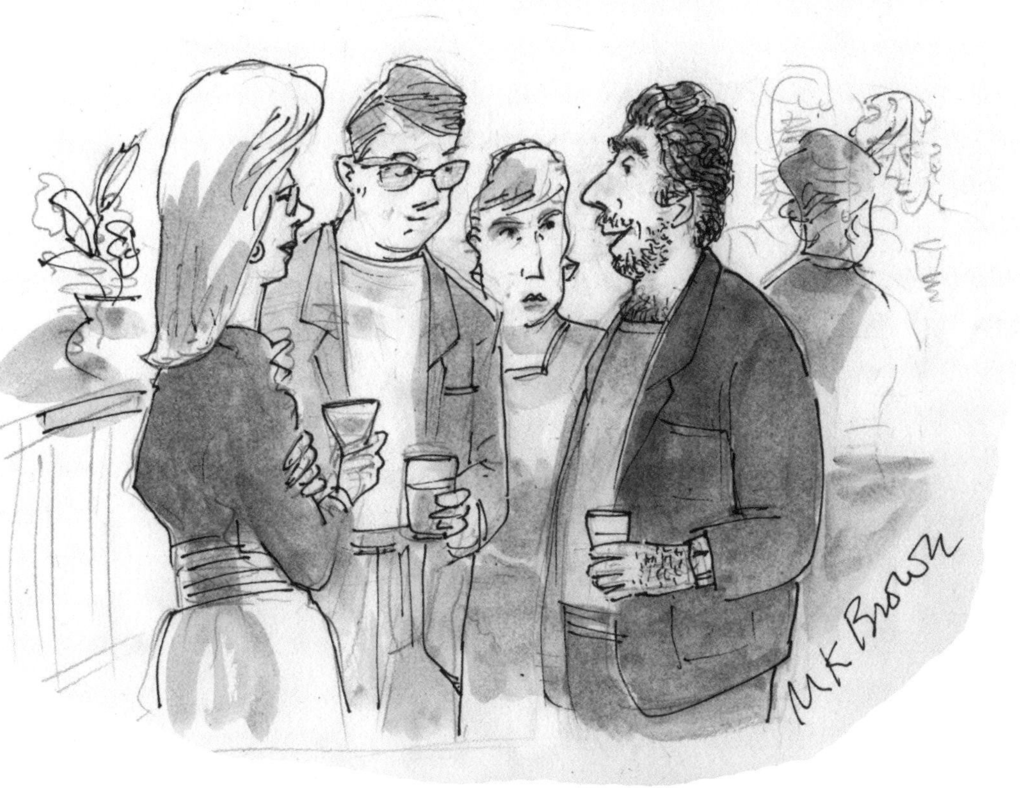
MK Brown

My name's Larry, but my friends call me Harry.

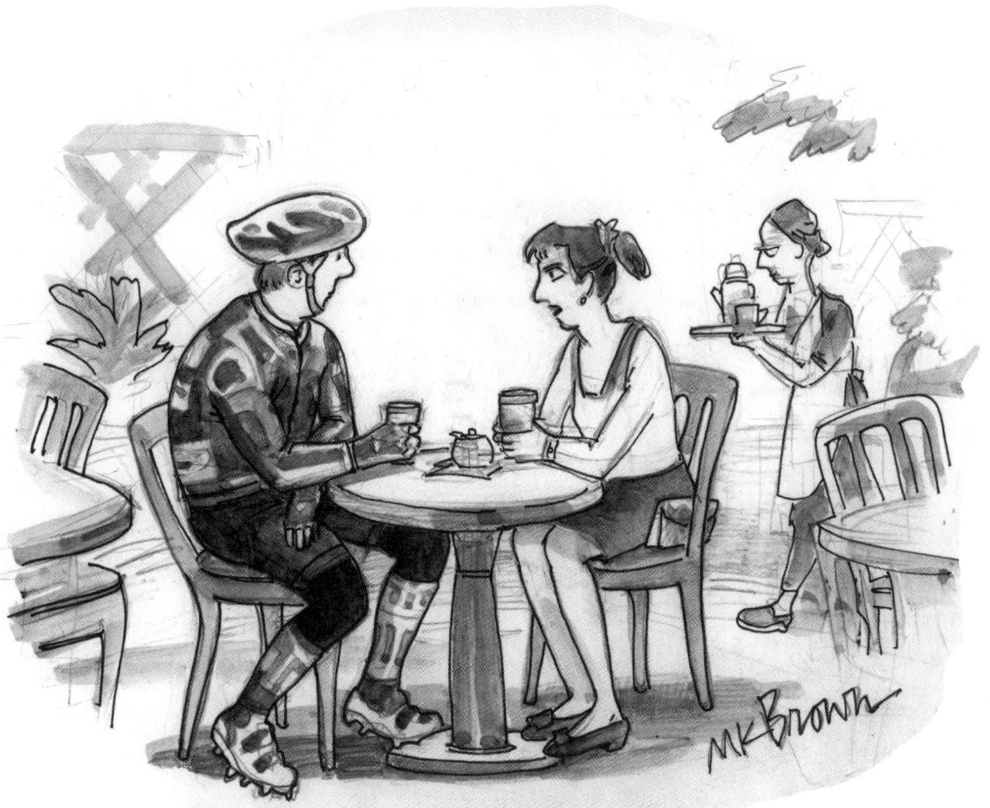
MK Brown

Seriously, Dick, you really should get a bicycle.

AT THE MEAT MUSEUM

M.K. Brown

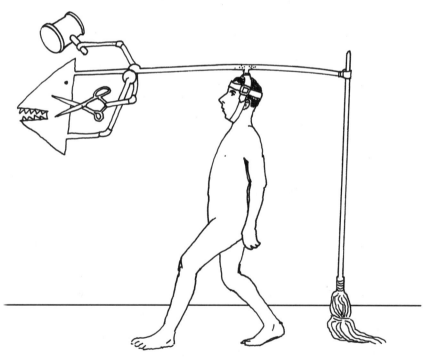

M.K. Brown

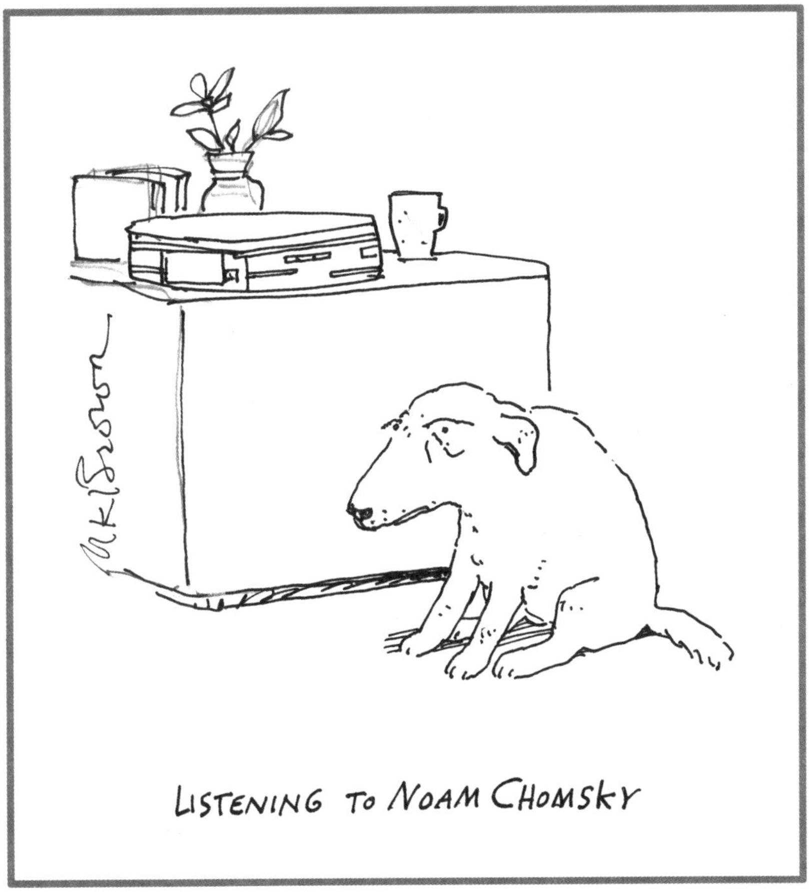

LISTENING TO NOAM CHOMSKY

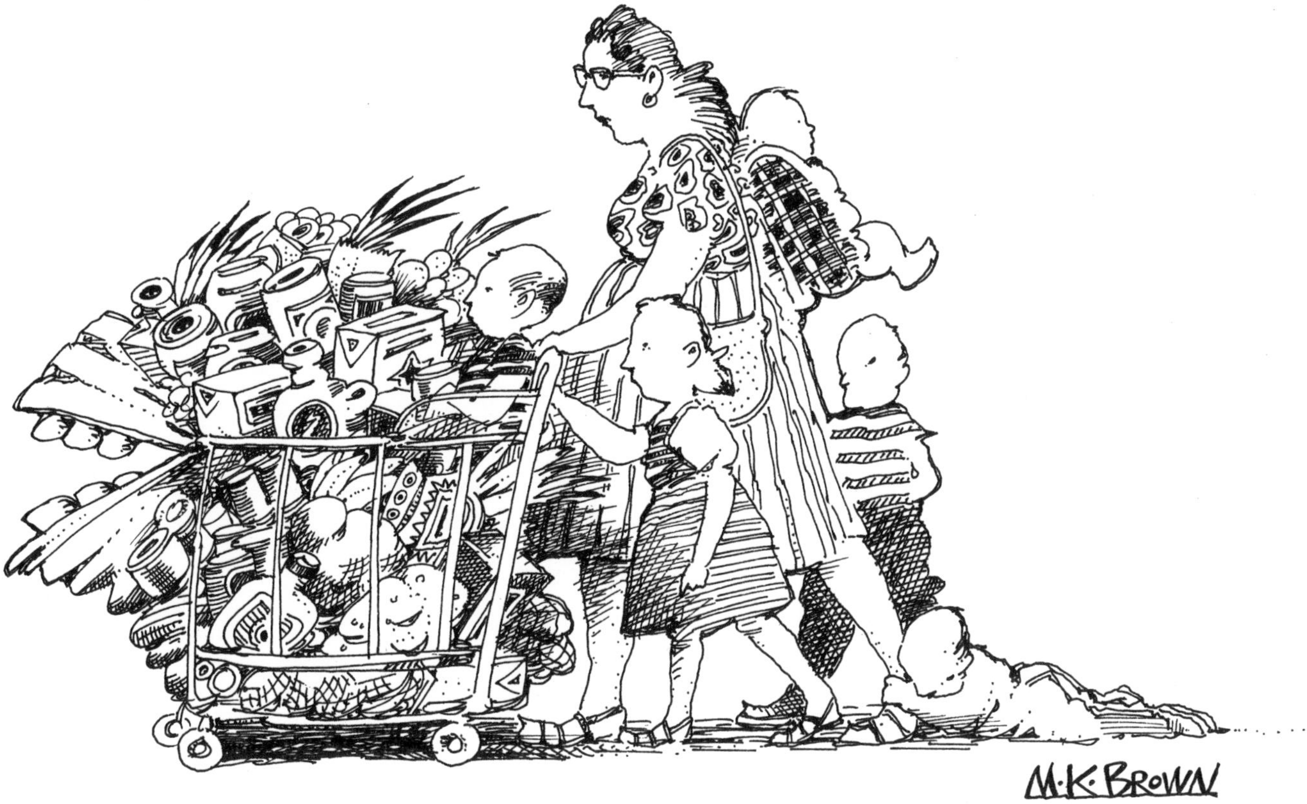
M.K. BROWN

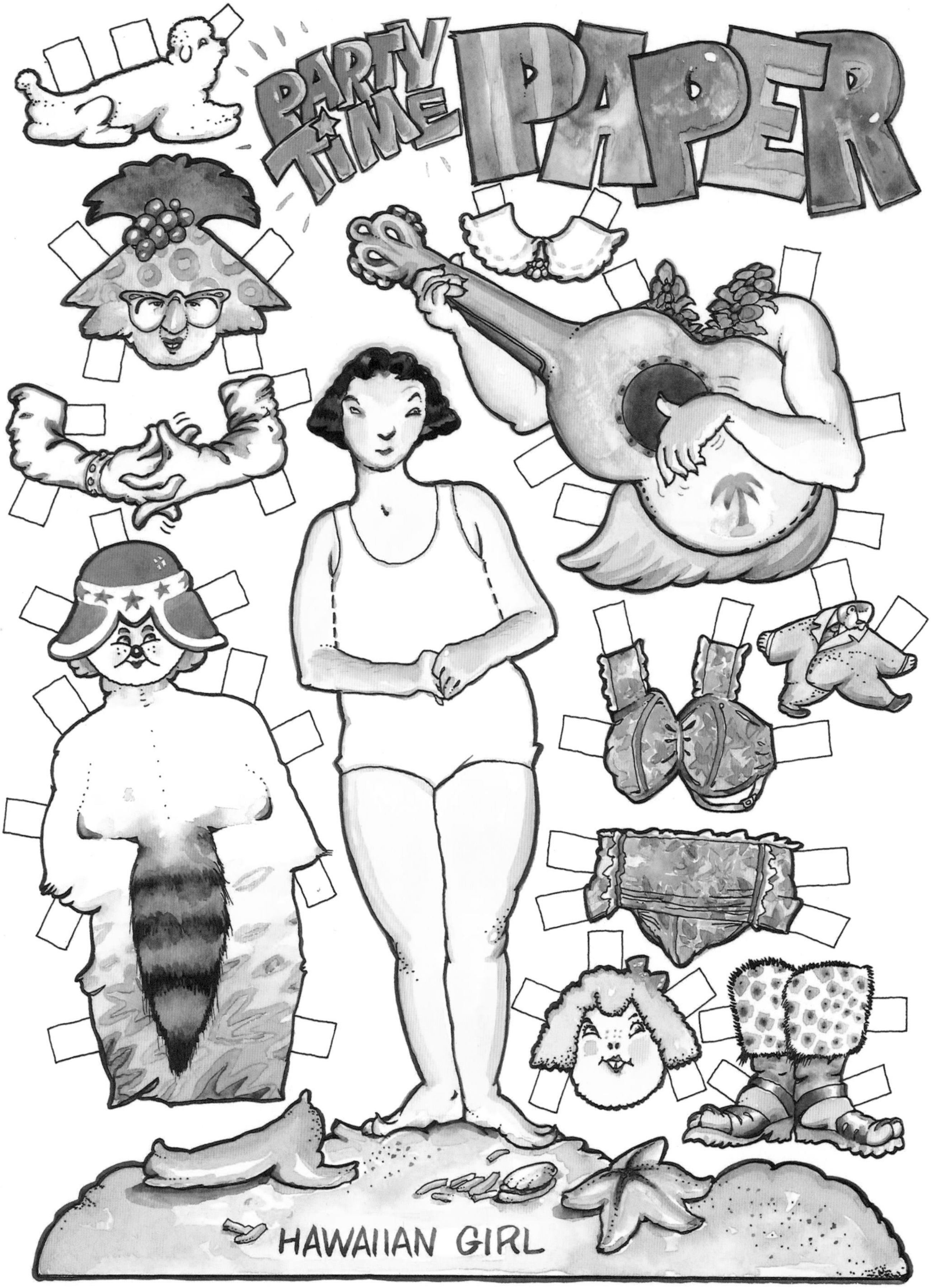
PARTY TIME PAPER
HAWAIIAN GIRL

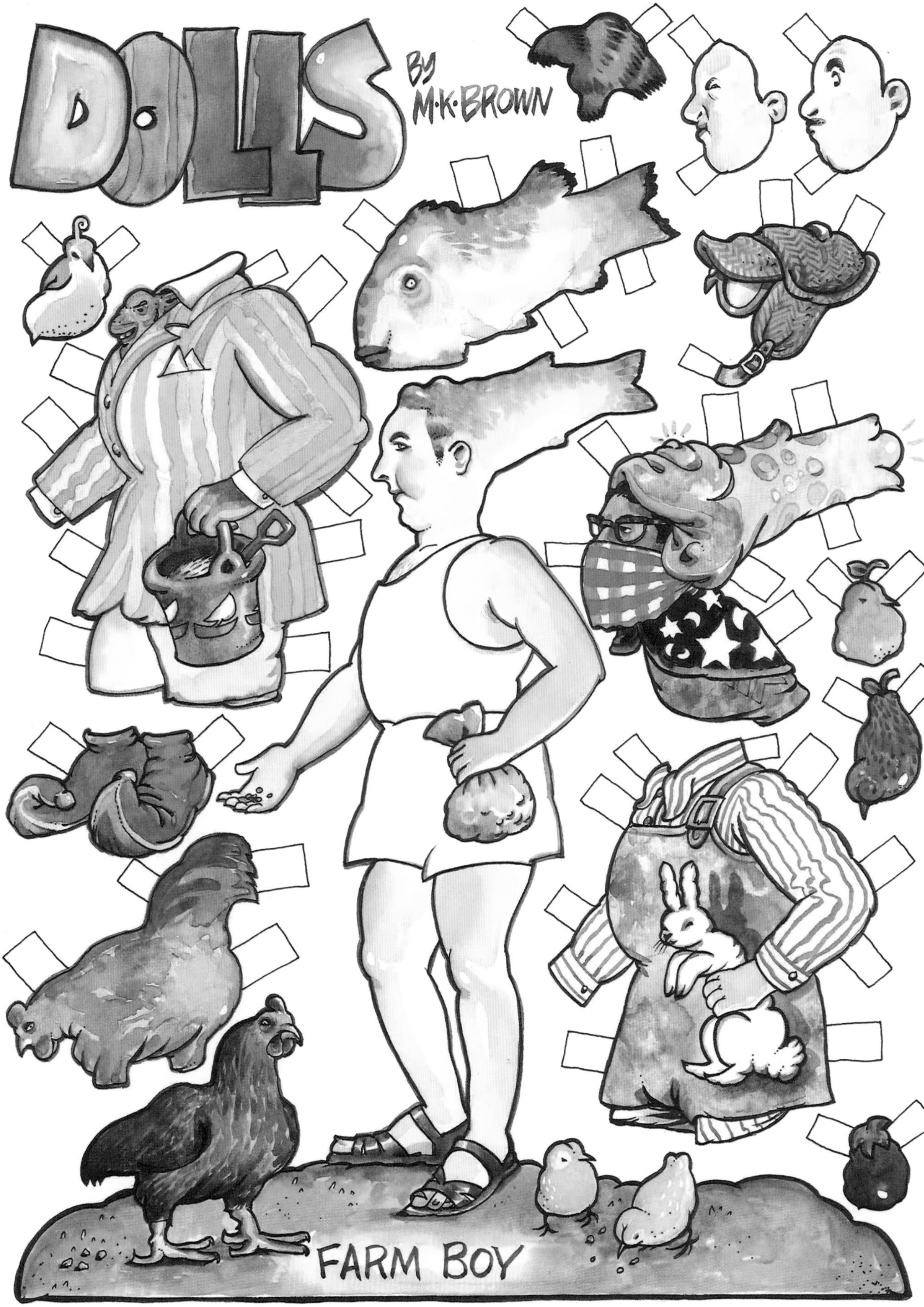
DOLLS
BY M·K·BROWN
FARM BOY

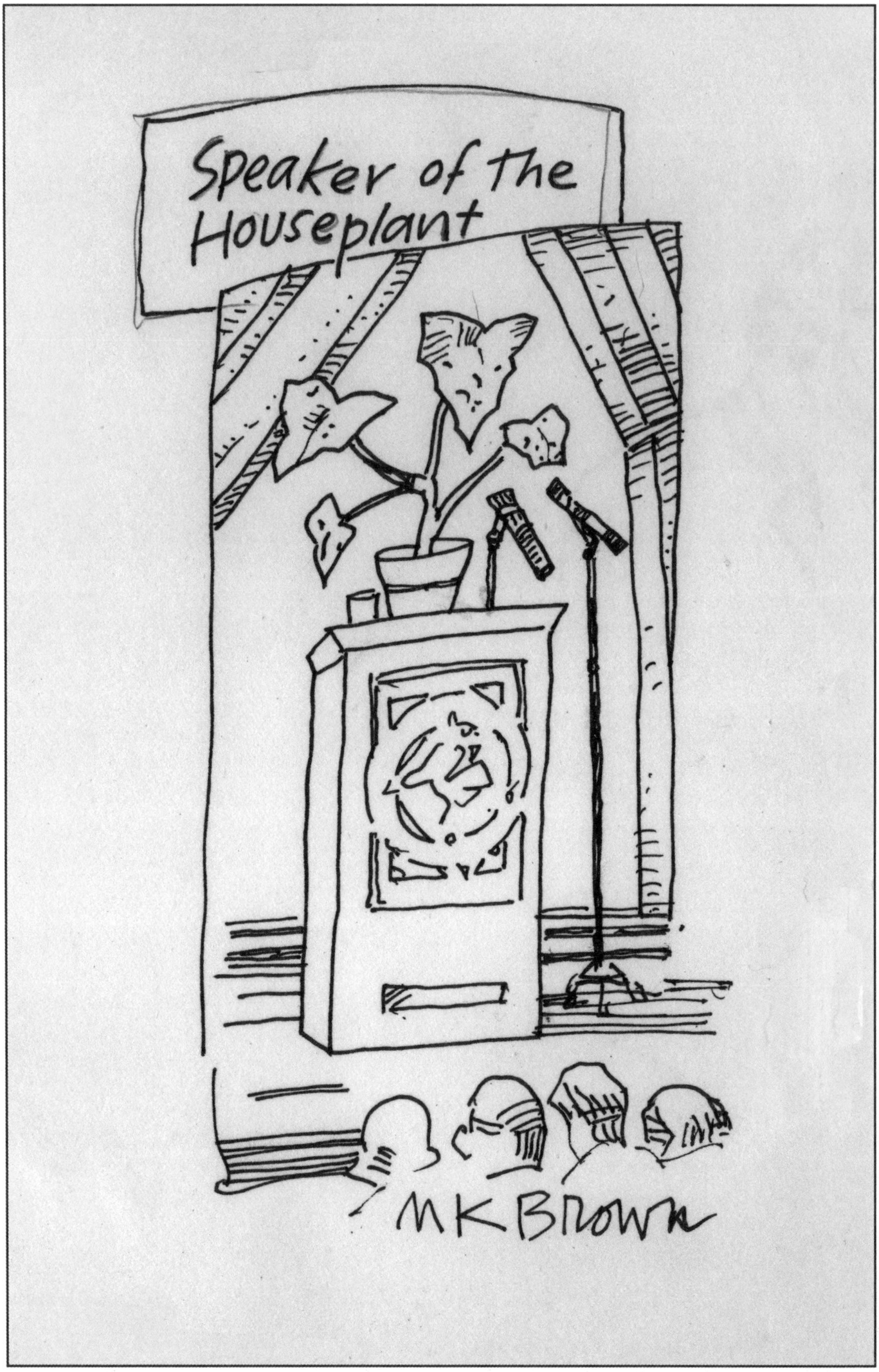
Speaker of the Houseplant
MK Brown

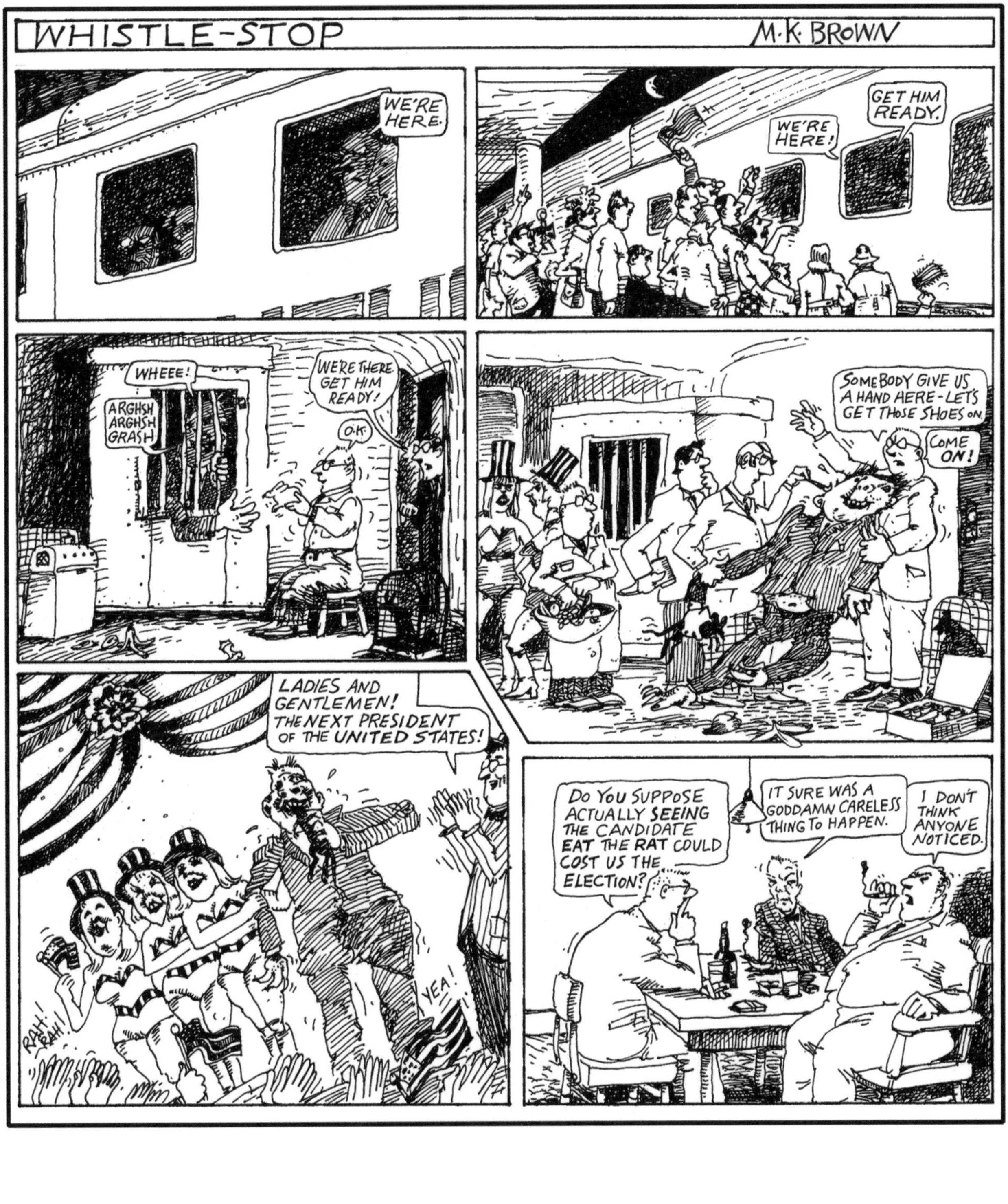
WHISTLE-STOP
M·K·BROWN
WE'RE HERE.
WE'RE HERE!
GET HIM READY.
WHEEE!
ARGHSH ARGHSH GRASH
WE'RE THERE. GET HIM READY!
O.K.
SOMEBODY GIVE US A HAND HERE - LET'S GET THOSE SHOES ON
COME ON!
LADIES AND GENTLEMEN! THE NEXT PRESIDENT OF THE UNITED STATES!
RAH! RAH!
YEA!
DO YOU SUPPOSE ACTUALLY SEEING THE CANDIDATE EAT THE RAT COULD COST US THE ELECTION?
IT SURE WAS A GODDAMN CARELESS THING TO HAPPEN.
I DON'T THINK ANYONE NOTICED.

First published in *Watergate Times*, "Whistle-Stop" was included in 1988's "America's Best Political Cartoons" (a supplemental booklet in *Mother Jones* magazine) and has appeared on many websites ever since. Unfortunately, it still seems generally appropriate.

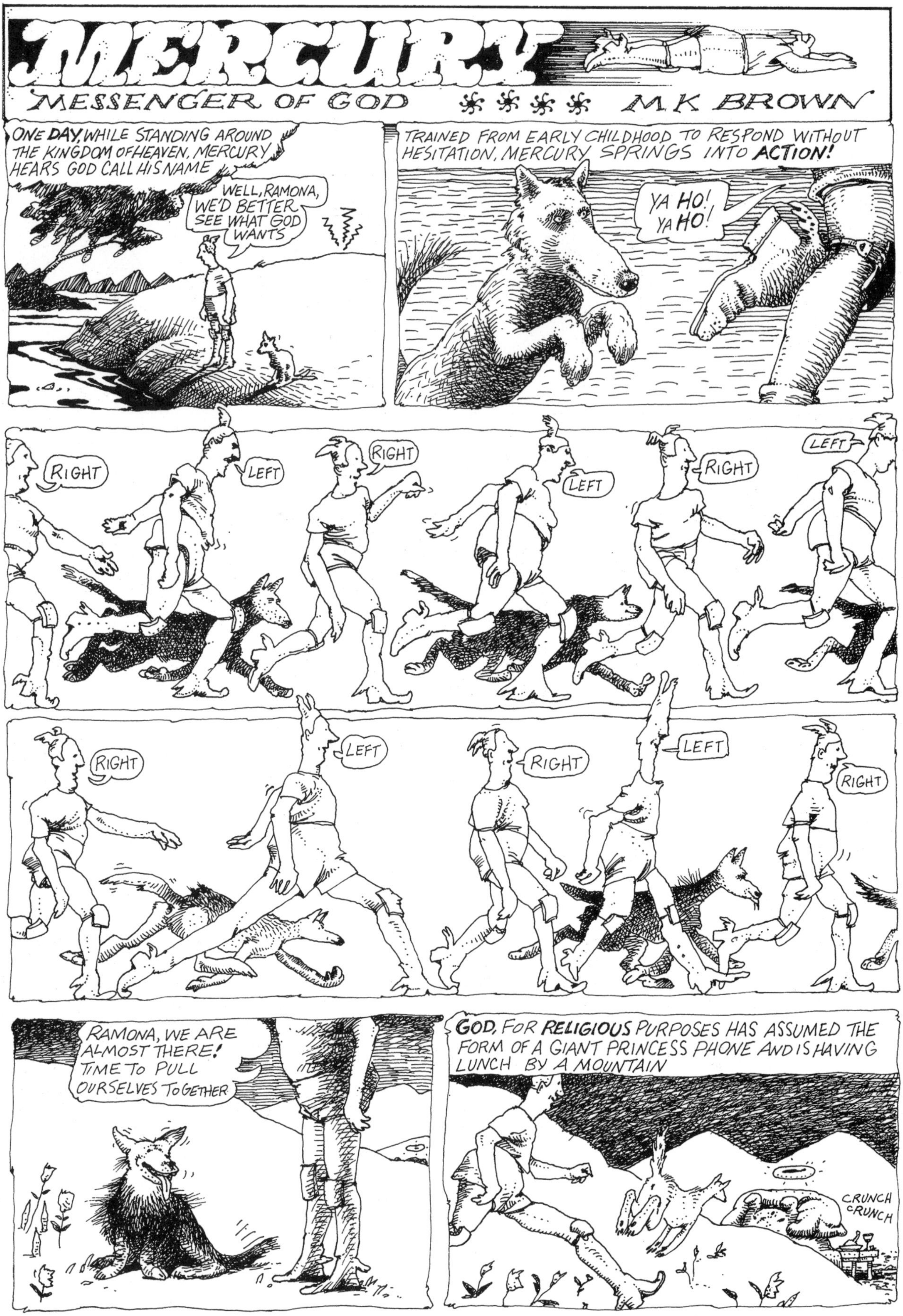
MERCURY
MESSENGER OF GOD
M.K BROWN
ONE DAY, WHILE STANDING AROUND THE KINGDOM OF HEAVEN, MERCURY HEARS GOD CALL HIS NAME
WELL, RAMONA, WE'D BETTER SEE WHAT GOD WANTS
TRAINED FROM EARLY CHILDHOOD TO RESPOND WITHOUT HESITATION, MERCURY SPRINGS INTO ACTION!
YA HO! YA HO!
RIGHT
LEFT
RIGHT
LEFT
RIGHT
LEFT
RIGHT
LEFT
RIGHT
LEFT
RIGHT
RAMONA, WE ARE ALMOST THERE! TIME TO PULL OURSELVES TOGETHER
GOD, FOR RELIGIOUS PURPOSES HAS ASSUMED THE FORM OF A GIANT PRINCESS PHONE AND IS HAVING LUNCH BY A MOUNTAIN
CRUNCH
CRUNCH

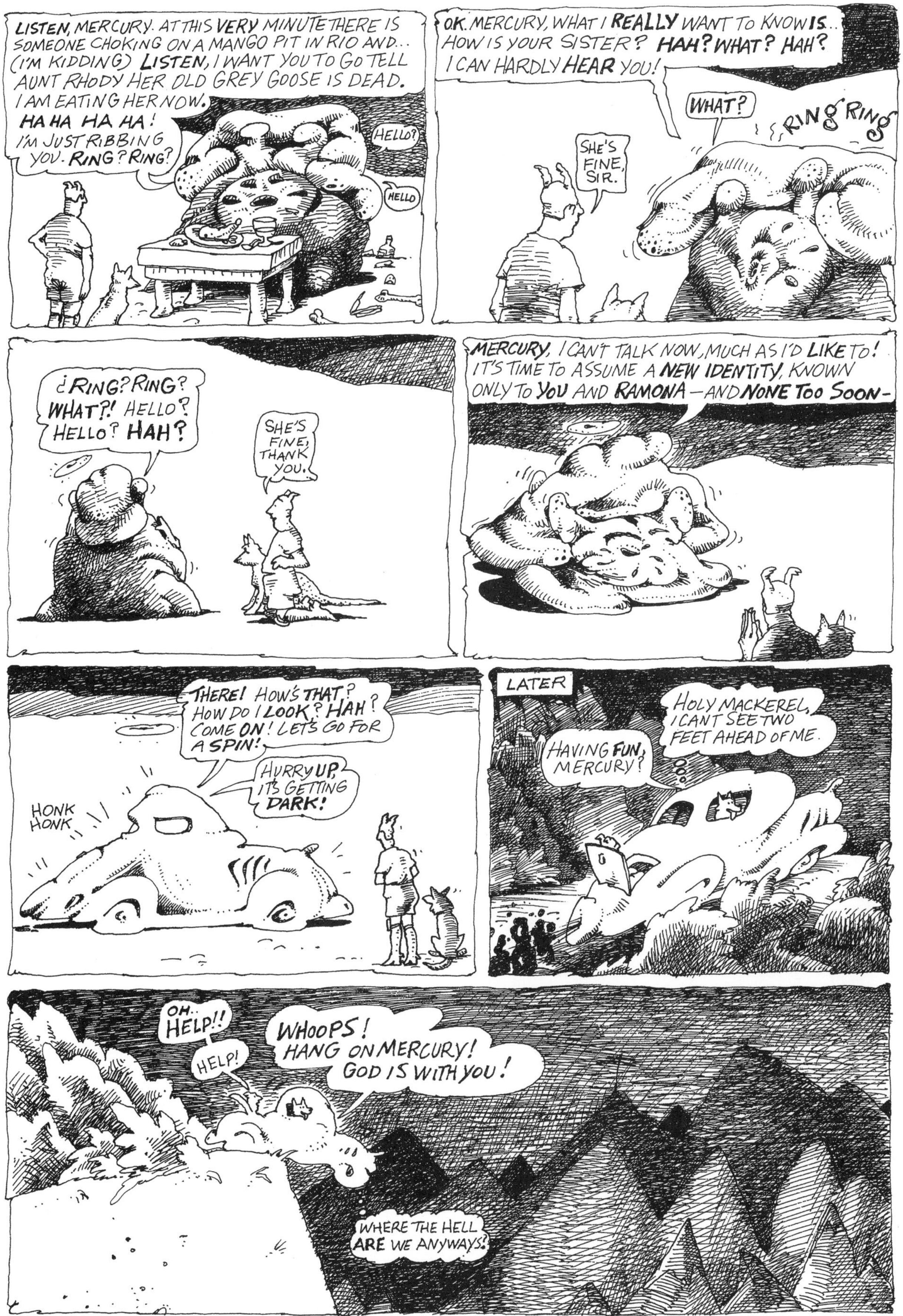
LISTEN, MERCURY. AT THIS VERY MINUTE THERE IS SOMEONE CHOKING ON A MANGO PIT IN RIO AND... (I'M KIDDING) LISTEN, I WANT YOU TO GO TELL AUNT RHODY HER OLD GREY GOOSE IS DEAD. I AM EATING HER NOW.
HA HA HA HA! I'M JUST RIBBING YOU. RING? RING?
HELLO?
HELLO
OK. MERCURY, WHAT I REALLY WANT TO KNOW IS... HOW IS YOUR SISTER? HAH? WHAT? HAH? I CAN HARDLY HEAR YOU!
WHAT?
RING RING
SHE'S FINE, SIR.
¿RING? RING? WHAT?! HELLO? HELLO? HAH?
SHE'S FINE, THANK YOU.
MERCURY, I CAN'T TALK NOW, MUCH AS I'D LIKE TO! IT'S TIME TO ASSUME A NEW IDENTITY, KNOWN ONLY TO YOU AND RAMONA — AND NONE TOO SOON —
THERE! HOW'S THAT? HOW DO I LOOK? HAH? COME ON! LET'S GO FOR A SPIN!
HURRY UP, IT'S GETTING DARK!
HONK HONK
LATER
HAVING FUN, MERCURY?
HOLY MACKEREL, I CAN'T SEE TWO FEET AHEAD OF ME.
OH.. HELP!!
HELP!
WHOOPS! HANG ON MERCURY! GOD IS WITH YOU!
WHERE THE HELL ARE WE ANYWAYS!
TO BE CONTINUED......

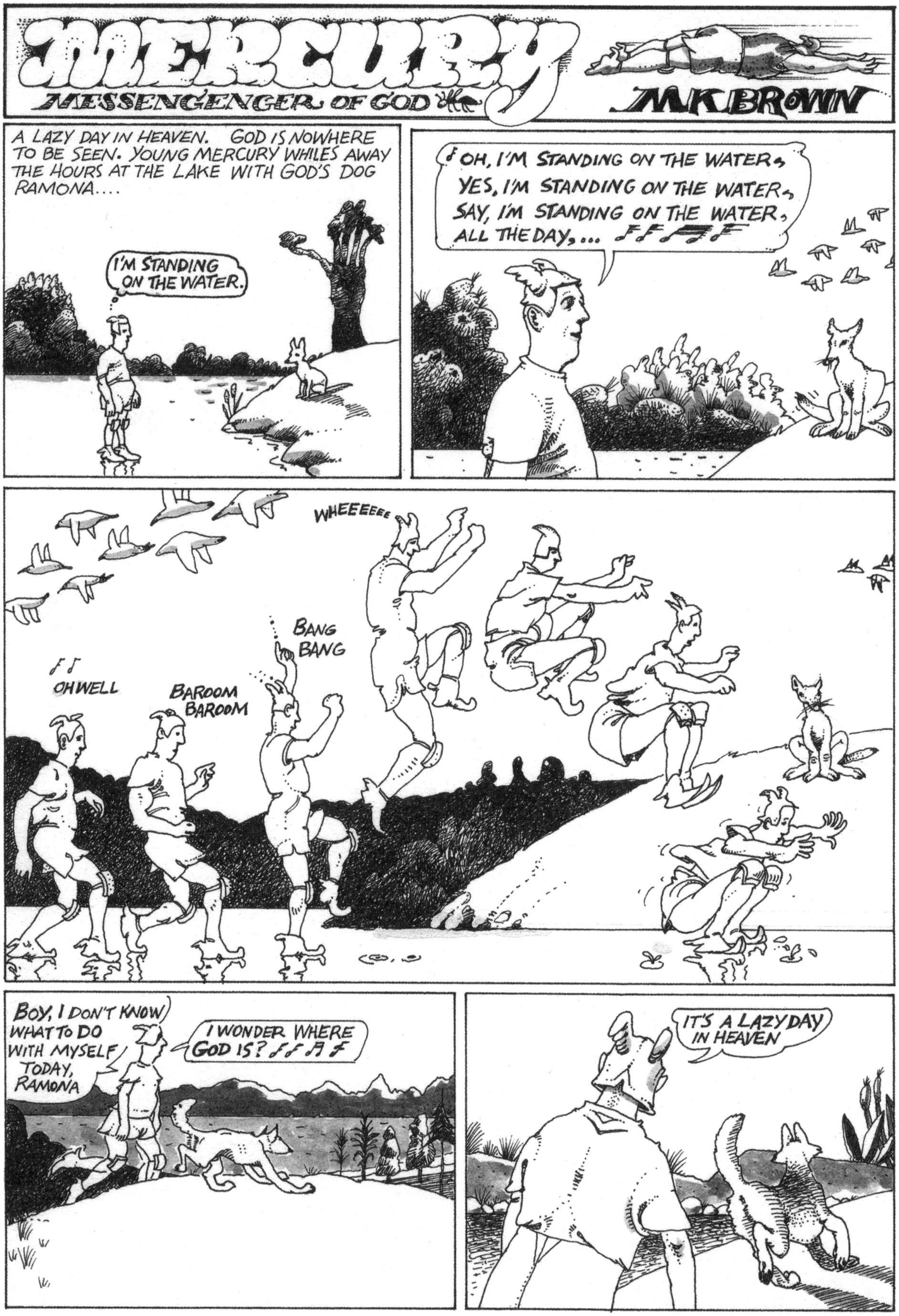
MERCURY
MESSENGENGER OF GOD
MK BROWN
A LAZY DAY IN HEAVEN. GOD IS NOWHERE TO BE SEEN. YOUNG MERCURY WHILES AWAY THE HOURS AT THE LAKE WITH GOD'S DOG RAMONA....
I'M STANDING ON THE WATER.
OH, I'M STANDING ON THE WATER, YES, I'M STANDING ON THE WATER, SAY, I'M STANDING ON THE WATER, ALL THE DAY, ...
OH WELL
BAROOM BAROOM
BANG BANG
WHEEEEEE
BOY, I DON'T KNOW WHAT TO DO WITH MYSELF TODAY, RAMONA
I WONDER WHERE GOD IS?
IT'S A LAZY DAY IN HEAVEN

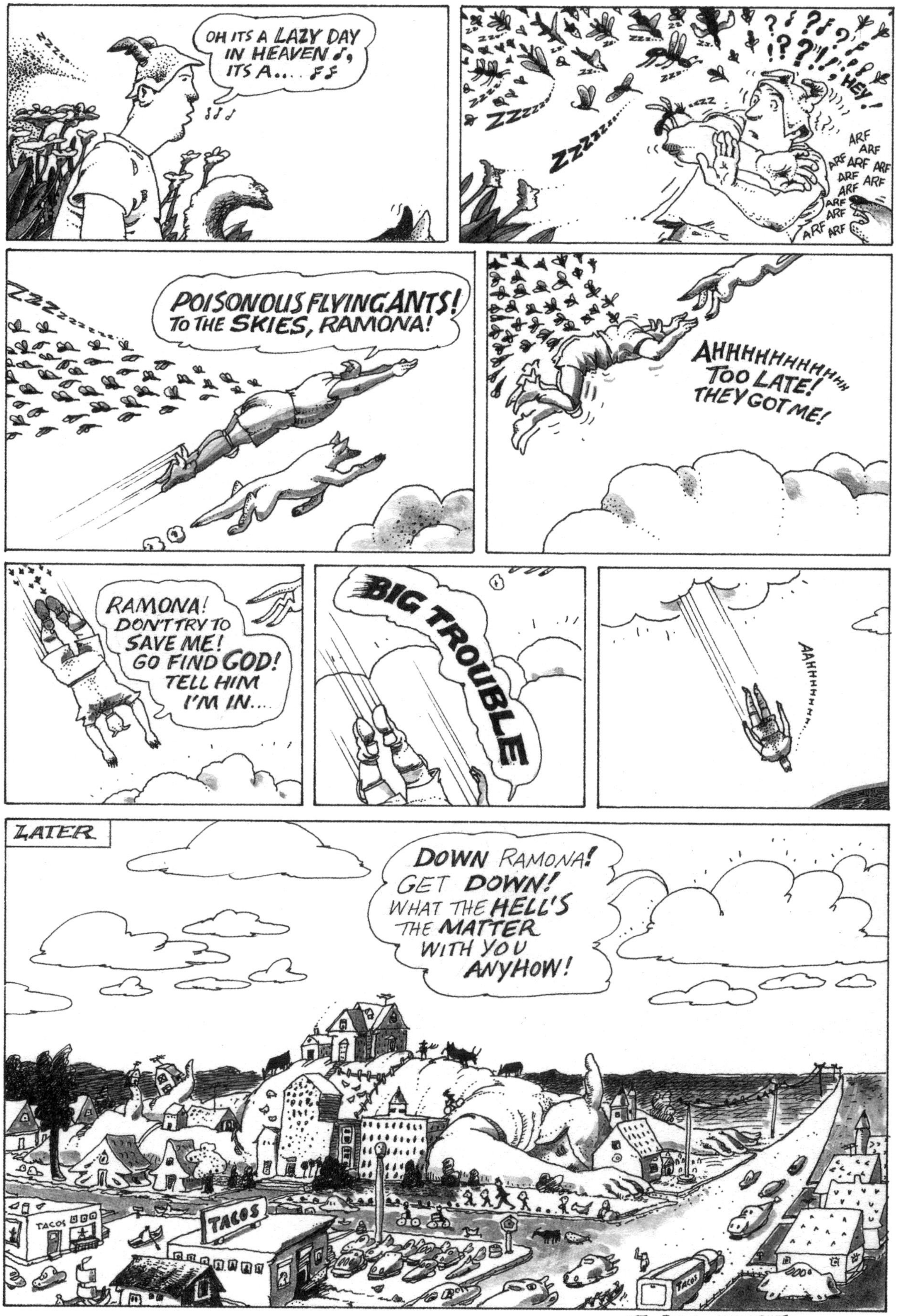

OH ITS A LAZY DAY IN HEAVEN, ITS A....
ZZZZ
!?? HEY!
ARF ARF ARF ARF ARF ARF ARF ARF ARF ARF ARF
POISONOUS FLYING ANTS! TO THE SKIES, RAMONA!
AHHHHHHHHHHH TOO LATE! THEY GOT ME!
RAMONA! DON'T TRY TO SAVE ME! GO FIND GOD! TELL HIM I'M IN...
BIG TROUBLE
AHHHHHHH
LATER
DOWN RAMONA! GET DOWN! WHAT THE HELL'S THE MATTER WITH YOU ANYHOW!
TACOS
TACOS
TO BE CONTINEUED

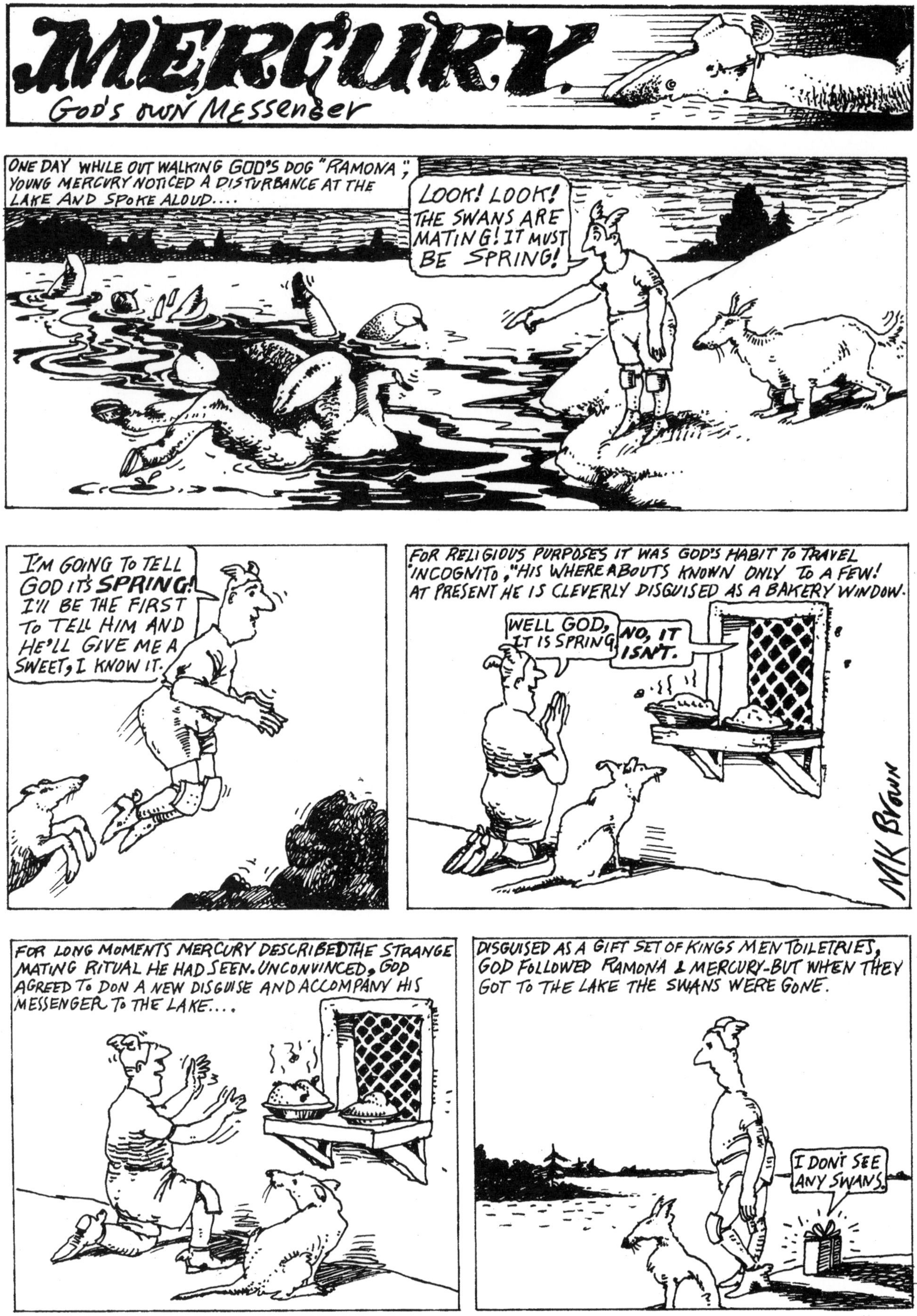
MERCURY
God's own Messenger
ONE DAY WHILE OUT WALKING GOD'S DOG "RAMONA", YOUNG MERCURY NOTICED A DISTURBANCE AT THE LAKE AND SPOKE ALOUD....
LOOK! LOOK! THE SWANS ARE MATING! IT MUST BE SPRING!
I'M GOING TO TELL GOD IT'S SPRING! I'LL BE THE FIRST TO TELL HIM AND HE'LL GIVE ME A SWEET, I KNOW IT.
FOR RELIGIOUS PURPOSES IT WAS GOD'S HABIT TO TRAVEL "INCOGNITO," HIS WHEREABOUTS KNOWN ONLY TO A FEW! AT PRESENT HE IS CLEVERLY DISGUISED AS A BAKERY WINDOW.
WELL GOD, IT IS SPRING.
NO, IT ISN'T.
MK BROWN
FOR LONG MOMENTS MERCURY DESCRIBED THE STRANGE MATING RITUAL HE HAD SEEN. UNCONVINCED, GOD AGREED TO DON A NEW DISGUISE AND ACCOMPANY HIS MESSENGER TO THE LAKE....
DISGUISED AS A GIFT SET OF KINGS MEN TOILETRIES, GOD FOLLOWED RAMONA & MERCURY-BUT WHEN THEY GOT TO THE LAKE THE SWANS WERE GONE.
I DON'T SEE ANY SWANS.

Travel and Nature

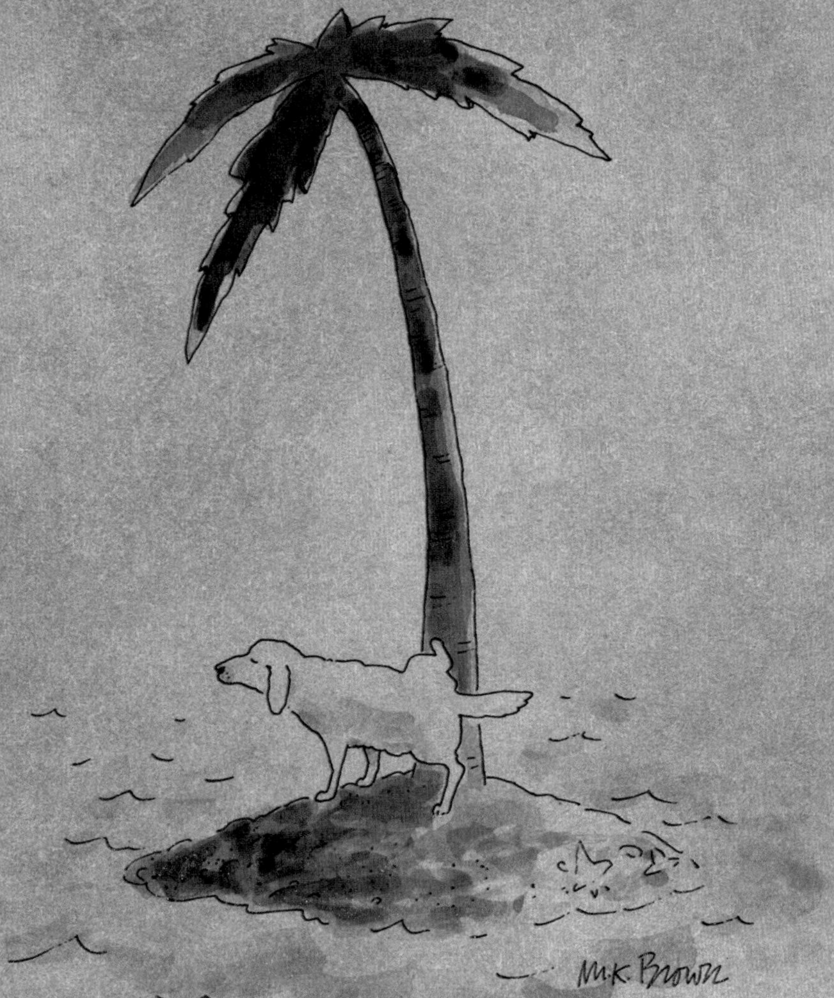
M.K. Brown

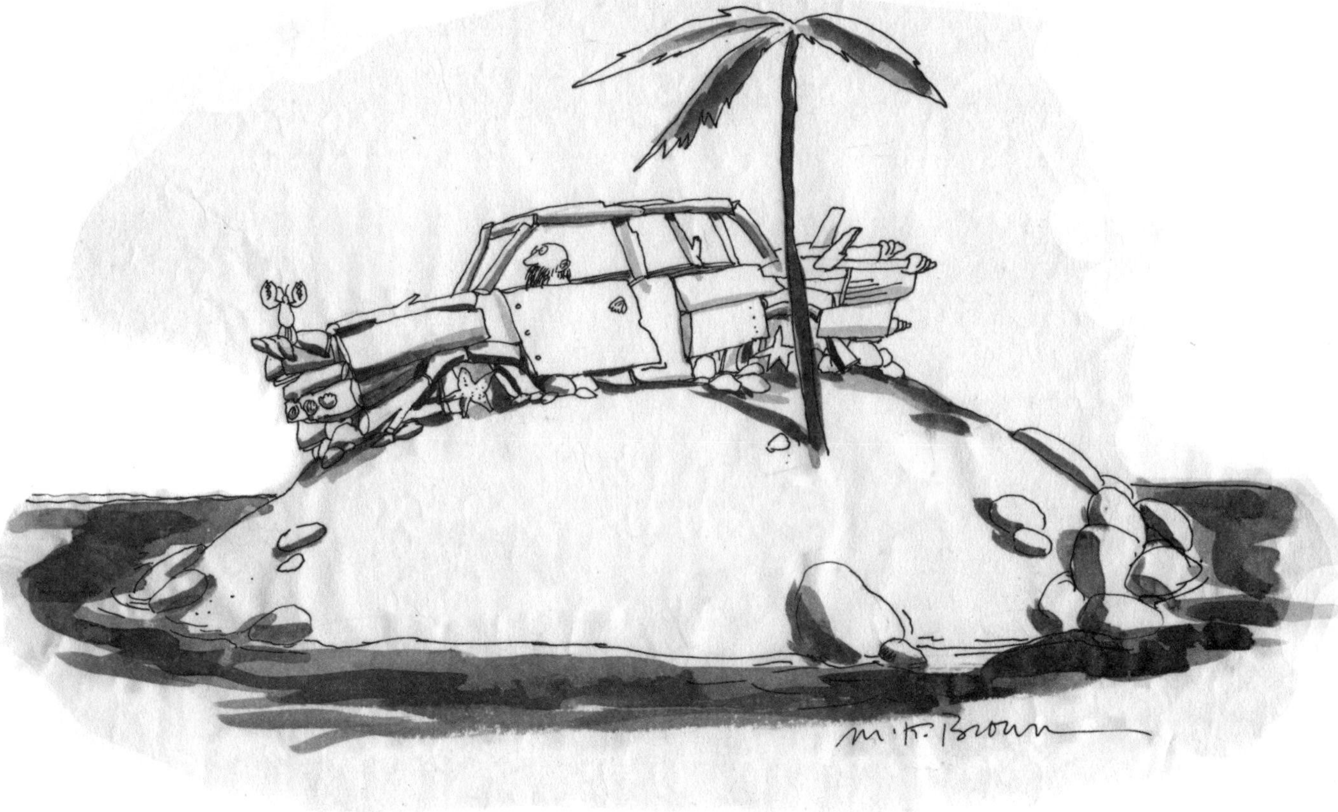
M.K. Brown

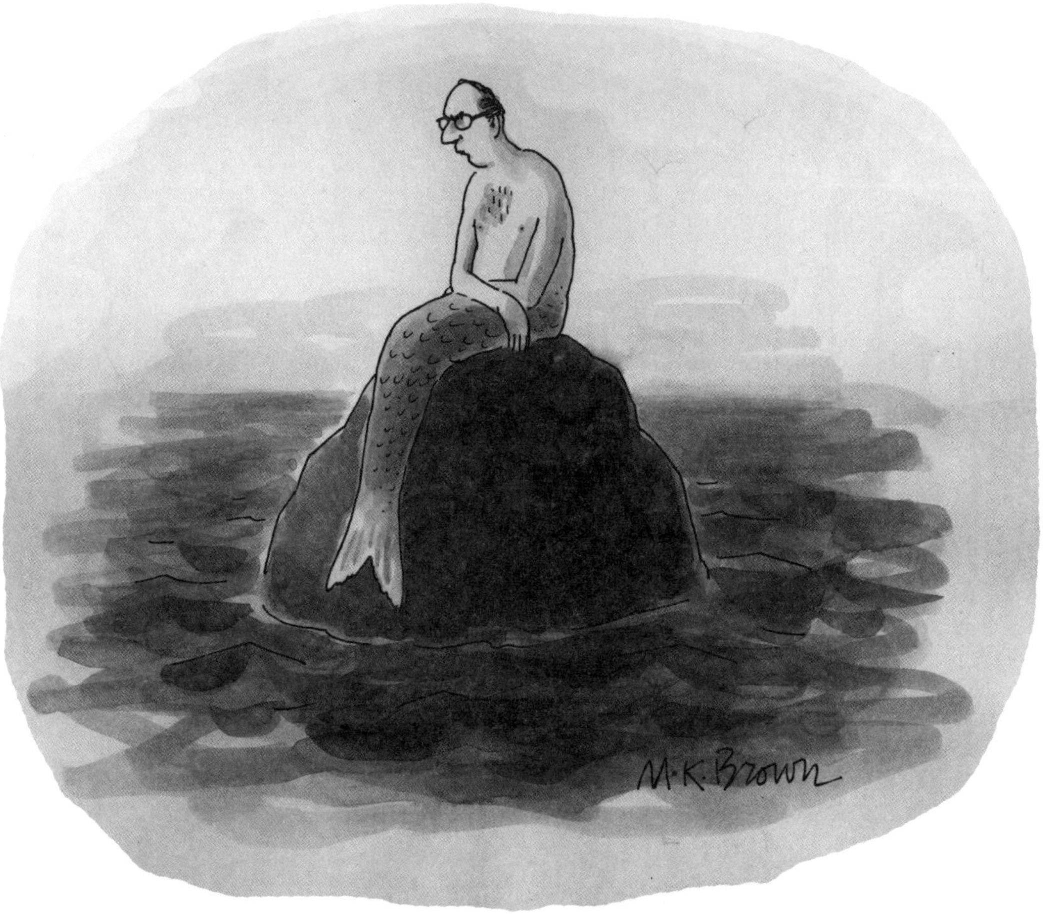
M.K. Brown

I went with friends to see the Mayan temples in Tikal and then made the following cartoon. By the way: there really was an insect like this in the jungle, and there really was a face in the banana cream pie—a face of doom as it turned out.

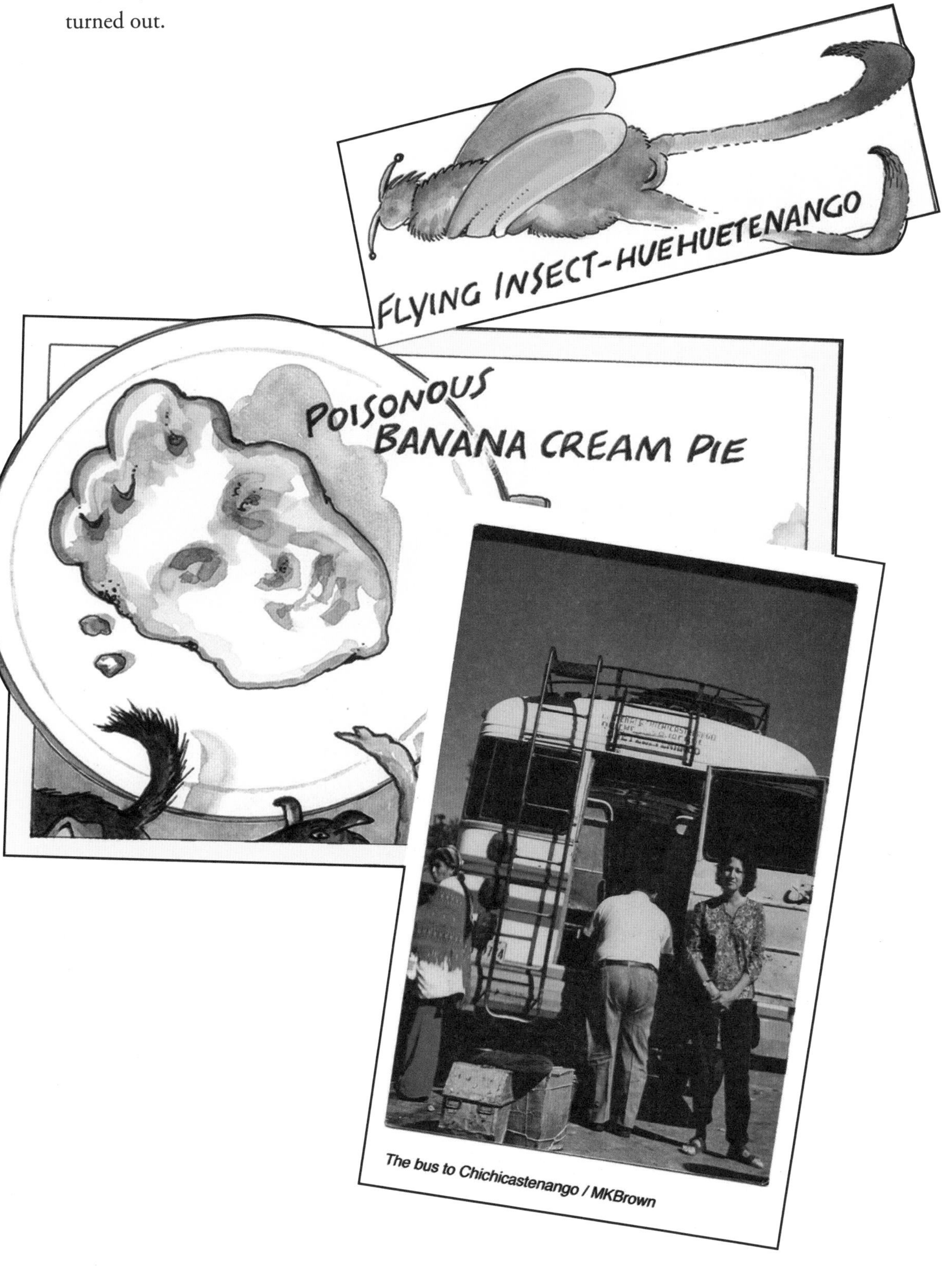
FLYING INSECT-HUEHUETENANGO
POISONOUS BANANA CREAM PIE

The bus to Chichicastenango / MKBrown

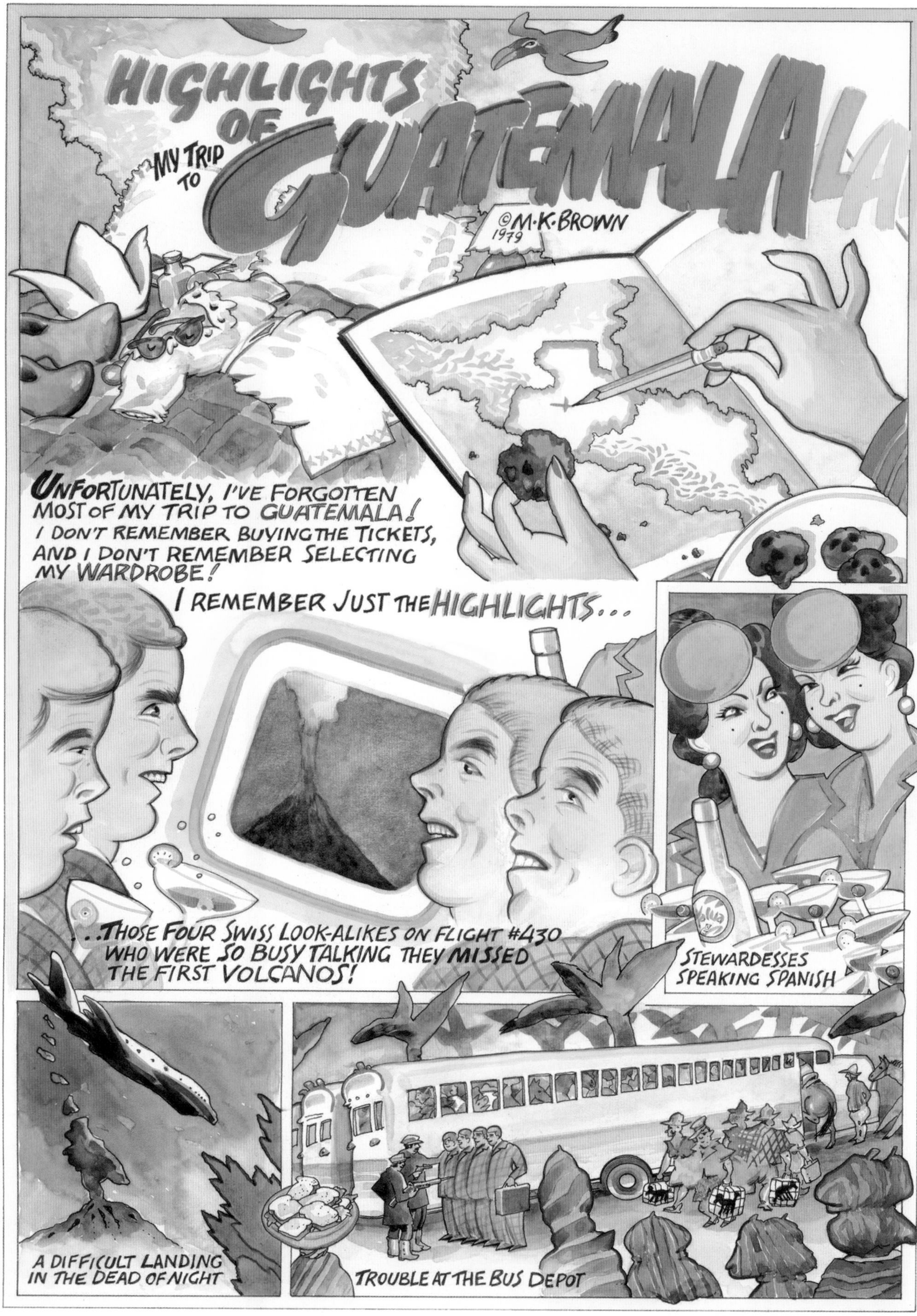
HIGHLIGHTS OF GUATEMALALA
MY TRIP TO
©M.K. BROWN 1979
UNFORTUNATELY, I'VE FORGOTTEN MOST OF MY TRIP TO GUATEMALA! I DON'T REMEMBER BUYING THE TICKETS, AND I DON'T REMEMBER SELECTING MY WARDROBE!
I REMEMBER JUST THE HIGHLIGHTS...
..THOSE FOUR SWISS LOOK-ALIKES ON FLIGHT #430 WHO WERE SO BUSY TALKING THEY MISSED THE FIRST VOLCANOS!
STEWARDESSES SPEAKING SPANISH
A DIFFICULT LANDING IN THE DEAD OF NIGHT
TROUBLE AT THE BUS DEPOT

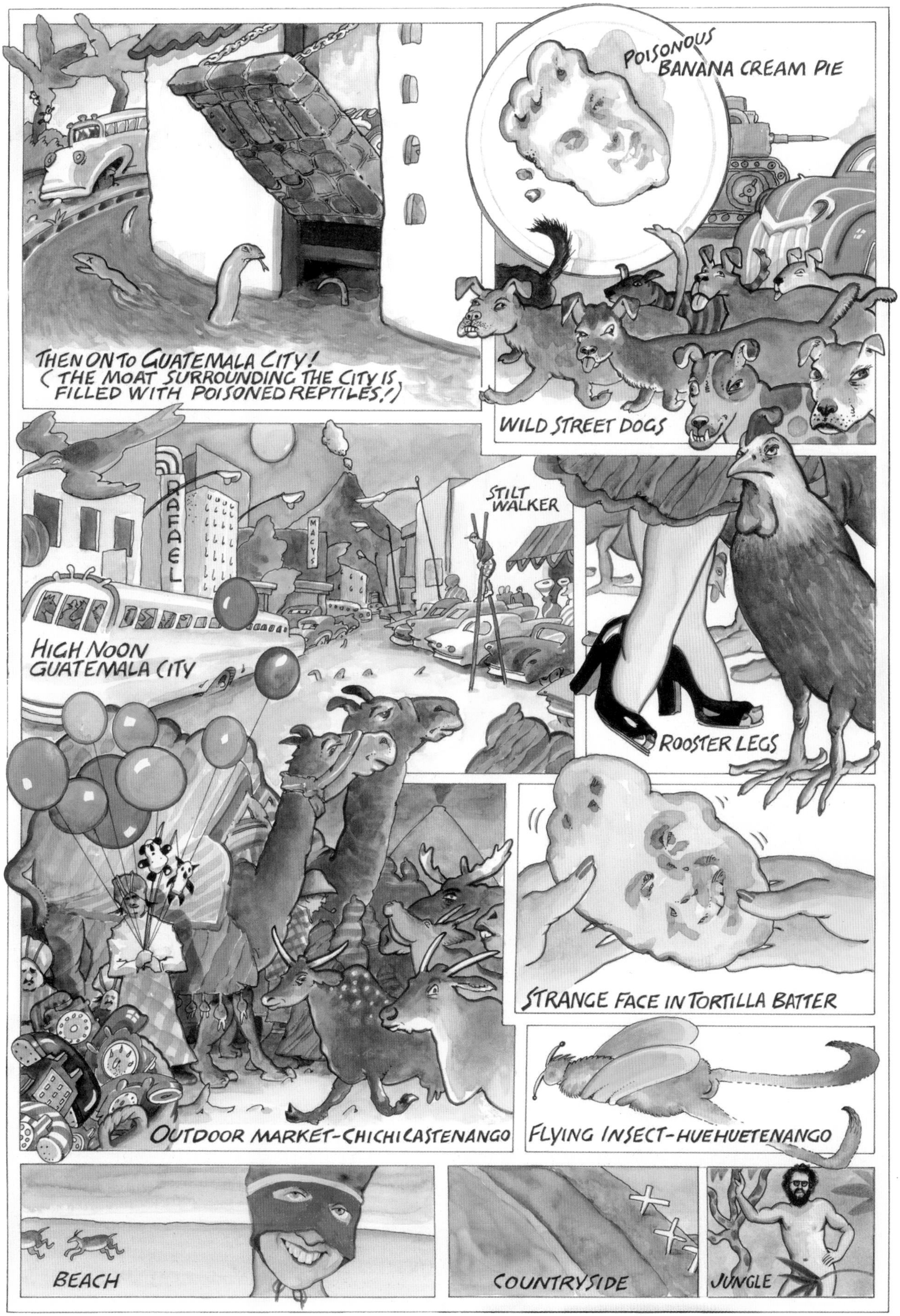
THEN ON TO GUATEMALA CITY!
(THE MOAT SURROUNDING THE CITY IS FILLED WITH POISONED REPTILES!)
POISONOUS BANANA CREAM PIE
WILD STREET DOGS
RAFAEL
MACY'S
STILT WALKER
HIGH NOON GUATEMALA CITY
ROOSTER LEGS
STRANGE FACE IN TORTILLA BATTER
OUTDOOR MARKET-CHICHICASTENANGO
FLYING INSECT-HUEHUETENANGO
BEACH
COUNTRYSIDE
JUNGLE

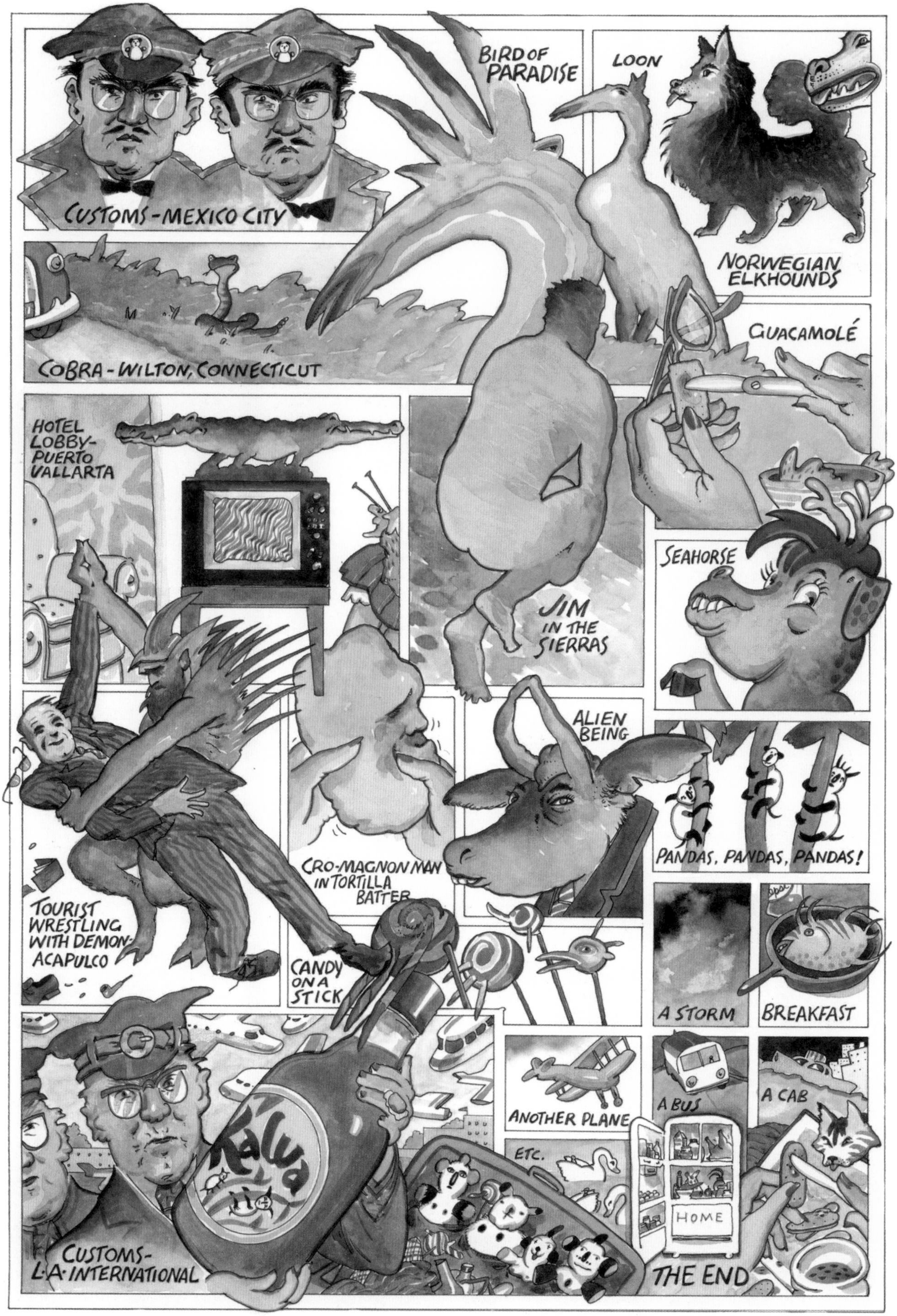
CUSTOMS - MEXICO CITY
BIRD OF PARADISE
LOON
NORWEGIAN ELKHOUNDS
COBRA - WILTON, CONNECTICUT
GUACAMOLÉ
HOTEL LOBBY- PUERTO VALLARTA
JIM IN THE SIERRAS
SEAHORSE
ALIEN BEING
PANDAS, PANDAS, PANDAS!
CRO-MAGNON MAN IN TORTILLA BATTER
TOURIST WRESTLING WITH DEMON- ACAPULCO
CANDY ON A STICK
A STORM
BREAKFAST
ANOTHER PLANE
A BUS
A CAB
ETC.
HOME
Kalua
CUSTOMS- L.A. INTERNATIONAL
THE END

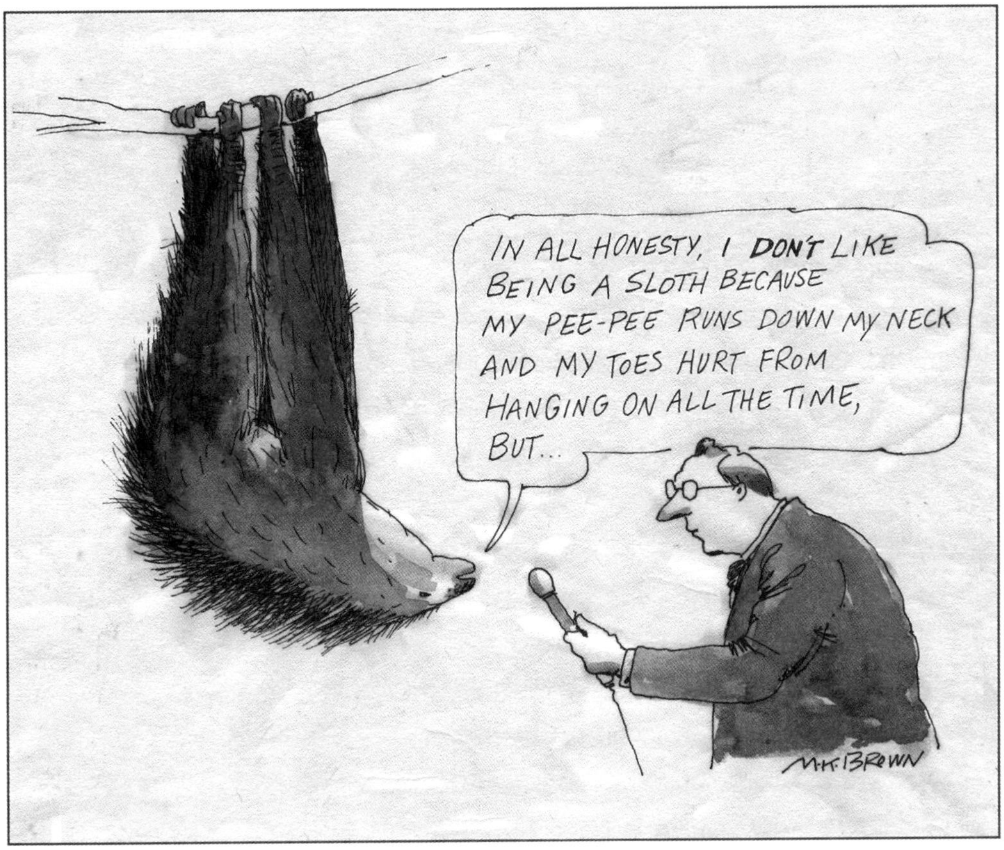
IN ALL HONESTY, I DON'T LIKE BEING A SLOTH BECAUSE MY PEE-PEE RUNS DOWN MY NECK AND MY TOES HURT FROM HANGING ON ALL THE TIME, BUT...
M.K. BROWN

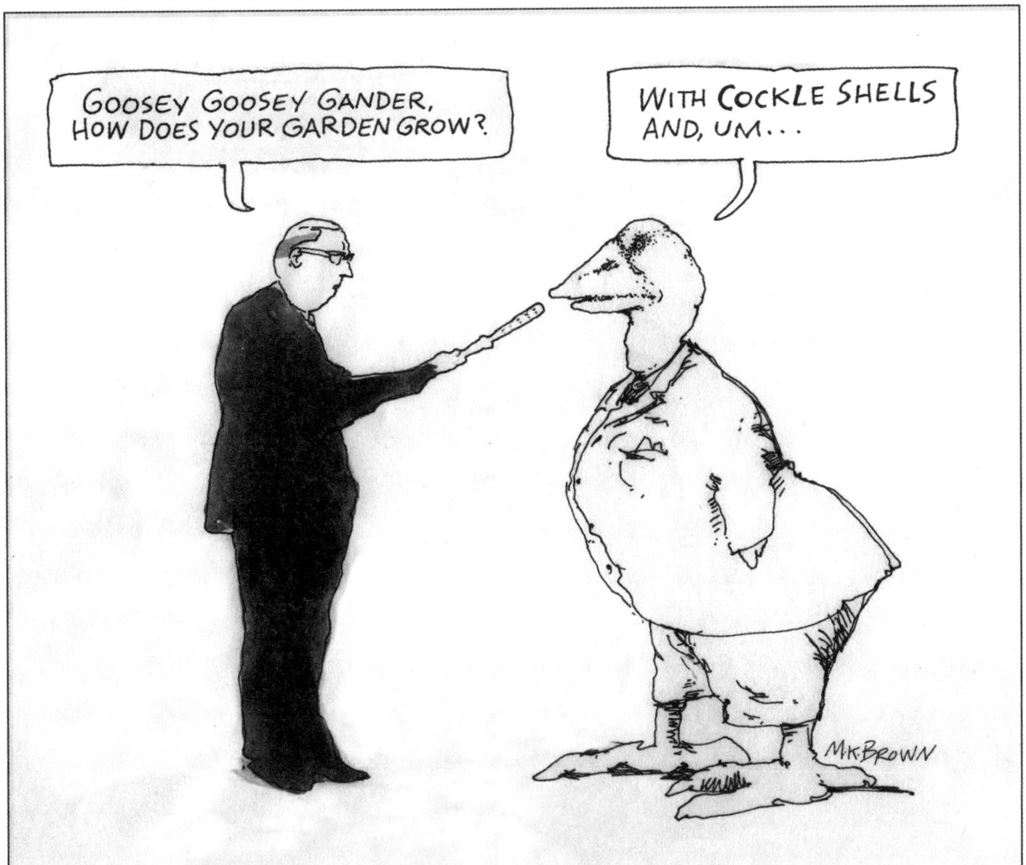
GOOSEY GOOSEY GANDER, HOW DOES YOUR GARDEN GROW?
WITH COCKLE SHELLS AND, UM...
M.K. BROWN

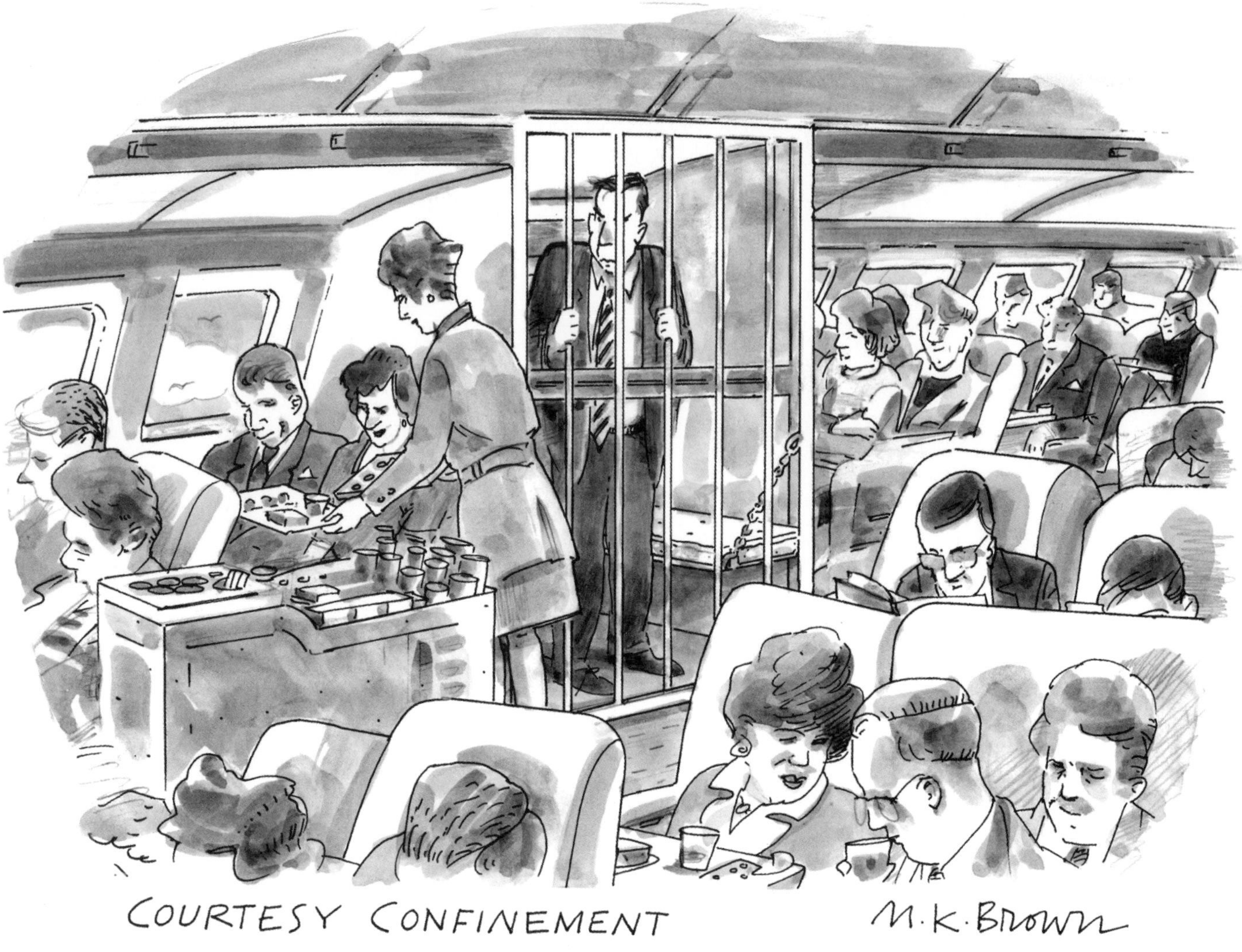
COURTESY CONFINEMENT
M.K. BROWN

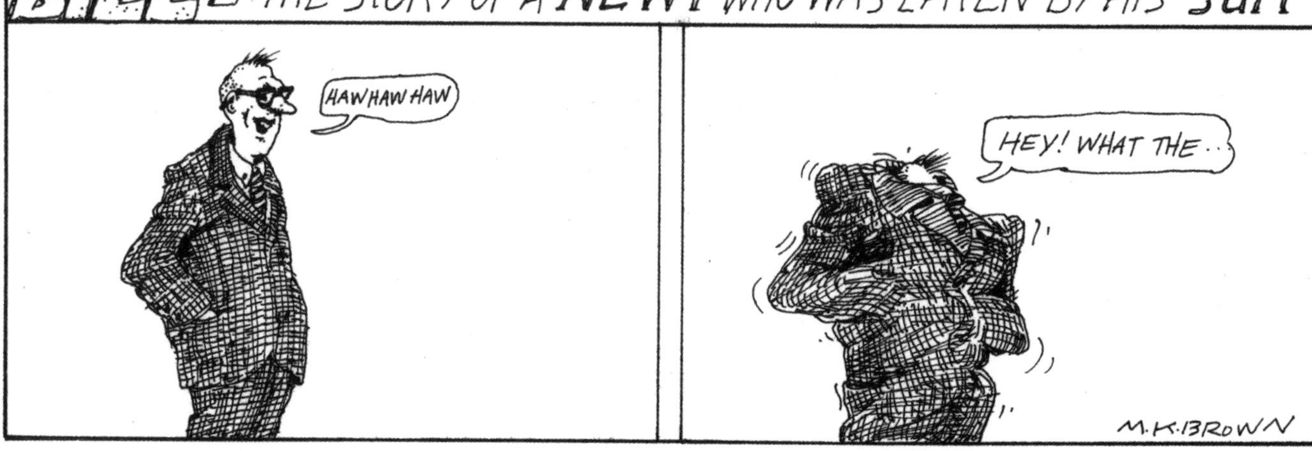
BILL ▫ THE STORY OF A NEWT WHO WAS EATEN BY HIS SUIT
HAWHAW HAW
HEY! WHAT THE..
M.K.BROWN

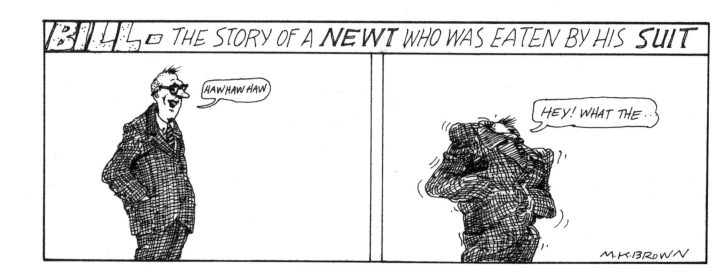

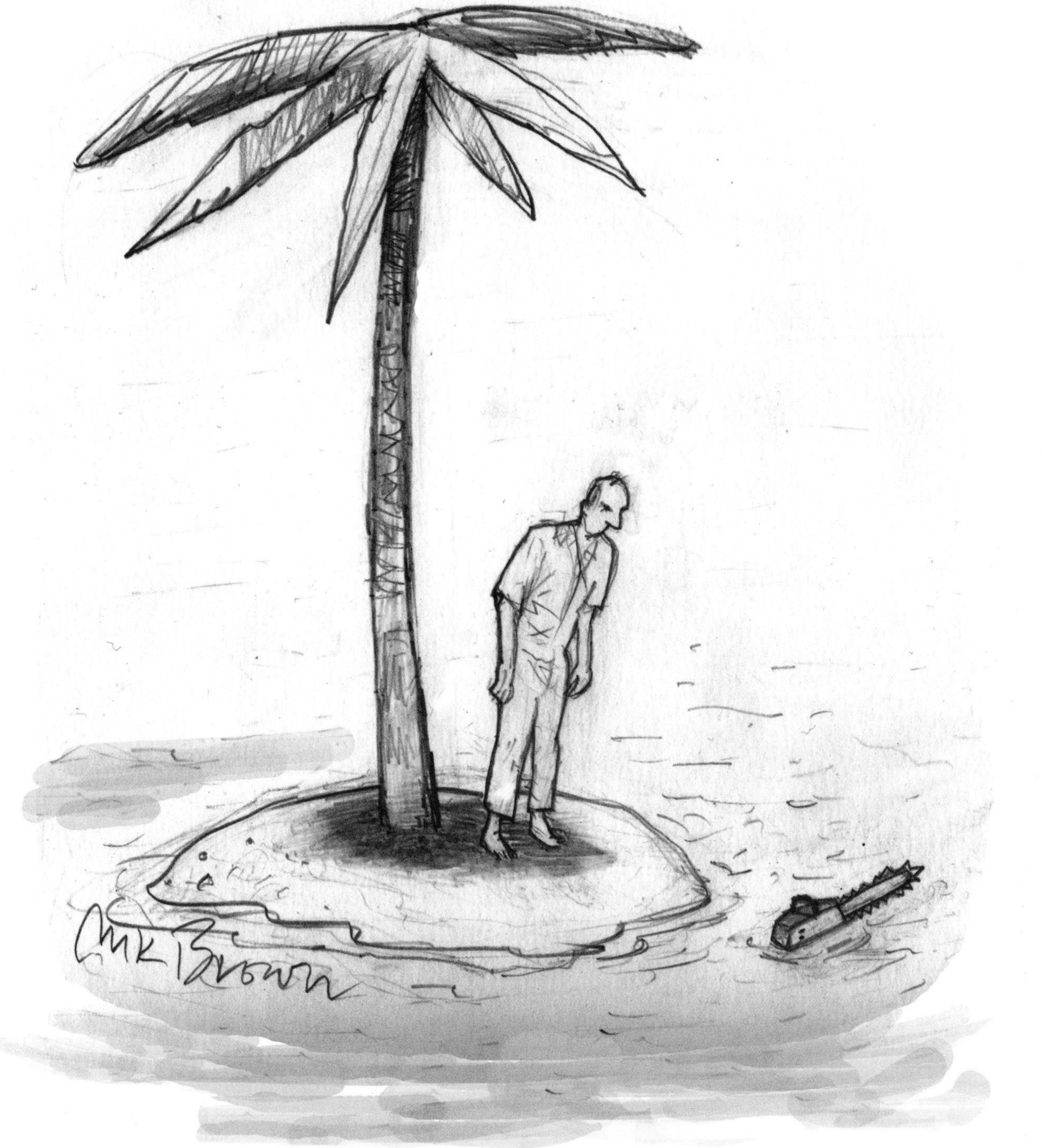

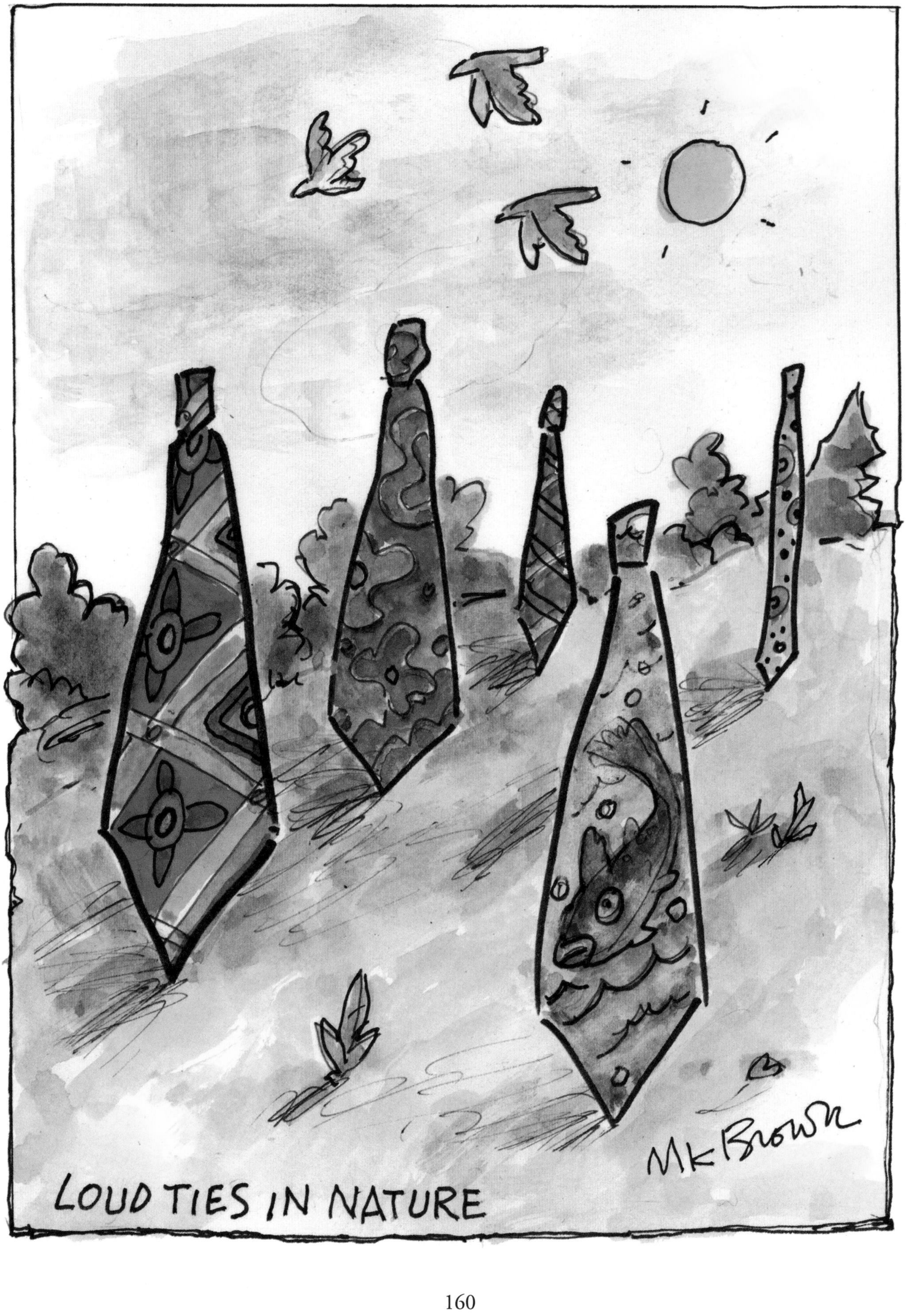
LOUD TIES IN NATURE
MK Brown

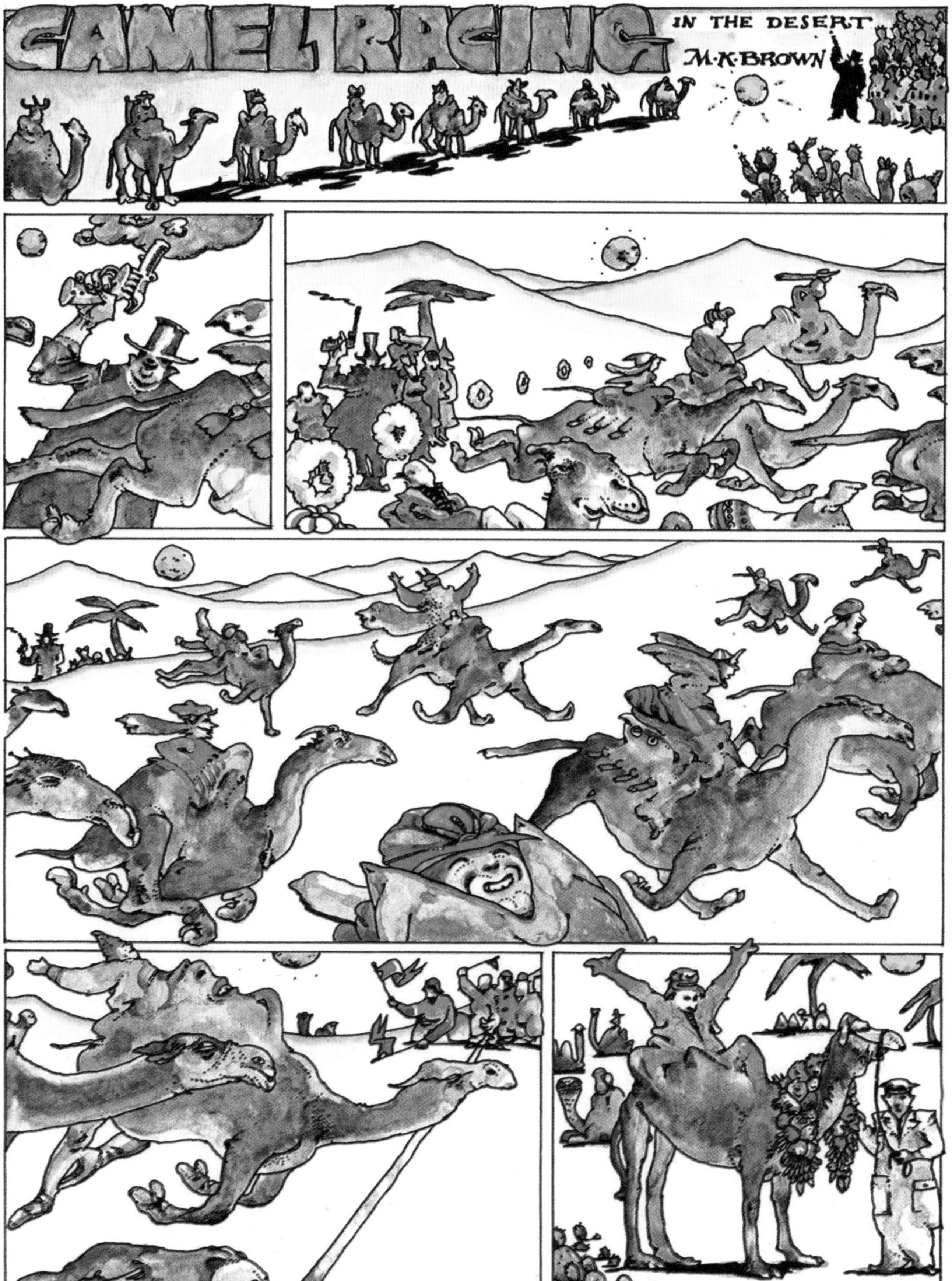
CAMEL RACING
IN THE DESERT
M·K·BROWN

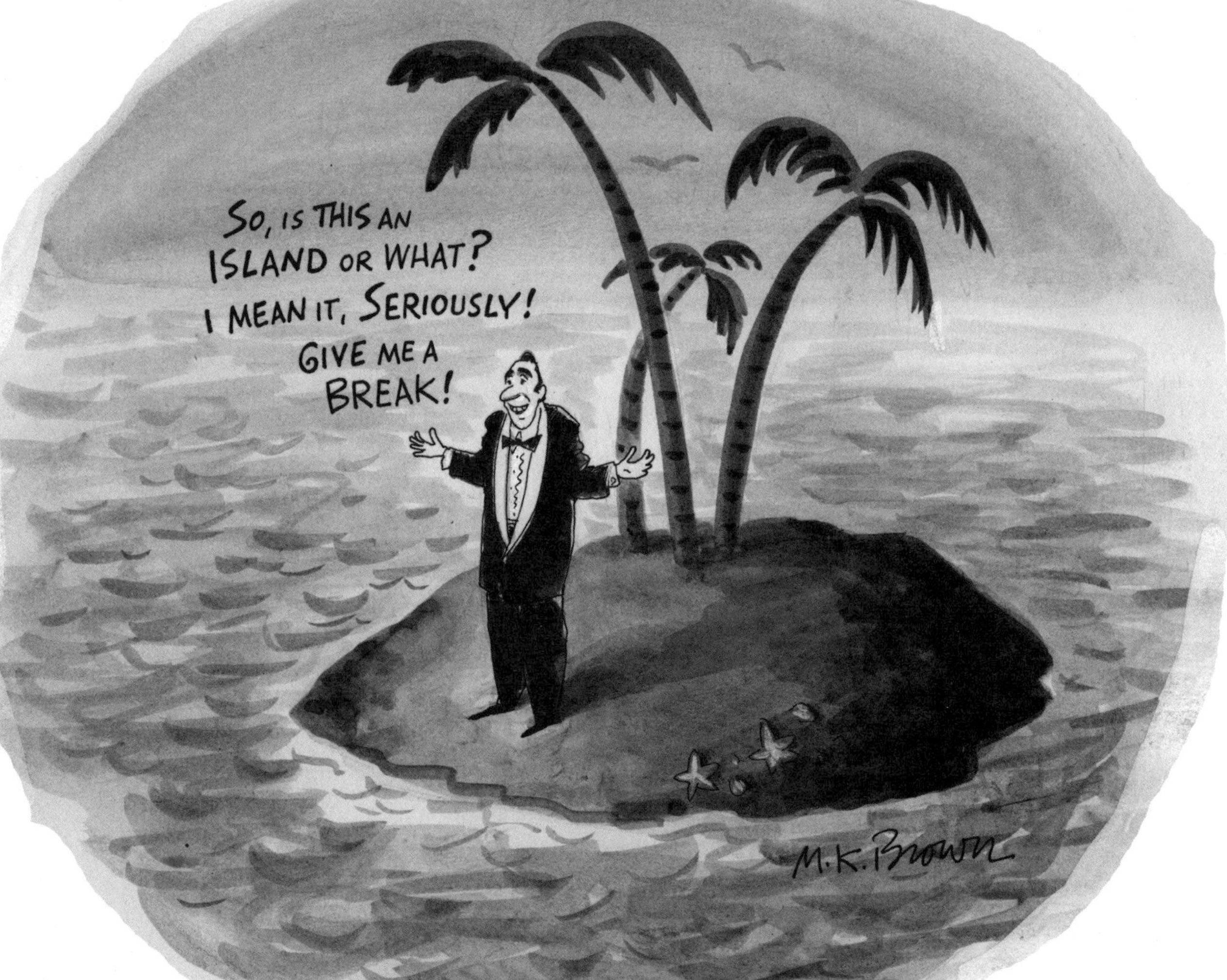
So, is THIS AN ISLAND OR WHAT? I MEAN IT, SERIOUSLY! GIVE ME A BREAK!
M.K. Brown

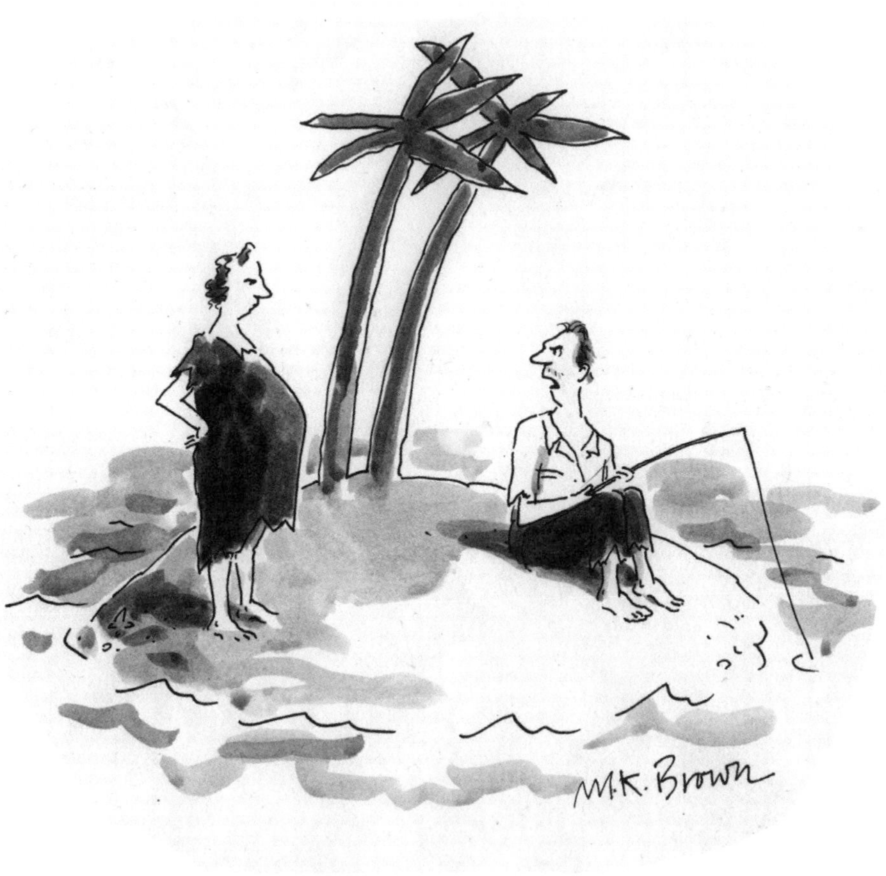
M.K. Brown

You're *what*?

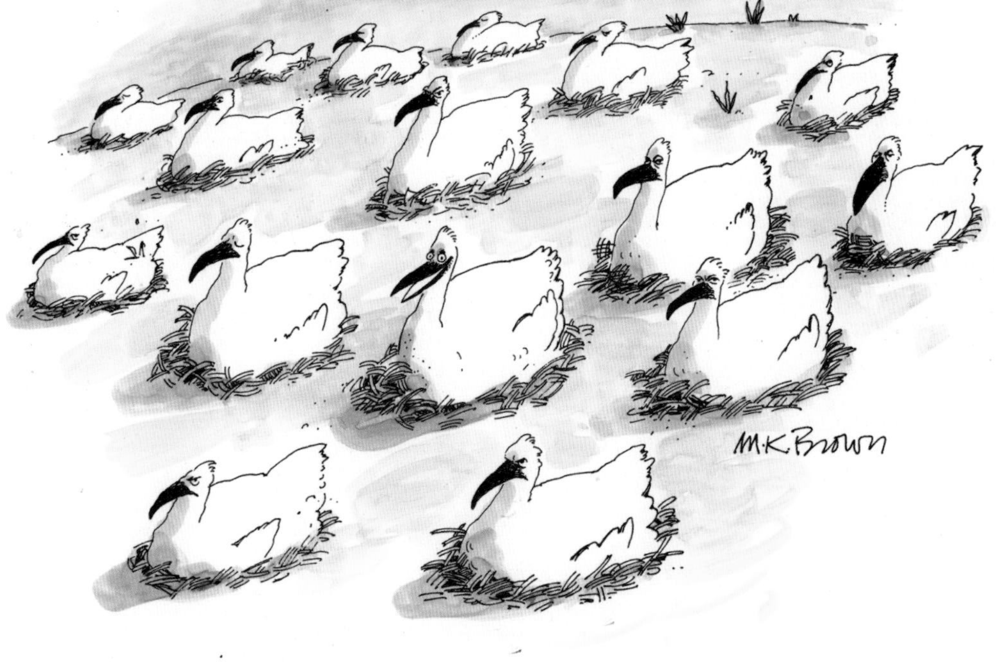
M.K. Brown

So then, Howard came along. He was Canadian, but couldn't make a nest to save his soul, poor thing. But we had a lot of laughs, Howard and I. I remember one time...

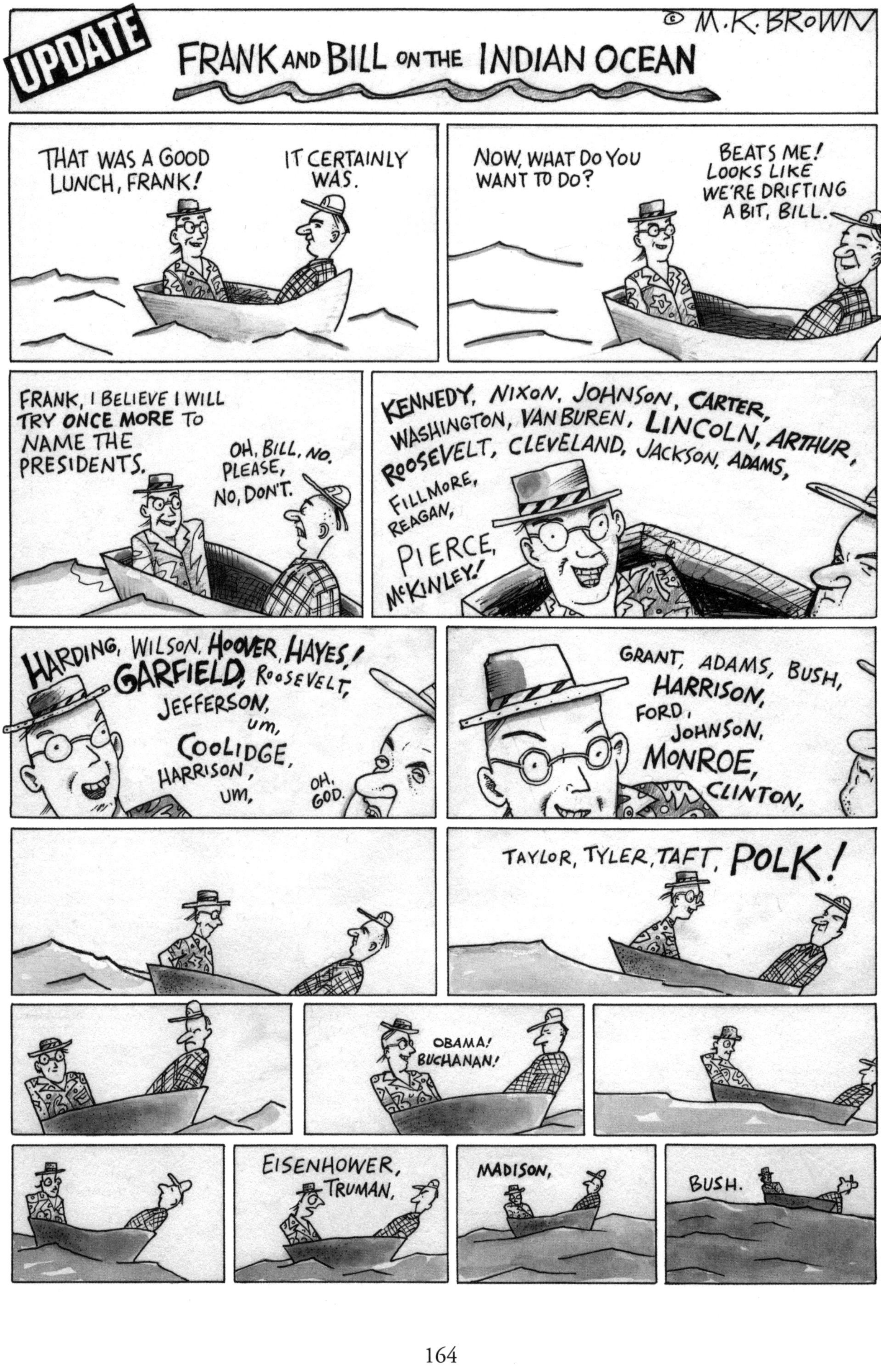
UPDATE
© M.K. BROWN
FRANK AND BILL ON THE INDIAN OCEAN
THAT WAS A GOOD LUNCH, FRANK!
IT CERTAINLY WAS.
NOW, WHAT DO YOU WANT TO DO?
BEATS ME! LOOKS LIKE WE'RE DRIFTING A BIT, BILL.
FRANK, I BELIEVE I WILL TRY ONCE MORE TO NAME THE PRESIDENTS.
OH, BILL, NO. PLEASE, NO, DON'T.
KENNEDY, NIXON, JOHNSON, CARTER, WASHINGTON, VAN BUREN, LINCOLN, ARTHUR, ROOSEVELT, CLEVELAND, JACKSON, ADAMS, FILLMORE, REAGAN, PIERCE, McKINLEY!
HARDING, WILSON, HOOVER, HAYES! GARFIELD, ROOSEVELT, JEFFERSON, um, COOLIDGE, HARRISON, um,
OH, GOD.
GRANT, ADAMS, BUSH, HARRISON, FORD, JOHNSON, MONROE, CLINTON,
TAYLOR, TYLER, TAFT, POLK!
OBAMA! BUCHANAN!
EISENHOWER, TRUMAN,
MADISON,
BUSH.

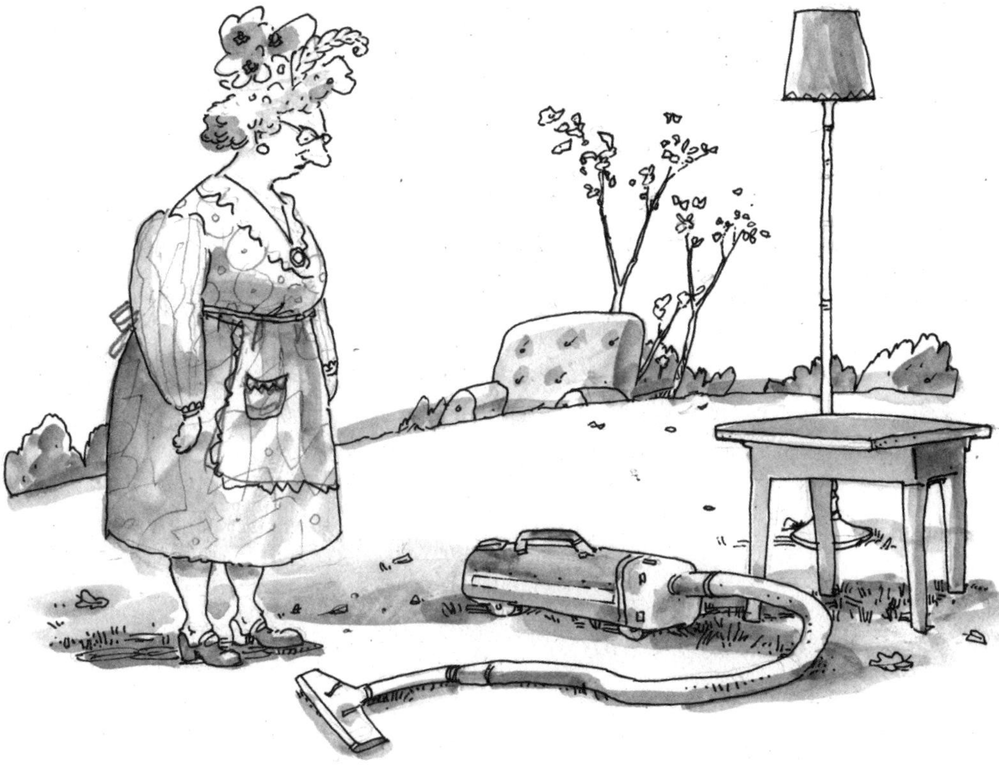

MOTHER NATURE ABHORRING A VACUUM • MKBrown

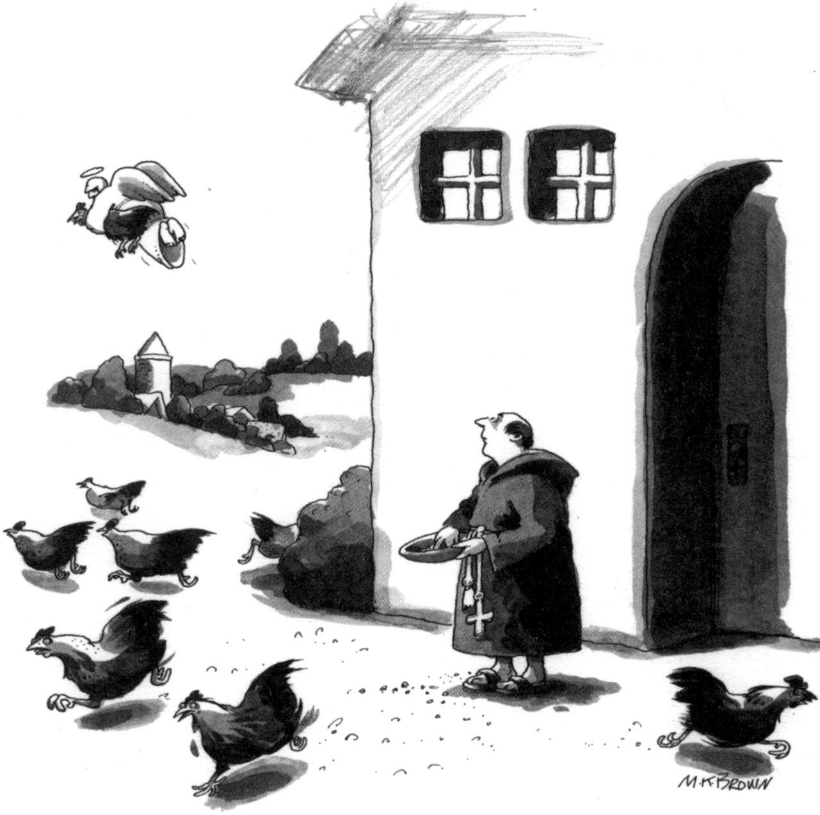

MKBROWN

The original Dr. N'Godatu was inspired by tales of distant relatives who were missionaries in Africa and were chased out of town by the Mau Mau. LIFE magazine published an article about it, which I read as a teenager in Darien, Connecticut.

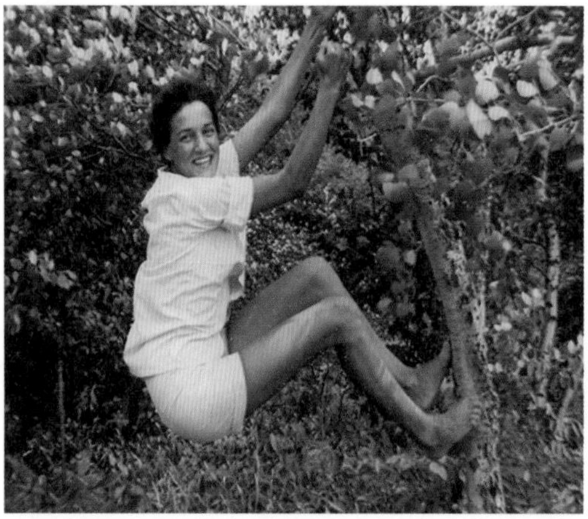

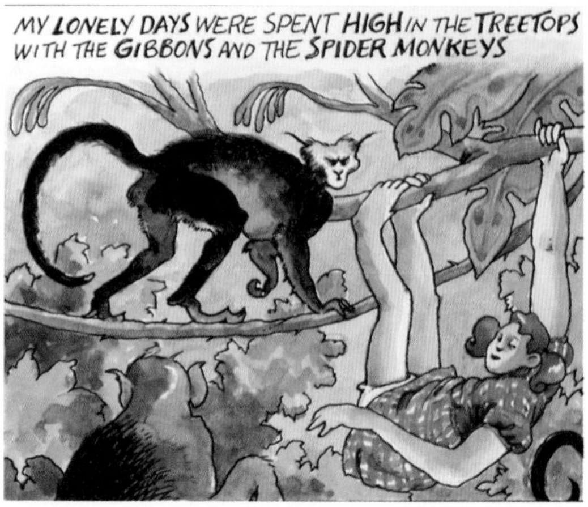
MY LONELY DAYS WERE SPENT HIGH IN THE TREETOPS
WITH THE GIBBONS AND THE SPIDER MONKEYS

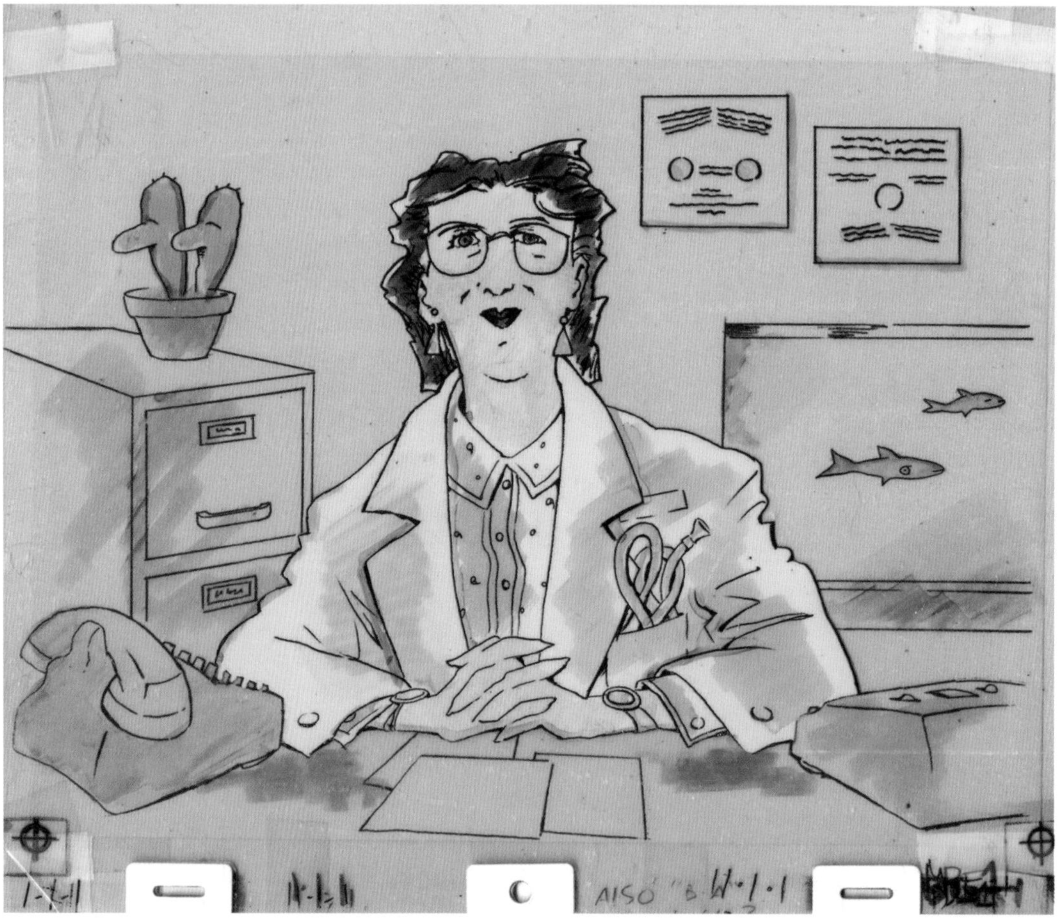

An animated version of Dr. N'Godatu appeared on the first season of the *Tracey Ullman Show* and The Third Animation Celebration.

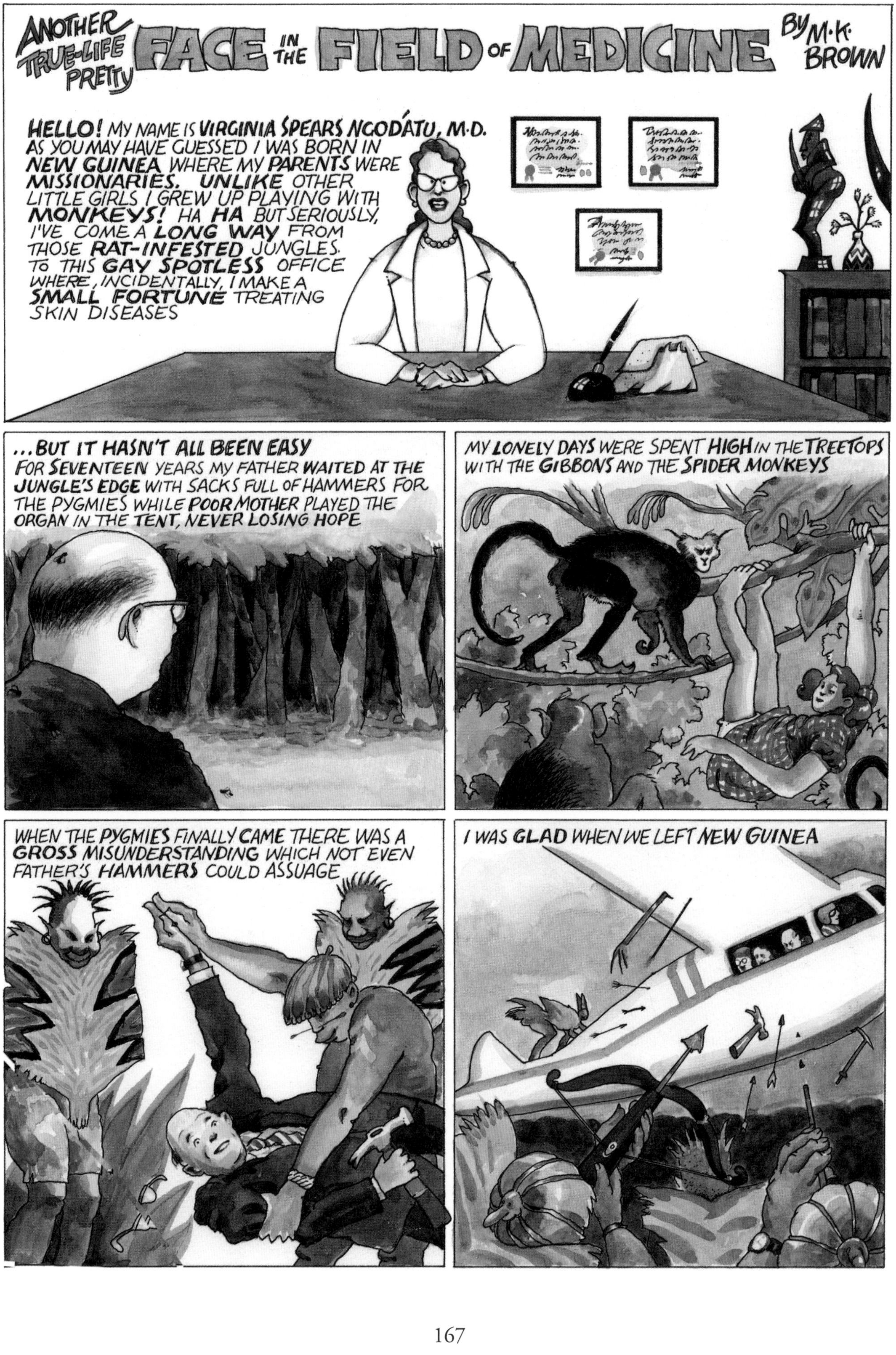
ANOTHER TRUE-LIFE PRETTY FACE IN THE FIELD OF MEDICINE
BY M.K. BROWN
HELLO! MY NAME IS VIRGINIA SPEARS NGODÁTU, M.D. AS YOU MAY HAVE GUESSED I WAS BORN IN NEW GUINEA WHERE MY PARENTS WERE MISSIONARIES. UNLIKE OTHER LITTLE GIRLS I GREW UP PLAYING WITH MONKEYS! HA HA BUT SERIOUSLY, I'VE COME A LONG WAY FROM THOSE RAT-INFESTED JUNGLES. TO THIS GAY SPOTLESS OFFICE WHERE, INCIDENTALLY, I MAKE A SMALL FORTUNE TREATING SKIN DISEASES
...BUT IT HASN'T ALL BEEN EASY
FOR SEVENTEEN YEARS MY FATHER WAITED AT THE JUNGLE'S EDGE WITH SACKS FULL OF HAMMERS FOR THE PYGMIES WHILE POOR MOTHER PLAYED THE ORGAN IN THE TENT, NEVER LOSING HOPE
MY LONELY DAYS WERE SPENT HIGH IN THE TREETOPS WITH THE GIBBONS AND THE SPIDER MONKEYS
WHEN THE PYGMIES FINALLY CAME THERE WAS A GROSS MISUNDERSTANDING WHICH NOT EVEN FATHER'S HAMMERS COULD ASSUAGE
I WAS GLAD WHEN WE LEFT NEW GUINEA

GLAD AT LONG LAST TO BE "JUST ANOTHER GIRL" AT A LEADING UNIVERSITY

GLAD AFTER GRUELING YEARS OF MEDICAL SCHOOL TO FINALLY HEAR THOSE WORDS

DR. NGODÁTU! PAGING DR. NGODÁTU!

WHY, THAT'S ME!

TO THIS DAY I REMEMBER MY FIRST CASE AND HOW VERY NERVOUS I WAS... A RETIRED ARMY COLONEL WITH A NASTY RASH. HIS HEAD WAS INSIDE A BOTTLE, SO YOU CAN IMAGINE HOW DIFFICULT THAT WAS TO TREAT

AND THEN THERE WAS THE YIPPIE WHO HAD EATEN TOO MUCH CHOCOLATE! HE FELL INTO A TRANCE AND HAD A VISION RIGHT THERE IN MY OFFICE

ALL MANNER OF PEOPLE HAVE PASSED THROUGH THIS WAITING ROOM: MOVIE STARS, POLITICIANS, KOOKS, CRIMINALS, NOBODIES. I TREAT THEM ALL! WHAT DO I CARE?

LIFE IS WONDERFUL. I LOVE BEING A DOCTOR! I LOVE SITTING AT THIS GIGANTIC DESK, DRESSED ALL IN WHITE, CLEAN INSIDE AND OUT LIKE A QUEEN WAITING FOR MY NEXT PATIENT. MAYBE IT WILL BE A MOVIE STAR — OR A JOCKEY!

WHAT MORE COULD A GIRL WANT?

END

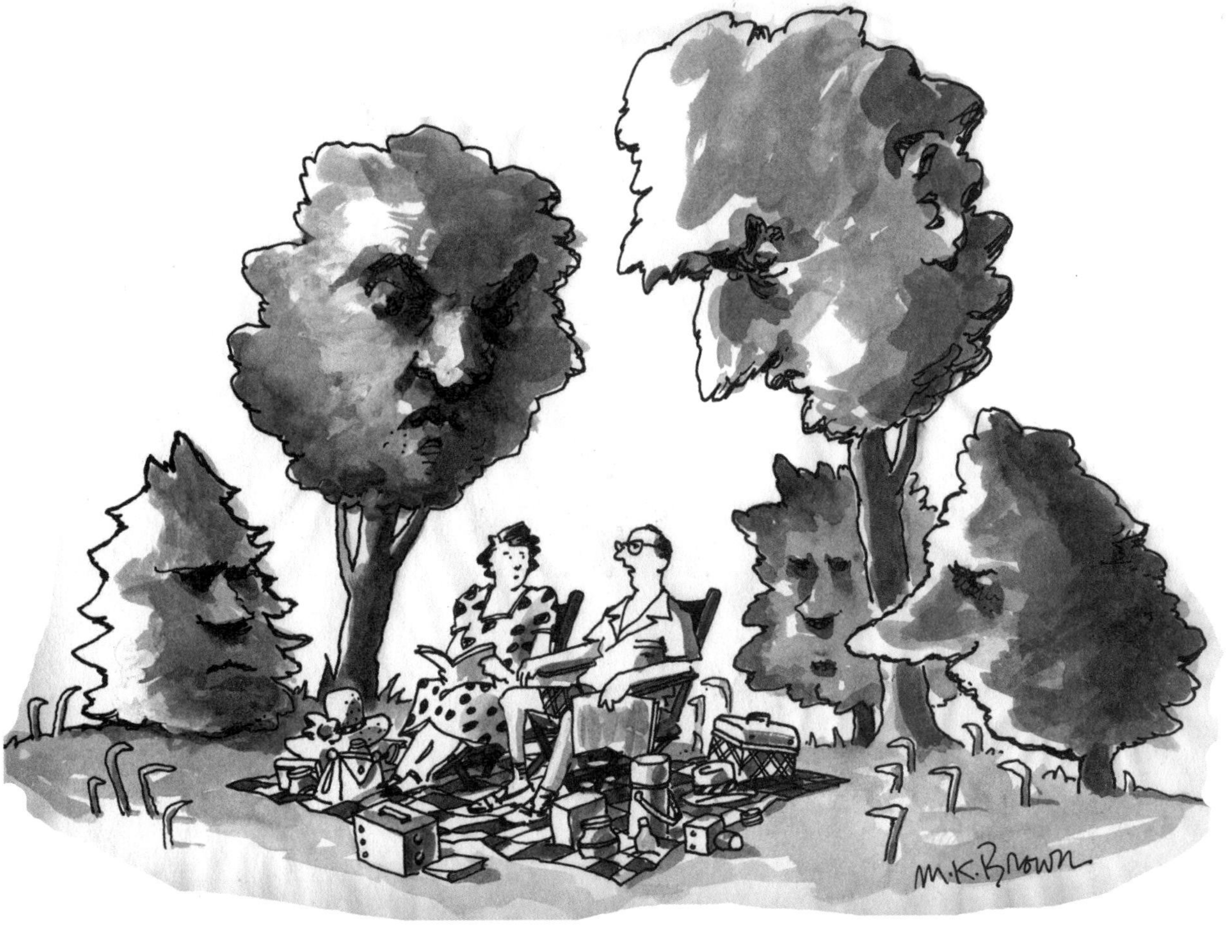
M.K.Brown

I don't like it here.

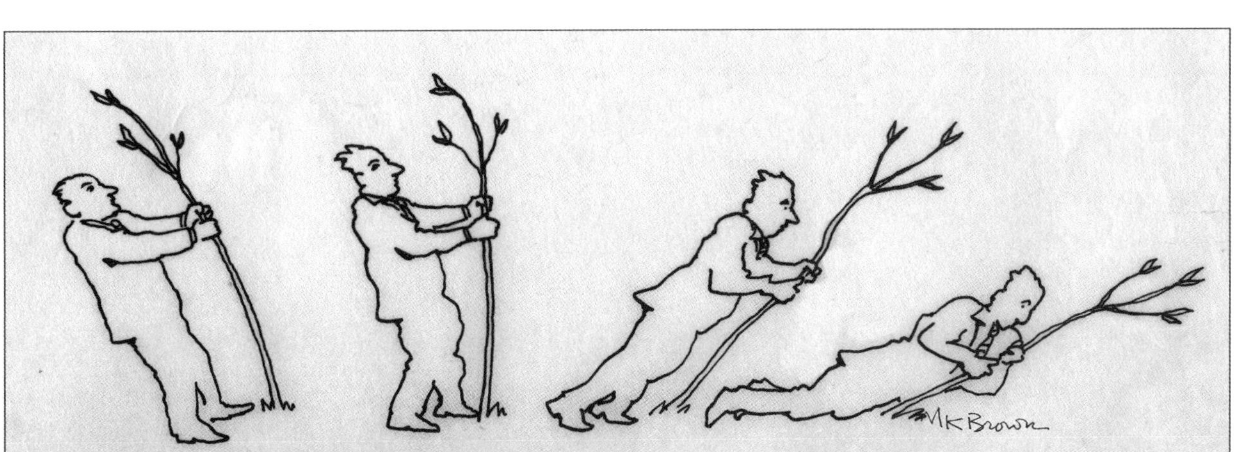
MKBrown

Sometime in the '70s, I read a report about two fishermen in Louisiana who were taken up into a spaceship for many hours, then released "physically unharmed, yet emotionally shaken." Under separate hypnosis, they told a matching and harrowing tale about being abducted and examined by beings from another planet. To assuage my fears, I made a cartoon about it for *National Lampoon*. This is exactly how the extraterrestrials looked in my imagination.

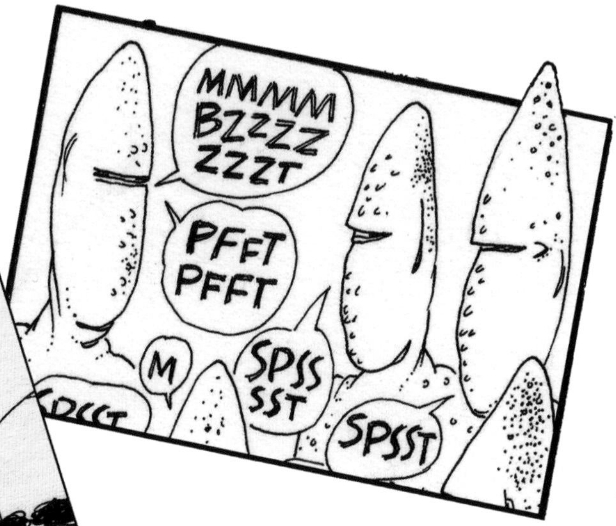
MMMM
BZZZZ
ZZZT
PFFT
PFFT
M
SPSS
SST
SPSST

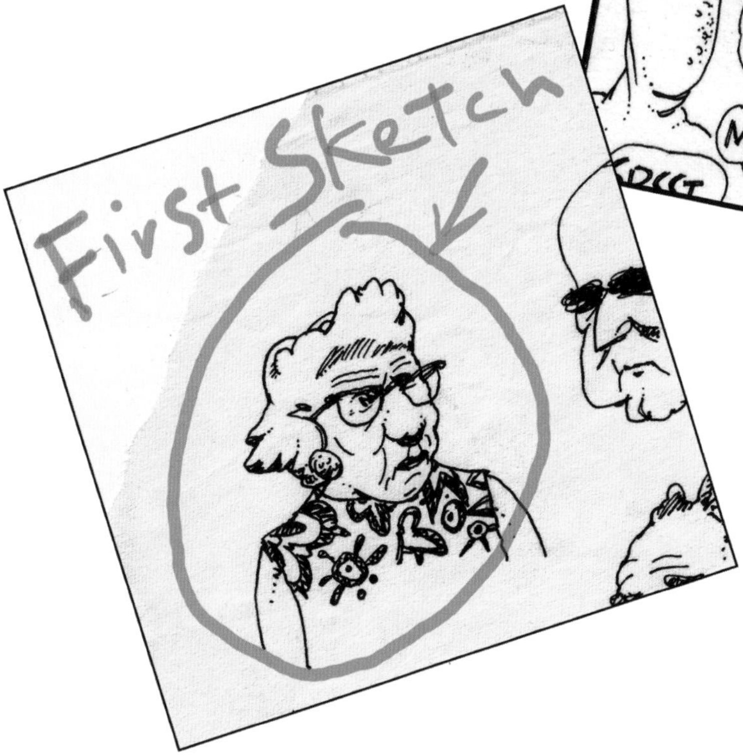
First Sketch

The inspiration for Dr. Woo was a woman on British TV on a show about gardening or politics. Her cranky face and personality appealed to me, so I used her in "They Came from Space."

Later, she and her twin sister, Mary, starred in the feature *Aunt Mary's Kitchen*, which ran for four years in *National Lampoon*, then in *Aunt Mary's Kitchen Cookbook*. A future collection is planned, but this is how it all began.

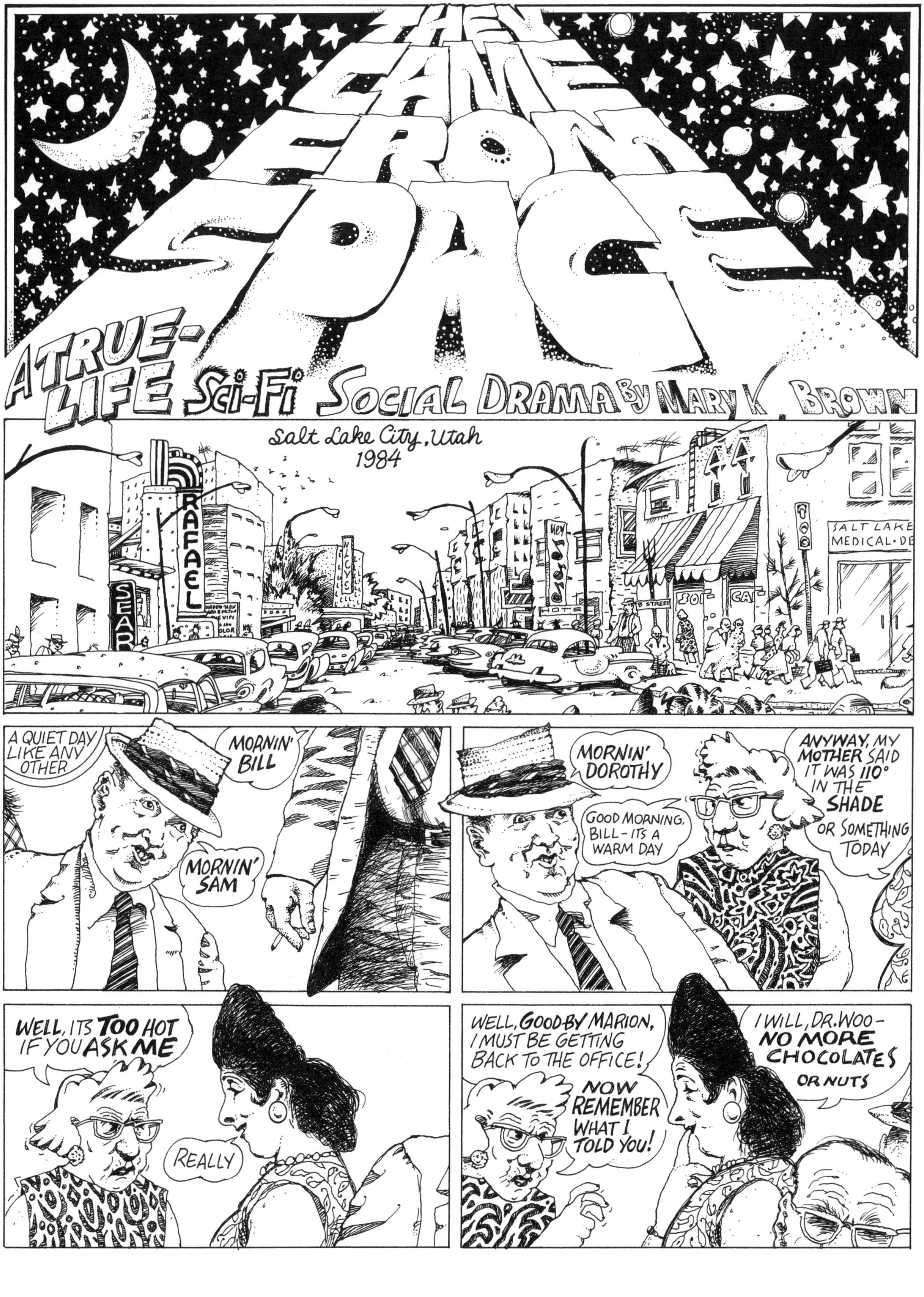
THEY CAME FROM SPACE
A TRUE-LIFE Sci-Fi SOCIAL DRAMA By MARY K. BROWN
Salt Lake City, Utah 1984
RAFAEL
SEARS
SALT LAKE MEDICAL·DE
B STREET
A QUIET DAY LIKE ANY OTHER
MORNIN' BILL
MORNIN' SAM
MORNIN' DOROTHY
GOOD MORNING, BILL - ITS A WARM DAY
ANYWAY, MY MOTHER SAID IT WAS 110° IN THE SHADE OR SOMETHING TODAY
WELL, ITS TOO HOT IF YOU ASK ME
REALLY
WELL, GOOD-BY MARION, I MUST BE GETTING BACK TO THE OFFICE!
NOW REMEMBER WHAT I TOLD YOU!
I WILL, DR. WOO - NO MORE CHOCOLATES OR NUTS

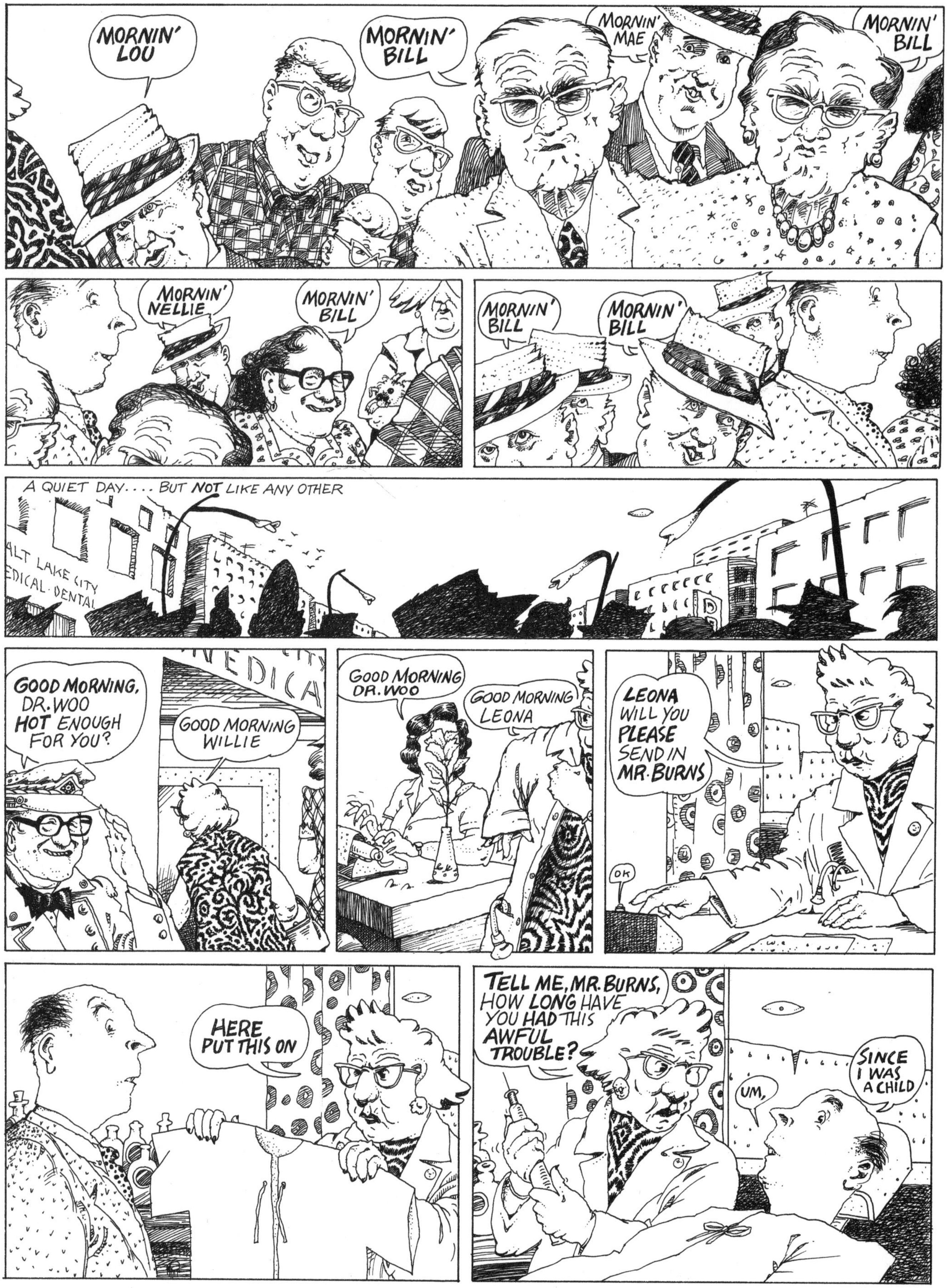

MORNIN' LOU
MORNIN' BILL
MORNIN' MAE
MORNIN' BILL
MORNIN' NELLIE
MORNIN' BILL
MORNIN' BILL
MORNIN' BILL
A QUIET DAY.... BUT NOT LIKE ANY OTHER
ALT LAKE CITY EDICAL·DENTAL
GOOD MORNING, DR. WOO HOT ENOUGH FOR YOU?
GOOD MORNING WILLIE
GOOD MORNING DR. WOO
GOOD MORNING LEONA
LEONA WILL YOU PLEASE SEND IN MR. BURNS
OK
HERE PUT THIS ON
TELL ME, MR. BURNS, HOW LONG HAVE YOU HAD THIS AWFUL TROUBLE?
UM,
SINCE I WAS A CHILD

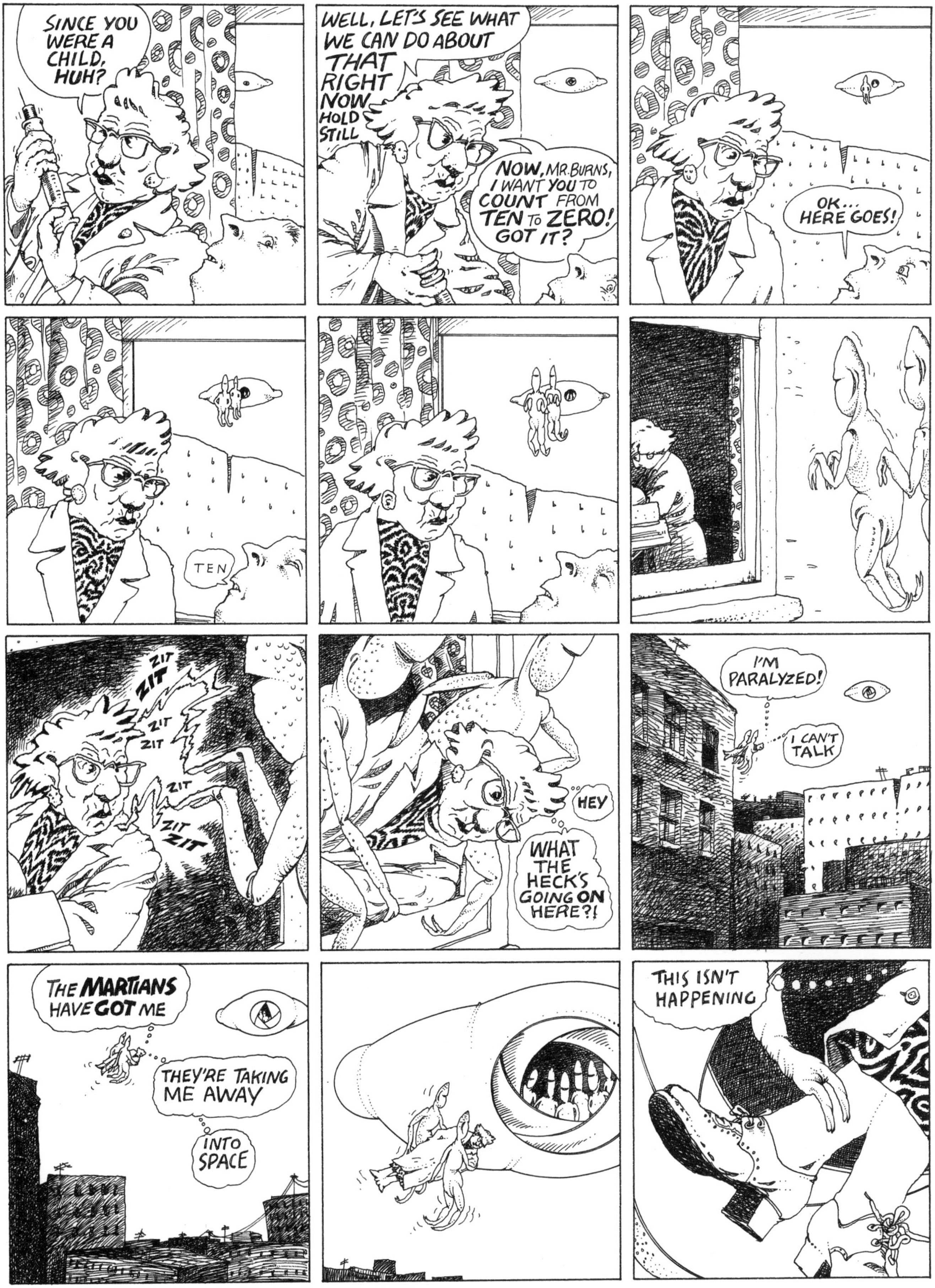

SINCE YOU WERE A CHILD, HUH?
WELL, LET'S SEE WHAT WE CAN DO ABOUT THAT RIGHT NOW HOLD STILL
NOW, MR. BURNS, I WANT YOU TO COUNT FROM TEN TO ZERO! GOT IT?
OK... HERE GOES!
TEN
ZIT ZIT ZIT ZIT ZIT ZIT ZIT
HEY
WHAT THE HECK'S GOING ON HERE?!
I'M PARALYZED!
I CAN'T TALK
THE MARTIANS HAVE GOT ME
THEY'RE TAKING ME AWAY
INTO SPACE
THIS ISN'T HAPPENING

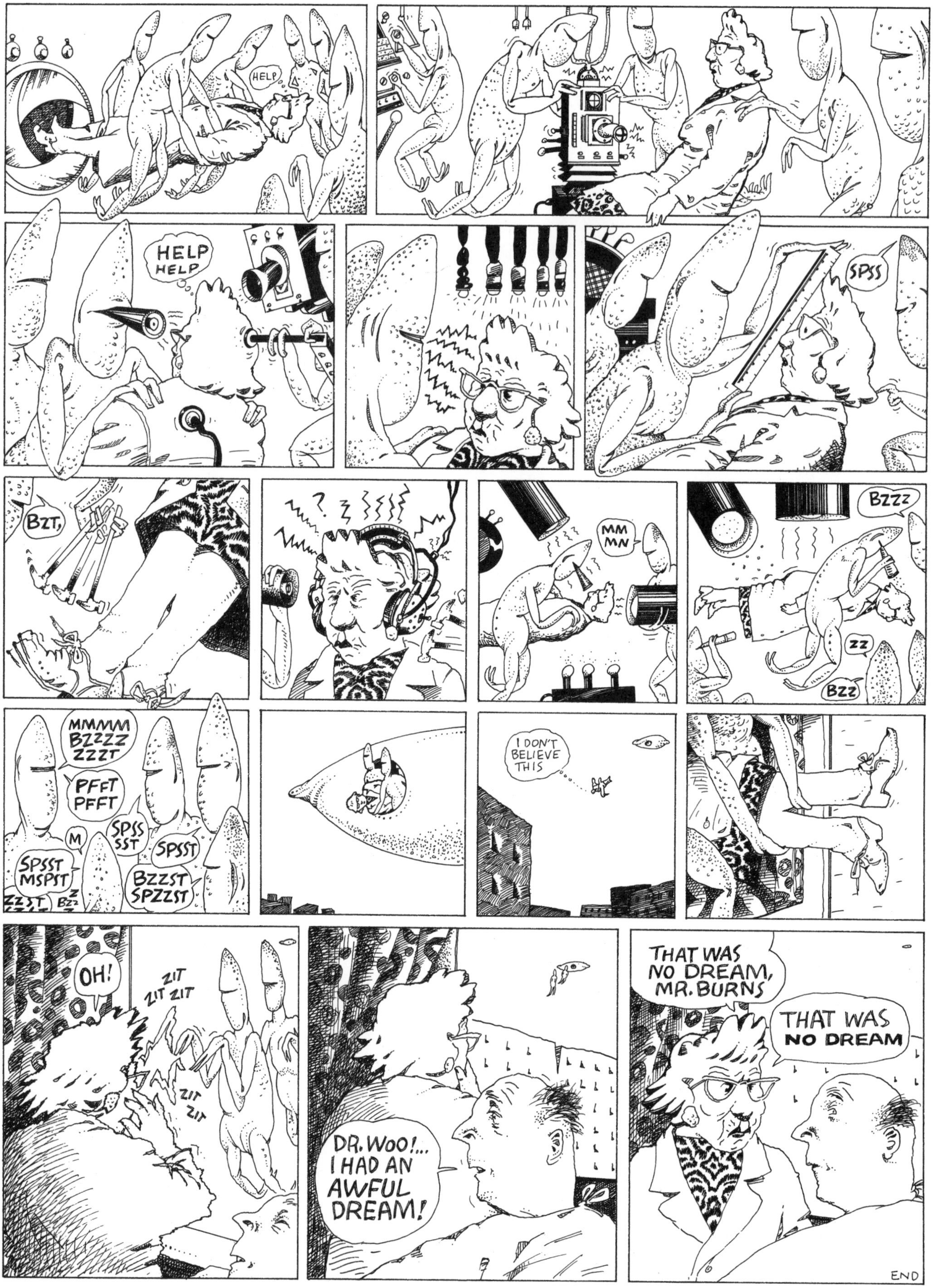

HELP
HELP
HELP
SPSS
BZT,
MM
MN
BZZZ
ZZ
BZZ
MMMM
BZZZZ
ZZZT
PFFT
PFFT
M
SPSS
SST
SPSST
SPSST
MSPST
BZZST
SPZZST
I DON'T
BELIEVE
THIS
OH!
ZIT
ZIT ZIT
ZIT
ZIT
DR. WOO!...
I HAD AN
AWFUL
DREAM!
THAT WAS
NO DREAM,
MR. BURNS
THAT WAS
NO DREAM
END

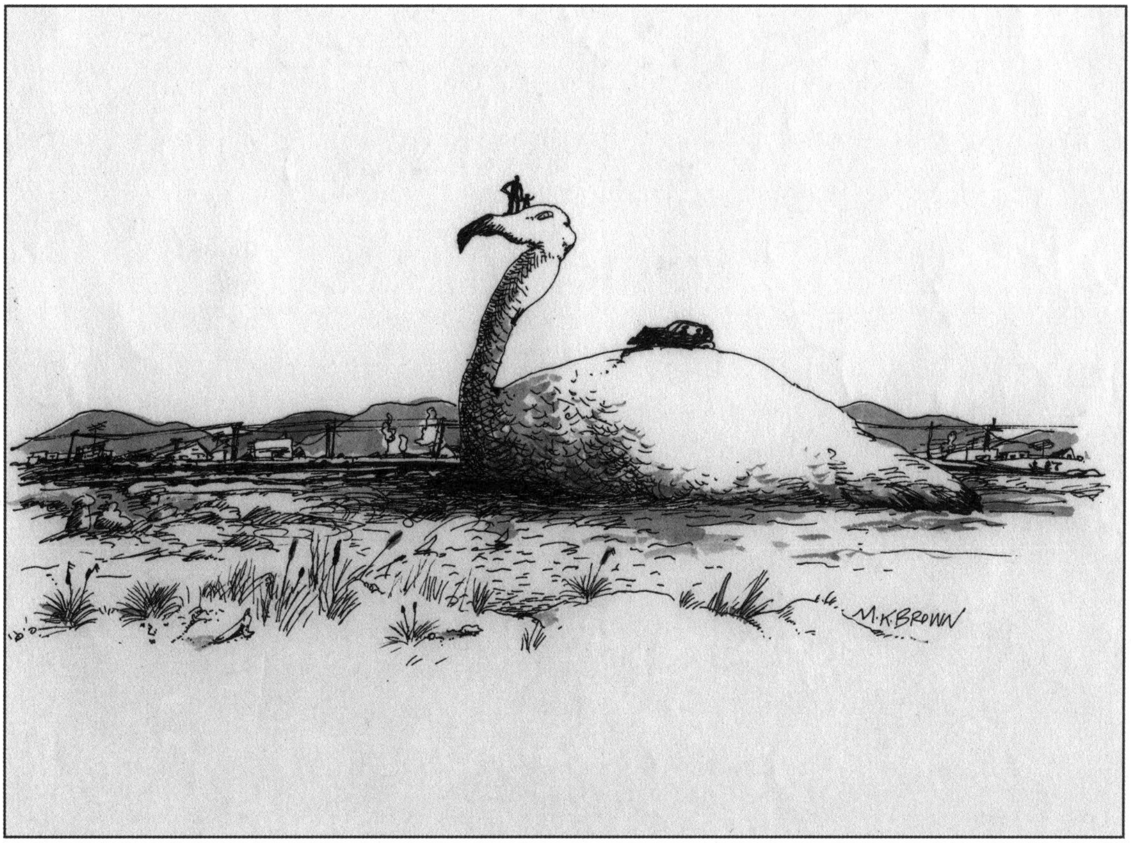
M.K.BROWN

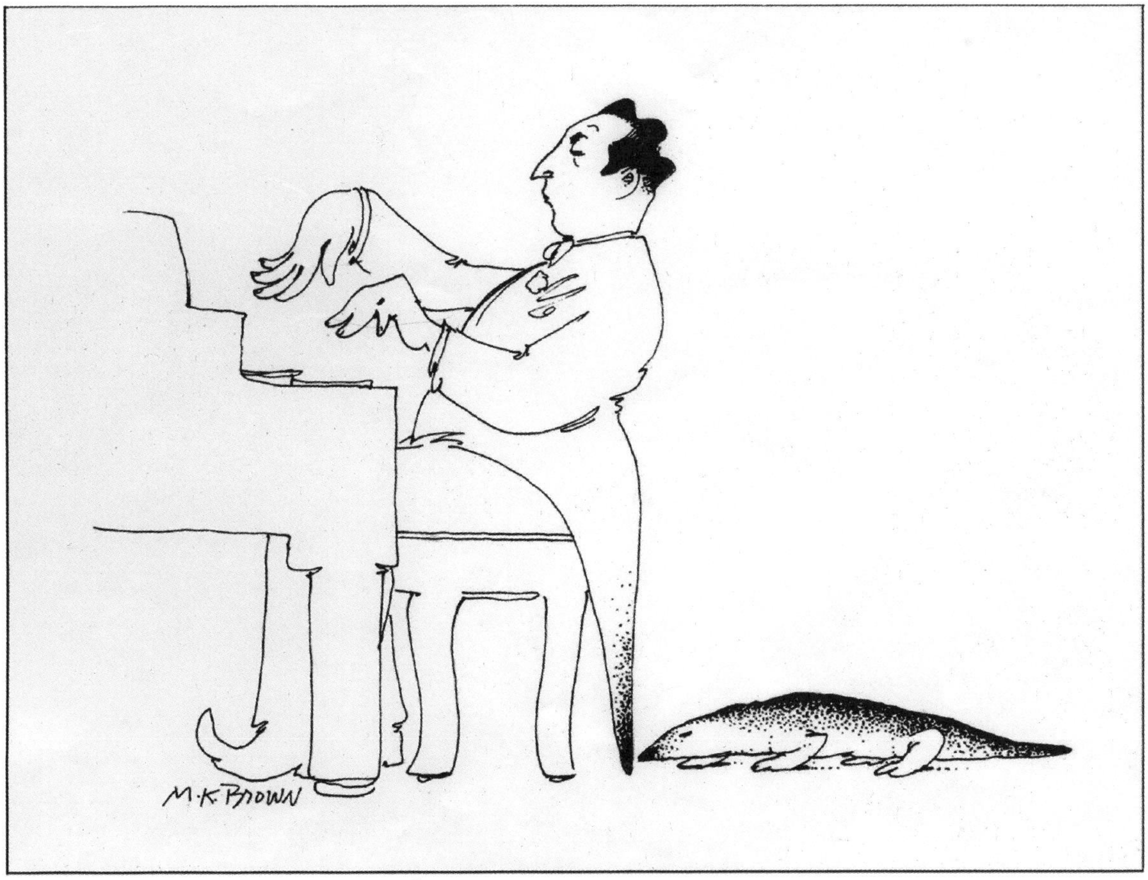
M.K.BROWN

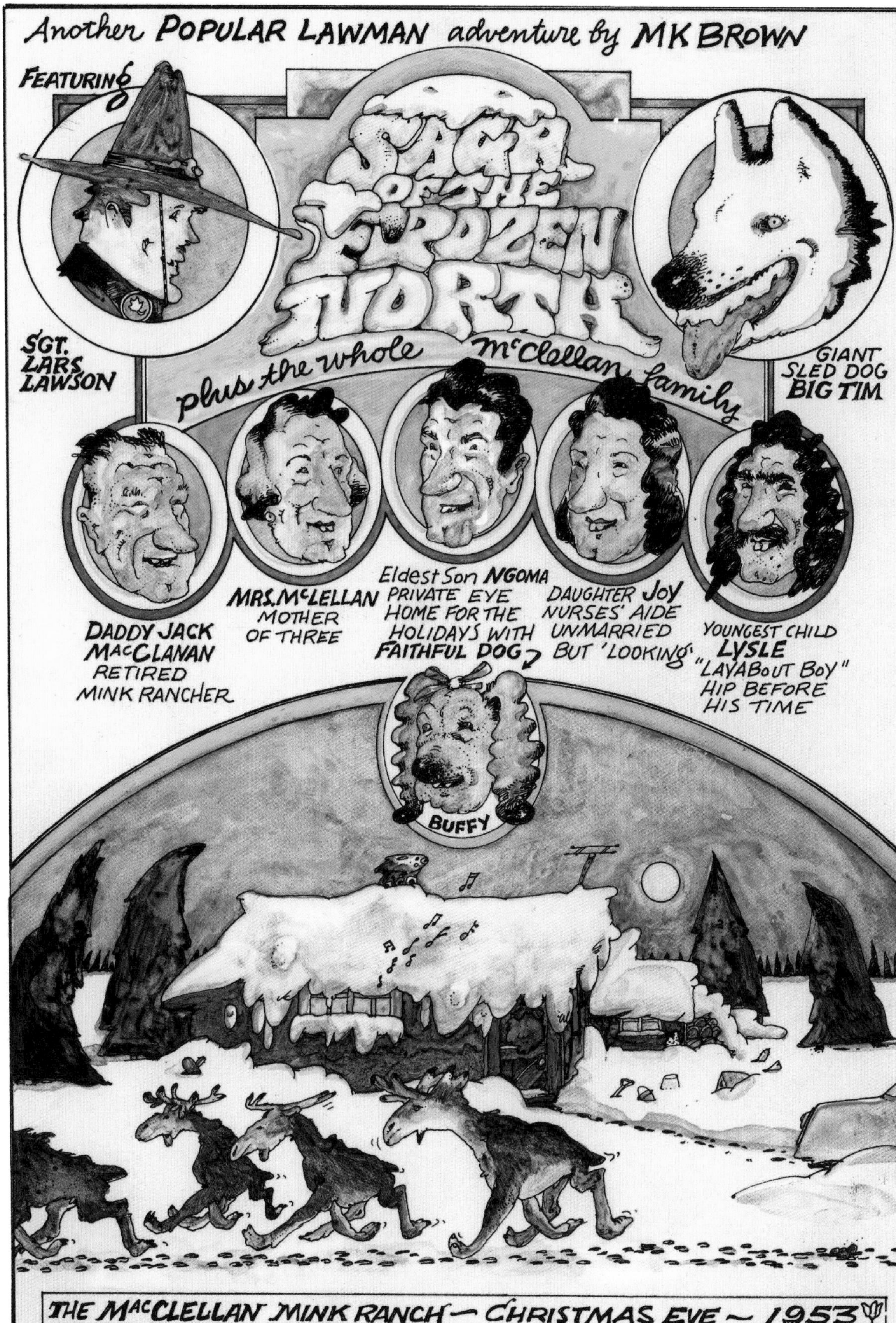
Another POPULAR LAWMAN adventure by MK BROWN
FEATURING
SAGA OF THE FROZEN NORTH
SGT. LARS LAWSON
plus the whole McClellan family
GIANT SLED DOG BIG TIM
DADDY JACK MacCLANAN RETIRED MINK RANCHER
MRS. McLELLAN MOTHER OF THREE
Eldest Son NGOMA PRIVATE EYE HOME FOR THE HOLIDAYS WITH FAITHFUL DOG
DAUGHTER JOY NURSES' AIDE UNMARRIED BUT 'LOOKING'
YOUNGEST CHILD LYSLE "LAYABOUT BOY" HIP BEFORE HIS TIME
BUFFY
THE MacCLELLAN MINK RANCH — CHRISTMAS EVE ~ 1953

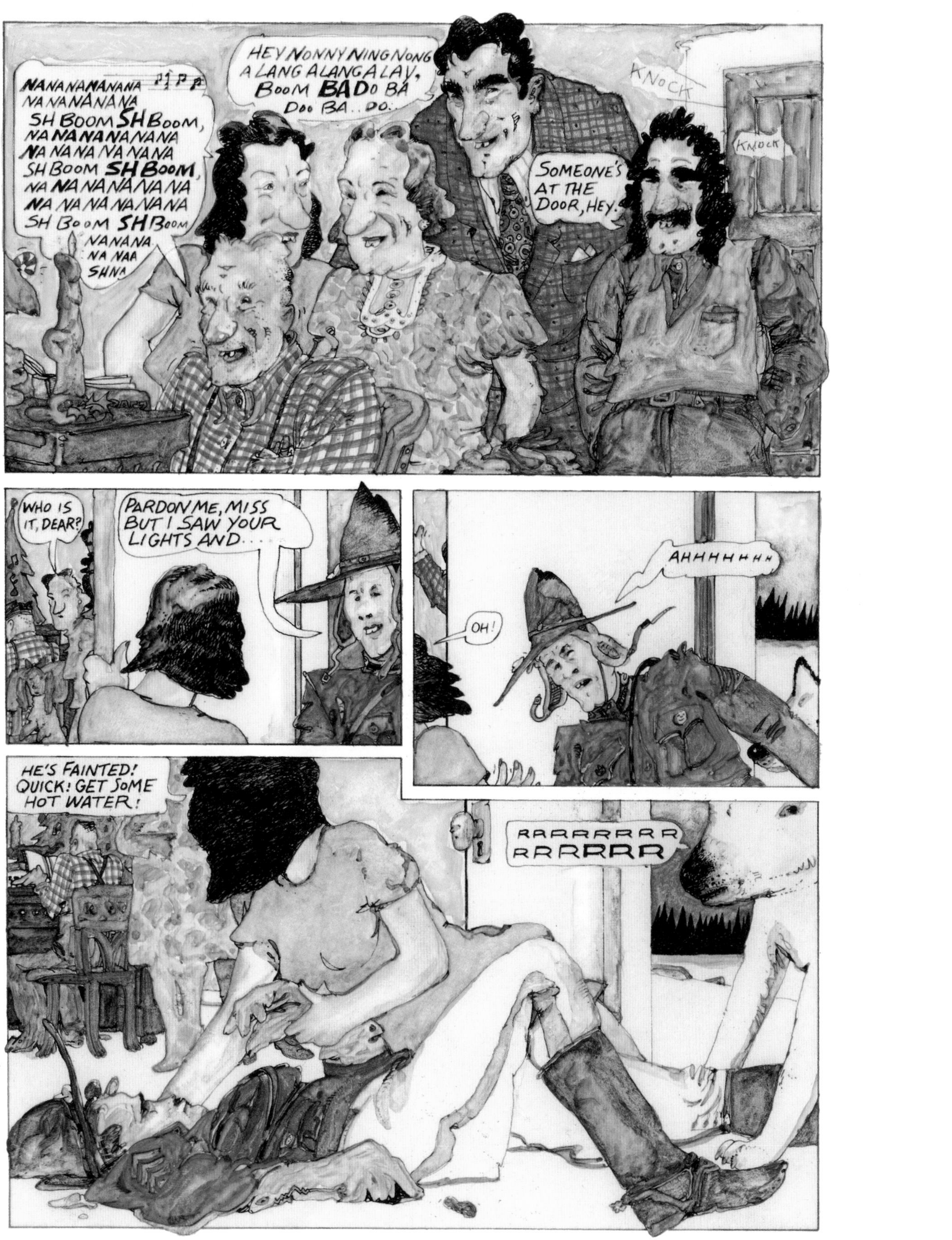

NANANANANANA NANANANANA SH BOOM SH BOOM, NANANANANANA NANANANANANA SH BOOM SH BOOM, NANANANANANA NANANANANANA SH BOOM SH BOOM NANANA NA NAA SHNA
HEY NONNY NING NONG A LANG ALANG ALAY, BOOM BADO BA DOO BA.. DO..
KNOCK
KNOCK
SOMEONE'S AT THE DOOR, HEY.
WHO IS IT, DEAR?
PARDON ME, MISS BUT I SAW YOUR LIGHTS AND.....
AHHHHHHH
OH!
HE'S FAINTED! QUICK: GET SOME HOT WATER!
RRRRRRRRR RRRRRRR

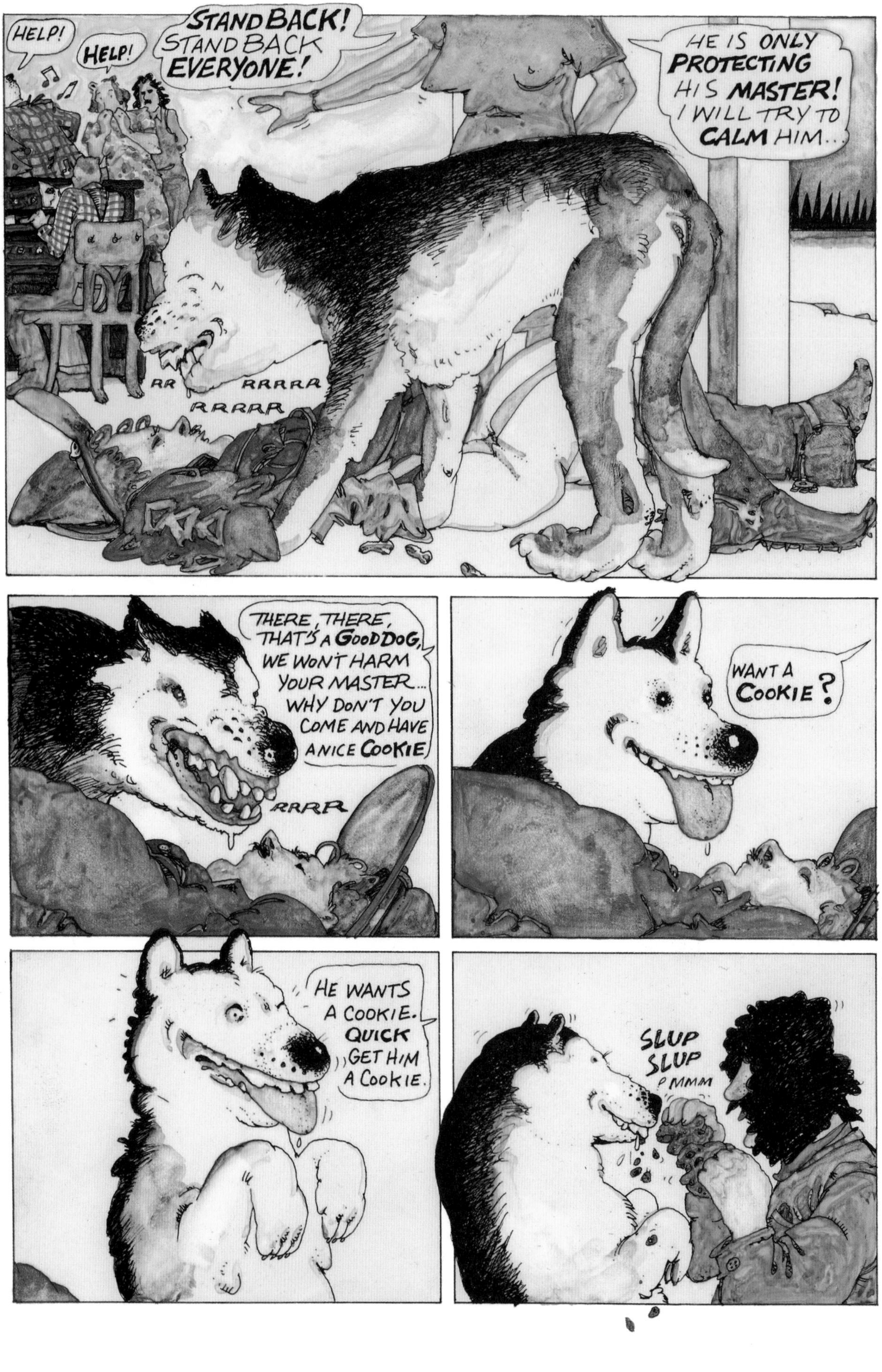
HELP!
HELP!
STAND BACK! STAND BACK EVERYONE!
HE IS ONLY PROTECTING HIS MASTER! I WILL TRY TO CALM HIM...
RR RRRRR
RRRRR
THERE, THERE, THAT'S A GOOD DOG, WE WON'T HARM YOUR MASTER... WHY DON'T YOU COME AND HAVE A NICE COOKIE
RRRR
WANT A COOKIE?
HE WANTS A COOKIE. QUICK GET HIM A COOKIE.
SLUP SLUP
MMM

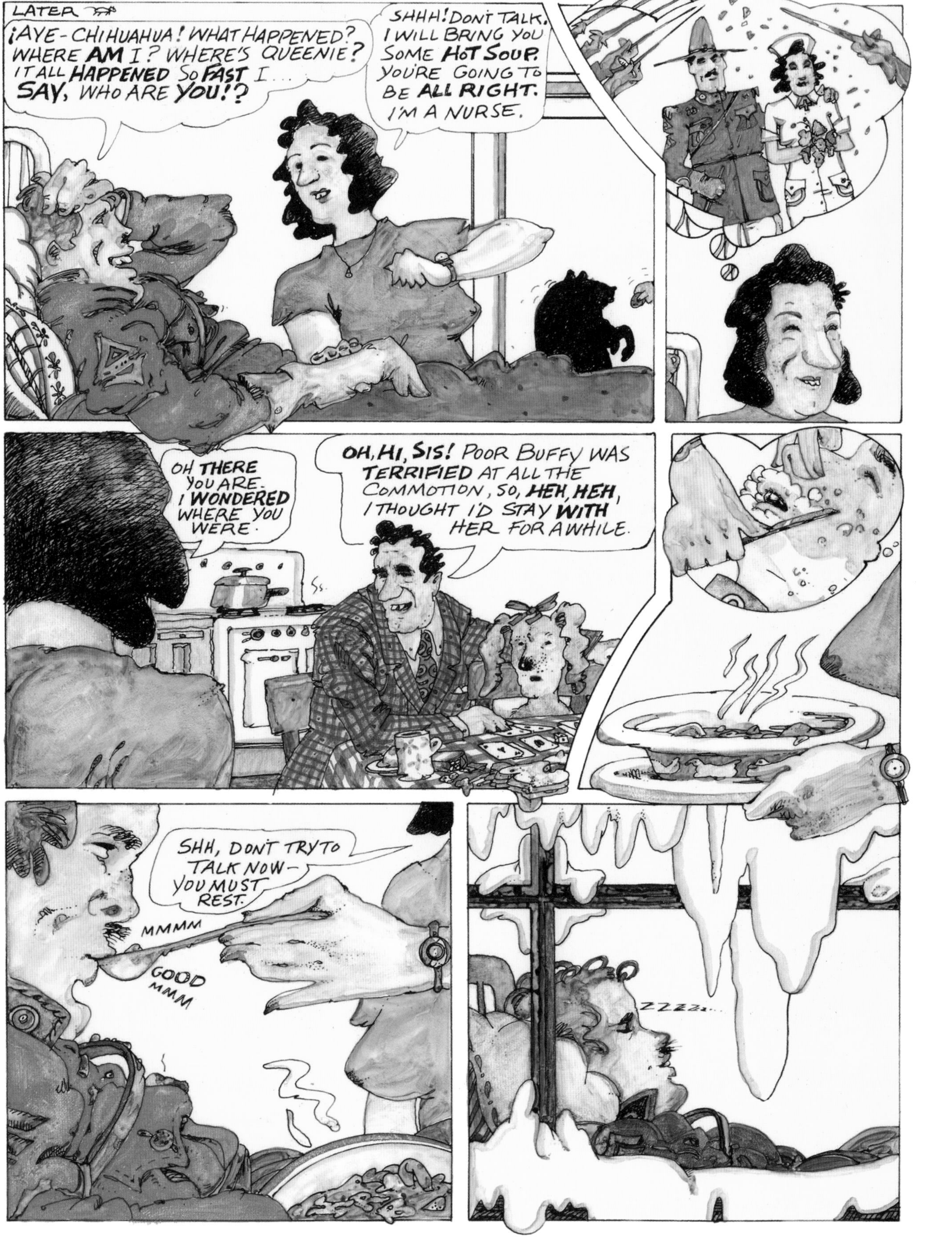
LATER
¡AYE-CHIHUAHUA! WHAT HAPPENED? WHERE AM I? WHERE'S QUEENIE? IT ALL HAPPENED SO FAST I... SAY, WHO ARE YOU!?
SHHH! DON'T TALK. I WILL BRING YOU SOME HOT SOUP. YOU'RE GOING TO BE ALL RIGHT. I'M A NURSE.
OH THERE YOU ARE. I WONDERED WHERE YOU WERE.
OH, HI, SIS! POOR BUFFY WAS TERRIFIED AT ALL THE COMMOTION, SO, HEH, HEH, I THOUGHT I'D STAY WITH HER FOR AWHILE.
SHH, DON'T TRY TO TALK NOW— YOU MUST REST.
MMMM
GOOD MMM
ZZZZ...

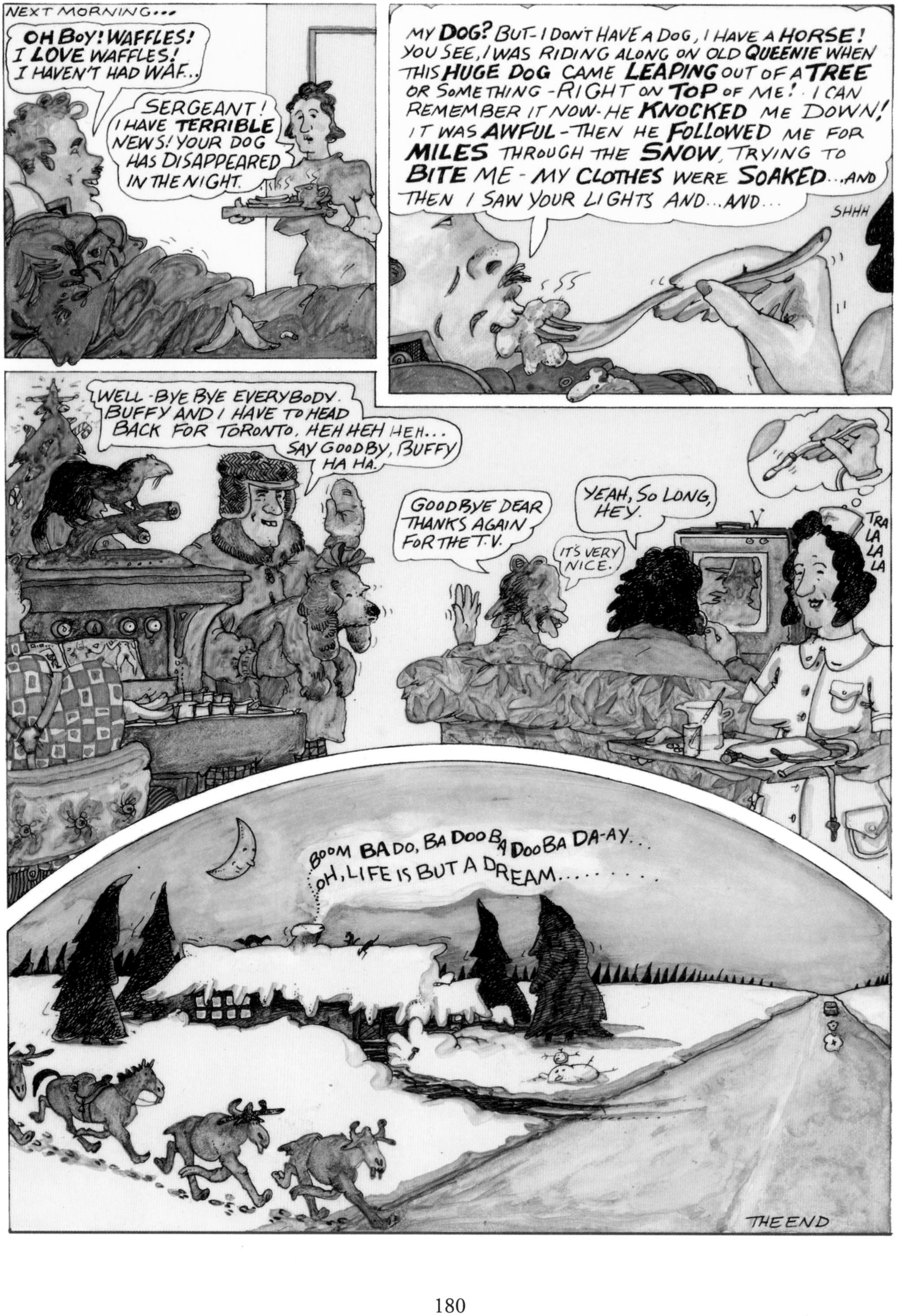
NEXT MORNING...
OH BOY! WAFFLES! I LOVE WAFFLES! I HAVEN'T HAD WAF...
SERGEANT! I HAVE TERRIBLE NEWS! YOUR DOG HAS DISAPPEARED IN THE NIGHT.
MY DOG? BUT- I DON'T HAVE A DOG, I HAVE A HORSE! YOU SEE, I WAS RIDING ALONG ON OLD QUEENIE WHEN THIS HUGE DOG CAME LEAPING OUT OF A TREE OR SOMETHING - RIGHT ON TOP OF ME! I CAN REMEMBER IT NOW - HE KNOCKED ME DOWN! IT WAS AWFUL - THEN HE FOLLOWED ME FOR MILES THROUGH THE SNOW, TRYING TO BITE ME - MY CLOTHES WERE SOAKED...AND THEN I SAW YOUR LIGHTS AND...AND...
SHHH
WELL - BYE BYE EVERYBODY. BUFFY AND I HAVE TO HEAD BACK FOR TORONTO, HEH HEH HEH... SAY GOODBY, BUFFY HA HA.
GOODBYE DEAR THANKS AGAIN FOR THE T.V.
YEAH, SO LONG, HEY.
IT'S VERY NICE.
TRA LA LA LA
BOOM BA DO, BA DOO BA DOO BA DA-AY... OH, LIFE IS BUT A DREAM.........
THE END

Way Out West

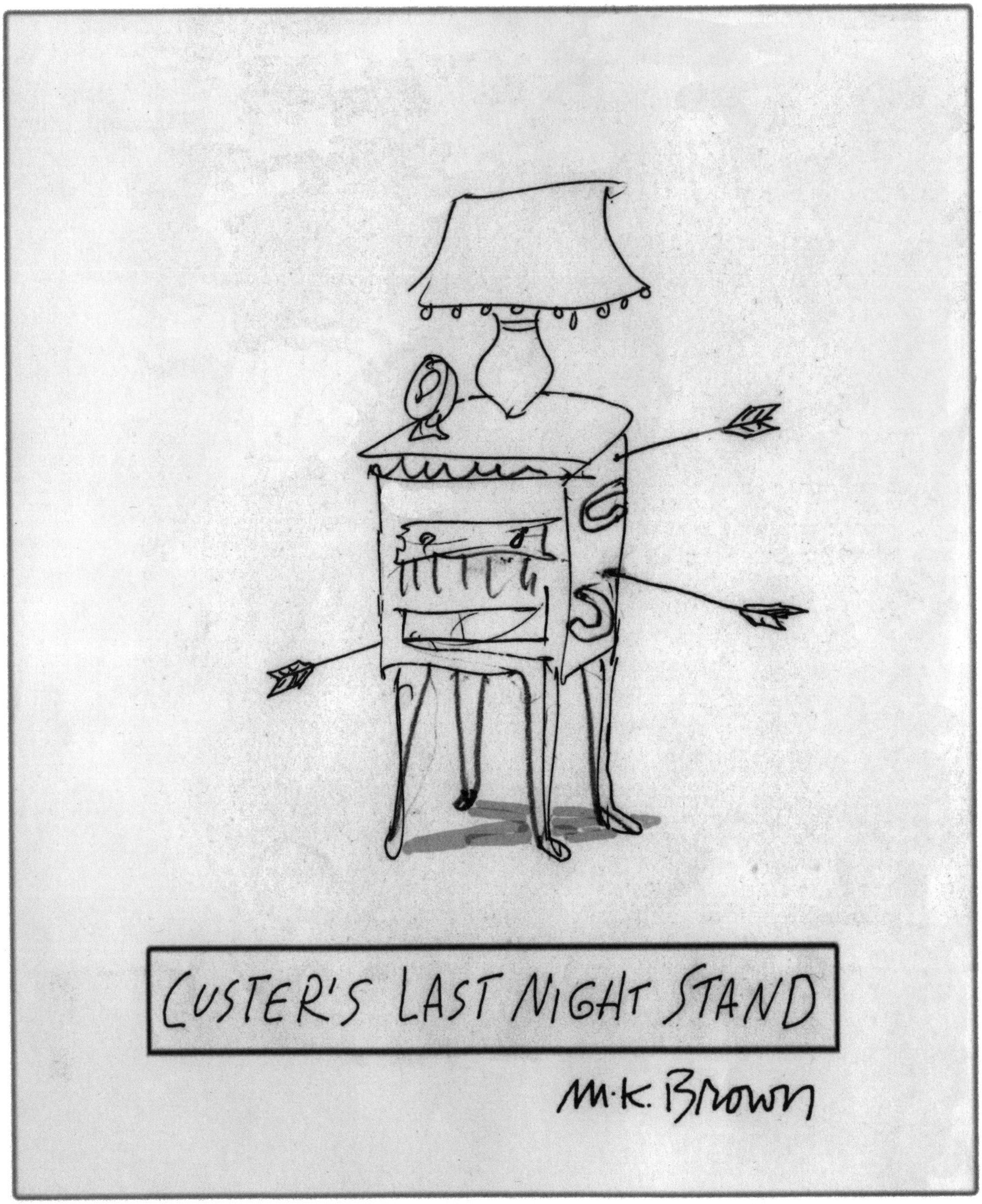
CUSTER'S LAST NIGHT STAND
M.K. Brown

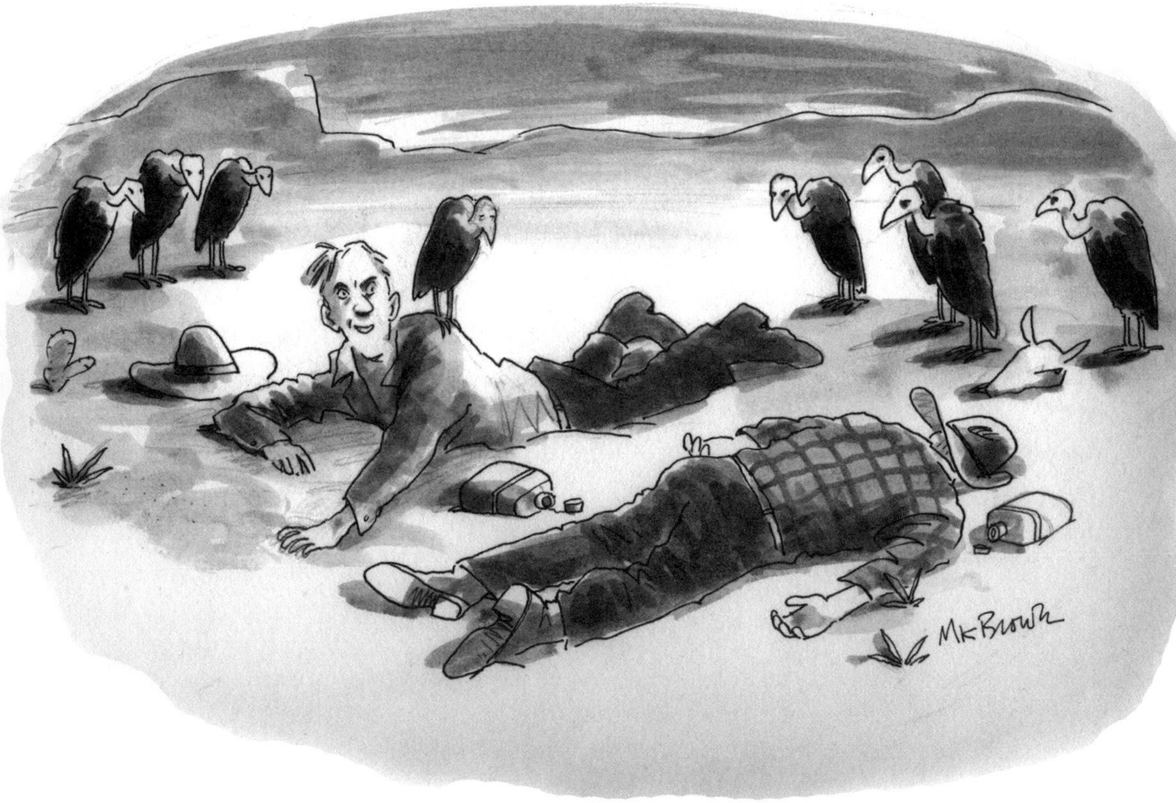
M.K. Brown

I just got this great idea for a screenplay.

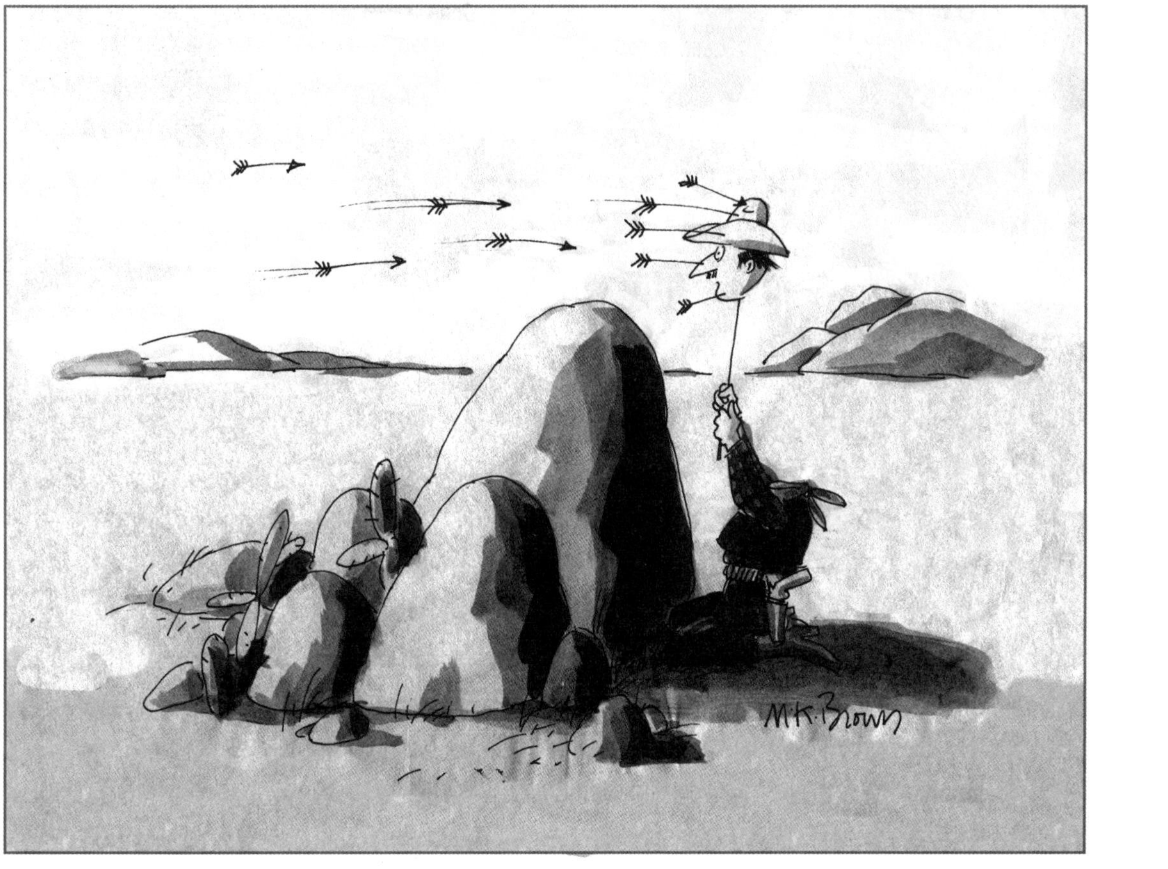
M.K. Brown

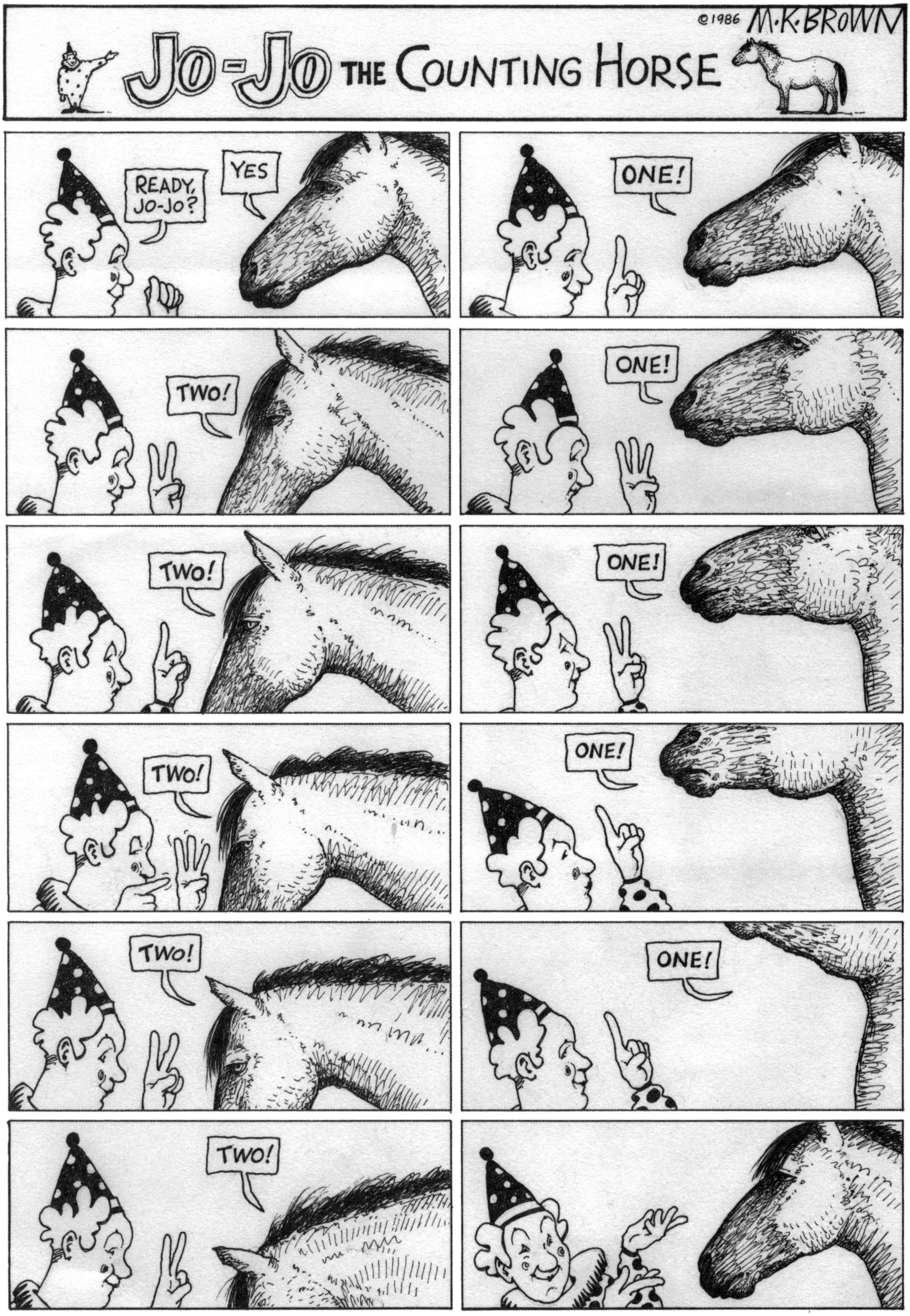
©1986 M.K.BROWN
JO-JO THE COUNTING HORSE
READY, JO-JO?
YES
ONE!
TWO!
ONE!
TWO!
ONE!
TWO!
ONE!
TWO!
ONE!
TWO!

"Western Romance" emerged when I had a horse and rode almost every day. Since I tend to draw what is currently happening around me, my cartoons became quite horsey for many years. We were living just outside San Francisco with a stable nearby and access to trails on open-space lands. One could ride all the way to the ocean, which I did on one occasion (underground hornet's nest, loose bulls, broken collarbone (not mine), sheriff's posse, etc.). Most of the time, however, there were long, relaxing rides on the California hills with plenty of time for fantasizing.

India   oil on panel   MK Brown

Western Romance

Part one

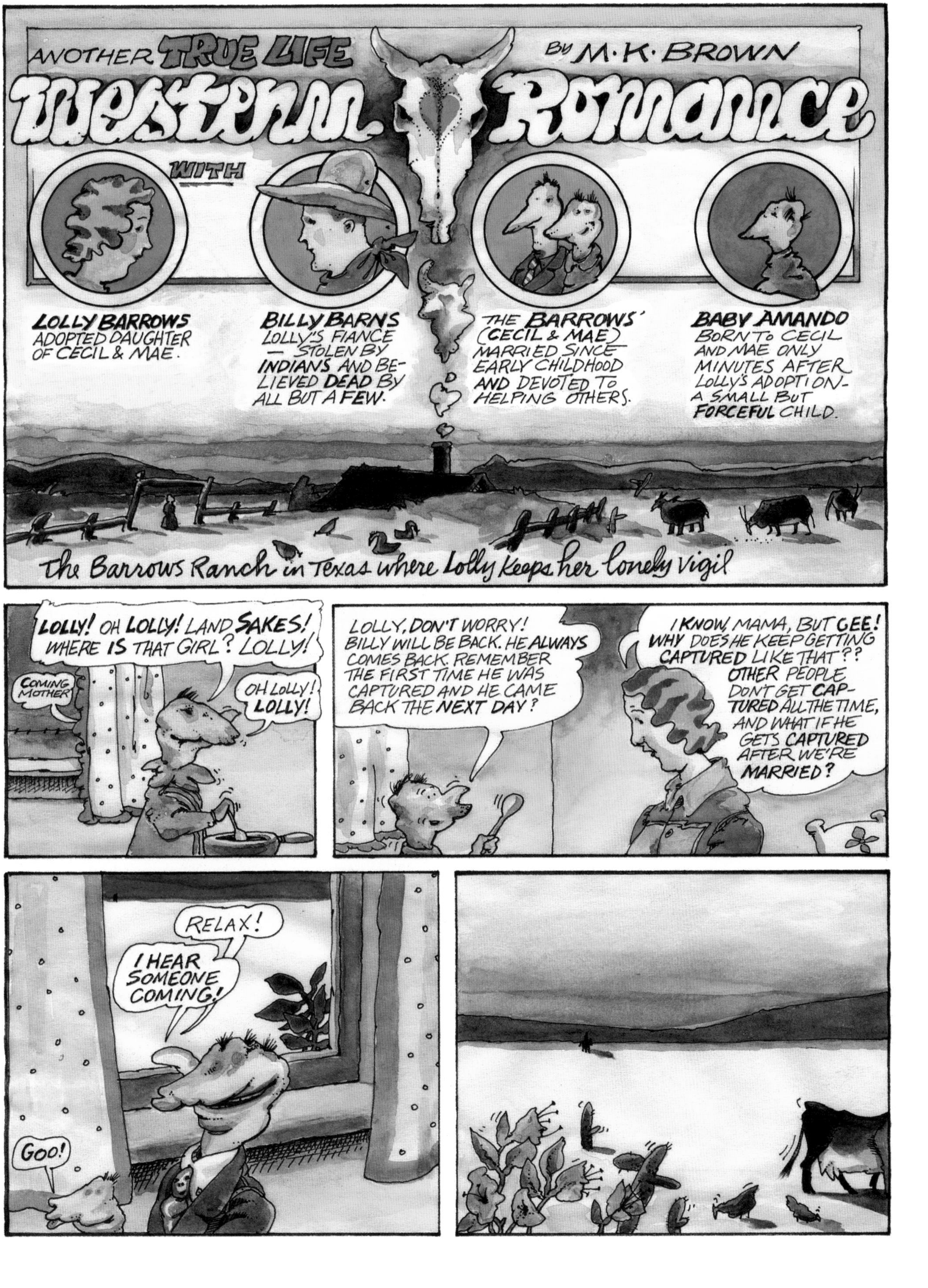
ANOTHER TRUE LIFE
BY M·K·BROWN
Western Romance
WITH
LOLLY BARROWS ADOPTED DAUGHTER OF CECIL & MAE.
BILLY BARNS LOLLY'S FIANCE — STOLEN BY INDIANS AND BELIEVED DEAD BY ALL BUT A FEW.
THE BARROWS' (CECIL & MAE) MARRIED SINCE EARLY CHILDHOOD AND DEVOTED TO HELPING OTHERS.
BABY AMANDO BORN TO CECIL AND MAE ONLY MINUTES AFTER LOLLY'S ADOPTION - A SMALL BUT FORCEFUL CHILD.
The Barrows Ranch in Texas where Lolly keeps her lonely vigil
LOLLY! OH LOLLY! LAND SAKES! WHERE IS THAT GIRL? LOLLY!
COMING MOTHER
OH LOLLY! LOLLY!
LOLLY, DON'T WORRY! BILLY WILL BE BACK. HE ALWAYS COMES BACK. REMEMBER THE FIRST TIME HE WAS CAPTURED AND HE CAME BACK THE NEXT DAY?
I KNOW, MAMA, BUT GEE! WHY DOES HE KEEP GETTING CAPTURED LIKE THAT?? OTHER PEOPLE DON'T GET CAPTURED ALL THE TIME, AND WHAT IF HE GETS CAPTURED AFTER WE'RE MARRIED?
RELAX!
I HEAR SOMEONE COMING!
GOO!

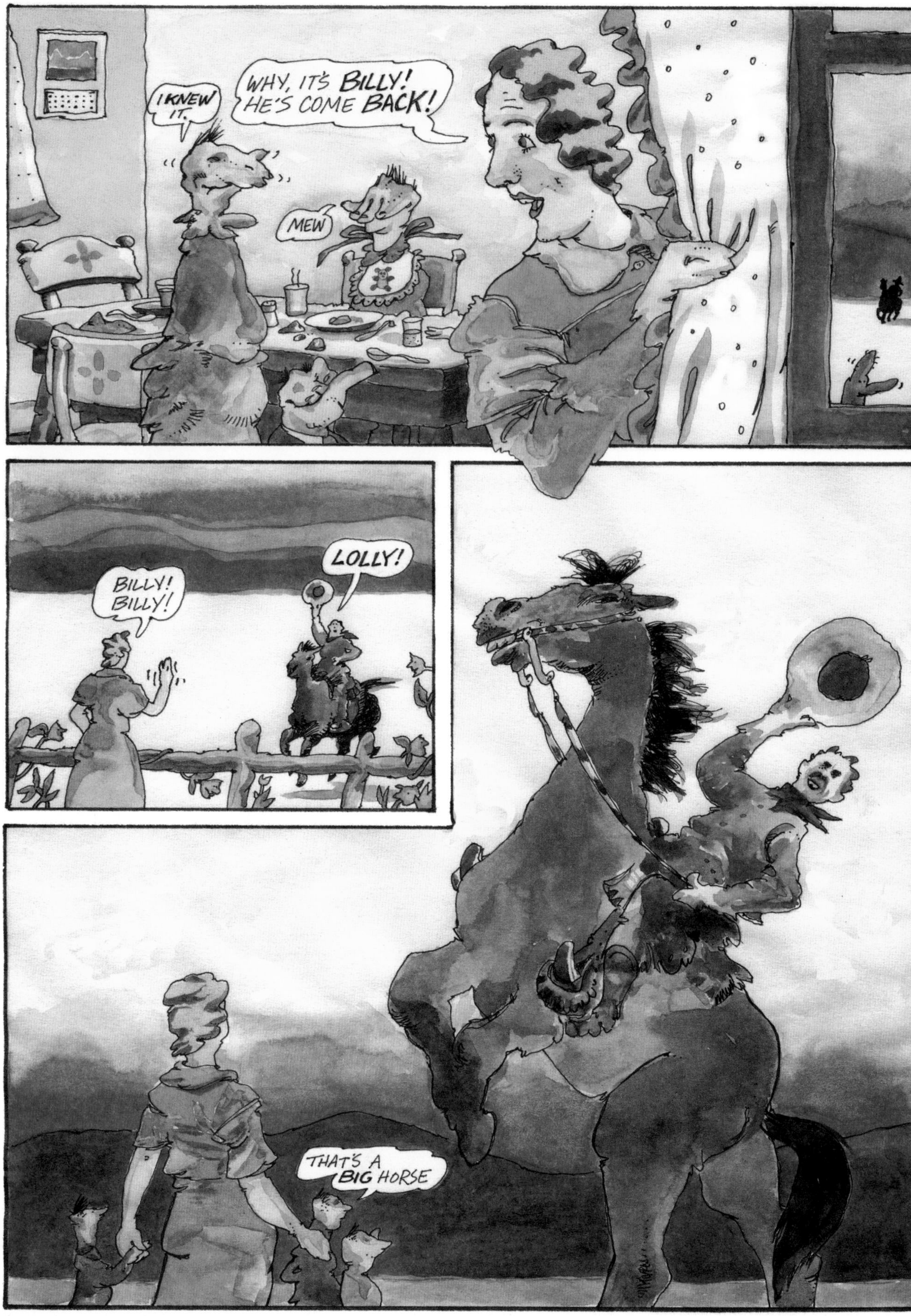
I KNEW IT.
WHY, IT'S BILLY! HE'S COME BACK!
MEW
BILLY! BILLY!
LOLLY!
THAT'S A BIG HORSE

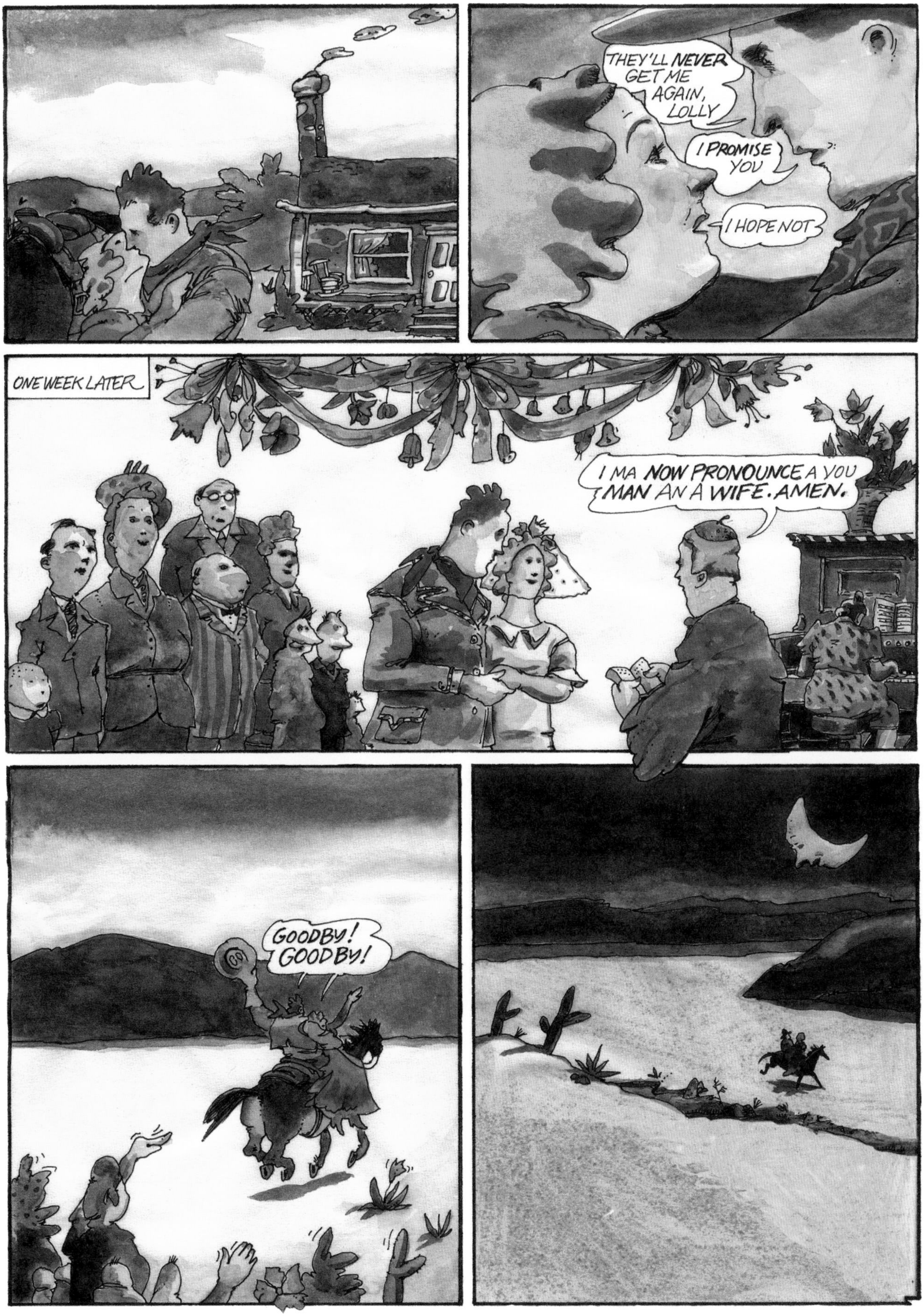
THEY'LL NEVER GET ME AGAIN, LOLLY
I PROMISE YOU
I HOPE NOT
ONE WEEK LATER
I MA NOW PRONOUNCE A YOU MAN AN A WIFE. AMEN.
GOODBY! GOODBY!

TO BE CONTINUED

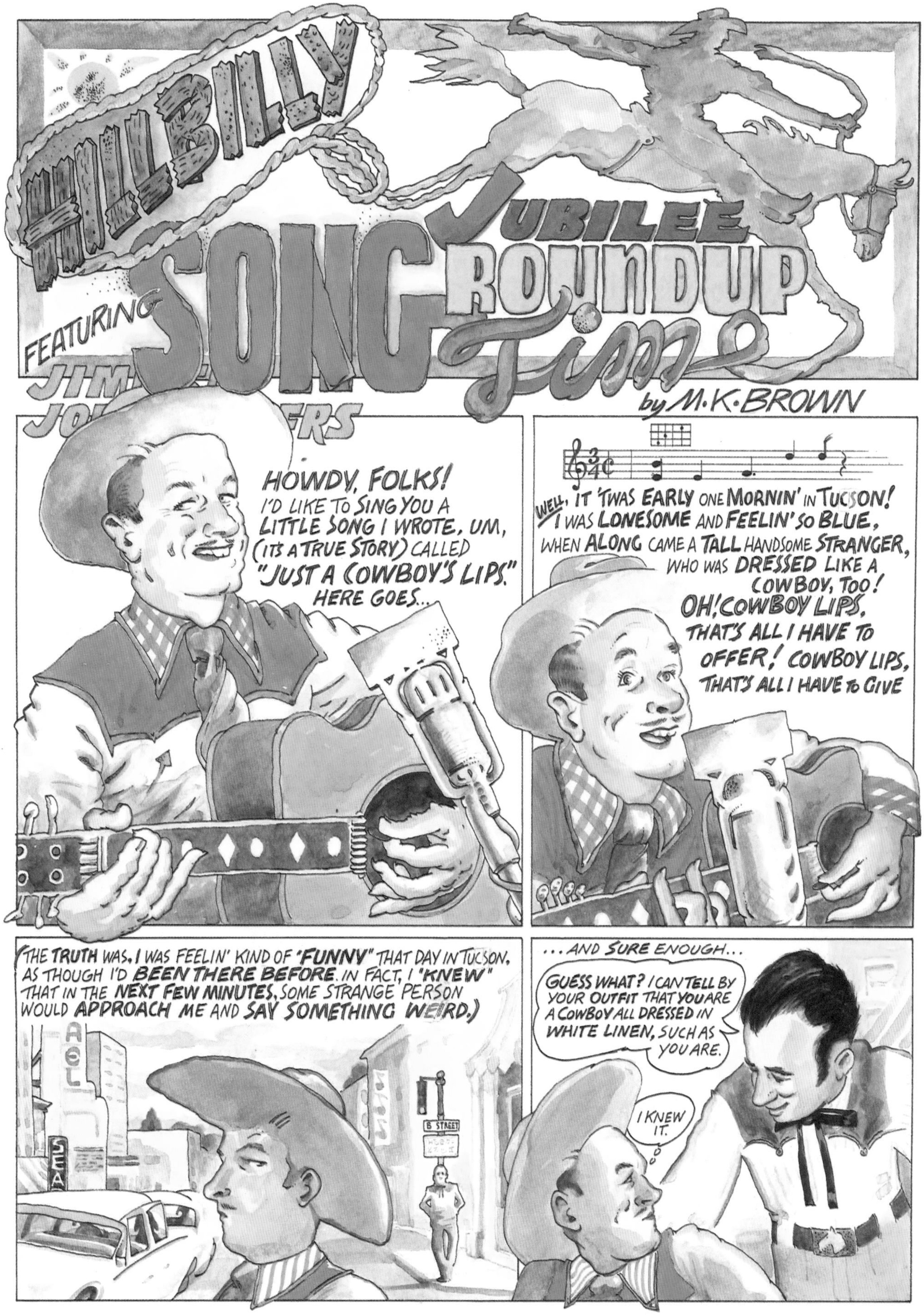

HILLBILLY JUBILEE
SONG ROUNDUP TIME
FEATURING JIM... JO...ERS
by M.K. BROWN
HOWDY, FOLKS! I'D LIKE TO SING YOU A LITTLE SONG I WROTE, UM, (IT'S A TRUE STORY) CALLED "JUST A COWBOY'S LIPS." HERE GOES...
WELL, IT 'TWAS EARLY ONE MORNIN' IN TUCSON! I WAS LONESOME AND FEELIN' SO BLUE, WHEN ALONG CAME A TALL HANDSOME STRANGER, WHO WAS DRESSED LIKE A COWBOY, TOO!
OH! COWBOY LIPS, THAT'S ALL I HAVE TO OFFER! COWBOY LIPS, THAT'S ALL I HAVE TO GIVE
(THE TRUTH WAS, I WAS FEELIN' KIND OF "FUNNY" THAT DAY IN TUCSON, AS THOUGH I'D BEEN THERE BEFORE. IN FACT, I "KNEW" THAT IN THE NEXT FEW MINUTES, SOME STRANGE PERSON WOULD APPROACH ME AND SAY SOMETHING WEIRD.)
B STREET
...AND SURE ENOUGH...
GUESS WHAT? I CAN TELL BY YOUR OUTFIT THAT YOU ARE A COWBOY ALL DRESSED IN WHITE LINEN, SUCH AS YOU ARE.
I KNEW IT.

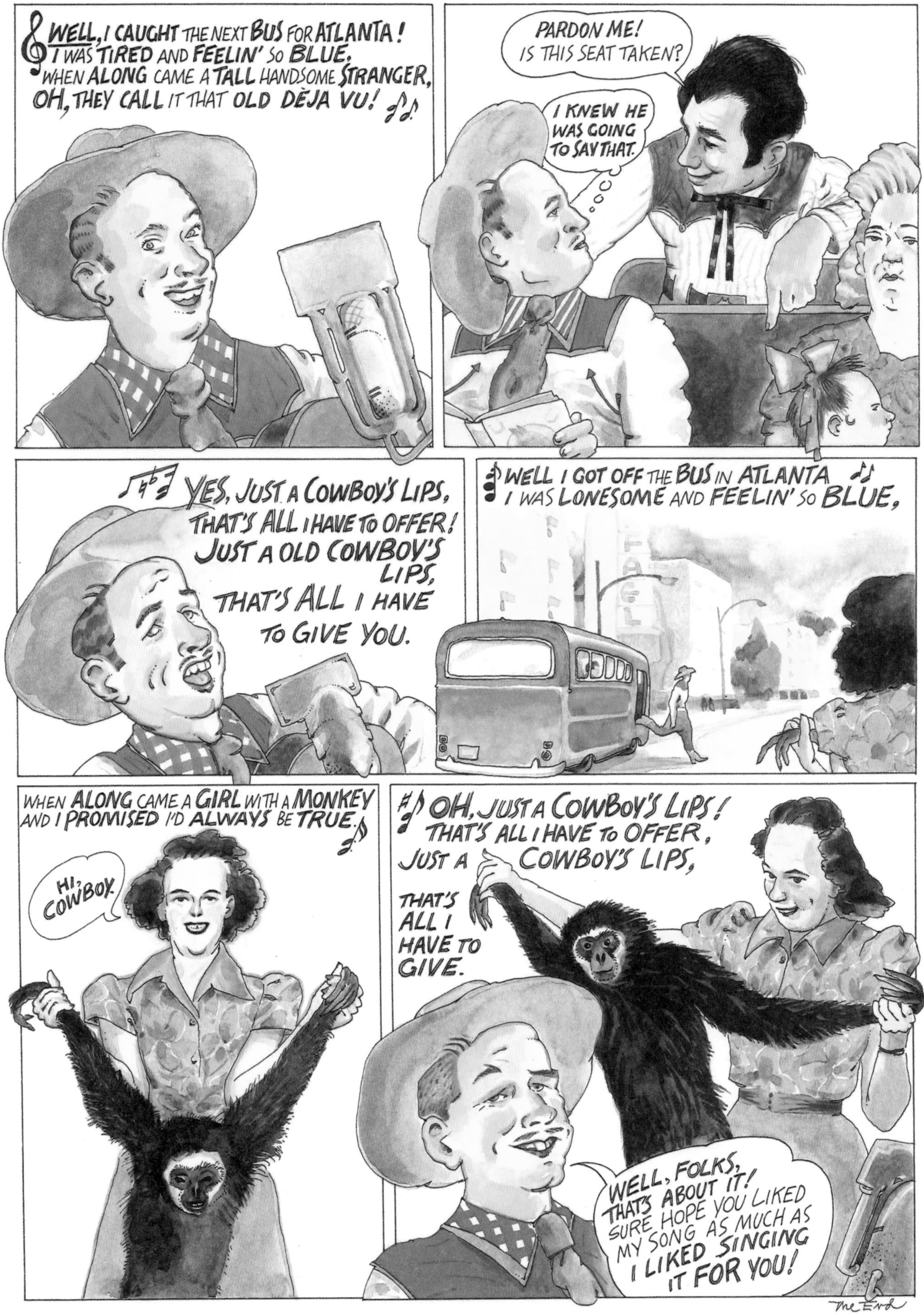
WELL, I CAUGHT THE NEXT BUS FOR ATLANTA! I WAS TIRED AND FEELIN' SO BLUE. WHEN ALONG CAME A TALL HANDSOME STRANGER, OH, THEY CALL IT THAT OLD DÈJA VU!
PARDON ME! IS THIS SEAT TAKEN?
I KNEW HE WAS GOING TO SAY THAT.
YES, JUST A COWBOY'S LIPS, THAT'S ALL I HAVE TO OFFER! JUST A OLD COWBOY'S LIPS, THAT'S ALL I HAVE TO GIVE YOU.
WELL I GOT OFF THE BUS IN ATLANTA I WAS LONESOME AND FEELIN' SO BLUE,
WHEN ALONG CAME A GIRL WITH A MONKEY AND I PROMISED I'D ALWAYS BE TRUE.
HI, COWBOY.
OH, JUST A COWBOY'S LIPS! THAT'S ALL I HAVE TO OFFER, JUST A COWBOY'S LIPS, THAT'S ALL I HAVE TO GIVE.
WELL, FOLKS, THAT'S ABOUT IT! SURE HOPE YOU LIKED MY SONG AS MUCH AS I LIKED SINGING IT FOR YOU!
The End

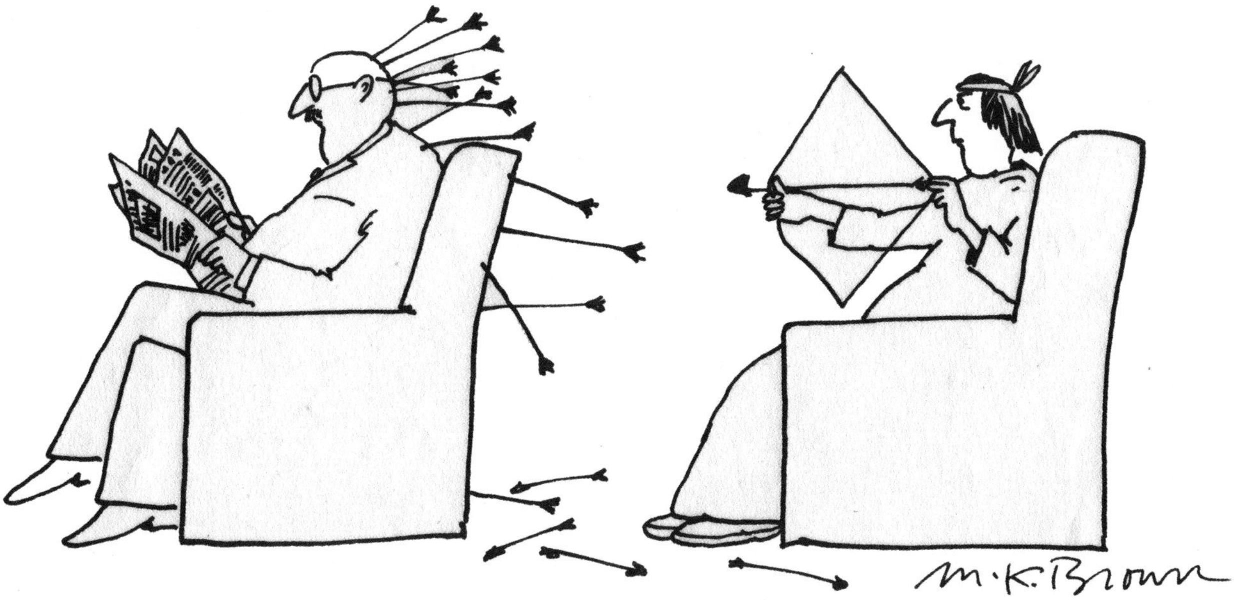
M.K.Brown

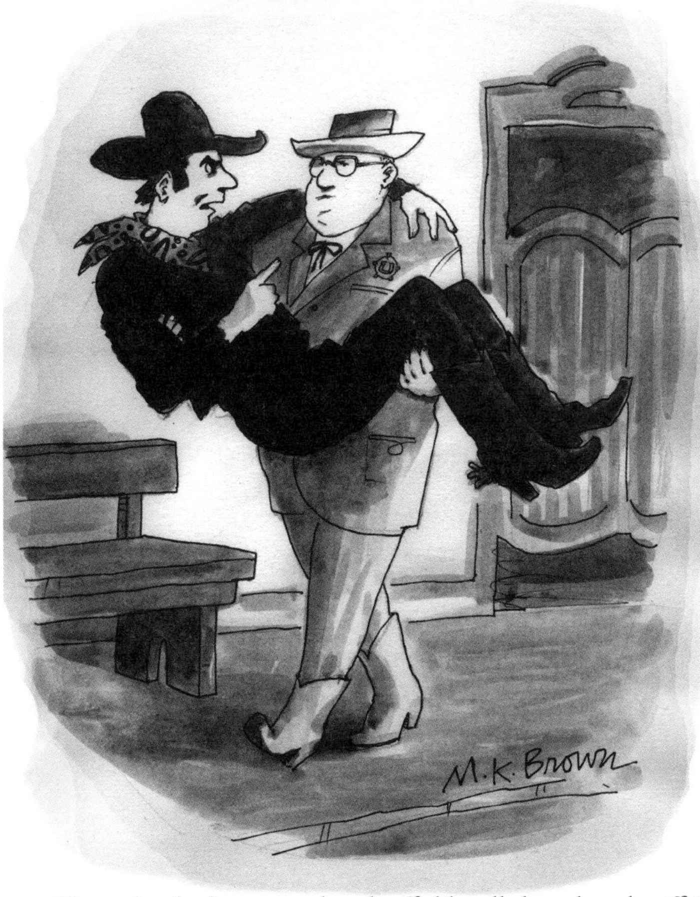
M.K.Brown

Hey, why don't you use handcuffs like all the other sheriffs?

Western Romance

Part two

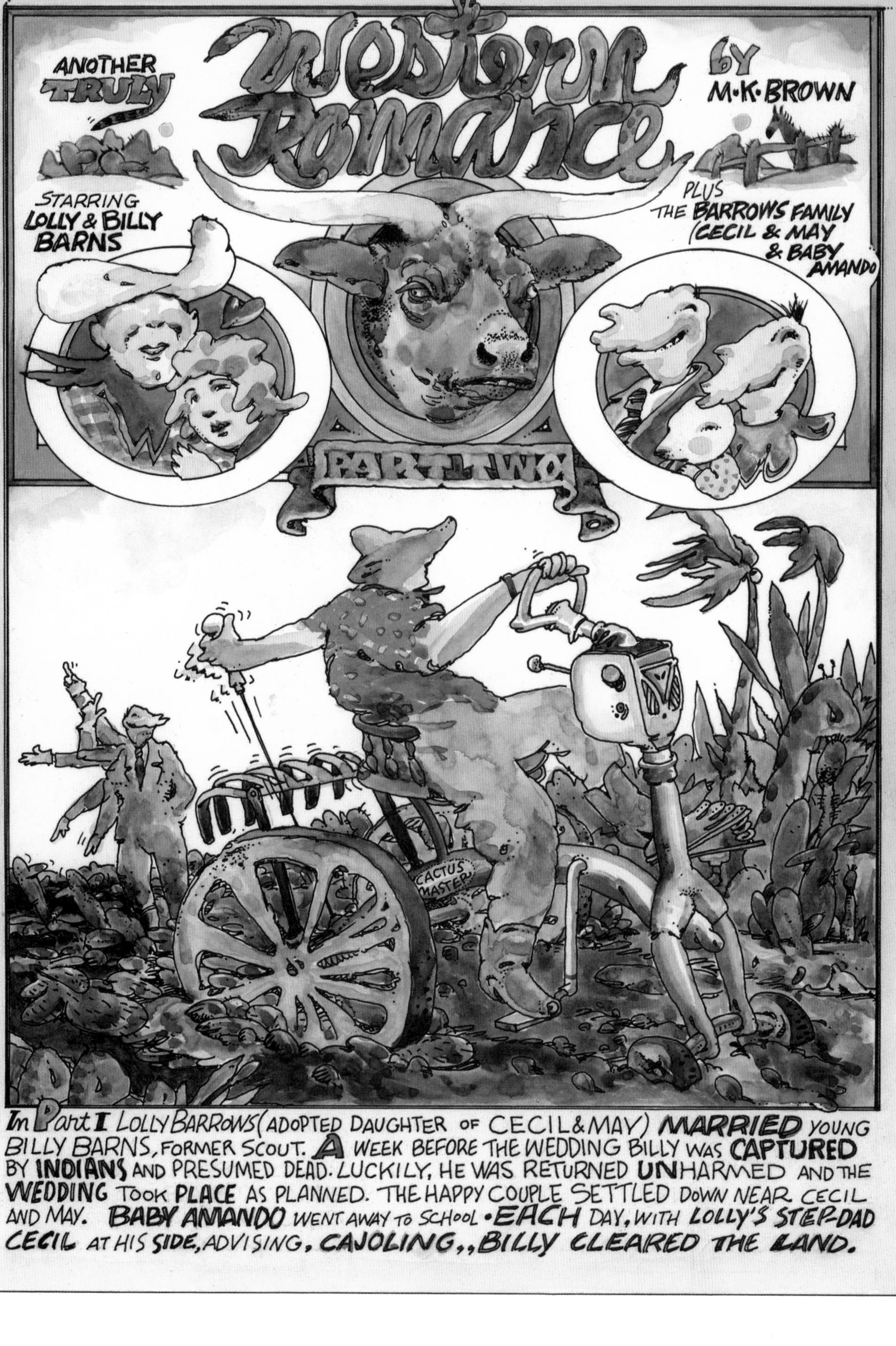
ANOTHER TRULY
Western Romance
BY M·K·BROWN
STARRING LOLLY & BILLY BARNS
PLUS THE BARROWS FAMILY (CECIL & MAY & BABY AMANDO
PART TWO
CACTUS MASTER
In Part I LOLLY BARROWS (ADOPTED DAUGHTER OF CECIL & MAY) MARRIED YOUNG BILLY BARNS, FORMER SCOUT. A WEEK BEFORE THE WEDDING BILLY WAS CAPTURED BY INDIANS AND PRESUMED DEAD. LUCKILY, HE WAS RETURNED UNHARMED AND THE WEDDING TOOK PLACE AS PLANNED. THE HAPPY COUPLE SETTLED DOWN NEAR CECIL AND MAY. BABY AMANDO WENT AWAY TO SCHOOL • EACH DAY, WITH LOLLY'S STEP-DAD CECIL AT HIS SIDE, ADVISING, CAJOLING,, BILLY CLEARED THE LAND.

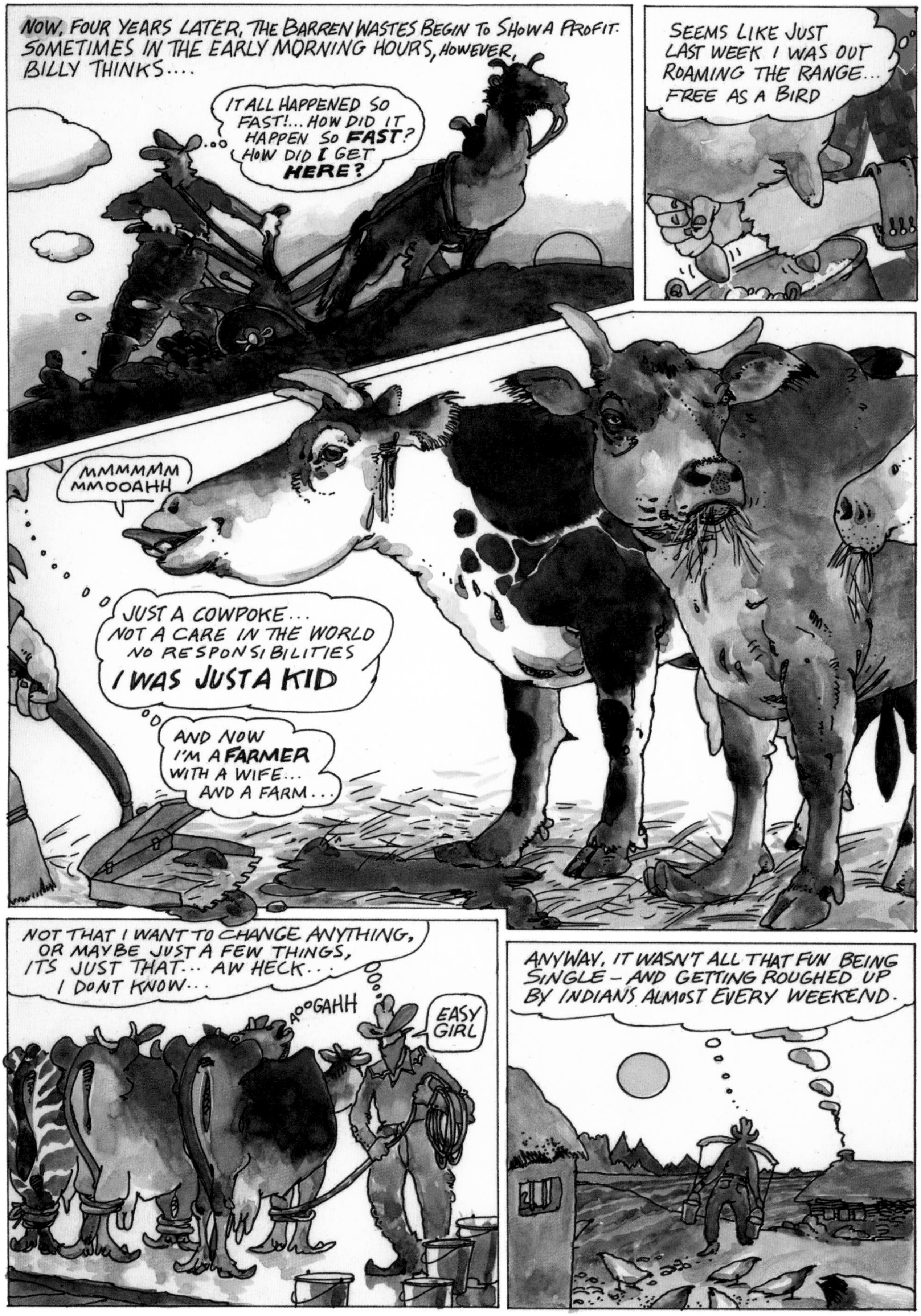
NOW, FOUR YEARS LATER, THE BARREN WASTES BEGIN TO SHOW A PROFIT. SOMETIMES IN THE EARLY MORNING HOURS, HOWEVER, BILLY THINKS....
IT ALL HAPPENED SO FAST!... HOW DID IT HAPPEN SO FAST? HOW DID I GET HERE?
SEEMS LIKE JUST LAST WEEK I WAS OUT ROAMING THE RANGE... FREE AS A BIRD
MMMMMM MMOOAHH
JUST A COWPOKE... NOT A CARE IN THE WORLD NO RESPONSIBILITIES I WAS JUST A KID
AND NOW I'M A FARMER WITH A WIFE... AND A FARM...
NOT THAT I WANT TO CHANGE ANYTHING, OR MAYBE JUST A FEW THINGS, ITS JUST THAT... AW HECK... I DONT KNOW...
AOOGAHH
EASY GIRL
ANYWAY, IT WASN'T ALL THAT FUN BEING SINGLE - AND GETTING ROUGHED UP BY INDIANS ALMOST EVERY WEEKEND.

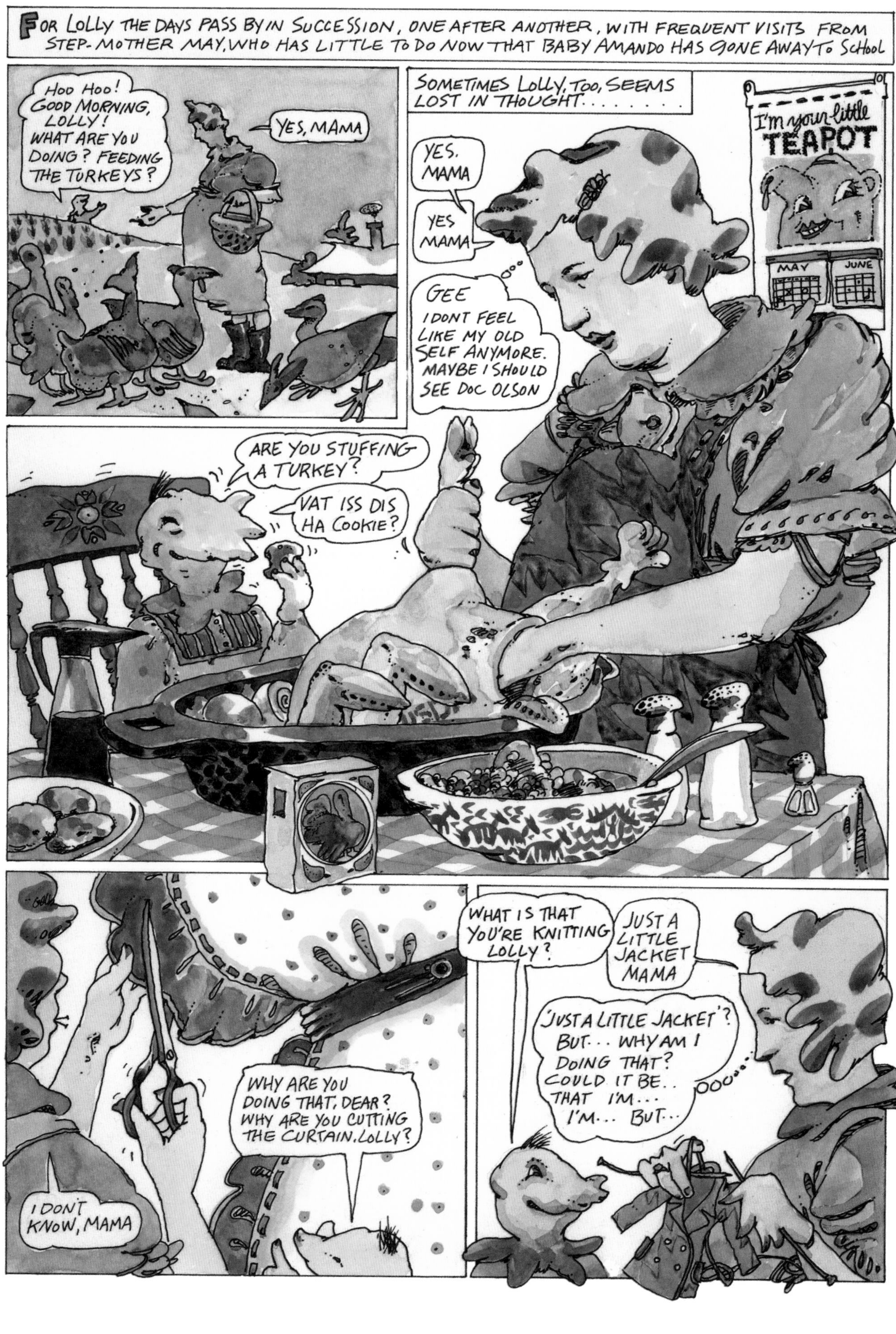

FOR LOLLY THE DAYS PASS BY IN SUCCESSION, ONE AFTER ANOTHER, WITH FREQUENT VISITS FROM STEP-MOTHER MAY, WHO HAS LITTLE TO DO NOW THAT BABY AMANDO HAS GONE AWAY TO SCHOOL
HOO HOO! GOOD MORNING, LOLLY! WHAT ARE YOU DOING? FEEDING THE TURKEYS?
YES, MAMA
SOMETIMES LOLLY, TOO, SEEMS LOST IN THOUGHT.........
YES. MAMA
YES MAMA
GEE I DONT FEEL LIKE MY OLD SELF ANYMORE. MAYBE I SHOULD SEE DOC OLSON
I'm your little TEAPOT
MAY
JUNE
ARE YOU STUFFING A TURKEY?
VAT ISS DIS HA COOKIE?
I DONT KNOW, MAMA
WHY ARE YOU DOING THAT, DEAR? WHY ARE YOU CUTTING THE CURTAIN, LOLLY?
WHAT IS THAT YOU'RE KNITTING LOLLY?
JUST A LITTLE JACKET MAMA
'JUST A LITTLE JACKET'? BUT... WHY AM I DOING THAT? COULD IT BE.. THAT I'M... I'M... BUT...

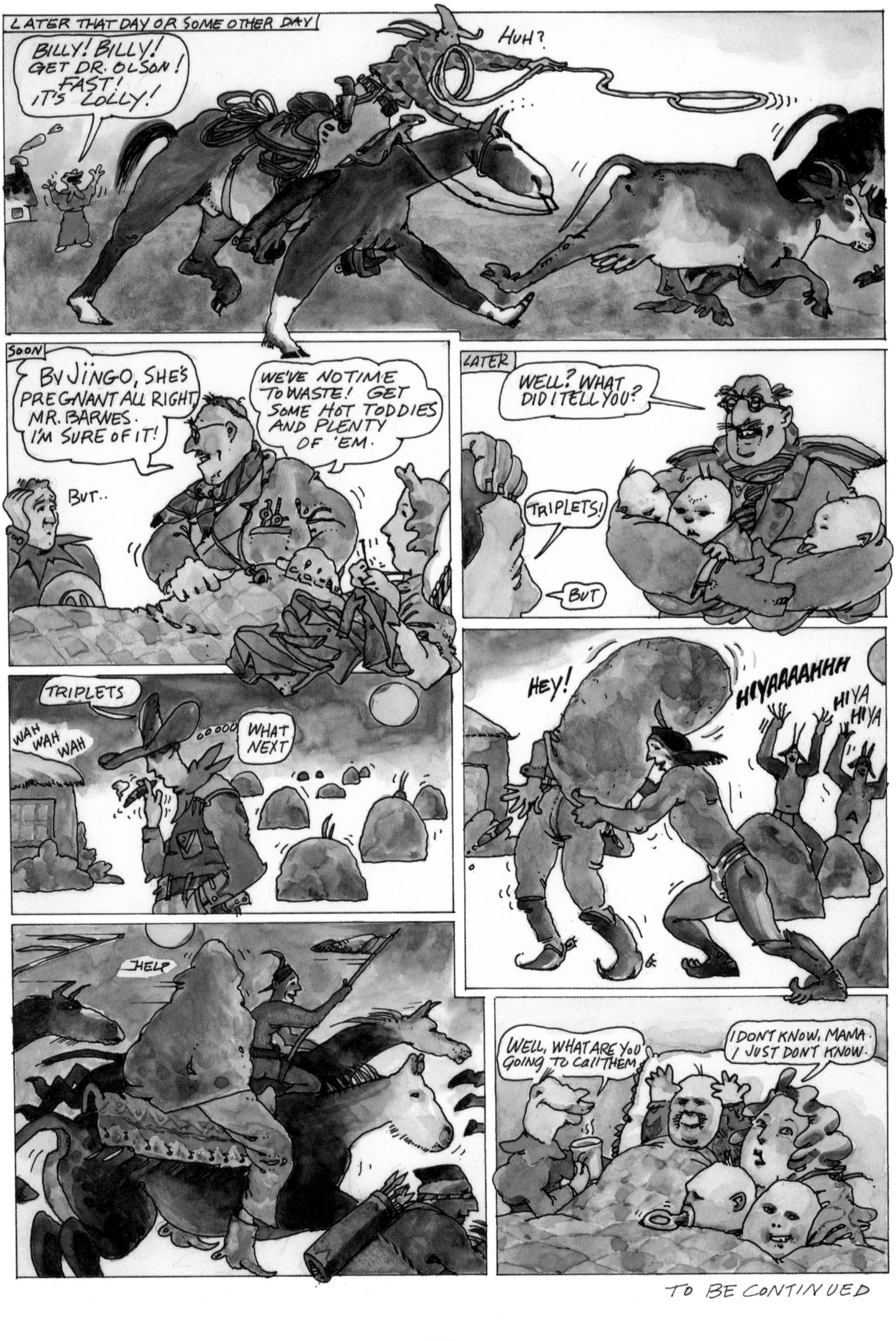
LATER THAT DAY OR SOME OTHER DAY
BILLY! BILLY! GET DR. OLSON! FAST! IT'S LOLLY!
HUH?
SOON
BY JINGO, SHE'S PREGNANT ALL RIGHT MR. BARNES. I'M SURE OF IT!
WE'VE NO TIME TO WASTE! GET SOME HOT TODDIES AND PLENTY OF 'EM.
BUT..
LATER
WELL? WHAT DID I TELL YOU?
TRIPLETS!
BUT
TRIPLETS
WAH WAH WAH
OOOOO
WHAT NEXT
HEY!
HIYAAAAHHH
HIYA HIYA
HELP
WELL, WHAT ARE YOU GOING TO CALL THEM
I DON'T KNOW, MAMA. I JUST DON'T KNOW.

TO BE CONTINUED

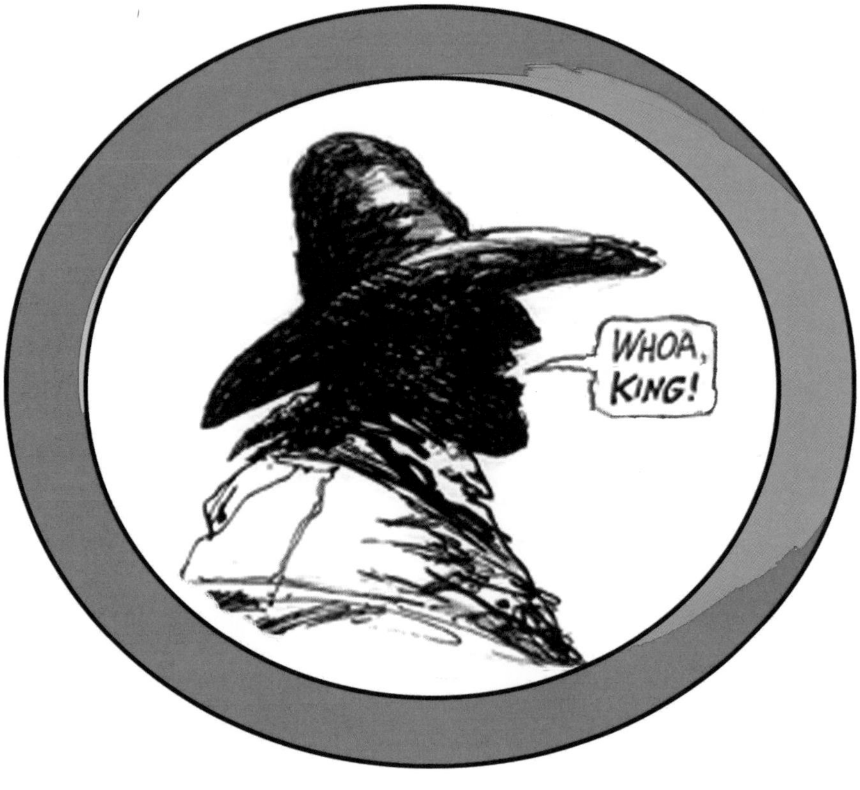
WHOA, KING!

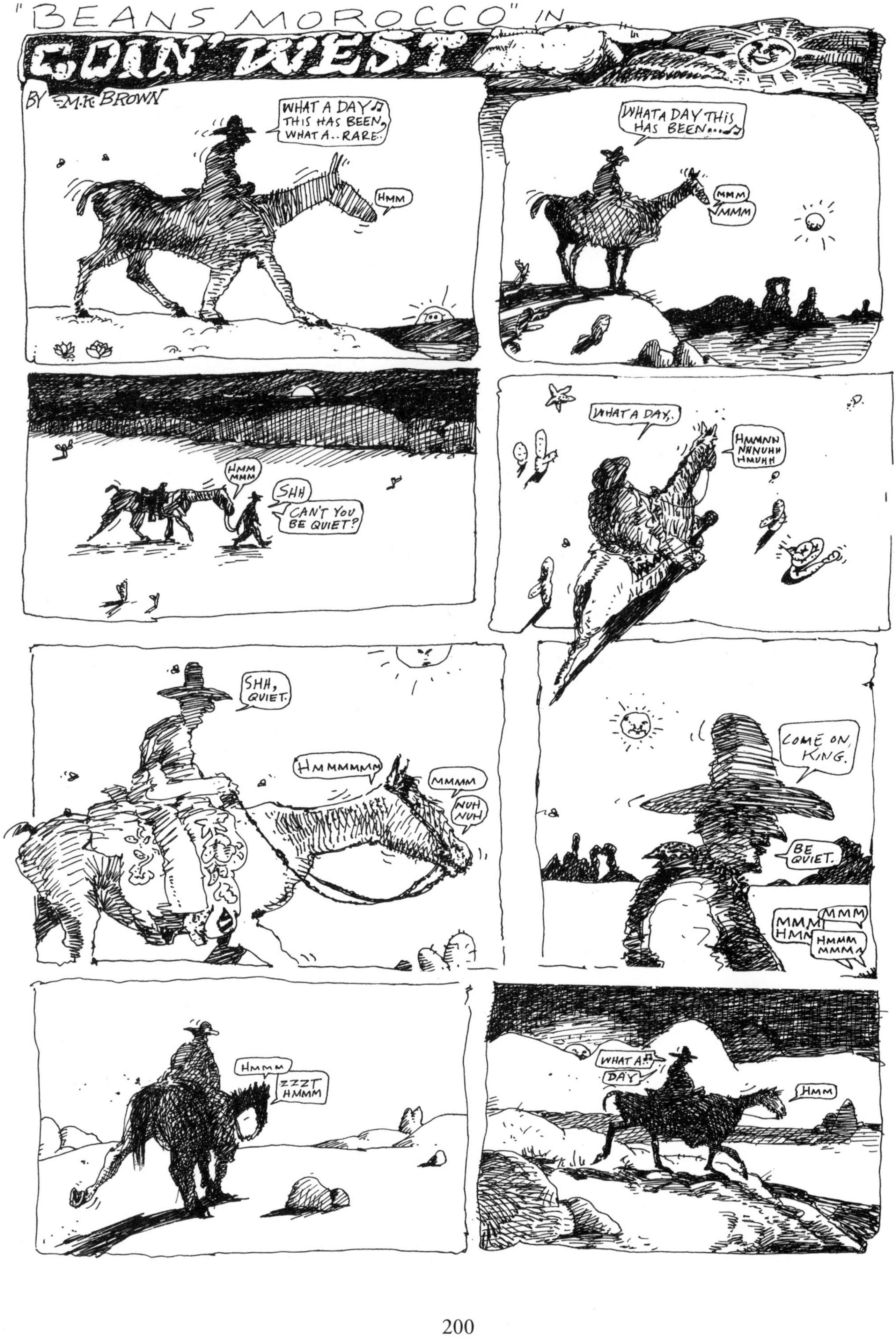
"BEANS MOROCCO" IN
GOIN' WEST
BY M.K. BROWN
WHAT A DAY♫ THIS HAS BEEN, WHAT A.. RARE.
HMM
WHAT A DAY THIS HAS BEEN...♫
MMM MMM
HMM MMM
SHH
CAN'T YOU BE QUIET?
WHAT A DAY,
HMMNN NNNUHH HMUHH
SHH, QUIET.
HMMMMMM
MMMM
NUH NUH
COME ON, KING.
BE QUIET.
MMM HMM
MMM
HMMM MMMA
HMMM
ZZZT HMMM
WHAT A♫ DAY
HMM

...CONTINUED

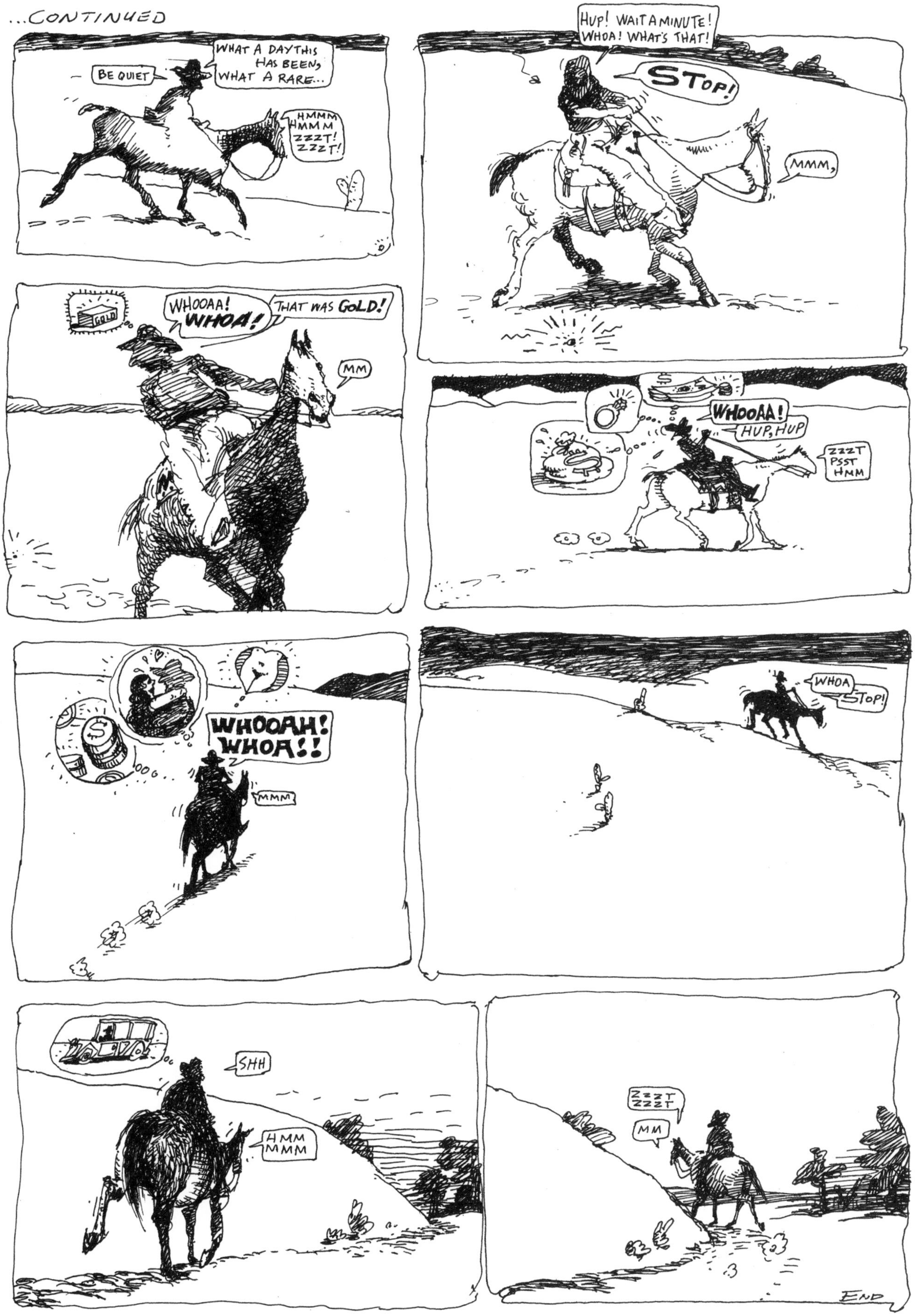

WHAT A DAY THIS HAS BEEN, WHAT A RARE...
BE QUIET
HMMM HMMM ZZZT! ZZZT!
HUP! WAIT A MINUTE! WHOA! WHAT'S THAT!
STOP!
MMM,
GOLD
WHOOAA! WHOA!
THAT WAS GOLD!
MM
WHOOAA!
HUP, HUP
ZZZT PSST HMM
WHOOAH! WHOA!!
MMM
WHOA
STOP!
SHH
HMM MMM
ZZZT ZZZT
MM
END

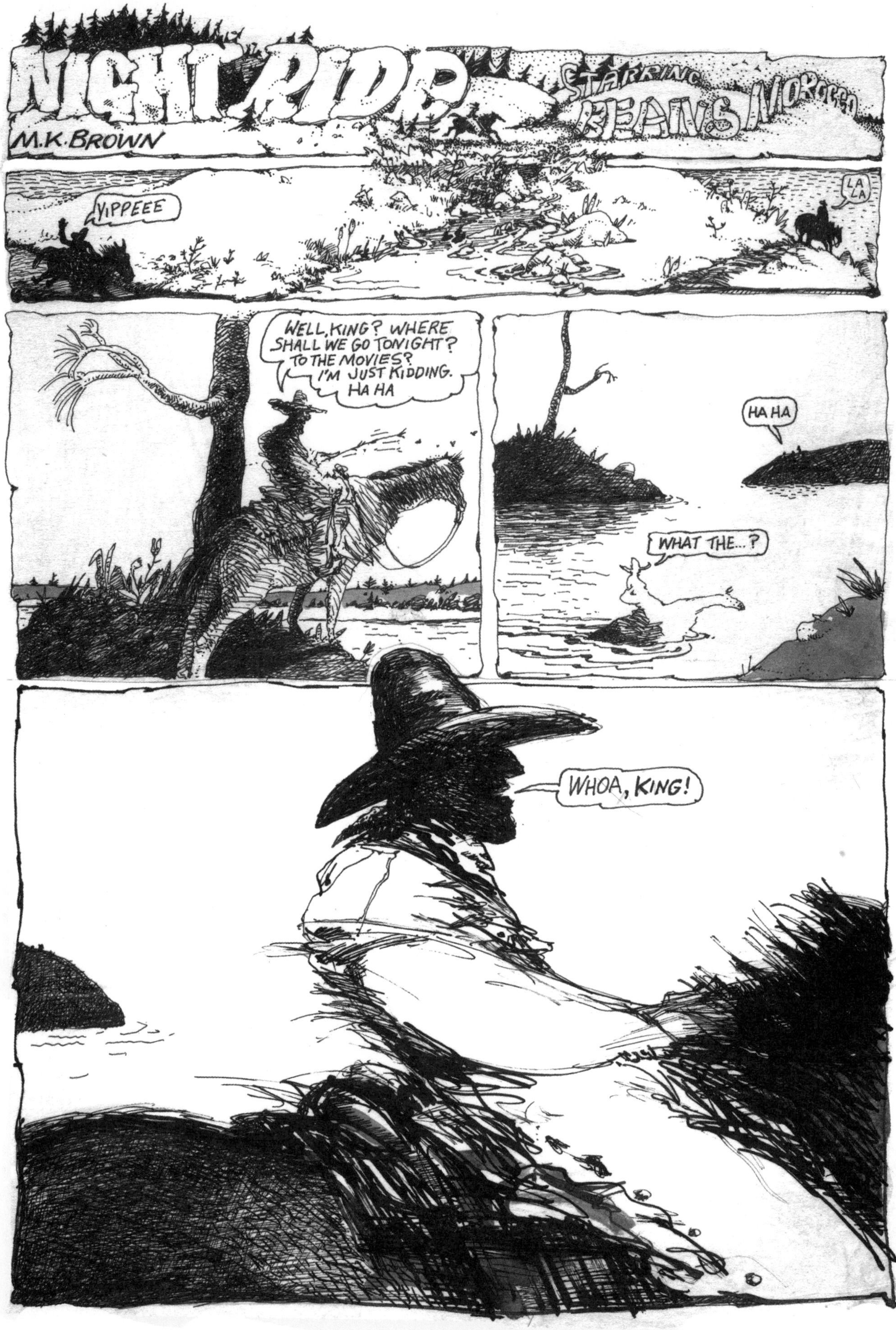

NIGHT RIDE
STARRING BEANS MOROCCO
M.K. BROWN
YIPPEEE
LA LA
WELL, KING? WHERE SHALL WE GO TONIGHT? TO THE MOVIES?
I'M JUST KIDDING. HA HA
HA HA
WHAT THE...?
WHOA, KING!

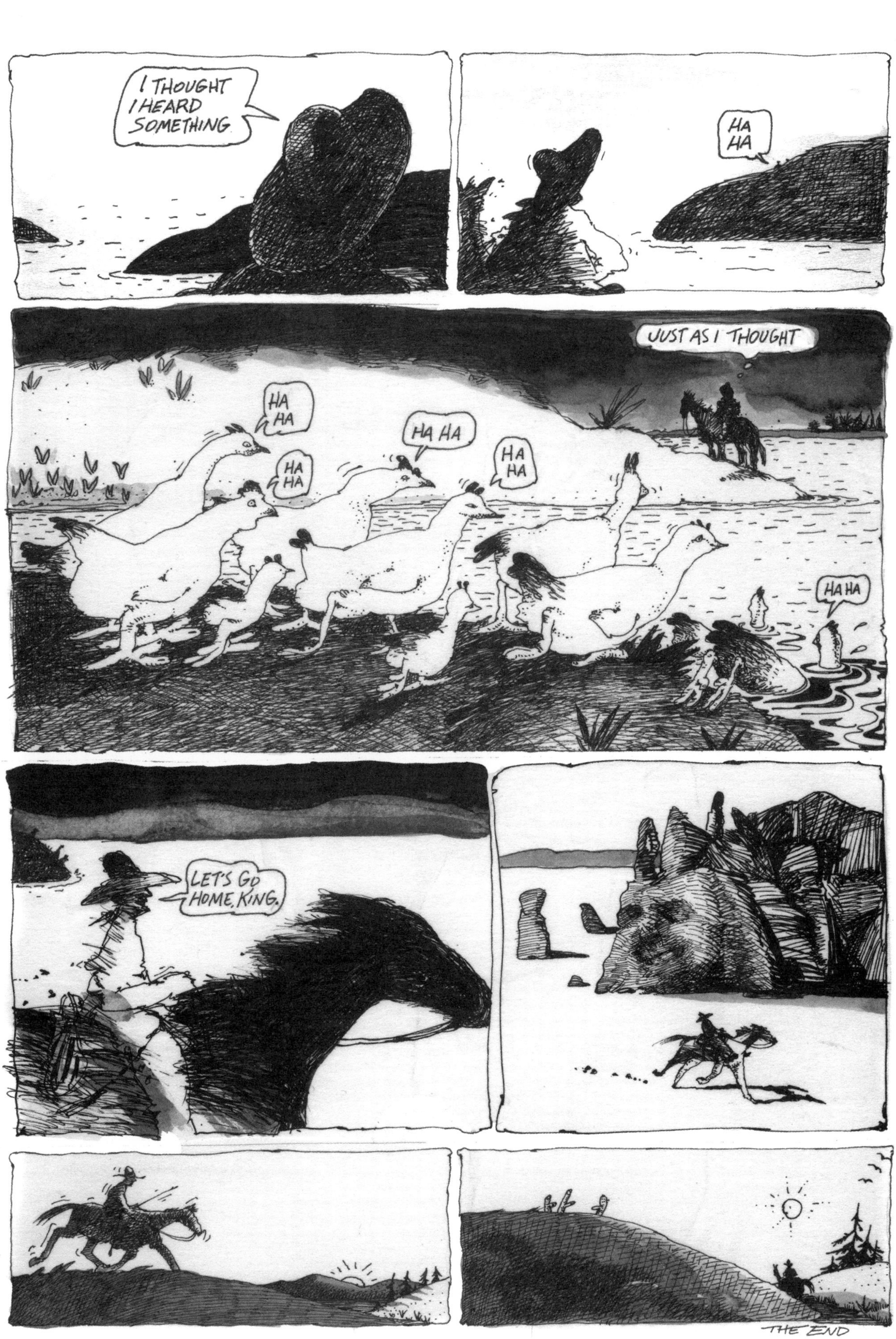
I THOUGHT I HEARD SOMETHING
HA HA
JUST AS I THOUGHT
HA HA
HA HA
HA HA
HA HA
HA HA
LET'S GO HOME, KING.
THE END

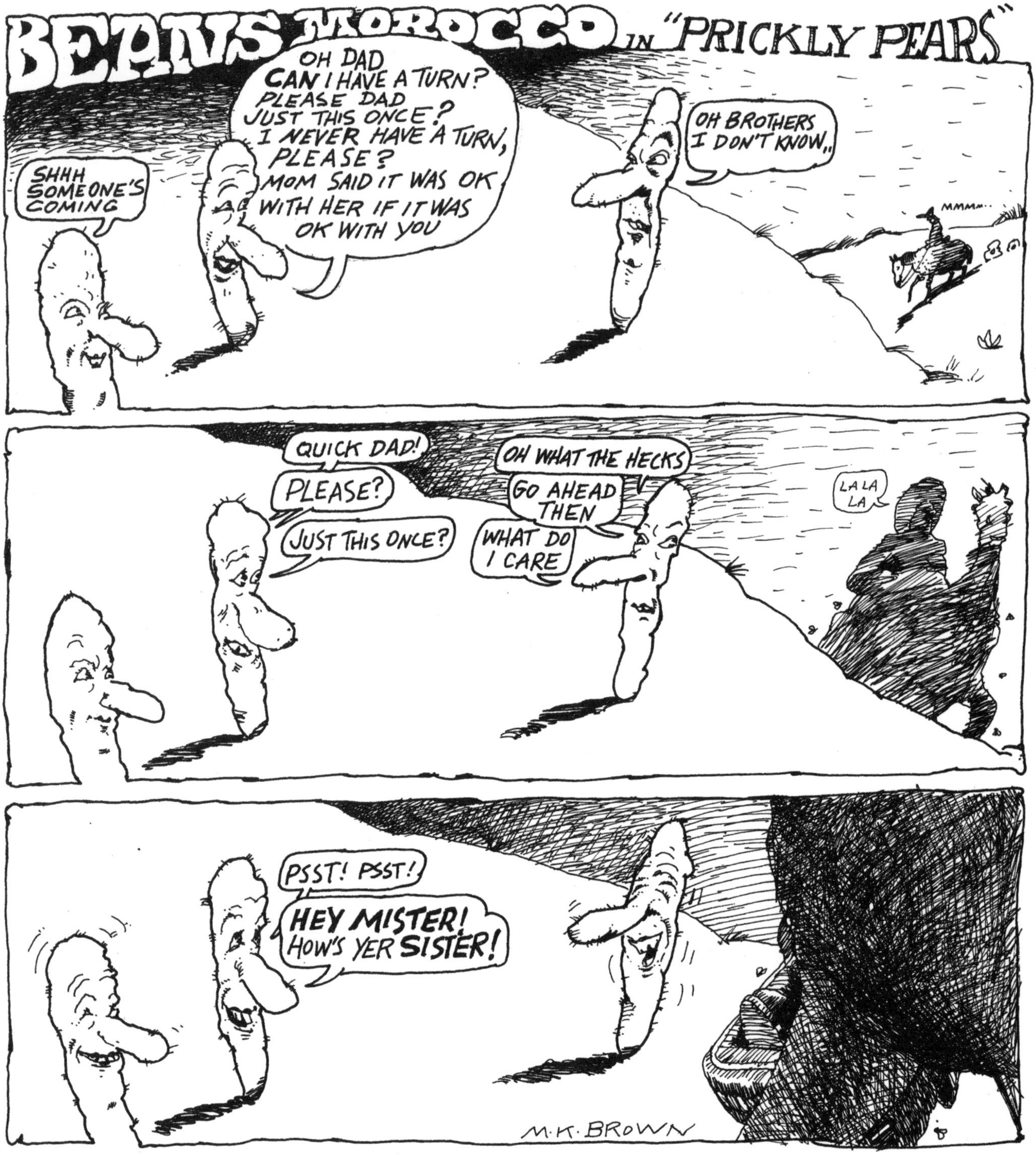
BEANS MOROCCO IN "PRICKLY PEARS"
SHHH SOMEONE'S COMING
OH DAD CAN I HAVE A TURN? PLEASE DAD JUST THIS ONCE? I NEVER HAVE A TURN, PLEASE? MOM SAID IT WAS OK WITH HER IF IT WAS OK WITH YOU
OH BROTHERS I DON'T KNOW..
MMMM...
QUICK DAD!
PLEASE?
JUST THIS ONCE?
OH WHAT THE HECKS
GO AHEAD THEN
WHAT DO I CARE
LA LA LA
PSST! PSST!
HEY MISTER! HOW'S YER SISTER!
M.K. BROWN

Western Romance

Part three

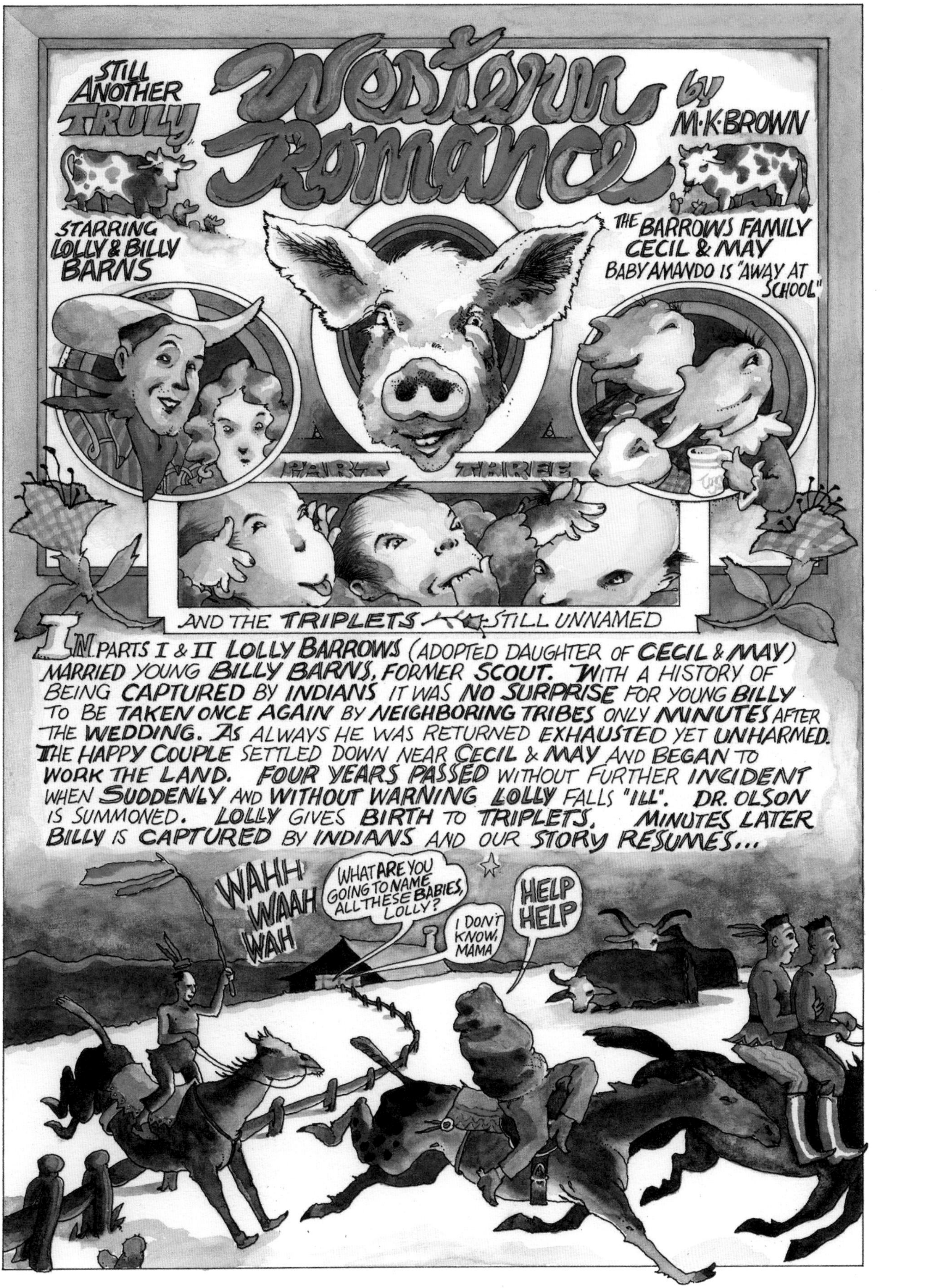
STILL ANOTHER TRULY
Western Romance
by M·K·BROWN
STARRING LOLLY & BILLY BARNS
THE BARROWS FAMILY CECIL & MAY
BABY AMANDO IS "AWAY AT SCHOOL"
PART THREE
AND THE TRIPLETS STILL UNNAMED
IN PARTS I & II LOLLY BARROWS (ADOPTED DAUGHTER OF CECIL & MAY) MARRIED YOUNG BILLY BARNS, FORMER SCOUT. WITH A HISTORY OF BEING CAPTURED BY INDIANS IT WAS NO SURPRISE FOR YOUNG BILLY TO BE TAKEN ONCE AGAIN BY NEIGHBORING TRIBES ONLY MINUTES AFTER THE WEDDING. AS ALWAYS HE WAS RETURNED EXHAUSTED YET UNHARMED. THE HAPPY COUPLE SETTLED DOWN NEAR CECIL & MAY AND BEGAN TO WORK THE LAND. FOUR YEARS PASSED WITHOUT FURTHER INCIDENT WHEN SUDDENLY AND WITHOUT WARNING LOLLY FALLS "ILL". DR. OLSON IS SUMMONED. LOLLY GIVES BIRTH TO TRIPLETS. MINUTES LATER BILLY IS CAPTURED BY INDIANS AND OUR STORY RESUMES...
WAHH WAAH WAH
WHAT ARE YOU GOING TO NAME ALL THESE BABIES, LOLLY?
I DON'T KNOW, MAMA
HELP HELP

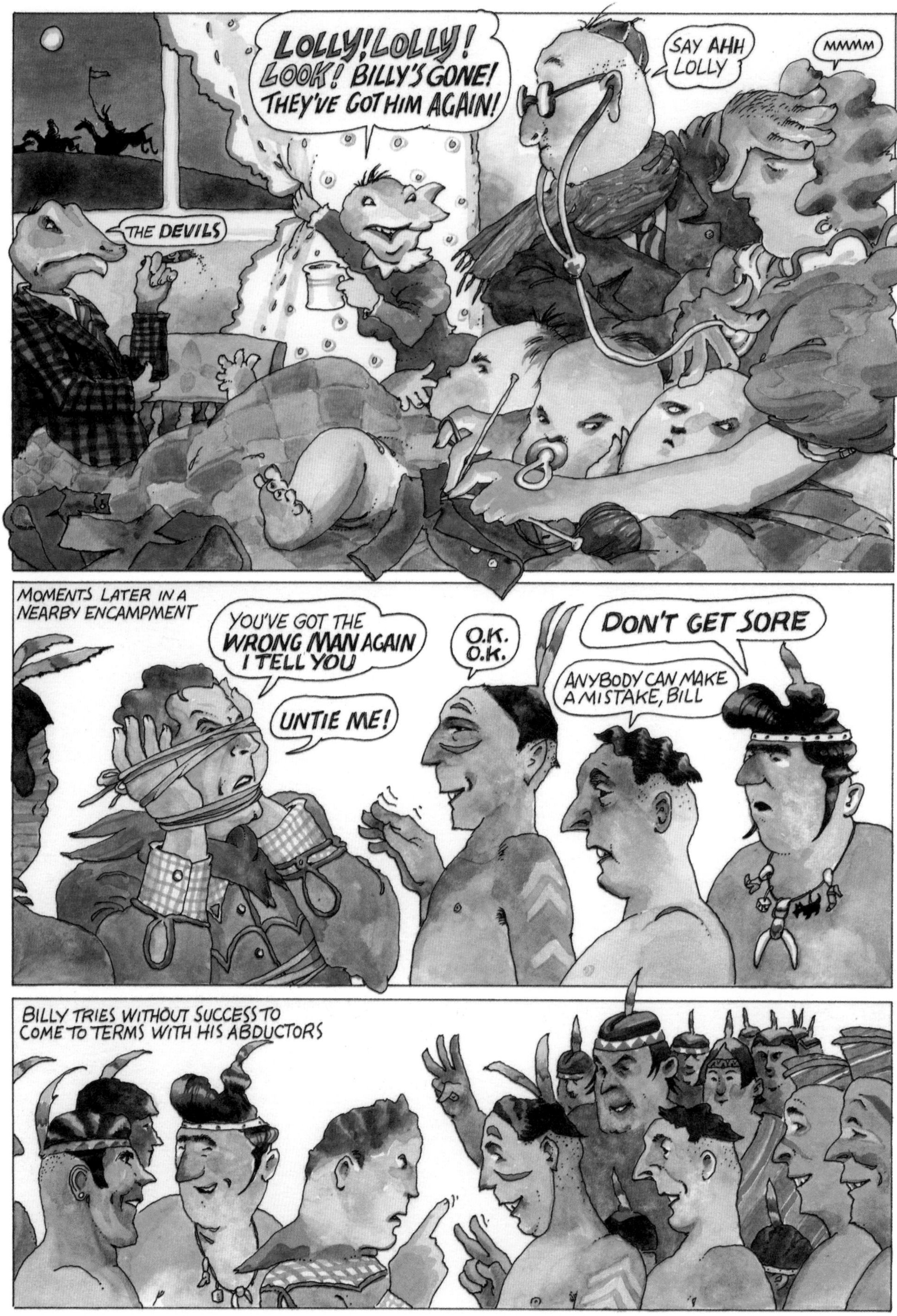

LOLLY! LOLLY! LOOK! BILLY'S GONE! THEY'VE GOT HIM AGAIN!
SAY AHH LOLLY
MMMM
THE DEVILS
MOMENTS LATER IN A NEARBY ENCAMPMENT
YOU'VE GOT THE WRONG MAN AGAIN I TELL YOU
UNTIE ME!
O.K. O.K.
DON'T GET SORE
ANYBODY CAN MAKE A MISTAKE, BILL
BILLY TRIES WITHOUT SUCCESS TO COME TO TERMS WITH HIS ABDUCTORS

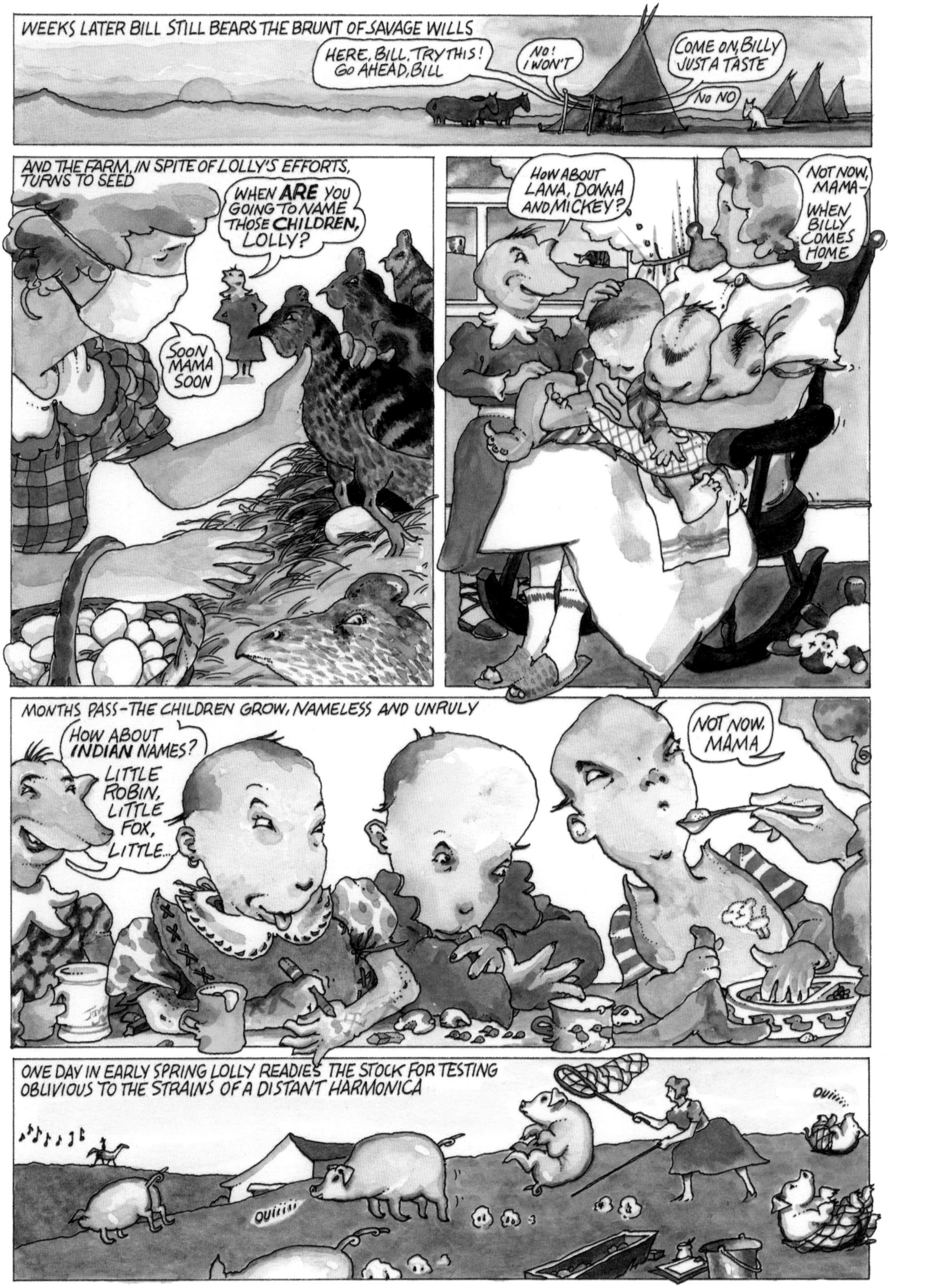

WEEKS LATER BILL STILL BEARS THE BRUNT OF SAVAGE WILLS
HERE, BILL, TRY THIS! GO AHEAD, BILL
NO! I WON'T
COME ON, BILLY JUST A TASTE
NO NO
AND THE FARM, IN SPITE OF LOLLY'S EFFORTS, TURNS TO SEED
WHEN ARE YOU GOING TO NAME THOSE CHILDREN, LOLLY?
SOON MAMA SOON
HOW ABOUT LANA, DONNA AND MICKEY?
NOT NOW, MAMA- WHEN BILLY COMES HOME
MONTHS PASS-THE CHILDREN GROW, NAMELESS AND UNRULY
HOW ABOUT INDIAN NAMES? LITTLE ROBIN, LITTLE FOX, LITTLE...
NOT NOW, MAMA
ONE DAY IN EARLY SPRING LOLLY READIES THE STOCK FOR TESTING OBLIVIOUS TO THE STRAINS OF A DISTANT HARMONICA
OUI!!!!
OUI!!!!

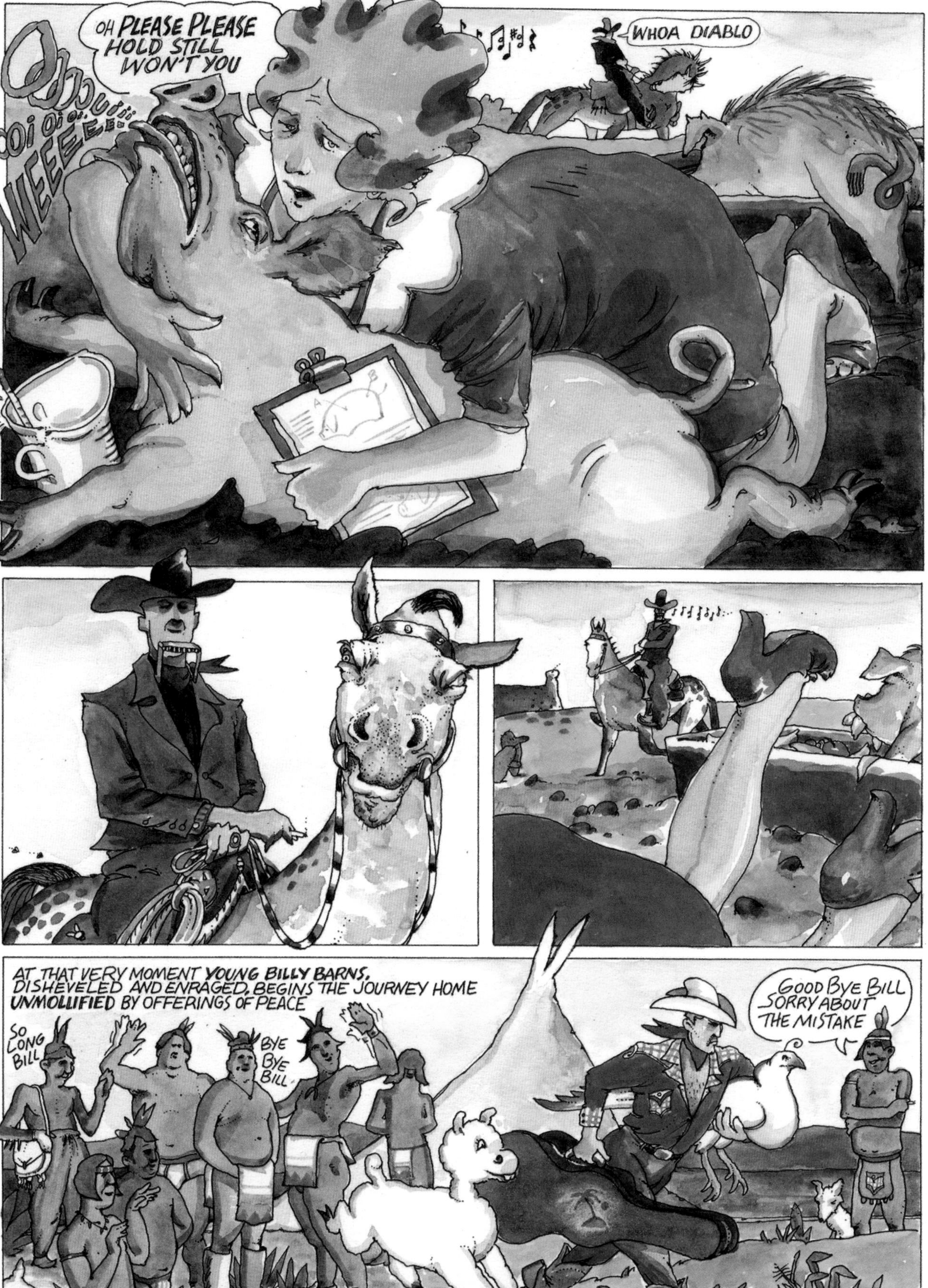

OH PLEASE PLEASE HOLD STILL WON'T YOU
OOI OI OI
WEEEEE
WHOA DIABLO
AT THAT VERY MOMENT YOUNG BILLY BARNS, DISHEVELED AND ENRAGED, BEGINS THE JOURNEY HOME UNMOLLIFIED BY OFFERINGS OF PEACE
SO LONG BILL
BYE BYE BILL
GOOD BYE BILL SORRY ABOUT THE MISTAKE

TO BE CONTINUED

Western Romance

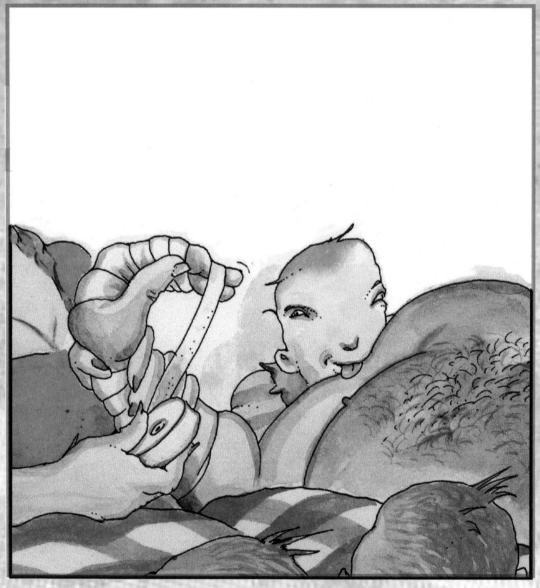

Part four

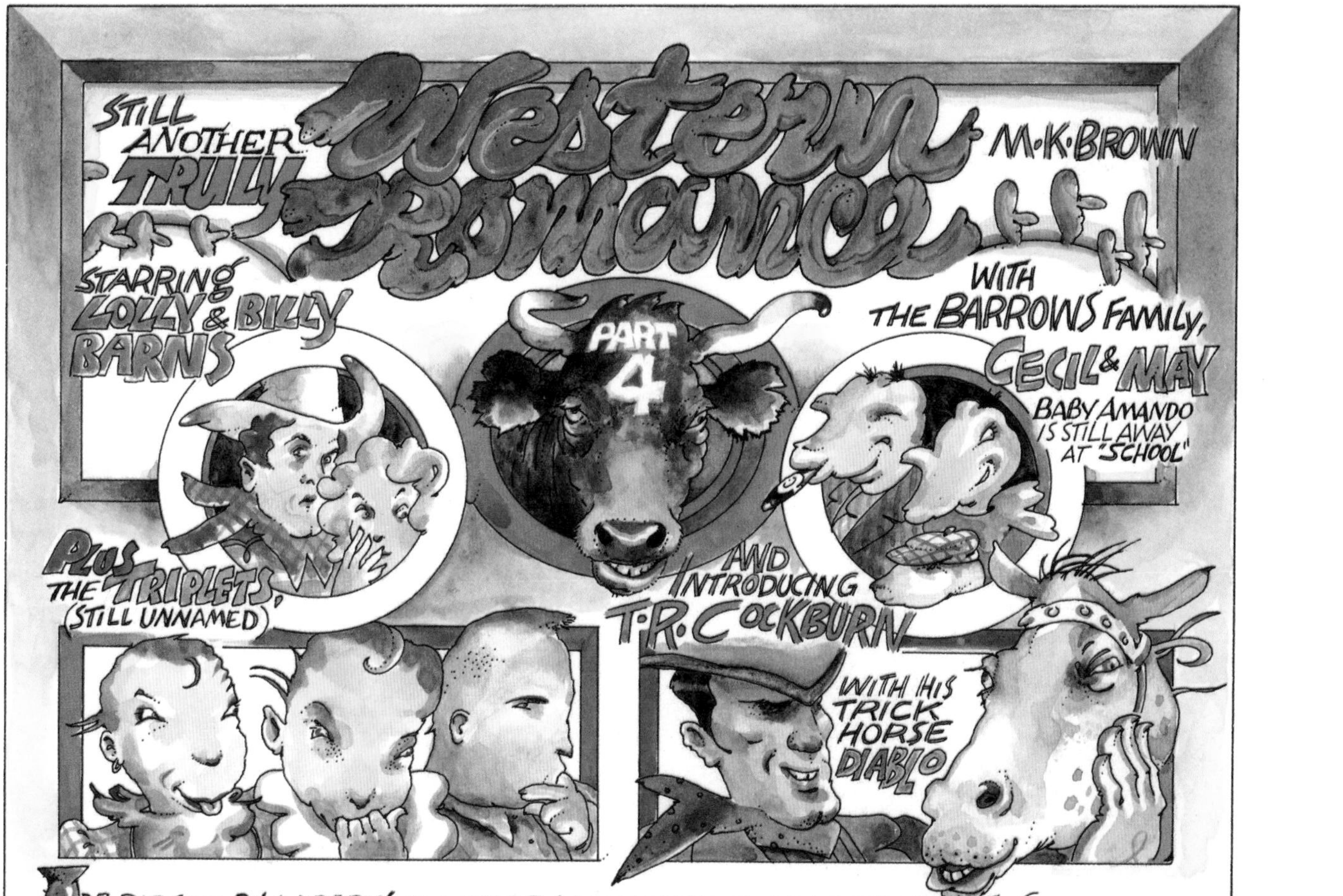
STILL ANOTHER TRULY
Western Romance
M·K·BROWN
STARRING LOLLY & BILLY BARNS
PART 4
WITH THE BARROWS FAMILY, CECIL & MAY
BABY AMANDO IS STILL AWAY AT "SCHOOL"
PLUS THE TRIPLETS, (STILL UNNAMED)
AND INTRODUCING T·R·COCKBURN
WITH HIS TRICK HORSE DIABLO

IN PART III BILLY BARNS HAS ONCE AGAIN BEEN TAKEN BY INDIANS (ONLY MINUTES AFTER LOLLY GIVES BIRTH TO TRIPLETS). THE FARM, IN BILLY'S ABSENCE AND IN SPITE OF LOLLY'S EFFORTS, FALLS TO RUIN. THE CHILDREN GROW, NAMELESS AND UNRULY. CECIL & MAY, LOLLY'S FOSTER PARENTS LIVING ON A NEARBY FARM, DO THEIR VERY BEST TO HELP. WHEN, THAT AUTUMN, BILLY STILL HAS NOT RETURNED, LOLLY TACKLES ALONE THE MONSTROUS JOB OF "TESTING THE STOCK," A TASK WHICH NORMALLY REQUIRES THE STRENGTH OF MANY MEN. LUCKILY, A "PASSING COWPOKE" SEES HER PLIGHT AND STOPS TO OFFER HIS ASSISTANCE. AT THAT VERY MOMENT, MILES AWAY, YOUNG BILLY BARNS, DISHEVELED & ENRAGED, IS SET FREE AT LAST. LADEN WITH GIFTS FROM THE 'INDIANS' HE EMBARKS ONCE MORE UPON THE GRUELING JOURNEY HOME.

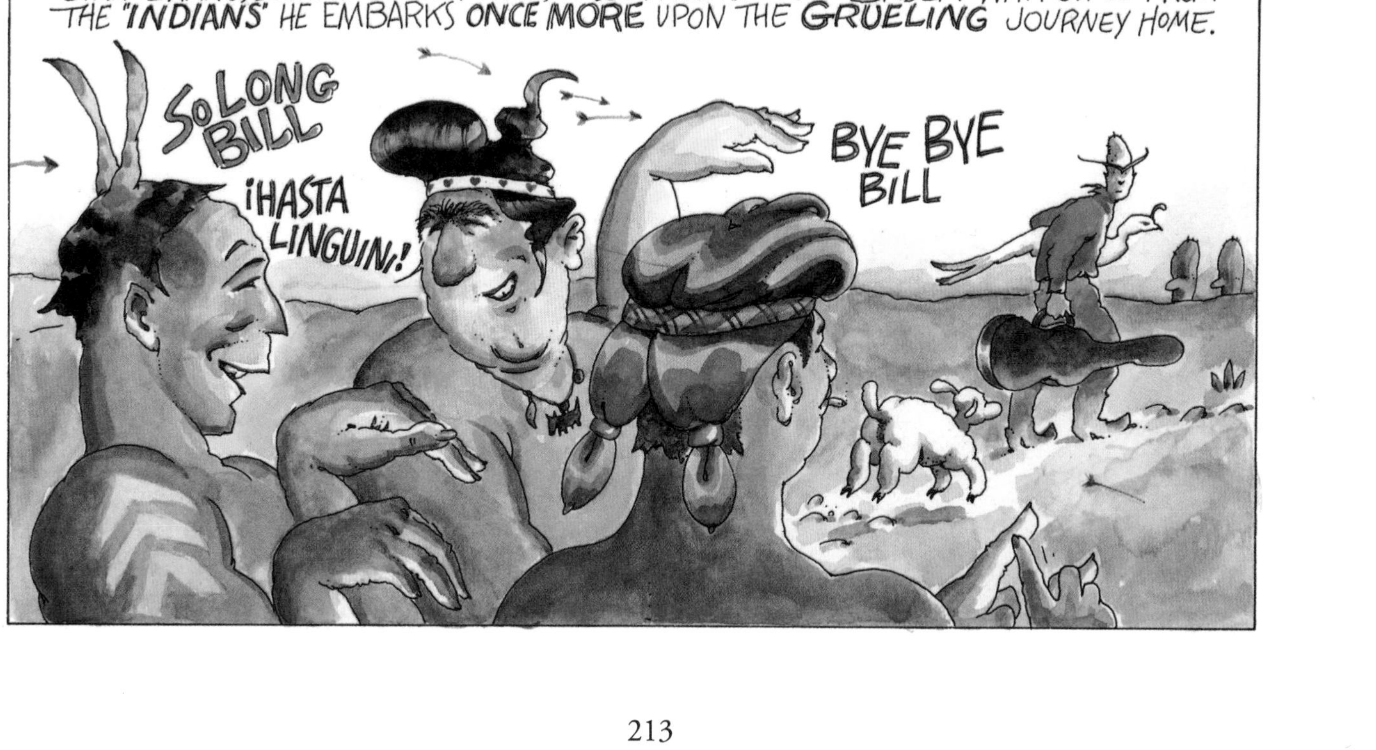
SO LONG BILL
¡HASTA LINGUINI!
BYE BYE BILL

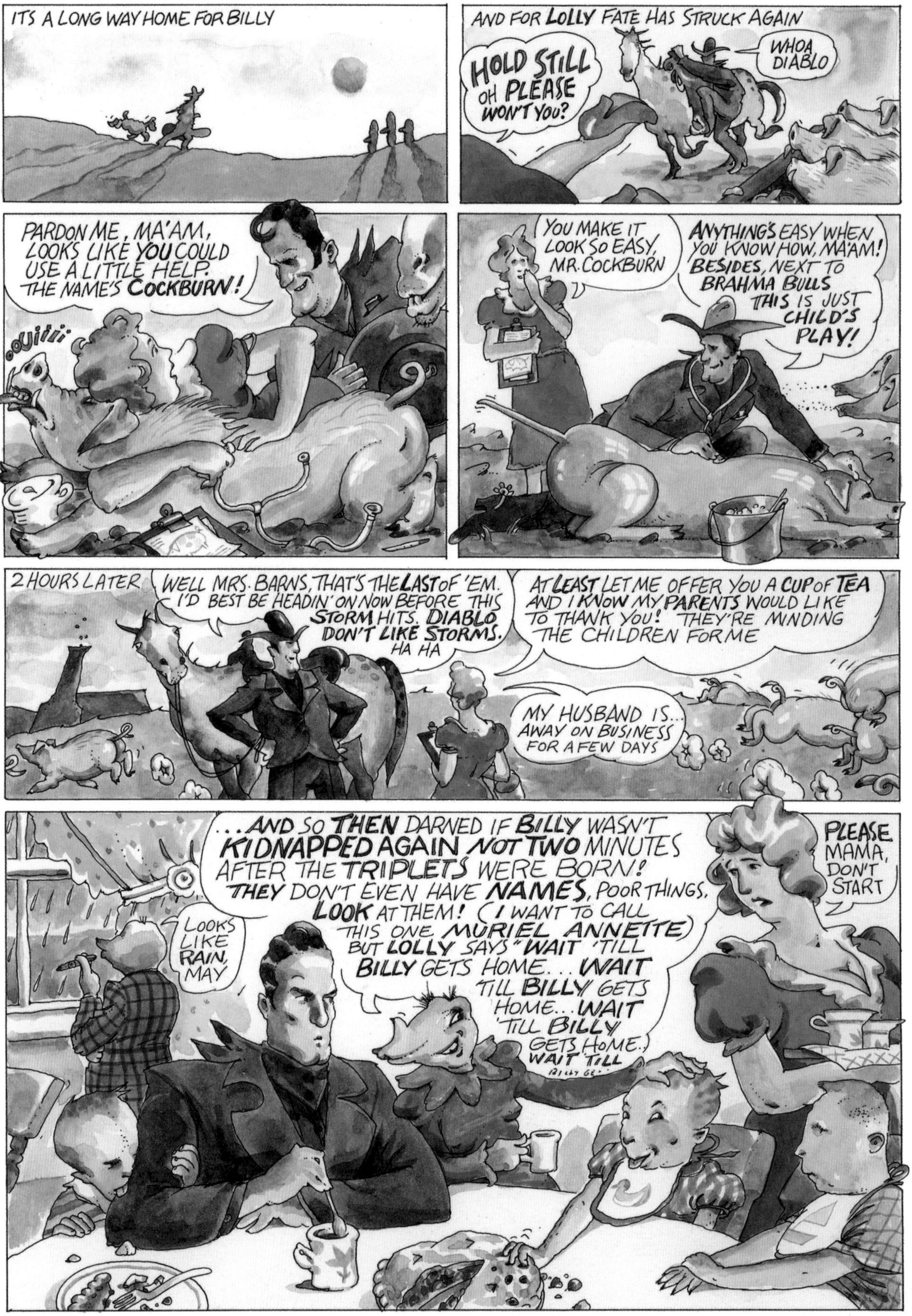
ITS A LONG WAY HOME FOR BILLY
AND FOR LOLLY FATE HAS STRUCK AGAIN
HOLD STILL OH PLEASE WON'T YOU?
WHOA DIABLO
PARDON ME, MA'AM, LOOKS LIKE YOU COULD USE A LITTLE HELP. THE NAME'S COCKBURN!
OUIII
YOU MAKE IT LOOK SO EASY, MR. COCKBURN
ANYTHING'S EASY WHEN YOU KNOW HOW, MA'AM! BESIDES, NEXT TO BRAHMA BULLS THIS IS JUST CHILD'S PLAY!
2 HOURS LATER
WELL MRS. BARNS, THAT'S THE LAST OF 'EM. I'D BEST BE HEADIN' ON NOW BEFORE THIS STORM HITS. DIABLO DON'T LIKE STORMS. HA HA
AT LEAST LET ME OFFER YOU A CUP OF TEA AND I KNOW MY PARENTS WOULD LIKE TO THANK YOU! THEY'RE MINDING THE CHILDREN FOR ME
MY HUSBAND IS... AWAY ON BUSINESS FOR A FEW DAYS
...AND SO THEN DARNED IF BILLY WASN'T KIDNAPPED AGAIN NOT TWO MINUTES AFTER THE TRIPLETS WERE BORN! THEY DON'T EVEN HAVE NAMES, POOR THINGS. LOOK AT THEM! (I WANT TO CALL THIS ONE MURIEL ANNETTE) BUT LOLLY SAYS "WAIT 'TILL BILLY GETS HOME... WAIT 'TILL BILLY GETS HOME... WAIT 'TILL BILLY GETS HOME.) WAIT 'TILL BILLY GE...
PLEASE MAMA, DON'T START
LOOKS LIKE RAIN, MAY

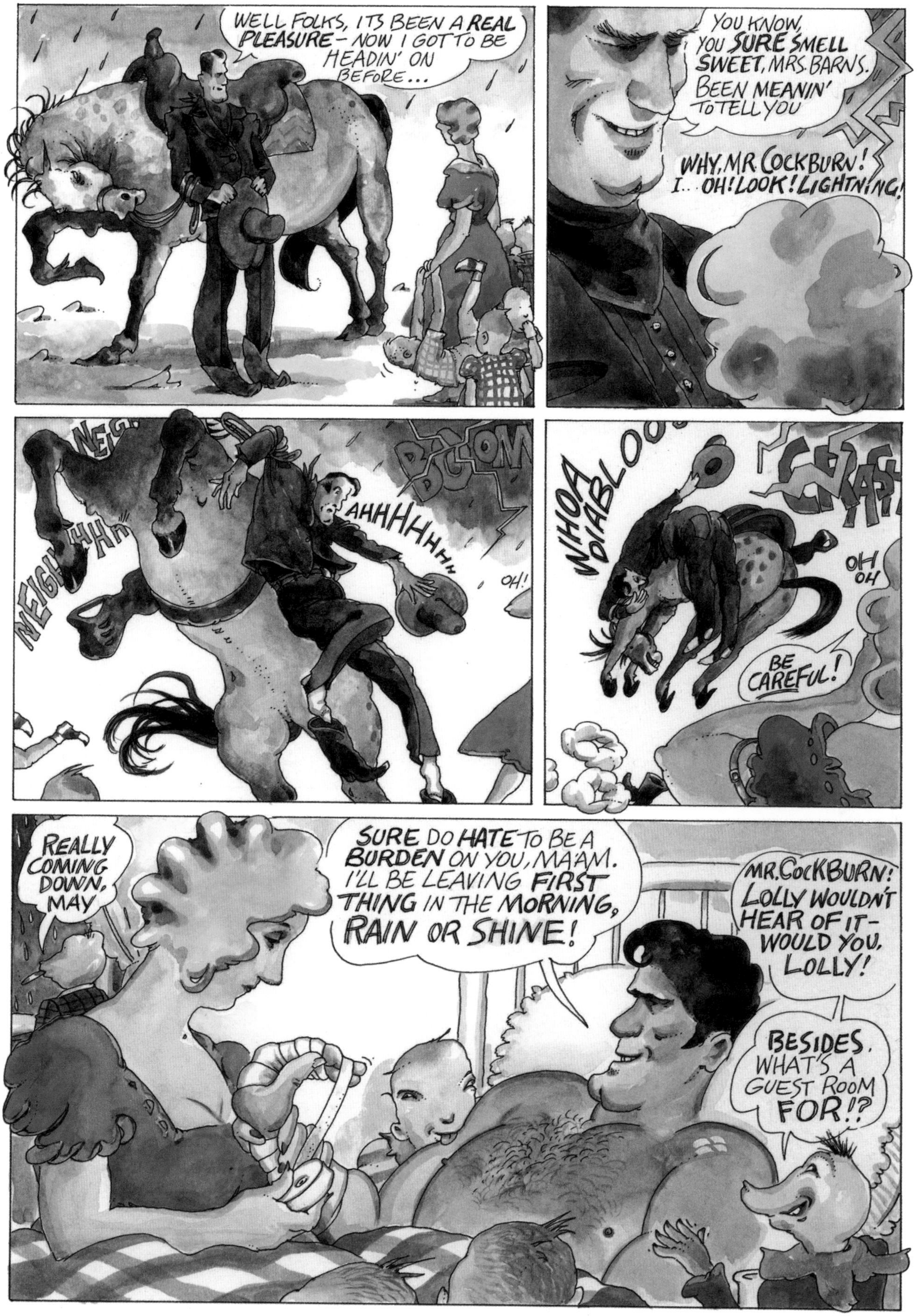
WELL FOLKS, ITS BEEN A REAL PLEASURE - NOW I GOT TO BE HEADIN' ON BEFORE...
YOU KNOW, YOU SURE SMELL SWEET, MRS. BARNS. BEEN MEANIN' TO TELL YOU
WHY, MR. COCKBURN! I... OH! LOOK! LIGHTNING!
NEIGHHHH
BOOM
AHHHHHhhh
OH!
WHOA DIABLO
CRASH
OH OH
BE CAREFUL!
REALLY COMING DOWN, MAY
SURE DO HATE TO BE A BURDEN ON YOU, MA'AM. I'LL BE LEAVING FIRST THING IN THE MORNING, RAIN OR SHINE!
MR. COCKBURN! LOLLY WOULDN'T HEAR OF IT - WOULD YOU, LOLLY!
BESIDES, WHAT'S A GUEST ROOM FOR!?

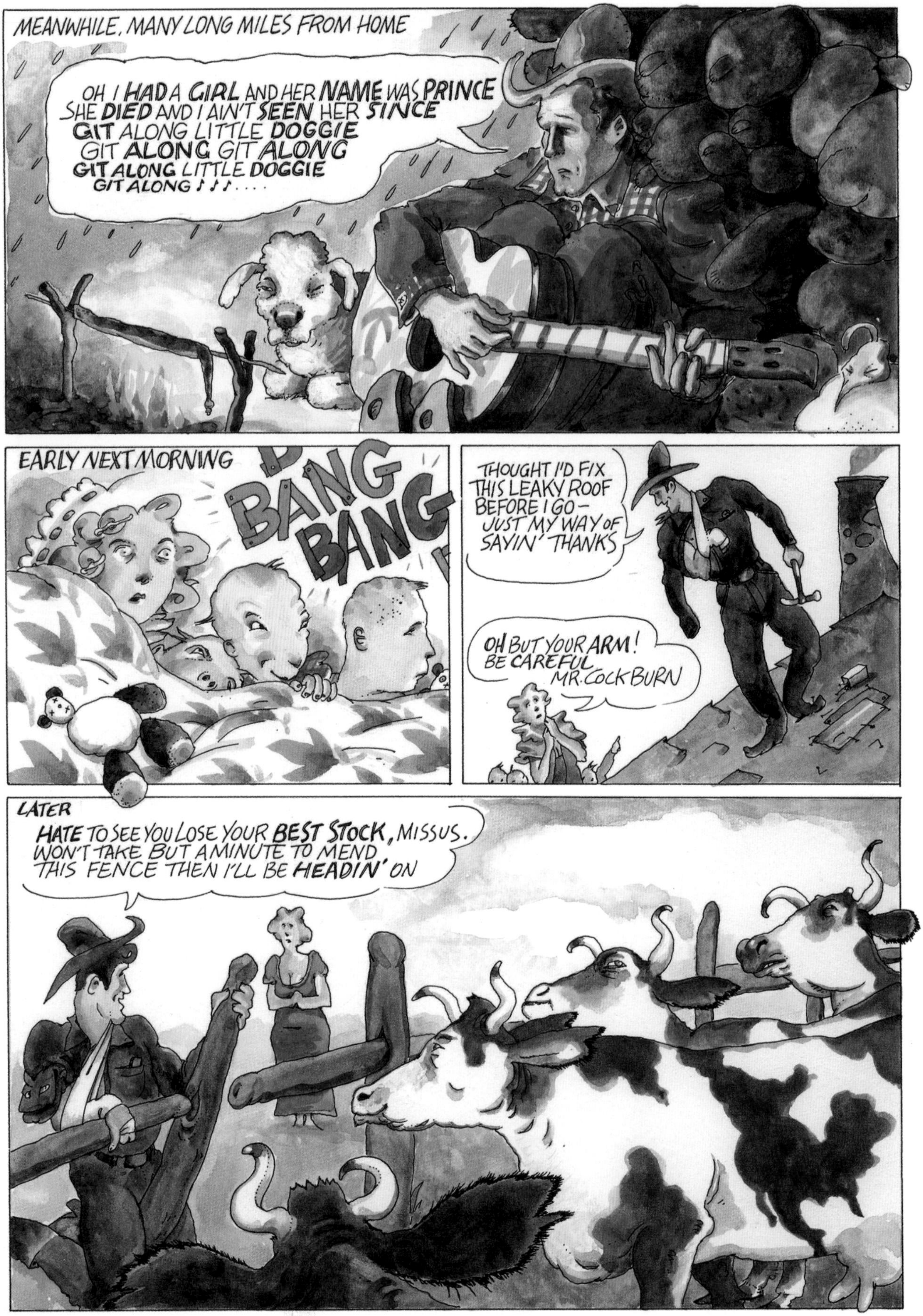
MEANWHILE, MANY LONG MILES FROM HOME
OH I HAD A GIRL AND HER NAME WAS PRINCE SHE DIED AND I AIN'T SEEN HER SINCE GIT ALONG LITTLE DOGGIE GIT ALONG GIT ALONG GIT ALONG LITTLE DOGGIE GIT ALONG ♪♪♪....
EARLY NEXT MORNING
BANG BANG
THOUGHT I'D FIX THIS LEAKY ROOF BEFORE I GO - JUST MY WAY OF SAYIN' THANKS
OH BUT YOUR ARM! BE CAREFUL MR. COCKBURN
LATER
HATE TO SEE YOU LOSE YOUR BEST STOCK, MISSUS. WON'T TAKE BUT A MINUTE TO MEND THIS FENCE THEN I'LL BE HEADIN' ON

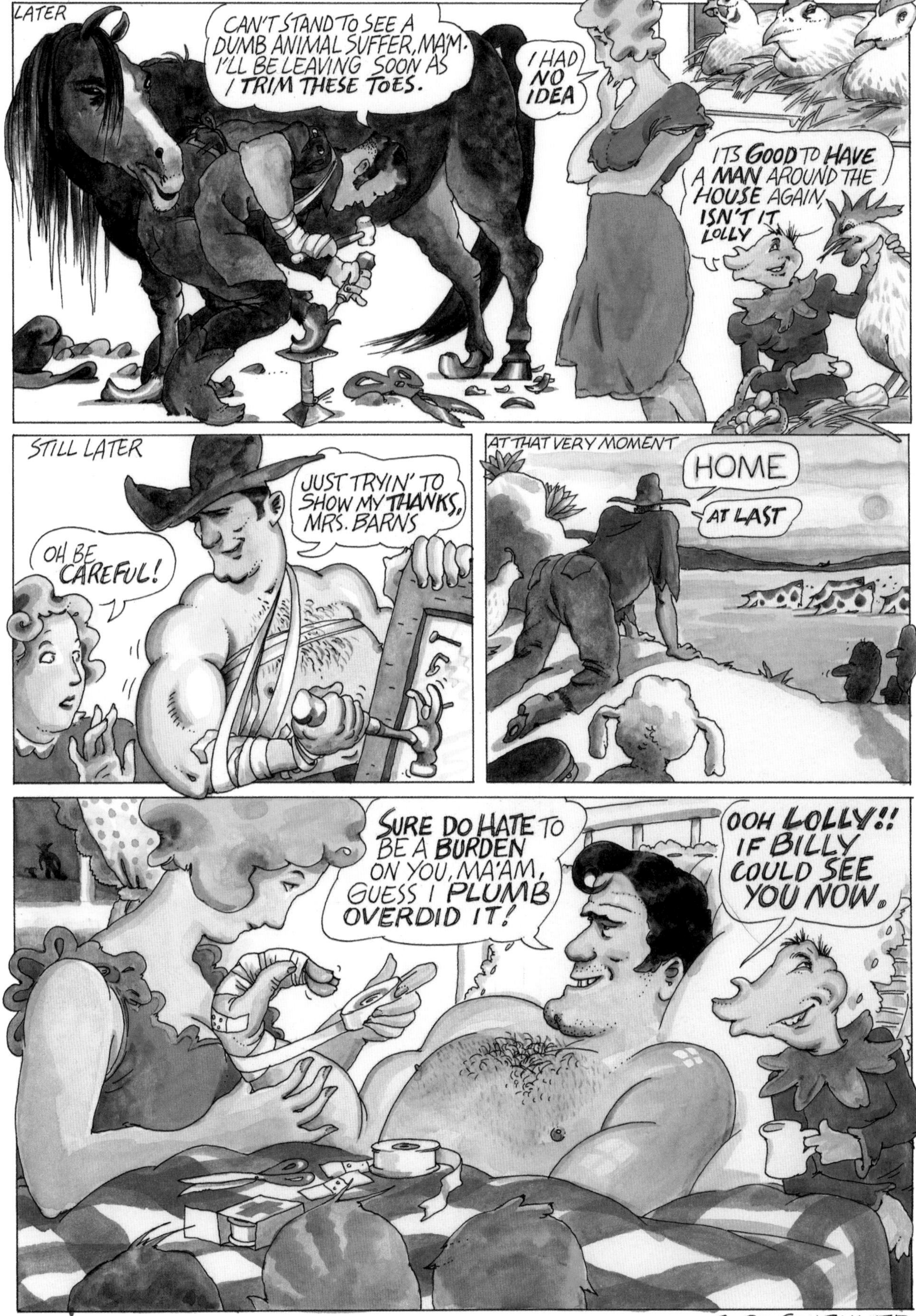
LATER
CAN'T STAND TO SEE A DUMB ANIMAL SUFFER, MA'M. I'LL BE LEAVING SOON AS I TRIM THESE TOES.
I HAD NO IDEA
ITS GOOD TO HAVE A MAN AROUND THE HOUSE AGAIN, ISN'T IT LOLLY
STILL LATER
JUST TRYIN' TO SHOW MY THANKS, MRS. BARNS
OH BE CAREFUL!
AT THAT VERY MOMENT
HOME
AT LAST
SURE DO HATE TO BE A BURDEN ON YOU, MA'AM, GUESS I PLUMB OVERDID IT!
OOH LOLLY!! IF BILLY COULD SEE YOU NOW.
TO BE CONTINUED

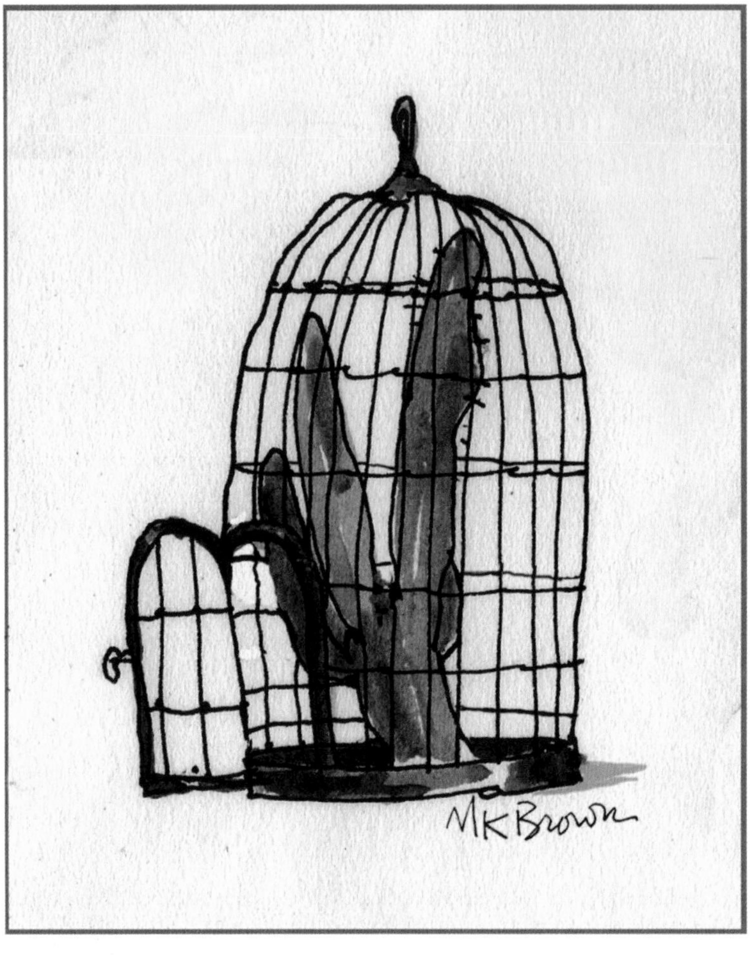
MK Brown

FOR THE BICENTENNIAL ISSUE of *National Lampoon*, art director Michael Gross envisioned a spread on vintage weaponry and asked if I could draw guns. I said I could, of course, although guns and cars, fistfights, and explosions have never been my strong suit. I am convinced, however, that by drawing without fear, regardless of any real knowledge of the subject, a better understanding will be achieved.

*Captions by Tony Hendra

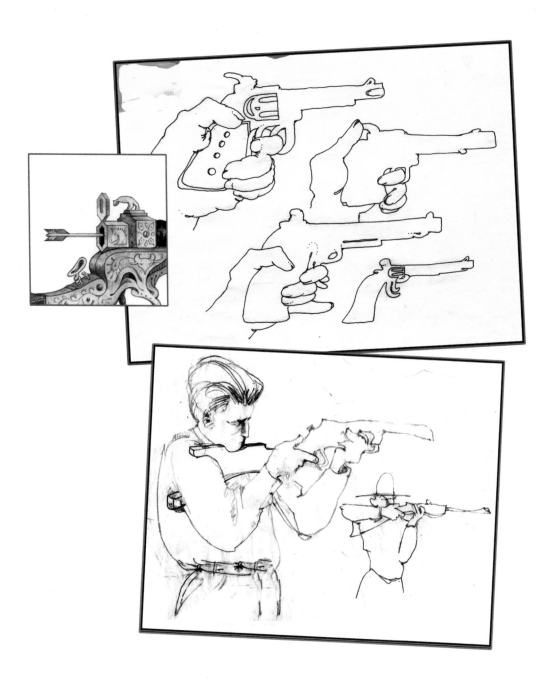

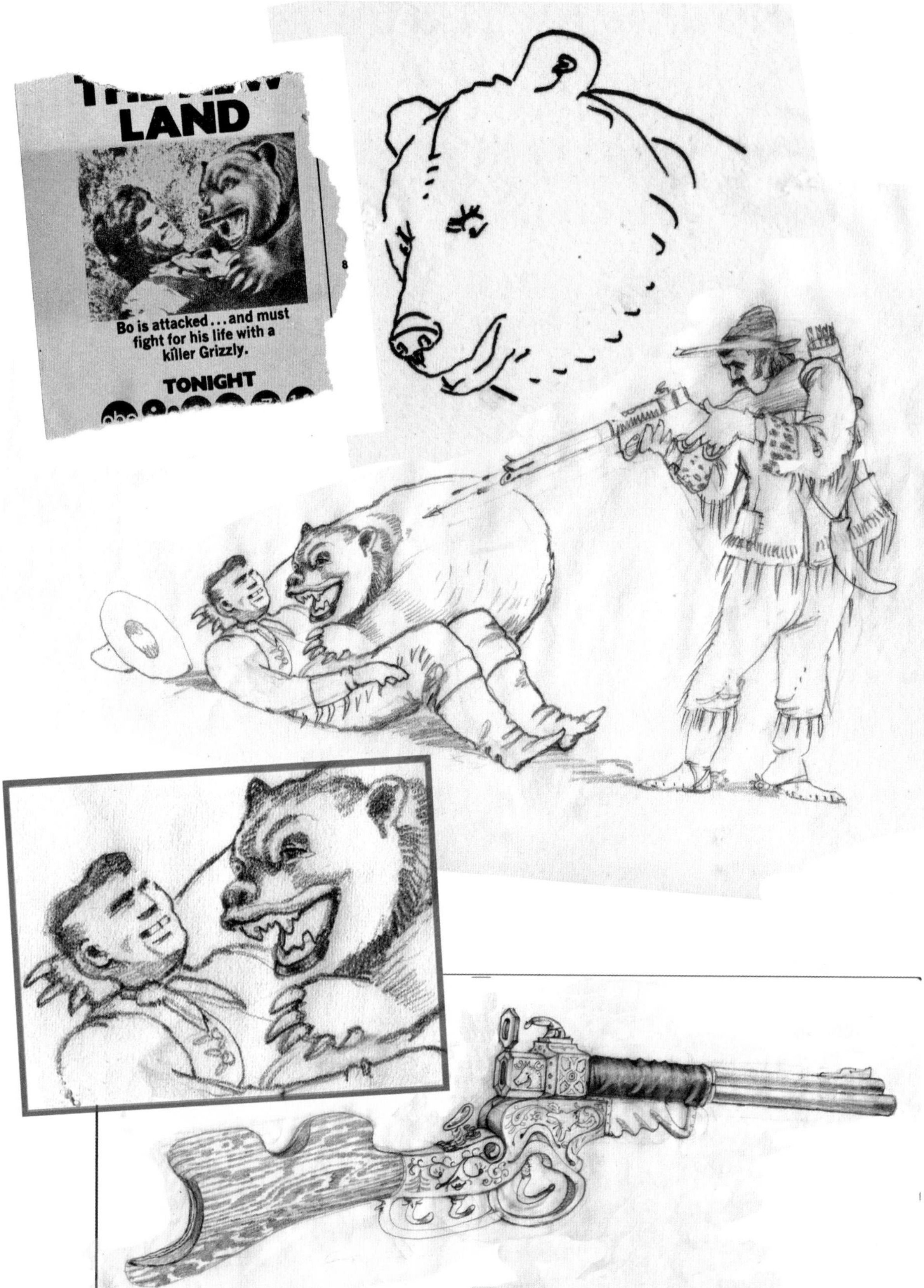
LAND
Bo is attacked...and must fight for his life with a killer Grizzly.
TONIGHT

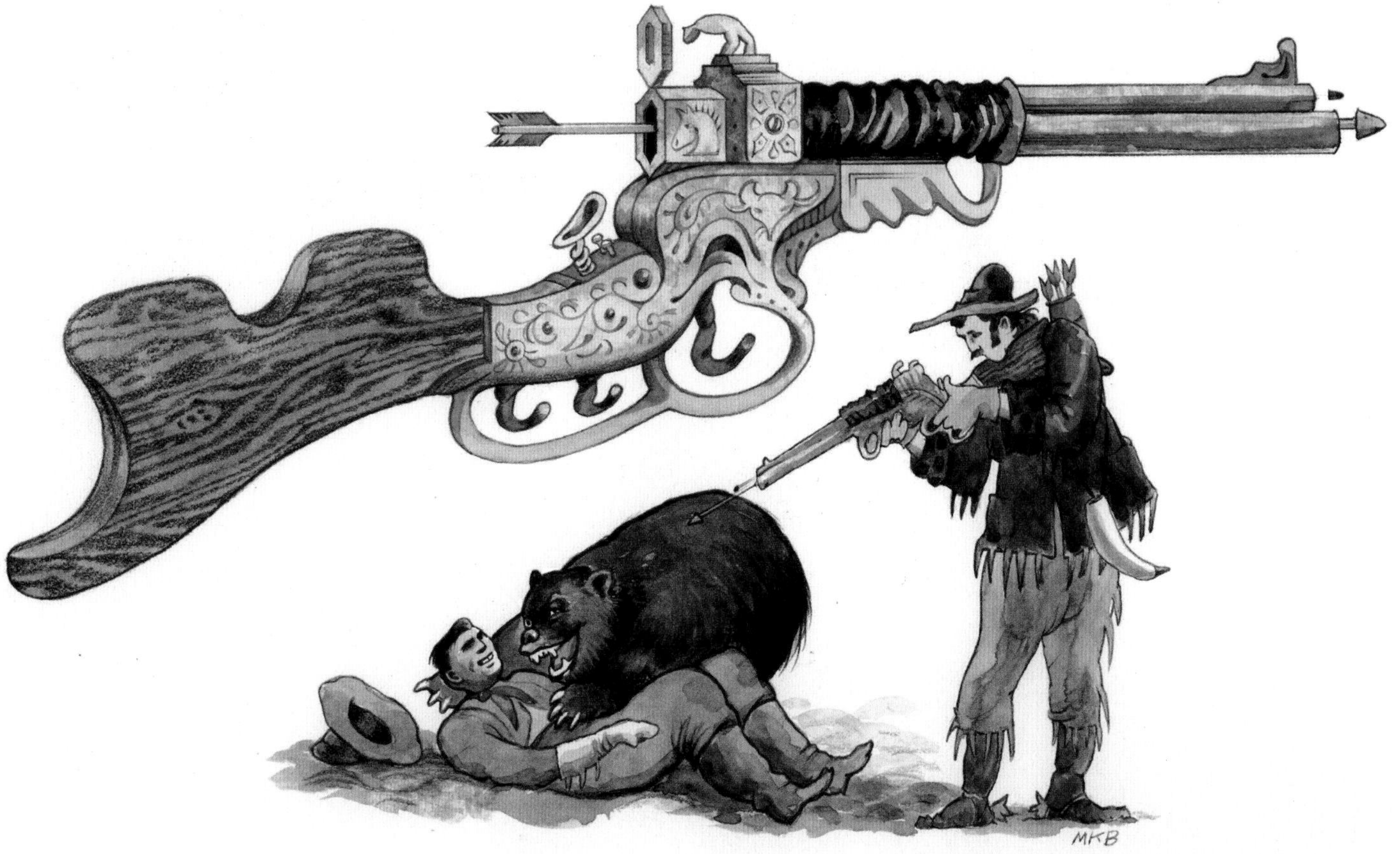
MKB

Dual-purpose Backwoodsman's Longbore Rifle, "Half-Breed's Delight." 1825

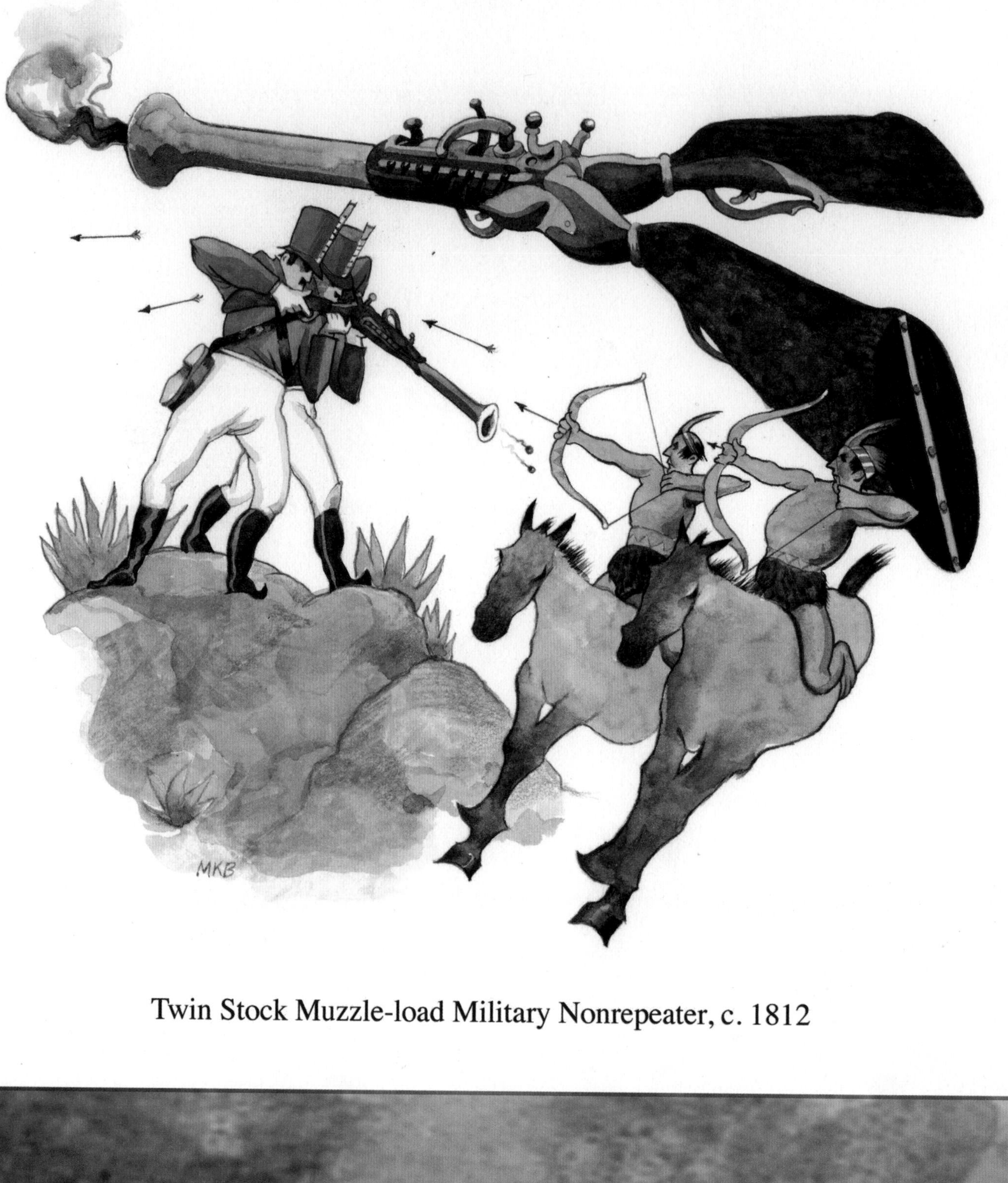
MKB

Twin Stock Muzzle-load Military Nonrepeater, c. 1812

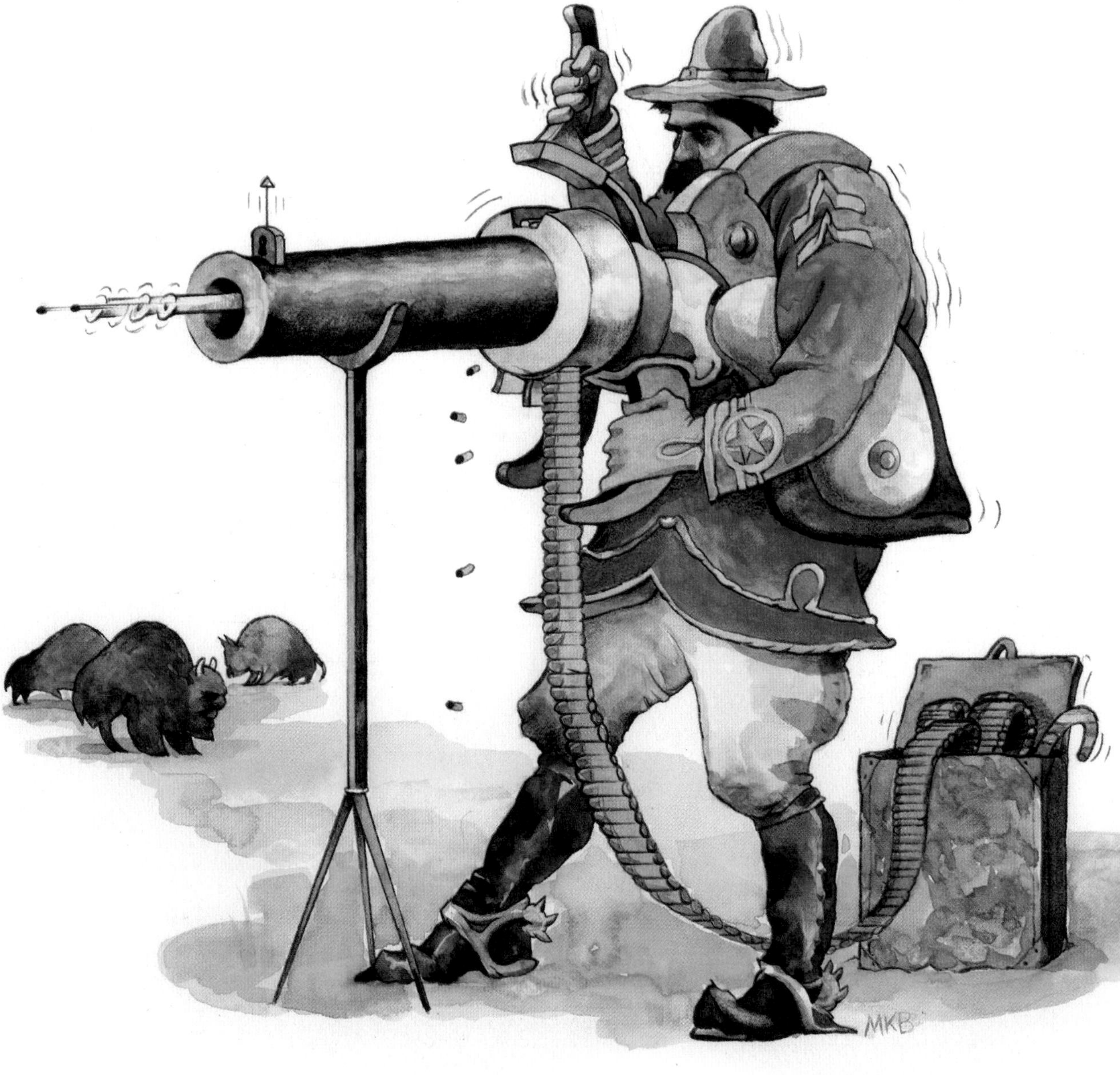
MKB

Heavy-duty Pearl Handled Cavalry-issue Machine Gun, "Old Talkative," c.1870

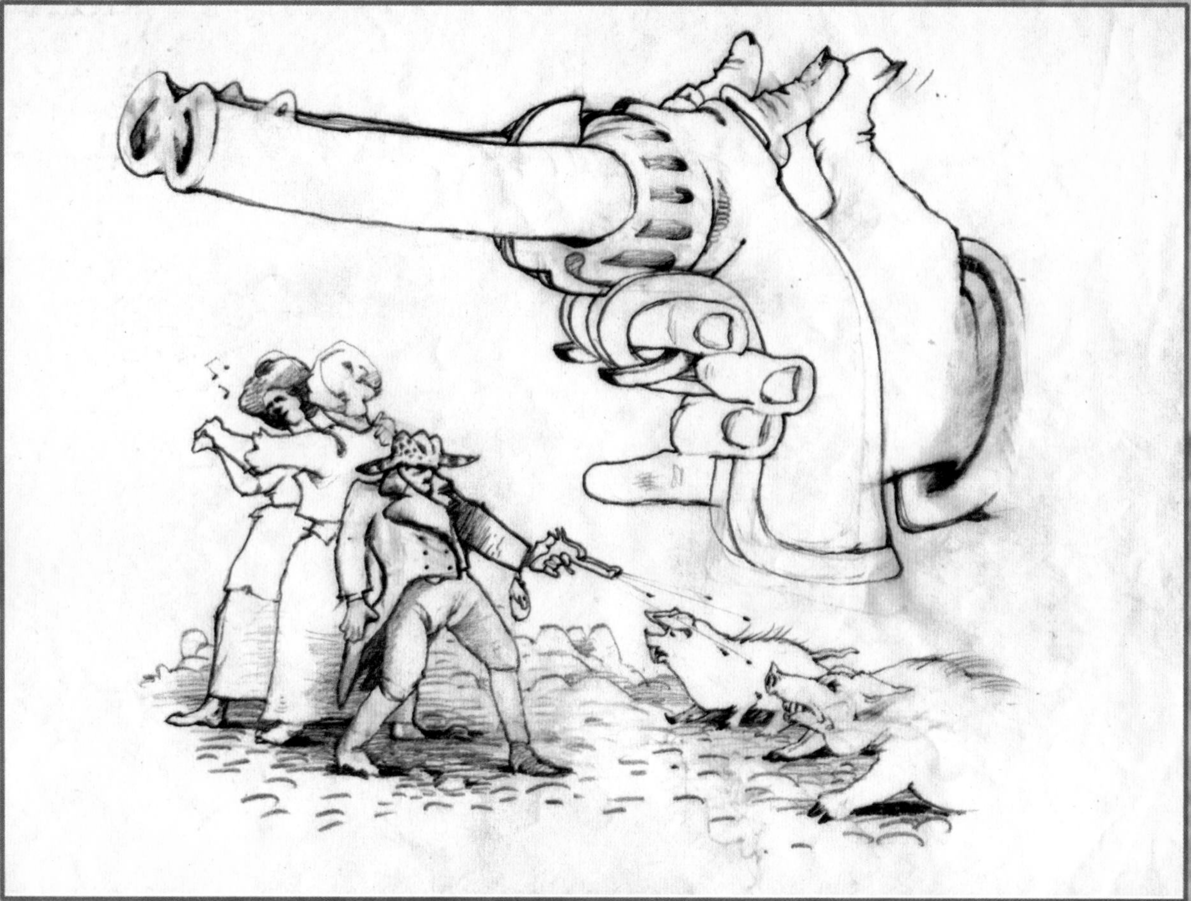

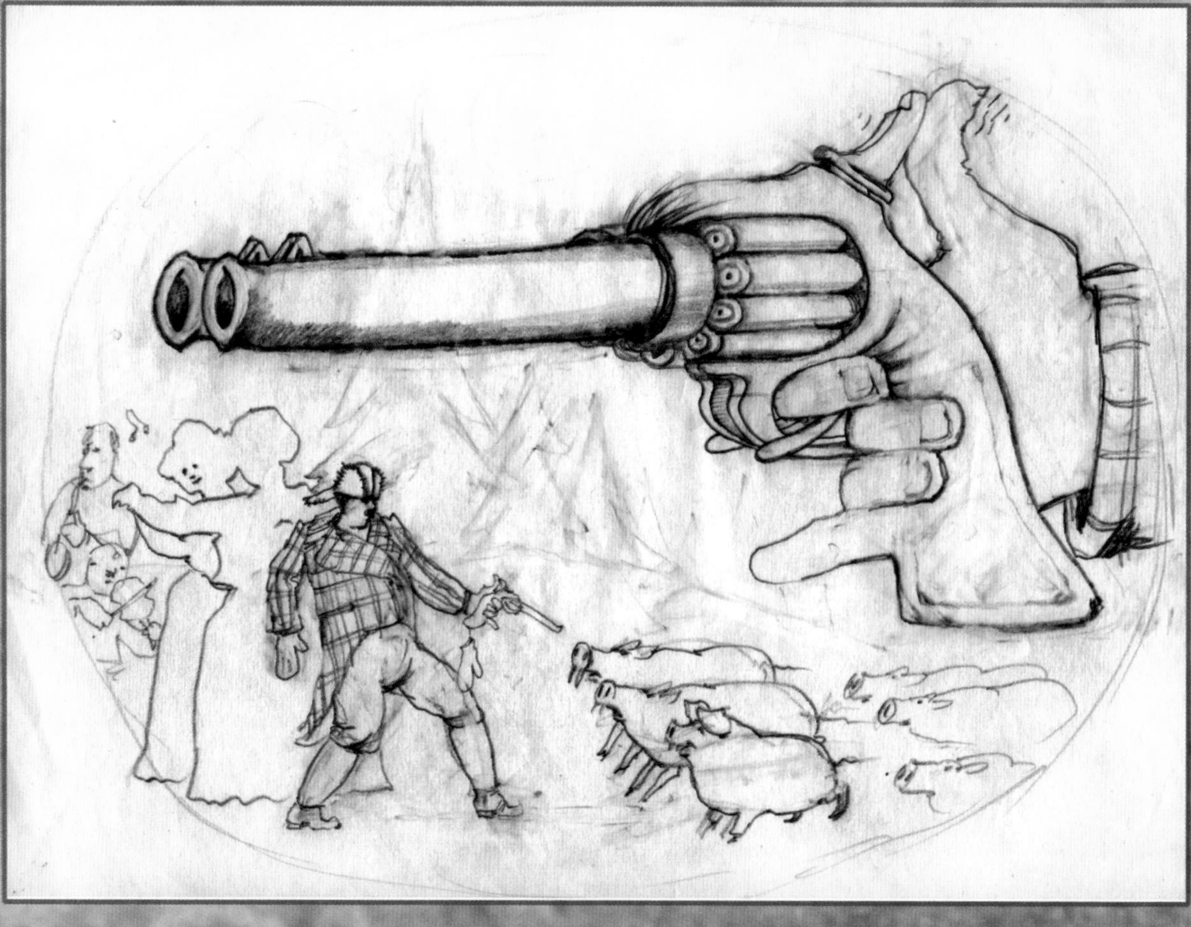

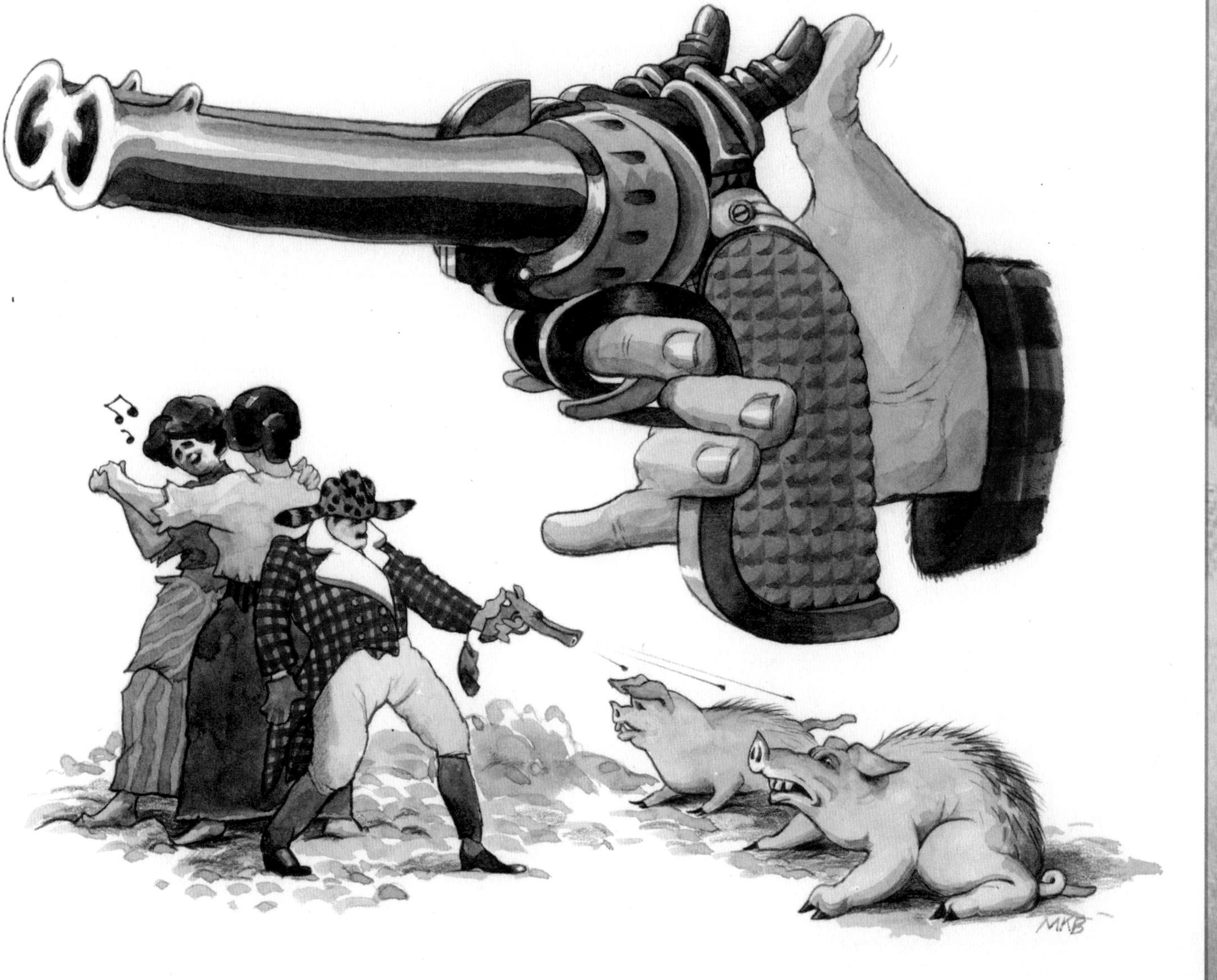
MKB

French Trader Thumb-action Wild Hog Pistol, "Le Chef du Pate," c.1825

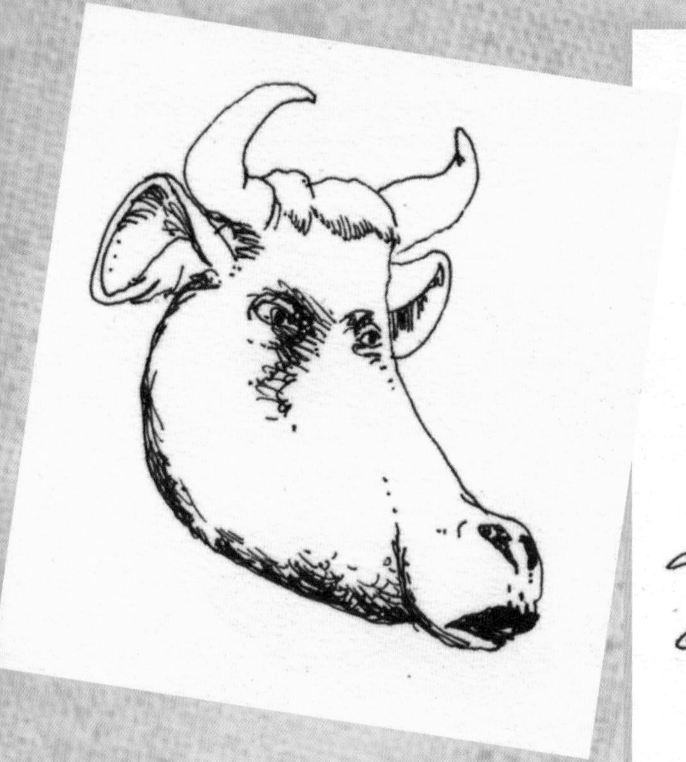

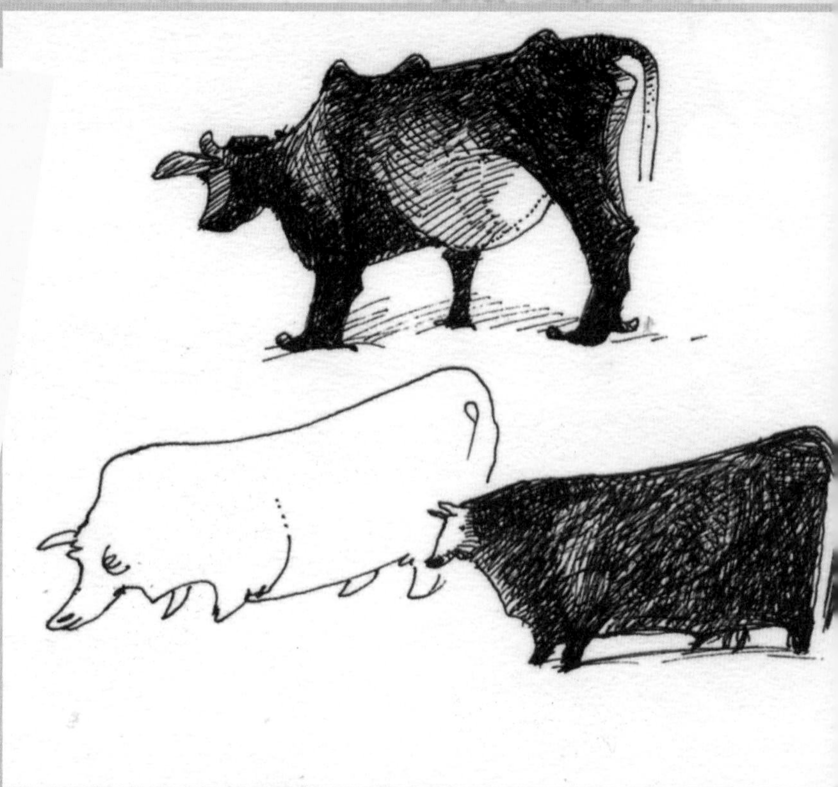

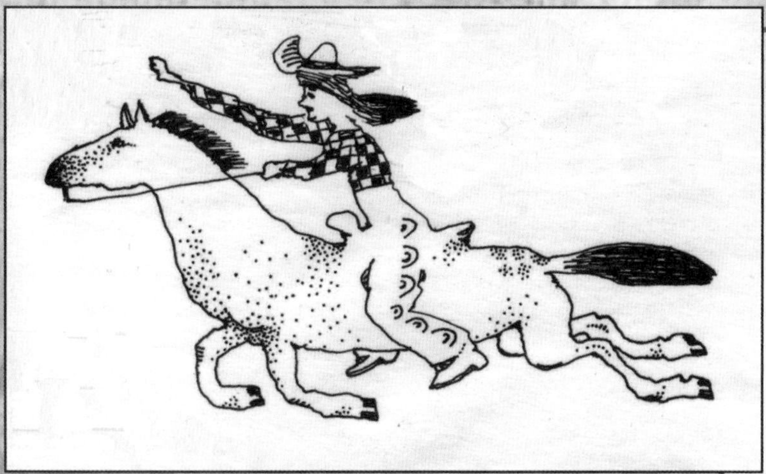

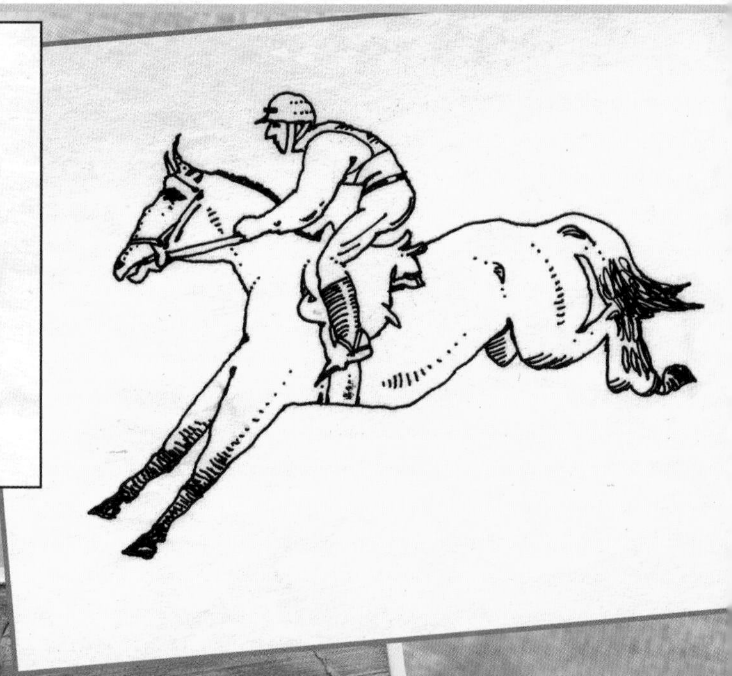

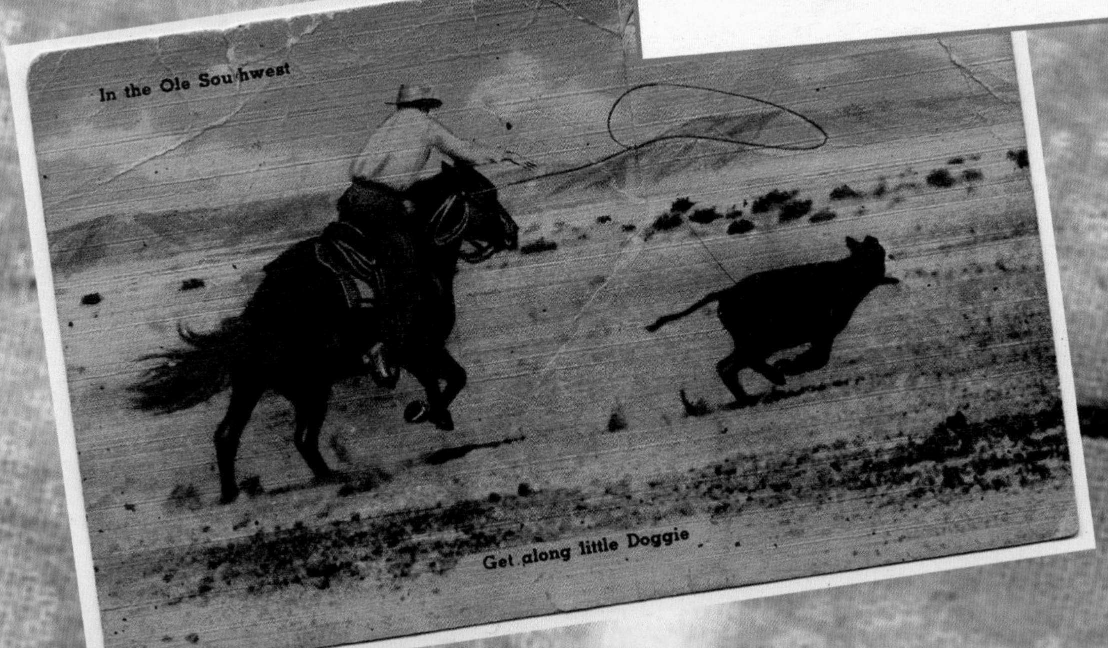
In the Ole Southwest
Get along little Doggie

Western Romance

Part five

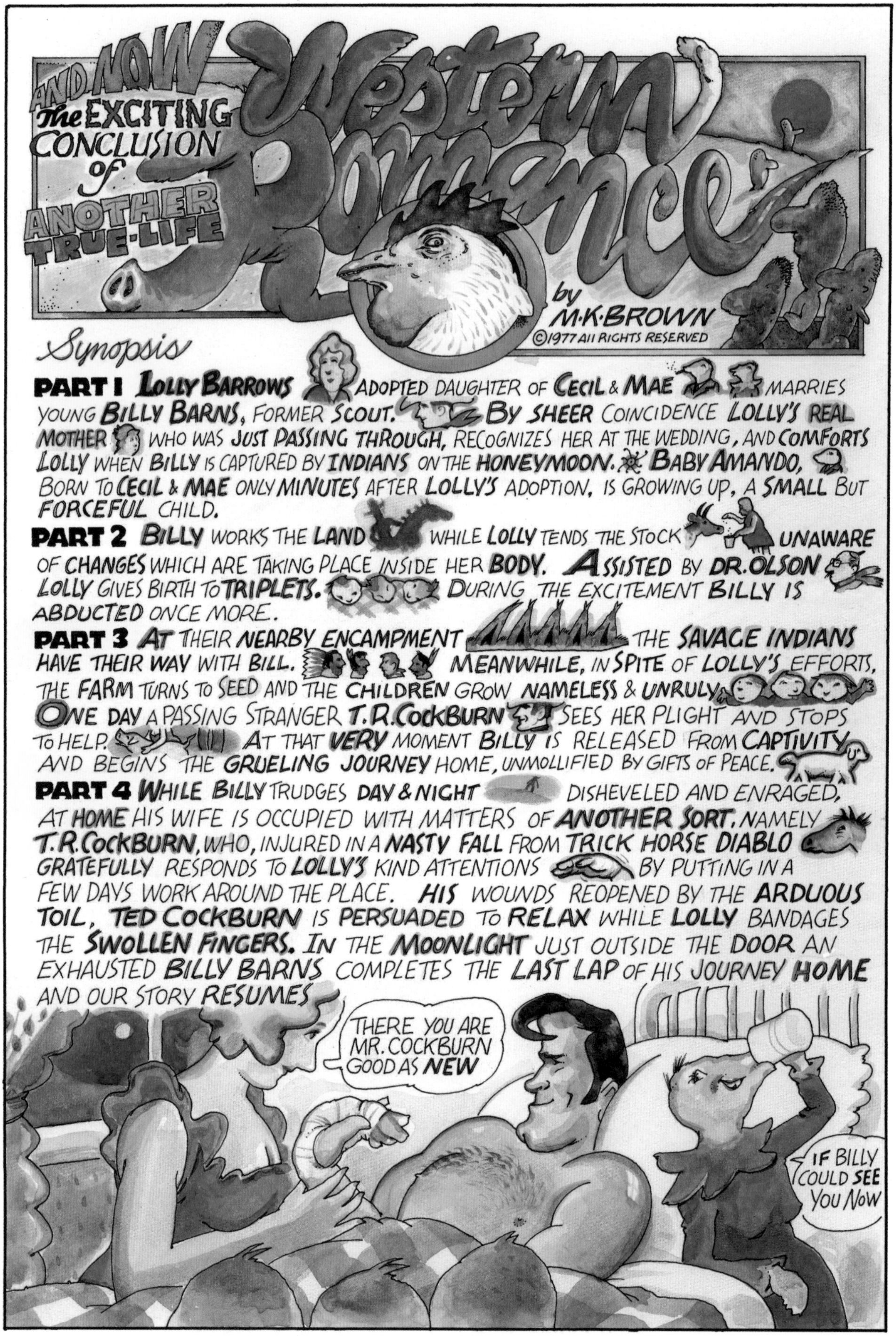
AND NOW The EXCITING CONCLUSION of ANOTHER TRUE-LIFE
Western Romance
by M·K·BROWN
©1977 All RIGHTS RESERVED
Synopsis
PART 1 LOLLY BARROWS ADOPTED DAUGHTER OF CECIL & MAE MARRIES YOUNG BILLY BARNS, FORMER SCOUT. BY SHEER COINCIDENCE LOLLY'S REAL MOTHER WHO WAS JUST PASSING THROUGH, RECOGNIZES HER AT THE WEDDING, AND COMFORTS LOLLY WHEN BILLY IS CAPTURED BY INDIANS ON THE HONEYMOON. BABY AMANDO, BORN TO CECIL & MAE ONLY MINUTES AFTER LOLLY'S ADOPTION, IS GROWING UP, A SMALL BUT FORCEFUL CHILD.
PART 2 BILLY WORKS THE LAND WHILE LOLLY TENDS THE STOCK UNAWARE OF CHANGES WHICH ARE TAKING PLACE INSIDE HER BODY. ASSISTED BY DR. OLSON LOLLY GIVES BIRTH TO TRIPLETS. DURING THE EXCITEMENT BILLY IS ABDUCTED ONCE MORE.
PART 3 AT THEIR NEARBY ENCAMPMENT THE SAVAGE INDIANS HAVE THEIR WAY WITH BILL. MEANWHILE, IN SPITE OF LOLLY'S EFFORTS, THE FARM TURNS TO SEED AND THE CHILDREN GROW NAMELESS & UNRULY. ONE DAY A PASSING STRANGER T.R. COCKBURN SEES HER PLIGHT AND STOPS TO HELP. AT THAT VERY MOMENT BILLY IS RELEASED FROM CAPTIVITY AND BEGINS THE GRUELING JOURNEY HOME, UNMOLLIFIED BY GIFTS OF PEACE.
PART 4 WHILE BILLY TRUDGES DAY & NIGHT DISHEVELED AND ENRAGED, AT HOME HIS WIFE IS OCCUPIED WITH MATTERS OF ANOTHER SORT, NAMELY T.R. COCKBURN, WHO, INJURED IN A NASTY FALL FROM TRICK HORSE DIABLO GRATEFULLY RESPONDS TO LOLLY'S KIND ATTENTIONS BY PUTTING IN A FEW DAYS WORK AROUND THE PLACE. HIS WOUNDS REOPENED BY THE ARDUOUS TOIL, TED COCKBURN IS PERSUADED TO RELAX WHILE LOLLY BANDAGES THE SWOLLEN FINGERS. IN THE MOONLIGHT JUST OUTSIDE THE DOOR AN EXHAUSTED BILLY BARNS COMPLETES THE LAST LAP OF HIS JOURNEY HOME AND OUR STORY RESUMES
THERE YOU ARE MR. COCKBURN GOOD AS NEW
IF BILLY COULD SEE YOU NOW

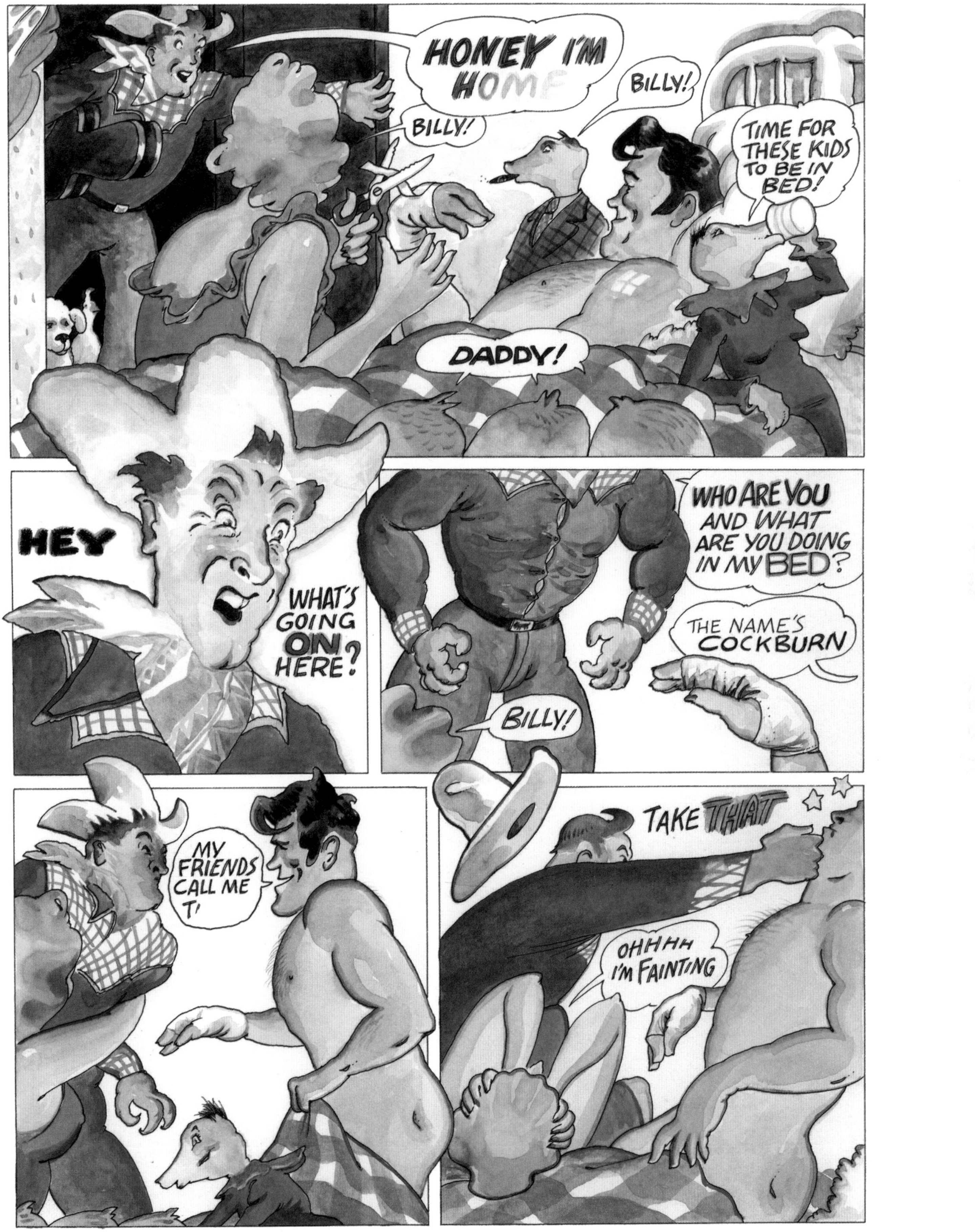
HONEY I'M HOME
BILLY!
BILLY!
TIME FOR THESE KIDS TO BE IN BED!
DADDY!
HEY
WHAT'S GOING ON HERE?
WHO ARE YOU AND WHAT ARE YOU DOING IN MY BED?
THE NAME'S COCKBURN
BILLY!
MY FRIENDS CALL ME T'
TAKE THAT
OHHHH I'M FAINTING

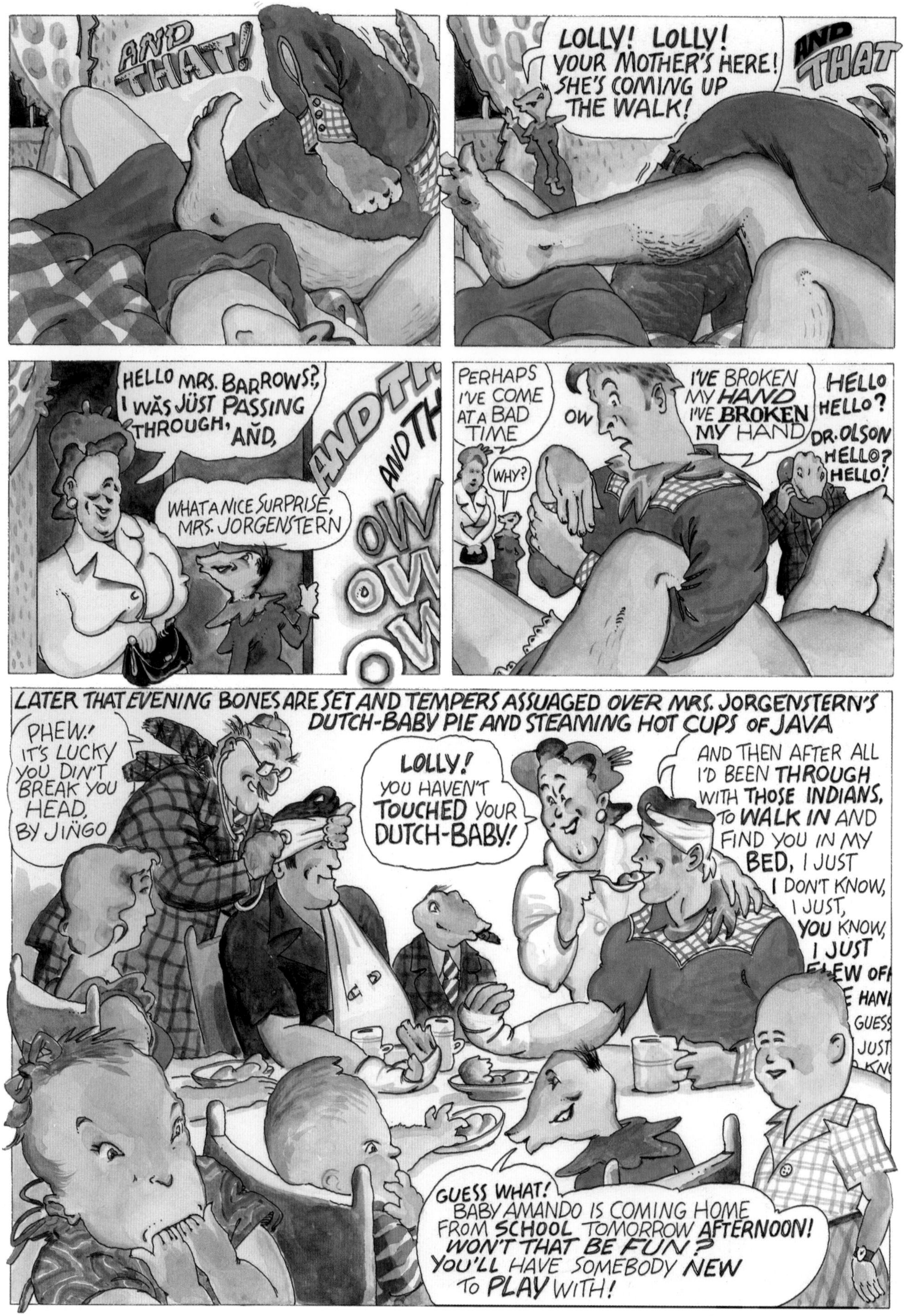
AND THAT!
LOLLY! LOLLY! YOUR MOTHER'S HERE! SHE'S COMING UP THE WALK!
AND THAT
HELLO MRS. BARROWS?, I WAS JUST PASSING THROUGH, AND,
WHAT A NICE SURPRISE, MRS. JORGENSTERN
PERHAPS I'VE COME AT A BAD TIME
WHY?
OW
I'VE BROKEN MY HAND I'VE BROKEN MY HAND
HELLO HELLO? DR. OLSON HELLO? HELLO!
LATER THAT EVENING BONES ARE SET AND TEMPERS ASSUAGED OVER MRS. JORGENSTERN'S DUTCH-BABY PIE AND STEAMING HOT CUPS OF JAVA
PHEW! IT'S LUCKY YOU DIN'T BREAK YOU HEAD, BY JINGO
LOLLY! YOU HAVEN'T TOUCHED YOUR DUTCH-BABY!
AND THEN AFTER ALL I'D BEEN THROUGH WITH THOSE INDIANS, TO WALK IN AND FIND YOU IN MY BED, I JUST I DON'T KNOW, I JUST, YOU KNOW, I JUST
GUESS WHAT! BABY AMANDO IS COMING HOME FROM SCHOOL TOMORROW AFTERNOON! WON'T THAT BE FUN? YOU'LL HAVE SOMEBODY NEW TO PLAY WITH!

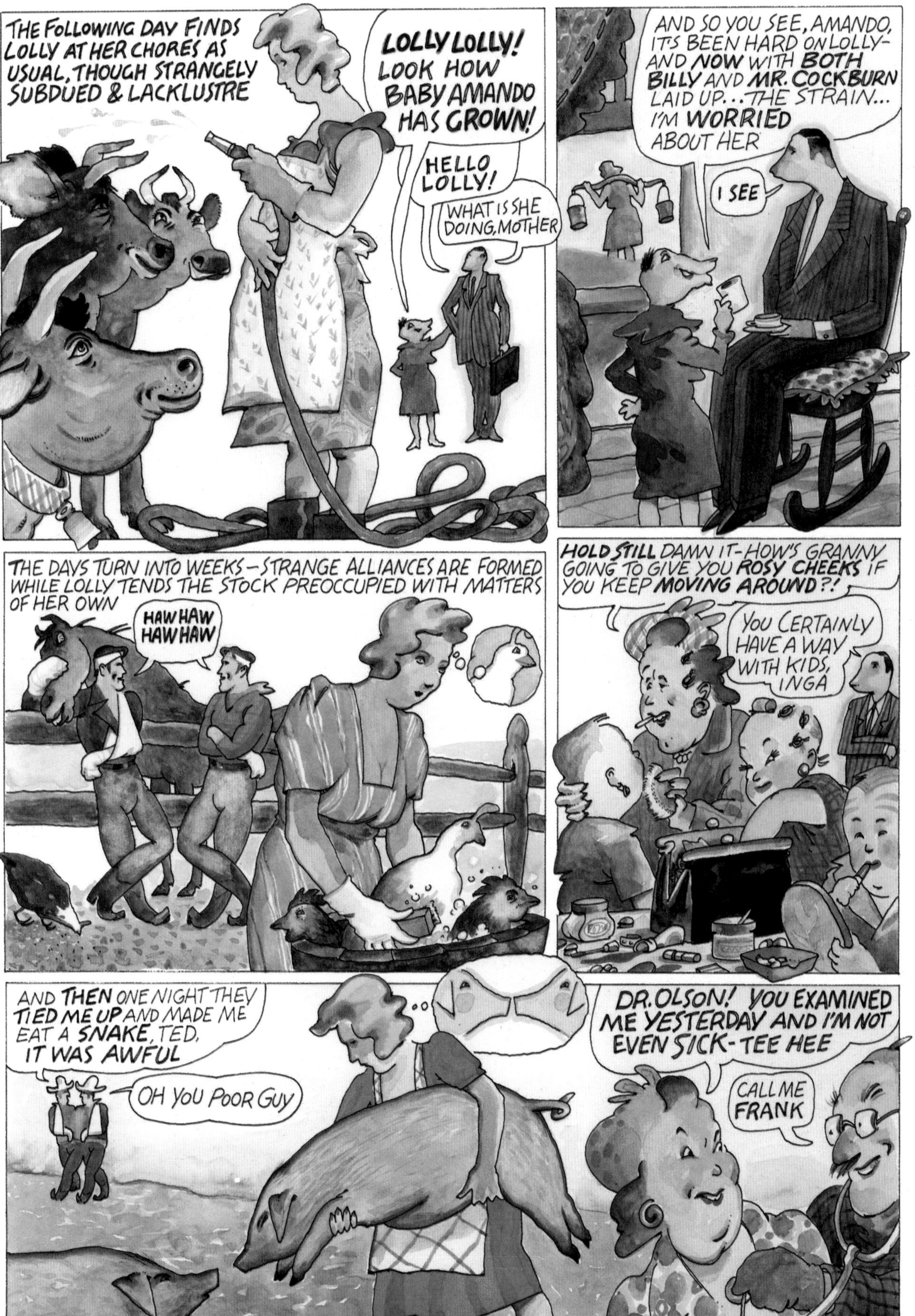

THE FOLLOWING DAY FINDS LOLLY AT HER CHORES AS USUAL, THOUGH STRANGELY SUBDUED & LACKLUSTRE
LOLLY LOLLY! LOOK HOW BABY AMANDO HAS GROWN!
HELLO LOLLY!
WHAT IS SHE DOING, MOTHER
AND SO YOU SEE, AMANDO, IT'S BEEN HARD ON LOLLY- AND NOW WITH BOTH BILLY AND MR. COCKBURN LAID UP... THE STRAIN... I'M WORRIED ABOUT HER
I SEE
THE DAYS TURN INTO WEEKS—STRANGE ALLIANCES ARE FORMED WHILE LOLLY TENDS THE STOCK PREOCCUPIED WITH MATTERS OF HER OWN
HAW HAW HAW HAW
HOLD STILL DAMN IT-HOW'S GRANNY GOING TO GIVE YOU ROSY CHEEKS IF YOU KEEP MOVING AROUND?!
YOU CERTAINLY HAVE A WAY WITH KIDS, INGA
AND THEN ONE NIGHT THEY TIED ME UP AND MADE ME EAT A SNAKE, TED, IT WAS AWFUL
OH YOU POOR GUY
DR. OLSON! YOU EXAMINED ME YESTERDAY AND I'M NOT EVEN SICK-TEE HEE
CALL ME FRANK

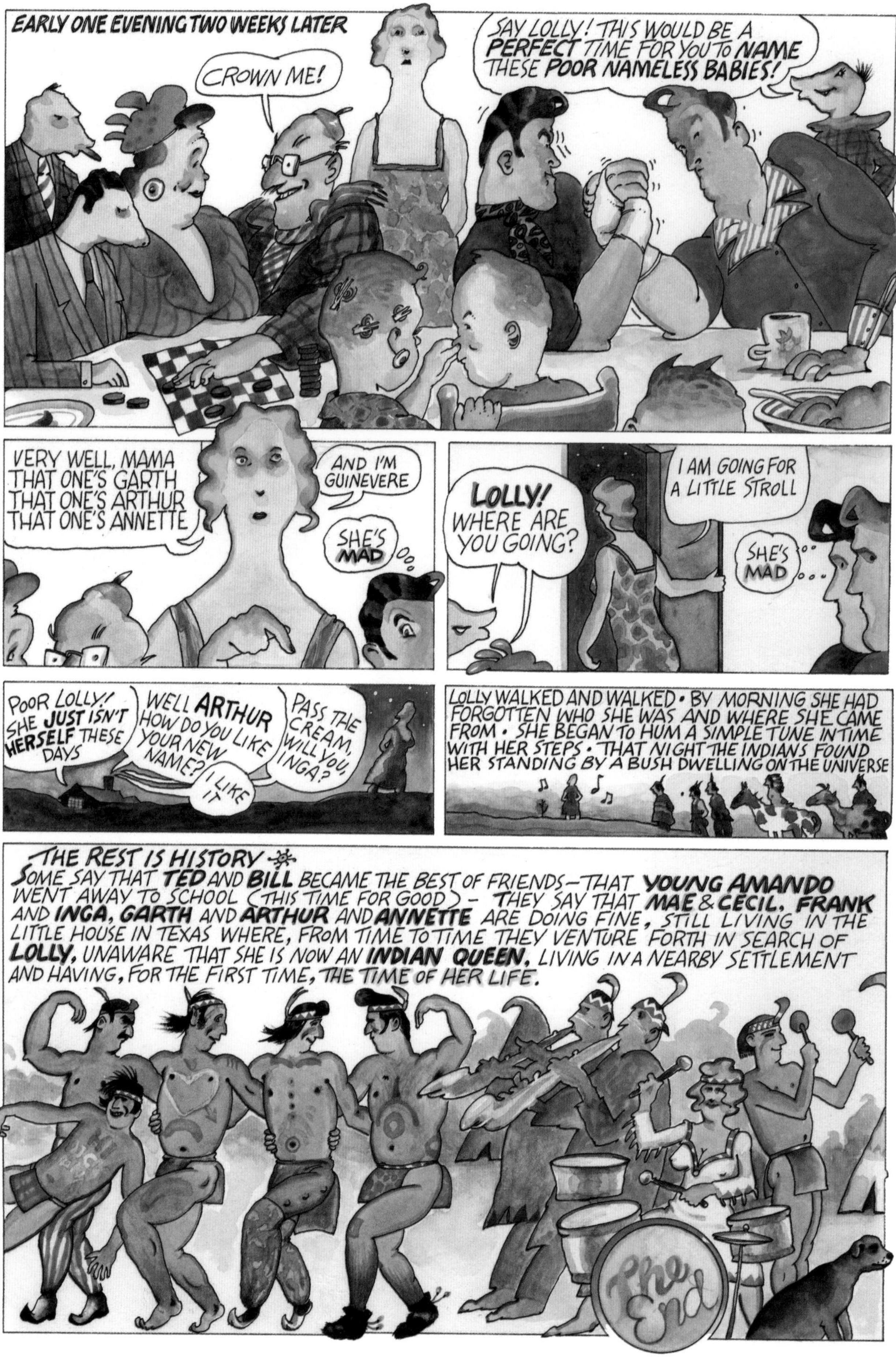
EARLY ONE EVENING TWO WEEKS LATER
CROWN ME!
SAY LOLLY! THIS WOULD BE A PERFECT TIME FOR YOU TO NAME THESE POOR NAMELESS BABIES!
VERY WELL, MAMA THAT ONE'S GARTH THAT ONE'S ARTHUR THAT ONE'S ANNETTE
AND I'M GUINEVERE
SHE'S MAD
LOLLY! WHERE ARE YOU GOING?
I AM GOING FOR A LITTLE STROLL
SHE'S MAD
POOR LOLLY! SHE JUST ISN'T HERSELF THESE DAYS
WELL ARTHUR HOW DO YOU LIKE YOUR NEW NAME?
I LIKE IT
PASS THE CREAM, WILL YOU, INGA?
LOLLY WALKED AND WALKED • BY MORNING SHE HAD FORGOTTEN WHO SHE WAS AND WHERE SHE CAME FROM • SHE BEGAN TO HUM A SIMPLE TUNE IN TIME WITH HER STEPS • THAT NIGHT THE INDIANS FOUND HER STANDING BY A BUSH DWELLING ON THE UNIVERSE
THE REST IS HISTORY
SOME SAY THAT TED AND BILL BECAME THE BEST OF FRIENDS—THAT YOUNG AMANDO WENT AWAY TO SCHOOL (THIS TIME FOR GOOD) – THEY SAY THAT MAE & CECIL, FRANK AND INGA, GARTH AND ARTHUR AND ANNETTE ARE DOING FINE, STILL LIVING IN THE LITTLE HOUSE IN TEXAS WHERE, FROM TIME TO TIME THEY VENTURE FORTH IN SEARCH OF LOLLY, UNAWARE THAT SHE IS NOW AN INDIAN QUEEN, LIVING IN A NEARBY SETTLEMENT AND HAVING, FOR THE FIRST TIME, THE TIME OF HER LIFE.
The End

When things go up on my wall, they often appear later in cartoons. One day this postcard arrived from a friend. On the back it said, "I still remember the wind blowing through your hair at Skateland. Love, Moris." We'd been roller-skating in San Rafael, unsuccessfully, and had survived. I put the postcard on my wall.

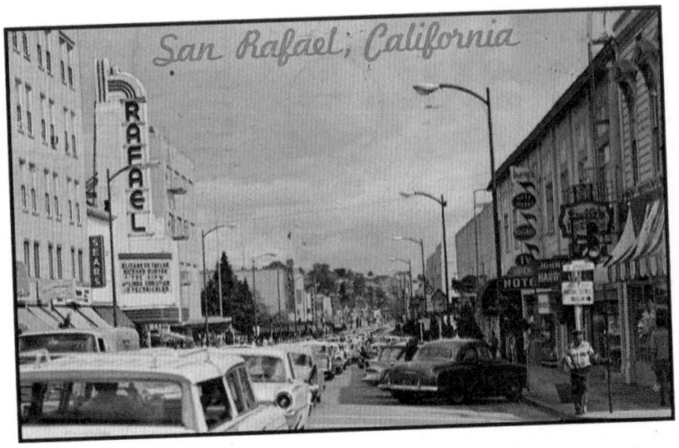
San Rafael, California
RAFAEL

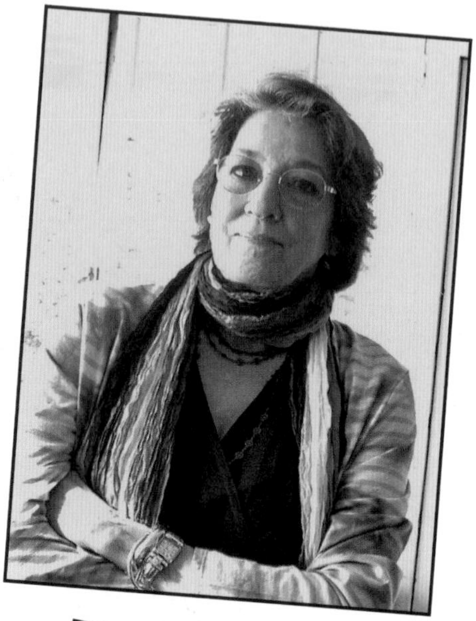

At that same time, I was working on "Self-Portrait" for *Arcade Comics* and needed a reference picture for a street in Hamburg, Germany. Not having one, I copied the postcard and it worked just fine, so from then on, whenever I have needed a downtown city street, I draw this one.

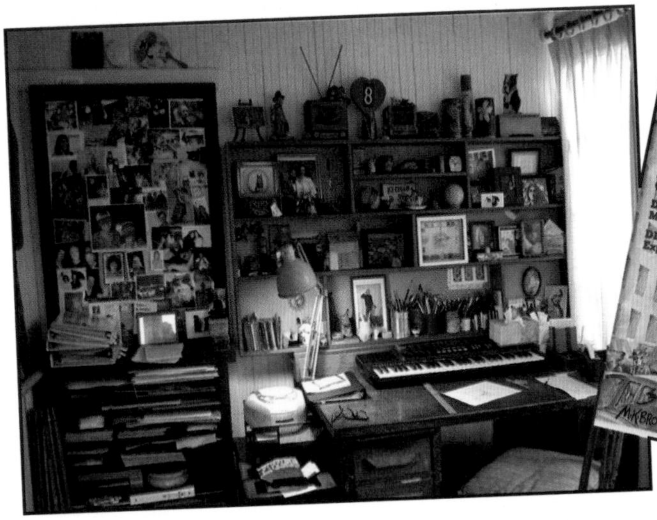

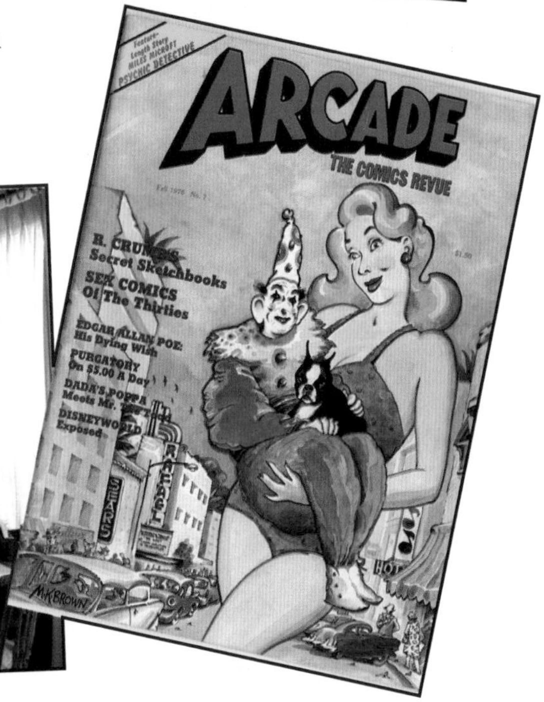
PSYCHIC DETECTIVE
ARCADE
THE COMICS REVUE
Secret Sketchbooks
SEX COMICS
Of The Thirties
EDGAR ALLAN POE:
His Dying Wish
PURGATORY
On $5.00 A Day
DISNEYWORLD
Exposed
RAFAEL
M.K.BROWN

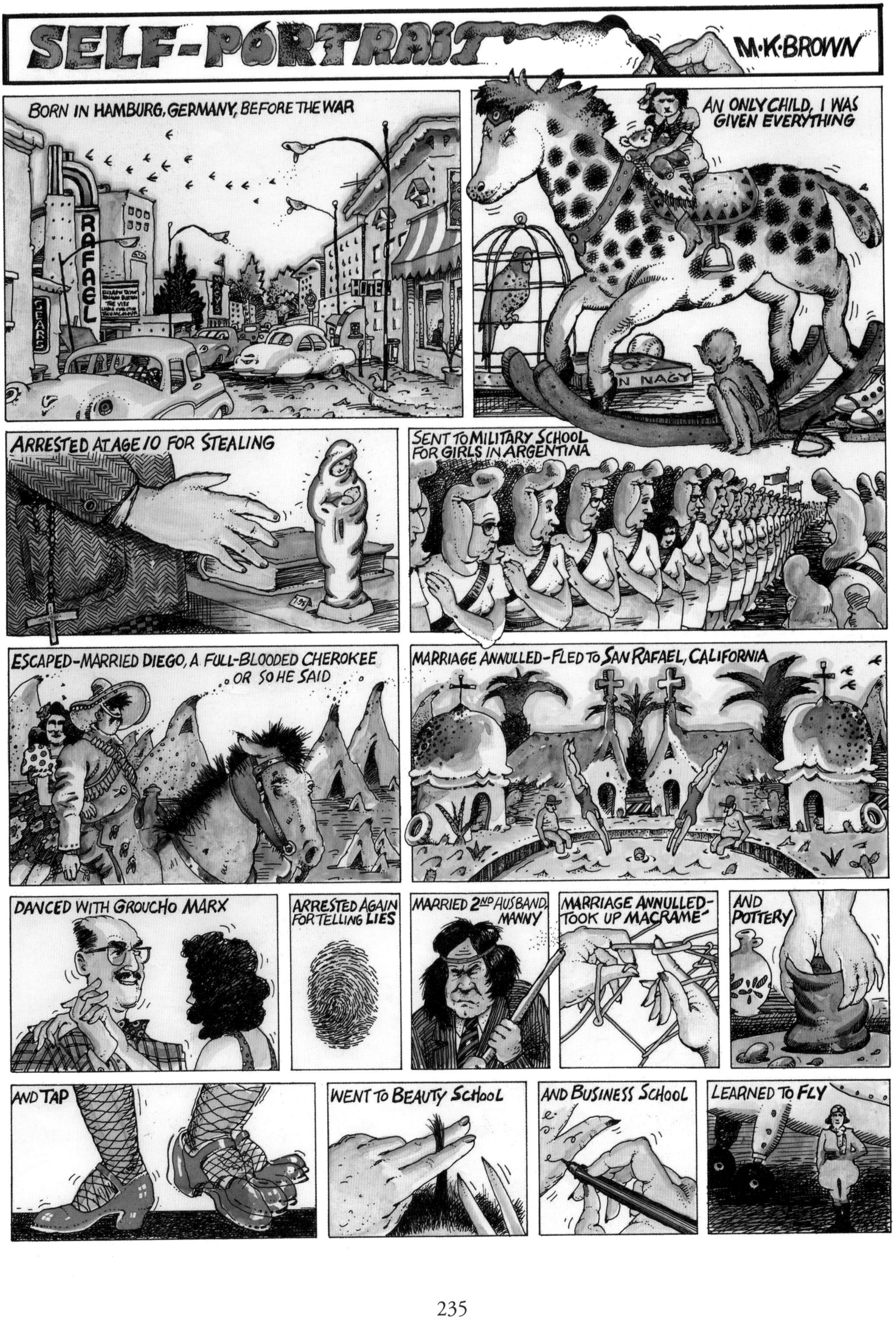
SELF-PORTRAIT
M·K·BROWN
BORN IN HAMBURG, GERMANY, BEFORE THE WAR
AN ONLY CHILD, I WAS GIVEN EVERYTHING
ARRESTED AT AGE 10 FOR STEALING
SENT TO MILITARY SCHOOL FOR GIRLS IN ARGENTINA
ESCAPED-MARRIED DIEGO, A FULL-BLOODED CHEROKEE
...OR SO HE SAID
MARRIAGE ANNULLED-FLED TO SAN RAFAEL, CALIFORNIA
DANCED WITH GROUCHO MARX
ARRESTED AGAIN FOR TELLING LIES
MARRIED 2ND HUSBAND, MANNY
MARRIAGE ANNULLED-TOOK UP MACRAME
AND POTTERY
AND TAP
WENT TO BEAUTY SCHOOL
AND BUSINESS SCHOOL
LEARNED TO FLY

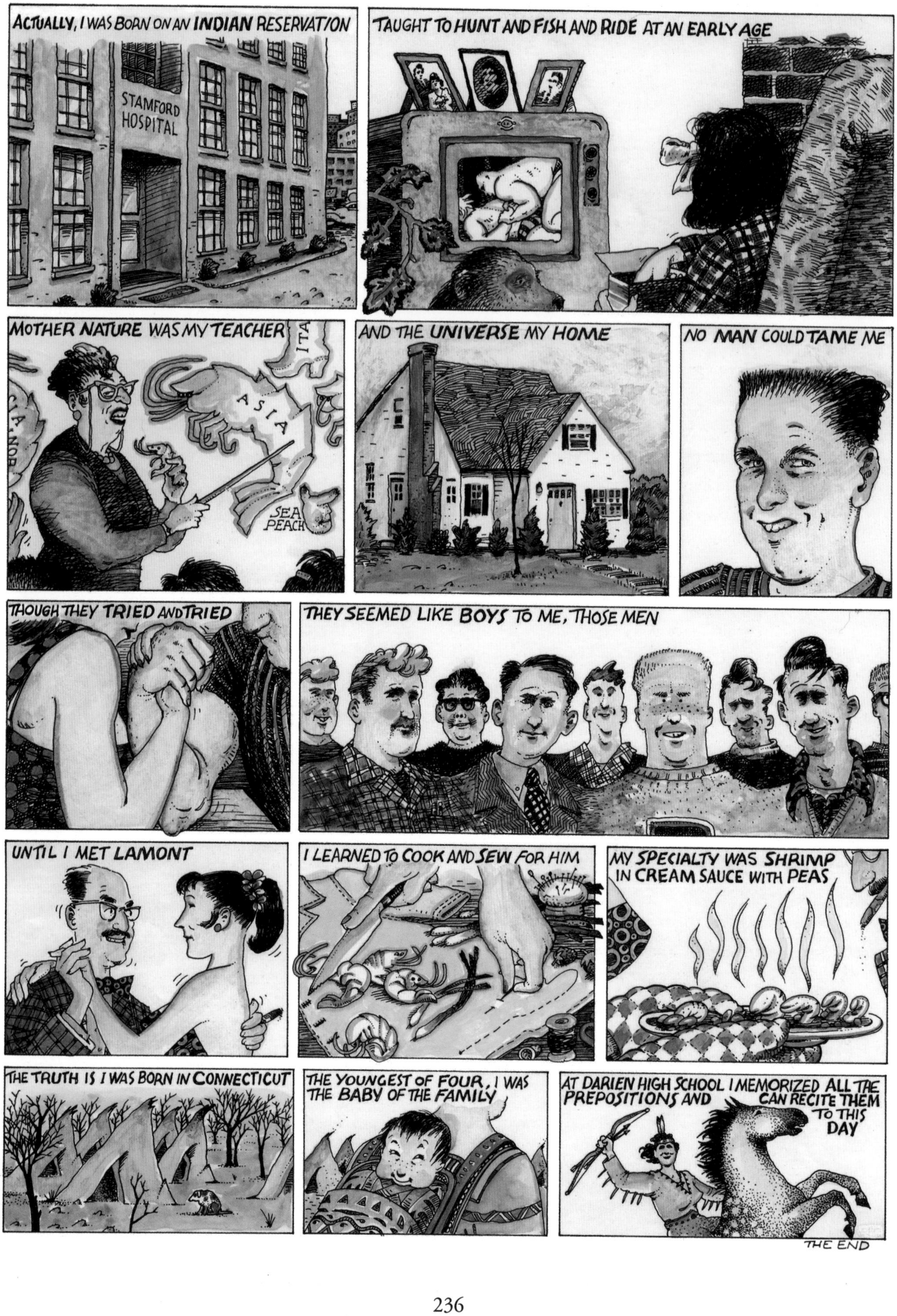
ACTUALLY, I WAS BORN ON AN INDIAN RESERVATION
STAMFORD HOSPITAL
TAUGHT TO HUNT AND FISH AND RIDE AT AN EARLY AGE
MOTHER NATURE WAS MY TEACHER
ASIA
SEA PEACH
AND THE UNIVERSE MY HOME
NO MAN COULD TAME ME
THOUGH THEY TRIED AND TRIED
THEY SEEMED LIKE BOYS TO ME, THOSE MEN
UNTIL I MET LAMONT
I LEARNED TO COOK AND SEW FOR HIM
MY SPECIALTY WAS SHRIMP IN CREAM SAUCE WITH PEAS
THE TRUTH IS I WAS BORN IN CONNECTICUT
THE YOUNGEST OF FOUR, I WAS THE BABY OF THE FAMILY
AT DARIEN HIGH SCHOOL I MEMORIZED ALL THE PREPOSITIONS AND CAN RECITE THEM TO THIS DAY
THE END

AFTERWORD

I first encountered M.K. Brown's cartoons in the *National Lampoon* in the early 1970s: back when it was a groundbreaking, intelligent, and incredibly hilarious humor magazine. In every issue, there was always something that made me laugh. But the part I always looked forward to reading more than anything else in the magazine was the last section: something called the "Funny Pages." The Funny Pages were made up of cartoon strips unlike any others I'd ever seen. They didn't look like newspaper comic strips, which almost always depressed me—they were so tired and hacky. Also, were these jokes? If so, why wasn't I laughing? But they weren't quite like underground comics, either, with their druggy (let's always be soooo stoooned, man...), ultra-sexual (huh...these frogs have huge human penises. That's totally hilarious, I guess...), misogynistic (women aren't real people...I thought we were, but I see now that I was mistaken...) sensibility. In the Funny Pages, I saw something new. For one thing, everyone had his or her own voice, not only in terms of drawing style, but also in his or her sense of humor. I found this very appealing, and also very encouraging as a young cartoonist. In the Funny Pages, I sensed that the cartoonists were writing and drawing for themselves. Their drawings were personal and idiosyncratic: and most of all, funny. You have to remember: I'm talking about the dark days, when comics were pretty much either corny newspaper strips ("The Clobbersons! The husband's a moron! The wife is a shrew! It's a laff riot!"), underground stuff (giant-penised frogs, etc.), and superhero comic books ("Will our muscle-bound hero outwit the evil Flarboni this time? One wonders.") These strips were a breath of fresh air. But I'm getting off topic. Sorry.

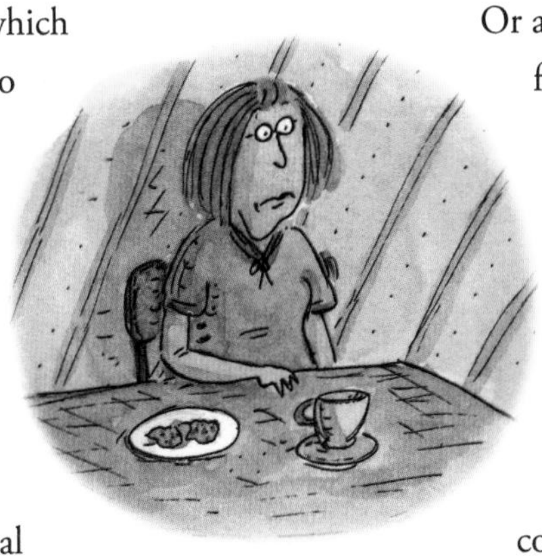

In the Funny Pages, I noticed M.K. Brown's cartoons right away. I'd never seen an artist who drew like that, or who thought like that. Who *were* these people? Who were these cowboys and housewives and policemen and Hollywood agents, and women in cat-eye glasses and jackets that bulged with shoulder pads, and men with strange teeth—and even stranger haircuts? What planet did these anthropomorphic apple pies, lamps, checkered tablecloths, and smiling teacups come from? What the hell was that creature in the corner of the panel with that pointy and deeply peculiar face? Was it human? Or an animal of some sort? What was this fascination with the West, and why did her drawings make me suddenly have a fascination with the West, too? What were these stories that veered this way and that, in the way of a pleasant but slightly disturbing and yet funny dream? What *was* this hilarious, surreal, and completely and totally original work?

When you read M.K. Brown's cartoons, her enormous talents draw you into her world. She not only draws (and paints) beautifully, but she has a wonderful ear for language. You can sense that she takes delight in ordinary conversations between human beings: conversations about ordinary stuff like Corian countertops or meatloaf and peas that, in her parallel universe, become a little spooky, a lot funny, and otherworldly. Her facial expressions are nuanced and wonderful. In one drawing, you might see 10 different kinds of smiles—delight, self-satisfaction, fake politeness, fright, meanness....Her peoples' faces are rubbery and expressive. In fact, everything she draws is a little rubbery and expressive, even the inanimate objects.

M.K. Brown is one of the most gifted and observant comic writers and artists around. And these two talents together are what make her work brilliant and unique.

-Roz Chast